John Bull's Other Homes

John Bull's Other Homes

State Housing and British Policy in Ireland, 1883 – 1922

Murray Fraser

LIVERPOOL UNIVERSITY PRESS

First published 1996 by
LIVERPOOL UNIVERSITY PRESS
Liverpool, L69 3BX

Copyright © 1996 Liverpool University Press

All rights reserved. No part of this volume may be reproduced,
stored in a retrieval system, or transmitted, in any form or by
any means, electronic, mechanical, photocopying, recording or
otherwise without the prior written permission of the
publishers.

British Library Cataloguing-in-Publication Data
A British Library CIP record is available

0–85323–670–4 cased
0–85323–680–1 paper

Set in $10\frac{1}{2}$ on $12\frac{1}{2}$ Meridien by
Wilmaset Limited, Birkenhead, Wirral
Printed and bound in the United Kingdom by
Bell & Bain Limited, Glasgow

For Helen, Callum and Liam

Frontispiece: H. Clarke, 'The last hour of the night'

CONTENTS

List of Figures, Diagrams and Tables   ix

Acknowledgements   xiv

Introduction   1

1. **Rural Housing and the State in Ireland before the First World War**   21
   The Irish Land Acts and the background to the Labourers Act; The first phase of the Irish Labourers Acts from 1883 to 1906; Political influences on the first phase of the Labourers Acts; The design of early Labourers Acts cottages; The second phase of the Labourers Acts from 1906 to 1914; Housing design in the second phase of the Labourers Acts; The decline of the Labourers Acts programme

2. **Urban State Housing in Ireland before 1914**   61
   Urban housing reform in Ireland; Early municipal housing in urban Ireland; Nationalism and municipal housing in Ireland from 1890; The Irish Party and urban housing after 1906; The results of the 1908 Irish Housing Act; Housing design in pre-war municipal schemes; Responses to the inadequacy of the Irish Housing Fund; The 1913–14 Dublin Lock-out and the housing issue; The 1913–14 Dublin Housing Inquiry

3. **The Influence of Early Irish State Housing on British Policy**   116
   Pre-war British reactions to the Irish Labourers Acts; The attitude of the Conservative Party to the Labourers Acts; The attitude of the Liberal Party to the Labourers Acts; The reaction in Westminster to the Dublin Housing Inquiry; The 1914 Budget and Irish urban housing subsidy; The aftermath of the rejection of the Dublin Housing Inquiry

4. **Home Rule and Garden Suburb Ideals in Ireland before 1914**   132
   The beginnings of the town planning movement in Ireland; Reactions to town planning ideals in pre-war Ireland; The intensification of the town planning campaign in 1913–14; The outcome of the planning crusade in pre-war Ireland

viii   *Contents*

5. **War-time Housing and Reconstruction after the 1916 Easter Rising**   148
   War-time retrenchment in Irish urban housing policy; The aftermath of the 1916 Easter Rising; War-time housing design in Dublin Corporation schemes; Plans for Irish reconstruction and housing; The 1917–18 Irish Convention and state housing proposals; Preparations for the post-war Irish housing campaign

6. **The Post-war Housing Campaign in Ireland**   185
   Initial British proposals for the Irish housing campaign; The 1919 Irish Housing Act and reactions in Ireland; Efforts to implement the post-war Irish housing campaign; Design standards for the Irish housing campaign; The collapse of the post-war Irish housing campaign; Housing policy at the end of British rule in Ireland

7. **Post-war Housing for Irish Ex-servicemen**   240
   Preparations for the 1919 Irish Land Act; The implementation of the 1919 Irish Land Act; Ex-servicemen's housing and the transfer of power in Ireland; The creation of the Irish Sailors' and Soldiers' Land Trust

8. **State Housing in Northern Ireland and the Irish Free State**   272
   Post-devolution housing policy in Northern Ireland; Municipal housing in Belfast from 1919; Post-independence housing policy in the Irish Free State; Municipal housing in Dublin from 1919

Conclusion	292
Diagrams and Tables	303
References	314
Bibliography	390
Index	409

LIST OF FIGURES, DIAGRAMS AND TABLES

FIGURES

Frontispiece: H. Clarke, 'The last hour of the night'
[Sir L. P. Abercrombie et al., *Dublin of the Future*, 1924: by permission of the British Library]

1. Map of Ireland, showing the provinces and principal urban centres
[author's drawing: information from R. D. Edwards, *An Atlas of Irish History (2nd Edition)*, 1981]
2. W. A. Scott: Spiddal Church in Co. Galway (1904–07)
[*Builder*, 8 December 1904; by permission of the British Library]
3. W. A. Scott: foremen's cottages at 'Kilkenny Garden Village' (1907)
[*Irish Builder*, 30 November 1907: by permission of the British Library]
4. Irish Board of Works: recommended two-storey, four-room type (1869)
[IBoW, *Land Improvement*, 1869, design no. 4: by permission of the National Library of Ireland]
5. Congested Districts Board: recommended single-storey, three-room type (1914)
[CDB, *Plans for Houses*, 1914, plan no. 2: by permission of the National Library of Ireland]
6. Congested Districts Board: recommended two-storey, four-room type (1914)
[ibid., plan no. 6: by permission of the National Library of Ireland]
7. Midleton RDC, Co. Cork: single-storey pre-1906 Labourers Act cottage
[W. Thompson, *The Housing Handbook*, 1903: by permission of the British Library]
8. Carrick, Co. Wexford: typical two-storey pre-1906 Labourers Act cottage
[author's photograph]
9. W. J. Fennell: romanticised 'Irish' alternatives to the ILGB designs (1907)
[Irish International Exhibition, *Irish Rural Life and Industry*, 1907: by permission of the National Library of Ireland]
10. ILGB: recommended 'Type A' single-storey Labourers Act Cottage (1907), based on winning entry for 1906 competition by S. Moss
[ILGB, *Labourers (Ireland) Acts 1883 to 1906: Model Plans of Labourers' Cottages*, 1907: by permission of the British Library]
11. ILGB: recommended 'Type C' single-storey Labourers Act cottage (1907), based on third-place entry for 1906 competition by T. M. Deane
[ibid.: by permission of the British Library]

12. ILGB: recommended 'Type F' two-storey Labourers Act cottage (1907)
    [ibid.: by permission of the British Library]
13. ILGB: recommended 'Type G' two-storey Labourers Act cottage (1907)
    [ibid.: by permission of the British Library]
14. Roscrea RDC: two-storey 'urban' type built under Labourers Act (1913–14)
    [author's photograph]
15. T. J. Byrne/South Dublin RDC: typical single-storey post-1906 Labourers Act cottages at Templeogue Road, Templeogue
    [author's photograph]
16. T. J. Byrne/South Dublin RDC: Woodview Cottages, Rathfarnham
    [author's photograph]
17. T. J. Byrne/South Dublin RDC: 'garden village' at Shankhill, Co. Dublin
    [author's photograph]
18. Photograph of a typical Dublin tenement slum in the early-twentieth century
    ['Darkest Dublin Collection': by permission of the Royal Society of Antiquaries of Ireland]
19. Guinness Trust: the Bull Alley scheme (1899–1905), and adjacent; Dublin Corporation: the scheme at Brides' Alley (1901–11)
    [author's photograph]
20. Waterford Corporation: the first terrace at Green Street, Ballybricken (1879)
    [author's photograph]
21. Dublin Corporation: the Benburb Street [Barrack Street] scheme (1886–87)
    [author's photograph]
22. Cork Corporation: typical municipal terrace plans (1886/1905)
    [P. C. Cowan, *Report on Dublin Housing*, 1918, nos 12 and 13: by permission of the Dublin Corporation Archives]
23. Cork Corporation: Roche's Buildings (1892) and Sutton's Buildings (1905)
    [author's photograph]
24. Limerick Corporation: wide-fronted terrace plans with front dormers (1912)
    [P. C. Cowan, op. cit., nos 18 and 19: by permission of the Dublin Corporation Archives]
25. Chillingworth and Levie: winning entry for Belfast competition (1913)
    [*Irish Builder*, 1 March 1913: by permission of the British Library]
26. P. Abercrombie: winning entry in the 1914 Dublin Town Plan Competition
    [Sir L. P. Abercrombie et al., *Dublin of the Future*, 1923: by permission of the British Library]

List of Figures, Diagrams and Tables xi

27. P. Abercrombie: proposal for civic improvements in central Dublin (1914)
    [ibid.: by permission of the British Library]
28. P. Abercrombie: proposal for neo-Georgian suburban housing (1914)
    [ibid.: by permission of the British Library]
29. P. Geddes and R. Unwin: perspective of the proposal for the Marino Estate (1914)
    [Geddes/Unwin Report: by permission of the Dublin Corporation Archives]
30. G. O'Connor/Pembroke UDC: Harmony Avenue, Donnybrook (1916)
    [author's photograph]
31. T. J. Byrne/Dublin Corporation: site plan of the McCaffrey Estate (1915)
    [P. C. Cowan, op. cit.: by permission of the Dublin Corporation Archives]
32. T. J. Byrne/Dublin Corporation: four-room type at the McCaffrey Estate
    [ibid.: by permission of the Dublin Corporation Archives]
33. T. J. Byrne/Dublin Corporation: 'street picture' at the McCaffrey Estate
    [author's photograph]
34. Dublin Corporation: perspective of the Church Street scheme (1916)
    [P. C. Cowan, op. cit.: by permission of the Dublin Corporation Archives]
35. Dublin Corporation: site plan and five-room type at Fairbrothers Fields (1918)
    [*Architect*, 29 November 1918: by permission of the British Library]
36. Dublin Corporation: various four-room types at Fairbrothers Fields
    [ibid.: by permission of the British Library]
37. Typical competition entry from the 1919 RIAI/ILGB Housing Competition
    [ILGB, *Housing of the Working Classes in Ireland*, 1919: by permission of the National Library of Ireland]
38. ILGB: recommended 'Type A' four-room plan from the 1919 circular
    [ibid.: by permission of the National Library of Ireland]
39. ILGB: recommended 'Type B' four-room plan from the 1919 circular
    [ibid.: by permission of the National Library of Ireland]
40. ILGB: recommended 'Type C' five-room plan from the 1919 circular
    [ibid.: by permission of the National Library of Ireland]
41. ILGB: recommended 'Type C/D/E/F' plans from the 1919 circular
    [ibid.: by permission of the National Library of Ireland]
42. F. Mears/ILGB: site plan of the Killester Estate (1920–22)
    [PRO/HO.45/14659, ISSLT, *First Report*, 1927, scheme 114: Crown copyright, by permission of the Controller of Her Majesty's Stationery Office]
43. F. Mears/ILGB: photograph of the Killester Estate in the late-1920s
    [ibid.: Crown copyright, by permission of the Controller of Her Majesty's Stationery Office]

xii *John Bull's Other Homes*

44. F. Mears/ILGB: photograph of the Killester Estate now
    [author's photograph]
45. Irish Board of Works: 'Type 2^A' four-room cottage for ex-servicemen
    [PRO/HO.45/14659, op. cit.: Crown copyright, by permission of the Controller of Her Majesty's Stationery Office]
46. Irish Board of Works: 'Type 3' four-room cottage for ex-servicemen
    [ibid.: Crown copyright, by permission of the Controller of Her Majesty's Stationery Office]
47. ISSLT: photograph of the Shantallow Estate, Co. Londonderry
    [ibid.: Crown copyright, by permission of the Controller of Her Majesty's Stationery Office]
48. ISSLT: 'Type Z.1' two-storey five-room cottage as used at Shantallow
    [ibid.: Crown copyright, by permission of the Controller of Her Majesty's Stationery Office]
49. ISSLT: 'Type D' two-storey four-room cottage as used in the Irish Free State
    [ibid.: Crown copyright, by permission of the Controller of Her Majesty's Stationery Office]
50. Belfast Corporation: parlour houses on the Wandsworth Road Estate (1922–24)
    [Belfast Corporation, *Belfast Book*, 1929: by permission of the National Library of Ireland]
51. Dublin Corporation: the Fairbrothers Fields Estate as completed (1921–27)
    [author's photograph]
52. H. T. O'Rourke/Dublin Corporation: first design for the Marino Estate (1920)
    [*Builder*, 27 February 1920: by permission of the British Library]
53. H. T. O'Rourke/Dublin Corporation: first house-types for the Marino Estate
    [ibid.: by permission of the British Library]
54. F. G. Hicks/Dublin Corporation: final site plan of the Marino Estate (1923–27)
    [H. T. O'Rourke et al., *Dublin Civic Survey Report*, 1925: by permission of the British Library]
55. F. G. Hicks/Dublin Corporation: the Marino Estate as completed
    [author's photograph]

DIAGRAMS

A. Annual total of Labourers Acts loans
   [ILGB/IBoW/Irish Land Commission Annual Reports]
B. Annual total of Labourers Acts houses built
   [ILGB Annual Reports]

C. Cumulate total of Labourers Acts loans
   [ILGB/IBoW/Irish Land Commission Annual Reports]
D. Annual total of Irish urban housing loans
   [IBoW Annual Reports]
E. Cumulate total of loans advanced under the Housing of the Working Classes (Ireland) Acts
   [ibid.]

TABLES

1. Abstract of loans sanctioned and houses built under the 1883–1919 Labourers Acts, from 1884/85
   [ILGB Annual Reports]
2. Abstract of loans advanced for rural housing under the Labourers Acts, from 1885/86
   [IBoW/Irish Land Commission Annual Reports]
3. Abstract of regional differences under the 1883–1919 Labourers Acts
   [IBoW/ILGB Annual Reports]
4. Abstract of loans advanced under all urban housing codes in Ireland, from 1882/83
   [IBoW Annual Reports]
5. Abstract of loans advanced under the 1885–1919 Housing of the Working Classes (Ireland) Acts, from 1885/86
   [ibid.]
6. Proportions of rural and urban housing loans in relation to total public loans advanced in Ireland, from 1903/04
   [ibid.]

ACKNOWLEDGEMENTS

This book is based on a doctoral thesis submitted to the University of London. Only a few relatively minor alterations have been made to the text in preparing it for publication. My greatest intellectual debt is to Adrian Forty and Mark Swenarton, who were the supervisors for my thesis. I am also indebted to my examiners, Mary Daly and Martin Daunton, for their constructive comments and their help in enabling my research to be published. The book would not have been possible without the patience and professionalism of Robin Bloxsidge at Liverpool University Press. Any errors and shortcomings that remain are, of course, entirely my responsibility. A number of other scholars and colleagues have generously provided me with specific information and encouragement, notably Frederick Aalen, but also Mary Clark, Harry Connor, Christopher Cross, Brian Finnimore, John Graby, Dennis Hardy, Joe Kerr, Bill Licken, Yvette Marin, Bill Menking, Shane O'Toole, Ruth Owens, Andrew Saint and Stephen Ward. My family have been a constant source of strength and so I extend my thanks to Ann, Leslie, Ross and Rowan Fraser.

I would like to praise the unsung work of the staff of the following libraries: the Bodleian Library, British Library (including Manuscripts, Newspaper Library and Official Publications Library), Columbia University (Avery Library), Dublin Corporation Archives, House of Lords Library, Imperial War Museum, Irish Architectural Archive, National Library of Ireland (including Manuscripts), National Library of Scotland, Public Records Office (Kew), Public Records Office of Northern Ireland, Royal Institute of Architects of Ireland, Royal Institute of British Architects, Royal Society of Antiquaries of Ireland, State Paper Office (Dublin), Trinity College Dublin, University College Dublin, University College London (including Bartlett), University of London (Senate House), and the Wiltshire Record Office. I am grateful to Baron Merrivale and Mrs Patricia Medley for their permission to consult, respectively, the Duke Papers and the Birrell Papers (Medley Deposit) in the Bodleian Library. My research has benefited greatly from financial assistance given by the Central Research Fund of the University of London and the Research Fund of Oxford Brookes University. I also wish to record my thanks to the following libraries for permission to reproduce photographs and drawings: the British Library (including Newspaper Library), Dublin Corporation Archives, National Library of Ireland, Public Records Office (Kew), and the Royal Society of Antiquaries of Ireland.

I have deliberately kept my most heartfelt acknowledgement until last. My wife and friend, Helen Hughes, has been behind this book from the start, and the finished article bears her stamp in manifold ways. Since my research began, we have brought into the world two delightful and beautiful boys, Callum and Liam Fraser. I am sure that Helen will be honoured if I include our sons in my debt to her.

INTRODUCTION

State housing played an integral role in the relationship between Ireland and Great Britain from the 1880s until the early-1920s, during the period when the 'Irish Question' was the major issue in the domestic politics of the United Kingdom. The basis of state housing policy as it was to develop subsequently in Great Britain, namely direct central subsidy and recommended plan types, originated in Ireland. Yet the significance of early state housing in Ireland has not been fully appreciated by Irish historians, and in Britain the subject remains virtually unknown. This book will therefore set out to explain the complex interplay of ideas about Irish housing policy and design, and in doing so will place most emphasis on the moments when either Ireland or Great Britain came to influence the other party decisively.

Three types of historiographical questions present themselves immediately. Did the relationship with Britain determine or simply reflect Irish social conditions? In what ways did cultural interaction influence the framework of architectural practice in Ireland? And how does the subject of Irish state housing fit into the established account of housing developments in Britain? This introduction will deal with each of these issues in turn.

In terms of analysing the influence of Britain on Ireland, the concepts that are of most importance to this study are those of 'modernisation' and 'nationalism'. Modernisation is understood here as the transformation from an agricultural society governed by a small landowning elite, to a functionally specialised and (usually) capitalist industrial society, committed (at least in theory) to democratic participation and an open meritocracy. Ireland does not conform to this pattern in that it remained—with the exception of an industrial enclave in North-East Ulster—an essentially agricultural economy. Problems of interpretation therefore stem from the fact that historians have differing views as to what extent, if at all, Ireland went through a process of modernisation. Nevertheless, a number of general points need to be made. First, modernisation in the Irish context means in essence the response to the *modernisation of England*, since it was the latter nation that produced not only the first capitalist industrial system, but also developed an effective colonising strategy that culminated in worldwide empire-building.[1] Wales was the first territory to be economically and politically assimilated, followed by union with Scotland in 1707. The slow conquest of Gaelic Ireland had begun with the Norman feudal expansionism of the twelfth century (establishing the colonial region around Dublin known as the 'Pale'), but it was not until the sixteenth and seventeenth centuries that colonisation was pursued with sustained purpose (see Fig. 1).[2] From this period, the consolidation of an Anglican Anglo-Irish 'Ascendancy' as a ruling landowning class throughout the land, along with the intensive 'plantations' of both Anglicans and Presbyterians in Ulster, served to cement the dominance of British interests over those of the native Roman Catholic

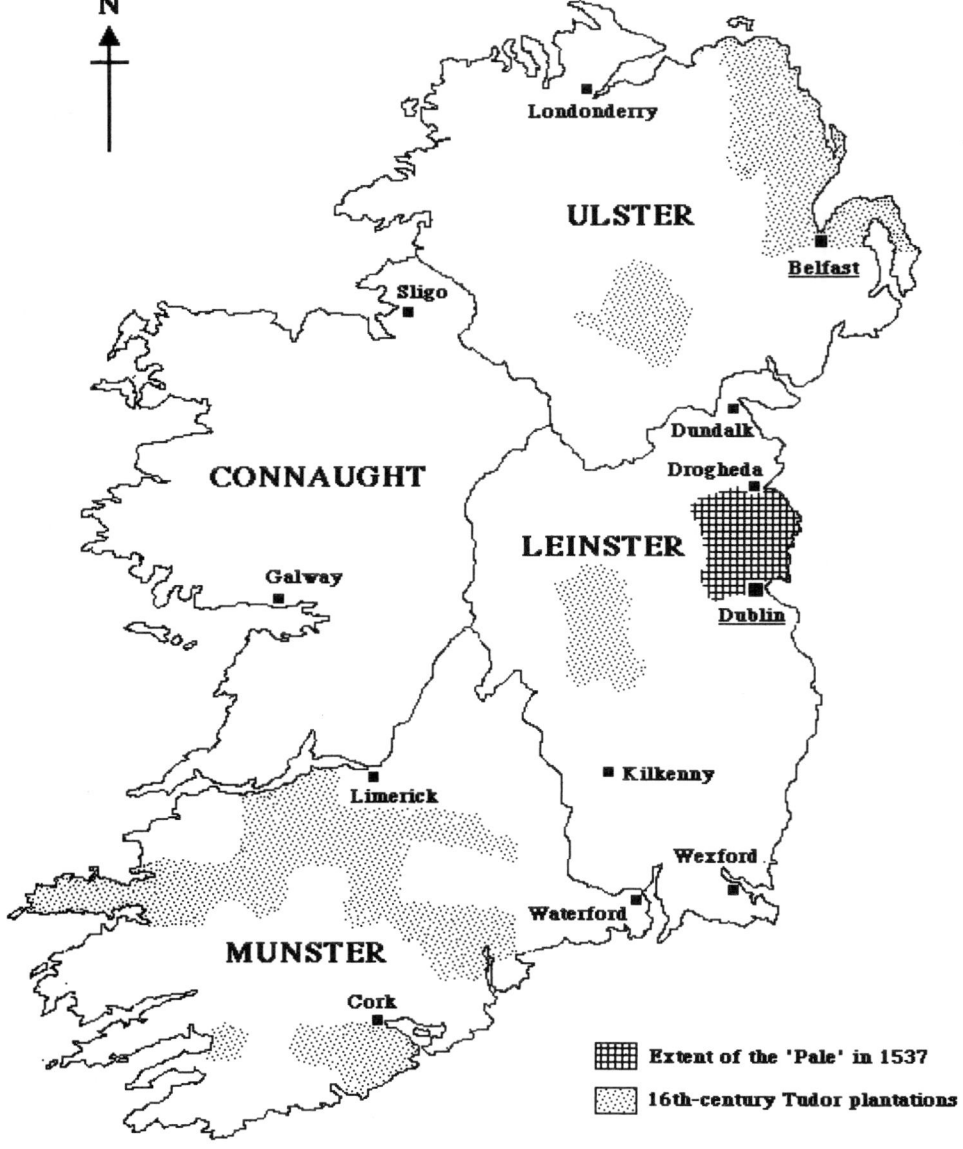

Fig 1. Map of Ireland, showing the provinces and principal urban centres

majority (nineteenth-century statistics consistently showed that Catholics accounted for around 75 per cent of the total population of Ireland; while in Ulster, Protestants of all denominations comprised some 56 per cent of the population, rising to 66 per cent in the six North-Eastern counties). Catholics were now mostly reduced to the status of tenant-farmers and labourers. An Irish Parliament governed the kingdom under the authority of the English Crown, and after the Battle of the Boyne in 1690 passed a sequence of legal and civil restrictions over Catholics known as the 'Penal Laws', which were to remain in force for most of the eighteenth century. There were two reasons why Britain felt it necessary to maintain its rule over a disaffected and often hostile population. The first was the desire to create an enlarged economic market based on the supply of Irish agricultural produce and the reciprocal consumption of British manufactures; the second was a continual concern to protect the expanding British state from the strategic threat that a potentially disloyal Ireland might pose as an invasion route. These goals were jeopardised in the late-eighteenth century by the growing demands for colonial autonomy from the Irish Parliament, and then by the 1798 Rebellion of the United Irishmen. The government of William Pitt the Younger could no longer rely with confidence on the Ascendancy class to preserve Ireland as a bulwark against foreign invasion, and hence it introduced the Act of Union in 1800–01 to create the United Kingdom of Great Britain and Ireland. This was a watershed in modern political relations between the countries, since it appeared to give Ireland the status of a *province*, rather than an *imperial colony* of Britain. However, unlike the incorporation of Wales and Scotland into the United Kingdom, the lack in Ireland of popular support for unification, outside a few counties in North-East Ulster, meant that it remained an unhappy and resented marriage of convenience. The outcome was a conflict, found at all levels, between pressures that tended towards integration and those that tended towards separation.

Tensions over economic matters were evident in the eighteenth century, but took on increasing importance from the early-nineteenth century. Already by 1800, Ireland had become an integral part of the imperial economic system: some 80 per cent of Irish imports came from Britain, and 85 per cent of its exports flowed in the other direction.[3] The Act of Union intensified this trend through the abolition of the Irish Exchequer in 1816, the removal of customs duties in 1820, and monetary unification in 1826. However, closer dependency never brought about real equality for Ireland. 'A condition of genuine market unification existed', one historian has written, '. . . but Britain was clearly the richer, more powerful and more populated of the two.'[4] Ireland in general became ever more specialised as the supplier of agricultural goods (particularly cattle products) to the burgeoning British urban population. It remained essentially a colonial economy, and hence the least developed and poorest part of the United Kingdom. It was the entrenchment of a 'pre-industrial' agricultural society in the majority of Ireland, and its growing identification with

Nationalist and Catholic values, that prevented the modernisation of Ireland in parallel with Britain.[5] Indeed, by the nineteenth century Britain had all but abandoned direct attempts to alter the predominant social system in Ireland. Catholicism was too far rooted in areas outside Ulster for proselytisation or repression to have a chance, and the incidence of Irish-speaking was declining of its own accord. What there was instead was a steady wave of racial propaganda from Britain which denigrated 'backward' Irish culture, as if somehow assertions of British superiority would indirectly make people in Ireland wish to become more like their rulers.[6] No such message was needed in North-East Ulster, where a much closer economic integration with Britain was found in the industrial region centred on the Lagan valley. This underpinned the political and cultural loyalty of the Protestant and Presbyterian majority in the region: it was no coincidence that the Union was defended most virulently by capitalist businessmen who realised that their economic well-being depended on the British connection.

It was at the political level, however, that the conflict in Ireland between integration and separation was revealed with most clarity. The Union had in principle made uniform the political structure of the United Kingdom, since Irish Members now sat in the Westminster Parliament as provincial representatives. Yet the myth of a unified Parliament was always to prove a chimera, since, as MacDonagh has observed, 'in the case of Ireland its fundamental objective was the maintenance of imperial control'.[7] Thus the policies of Parliament could in Ireland only be implemented by a unique quasi-colonial administration in Dublin Castle. The Castle Administration sat nominally under the rule of a politically appointed Lord Lieutenant, but in reality it was increasingly controlled by the Chief Secretary of Ireland—a figure who usually, though not always, was also a member of the British Cabinet.

In its attempt to achieve the political integration of two countries with very different levels of development, the British Government was forced to rely in Ireland on an unparalleled degree of centralised state intervention. The aim was to ameliorate the worst social and economic consequences of uneven modernisation, and in most instances hinged on policies designed to improve agricultural performance. The instinctive starting point for British policy in Ireland was the same as that for the mainland, where the *laissez-faire* doctrine of 'political economy' (as first put forward by the classical economists) remained essentially intact, if somewhat dented, in the period up to the First World War.[8] However, the few policies that were actually transferred to Ireland unaltered, such as the Poor Law system in 1838, proved so disastrous in operation that soon it became the accepted principle that special treatment was inevitable. It was this realisation that prompted some radical British intellectuals, such as John Stuart Mill, to modify their economic theories. 'Finding Irish solutions to Irish problems', O'Tuathaigh has written, 'became part of the strategy of government pursued by various British cabinets during the second half of the nineteenth century.'[9] The result was a number of 'exceptional' social policies which appeared to anticipate the subsequent introduction of similar policies in Britain: examples included a national police force (1836; Dublin retained its own force), a national elementary education system (1831), and, as will be seen, a greater involvement in state housing. The reason for this degree of quasi-collectivist state intervention in Ireland has been the subject of much historical debate. One theory has argued that Ireland formed a 'social laboratory' in which experiments to solve particular social or economic problems could be tested out, and if successful, could then be transferred to Britain.[10] However, there are undoubted difficulties with this viewpoint.[11] There is no evidence that any strategy was tried out with the conscious intention of it being intended for Britain, nor indeed did any policy of collectivism exist to form the hypothesis for an experiment. Most historians tend to the view that British intervention was instead a series of reactive, *ad hoc* expedients, hastily conceived and with uncertain long-term consequences. The notion of Ireland as a 'social laboratory' can only be, at best, an explanation that is applied in retrospect and not one that was perceived at the time. State intervention in Ireland, as will be seen, remained in British eyes in principle a necessary evil.

Nothing more starkly prevented the political integration of Britain and Ireland than the complex strands of the Irish Nationalist movement. At heart, Irish Nationalism was motivated by a desire for greater autonomy from Britain and the emasculation of the Protestant Ascendancy landed class, whose *raison d'être* as a colonial governing elite had been made theoretically irrelevant by the Act of Union. Nationalist demands varied throughout the nineteenth century, and the movement changed from one with a cross-denominational base to a narrower ethnic position in which the tendency was, as Townshend has noted, 'for Irish Nationalism to be seen as a Roman Catholic movement posing both economic and moral threats to Protestants'.[12] After the campaign for religious equality led by Daniel O'Connell which resulted in the 1829 Catholic Emancipation Act (and the disestablishment of the Anglican Church of Ireland 40 years later), in the 1840s the more militant Romantic nationalism of 'Young Ireland' began to foster a keen interest in cultural separateness. The greatest possible emotional charge was given to Nationalist sentiment by the cataclysmic Irish Famine of 1845–49. It is estimated that around a million people died and the same number or more were forced to emigrate: blame was placed squarely on the British Government, and large-scale exodus became a persistent trauma thereafter. In the late-1860s the Fenians preached the use of out-and-out physical force. Yet just over a decade later a 'New Departure' in the Nationalist movement, led by Charles Stewart Parnell and the Irish Parliamentary Party, allied a constitutional demand for self-government with the campaign by Irish tenant-farmers for land reform in the wake of the severe agricultural slump and 'Land War' of 1879–82. Land redistribution was now to be the economic 'engine' that was to drag in its train the political demand for 'Home Rule' (or, more precisely, a greater autonomy for Ireland over non-strategic matters within the United Kingdom). The implication of this parliamentary strategy, once William Gladstone had committed the Liberal Party to Home Rule, and total opposition had been registered by the Unionist heartland of North-East Ulster and the Conservative Party in Britain, was that the 'Irish Question' came to dominate domestic politics for the next 35 years. The failure of Gladstone's famous Home Rule Bills in 1886 and 1893 made disenchanted Irish intellectuals opt increasingly for, on one hand, an anglophobic 'cultural nationalism' as the basis for political mobilisation (initiatives included the formation of the Gaelic Athletic Association in 1884 to promote native Irish sports, and the Gaelic League in 1893 to revive the use of the Irish language and the study of medieval Irish literature); and, on the other hand, the formation of more radical political groupings. Amongst the latter was the creation in 1900 of the minority separatist party that was to become Sinn Fein, with its policy of abstention from the Imperial Parliament and its advocation of the establishment of Ireland as a distinct nation under the British Crown, on the Austro-Hungarian precedent of 'dual monarchy'. Taken together, these new initiatives produced a veritable 'alternative history' to the mainstream path of constitutional Nationalism.[13] Yet for all its intended radicalism and the heroic status it was later awarded in the Republican pantheon, separatist Nationalism was at heart only another facet of the same rejection of British rule in Ireland.

It is the explanation for the growth of Irish Nationalism, and particularly its relation to the modernisation process in Ireland, that has caused perhaps greatest disagreement amongst historians.[14] The process by which nation-states are formed has been of great interest ever since the writings of sociologists such as Max Weber at the turn of the century, and much analysis has been focused on the ways in which a powerful state-building 'core' seeks to enlarge by incorporating territories on its 'periphery'.[15] Sometimes territorial expansion has produced viable and augmented states; other times it has merely produced a resented manifestation of imperialism. In the specific case of Ireland, some observers such as Michael Hechter have argued that Irish Nationalism was the political reaction to persistent regional inequalities created by the uneven pattern of modernisation within the United Kingdom.[16] The problem, however, remains as to how far an 'anglicised' model of modernisation, defined as a process resulting from industrialisation, can ever adequately cover the social complexities of Ireland. Indeed, other historians have poured doubt on a correlation between economic modernisation and the growth of Irish Nationalism, by pointing out that what the 'Land War' did was to usher in a new phase of a movement whose ideas and historical pattern had been developing ever since O'Connell's campaign for religious equality in the 1820s.[17] This reminder of the complex interaction between British influence and Nationalist counter-struggle is useful: not least in the fact that, as has been pointed out, the strategies of constitutional Nationalists and even the most separatist of 'Irish-Irelanders' were so deeply infused with British values of liberal democracy and modernisation, that they themselves contributed to the 'anglicisation' of the country.[18]

Another complicating factor within the Anglo-Irish relationship was the instances where so-called 'peripheral' political groups in Ireland were able to affect developments in the dominant 'core' nation of Britain. The best-known example was O'Connell's campaign which secured Catholic emancipation not just for Ireland but for the whole of the United Kingdom. This intriguing cross-influence of the Celtic fringes on the 'core' has prompted some recent cultural writers to look to Antonio Gramsci's idea of a 'hegemonic' ideological struggle between social classes, and to argue for a more refined model in which the dependent country also forces the dominant nation to modify its way of thinking.[19] It is illuminating that nineteenth-century English observers frequently defined themselves in terms of the rational, civilised 'opposite' of the under-developed Celtic periphery. The perceived 'backwardness' of Ireland was therefore essential for Britain, both in the economic and the ideological realms, as part of the latter's need to justify claims of cultural superiority and imperial 'advancement'. It formed the ideological underpinning for the so-called 'civilising mission'. This important cross-influence between ruler and ruled was never likely to result in genuine cultural integration, but it does reveal that there was more than a simple one-way domination of the 'core' over the 'periphery'. In this study, it is necessary therefore to look at not only the direct impact of British policies on Ireland, but also the extent to which the mainland country came itself to be changed by Irish developments.

The interplay of British modernisation and Irish Nationalism thus forms the background to the developments discussed in this study. What, then, of the second area of historiographical investigation: that is, to what extent did Britain exercise a cultural hegemony over Irish architecture? In nineteenth-century Ireland, architectural practice continued to be centred in Dublin, although provincial towns such as Cork, Waterford, Limerick, and above all Belfast, began to develop their own local networks of architects.[20] Indeed the leading Irish practice of the mid-nineteenth century, that of Sir Thomas Deane and Benjamin Woodward, came from Cork. Regional diffusion did little to alter the fact that, compared with Britain, architecture remained an insignificant occupation. The first moves towards professional organisation in Ireland generally followed in the wake of those on the mainland. The Royal Institute of Architects of Ireland (hereafter RIAI) was formed in 1839, partly through the efforts of an English architect, George Papworth, who had links with those who had five years earlier set up the Institute of British Architects (soon to become the Royal Institute of British Architects; hereafter RIBA). In 1859 the fortnightly *Dublin Builder* was first published in emulation of its namesake in Britain: by 1867 it was renamed the *Irish Builder*, and it was to prove the principal source of architectural information and analysis over the next century.[21] The Architectural Association of Ireland was briefly set up in Dublin in the 1860s as a pale imitation of its famous London precedent. The association lay moribund until it was revived in 1896, largely at the initiative of a recent British arrival, Harry Allberry, for the similar purpose of providing an informal education for young architects. Yet the weakness and disorganisation of the Irish profession were continually demonstrated by the ineffectuality of the RIAI. 'The Irish Institute has been for a long time little more than a name,' wrote the *Irish Builder* in the late-1870s, and there was no dramatic change thereafter.[22] Membership stood at about 65 architects in the 1880s, and this barely rose to around 100 members in the period just before the First World War.[23] The business of the RIAI was riven from the turn of the century by a growing division with a splinter association in Belfast, the Ulster Society of Architects, and by a fruitless obsession with the idea of securing compulsory legal registration for the use of the title of 'architect'. One way for the RIAI to augment itself was to attach itself to the much stronger English institute, and thereby to become a regional branch of a 'trade union' across the whole United Kingdom. However, a complete merger had been ruled out in 1889 in favour of a formal alliance with the RIBA. This link was praised by the incumbent RIAI President in 1898 because it 'strengthens uniformity of practice between ourselves and our brethren across the water, and strengthens our hands'.[24] Nowhere was the attempt at parallelism more clearly shown than in the matter of architectural education. In 1889 the RIAI introduced the RIBA professional examination, and then, after overcoming the objections of the English institute, began in 1905 to set its own equivalent entrance exam. By this point many Irish architects believed that professional salvation lay in the foundation of a university school of architecture on the academic Beaux-Arts model, as first formulated in the USA and subsequently introduced to Britain at Liverpool University. A Chair of Architecture was duly established in 1909 at the new 'Catholic' institution of University College Dublin.[25] However, this remained in reality only a professorship during the period of the first two incumbents, Sir Thomas Drew and William Scott. It was not until the mid-1920s that a proper architectural course can been said to have started.

The desire of Irish architects to found a university course was not just based on a concern to bolster the profession, but also reflected a deep insecurity about their relationship with Britain. In the nineteenth and early-twentieth centuries it was obvious that British architecture set the lead. The *Irish Builder* repeatedly described Irish architecture as a 'colourless imitation' of that on the mainland, and in 1909 wrote of Ireland's future prospects that 'the probability is that she will continue to follow England, as heretofore, at a respectful distance—the habit of imitativeness is too ingrained to be readily cast off'.[26] A little over a decade later the same journal observed that 'It must be confessed that the illustrated English building journals have wholly set our fashion for sixty or seventy years'.[27] Dependence on Britain brought undoubted benefits. Many of Ireland's leading architects at the turn of the century were Britons who had settled there, and several native practitioners had trained in offices on the mainland. There was also a healthy cross-flow of commissions between the two countries, even if it was British architects who tended to benefit most. The two outstanding examples of reciprocation date from the High Victorian Gothic

Revival, and were—respectively—William Burges' St Fin Barr's Cathedral in Cork (1862–78), and Deane and Woodward's Oxford Museum (1855–60). Although there are no statistics available on the religious affiliation of Irish architects, it is probable that the high proportion of Protestants found in professions in Ireland at the time would have tended to make architects as a group more sympathetic to British values and the Imperial connection.[28] It was not uncommon for Irish architects, such as the RIAI President in 1900, Sir Thomas Drew, to welcome the 'friendly invasion' of English architects if in return there was the chance to obtain work in Britain and the Empire.[29]

Cultural dependence, however, also bred resentment and feelings of inferiority. The esteemed poet William Butler Yeats could therefore deride the profession in 1915 by observing that 'we have no Irish architect whom anybody suspects of remarkable talent'.[30] Nor would architectural practitioners have necessarily disagreed. 'I do not think that we have had in Ireland . . . any architect who can be called first-class or of international repute', bemoaned one architect in 1924.[31] Irish resentment usually came to the surface when a plum public commission went to a British architect, notably in the controversies over the appointment of Sir Aston Webb for the College of Science in Dublin (1904–13; the Irish architect Thomas Manly Deane was brought in as collaborator), and Hugh Lane's nomination of Edwin Lutyens to design the new Dublin Municipal Art Gallery (1912–13; unexecuted). Yet an even greater problem brought on by British domination was the confusion produced in Irish architects when they tried to wrestle with the concept of 'national style'—the holy grail that permeated nineteenth-century architectural thinking in Europe generally, and was so frequently linked with medieval revivalism. 'What chance is there of a distinctly national style being produced amongst us?', asked the then President of the RIAI in 1874.[32] But within Ireland's specific historical context, this of course meant that architects had to decide whether or not to directly embrace a Nationalist position. An alignment with Nationalism had been made with notable success in the field of literature, from the 'Young Ireland' Romantic movement of the 1840s through to the avant-garde Celtic Literary Revival (the so-called 'Irish Renaissance') led by Yeats at the turn of the century.[33] In the case of Irish architecture, the decision was to prove more difficult for two reasons. Firstly, unless architects chose to confine themselves to visionary projects (such as those produced by *Ancien Régime* architects after the French Revolution), then they had to compromise with clients who controlled the means of building production in Ireland and who were likely to support the status quo. Put another way, it was far easier and cheaper to write a book or join a society than to build a monument to Nationalism. Secondly, the oral tradition of Irish language and literature was diminished but definitely still alive in the nineteenth century, particularly in the remote Western areas. It could therefore be more easily revived than the tradition of Irish building which, with the possible exception of the continual and repetitive production of vernacular housing, was generally perceived to have died out. 'There is no real Irish national style of architecture . . . practically no good architecture was produced in Ireland after the coming of the English', was the view of one extremist.[34]

How then did Irish architects respond to the dilemma created by the idea of a 'national style'? Here it is useful to borrow the framework devised by Lyons for his analysis of Irish literature in the period.[35] At one extreme lay those architects who from the 1840s believed in the possibility of a distinctively 'Irish' national architecture.[36] Usually, though not necessarily, committed Nationalists, the first of note within this group was J. J. McCarthy. McCarthy was the leading Gothic Revivalist in the mid-nineteenth century and a supporter of the 'Young Ireland' movement, but his call for a national style based on Irish Gothic was seen by others as problematic because the source buildings dated from after the first colonisation and were therefore 'tainted' by British influence. Hence by the late-1860s the preferred Nationalist style was almost always the pre-colonial Hiberno-Romanesque.[37] While the nineteenth-century Irish Romanesque Revival did produce a few significant church designs, more commonly it resulted in the superficial application of romanticised Celtic symbolism such as round-towers, shamrocks, harps, wolfhounds, and Celtic crosses. This sham tendency was even more pronounced in the Nationalist applied arts of the period, and not surprisingly was repeatedly criticised. A more imaginative approach appeared to be introduced into the Hiberno-Romanesque style at the turn of the century by the talented young architect, William Scott. He designed a series of bold, and often polemically Nationalist buildings such as St Enda's Church in Spiddal, Co. Galway (1904–07; see Fig. 2).[38] At one level, Scott can be said to have been the nearest to an architectural equivalent of the Celtic Literary Revival: for instance, it was he who refurbished Yeats' famous Ballylee Tower in Co. Galway (1917–18). However, Scott was never a zealous Romanesque Revivalist. Rather, as will be seen below, it was his commitment to the English Arts and Crafts that allowed him to use a free-style Romanesque when he felt it appropriate. All in all, the structure of British cultural domination appears to have been too strong for would-be Nationalist architects to overcome. In the early-1920s, the *Irish Builder* wrote in retrospect:

> It is thirty years now since the beginning of the modern Irish renaissance in Literature and Art, and much has been achieved in that period, notably in dramatic art, but architecture has been left out in the cold.[39]

It is a view echoed by recent historians. 'The hopes of those who had wished for a distinctly Irish style of architecture to emerge from the Celtic Revival were not realized,' Sheehy has observed.[40] For example, there was certainly nothing like the innovative and romantic variant of Neo-Classical architecture found in turn-of-the-century Finland in the designs of Lars Sonck and Eliel Saarinen, produced as the result of cultural Nationalism in another peripheral European nation in response to domination by a powerful political neighbour. And as a postscript from Ireland in the 1920s, whenever triumphant Nationalists

Fig 2. W. A. Scott: Spiddal Church in Co. Galway (1904–07)

(including a few Government ministers) called on architects to create a national style for the new Irish Free State, their calls fell on deaf ears. 'No country has a style of architecture which can be classed entirely as its own', wrote one architect dismissively in 1923; 'all it can do is to dress a tradition in a national garb.'[41]

If the latter represented the dominant view amongst Irish architects, there remained the question of which tradition to follow. Lyons has described a position within Irish literary circles which sought to bypass the reality of British domination by looking for 'cosmopolitan' inspiration from countries beyond. 'Should Ireland try to establish a purely native school of building or should she open her doors to the art of the world?', inquired the Unionist *Irish Times* in 1922; '. . . The best way to encourage the development of Irish genius is to feed it on universal beauty.'[42] However, it is difficult to find any substantial evidence of cosmopolitanism in Irish architecture. One possible source of inspiration was of course the USA, with its large population of Irish immigrants, but no substantive architectural links can be traced. Indeed, it tended to be English architects who promoted the virtues of American Beaux-Arts architecture and town planning.[43] The example of Continental Europe was nearer to hand, but not till after the formation of the independent Irish Free State in 1922 were even the first hesitant connections made. William Butler Yeats, now a distinguished senator, went to Stockholm in 1924 to collect the Nobel Literature Prize. On his return he recommended to Irish architects that they strive for an approach similar to that found in Romantic Nationalist buildings in Sweden.[44] Yeats, however, could offer no real direction beyond a vague assertion that what was needed somehow was a balance between architectural tradition and innovation. Quite simply, there was in Ireland no framework for the type of cosmopolitanism that enabled, for example, Josef Chochol and a few colleagues in Prague before the First World War to look to Parisian Cubism as an architectural style that could finally erase Viennese domination. In Ireland it was not until the late-1920s that interest first grew in European Modernism, and even then it took a further decade and the continuing influence of British practitioners before the new approach amounted to a significant movement.[45]

Instead, most Irish architects in the late-nineteenth and early-twentieth centuries supported a position that Lyons has described as an 'Anglo-Irish' cultural identity. This bi-partisan approach sought consciously to create an Irish dimension that was based on acknowledged English precedent. It demonstrated above all a pragmatic acceptance of British influence in Ireland, and thereby could appeal to Unionists as well as non-militant Nationalists. The fundamental tenet was that the search for a 'national Irish' or even a 'cosmopolitan' approach was inherently misguided, since any genuine architectural style could not be instantly adopted but had to be evolved over a long period of time.[46] This of course immediately closed down many options. It meant, in effect, that the field was open to re-enact the battle then raging within British architecture between the Neo-Vernacular Arts and Crafts movement, which was in notable decline after 1900, and those who supported the Neo-Classical Revival, which was in the ascendant in Britain from around 1906. Irish architects in the Arts and Crafts camp argued not for a simple copying of English mentors such as Richard Norman Shaw or his followers, but rather a development of the Vernacular Revival approach that was 'based upon our own climate, our own materials, our own way of life, and our own landscape'.[47] Here the most talented exponent was once again William Scott, who, after a spell at the prestigious Architects Department of the London County Council where he designed Arts and Crafts fire-stations at West Hampstead (1901) and elsewhere, returned to Ireland in 1902. His subsequent work was predominantly in a Neo-Vernacular manner which relied heavily on the work of two leading British exponents, Charles Voysey and William Lethaby. Examples of Scott's designs include the eclectic, thatched dwellings for a model industrial 'garden village' at Sheestown, Co. Kilkenny (1907 – see Fig. 3), and, as will be seen in Chapter 1, his contribution to the pre-war labourers' cottages that were built in South Co. Dublin.[48]

As in Britain, supporters of the Arts and Crafts in Ireland increasingly came under attack from Neo-Classical partisans both before and after the First World War. Joining in the assault were such distinguished British classicists as Professor Charles Reilly, head of the Liverpool University School of Architec-

Fig 3. W. A. Scott: foremen's cottages at 'Kilkenny Garden Village' (1907)

ture, and Albert Richardson, who gave high praise to the undoubtedly impressive public buildings of Georgian Dublin in his major tome, *Monumental Classic Architecture in Great Britain and Ireland in the Eighteenth and Nineteenth Centuries* (1914). Richardson took up a professorial role in 1919 as head of the Bartlett School of Architecture at University College London, and on a subsequent visit to Dublin he asked his audience:

> Why is it necessary for Irish architects to follow the prevalent fashion of England [Arts and Crafts], and import ideas of hooded gables and half-baked systems of tile-hanging . . . when such excellent material exists as that offered by the Irish section of the national tradition?[49]

The last phrase was a calculated attempt to capitalise on the pride felt by the Irish cultured elite in the Anglo-Irish Ascendancy's contribution to eighteenth-century Neo-Classicism. The Irish Georgian Society had been formed in 1908, and fed on the popular and nostalgic myth that the buildings from the time of 'Grattan's Parliament' were the symbols of a halcyon period of national independence prior to the Act of Union.[50] A more contemporary Neo-Classical argument was put forward by Charles Reilly when he declared that Beaux-Arts design, learned along the lines of the American university system, was the only way out of the morass of Arts and Crafts amateurism and individualism. It was a message that appealed especially to the leading Neo-Classical propagandist in Ireland, R. M. Butler. Editor of the *Irish Builder* between 1899 and 1935, and also Albert Richardson's guide on his visits to Dublin, Butler realised his ambition when in 1924 he was appointed as Professor of Architecture at University College Dublin. It was he who set up the basis for a Neo-Classical course in emulation of his mentors, Richardson and Reilly, writing that:

> This means that the ideal set before the future students of architecture in Ireland is an academic one, conforming in time to the model of Liverpool University, the Ecole des Beaux-Arts, and the American University schools . . . ultimately this will lead to the establishment in Ireland of a strong, efficient 'School' of architecture.[51]

Thus in Ireland, as in Britain, the battle had been all but won by the Neo-Classicists after the First World War. One area of agreement amongst Irish practitioners lay in the belief that the best architecture in Ireland was, as a result of economic and climatic factors, distinguished by an austere simplicity. 'In their massive buildings, their simple roofs, and their quiet but effective grouping of blocks of buildings, there is much to be admired and followed as a lead at the present time . . . Their decoration was simple, but not the less effective', declared William Scott of the ancient builders of Ireland. From a different perspective, R. M. Butler expressed the view that the new Irish Neo-Classical school should, 'in view of our native building materials, our resources, and our traditions, be of a very simple style, bold and vigorous, but very refined—indeed almost severe'.[52] These attempts to posit an ideology of essential simplicity in Irish architecture were not to be without significance in the design of early state housing. Yet it was, however, to prove to be only a minor graft on to a condition in which British ideas were clearly dominant.

Turning now to the third historiographical issue, there is a clear discrepancy between the abundance of published research on housing history in Britain and the paucity of work on the same subject in Ireland. In general, this is because of a long-standing interest in Britain in the historical development of the urban working class. This has in turn prompted much analysis of the process by which (however reluctantly) the British Government in 1919 took over the primary responsibility for housing this class and introduced subsidised rents. The first histories of British state housing were written from the perspective of the post-war Keynesian Welfare State. As such, they adopted a teleological construct in which an apparently inevitable and linear process of state intervention was set in motion in the mid-nineteenth century by a growing perception that private enterprise could no longer provide for those at the bottom of the rent spectrum.[53] The outlines of this teleological story are familiar enough now. State regulation over public health standards gave way in the large cities to Victorian semi-philanthropic housing companies, which used either multi-storey tenement blocks or, for suburban schemes, the more traditional English model of two-storey terraced houses. In turn, these companies were superseded by local authority housebuilding, which came to be subsidised after the First World War in order to build low-density suburban cottage estates. This policy gave way to slum clearance and inner-city flats in the 1930s, and the ground was set for the realisation of the mass housing programme of the Welfare State. As explanations of Welfarism, these studies tended to combine what Derek Fraser has termed a 'whig' (i.e. liberal-progressivist) interpretation of evolutionary growth, and a 'pragmatic' or 'bureaucratic' justification of the process by which the state came to acquire incrementally new housing responsibilities.[54] The liberal-progressivist analysis was, however, shown to be increasingly inadequate by the new British socio-economic history initiated by the urban history of Jim Dyos in the early-1960s, and by Gareth Stedman Jones' classic study of working-class housing as an aspect of late-Victorian class relations in the East End of London.[55] The economic insights provided by such analyses had by the early-1980s fed through to a new phase of housing history which, appropriately for the time at which the Welfare State was being dismantled in Britain, specifically rejected the notion of evolutionary development. 'There was no inevitability in the acceptance of subsidised public housing as the end result of policy, as the experience of other countries makes perfectly clear', Martin Daunton has written; 'The historian should ask why one particular solution to the housing problem was selected from the wide range of possibilities.'[56] Hence attention became focused on explaining the decisive moment, some time around the First World War, when the British Government first committed itself to a policy of subsidised state housing. Before looking at current historical explanations of this development, it is worth restating just why this moment is seen as so important.

It has often been pointed out that there was some degree of financial assistance implicit in all British housing legislation ever since the first Shaftesbury Housing Acts of 1851. However, financial help to housing agencies in Britain prior to 1914 remained minimal, and was limited to two specific forms. Firstly, the provision of public loans from the Exchequer at interest rates slightly below the general 'market-rate' was contained in both the 1875 Cross Act and the 1890 Housing Act. But at no point before the First World War did the Treasury ever incur a loss by permitting housing loans to be granted at rates lower than it could borrow itself, since to have done so would have meant a centralised subsidy. Indeed, when such a possibility was mooted during the lengthy preparations for the 1909 Housing and Town Planning Act, it was rejected outright by the incumbent Liberal Government. The second form of financial assistance did involve an actual capital loss, but, importantly, this was a loss only to the rate income of local authorities and definitely not to the Exchequer. For example, the 1875 Cross Act allowed local authorities to sell land to semi-philanthropic housing companies at a sum below that necessary to meet the expense of site acquisition. This 'writing-down' of site costs was intended to help ensure that the joint-stock companies could pay their stipulated 5 per cent dividend to investors, and hence, for ideological purposes, to sustain the belief that working-class housebuilding represented an economic proposition. The aim was never to provide cheaper rents for tenants, and for this reason it has been described by Merrett as being at best a fallacious 'indirect subsidy'.⁵⁷ Another instance was the decision by Liverpool Corporation in the early-1880s to deliberately set rent levels that would not be sufficient to cover the capital expenditure on housing schemes. It was a policy that Pooley has called 'local subsidy'.⁵⁸ But, significantly, it must be remembered that in both instances the loss had to be met by a compensating increase in local rates, and that the rates, as historians have pointed out, constituted a notoriously regressive tax system.⁵⁹ Hence the net effect would have been simply to worsen the financial burden on the working classes in the city, possibly even on those who were actually being rehoused. This explains why such ventures were rare, and why they cannot be regarded as being a genuine subsidy. They were certainly not perceived as subsidy at the time, as will be seen in Chapter 3 when examining British reactions to precedents in Irish housing policy. Rather, following the writings of that early evangelist of 'municipal socialism', Sydney Webb, a necessary distinction has been given to those state policies that are not merely collectivist but are geared explicitly to effect a redistribution of wealth to the working class.⁶⁰ Thus the term 'subsidy' should be used only to describe the point when national wealth that has been *collected centrally* via a system of *progressive taxation* (however imperfect), is then *redistributed centrally* as a net gain to the working class through subsidised rents on new dwellings.

Three revisionist theories were put forward in the early-1980s to explain why the British Government had decided to introduce centralised subsidy for working-class housing through the mechanism of the 1919 Addison Housing Act. The first, by Avner Offer, argues that state intervention was the result of an inherent contradiction in the capitalist housing market, first recognised by Frederick Engels in the 1870s, and which by the property slump of 1905–12 had created an endemic crisis.⁶¹ Housing capitalists, whether speculative builders or private landlords, now found that the profit return on working-class dwellings had been eroded by a range of factors. On the supply side, the higher construction standards imposed by late-Victorian public health legislation, and the rising interest rates on loans, pushed up the cost of housebuilding and maintenance. On the demand side, the pressure within the capitalist economy to keep wages low (to allow the extraction of surplus value of labour), and the punitive effect of increased local taxation from municipalities starved of central funds, meant that there was little capacity for the working class to pay higher rents. The potential profit available from housing the poorer sections of the working class was now minimal compared with that from housing the better-paid classes. One solution might have been for the Conservative Party, the traditional bastion of property interests, to have come to the financial aid of housebuilders and landlords. However, the deliberate politicisation of the whole issue of land and property ownership by the pre-war Liberal Party ensured that no political group was willing to defend the marginalised and unpopular sector of housing capitalists. The result, Offer argues, was that even before the First World War the Liberal Government was in the position of being forced to intervene itself.⁶² The introduction of rent controls on working-class dwellings under the 1915 Rent Act simply intensified the structural crisis, and meant that in the post-war period the desperate need to maintain the 'reproduction of labour power' forced the state to intervene decisively. This interpretation is of course essentially economic, and is echoed by the writings of Marxist economists on more contemporary housing issues.[63] It is an example of a 'capitalistic' theory that sees the development of Welfarism in Britain as a product of the state being forced to mediate in class relations in order to sustain the prevailing economic system.[64]

A second, slightly different explanation is given by David Englander.[65] This theory is based on similar economic analysis, but places far more emphasis on the social tensions that had been created by 1914 as the result of the growing political power of working-class tenants. Englander argues that tenants' organisations in several British cities were instrumental in swinging the pendulum of political influence away from what were seen as exploitative landlords: hence it was mass action that effectively undermined the economic basis of the private housing market. The most decisive front was fought in Glasgow, notably in the militancy that provoked the 1915 Rent Act. It was the British Government's inability to repeal this legislation in the volatile post-war political climate (indeed, rent control was extended to cover the lower middle classes), that made it decide reluctantly to temporarily subsidise new working-class housing. This account of early Welfarism blends the 'capitalistic' theory with a more 'democratic' perspective that gives a decisive role to mass consumer demand.[66] A third interpretation has been put forward by Mark Swenarton, and sees the state housing campaign after the First World War as being motivated principally by political ideology.[67] Swenarton argues that the overriding concern of the British Government was to maintain social stability. Returning servicemen had to be convinced that their best interests lay in a continuation of the current social system, rather than its overthrow as had happened in Russia. Subsidised state housing thus formed an *ad hoc* 'insurance against revolution', designed and implemented from above as an instrument of political control over the working class. The dramatic termination of the initial post-war campaign in July 1921 was prompted by the Government's realisation that social revolution was now unlikely, given that the threat from labour power had collapsed along with the post-war economic boom. Swenarton also accounts for another important aspect of post-war housing that is not dealt with in other theories. Central to Swenarton's case is that the *qualitative* improvement in design standards of post-war housing was conceived as a tangible demonstration of the irrelevance of revolutionary action. It is the only explanation that links policy developments with architectural ideas, and in so doing demonstrates that early state housing was the product not only of economic and political factors, but also of the ideological nature of design. In general, Swenarton's thesis augments the 'capitalistic' theory of Welfarism by introducing what Fraser has termed a 'conspiratorial' use of state ideology to delude the working class into supporting the existing social order.[68]

Martin Daunton has for the last decade been the principal interpreter of British housing history. He has suggested that the three explanations outlined above might not necessarily be mutually exclusive, and at the same time has raised serious questions about each.[69] Daunton has pointed out, in relation to Offer's analysis, that it is far from certain that profit erosion in the working-class sector of the housing market was seen at the time as (or indeed really was) a terminal structural crisis, rather than a temporary cyclical slump. The emphasis on tenant militancy in Englander's explanation seems to over-estimate its influence on pre-war attitudes to housing capitalists, and on the reasons why rent control was so staunchly maintained after the war. Daunton has countered the Swenarton theory by arguing that the use of state housing as a primary instrument of social legitimation was unlikely given that it was slow, expensive, and cumbersome to implement. He has also suggested that the working class was by this point too organised for such a blatant ideological manoeuvre to be effective: social legitimation might have been a secondary benefit of the housing campaign, but not its primary cause. Instead, Daunton has argued that the history of early state housing must be dealt with on a much broader canvas. On one hand, this involves concentrating much less on the atypical or 'pathological' elements of the housing market (local authorities and semi-philanthropic housing companies had built less than one per cent of Britain's housing stock by 1914), and placing much more emphasis on the dominant private speculative sector.[70] Comparative studies with other countries can also be used to throw light on to specific developments in the housing of the working classes in Britain.[71] And in terms of state housing policy, Daunton has called for a broader analysis of economic policy and the relationship between political parties. He has thus stressed that the post-war Coalition Government intended subsidised housing to be a short-term response while rent control continued, and that the policy was always subordinate to the real aim of economic deflation and a return to the 'Gold Standard'. The Government began the policy shift by cutting the post-war housing campaign in mid-1921, but when it was subsequently found to be politically impossible to terminate rent control legislation, then even the Conservative Party was forced reluctantly to retain subsidised local authority housing as a residual activity. The Labour Party by this point formed the principal opposition, and had clearly accepted its role as the champion of ameliorative social democratic reforms within a British state that now consciously portrayed an image of class neutrality. But in reality, the growth trend in housing subsidy in the inter-war period was the Conservative Party's stimulation of middle-class house-ownership through mortgage relief.[72] However, while Daunton's work clearly brings an important breadth to the subject of housing history, the corollary is that he loses sight of two central questions: why precisely did the British Government intervene in working-class housing in 1919, and why did it do so by using such distinctive house designs?

Academic interest in early state housing in Ireland has been far more limited.

The sole pioneer in the field has been Frederick Aalen, a social geographer at Trinity College Dublin.[73] His work has covered almost the entire span of early housing history in Ireland, in particular looking at the semi-philanthropic housing companies of nineteenth-century Dublin, and at local authority housing in both town and country prior to the First World War. Aalen's methodology, however, is essentially descriptive and fragmentary, and has not advanced an adequate *historical* explanation of why Irish state housing developed as it did. His writings have not examined the involvement of the British Government in the process, nor have they pursued the cross-influence with housing policy in Britain. There have in addition been a number of books by other authors that have dealt with wider aspects of housing in Ireland, and these have sometimes contained material on early state housing. Rural authority housing crops up briefly in general studies of Irish vernacular dwellings, and information on early urban schemes has been included as a background for analyses of modern problems such as housing policy in sectarian Belfast.[74] Furthermore, there has been fragmentary coverage of Irish state housing in associated historical disciplines. Studies of social policy have given an overview of the pattern of housing history in Northern Ireland and in the Irish Free State after independence and partition in 1922.[75] Probably the most interesting work has come from socio-economic historians, notably Joseph O'Brien and Mary Daly, and their concern with working-class housing as a key part of wider problems in Dublin prior to the First World War.[76] Attention to early state housing has also resulted from the attempt by Michael Bannon and associates to inaugurate the subject of planning history in Ireland: the problem with this approach, as will be seen in Chapter 4, is that it tends to distort the explanation of housing issues.[77] In the field of architectural history, the two Irish writers who have concentrated on the nineteenth and early-twentieth centuries, Jeanne Sheehy and Sean Rothery, have all but ignored the subject of state housing.[78]

Thus, this study represents the first synthesised historical account of early state housing in Ireland, and it is certainly the only one to draw on source material in both Ireland and Westminster. The methodology used here is based on the innovative approach to architectural history developed in the early-1980s by Adrian Forty and Mark Swenarton at the Bartlett School of Architecture.[79] In emulation of the methodological advances made in other historical disciplines, the intention is to explain changes in architectural design as part of the broader social, economic, and political transformations in society as a whole. Therefore the reader of this book will find that discussions of housing policy and design are consciously interwoven throughout, and that there is an attempt to represent the widest possible range of views of political and economic interest groups in Ireland and Britain. Only in this way can the multifarious influences on Irish state housing be examined within a complex structure of modernisation and Nationalism, and within a condition of cultural reliance on British ideas. Unlike mainland Britain, rural housing was as much a subject of state policy as urban housing, and indeed in the 1880s received far more attention than the problem in Irish towns. The result was that housing policy in late-nineteenth-century Ireland was split into distinct rural and urban initiatives, with the former initially dominant. Chapter 1 therefore looks at pre-war rural housing, and the introduction of the first state subsidies under the Irish Labourers Act. Chapter 2 studies the urban housing question, and the reasons why this issue had become of paramount importance by the First World War, particularly during the Dublin labour crisis of 1913–14. Two short chapters then round off the period before 1914. Chapter 3 traces the influence of Irish state housing precedent on British policy, while the next chapter returns to Dublin to examine the pre-war crusade by supporters of British garden suburb ideals. Chapter 5 then deals with developments in policy and design during the First World War, in light of critical events such as the 1916 Easter Rising and the 1917–18 Irish Convention. The next chapter traces the course of the much disrupted post-war housing campaign in Ireland, while Chapter 7 details the unique programme from 1919 to build cottages directly for ex-servicemen. Then, as a deliberate counterpoint to the preceding analysis, Chapter 8 provides a brief account of housing in Northern Ireland and the Irish Free State after 1922. A final conclusion will draw together the underlying themes raised by the study.

Chapter 1

RURAL HOUSING AND THE STATE IN IRELAND BEFORE THE FIRST WORLD WAR

Any account of Irish state housing must begin with the rural issue. By 1914 a total of nearly 50 000 cottages had been built for agricultural labourers, mostly with subsidy from the Imperial Exchequer. The programme was the result of nationalist agitation by the Irish Parliamentary Party from the early-1880s, and was linked to the demand for redistribution of landownership to tenant-farmers. This chapter will examine the rural housing campaign in light of the complex structural changes in agricultural Ireland. Particular emphasis will be given to the major turning point in 1906, when a substantial increase in rural subsidy was accompanied by the publication of the first official manual of recommended type-plans for state housing.

The nineteenth century saw the confirmation of Ireland as an essentially agricultural nation, with the exception of North-East Ulster. Population growth had been checked (and had probably already begun to reverse), when successive failures of the potato crop during the Great Famine (1845–49) precipitated a dramatic fall from over 8 200 000 people in 1841 to only around 5 200 000 forty years later. Net migration to towns remained slow: in 1881 nearly 75 per cent of Irish people still lived in rural areas.[1] The Famine also appears to have accelerated a major transformation already under way in Irish agriculture.[2] At the start of the nineteenth century, the predominant landownership structure had been that of the Anglo-Irish Protestant Ascendancy letting out parcels of their estates to so-called 'middlemen', who would then sub-let to a farming class of Catholic tenant small-holders (1–15 acres) or marginal cottiers (less than one acre). The farming pattern was labour-intensive tillage of high-yield crops, such as the potato, which could feed a large workforce. This system was showing signs of strain by the 1820s, but it was undoubtedly the chronic manpower shortage after the Famine that speeded up a switch towards larger holdings (15–30 acres, or over) and labour-extensive livestock farming. This created a new structure of small to medium tenant-farmers leasing directly from Ascendancy landowners. Not only were the 'middlemen' finally eliminated, but there was also a dramatic decline in the number of rural labourers available for hire. The degree of agricultural restructuring varied across Ireland. It was most noticeable in the southern and eastern provinces of Munster and Leinster, and could also be detected in rural Ulster.[3] The only real exception was in the poorest western seaboard counties of Connaught, where there persisted a pattern of subsistence cottier farming coupled with seasonal migration to work in Ulster or Britain.

What did not change was the negligible extent of owner-occupation. In 1870 still only 3 per cent of Irish farmers owned their land, and amongst the Ascendancy landlords, fewer than 800 owned half the country.[4] The post-Famine transformation in rural Ireland therefore provided a new focus for the political challenge to the Anglo-Irish Ascendancy. Large landowners were consistently portrayed in Nationalist lore as being mainly absentee, unwilling to invest in land improvements, and rapacious in their pursuit of extortionate rents. Revisionist scholarship has shown much of this to have been overstated: the Ascendancy landownership system does not appear to have held back economic development to the extent claimed, and rent increases and evictions of tenant-farmers were if anything rather on the low side. However, the reality was less relevant than the ideological battle. Thus, while many nineteenth-century Irish landowners like the Duke of Leinster or the Duke of Devonshire did in fact built model cottages for estate workers (and were even encouraged to do so by an annual design prize offered by the Royal Agricultural Society of Ireland), these efforts won few friends. 'Irish landlords as a class have done comparatively little for the comfort of their tenants, whether small cottier farmers or labourers', adjudged the *Irish Builder* in 1871.[5]

Rural class tensions in Ireland could not be ignored by the British Government. 'The role of Irish agriculture', Bew has written, 'was to supply the British market, regardless of broader social and national considerations.'[6] Nearly two-thirds of Irish exports to Britain consisted of agricultural produce, principally the livestock and dairy goods that helped to feed the mainland urban population. The initial concern of successive British Governments after the Famine was to instil free-trade principles into Irish agriculture. It was believed that this would increase productivity and wages, and thereby stifle endemic rural unrest. The Imperial Parliament thus passed the Encumbered Estates Acts to encourage the sale or lease of large holdings to more entrepreneurial farmers. And in addition, the Land Improvement Acts (which began in 1847 as an emergency relief measure) offered low-interest loans from the Irish Board of Works to landowners or farmers, for investment in drainage, land reclamation, and the like.[7] One activity not eligible under the early Land Improvement Acts was housing, and it is necessary to explain why.

Before the Famine, rural housing conditions in Ireland had been truly appalling, and easily amongst the worst in Europe. The 1841 Census showed that 470 000 dwellings, around 40 per cent of the rural housing stock, had only one room.[8] These hovels were commonly known as 'cabins', and were poorly constructed with walls usually of wattle and mud, and roofs of turf or thatch. Most had straw floors since livestock were kept indoors, and chimneys and windows were rare. The next category of dwelling identified by the 1841 Census included modest cottages of between two and four rooms, and these accounted for another 490 000 units (42 per cent of the stock). However, even these apparently better dwellings were prone to overcrowding, and thus the Census also recorded separately the pattern of occupation. Using this indicator, then, a total nearer 540 000 dwellings (44 per cent of the stock) in rural Ireland fell into the lowest category of '4th Class' accommodation. The highest proportion of substandard dwellings was to be found in Connaught, but much of Munster was also wretched. In Co. Cork alone, in 1841 there were some 16 000 one-room 'cabins', and in the very poorest districts this type of dwelling formed 80 per cent of all dwellings.[9] It was a desperate situation much commented upon at the time. As early as the mid-1830s, a Royal Commission examining the conditions of the rural poor recommended that the mud 'cabin' which littered the Irish countryside be replaced by healthy cottages.[10] A similar view was expressed by an official inquiry into Irish agriculture in 1843–44, and in the same decade Frederick Engels observed that in Ireland most rural workers 'live in single-roomed cabins built of mud . . . which are hardly fit for animals'.[11] However, the decimation of the population by the Famine had a striking effect. Reduced demand for housing meant that the worst hovels could be abandoned, and a period of rising Irish rural prosperity during the 1850s also saw a modest revival in investment in estate improvement and rural housing.[12] By 1861 the number of one-room 'cabins' had plunged to 85 000 (10 per cent of the stock), and the proportion of '4th Class' accommodation now formed only 15 per cent of rural dwellings.

Yet although the Famine took away much of the urgency of the rural housing problem, there was a by-product of the British Government's free-trade strategy in the 1850s that needed to be addressed. If larger farm units were to be created, then in some cases this would require new dwellings to be built if none were otherwise available. Hence the Land Improvement Acts were extended in 1860 to allow public loans (at 6.5 per cent interest over 22 years) to landowners or lessees, in order to build homes for themselves and their labourers. To accompany the new borrowing powers, in 1869 the Irish Board of Works published a full set of suggested plans, plus details and specifications, for dwellings ranging from humble cottages to substantial farmhouses.[13] This manual was an official version of the books on model rural housing written by English architects from the late-eighteenth century, and it is significant that the designs it contained ignored the Irish vernacular (the latter was typically an unadorned single-storey cottage, one room deep, and built of rendered mass stone walling with a sod grass or thatched timber roof).[14] Instead, the four recommended plans for labourers' cottages given by the Irish Board of Works all had a layout closer to the English model (see Fig. 4). One half of the dwelling comprised a double-height living room/kitchen, and also contained the entrance (in all but one case this had a lobby) and a central chimney. The other half was two rooms deep, and had a first floor level reached by a ladder-stair from the living room below. This allowed the possibility of either three or four bedrooms, and in general the space standards envisaged were much more generous than in the usual Irish cottage. The living

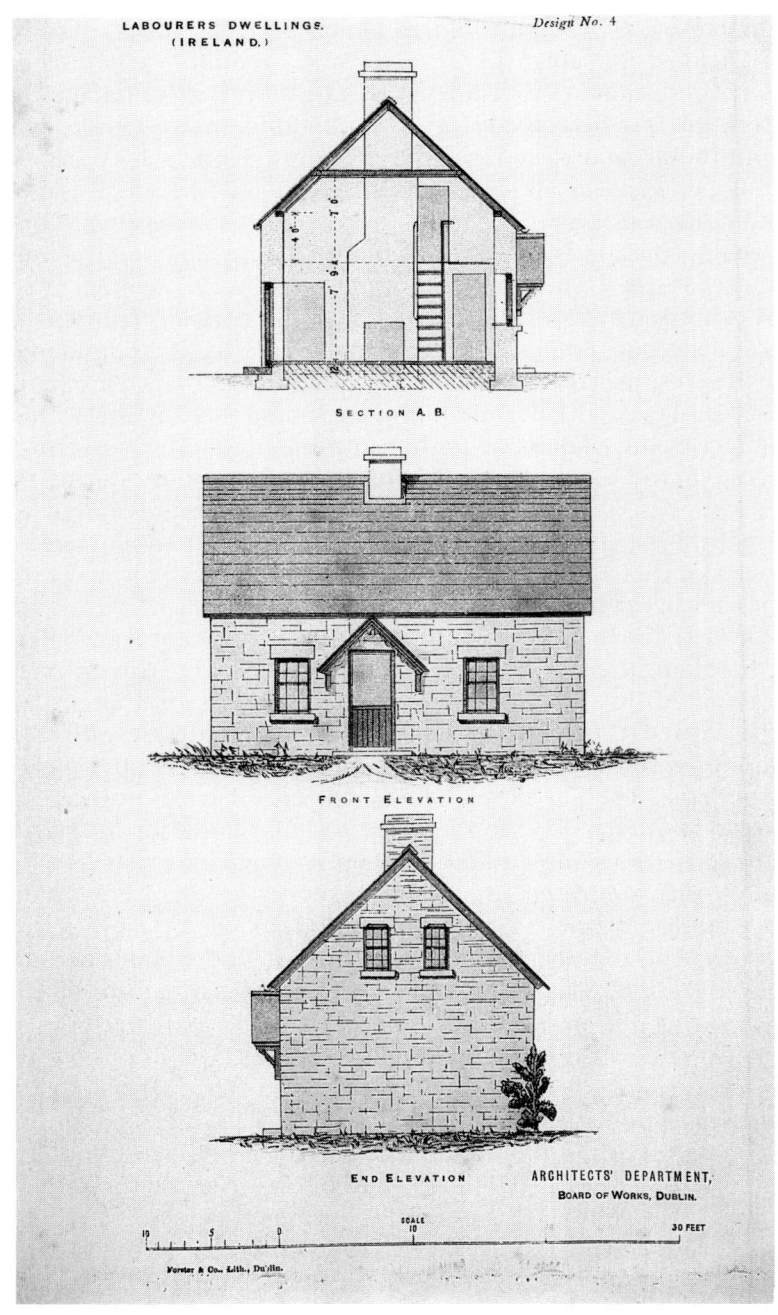

Fig 4. Irish Board of Works: recommended two-storey, four-room type (1869)

room/kitchen ranged between 156 and 288 square feet in area, and bedrooms from 72 to 120 square feet. Construction was likewise atypical, being of unrendered masonry or brickwork with a slate roof. Indeed, the watered-down blend of Gothic Revival and Neo-Vernacular styles in the elevations showed clearly the reliance on conceptions of the English Picturesque.[15] Features such as ornamental bargeboards and front porches were obvious anglicisations, and in using them the Irish Board of Works emulated the trend towards a non-Irish character displayed in the 'improved' estate cottages built by Anglo-Irish landowners at Enniskerry, Co. Wicklow, and elsewhere.[16] In the 1870s, some designs by Edward Townshend for estate labourers' dwellings in Co. Galway and Co. Mayo shared strong similarities with one of the recommended alternatives of the Irish Board of Works.[17] But it is hardly surprising that this early attempt to 'anglicise' rural housing found little support in Nationalist Ireland. In the event, the policy of housing loans under the Land Improvement Acts (like the whole strategy of the British Government to attract entrepreneurial farmers) was an almost complete failure. A later official estimate was that the 1860 Act produced only between 600 and 800 cottages in all of Ireland; activity in Ulster appears to have been particularly sparse.[18] The measure soon lay all but forgotten.

THE IRISH LAND ACTS AND THE BACKGROUND TO THE LABOURERS ACT

In 1870 the Liberal Government led by William Gladstone reacted to rural grievances in the wake of Fenianism, by passing the first of a wave of Irish Land Acts.[19] The measure gave greater protection of tenure and rent to tenant-farmers, and implied a possible 'dual ownership' whereby property might be shared with landowners. The 1870 Act itself had little effect, but an ensuing period of moderate prosperity in rural Ireland led to a brief respite in agitation. This situation was soon drastically reversed by the 'great depression' that hit Europe in the late-1870s and lasted for a decade. In agriculture, the causes lay in a series of poor harvests in countries such as Ireland, and a collapse in prices due to the influx of cheap grain and beef from the USA.[20] Conditions were especially severe for farmers in the poorest western regions in Connaught and Munster, and it was these areas that fuelled the famous 'Land War' waged by Michael Davitt and the Land League from 1879 to 1882.[21] Out of this bitter struggle against the British Government and the Ascendancy elite, came the so-called 'New Departure' of Irish Nationalism in the early-1880s. The most influential strand was now the constitutional approach advocated by the Irish Parliamentary Party (hereafter the Irish Party, or IPP). The party's organisational machine, the National League, soon dominated Irish politics outside Ulster, and skilfully blended a heterogeneous mix of tenant-farmers, shop-keepers, urban professionals, and support from the Catholic clergy. In the Imperial Parliament in Westminster, the Irish Party under the leadership of

Charles Stewart Parnell employed obstructionary tactics to advance the key demands of Home Rule plus land reform.

In 1881 the new Gladstone Government, under pressure from the IPP, passed a far more ambitious Land Act. This measure successfully undermined the Land League by granting fair-rent control, fixity of tenure on leases, and freedom of sale; all to be overseen by a new Irish Land Commission. 'Dual ownership' of land had now replaced free trade as the guiding principle, and in holding down rents during a period of low agricultural prices, the result was a squeeze on landowners' profits.[22] Soon there would be little other alternative for landowners than to sell off land. Thus the 1881 Act also tentatively conceded the need for state participation in the redistribution of Irish landownership. There was no subsidy, but public loans for up to 75 per cent of the purchase price were made available to tenant-farmers (at 5 per cent interest over 35 years), if the owner was willing to sell. A further consequence of eroded landowners' profits was the depletion of new housing for agricultural labourers. As a leading Conservative peer put it, the 1881 Land Act had 'destroyed, to a great extent, in Ireland the only person who was in the habit of building cottages—namely, the landlord'.[23] But although some minor clauses in the 1881 Act (and in a further measure the next year) allowed public loans for labourers' cottages, the terms were too limited and found only minimal application.[24]

The half-heartedness shown towards labourers' housing by the 1881 Land Act was symptomatic of the fact that Irish rural labourers had been little involved in the 'Land War'. Indeed, the post-Famine transformations in Irish agriculture were causing a steady 'disappearance' of this class. From 1841 to 1881 the number of agricultural labourers fell from just under 900 000 (56 per cent of the rural workforce) to around 360 000 (38 per cent of the workforce).[25] Equally important, it would also appear that the greatest decline was amongst labourers who leased some land; since they, being slightly better off, were more able to turn themselves into farmers, or else to emigrate to the USA. Labourers with no access to land were in a worse position. Clark has estimated that 'landless' labourers thus formed a consistent 25 per cent of the rural workforce in late-nineteenth-century Ireland, and as a class came to account for nearly 70 per cent of all agricultural labourers by 1881.[26] The outcome in areas where poor landless labourers were most concentrated, such as Co. Limerick and Co. Cork, was a heightened class differentiation between farmer and labourer. This forced the Land League to address labourers' grievances, and in particular the Irish Party began to realise that sectional rural conflict posed a threat to its aim of building broad-based support for parliamentary Nationalism around the issue of land redistribution.[27] At the National Convention in September 1881, Parnell called on Irish labourers to stand alongside the tenant-farmers, and he is reputed to have become further converted to the labourers' cause during his imprisonment in Kilmainham Jail the following year. Under the terms of the famous pact that he signed with Gladstone, the renunciation of extra-parliamentary agitation was to be repaid by further land reforms in Ireland. On release, Parnell declared at the foundation of the Irish Labour and Industry Union in August 1882 that 'the national credit is pledged to securing for the Irish labourers some such amelioration in their own condition as they have so loyally striven to bring about in the condition of the tenant-farmers'.[28] It would appear that the twin demands of labourers at the time were for a decent home and a small piece of land at a fair rent.[29] The latter was potentially divisive, since tenant-farmers with their eyes on purchase clearly did not want to give any land away. Parnell tried to get round this problem by promising plots of unwanted semi-waste land to landless labourers, but it was hardly an appealing offer.[30] Better housing was a far less controversial concession.

It was also the case that the post-Famine structural changes in rural Ireland had by the 1880s both intensified and highlighted the relative housing hardship of landless workers. The 1881 Census showed that there remained only about 40 000 one-room 'cabins' (5 per cent of the rural housing stock). Overcrowded '4th Class' accommodation now formed just 7 per cent of all dwellings; only in Co. Kerry and Co. Limerick in west Munster did the figure still exceed 10 per cent. Yet it was exactly this worst type of cottage in which an estimated 60 000 agricultural labourers and their families were still compelled to live.[31] The squalor of such dwellings prompted the *Irish Builder* to call for the application of modern sanitary science to rural housing design.[32] And one American observer wrote in 1882 that:

> In some parts of the South and West one often finds the people living in small mud huts one storey high, often with no floor, window or chimney, and the poorest conceivable sort of furniture. In these wretched huts the man and his wife and children live with the pigs and chickens, the cow and the donkey, if the family are rich enough to own these animals. The manure heap and green pool are sometimes so near the door that one has difficulty in entering. The inside is often much more like a very poor stable than a human habitation.[33]

Concern about the special plight of the Irish rural labourer even surfaced in the House of Lords, with one peer noting that this class 'had always been very poorly paid, fed, clothed and housed'.[34] Yet the persistence of bad rural housing in Ireland in the 1880s must not be overstated: equally appalling conditions could have been found in the poorest English counties of the West Country and East Anglia.[35] What was different about rural Ireland was the determination of the Irish Party to win the landless labourers over to constitutional Nationalism through the offer of better housing. The Liberal Government was also willing to concede this social improvement so as to mediate the conflict between farmers and labourers. Thus, ultimately, action to improve the dwellings of Irish rural workers in the early 1880s was due to political factors rather than a perceived shortage or housing need *per se*.

THE FIRST PHASE OF THE IRISH LABOURERS ACTS FROM 1883 TO 1906

Rural housing from the 1880s was dealt with under a distinct legislative code known as the Irish Labourers Acts. There were in fact two distinct phases of the Labourers Acts prior to the First World War, as was later pointed out in a wartime report by a British official.[36] The initial period lasted from 1883 to 1906; the second, and far more comprehensive phase, from 1906 to 1914.

In 1883 the Irish Party brought in a private members Bill which, with the support of the Opposition Tories and the Gladstone Government, became the first Irish Labourers Act.[37] Intended by the IPP as proof of the validity of the parliamentary approach, what the measure did was to extract the relevant clauses out of the Land Acts and create a corollary rural housing code.[38] Twelve or more local ratepayers could now apply to the local Board of Guardians (then responsible for rural sanitation) to ask them to carry out a housing scheme for labourers in the vicinity. If a proposal was approved by the Irish Local Government Board (hereafter ILGB), and then sanctioned by Parliament, the Guardians could apply to the Irish Board of Works for a public loan over a maximum period of 60 years. The model used by the Irish Party was that of contemporary British urban housing legislation, i.e. the 1866 Torrens Act and the 1875 Cross Act. Indeed, the intention was simply to extend these measures, which hitherto had applied only to the five largest Irish cities, to rural districts.[39] This led to a curious situation whereby powers devised initially to facilitate slum clearance in London were applied on behalf of Irish rural labourers. Certainly the incumbent Chief Secretary for Ireland was worried about setting a precedent which might then be demanded for rural Britain, and he consulted the Treasury about the likely cost.[40] Alarm about the implication of the 1883 Labourers Act was greatest in the House of Lords, where one peer complained that if 'the State built houses for the working classes, he did not see why they should not undertake to clothe them also'.[41] Another warned that, by killing off private enterprise in Irish rural housing, soon 'they would be obliged to proceed more upon what were called socialistic principles, and to insist on local authorities building cottages'.[42] To allay such fears, tight controls were imposed. The maximum rate that could be levied for housing was set at 1s in the £1; the 1883 Act had a five-year limit; and only bona fide agricultural labourers could be housed. Importantly, each cottage was given a half-acre of land to supplement the tenant's income, meaning that the British Government was helping to create a quasi-cottier class.

Given that the first Labourers Act was based on slum legislation, it soon proved to be cumbersome in practice. In 1884 a parliamentary committee, including Parnell and other IPP members, decided that easier legal procedure and more favourable loan terms were needed.[43] In 1885 the new Tory Government (at that point exploring the possibility of an alliance with the Irish Party) demonstrated their support for Irish rural amelioration by pushing through an amending Labourers Act.[44] The 1885 Act made the Irish Privy Council rather than the Imperial Parliament the final appeal body, and allowed Boards of Guardians to repair existing cottages as well. The loan terms from the Treasury were also improved.[45] The popularity of the policy in Ireland was undoubted. Rural labourers helped the Irish Party to sweep to a convincing victory throughout most of Ireland in the 1885 General Election.[46] This prompted the IPP to push for further concessions. The Labourers Act of 1886 extended housing eligibility to anyone who worked part-time as an agricultural labourer, but might otherwise have another trade. Together these stimuli resulted in the first peak in output in the late-1880s, with a total of 2188 cottages being built in 1888–89 (see Diagram B and Table 1).[47] By the early 1890s, after a decade of operation, 94 out of 161 rural Poor Law Unions had either completed or at least begun housing schemes.[48]

A striking feature of the first phase of the Labourers Acts was the consistent regional disparity in activity (Table 3). Around three out of every five cottages built were in the south-western province of Munster, where there was a high proportion of low-paid labourers. Virtually all the other two-fifths were in Leinster, where agricultural wages were slightly higher. Within these two southern provinces, it would appear that schemes were most likely in districts where local labourers' associations, at the urging of the Irish Party, were best organised.[49] The converse was that only negligible numbers of cottages were built in Connaught or Ulster. Connaught was the poorest province. Rural authorities were handicapped by extremely low rate incomes, and the prevalence of the cottier system meant that there were relatively few eligible agricultural labourers.[50] Wages were higher in Ulster, but here the Unionist rural authorities were notoriously reluctant to burden the rates, and were generally opposed to legislation so clearly associated with the Nationalist cause. By 1892 only two Ulster rural authorities in Ballycastle and Ballymena had acted, and they had built just 26 cottages between them.[51]

POLITICAL INFLUENCES ON THE FIRST PHASE OF THE LABOURERS ACTS

In the late-1880s the Labourers Acts became, like all other matters, overshadowed by the political polarisation in both Ireland and Britain over the issue of Irish self-government. The key question asked in Ireland about any initiative was whether it would help or hinder British rule. In 1886 the Irish Party for the first time held the balance of power in the House of Commons. Gladstone, previously intransigent, now underwent a complete conversion and introduced the first Home Rule Bill. This measure envisaged that Ireland would remain firmly within the United Kingdom, yet with greater autonomy over domestic policy (though not over key areas such as defence, or customs and excise). In the event Gladstone's Bill and its successor in 1893 were humiliatingly defeated by the combined opposition of Ulster Unionists,

Conservatives, and Liberal Unionists (several leading Liberals, notably Joseph Chamberlain, crossed the floor of the Commons over the issue). The failure of Home Rule fuelled the resumption of land agitation in the 'Plan of Campaign' of 1886–91, and aggravated the split within the Irish Party that followed Parnell's fall in 1891. The rift was not healed until the rapid growth of a rival United Irish League amongst western small-holders prompted the IPP's new leader, John Redmond, to reunite most of the Nationalists' factions in 1900.

Meanwhile, the Conservative Party, now calling themselves Unionists, enjoyed an unbroken spell of rule from 1893 to 1905. In response to the policy of Home Rule, the Conservatives developed a balanced strategy known as 'constructive Unionism'. State intervention in Irish economic and social reform was used to prove that Ireland's best future progress lay with Britain. Opponents derided the policy as trying to 'kill Home Rule by kindness', yet more likely the Tory Cabinet wanted to give British rule the best possible image, and thereby to reassure waverers amongst the Tory Party and Liberal Unionists of the need to reject any manifestation of Home Rule.[52] The detailed policy of 'constructive Unionism' was worked out in Dublin Castle during the stints as Chief Secretary of the future Prime Minister, Arthur Balfour (1887–91), his brother Gerald Balfour (1895–1900), and lastly George Wyndham (1900–1905). The most conspicuous legacy was the reform of Irish local government in 1898 along the lines of the new British model. Also important were unique new official bodies such as the Department of Agriculture and Technical Instruction, and, in 1891, the Congested Districts Board.

The Congested Districts Board was a quasi-autonomous development agency set up to provide relief and stimulate economic growth in western Ireland.[53] The area of operation was restricted to the poorest rural areas with an average rateable value of less than 30s per head, which in actuality meant the unproductive small-holdings of Connaught. The Board's dominion at first covered 3 500 000 acres and 500 000 people; later, in 1909, it was doubled to incorporate nearly a third of Ireland, including parts of Munster (and was given control over land purchase to consolidate farm holdings). Yet for all the money and effort that went into projects such as drainage schemes, road building, and fisheries, the success of the Congested Districts Board in stimulating economic growth was far more limited than its supporters claimed.[54] This was clearly the case in terms of the powers given to the Board to build or renovate cottages, wherever land reorganisation required it.[55] Housing remained a minor part of the Congested Districts Board's activities, and those dwellings that were provided—mostly in the very poorest coastal areas—were generally for small farmers and cottiers rather than labourers. By 1919, after nearly three decades, it had built barely more than 3000 new cottages itself, and had given grants to occupants for the rebuilding of a similar number.[56] Such was the apparent inertia that a Royal Commission in 1906 even considered the possibility that the Board be given a share of Labourers Acts funds, in order to be forced to take on the major housing responsibility in its area.[57]

The relative disinterest of the Congested Districts Board in rural housing was reflected in the oft-remarked utilitarianism of its cottages. In 1903 the Board's Estates Department followed the example of the Irish Board of Works in the late-1860s, and produced a series of recommended plans; these were subsequently amended slightly, and reissued in 1914.[58] Since the cottages were intended for small farmers or cottiers, space standards were higher than for those under the Labourers Acts. Living rooms varied from 169 to 249 square feet, and bedrooms between 79 and 229 square feet. Yet the eight layouts given by the Board were of an extremely basic design. There were two principal types (Figs 5–6). The cheaper was a single-storey detached bungalow, with two bedrooms and a large living room/kitchen containing a further bed recess. The other type was a double-storey detached cottage with three bedrooms (or two bedrooms plus a parlour). The latter type were generally built in the slightly more prosperous inland districts and, after 1909, in south-west Munster. Hearths were central, and in most cases a dairy was attached. Elevations were of plain, rendered masonry walls and simple slate roofs to ward off the harsh western climate. A decorated bargeboard might be provided on flank walls, but the overall severity of the dwellings can be seen from contemporary photographs of Co. Roscommon and elsewhere.[59] The *Irish Builder* described the Congested Districts Board cottages as 'hideously ugly, in many cases badly built, and always a blot on the landscape'.[60]

Returning now to the mainstream Labourers Acts, the policy of 'constructive Unionism' also indirectly influenced the housing programme as a consequence of further Irish Land Acts. The Conservative Government from the 1890s now offered state compensation to induce Ascendancy landowners to sell land to tenants. Following a special cross-party Land Conference in late 1902, the revolutionary 1903 Wyndham Act provided even more generous subsidy terms. Bonuses were paid to landlords on sale, and tenants were wooed by interest repayments that worked out at 20 per cent less than their rent had been hitherto.[61] The result was the formation of a new peasant proprietorship and the steady extinction of the Anglo-Irish landed class. Whereas in 1870 only 3 per cent of Irish farmers had owned their land, by 1908 this had leapt to almost 50 per cent (by the early 1920s the figure was nearly 70 per cent, and independence saw the process completed).[62] The Tory Party showed far less concern for the issue of Irish rural housing, but it was realised that the process of land transfer had secondary economic consequences. 'Owner-occupation cannot be created throughout rural districts without regard to the proper accommodation of necessary labour', noted one champion of 'constructive Unionism'.[63]

The problem for the Salisbury Government in the early-1890s was a noticeable slump in activity under the Labourers Acts; just one of the repercussions of an estimated 20 per cent fall in Irish agricultural output and prices (see Diagram A and Table 1).[64] Their response was an improvement in the financial terms for rural housing. In 1890 the Chief Secretary, Arthur Balfour,

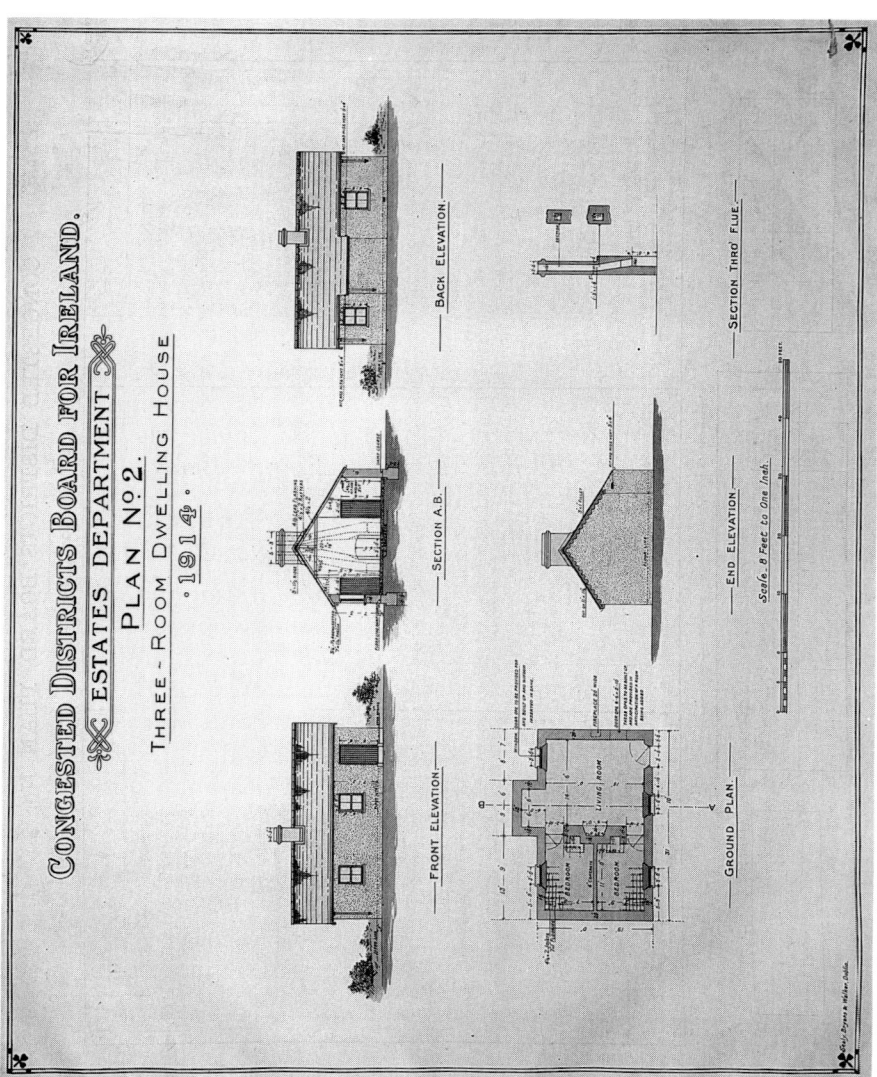

Fig 5. Congested Districts Board: recommended single-storey, three-room type (1914)

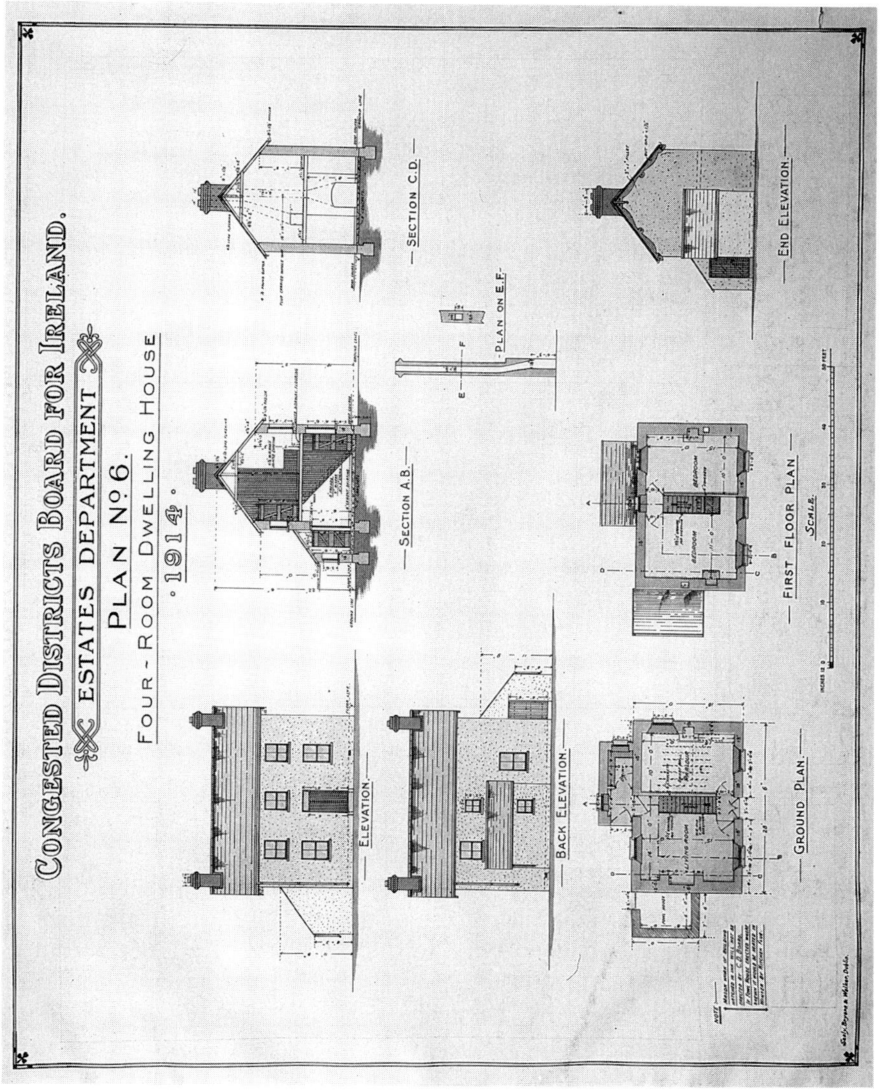

Fig 6. Congested Districts Board: recommended two-storey, four-room type (1914)

proposed as part of an innovative Irish Land Bill that the proceeds of an unused land purchase reserve could be used as a small 'experimental' housing subsidy to help rural authorities. Balfour's intention was to drive a wedge into the coalition of agricultural labourers and the Irish Party. He declared provocatively that he wanted 'to do something—and something substantial—for the labouring classes, who have been excluded absolutely from the benefits of every other Bill ever proposed'.[65] Stung by this direct attack on the Labourers Acts code, an Irish Party spokesman rejected Balfour's subsidy proposal 'because we believe that it is not likely to succeed, and we object to the employment of Irish funds for any experiment of the kind'.[66] However, it could not sustain this line, given the party's general commitment to secure any possible financial redress for Ireland that could be extracted from the Imperial Parliament. The IPP countered by introducing a private members Labourers Bill which proposed an alternative source of funding (from the residue of the Church Surplus Fund), but this was never likely to prevail. Instead the Irish Party had to content itself by persuading Chief Secretary Balfour to turn the subsidy contained in the 1891 Land Act into a more permanent feature (initially Balfour had simply envisaged a discretionary and occasional allowance). Following discussions between the ILGB and the Treasury, an initial grant of £40 000 was divided between all the counties in Ireland, and was then given to local authorities, pro rata to the number of cottages built, to offset the repayment of capital on housing loans. In counties where the grant was not fully expended (notably in Ulster), the surplus was put into a special account, totalling just under £15 000, and then re-allocated. It was a purely *ad hoc* solution to a specific problem, but it qualifies as the first direct housing subsidy from central government. Furthermore, it had also been agreed in 1891 that for the following five years the same £40 000 annual surplus from the Land Acts should be invested in a special account. Correspondingly, a reserve fund of £200 000 (plus accrued interest) was created by 1896, and after this date the annual proceeds from this fund, amounting to just under £37 000 per year, were ear-marked as an on-going subsidy under the Labourers Acts.[67]

During the 1890s, the Conservative Government also provided better public loan terms for Irish rural housing.[68] Procedure was eased. A new Labourers Act in 1891 permitted agricultural labourers themselves to be counted amongst the 12 representatives needed to initiate a scheme, and gave the ILGB powers to act in default if a rural authority failed in its duty.[69] The following year there was an increase in the maximum area of land that could be given, up from half an acre to one acre. A further Act in 1896 allowed rural authorities to sell off cottages if no longer required for labourers. However, it is doubtful whether the advent of partial state subsidy and increased powers in themselves did much to stimulate activity. There was a slight, temporary upturn under the Labourers Acts from the mid-1890s, but even then the completion rate still remained below 1000 dwellings a year (see Diagram A and Table 1).

Far more significant for the first phase of the Labourers Acts was the introduction of a universal franchise and a modern administrative hierarchy (i.e. County Councils, Urban District Councils, and Rural District Councils) under the 1898 Irish Local Government Act. One direct outcome was the completion of the transfer of local power in rural Ireland, in regions outside Ulster, to Nationalist tenant-farmers and shopkeepers. Another consequence of the 1898 Act, as the ILGB observed, was that by giving labourers the vote it forced rural authorities to pay greater attention to the demand for Labourers Act dwellings.[70] Certainly, there was a significant surge in loans sanctioned in 1901–02, which would have been an appropriate time-lag for newly elected councils to get schemes ready. There followed a rise in cottage building, peaking in 1904–05 with the completion of 1750 new dwellings (see Diagram B and Table 1). By this point, 20 years after the first Labourers Act, a total of just over 19 000 cottages had been achieved.[71] Another revealing statistic was that in 1900 over 80 per cent of the total debt incurred by rural authorities was for Labourers Acts loans; this proportion rose to an average of 90 per cent in the provinces of Munster and Leinster.[72] Progress was steady but not yet spectacular.

The inherent limitation on the first phase of the Labourers Act was that, ultimately, the Conservative Party's allegiance lay with Irish landowners rather than rural labourers. It was a dilemma epitomised by George Wyndham, the last Tory Chief Secretary to practise 'constructive Unionism'. The report of the 1902 Land Conference called for greater action on connected issues such as labourers' housing on the grounds that, as Wyndham noted, the 'transfer of property under the Land Act makes it necessary to deal now with these questions'.[73] Wyndham had only secured the Irish Party's support for the 1903 Land Act by promising an equally bold new Labourers Bill to follow. Rural housing reform also fitted in with his moral support for the 'National Efficiency' movement that swept Britain in the face of the Boer War defeat and the growing threat from Germany, and which regarded the decline of the rural labourer (hitherto assumed to be the stout backbone of the country) as the most serious problem. Within this ideological framework, the pressing need in Ireland was to overcome what was perceived as social and cultural backwardness. 'If the Irish Nation is to be healthy, energetic, hopeful and independent', wrote Wyndham, then up to a third of the population would have to be rehoused.[74] Wyndham, however, was also faced with the stark reality that Anglo-Irish landowners objected to a further augmentation of housing powers being given to rural authorities which they detested as not only virulently Nationalist, but also corrupt and profligate. As Wyndham complained to the Prime Minister, Arthur Balfour, in March 1904:

> It is very difficult to run my policy in Ireland—which is your policy and that of the Cabinet and party—if we are to revert to the view that the Irish County Councils are unfit for the duties which devolve upon them . . . [Unionist intransigence] will go far to destroy such influence

as I have over the Irish Party and to supply an excuse for declaring that I have closed the experiment of conciliation over agrarian problems.[75]

Despite his pleas, the most that Wyndham was allowed to offer as a new Labourers Bill in 1904 was a slight improvement of legal clauses, and a requirement that the ILGB carry out a survey of rural housing needs. Not surprisingly, the Irish Party regarded this proposal as a betrayal of his earlier promise, and sabotaged the initiative.[76] In 1905, both Wyndham's career and 'constructive Unionism' lay in ruins when a plan to grant a very limited degree of Irish self-administration ended in fiasco. The incoming Tory Chief Secretary, Sir Walter Long, returned to the older policy of imposing law and order. It was a political impasse that heralded the end of the first phase of the Labourers Acts.

What had been the economic consequences of partial subsidy for Irish rural housing from the early-1890s? The Land League veteran, Michael Davitt, went so far as to declare in 1904 that the Labourers Acts constituted 'a rational principle of state socialism'.[77] The reality was far less heroic, but nevertheless provided a useful case study for British and Irish observers to examine the results of a deviation from classical *laissez-faire* economics. Many contemporaries were interested in whether state intervention had killed off private housebuilding in rural Ireland; but the general consensus was that this question could not be proved one way or the other, given that the Irish Land Acts had probably already ended the provision of labourers' cottages by landowners.[78] The other important question at the time was whether the granting of a subsidised cottage had, as the theory of Liberal political economy held, served merely to hold down labourers' wages. Here the Irish statistics, though problematic in detail, were seen by many contemporary writers as disproving the old canard. A scarcity of labour and rising agricultural prosperity after the Famine had seen the average agricultural wage in Ireland rise gradually to a level in the early-1880s of around 8–9s per week.[79] Subsidy under the Labourers Acts did nothing to halt this trend, and in 1906 the estimate of the Castle Administration was that the typical wage for a rural labourer was now 10s 11d a week. It was not a uniformly rosy picture: there was considerable regional variation (the highest wages were in Ulster, Munster, and around Dublin; the lowest in Connaught and south-east Leinster), and the Irish level remained stubbornly 33 per cent lower than the average farm worker's pay in England.[80]

Nevertheless, there seems to have been a genuine improvement in real income and living conditions for rural workers in late-nineteenth-century Ireland.[81] And undoubtedly cheaper housing under the Labourers Acts played its part. The typical rent for a cottage in 1906 was the same as at the outset of the programme, i.e. 11–12d per week (around 1s 1d including rates) for a dwelling with half an acre of land, and 1s 3d per week (1s 5d with rates) for a one-acre plot. The range of rents varied from 4d a week in remote districts, to a maximum of 2s 6d in the districts around Dublin, such as Rathdown, which had the highest wage levels. At the turn of the century, therefore, the Labourers Acts were providing decent new dwellings for only 10–14 per cent of farm labourers' incomes: in meeting the needs of the class for which they were intended, they were notably more successful than early local authority housing in Britain. The problem for Irish rural authorities, however, was that rents of around 1s per week were insufficient to meet loan charges given an average 'all-in' cost, including land, of £100 per cottage. Since there was only a limited amount of subsidy available before 1906, the prospect was another burden on already high local rates. Where land was cheap and plentiful this was less of a problem. But in agricultural districts close to cities such as Dublin, Cork, and Limerick, even with higher rent levels there was a 'housing rate' under the Labourers Acts of anything up to 8d in the £1.[82] There remained a powerful disincentive to the building of rural dwellings.

THE DESIGN OF EARLY LABOURERS ACTS COTTAGES

The Castle Administration brushed aside all calls for the issue of standard plans for the 1883 Labourers Act (hence taking a very different line to that of the Irish Board of Works in the late-1860s). An ILGB circular in November 1883 declared that 'the Board desire to interfere as little as possible with the discretion of Sanitary Authorities in regard to the plans and designs of such houses'.[83] Instead, the ILGB simply stipulated a few basic requirements. There was to be a minimum ceiling height of 8 feet (reduced to 7 feet for attic bedrooms); a window area in every habitable room of at least one-twelfth of the floor area; an external WC located at least 10 feet away from the dwelling; and no cottage could be less than 15 feet from a main road. Each dwelling was to have a single room for living and cooking, and at least two bedrooms. The ILGB did not rule out the possibility of a third bedroom, but pointedly warned that this would add a further £10–15 on to the anticipated building cost of £65–70 per cottage.[84] Beyond this, all the ILGB could suggest was that plans submitted to them for approval 'may be prepared by the architect or builder employed by the Sanitary Authorities'.[85]

Given this *laissez-faire* attitude during the first phase of the Labourers Acts, perhaps not surprisingly the quality of design was seen as leaving much to be desired.[86] The vast majority of cottages plus plots were built along the roadside, either as isolated units or in small linear groups, in order to be close to the farms where the tenant worked.[87] And in contrast to the Irish Board of Works in 1869, the typical detached cottage tended to be simply a reworking of the indigenous single-storey vernacular preferred by rural labourers. On one side of the dwelling a single large living room/kitchen, containing a central hearth, gave access to two bedrooms (or, occasionally, three bedrooms). Wherever dwellings were built as a semi-detached pair, the same plan would be handed. Internal space provision was in the order of 400–480 square feet in total,

MUNICIPAL COTTAGES FOR IRISH LABOURERS.

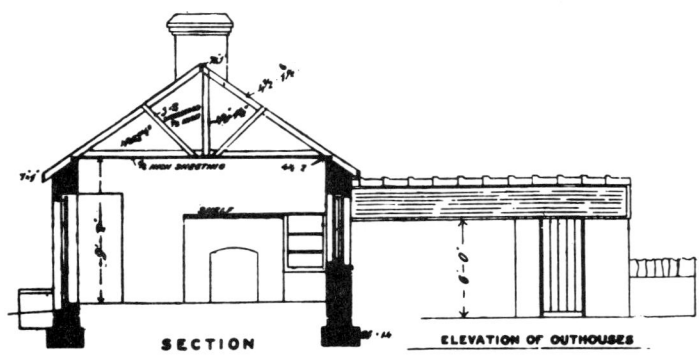

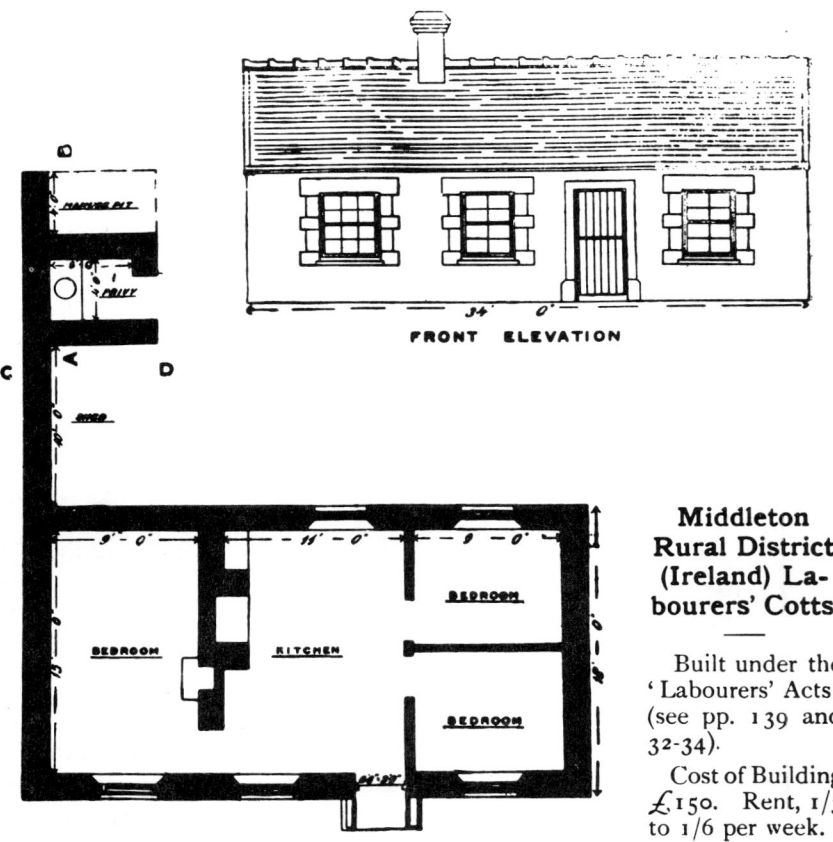

Middleton Rural District (Ireland) Labourers' Cotts.

Built under the 'Labourers' Acts' (see pp. 139 and 32-34).

Cost of Building £150. Rent, 1/3 to 1/6 per week.

Fig 7. Midleton RDC, Co. Cork: single-storey pre-1906 Labourers Act cottage

which, although hardly generous, was a clear improvement on the traditional rural 'cabin'. A typical early Labourers Act plan could be seen in the rendered stone cottages built by Midleton RDC in Co. Cork (see Fig. 7).[88] Sometimes, however, two-storey cottages were built on the Irish Board of Works' model. Examples can be found in Co. Wexford or in Tallaght near Dublin, but even here the upper storey generally consisted of attic bedrooms with windows in the end walls, so that an appearance of a single-storey dwelling could be maintained.[89] For the reality was, as the *Irish Builder* noted, that 'two-storey cottages are very unpopular with the labouring classes in rural districts in Ireland. Considerable objection is expressed to stairs'.[90] As will be seen later, it was not until after 1906 that the building of two-storey dwellings became a more regular feature.

Aesthetically the early Labourers Acts cottages were also closer to the simple vernacular tradition, with their roughcast-rendered masonry walls and plain roofs (albeit in slate) (see Fig. 8). Some designs introduced minimal brick details such as window dressings and quoins, to a pleasant effect.[91] But most were undecorated and architecturally modest. As one participant commented, the dwellings were 'not intended to ornament a gentleman's property, so that there is no reason why they should build any fancy cottages'.[92] There was, however, a counter-lobby from the Royal Institute of Architects of Ireland (RIAI) and the *Irish Builder*, which demanded the mandatory employment of

Fig 8. Carrick, Co. Wexford: typical two-storey pre-1906 Labourers Act cottage

architects in order to improve the standard of cottage design. The RIAI sent a deputation to Dublin Castle in June 1901 to demand a stricter control over those carrying out Labourers Acts schemes, but given its political ineffectiveness, the suggestion went unheeded.[93] By leaving the design of labourers' dwellings entirely in the hands of rural authorities up until 1906, successive British Governments were taking a hands-off approach that was less likely to antagonise Nationalist councils. The result was cottages that were simplified and rationalised versions of vernacular types, but were regressive rather than innovative.

THE SECOND PHASE OF THE LABOURERS ACTS FROM 1906 TO 1914

The turning point for the Labourers Acts programme came in December 1905, when the Liberal Party won a landslide election and held power for the next decade. The motives in the second phase were very different to those of 'constructive Unionism', and arose from the need to appease the Irish Party in lieu of dealing with the thornier question of self-government. The Liberal Government (first under Henry Campbell-Bannerman, and from 1908 under Henry Asquith) decided not to attempt to pass Home Rule, realising that it would simply be vetoed by the House of Lords. Instead the Cabinet concentrated on the populist social reform legislation of 'New Liberalism' advocated by young radicals like David Lloyd George, who preferred to keep Ireland down the political agenda.[94] Various Irish measures were also put forward to keep the IPP more or less loyal until such a time as Home Rule might be introduced. Thus a further Land Act in 1909 provided more funds and made sale compulsory if the tenant wanted to purchase, and innovative mainland policies, such as the old age pensions scheme copied from Bismarckian Germany, were extended to Ireland.

Likewise, the Irish Party was forced to turn attention to social legislation in face of its inability to deliver Home Rule.[95] Winning improvements in Irish social conditions at least enabled it both to defend the legitimacy of constitutional Nationalism (against, say, the abstentionist approach of Sinn Fein), and to deter the development of an independent working-class political party in Ireland. The IPP was determined to make housing reform a key plank of the social concessions it extracted from the Liberal Government, and indeed used the demand for increased rural subsidy as a central issue in the 1905 election campaign. By February 1906, the IPP's deputy leader was confiding to his superior, John Redmond, that in the secret negotiations with the Liberal Government, 'we have so far got nothing beyond the hope of a satisfactory Labourers' Bill, and even as regards that there is no definite promise'.[96] The pressure was kept up, and a few months later Redmond could publicly declare that he had told the new Chief Secretary, James Bryce:

that the first business of the Government would be the introduction of a satisfactory Labourers Bill, and . . . I have myself, on behalf of the Irish Party, been PRACTICALLY IN DAILY COMMUNICATION WITH MR BRYCE and the other men responsible for the Government of Ireland, pressing upon him and them the full claims of the Irish labourers.[97]

Privately in April 1906, Bryce warned the Prime Minister that given the absence of Home Rule proposals, the IPP was likely to stir up unrest in Westminster and Ireland over the coming year unless alternative victories were provided. The Chief Secretary added that 'they are very eager and pressing about the Labourers' Bill, wanting a Treasury Grant to work it: and I fear this is necessary, if quiet is to be preserved'.[98] Bryce duly got Cabinet approval, and at once set about pushing through a new Labourers Act.[99] The second phase had begun, and once again the impetus was political. Indeed the genuine demand for improved rural housing in Ireland was even lower in 1906 than it had ever been. The number of farm labourers had continued to decline as a result of rural depopulation and emigration, and the 1901 Census showed that there remained just over 9000 one-room 'cabins'; this represented a mere 1 per cent of the rural housing stock. Only 2 per cent of the stock could be classified as '4th Class' accommodation, whereas now nearly two-thirds of rural dwellings were substantial cottages with up to four rooms.[100]

The 1906 Labourers Act was remarkable for its financial features. It not only extended to rural housing the generous public loan terms of the 1903 Irish Land Act (interest at 3.25 per cent including sinking fund over 68.5 years), but it also created a dedicated loan fund of £4 250 000. The fund was to be administered by the Irish Land Commissioners and not, as previously, by the Irish Board of Works. And, most importantly, the 1906 Act provided a massive direct subsidy whereby the state met 36 per cent of loan repayments: thus out of a typical repayment cost of £3 5s in £100, the Treasury contributed £1 4s and the rural authority £2 1s.[101] A maximum expenditure of £170 per cottage was also stipulated, based on an estimated £130 for building and £40 for land. Hence it was expected that the loan fund would produce some 25 000–30 000 new dwellings. There were also further procedural improvements, with for instance the ILGB now being able to issue provisional orders without having to seek Privy Council approval.

The 1906 Act was an exceptional innovation, which the Cabinet presented as an inevitable extension of the generous Wyndham Land Act. Chief Secretary Bryce pointed out that 'there were circumstances in this case which justified very exceptional measures'.[102] Even the then Chancellor of the Exchequer, Henry Asquith, known to be a staunch opponent of housing subsidy, was forced to concede that the terms 'were both financially sound and morally equitable, and he did not in the least degree recede from them'.[103] The Irish Party proclaimed the new Labourers Act as a 'radical and sweeping measure', and it is notable that it enjoyed full cross-party support from the Ulster Unionists and from Irish landowners.[104] Against the argument that it might be 'too socialistic', one Irish MP pointed out that private enterprise had failed in Irish rural housing and that because of the Land Acts there would soon be no landlords to build cottages in any case.[105] There were a few minor parliamentary disagreements. The IPP failed to get the definition of 'rural labourer' extended to include artisans and fishermen. Ulster Unionists tried unsuccessfully to get the subsidy allocated to counties on a fixed basis, so that less active Ulster authorities would not lose out. The House of Lords sought to emasculate the clauses which gave increased powers of compulsory acquisition. But against the broad consensual sweep, such disputes were insignificant.

When applied in Ireland, the financial benefits of the 1906 Labourers Act were immediately apparent. Rural authorities found that, although the average 'all-in' cost of £185 per cottage actually exceeded the stipulated limit, they could now build larger three-bedroom cottages and still let them at an average rent of just 1s 1d per week. From 1906 the majority of rents lay in a band from 1s–1s 6d per week, and the range was from only 4d in very rural areas to 2s 9d per week in districts around Dublin.[106] At a time when rural wages were continuing to rise, reaching an average of 11–12s a week in 1915, this meant that even higher standard housing was now being supplied for only 9 or 10 per cent of labourers' incomes. Furthermore, rural authorities could now build at no loss at all to the rates. Roscrea RDC, which from 1908 built 99 cottages for £160–170 each and let them at 1s 4d–1s 9d per week, even boasted of making a small profit out of the venture.[107] The terms were simply too good to refuse. As the Irish Party proudly pointed out, there was never any need after 1906 to place any compulsion on rural authorities to build dwellings. By the outbreak of the First World War, virtually every single one of the 213 RDCs in Ireland had acted, and perhaps most significantly, even the previously parsimonious authorities in rural Ulster could no longer restrain themselves. Hence, from having a negligible proportion of Labourers Acts cottages prior to 1906, by 1914 nearly 20 per cent of dwellings were to be found in Ulster (see Table 3). Indeed, in January 1913 the *Irish Builder* observed that the 'bulk of activity is now in the north, where formerly the vast benefits of these Acts were almost wholly ignored'.[108] There was also a new-found zeal amongst Ulster Unionists to press the Chief Secretary for further funds and to convince Northern authorities to undertake schemes. Altogether in Ireland there was a dramatic escalation following the 1906 Act. By March 1914, a total of 43 702 cottages had been built under the Labourers Acts, of which just over 23 000 were built in the previous eight years.[109] In the peak year of 1910–11, an unprecedented 6223 dwellings were completed (see Diagram B and Table 1). Such was the demand that by this point the original loan fund of £4 250 000 was virtually exhausted; the IPP soon obtained a new Labourers Act in 1911 with a further £1 000 000 to build 6000 more cottages.[110] This produced another noticeable surge in building activity just before the First World War (Diagram A and Table 1). Between 1906 and 1914, the one-room 'cabin' and indeed the housing demand from rural labourers were all but eradicated in Ireland. It is also clear that the Labourers Acts programme had by this point taken on a wider role. After 1906 many rural authorities ran out of farm labourers to rehouse and so instead built increasingly for those with marginal connections with agriculture. What was now being provided was suburban working-class housing close to towns. For instance, in 1913 the *Limerick Echo* reported a discussion of Limerick No. 1 RDC in which it was declared that if they evicted one tenant because he worked in the city and not on a farm, then 'a good deal' of their other tenants would have to go as well.[111]

The scope of the second phase of the Labourers Acts created a situation in Ireland where there was virtually unanimous support for state-subsidised housing. It was an attitude much remarked on by contemporary observers.[112] Only a few lonely voices, such as Nicholas Synnott, dared to criticise the Labourers Acts on the grounds that they had pauperised rural labourers and had ended private housebuilding.[113] The vast majority disagreed. The *Irish Builder* claimed that on 'the principle of State aid in the shape of Exchequer contributions and loans perfectly secured on the rates, there is no room for difference of opinion'; it later added that the result had been 'a bloodless social revolution in the condition of the Irish rural labourer . . . The operation of these Acts has literally changed the face of rural Ireland.'[114] Even members of the Catholic Church, a body generally opposed to state intervention, supported the Labourers Acts code.[115] Occasionally there was friction between farmers and labourers, in cases where the former objected to having land compulsorily purchased, or where the latter felt that schemes were being deliberately obstructed.[116] But by the turn of the century, both classes were united behind the Labourers Acts due to the efforts of the Irish Party and its new national organisation, the United Irish League. Nationalist justifications for the Labourers Acts were often fallacious, the chief myth being that the code had been instrumental in stopping rural depopulation and emigration. 'For every house you build you are keeping a family in the country and rooting them to the soil', opined an Independent Nationalist MP; '. . . You are not only building cottages, but you are building up the national character of the people.'[117] One architect stated a commonplace when he said that the code had 'done more than anything to combat the awful drain of emigration': an emotive message that went down well with Nationalist organisations in the USA.[118] In reality, the Labourers Acts seem to have done little to halt the decline in the rural population to around two-thirds of the total Irish figure at the outbreak of the First World War. Emigration was then still running at an average of almost 40 000 a year, and while this was less than in the 1880s, the fall was due mainly to economic recession and stricter immigration controls in the USA. If anything, rural labourers appear to have made up a higher proportion of Irish emigrants from the turn of the century, since, paradoxically, rising incomes meant that many could for the first time afford the cost of passage.[119]

Support in Ireland for the Labourers Acts was rooted more on political allegiance. The Irish Party never missed an opportunity to cite rural housing reform as part of the litany of its achievements. 'The Irish Labourers in these cottages are now the best housed in the world', boasted the United Irish League.[120] The IPP leader, John Redmond, told the Imperial Parliament that there was 'no work to which this House has ever set its hand which I think has been more beneficial to the people of Ireland than the erection of these cottages'; and similar sentiments were frequently expressed by his colleagues.[121] The IPP used the Labourers Acts for three specific political purposes. First, the code was a rallying point to fight what Nationalists saw as the continuing economic exploitation and over-taxation of Ireland. One leading MP said that the Labourers Acts were one of the few things 'that console one for the many unpleasant and mortifying incidents in the social and political history of Ireland', and another added that the payment of rural housing subsidy 'would only be paying back a very small instalment of the millions and millions that they [the British Government] have robbed from our country'.[122] Secondly, the Irish Party was always mindful of the dangers of appearing to be only acting in farmers' interests. Thus the housing programme also served as proof that rural labourers—linked to the IPP by the Irish Land and Labour Association, and its President, William Field—were an essential part of the movement. 'Believe me THE SAFETY OF THE LABOURERS' CAUSE depends to-day, as it always did, on the power and unity of the Irish Party', declared John Redmond. Another MP reassured them that there 'was no better Labour Party in the House of Commons than the Irish Party . . . there was no member of the Party who had not the interests of the labourer as much at heart as those of the farmer or any other class'.[123] Thirdly, the IPP continually used the Labourers Acts to highlight the relative impotence of other parties, whether they be Independent Nationalists, Sinn Fein, or Ulster Unionists.[124] In this manipulation of rural housing for political ends, the Irish Party received the steadfast support of its allies in the Liberal Government. In 1910 the Chief Secretary, Augustine Birrell, told the House of Commons that 'no money . . . was ever better spent, out of Imperial resources or Irish money, than for this rebuilding of the cottages of the labourers in Ireland'.[125] Of course, the other political parties in Ireland were forced to respond in kind. Unionists taunted the IPP that Home Rule would deprive Ireland of the very source of funds that made the Labourers Acts possible.[126] The most complex position was that of the Independent Nationalists. Their leader, William O'Brien, promoted a conciliatory Nationalism which sought compromise with Ascendancy landowners and Ulster Unionists, and he saw labourers' housing as a key issue around which differing parties could unite.[127] O'Brien had been in the Irish Party at the time of the 1902 Land Conference, and he repeatedly claimed that it had been his idea to extend land-purchase finance to rural dwellings. He even said that he had come to a secret agreement to this effect with the Castle Administration prior to the 1906 Labourers Act. Such claims were unlikely, but nevertheless Independent Nationalists tended to regard the rural housing programme as if it belonged to them and not the IPP. O'Brien wrote that the Labourers Acts were 'scarcely less wonder-working than the abolition of landlordism itself'. He told Parliament that after land redistribution, the code was 'the most vital requirement to the peace of Ireland', and 'the only matter in which Ireland ever got the best of a bargain with the Imperial Exchequer'.[128]

HOUSING DESIGN IN THE SECOND PHASE OF THE LABOURERS ACTS

The second phase of the Labourers Acts programme from 1906, which saw the provision of massive state subsidy, was also accompanied by a significant change in official attitude towards the quality of cottages. Housing standards were raised, most tangibly by the recommended inclusion of a third bedroom and a separate scullery. It was also made clear that rural authorities would now have to build in accordance with types issued by the ILGB, unless they obtained special approval for their own designs. This is significant, for it represented the imposition of the first centralised controls on the architectural form of working-class housing (by contrast, the plans issued by the Irish Board of Works in 1869 had been illustrative, and those used by the Congested Districts Board from 1903 were intended only for a minor aspect of that agency's work). The greater degree of design control was welcomed by Irish MPs from all parties, with one Unionist hoping that 'the cottages to be built under the Bill would be better and more substantial than many of those which he had examined'.[129] The Castle Administration had three aims in introducing standardised plans: first, to speed up the approval process; second, to ensure that no substandard schemes got through; and third, to reduce design costs. Thus, in 1906 Chief Secretary Bryce stated that the ILGB would 'issue model plans of cottages, under which architects' charges might be greatly reduced'.[130] The typical architectural fee at the time was 5 per cent of the contract sum, yet under the 1906 Labourers Act the ILGB imposed a 2 per cent maximum on the grounds that the use of standard plans meant that only routine contract supervision was required. Rural authorities were even encouraged to seek competitive fee bids in an attempt to reduce the figure even further. Indeed, some Irish Party MPs, including John Redmond, argued that it was unnecessary to use a qualified architect at all. The Nationalist *Freemans Journal* declared that 'the building of a plain four or five-roomed slate cottage is surely simple enough to allow the businessmen of Ireland who constitute the District Councils to arrange it for themselves'.[131]

The undermining of fee income and potential workload for its members caused the RIAI to complain bitterly, writing 'that the distribution of complete working drawings broadcast throughout the country will inflict a serious injury on the qualified Country Architect who would otherwise, probably, be employed to design and superintend schemes undertaken in his district'.[132] As a result of pressure from the RIAI and those Irish MPs who argued that the use of architects would be the most cost-effective strategy, the ILGB finally agreed to stipulate that rural authorities had to appoint either a qualified architect, engineer, or surveyor with proven experience in cottage-building.[133] Curiously, the *Irish Builder* welcomed this as the first official recognition of the need for compulsory registration of architects, on the grounds that 'for the first time in the history of dealings between their profession and the State, regard is had to the professional attainments and qualifications of the persons entrusted with . . . the design of structures built with public funds'.[134] But in fact the ILGB's clause posed a bigger dilemma for the RIAI in its campaign for professional protection, since rural authorities could obviously continue to employ non-architects who could now claim the reflected status of being the 'architect' for the project. Therefore, the RIAI tried fervently once more to persuade the new Chief Secretary, Augustine Birrell, to restrict employment to registered architects only. It was crushingly rebuffed when Birrell ruled in May 1907 that designing labourers' cottages 'does not require specialist knowledge . . . excellent work in connection with such schemes has been done at a moderate cost by men who did not claim in any way to be professional Architects'.[135] After this, the RIAI could only look on in impotence. From 1907 to 1912, there was a prolonged period of depression in the Irish building industry, during which time the *Irish Builder* repeatedly noted that the greatest area of activity was rural labourers' cottages, and yet Irish architects were being denied their full share of this work.[136] Numerous disputes arose in Labourers Acts schemes because of negligent site administration. An official report noted that 'the root cause of the bad quality of the work done is to be found in bad supervision . . . appointments have frequently been made of men who were wretchedly qualified, unreliable, and often morally unsound and not above accepting a five pound note from the contractor'.[137]

But having agreed the decision to adopt standardised designs, the ILGB then had to face the problem that there were simply no adequate models available. The CDB types were widely seen in Ireland as deficient, and the Local Government Board for England and Wales had issued no recommended plans (nor was it to do so until 1913).[138] So in November 1906 the ILGB organised the first official competition for the design of labourers' dwellings. The spur appears to have been dissatisfaction with the failure of the 1905 Cheap Cottages competition, held in Letchworth Garden City, to come up with a solution that would realistically cost less than £150.[139] The competition brief as set by the ILGB was to design an Irish cottage which could be built for £130 or less, and which required the minimum of skilled labour.[140] Some 386 architects entered from all over the United Kingdom. The results were announced in January 1907, the winner being a Lancashire architect, Sydney Moss. Runner-up was a Scot who was resident in Dublin, J. Roseman Burns, and in third place was the distinguished Irish architect, Thomas Manly Deane (the latter subsequently added a variant of his design, making four winning type-plans in all). All four designs were for detached single-storey cottages with three bedrooms, and, as Gailey has suggested, represented various attempts to recast vernacular idioms to meet modern planning needs.[141] The question, therefore, was how well had the architects understood Irish building traditions. There was widespread criticism of the competition from Irish architects, partly on the grounds that the £130 limit was too low, but also because the winning entries were seen as too picturesque and impractical for the Irish climate and building industry. The most outspoken opponent was the Belfast antiquarian and Nationalist, Joseph Biggar, who accused the designs of being too anglicised. Biggar and another critic, Robert Brown, both asked a Belfast architect, W. J. Fennell, to design alternatives in a romanticised 'Irish' vernacular (see Fig. 9).[142] This consituted a rare instance of Nationalist objection to the Labourers Acts, and certainly Biggar's vision was fired by a mythical notion of the 'native' Celtic home that was commonplace within the Gaelic Revival movement (and was later memorably satirised in Flann O'Brien's *The Poor Mouth*).

The ILGB simply ignored all criticisms. Indeed, when it issued the set of recommended plans in June 1907, included were not just the four winning competition proposals, but also a further four types designed by its own in-house architects which bore even less resemblance to vernacular precedent (see Figs 10–13).[143] Three of the ILGB suggestions were for two-storey cottages

INTERIOR OF ARTIZAN'S COTTAGE (B).

Fig 9. W. J. Fennell: romanticised 'Irish' alternatives to the ILGB designs (1907)

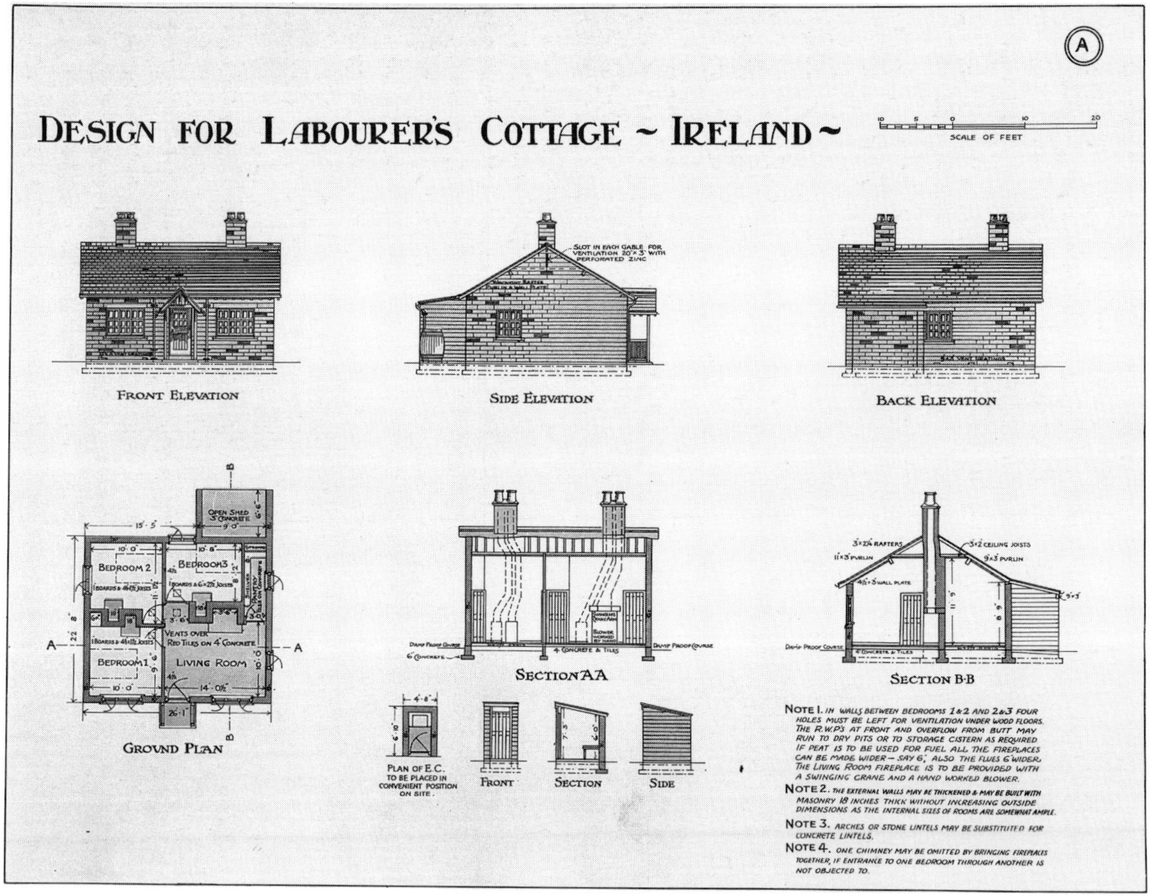

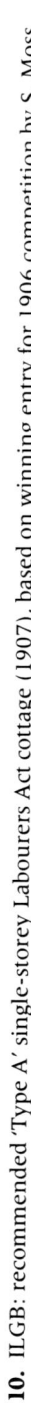

Fig 10. ILGB: recommended 'Type A' single-storey Labourers Act cottage (1907), based on winning entry for 1906 competition by S. Moss

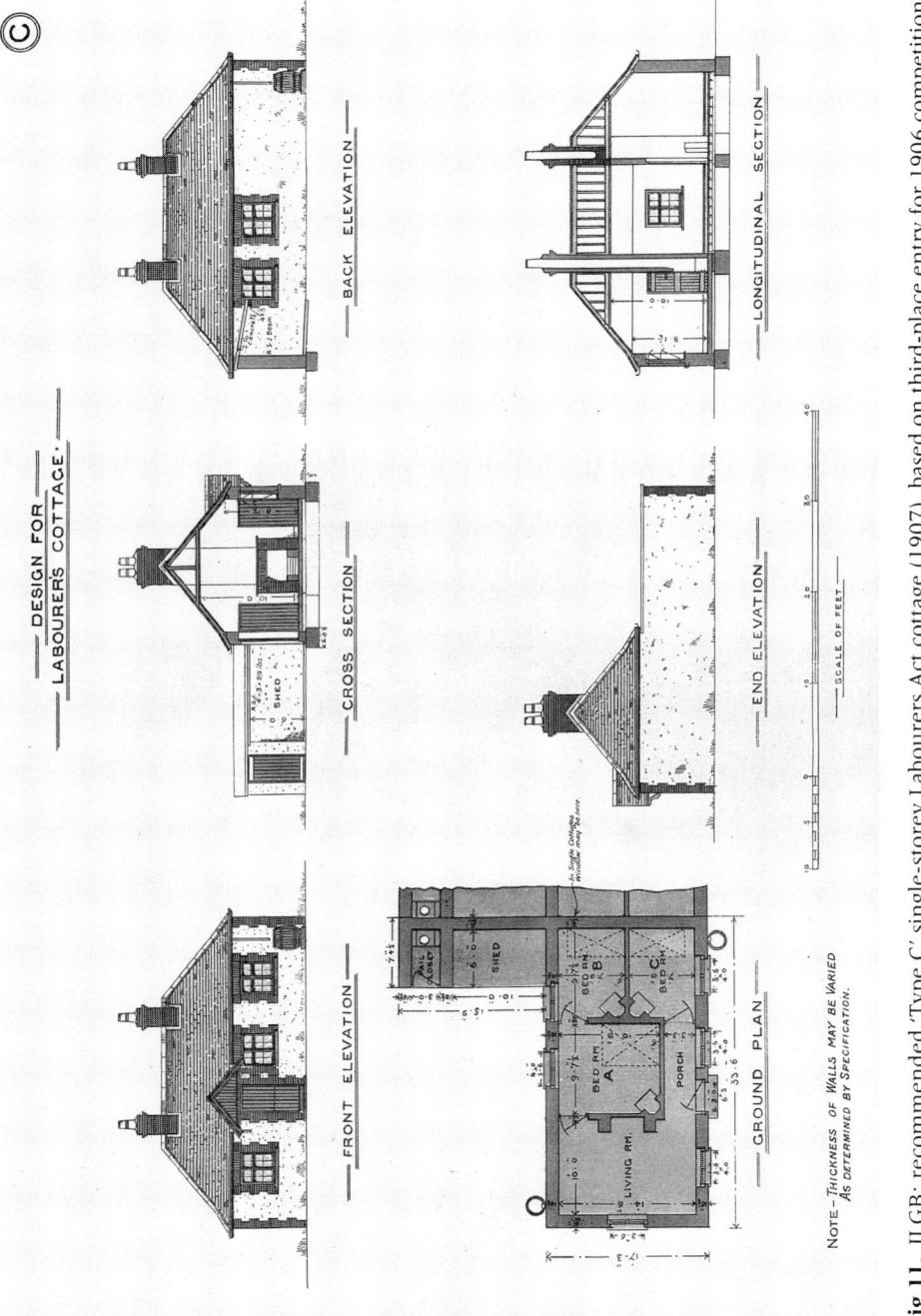

Fig 11. ILGB: recommended 'Type C' single-storey Labourers Act cottage (1907), based on third-place entry for 1906 competition by T. M. Deane

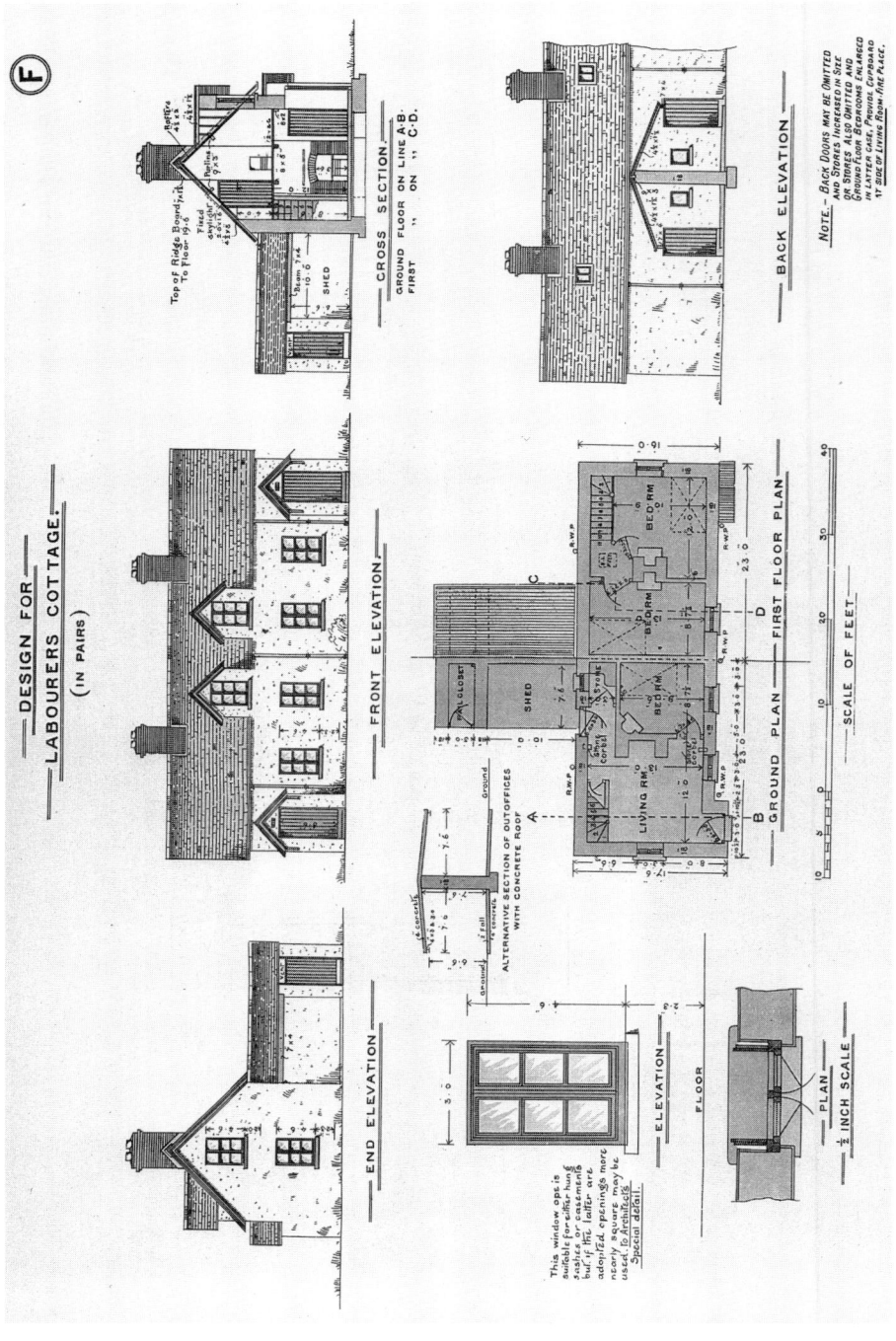

Fig 12. ILGB: recommended 'Type F' two-storey Labourers Act cottage (1907)

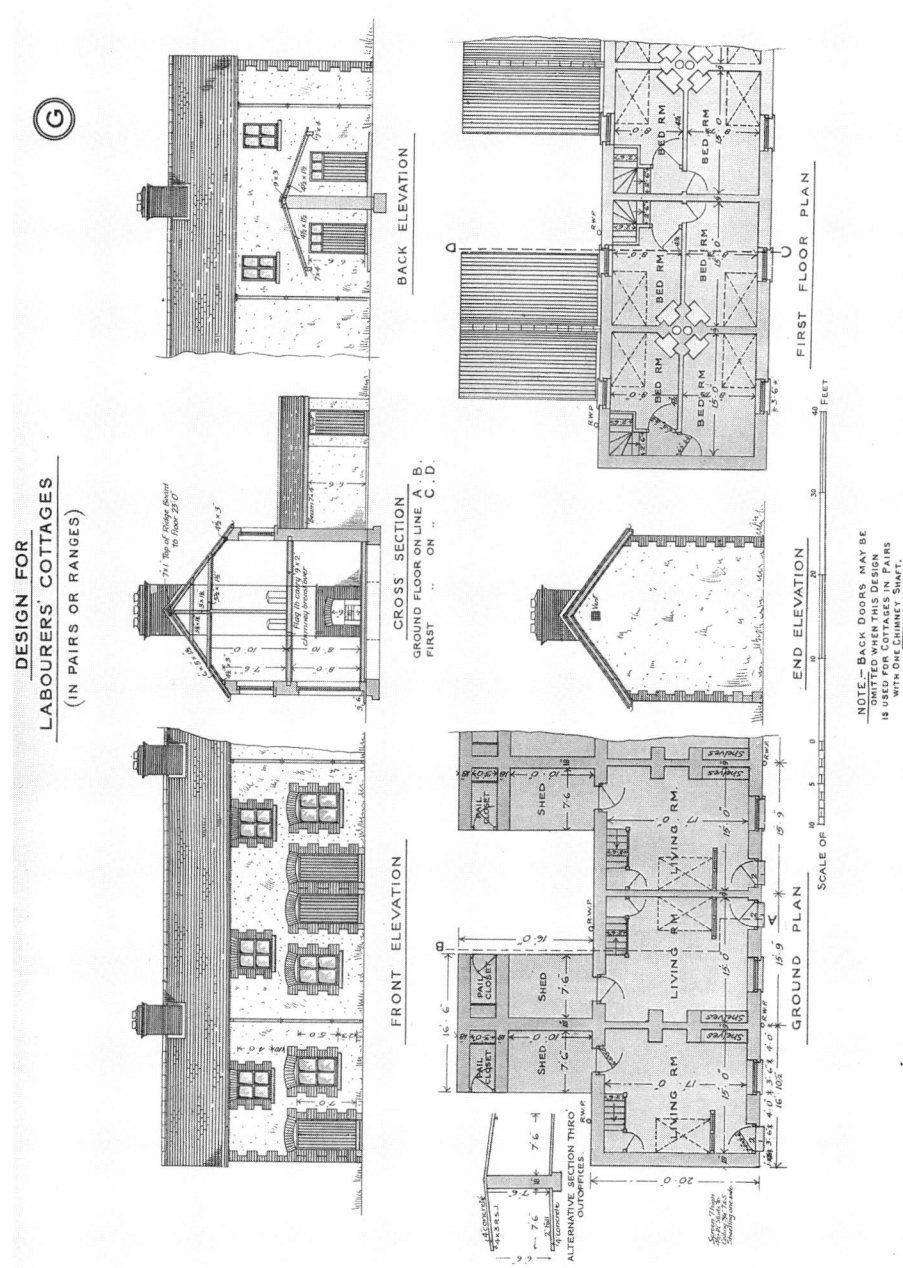

Fig 13. ILGB: recommended 'Type G' two-storey Labourers Act cottage (1907)

on the English model, two were for semi-detached arrangements (Types F and H), and one was even suitable for a terraced layout (Type G). Clearly these designs were intended for more suburban sites. To provide a range of sizes, two of the ILGB types had only two bedrooms (Types G and H). The sizes of rooms varied across the different plans, but nevertheless the ILGB issued recommended space standards for an average five-person cottage: a single living room/kitchen of between 1200 and 1400 cubic feet (i.e. 150–175 square feet in area); a main bedroom of at least 900 cubic feet (i.e. 110 square feet); and smaller bedrooms of between 600 and 800 cubic feet (i.e. 75–100 square feet). No parlour was envisaged. Ceiling heights were to be a minimum of eight feet, except on the first floor where an average of seven feet was allowed. An open shed was to be provided at the rear of the house. Elevations were generally plain, though in some cases monotony was relieved by using hipped roofs, dormer windows, brick window-dressings, quoins, etc. Servicing was extremely basic. All rooms had hearths located on internal walls. Mains water supply was not insisted upon, and an outside dry-earth closet at least 10 feet away from the house was preferred to a WC. Construction was also regulated by the issue of standard details and specifications. Roofs were to be slated, and wall construction was to depend on what was the cheapest local material. Permitted variants were for 18-inch solid masonry; 14-inch solid brickwork; 9-inch rendered brickwork; 11-inch cavity brickwork; 10-inch in-situ poured concrete walls; and 10-inch concrete blockwork. Thus, while construction was to be mainly traditional, the last two options allowed experimentation if brick or stone were scarce. There was support for this approach within the ILGB, notably from one inspector who recommended the pre-cast concrete system pioneered by the Liverpool City Engineer, J. A. Brodie, on the basis that 'all the advantages of modern factory methods and repetition work are available for cheapening the finished article'.[144] The ILGB also encouraged an English and an Irish contractor to build concrete block versions of the top two competition entries at the 1907 Irish International Exhibition in Dublin, in order to demonstrate the possibilities of this new form of construction.[145]

It would appear that from 1906 the majority of Irish rural authorities simply followed one or more of the ILGB's eight recommended plans. This can be seen for example in schemes by Mallow RDC, or Larne RDC in Ulster.[146] Also significant was that, as mentioned earlier, the search for new demand meant that the Labourers Acts now incorporated the role of a *suburban* housing programme. One leading British reformer noted that while 'at first the cottages were built near to farms on which the men were employed, the cottages in recent years have been built in village groups'.[147] Land, however, was more expensive on the outskirts of urban centres. Prices in Co. Dublin could be anything up to £100 per acre, compared with only £25–60 an acre in more rural districts. The consequence of higher site costs was that housing density needed to be increased. In turn, this meant the provision of smaller plots of accompanying land under the 1906 Act (as low as a quarter-acre in some cases), and the far greater use, as a visiting deputation observed in 1912, of 'two-storey semi-detached cottages of the English type, with bedrooms upstairs'.[148] The result in towns such as Roscrea was the replacement of existing single-storey thatched cottages by new terraces of double-storey, slated houses more reminiscent of an industrial town in Northern England (see Fig. 14).[149] Yet, irrespective of whether single- or double-storey types were used for schemes under the 1906 Act, the overriding aim of the ILGB was to keep building costs to an absolute minimum. Therefore it was common for observers to praise the general rise in housing standards from 1906, but to continue to disparage the aesthetic appearance of Labourers Act dwellings. The *Irish Builder* commented that in general the cottages 'cannot be said to boast any great architectural qualities'.[150] In 1909 an Irish Party MP called on Chief Secretary Birrell and the ILGB to 'introduce a little variety into these cottages by placing more artistic, but not more expensive, designs before the local authorities'.[151] Birrell at first prevaricated, but was later forced to concede that:

> They are not all of them architecturally beautiful. Some of them, I am sorry to admit, are hideous, but the greater part of them may be described as in themselves an addition to the landscape.[152]

The IPP leader, John Redmond, concurred that most of the cottage designs were plain, but added that once covered with creepers and climbing roses they

Fig 14. Roscrea RDC: two-storey 'urban' type built under Labourers Act (1913–14)

made a beautiful scenic contribution.[153] It was a romantic view echoed by the Independent Nationalist, William O'Brien, when he wrote fulsomely of 'the labourers' cottages which dot the landscape—prettier than the farmers' own homes—honeysuckles or jasmines generally training around the portico . . . a bunch of roses in the cheeks of the children clustering about the doorsteps'.[154]

However, it was not the case that all Labourers Act cottages after 1906 were architecturally undistinguished, or unthinkingly followed ILGB types. From the turn of the century, a number of eminent Irish architects derived a substantial part of their workload from rural cottage design. The entries for the 1906 ILGB competition by Thomas Manly Deane were mentioned earlier. There were also a number of other exceptional figures who worked for rural authorities, particularly in the areas around Dublin where the highest rents could be charged. Many had been wrestling with the problem of improving design quality even before the 1906 Labourers Act: after it, the generous subsidy and the switch towards larger and denser suburban schemes enabled them to be more ambitious. One such architect was R. M. Butler, who (as noted in the Introduction) was both the influential editor of the *Irish Builder* and a leading advocate of a sober Neo-Classical style. Butler's own work included cottage schemes for Rathdown No. 1 RDC, and in 1906 he gave a lucid analysis of the problem in hand. To be economical, Butler said, what were required were two-storey, semi-detached cottages, with three bedrooms and designed without ostentation: 'plans should be as simple and as nearly square as possible—all excrescences in the walls are costly and to be avoided, as are gabled structures in the roof'. He added:

> The external appearance should be extremely plain, and one must trust to a good outline for effect . . . Projecting porches, unnecessary gables, and ornament add to the cost . . . All the space within the walls should be devoted to kitchen and bedrooms. What the labouring man wants is *living accommodation*, pure and simple.[155]

This equation of architectural simplicity with good housing design (i.e. the rejection of unnecessary ornament, and the use of harmonious proportions) was thus being advocated in Ireland at exactly the same time as the more famous English exponents such as Raymond Unwin, Alexander Harvey, and Charles Ashbee.[156]

Another important Irish architect within this category was Anthony Scott, who sat at the head of a dynasty responsible for numerous labourers' cottages in the Dublin region. Anthony Scott worked for, among others, Navan RDC, Balrothery RDC, and South Dublin RDC. In his obituary the *Irish Builder* adjudged that 'he probably designed and superintended the building of far more houses for the working classes than any other architect in Ireland'.[157] In 1901 Scott handed over his position in South Dublin to Thomas Joseph Byrne, his ex-pupil and very soon to be his son-in-law. Byrne had worked from 1899 to 1901 with the prestigious LCC Architects Department, first in the section responsible for new fire stations, and then on the design of working men's hostels. He was extremely influenced by the innovative municipal housing being built in London, and for a while lived in a flat on the LCC's Millbank Estate in Pimlico.[158] On his return to Ireland, he served for 18 years as the full-time clerk and architect to South Dublin RDC, during which time he designed hundreds of Labourers Acts cottages in districts such as Rathfarnham, Tallaght and Chapelizod. Byrne's experience in England was important in two respects. First, he gained knowledge of the latest town planning principles and subsequently began to extol these ideas in Ireland. For instance, Byrne criticised the policy of providing scattered labourers' cottages, and instead urged the creation of 'garden villages' or 'garden hamlets' on the outskirts of towns and villages. Second, Byrne became an adherent of the Arts and Crafts approach associated with the LCC Architects Department, and was thus the first to apply this British model to the design of mass housing in Ireland. It is significant that for the design of the two major housing programmes carried out in South Dublin under the 1906 Labourers Act, Byrne brought in his talented and widely respected brother-in-law, William Scott, to assist him. Scott had also worked on fire station and housing design for the LCC between 1899 and 1902, and (as noted in the Introduction) in his subsequent domestic projects in Ireland had shown clearly the Neo-Vernacular influence of Charles Voysey and William Lethaby.

The first programme designed by Byrne, with help from Scott, was for a total of 223 cottages distributed over a large number of sites. Built between 1908 and 1912 at an average 'all-in' cost of £236 per dwelling (including a building cost of £145), these schemes reflected a conscious attempt to increase standards in light of the 1906 Act. Whereas previous housing by South Dublin RDC had generally consisted of two-bedroom cottages, now virtually every dwelling included a third bedroom. Byrne devised a repertoire of single-storey and wide-fronted types on rural sites, these being arranged as individual detached dwellings, symmetrical pairs, or even in short terraces. Double-storey cottages with narrower frontages and terraced layouts were used on more suburban schemes, and in some instances the front room on the ground floor became the parlour. Elevations were definitely intended to be better than the typical Labourers Act house. Many of the single-storey cottages, especially in the Tallaght area, contained simplified classical or vernacular details such as string courses, brick quoins, projecting gables, and front porches with semi-circular fanlights (see Fig. 15).[159] In one scheme for 20 cottages in the village of Templeogue, a striking semi-circular site layout was introduced. The strong influence of the English Arts and Crafts was even more pronounced in South Dublin RDC's second housing programme, under which 220 dwellings were built from 1912 to 1916. Byrne and Scott were now required in some cases to design suburban terraced schemes to notably higher densities, and this forced them to pay more attention to the issues of site aspect and the maximisation of sunlight within each dwelling (in keeping with advanced housing theory in

56   *John Bull's Other Homes*

Fig 15. T. J. Byrne/South Dublin RDC: typical single-storey post-1906 Labourers Act cottages at Templeogue Road, Templeogue

Britain). 'The essential factor determining the sanitary value of a building is . . . its orientation', declared Byrne.[160] The pinnacles of pre-war housing in South Dublin RDC were represented by two quite different schemes. The first was a design that Byrne singled out for special mention, which consisted of two terraces of eight dwellings at Woodview Cottages, off Church Lane in Rathfarnham. Here there was a careful blend of four-roomed parlour cottages (619 square feet in total area), with large bedrooms of between 104 and 162 square feet, along with smaller three-room cottages (520 square feet) containing a substantial living room/kitchen of 175 square feet (see Fig. 16). Elevationally the scheme demonstrated a sophisticated manipulation of materials. The houses had a rusticated stonework base made from hammer-dressed granite and an upper storey built of local Dolphins Barn brick. There were also projecting stone lintels over the front doors, and half-timber infilling to the gable ends. The overall feel is very much that of a smaller version of the pre-war LCC suburban estates such as White Hart Lane in Tottenham, or Norbury in Croydon. The second notable scheme by South Dublin RDC was a 'model village' for agricultural labourers at Shankhill, near Bray. Here just over 30 single-storey cottages were built to a much lower density, mostly in semi-detached pairs. What was innovative was the symmetrical arrangement of the dwellings around a central green, the latter being a formal device based on an idealised image of the English village as recommended in Raymond Unwin's

Fig 16. T. J. Byrne/South Dublin RDC: Woodview Cottages, Rathfarnham

Fig 17. T. J. Byrne/South Dublin RDC: 'garden village' at Shankhill, Co. Dublin

58 *John Bull's Other Homes*

Town Planning in Practice (1909) (see Fig. 17). Byrne's work was repeatedly eulogised in the press and in official reports. The *Irish Builder* observed that his simple but artistic designs 'are models of all that Irish labourers' cottages should be', and added that Byrne 'has transformed the entire face of entire districts of County Dublin, with his most admirable cottages'.[161] The quality of design in South Dublin RDC outshone all other pre-war Labourers Acts cottages, although it should be noted that there were also two attempts to create superior 'garden villages' at Tower, near Blarney in Co. Cork, and at Gorey in Co. Wexford.[162] In general, therefore, the standard of cottages in the second phase from 1906 was raised by a combination of recommended plans and closer monitoring by the ILGB. In the best suburban schemes by Thomas Byrne and William Scott there was a careful attention to efficient site layout, orientation, rationalised design, and picturesque elevations in the Arts and Crafts manner. The results resembled the low-density and 'close-to-nature' model reached in England by an entirely different route: i.e. the anti-urban social idealism of Ebeneezer Howard and Raymond Unwin.

THE DECLINE OF THE LABOURERS ACTS PROGRAMME

The Labourers Acts stemmed from Irish agitation but ultimately depended on support from the British Government. Hence it was political events in Westminster that signalled the end of the programme. The catalyst was the constitutional crisis of 1910–11, provoked when the House of Lords rejected Lloyd George's so-called 'People's Budget'. The re-elected Liberal Party, with the IPP and Labour Party now holding the balance of power, immediately passed legislation to reduce the Lords' veto to a delaying power only. The course was now open for the introduction of the third Home Rule Bill in 1912, a reworking of Gladstone's first two measures and therefore devolutionary rather than separatist.[163] There appears to have been little consideration of the form of the future Irish administration. The Irish Party simply assumed that eight new Irish Departments would replicate the existing structure of Dublin Castle, with a Ministry of Home Affairs taking over from the ILGB (thereby demonstrating the continued inability of Nationalists to break away from British models).[164] However, the major problem with the new Home Rule Bill was that it made no allowance for Ulster Unionism, despite the private warnings of some Cabinet ministers. Egged on by the Conservative Party, ferocious Unionist opposition led by Sir Edward Carson plunged the Government into an escalating 'Ulster Crisis' that was only resolved by the outbreak of war with Germany in August 1914. The Conservatives now agreed to a compromise whereby the Home Rule Bill was passed on condition that it be suspended for the duration of the war, and that it would never be implemented until Parliament had agreed an exclusion clause for Ulster. The failure of the Asquith Cabinet to deal effectively with the Ulster problem undoubtedly undermined its authority, and also paralysed the social policies of 'New

Liberalism'. Jalland has observed that, after the premature high-point of the 1911 National Insurance Act, 'the Liberal Government was unable to give the necessary attention to the demands of the radical elements within the party for increased state intervention in the interests of the working classes'.[165] Many of the party's supporters were alarmed at the time. The Yorkshire Liberal Association warned the Chancellor of the Exchequer, Lloyd George, that unless the 'Irish Question' was settled quickly, then 'we are wasting our time on land and housing'.[166] Lloyd George was only too aware of the problem, stating that the preoccupation with Home Rule 'has stayed in the way of settling great urgent problems which affect the lives and conditions of millions of people'.[167] The consequences seemed to be borne out by a string of disastrous by-election defeats for the Liberal Party in mid-1912, during which Conservatives ridiculed the Government's impotence over both Ireland and social legislation. Lloyd George responded by launching his diversionary 'Land Campaign', an ill-fated attempt to draw attention away from Ireland and to win support (particularly in rural areas) in case of a general election.[168]

The paralysis on social issues caused by the Home Rule controversy also affected the Irish Party from 1911. By March 1913 the loan funds under the Labourers Acts were again running out, but now the IPP was hamstrung by its need to maintain solidarity with the Liberal Government while the Home Rule Bill was steered through. This allowed William O'Brien and the Independent Nationalists to seize the initiative away from an embarrassed Irish Party.[169] Chief Secretary Birrell relieved the pressure on the IPP when he finally obtained Treasury agreement for a further £1 000 000 loan, but due to the urgency of other events, the 1914 Labourers Act was not passed until war had broken out. By this point, some £4 415 000 of rural housing loans had actually been advanced.[170] Since the total fund under the Labourers Acts now stood at £6 250 000, there appeared to be plenty of scope for action. However, as will be seen in Chapter Five, the imposition of war-time retrenchment by Treasury representatives prevented any revival. As early as 1912 the Treasury Remembrancer in Dublin Castle, Maurice Headlam, had been trying to wind down the rural housing programme and prune back the ILGB staff involved.[171] By the outbreak of war, the Treasury could justifiably declare that the Labourers Acts had done their job, and that sub-standard rural dwellings had been erased.[172] The question of rural housing reform in Ireland had now become a residual issue.

Thus the Irish Labourers Acts prior to 1914 had initiated the connected policies of direct state subsidy and official type-plans for local authority dwellings. The subsidy was sufficient to create a rare example of an initiative that actually housed the class for which it was intended. Indeed the success in rehousing agricultural labourers was shown by the increasing tendency from 1906 to also include low-paid workers who lived in suburban districts. The scale of the Labourers Acts programme produced a complete 'municipalisation' of new working-class dwellings in rural Ireland: an achievement that can still be seen today in the plethora of detached, usually single-storey, pre-war cottages dotted around Munster and Leinster.[173] There would appear to be a paradox in that the most advanced—or certainly the most 'socialised'—housing model came about in what was the least economically developed part of the United Kingdom. This, however, can be explained by seeing the Labourers Acts as a response to the economic and political problems engendered by an uneven process of modernisation. The initiative was therefore a product of the major socio-economic transformation in rural Ireland that, through legislation for land redistribution, was forming a peasant proprietorship. The specific impetus for the state to become the principal provider of rural cottages came from the desire of the Irish Party to absorb farm labourers into the parliamentary Nationalist movement. The political basis of the Labourers Acts was shown by the fact that this class was in severe decline, and that therefore nearly 50 000 new houses were supplied in a condition of diminishing demand. By 1914, a profusion of cheap dwellings had been provided and still the wages of agricultural labourers had continued to rise. Interest was stirred amongst British housing reformers, particularly in the best designed cottages such as those in south Co. Dublin. Yet the example of the Irish Labourers Acts only hardened the resistance of the pre-war Liberal Government and Imperial Treasury to the extension of central state subsidy to other sectors of the housing market. The strength of this resistance in Westminster, and the political battle it provoked in Ireland, forms the context for the next chapter on Irish urban housing.

Chapter 2

URBAN STATE HOUSING IN IRELAND BEFORE 1914

The last chapter showed that from the 1880s successive British Governments were compelled to intervene in Irish rural housing, as a result of the Irish Party's determination to use land reform as the engine for Home Rule. State intervention was deemed necessary because Ireland was an important agricultural supplier to the British market. But given the relative insignificance of Irish industry, what was the attitude of Westminster and Dublin Castle to the housing problem in Irish towns and cities? This chapter will show that, despite a relative absence of state support for Irish urban housing compared with the Labourers Acts programme, similar political pressure from constitutional Nationalists produced a turn-around in policy through the 1908 Irish Housing Act. From this point until the outbreak of the First World War, it was the urban housing question that became the most volatile social issue in Ireland.

There had been signs of early industrialisation in Ireland in the period prior to 1815, but after this date the spectacular growth of industrial capitalism in Britain had left most of the country relatively untouched. The causes of Irish industrial retardation are the subject of debate, but contributory factors included an absence of natural energy resources, a lack of risk investment in domestic industries, and an unfavourable geographical location on the periphery of European markets.[1] The domination by British capitalism also consumed a large proportion of potential Irish labour, particularly in the spheres of heavy industry and transport infrastructure. Large Irish immigrant communities formed in many of the great western ports and industrial centres of Britain, notably Liverpool, Manchester, Glasgow, and also in the metropolis of London. In 1861 nearly 9 per cent of the British workforce were Irish-born. The vast majority of this group worked as unskilled labourers, constituting a genuine lumpen-proletariat that was notoriously the lowest paid and worst housed sector of the working classes. As a result the Irish gained a stereotyped, not to say prejudiced, reputation for violence and drunkenness.[2] By the late-nineteenth century, Ireland and mainland Britain were virtual mirror-images in terms of their demographic structure. In 1881 only 25 per cent of the Irish population lived in towns, compared with about 70 per cent in Britain; even after the First World War, the figures were around 30 per cent and 80 per cent respectively.[3] Ireland before 1914 had in the region of 1 300 000 urban inhabitants. There were only two cities of any real size: Belfast, which by 1901 was the largest with a population of 350 000; followed by Dublin, with 305 000 citizens. The next in importance was Cork (76 000 population in 1901), followed by Londonderry and Limerick (both with just under 40 000), and then Waterford (under 25 000). These six cities accounted for nearly two-thirds of the entire urban population. A further 150 000 or so people lived in the disparate suburbs surrounding Dublin; the remainder in secondary ports or market towns such as Galway or Kilkenny.

Only Belfast was truly enmeshed with British industrial capitalism, importing vast quantities of coal and then exporting the products of its staple industries, linen and shipbuilding.[4] Yet even in Belfast the unique political and religious circumstances produced a distinctive character. Three-quarters of the city's population were Protestant (either Anglican or Presbyterian), and thus most of its capital was in the hands of Unionist businessmen determined to preserve the market connection with Britain against the threat of Home Rule. Belfast Corporation was a staunch defender of Unionist interests, modelling itself on the confident new British municipalities and in particular on the Conservative-controlled administration in Liverpool.[5] The Corporation successfully implemented the twin policies used in the nineteenth century by its British counterparts to increase municipal power. A steady process of boundary extension helped the population swell from 20 000 in 1801 to around 90 000 in 1851, and then to almost four times the latter figure by the turn of the century. Property revaluation in the first decade of this century also raised Belfast's rateable valuation to nearly £1 500 000, enabling the Corporation to cut the local rates to only 6s 1d in the £1.[6]

Belfast Corporation from the mid-1840s also introduced a series of local by-laws and improvement measures to ensure that the booming city had a sanitary housing stock. And because Belfast's industrial and suburban expansion began later than in comparable British cities, more of its dwellings conformed to the higher standards imposed by these building regulations. The Corporation acted as a locus of power for wealthy Unionist housebuilders, notably Sir Daniel Dixon and later Sir Robert McConnell. As in the industrial cities of Northern England during the late-nineteenth century, the supply of new speculative housing in Belfast generally kept pace with, and often exceeded, demand. The number of houses in Belfast rose from 12 342 units in 1851 to 67 108 in 1901, resulting in a fall in average occupancy to only five persons per dwelling. Housebuilding ran at a rate of around 1000 units a year in the 1880s, then boomed in the next decade at an annual average of nearly 2000 dwellings. Production reached a peak of 4500 new dwellings in 1898, before tailing off sharply. It was later estimated that in 1904 there were 9000 vacant dwellings in Belfast.[7] Most new houses were built for the working classes, and conformed to the repetitive 'by-law housing' found in English towns.[8] Rigidly laid out in monotonous terraces at a density of around 40 dwellings per acre, the typical Belfast home was a 'two-up-two-down' built of good quality red brick with a slate roof. A single-storey rear projection contained the scullery, and in the backyard was a coal store and dry privy (water closets were not common until

1911). Houses were carefully graded in size at rents between 2s 6d and 5s per week, thus catering for all sectors of the working classes. The smaller dwellings were colloquially known as 'kitchen houses', and had a single room for living and cooking plus three bedrooms; more expensive were 'parlour houses', which had the front room given over to this symbol of social respectability. Belfast's housing stock was of course not perfect: the persistence of a few slum spots around the docks and the Smithfield Market area continued to cause concern. Nevertheless, the Royal Commission on Working Class Housing in the mid-1880s found the housing situation in Belfast to be good, a view often reiterated. 'No city in the Kingdom has a better supply of smaller modern suburban houses at very moderate rents', wrote the *Irish Builder* in 1913.[9] Ulster Unionists and their supporters on the mainland capitalised on the belief that Belfast was the best housed city in the United Kingdom, portraying it as a vindication of Unionist values. Political opponents could not respond. 'In Belfast, the housing problem is not so urgent or so difficult as it is in other Irish centres', conceded the city's solitary Irish Party MP.[10] The inconsistency in the Unionist argument, however, was that other towns in Ulster did not match Belfast. For instance, Londonderry had a healthy rate of speculative building but was still riddled by decaying older dwellings; one-room tenements formed around 7 per cent of the town's housing stock in 1913, and housed the female workers for its low-wage textile industries. Smaller towns appear to have had the worst housing conditions in the province.[11]

Yet the problems in Ulster were nothing compared with Southern Ireland, where towns and cities acted principally as centres for the exchange and consumption of agricultural wealth.[12] The largest urban concentrations were ports that served the hinterland (aided by the railway boom from the late-1840s to the mid-1860s), and also contained associated export industries such as brewing or distilling. The coastal economy sustained a small mercantile middle class, both Protestant and Catholic. But given that trade was relatively constant, towns in the South remained economically stagnant. The example *par excellence* was Dublin, where a particularly unfortunate combination of economic, political and social factors created a housing situation that was in greatest contrast to Belfast.[13] In the eighteenth century Dublin had been the second city of the British Empire, but after the Act of Union the population barely grew despite a continuing role as the administrative, legal, banking, medical, and intellectual capital of Ireland. The 1911 Census revealed that 194 250 people, 63 per cent of the population, were classified as 'working class'. What was most alarming was that the city had a very small industrial base. 'Dublin is, in point of economic structure, the weakest city in the three kingdoms', declared a contemporary economics professor.[14] Some industries did well by exporting quality foodstuffs to Britain, notably the Guinness brewery and Jacobs biscuit factory. But despite a scattering of engineering works, only a fifth of male workers were in manufacturing. Instead there was a preponderance of low-paid casual labouring and carrying work centred on the docks: in 1911 some 20 per cent of Dublin's workers were classed as general labourers, and a further 15 per cent worked in the transport sector. Unskilled occupations accounted for around half of the workforce.[15] Structural unemployment was probably around 15 per cent (it was estimated at around 7000 in 1909), and under-employment undoubtedly affected many more.[16] Over 12 000 people received outdoor relief every year in the pre-war period, on top of the 32 000 or so who at any time resided in Dublin's workhouses. Wages crept up but slowly, with the average combined earnings for a Dublin family just before the First World War reaching only 22s 6d per week. Casual labourers earned just 18–20s, only 66–75 per cent of the average unskilled wage in Britain (skilled workers in pre-war Dublin fared slightly better, with a weekly take-home of around 36–40s).[17]

The most telling sign of extensive poverty in Dublin was the putrid slums, a widespread problem noted ever since the 1836 Poor Law Commission. In the mid-1840s, Frederick Engels described the city's poorer districts as 'among the ugliest and most revolting in the world'.[18] By the early-twentieth century, Dublin had a veritable 'cordon insanitaire' of slum-lands that encircled the city centre, with the exception of the wealthier south-east sector. 'The whole city', wrote the *Irish Builder* in 1913, 'outside a few leading streets is in a process of decay.'[19] Surviving photographs show a rash of ruined or demolished properties more akin to a modern war-torn city (see Fig. 18). Contemporaries searched for comparisons with the worst spots of Europe, such as Budapest, or with Imperial horrors like Calcutta. 'The slums of Dublin are the worst in the kingdom', opined *The Times*, adding later that such conditions 'would not be tolerated even in a modern Oriental city without desperate attempts to remedy so deplorable a state of things . . . Yet people die like flies in its squalid slums.'[20] By the turn of the century, Dublin's slums had replaced Irish rural dwellings as the most frequently cited social problem. As one Irish Party MP put it, 'the housing problem really touched Dublin in a more extraordinary way than any other city in the Empire'.[21] British politicians of all parties echoed the despair. The pre-war Chancellor of the Exchequer, Lloyd George, described the city as having 'the worst housing conditions in Europe'.[22] A leading Conservative MP stated that 'the point about Dublin is that it is infinitely the worst of all the great cities in the United Kingdom. It is not that it has got a few slums, but it seems to have got very little else.'[23] Much of the social concern about Dublin's slums focused on moralistic side-issues such as drunkenness, inefficiency, immorality and crime. One lurid description called the slum-lands 'a thing apart in the inferno of social degradation', and another declared the problem as 'sui-generis both in its extent, and the intensity of the evils which it involves'.[24] Yet in late-nineteenth-century Dublin, following developments such as Charles Booth's sociological survey in London, there was also a clearer understanding of the direct link between bad housing and the prevalence of low-paid casual labour. The influence of poverty on Dublin's slums was tentatively mentioned by the 1884–85 Royal Housing Commission, and became explicit in subsequent

Fig 18. Photograph of a typical Dublin tenement slum in the early twentieth century

inquiries such as the 1900 report into public health in the city.[25] By 1913 the *Freemans Journal* could write unequivocally that 'the question of the slums is not simply a question by itself, but is related to a much bigger problem—the problem of unemployment and of the uncertainty of work'.[26] A political edge to Dublin's social problems was provided by the exodus from the mid-nineteenth century of the professional and middle classes, including a large proportion of Protestants, to live in the southern suburbs.[27] Catholics by 1911 now accounted for 83 per cent of the city's population, and the administration of Dublin Corporation was left increasingly to Nationalists from the Catholic lower-middle class (predominantly merchants, shopkeepers and publicans). Unionist opposition from suburbs such as Rathmines and Pembroke emasculated boundary extension, and a property revaluation in the mid-1900s lifted the rateable valuation to only £1 180 000. Despite constantly high rates, set in 1911 at 10s 10d in the £1 for the north side of the city and 10s 6d for the south side, municipal debt soared to nearly £2 700 000 by 1914. The *Irish Builder* wrote that Dublin's financial difficulties, 'and the apparent insolubility of its housing problem, is undoubtedly to be found in the ever increasing tendency of the better-to-do classes to migrate to the suburbs'.[28]

The net result for Dublin was a housing stock shown by official reports to have improved only marginally from the 1880s up to the First World War. For the discussion here the most complete data, those from the 1911 Census, will be used.[29] The root problem was that speculative housebuilding in Dublin had virtually ceased for several decades. From 1891 to 1911 the population of the city grew by 20 600 and yet only another 2600 new dwellings were added: an average pre-war building rate of 130 dwellings per year.[30] Even in the suburbs comparatively little was built for the working classes, precluding suburbanisation, and forcing Dublin's labourers to make do with the existing stock. Thus of the 194 000 working-class citizens in 1911, only 32 000 lived in purpose-built new houses (most of these provided by semi-philanthropic or municipal bodies). A further 34 000 people were recorded as inhabiting older dwellings deemed to be satisfactory ('1st Class'). This left 128 000 people—66 per cent of the working classes, and around 40 per cent of the total population—in substandard housing. Around 10 000 of this category lived in self-contained '2nd Class' or '3rd Class' houses, which were either dilapidated single-storey cottages or jerry-built dwellings erected in the back-lots of the grand terraces of Georgian Dublin. The vast majority of Dublin's poor, some 118 000 people, were squeezed into just over 5000 so-called 'tenement houses'. These were not purpose-built tenements, as in say Glasgow, but instead Georgian houses that had been crudely converted into multi-occupancy flats with inadequate, or even no, sanitation. As early as the 1870s the *Irish Builder* remarked that 'the great majority of our working classes are housed in antiquated and ill-drained and ill-ventilated tenement houses', and that 'whole streets of houses once occupied by single families are now inhabited by several families, from basement to attic . . . It is a system of "flats" improvised, but not the Scotch system of "flats", built to order.'[31] In 1884 the Medical Officer of Health, Sir Charles Cameron, noted that the city:

> does not in the least resemble Belfast, Liverpool, Manchester, Glasgow, and most other British cities. The latter consist in the chief part of new buildings, but they differ from Dublin in the important point that their working population live in houses built specially for them, and adapted to their wants, whilst the Dublin artisans and labourers live chiefly in the decayed houses of former generations of people of superior rank.[32]

The pressure of living in even once-grand houses took its toll. By 1911, around 1500 of the worst tenement houses, containing 22 700 people, were technically defined as being totally unfit for habitation. Surplus demand also resulted in nearly 80 per cent of all tenement flats consisting of only one room. This was equal to a third of Dublin's housing stock, giving it easily the highest incidence of single-room units in the United Kingdom (next came Finsbury in London, with just under 28 per cent, and Glasgow with 20 per cent).[33] It meant that 22 108 families, nearly a quarter of the city's population, lived in one-room tenements (compared with around 14 per cent in Finsbury and 13 per cent in

Glasgow). Overcrowding was chronic. The average occupancy of a one-room flat in Dublin was five people, but many contained more. The proportion of families with over five members living in a single room was twice as high as that in Glasgow, the next worst case.[34] As one graphic example, *The Times* reported a harrowing Dublin court case in which the defendant lived in a one-room tenement with 'his brother and himself, his wife, his six children, and his brother's child, who was dying of consumption—ten persons in all.'[35] With virtually all of the other 20 per cent of tenement flats having only two rooms, by 1911 the average occupancy of what had been a single-family Georgian residence was now 22 persons. Official inquiries revealed houses with up to 98 people living in them!

Housing shortage also meant that rent levels in Dublin were higher than in other Irish towns. In 1912 the typical rent for a one-room tenement was 3s per week, a sum which in Belfast would pay for a three-room house. To move up to a two-room flat in Dublin, a tenant would pay between 3s and 4s 6d per week, and for a further room the rent would rise to 4–6s.[36] As a proportion of income spent on rent, the figures in Dublin do not appear to have been significantly different from the estimated 16 per cent paid on average by workers in large British cities.[37] More the problem was that Dublin tenants got far less for their money, and slum landlords were able to make more profit. By splitting a single Georgian house into six flats, an owner could increase the rent return on the property to nearly £1 per week, equivalent to a labourers' entire wages (it was a practice known in London as 'house-knackering'). Much of Dublin's pre-war housing, as in Britain, was owned in small parcels by a wide spectrum of petty-bourgeois and middle-class landlords. Yet there was also a wealthy stratum who owned extensive tenement property, and relied on middlemen to maximise profit through a complex pattern of sub-letting. The large property-owners enjoyed strong influence at the municipal level, causing political opponents such as *The Times* to allege that 'the Dublin Corporation is in the grip of the slum landlord'.[38] While there was a grain of truth in this charge, it was an over-statement given that Corporation members themselves owned less than 2 per cent of pre-war tenement houses. Perhaps the most chilling product of Dublin's pre-war housing problem was its contribution, along with poverty, to a persistently high annual death rate of 22 per 1000 people, and an appalling infant mortality rate of one in seven babies. Both figures were at least 25 per cent higher than in British cities, and indeed were surpassed only by the world's unhealthiest cities such as Moscow or Rio de Janeiro. From 1880, official reports on public health in Dublin increasingly pinned the primary blame on the overcrowded and insanitary tenement system.[39] By the turn of the century it was realised that the mortality rate for a Dublin labourer living in a congested tenement was twice as high as for a suburban professional. The worst fear was tuberculosis, with pre-war Dublin suffering from easily the highest incidence in the United Kingdom.

The economic and social problems of Dublin were repeated on a lesser scale in the other towns of Southern Ireland. The 1884–85 Royal Commission heard of woeful housing and poverty in Limerick, Cork, Waterford, Galway, New Ross, and in towns near to Dublin such as Kingstown (now Dun Laoghaire). Later investigations added numerous other centres, including Sligo, Drogheda, Tipperary, Wexford, and Howth, to a growing roll of dishonour.[40] Decayed Georgian dwellings were often shoddily converted into overcrowded tenements, and in smaller towns especially there were extensive single-storey cottages, poorly built in render and thatch, and not dissimilar to the worst rural housing. Limerick was the provincial town frequently described as having the worst housing conditions after Dublin. In 1913 there were 1050 tenement houses in Limerick, around 20 per cent of the housing stock, and the proportion of one-room flats was around 15 per cent.[41] Employment was mostly confined to casual labouring related to the docks and railways, and Limerick's rates in 1908 stood at 11s 6d in the £1. The Irish Board of Works noted that it was 'a backward town, and the housing accommodation for the poorer classes is of a squalid description'; the *Irish Builder* could think of nowhere 'with worse slum dwellings than Limerick or where proper houses for the poor are more necessary'.[42] It was part of a wider housing problem whose causes lay, as an Irish Party spokesman pointed out, 'in the poverty of the towns, in the high rates of the towns, and in the unwillingness of Parliament to give any assistance in the matter'.[43] It was the legacy that any housing reform movement in Ireland had to deal with.

URBAN HOUSING REFORM IN IRELAND

The crucial difference between urban housing reform in Britain and Ireland lies in timing. Economic depression and cholera outbreaks in England in the early-1830s prompted the first official health inquiries, and out of these came the partnership of public regulation and private charitable activity best symbolised by the semi-philanthropic housing companies set up from the 1840s by Lord Shaftesbury and others. Reform was more tardy in Scotland, not commencing until the 1860s, by which point urban municipalities had begun to take a more active role through innovative Improvement Acts.[44] Ireland, being mainly an agricultural country, followed such developments at one remove. The London-based *Builder* noted in the late-1870s that 'the Artisans' and Labourers' Dwellings movement in Dublin is very small in its dimensions'.[45] In a recent account, Daly has observed that in nineteenth-century Dublin there was a lack of public interest and charitable action on the issues of public health and housing.[46] Quite simply, the stratum of upper-class and middle-class society which provided the charitable reformers in Britain was narrower in Ireland, and was beset by social and religious differences. Unionist reformers were often treated as would-be proselytisers, and found it hard to bridge the gulf between themselves and the poor Catholic labourers who were the main source of concern. For their part, Catholic organisations preferred to deal with moral or temperance issues rather than concrete social problems. A rare example of ecumenical reformism was provided by Sir Charles Cameron, a Unionist who served as Dublin Corporation's Medical Officer of Health from the 1870s to the First World War. Cameron's aims were openly paternalistic, arguing that 'the wealthy classes must stand *in loco parentis* to the poorer and more dependent classes'.[47] Yet his attempts to bring together different Irish social groups on the issue of public health remained only partially successful.

It was cholera epidemics in Ireland in 1848/49 that prompted the pioneering investigations by two medical practitioners serving in the front line, namely Dr Malcolm in Belfast and Dr Willis in Dublin.[48] Medical alarm was simple and direct. 'A man going about with insufficient clothing would probably only injure himself, whereas if his house is in a filthy condition it may injure me, and as a means of protection I get his house put into a proper sanitary state', as Sir Charles Cameron was later to note.[49] Concern over a further cholera attack in Dublin in 1853/54 led to the building of a pair of single-men's lodging houses; one by a businessman, Thomas Vance, who also provided a small block off Lower Bridge Street for 30 families at rents of 1s–3s 6d per week.[50] Of more significance for Dublin's housing in the 1850s were the first schemes built by employers for their workforce. Over the next half century, housing was built for skilled workers in suburban areas, mostly by transport firms such as the Great Southern and Western Railway Company (142 cottages), the Midland Great Western Railway Company (83 cottages), and the Dublin United Tramway Company (104 cottages). From 1872, the Guinness Company also built a total of 180 dwellings in a mixture of tenement flats and higher-rent cottages. The economic rationale was the same as for British welfare industrialists: Sir Arthur Edward Guinness said that by providing these dwellings, the company's employees 'live in fresher air and are more healthy; there are fewer days in the year when they are unable to do their work, it saves in that way'.[51] But in a non-industrial city like Dublin, such efforts had limited effect.

The first sustained initiative for public health reform in Dublin occurred in the mid-1860s, at a time of sharp economic downturn and a further influx of disease epidemics from Britain.[52] In 1862, Nugent Robinson called for the establishment of semi-philanthropic housing companies, a sentiment echoed by Dr Edward Mapother following his appointment two years later as Dublin Corporation's first health officer.[53] By 1866 the Corporation had set up a Public Health Committee, with Robinson as its secretary, an initiative marred, however, by persistent laxity over cases where councillors used their influence to protect vested interests.[54] In the same year came Ireland's first housing legislation, the 1866 Labouring Classes (Lodging Houses and Dwellings) Act. It was a belated transference of British powers, combining Shaftesbury's two measures of 15 years previous, with a new measure to facilitate the building of individual dwellings for the working classes. The Irish Board of Works could now make public loans at 4 per cent interest over 40 years to private companies, and even municipalities, for up to half the cost of a housing scheme.[55] The outcome in 1866 was the Dublin Industrial Tenements Company, the first joint-stock housing body in Ireland on the British model whereby a reduced 5 per cent dividend was paid to investors. Most of the founders were Dublin businessmen, along with reformers such as Dr Mapother. In the event the company built only one scheme in Meath Street in 1867, consisting of plain four-storey brick tenement blocks with 50 small flats at rents of 1–4s per week. It soon became a well-known slum. Further activity under the 1866 Act was slow. By the time it was superseded 20 years later, a total of only £190 000 had been advanced and 3416 dwellings completed.[56] Even less use was made in Ireland of the 1868 Artisans and Labourers Dwellings Act (the Torrens Act), which gave local authorities powers to repair or demolish individual insanitary dwellings if owners failed to maintain them.

Economic revival in Dublin in the late-1860s reduced concern about public health, yet by now housing reform was established as an issue. In 1871, at a Corporation banquet, the Lord Lieutenant of Ireland called for an end to political agitation by wondering 'that more has not been done in this country to *improve the habitations of the poorer classes . . .* we require a time of peace and quiet in order to carry out these reforms'.[57] Other influential voices, notably the *Irish Builder* and reformers such as Charles Dawson, constantly promoted the need for semi-philanthropic housing companies.[58] The next impetus came from a devastating smallpox epidemic in Dublin in 1871–72 which killed an unprecedented total of 1650 people. A report by Dr Thomas Grimshaw (later to become Registrar-General for Ireland) drew links between fever outbreaks and the slums, and resulted in the formation in 1872 of the Dublin Sanitary Association. This soon became the most effective public health pressure group in Ireland, combining members of the medical profession, barristers, Protestant clergy, some wealthy Unionist businessmen, and a few Corporation councillors.[59] The Dublin Sanitary Association had two major results. Firstly, it ensured that Dublin Corporation was the first municipality to issue by-laws under the 1878 Irish Public Health Act, covering factors such as street widths, constructional standards, waste removal, and the usage of lodging-houses and tenements (other urban authorities in Ireland by comparison were slow to use these powers, not least because the ILGB failed to issue model by-laws until 1903). Secondly, it was lobbying by the Dublin Sanitary Association that secured the extension to Ireland of the Artisans and Labourers Dwellings Improvement Act of 1875 (the Cross Act).[60] This measure, inspired by Scottish Improvement Acts, was primarily intended to facilitate the clearance and redevelopment of London's slums. Urban authorities were offered public loans at 3.5 per cent over 50 years to clear insanitary sites, with the intention that the land would then be sold or leased to private companies to build new dwellings (municipalities were permitted to rehouse as a last resort, if no private body came forward). A key requirement was that the same number of people as displaced, though not necessarily the same people, had to be rehoused. Eligibility under the Cross Act was confined to towns with a population over

25 000: a threshold that made sense in Britain but, as Irish MPs pointed out, was nonsensical in Ireland since only five cities would be included. Calls to lower the population limit in Ireland were spuriously dismissed by the Conservative Home Secretary, Assheton Cross, on the grounds that 'he thought the Irish members wished England and Ireland to be treated alike'.[61] Subsequent amending legislation in 1879 and 1882 reduced the limit to 12 000 inhabitants, bringing more Irish towns into the frame, and removed the need to rehouse the same number of displaced people on the cleared site.

As well as providing the Irish Party with an inappropriate model for the first Labourers Act, as was noted in the last chapter, the 1875 Cross Act also boosted urban housing reform. Out of a housing conference organised by the Sanitary Association in early-1876 came the Dublin Artizans Dwellings Company (hereafter DADC). The DADC was to prove the only sizeable semi-philanthropic housing body in Ireland: not surprising given that it contained the city's Unionist business elite, including Sir Arthur Edward Cecil Guinness (its chairman, and later Lord Iveagh), Arthur Edward Guinness (later Lord Ardilaun), William La Touche, and John Jameson, as well as wealthy Anglo-Irish landowners such as the Earl of Pembroke and the Countess of Meath.[62] From the outset the DADC was run as an efficient business and paid a dividend of between 4 and 5 per cent to shareholders. 'The commercial principle must be upheld', declared Sir Arthur Guinness, 'and to succeed it must be made to pay' (significantly, many Guinness workers lived in DADC dwellings in south-west Dublin).[63] Yet the declaration of free-market principles cannot conceal the fact that the company received two forms of state assistance from national and local levels. Over its period of activity, the DADC obtained nearly half its capital expenditure, around £290 000, from public loans at interest rates that were slightly better than the general market rate. Furthermore, on two early clearance schemes under the Cross Act, the DADC also benefited at the ratepayer's expense when Dublin Corporation leased it sites for sums that did not cover the expensive acquisition costs.[64] Both sites were in south-west Dublin; the first, the Coombe, cost the Corporation in 1878 some £24 000 to buy and develop, and was then let to the DADC at an annual rent of nearly £200 per acre; the second, at Plunket Street, cost £37 000 in the early 1880s and was let at £133 per acre. However, the financial strain put on Dublin Corporation (by 1913 the Coombe scheme had lost over £26 000, and Plunket Street over £31 000) made the Corporation decide never to repeat the mistake, and so the partnership soon ended.[65] The loss sustained by the Corporation was by no means a subsidy for Dublin's poor, but simply helped to sustain the pretence that 5 per cent semi-philanthropic housing was financially viable.

The DADC built in total nearly 3600 dwellings, plus a few shops. Given that private housebuilding had virtually ended in Dublin, the DADC thus assumed the mantle of the major provider of new working-class dwellings. Its economic rationale determined both the type of housing built and the class of tenant catered for. The company's prestige provoked an interest in housing design hitherto lacking in Irish architects, with for instance Sir Thomas Drew acting as its first adviser.[66] In terms of design, the DADC concentrated on two strategies taken directly from London precedents. The first was to provide small flats with between one and three rooms in multi-storey blocks, on the lines of those by Sir Sydney Waterlow's Improved Industrial Dwelling Company. This strategy was used for early schemes where the DADC had to buy central sites at full market prices, such as the four-storey block in Echlin Street, and by fixing rents at only 2s–4s 3d per week was aimed at the poorer members of Dublin's working class. The DADC built in all some 454 model tenement flats, but then abandoned the policy because it was deemed unsuccessful both financially and morally (small flats did not allow for gender segregation in children's sleeping arrangements). Furthermore, the use of tenement blocks was strongly criticised by the *Irish Builder* and others.[67] Instead, as Sir Thomas Drew admitted at the outset, the DADC's real view was 'that cottages would be much better suited for Dublin than the barrack-system which was in vogue in England'.[68] Thus the vast majority of DADC dwellings, some 3130 units, were built as cottages in lower density layouts. The first major cottage estate was at the Coombe in 1880–82, with 210 mainly two-storey houses built around four squares in a spacious arrangement made possible because Dublin Corporation was shouldering the loss. The second Cross Act scheme at Plunket Street had 126 cottages and dated from the late-1880s. But from this date the DADC favoured the building of even larger estates on cheaper suburban land. Here the model was another London precedent, the General Industrial and Artisans Housing Company: the result was estates laid out in long, monotonous rows such as in Oxmanstown in north-west Dublin (900 dwellings built 1903–08), and outside the city in Rathmines (318 cottages), Bray, and Kingstown. The DADC's own architect, Charles Ashworth, developed a standard range of house types based on the typical speculative terrace, with frontages between 14 and 18 feet. The basic division was between single-storey and two-storey dwellings, but within each category there was a range of two to three rooms in the former, and three to five rooms in the latter. The relatively high cost and low density of cottage estates meant that, as the DADC always openly admitted, it was only able to rehouse better-paid skilled workers if it was to pay the required dividend. Standard rents for single-storey DADC cottages were thus from 3s 6d to 5s per week, and for two-storey dwellings from 6s to 8s. The DADC dwellings were renowned for housing the elite of the working classes, and indeed were made desirable by this fact. The DADC relied on the justification used by semi-philanthropic housing bodies in Britain, namely that by rehousing this sector there would be a 'filtering up' of the poor into vacated dwellings.[69] Yet even the single-minded business strategy of the DADC could not help when the pre-war slump in Dublin brought its building work to an abrupt end in 1907. The slump also put paid to the few other joint-stock housing companies that had laboured in the shadow of the DADC.[70]

Before looking at municipal housing reform, it is worth noting two further philanthropic models brought over from Britain during the 1890s and aimed at providing cheaper flats for the poorest citizens. The first was the Guinness Trust (later the Iveagh Trust), set up in April 1890 in emulation of the famous Peabody Trust, with a donation of £50 000 from Sir Arthur Edward Cecil Guinness.[71] The Guinness Trust provided 586 dwellings in all, the most important scheme for 250 flats, with between one and three rooms, in three five-storey blocks in the Bull Alley area next to St Patrick's Cathedral (see Fig. 19). The design showed considerable architectural care by the London practice of Josephs and Smithem, with 'Queen-Anne' style gables, dormers and chimneys used to enliven the elevations. The Bull Alley project later included a lodging-house, public baths, and recreation building, making it an enclave of Unionist social reform in a decaying Nationalist city. The second model imported to Dublin was that of the strictly managed lodging-houses pioneered by Octavia Hill. An isolated experiment had been tried in the 1870s; then in 1898–1900 three companies were set up, of which the most significant was the Association for Housing the Very Poor (formed after a special conference organised by Sir Charles Cameron on behalf of Dublin Corporation's Public Health Committee).[72] For its second scheme in 1905, the Association moved closer to the principles of Samuel Barnett's East End Dwellings Company and built a three-storey block of 118 very basic single-room flats. Yet even with public loans of £9000 from the sympathetic Irish Board of Works, and by increasing rents to 2s 6d–4s 6d per week, the scheme was a financial disaster.[73]

Fig 19. Guinness Trust: the Bull Alley scheme (1899–1905), and adjacent; Dublin Corporation: the scheme at Brides' Alley (1901–11)

It was another demonstration of the failure of semi-philanthropic housing to continue in the face of the pre-war building slump. Nevertheless, by the First World War this form of initiative had contributed some 4500 dwellings in Dublin, equivalent to around 15 per cent of the city's housing stock.[74] It was a substantial total, proportionately more than in London, though helped by the fact that there had been virtually no competition from private speculators. Over 75 per cent of semi-philanthropic dwellings were built by a single company, the DADC, yet as an essentially Unionist organisation it remained somewhat anachronistic in a Nationalist city. Victorian reform bodies such as the Statistical and Social Inquiry Society or the Philanthropic Reform Association persisted into the twentieth century, but became increasingly marginalised. Perhaps the most telling epitaph for the voluntary reform movement came in 1913, when *The Times* thundered: 'The reproach for the condition of Dublin must lie chiefly at the doors of the better classes of the city, whose apathy and lack of public spirit has so long permitted nearly a third of the population to live in an environment which should long ago have been dealt with'.[75]

EARLY MUNICIPAL HOUSING IN URBAN IRELAND

The remainder of this chapter is concerned with Irish municipal housing, which grew steadily to take over the primary housing role from 1907 when semi-philanthropic activity collapsed. Municipal action began in the wake of the 1875 Cross Act, but, paradoxically, it was the failure of this measure that proved to be the spur. As in Britain, the Cross Act itself was little used in practice: a total of only £81 000 was borrowed under its terms, and no schemes were started after 1885.[76] Instead, the first local authority in Ireland to build its own dwellings, Waterford Corporation, did so out of grievance. For it, alone out of the six county boroughs in Ireland, was ineligible under the Cross Act since its population was below 25 000 people. The Corporation owned a uniquely high proportion of land in Waterford, and this enabled it to follow the precedent that had been set in 1869 by Liverpool Corporation through the pioneering municipal scheme at St Martin's Cottages. In 1878–79 the Waterford Corporation, using a loan of £1700 under the 1866 Irish Housing Act, built 17 two-storey terraced houses, each with four rooms, at Green Street (then Green's Lane) in Ballybricken, to the west of the city centre (see Fig. 20).[77] Waterford was thus one of the first authorities to act anywhere in the United Kingdom, but it proved a chastening experience. Originally the Corporation had hoped to make a profit, but due to contractual problems and unforeseen building costs, rents had to be set at 4s 6d per week just to cover expenses. Although the figure was later dropped to 3s 6d, the cottages still lay beyond the reach of unskilled labourers in the town.

The scheme by Waterford Corporation marked the start of a wave of municipal activity during the widespread economic depression that hit cities such as Dublin in the late-1870s and persisted for over a decade. In Britain the

Urban State Housing before 1914 75

Fig 20. Waterford Corporation: the first terrace at Green Street, Ballybricken (1879)

depression heightened concern that semi-philanthropic companies were not catering for those most in need, the labouring poor, and the 1880s saw a near panic over the prospect of social breakdown in areas such as the East End of London.[78] Echoes of these fears were voiced by contemporary housing reformers in Ireland. In 1883 the *Irish Builder* claimed that Dublin's slums were 'a serious social problem, which must be solved before long, or dangers will arise which the Government may not be able to cope with . . . the sooner our statesmen recognise the fact and legislate with the view of minimising the evil, the better it will be for the common good and well-being of all classes in the State'.[79] The Registrar-General of Ireland, Dr Thomas Grimshaw, called for the eradication of slums because 'ill health produces poverty, that poverty produces crime, and that so long as this vicious circle exists we need not expect anything but social chaos'.[80] Irish MPs successfully lobbied for the 1884–85 Royal Commission on the Housing of the Working Classes to turn its attention to their country in its third volume of investigation. It proved, like in Britain, to be a desultory affair that revealed the extent of the slum problem but offered no real answers.[81] The minor legal adjustments incorporated into the 1885 Housing Act were paltry, particularly when compared with bold calls in Ireland for a far broader municipalisation of working-class housing. The Irish Party's representative on the Royal Commission, Edward Dwyer Gray, was an ex-Lord Mayor of Dublin Corporation, and in his 'minority report' he called for the wholesale purchase of urban land by local authorities. Michael Davitt, the hero of the 'Land War', and now a sworn enemy of urban landlordism, declared in 1886: 'I favour Corporate bodies building dwellings for the poor when decent ones will not or cannot be erected by private enterprise without over-renting the occupants'.[82] In January 1887 the Irish Party even introduced its first private members Bill to deal with urban housing. The measure, however, was dropped when its main proposer died suddenly.[83]

It was against this background that Sir Charles Cameron in late-1879 recommended that Dublin Corporation should itself rehouse the poor, rather than pursue any further disastrous schemes with the DADC. Cameron estimated that the Corporation could make a 4 per cent profit and yet still provide dwellings for 10 000 citizens at rents of up to 2s 6d per week.[84] There was much support for his view, particularly from a deputation of local labourers protesting about chronic unemployment in August 1882. The Artisans' and Labourers' Dwellings Committee of Dublin Corporation, which had hitherto dealt with Cross Act clearance work, sent an official to study early municipal schemes in Liverpool and Glasgow.[85] In February 1884, formal approval was given for the Corporation's first housing scheme at Benburb Street (then Barrack Street), to be carried out under the 1866 Act. The DADC protested on the grounds that rate revenue was being misused to compete unfairly with semi-philanthropic housing, but Dublin Corporation officials argued that their explicit intention was to build for 'those for whom no company would attempt to provide dwellings'.[86] The result was that Benburb Street was designed by the City Architect, D. J. Freeman, as consciously austere four-storey blocks in the manner of the tenements erected by the Glasgow Improvement Trust. Built in 1886–87 at a total cost of £27 920, the scheme contained 144 small flats with between one and three rooms at rents from 1s 6d to 5s per week (there was also a separate 72-bed lodging-house; see Fig. 21). The Benburb Street blocks were built to such a low sanitary and constructional standard that they needed constant remedial work.[87] A proposal to build cottages at Dublin Corporation's second site, Bow Lane, was rejected because rents would have been too high. The scheme built from 1888 to 1889 comprised 86 flats with two or three rooms, let at 2s to 4s 6d per week, in two-storey cottages (a model used by speculative builders in Newcastle, and later tried out by the LCC). The Bow Lane cottages were designed by Arthur Dudgeon to utilise the supposed economy of reinforced concrete floors, staircases, and flat roofs. They too ended up as a catalogue of building failures. Thus although Dublin Corporation built 230 dwellings in the 1880s aimed at housing the poorest labourers, cost-cutting had been at the expense of design standards.

In addition to Waterford and Dublin, evidence suggests that 11 other Irish municipalities built housing during the 1880s.[88] The largest number of dwellings outside Dublin was in Cork, where 90 houses were provided on disused land in two schemes at Madden's Buildings (1886) and Ryan's Buildings (1888). The plans for these four-room, two-storey dwellings were essen-

Fig 21. Dublin Corporation: the Benburb Street [Barrack Street] scheme (1886–87)

tially those of the speculative terrace, but were even more basic in that there was no scullery and the upper floor consisted of attic bedrooms lit by rooflights. From outside it gave the cottages the appearance of being single-storey (see Figs 22–23).[89] The 1885 Housing Act, by offering public loans at only 3.5 per cent over 50 years to urban authorities, also enabled smaller bodies such as Sligo UDC and the New Ross Town Commissioners to each build just over 25 dwellings at rents around 3s 3d per week.[90] In total, the 13 active Irish municipalities provided around 570 dwellings in the 1880s, proportionately more than the estimated 2400 dwellings built by 5 authorities in Britain prior to the 1890 Housing Act.[91] Ireland, with an urban population only 5 per cent of that in Britain, had produced nearly 25 per cent of Britain's stock of municipal dwellings. Even before 1890, Irish urban housing was comparatively more municipalised.

NATIONALISM AND MUNICIPAL HOUSING IN IRELAND FROM 1890

In Britain the reform impetus during the 1880s led to the famous 1890 Housing Act, and this was extended to Ireland despite protests from Irish MPs that they had not been consulted about its provisions.[92] The Act was mostly unadventurous: existing measures to clear insanitary areas were consolidated under the 'Part 1' clauses, those dealing with individual unhealthy dwellings under 'Part

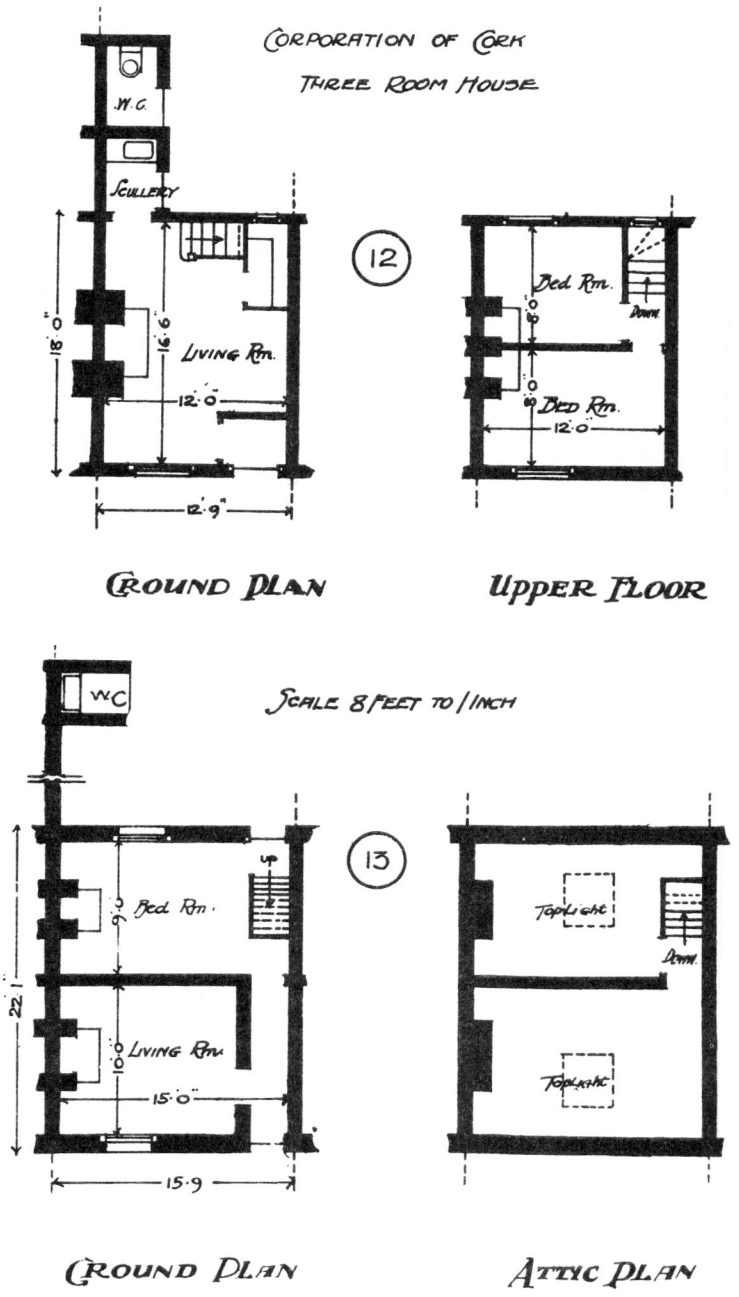

Fig 22. Cork Corporation: typical municipal terrace plans (1886/1905)

Fig 23. Cork Corporation: Roche's Buildings (1892) and Sutton's Buildings (1905)

2'. Yet a considerable widening of powers came in the 'Part 3' section, since it allowed local authorities for the first time to build new dwellings on virgin sites and thus remedy housing shortages as well as engage in slum replacement. The 1890 Act also improved public loan terms by fixing a 3.125 per cent rate of interest and extending repayment periods to up to 60 years. In Ireland it ushered in a distinct new phase in municipal housing. A realistic estimate is that by March 1901, a decade after the 1890 Act, a further 1500 dwellings had been added to make a cumulative total of nearly 2100 units. By the date of the next major legislation, the 1908 Housing Act, Irish urban authorities had probably built some 5000 dwellings.[93]

Also significant was that the middle-sized urban authorities had become more active.[94] Prior to 1890, this category had built only 30 per cent of urban municipal dwellings; by the mid-1900s it was nearer a half of the total. By 1906 some 70 out of the 125 Irish urban municipalities had begun housing work. Particularly prolific were a cluster of wealthier suburbs to the south of Dublin, now determined to eradicate slum pockets in their area.[95] Rathmines UDC, which remained staunchly Unionist, built 355 dwellings by 1908; Pembroke UDC, where Unionist domination dissipated after the 1898 Local Government Act, built 269 houses by the same date; and Kingstown UDC, a more distant railway suburb and passenger port, embarked in 1903 on over 300 dwellings. These three suburbs, with a combined population of around 85 000, produced nearly 1000 units (a fifth of all municipal housing in Ireland) before the 1908 Housing Act. Nearly half of the 5000 municipal stock were now in the capital or its environs, with Dublin Corporation remaining the single largest producer with around 1200 dwellings by 1908. Elsewhere the largest concentrations were to be found in Cork (515 cottages) and Waterford (260 cottages).

Less clear are the reasons behind fluctuations in activity by Irish municipalities under the 1890 Act. In Britain it has been argued that the rate of pre-war municipal housebuilding under 'Part 3' clauses was inversely related to the amount of empty housing stock (itself a product of economic cycles in speculative building), and was mediated by demands from local organisations of skilled labourers.[96] In Ireland, the 1890s were a period of relative prosperity in Dublin and other towns, but this was followed by a prolonged economic depression and a fall in real wages from 1904 to 1912. During this downturn, the slump in the British housebuilding industry spread to Ireland.[97] Although British economic cycles tended to have a lesser effect in agricultural Ireland, the effect of the pre-war Irish building slump could be seen in two ways. As noted earlier, from around 1907 it became financially unrewarding for semi-philanthropic companies like the DADC to build new schemes. And in Belfast, the only Irish city with an extensive private housebuilding sector, the boom of the late-1890s had plunged to a rate of only 622 new dwellings in 1906. Gradually the surplus of empty stock in Belfast was eaten away in the pre-war period.[98] Yet there was still no apparent pressure on Ulster municipalities to intervene. Londonderry Corporation provided nothing, and Belfast built only a 222-bed single-men's lodging hostel (1899–1903), as a reluctant contribution after it had been pushed by the ILGB into a small clearance scheme.[99] The activity of Irish urban authorities up to the pre-war building slump had been fairly consistent. From 1901 to 1903 advances to Irish municipalities soared to nearly 100 per cent of all public loans for urban housing. However, with the onset of slump in 1904, municipal building suddenly dipped substantially while private housing companies made a brief revival (see Diagram D and Table 5).[100]

Political factors appear to have been of more importance to Irish municipalities than economic pressures. By 1890 the growing interest of constitutional Nationalists in urban housing turned the issue from one of public health into a political demand that paralleled rural housing reform. This stemmed from the Irish Party's attempt to sustain a municipal hegemony (outside Ulster and a few southern Dublin suburbs) that depended on uniting a heterogeneous mix of lower-middle-class merchants, shopkeepers, publicans, professionals, and Catholic clergy.[101] As in rural areas, a continual concern of the IPP was to stress the Nationalist demand over labour issues and thereby to prevent the formation of an independent working-class political party as in Britain.[102] They were aided by the fact that the lack of industrialisation meant that the Irish labour movement was late to develop, and structurally weak even when it did.[103] Skilled trade unions were set up in the mid-nineteenth century, often as branches of British organisations, and from the 1880s started to form Trades

Councils in larger cities. These councils, however, were highly conservative, aiming to improve pay and working conditions for their skilled members rather than pursue militant political demands (a tendency confirmed with the formation of the Irish Trades Unions Council in 1894). Even in Belfast, which had formed the first Trades Council in 1881 and a local labour party in the next decade, an overriding concern with maintaining pay differentials plus sectarian rivalry led by Protestant skilled workers—Ireland's own 'aristocracy of labour'—caused fragmentation and stagnation.[104] The opposition of skilled trade unions also helped to defeat efforts in 1889–91 to organise the many unskilled labourers in Dublin and Cork on the lines of the so-called 'new unionism' in Britain.[105]

However, the flurry of excitement about 'new unionism' did inflame the divisions within the Irish Party following the fall of Parnell in late-1890. Both factions began to jockey for the favour of the urban working classes. The anti-Parnellites were led by the vocal champion of land and housing municipalisation, Michael Davitt, campaigning through his short-lived journal *Labour World*. On the other hand, the Parnellite rump believed, probably erroneously, that their strongest support lay in Irish towns. Hence Parnell, previously indifferent to urban labour issues, in the period up to his early death in October 1891 openly courted the labouring classes by advocating measures such as land acquisition to build municipal dwellings.[106] During the parliamentary debate in 1891 on rural housing subsidy, discussed in the last chapter, the Parnellite faction suddenly put forward an amendment to extend the financial benefit to Irish towns (though not the largest county boroughs). It was the first attempt to secure urban subsidy, but as Parnell told the Commons, 'there are no people in the world, certainly there are none in Ireland, whose dwellings stand more in need of improvement than those of the artisans and labourers in Irish towns'.[107] Chief Secretary Balfour was alarmed by a proposal which might have wrecked his Land Bill, and so asked 'whether it is quite fair to the Government to ask them to graft on to a Bill for land purchase in Ireland so novel and so wide-reaching a proposal, and one that would involve the employment of funds contributed by the British taxpayer for the erection of artisans' dwellings in the Irish towns?'. When the Parnellite MPs pointed out the inconsistency of this argument, in that the first-ever rural housing subsidy was already clumsily tacked on to the Irish Land Bill, Balfour fell back on to a line that had been first used by William Gladstone and which was to become the standard response for British Governments over the next quarter century:

> The Act for providing agricultural labourers with cottages is a very exceptional one; but, then, it is admitted that the condition of the agricultural labourers in many parts of Ireland is exceptional, and there is no analogy between their condition and that of the agricultural labourers in England and Scotland. But when we come to the towns,

can we make out a distinction whatever between the urban population of Ireland and the urban population of England or Scotland?[108]

Balfour's refusal of urban housing subsidy was not seriously challenged by either faction of the IPP, and the interest of constitutional Nationalists in urban issues faded when the organisation of unskilled unions failed to materialise. This possibly explains the slight downturn in municipal housebuilding in the early-1890s.[109] The next potential challenge to the Irish Party's dominance over labour interests came when the 1898 Irish Local Government Act extended the municipal franchise. The Dublin electorate increased five-fold, and Cork's four-fold; the outcome was the election of a few independent labour councillors in these cities. The new councillors, however, were members of skilled trade unions and showed no sign of social radicalism. Most were quickly absorbed into the constitutional Nationalist movement, but the Irish Party only achieved this assimilation by deliberately including the demands of urban labour within its social programme, in an attempt to ameliorate internal class conflict. Thus the 1898 Local Government Act appears to have stimulated municipal housing at the turn of the century, and forced the IPP to balance petty-bourgeois property interests along with those of the working classes.

Nowhere was the incorporation of urban housing reform into constitutional Nationalism after 1898 more clearly demonstrated than in Dublin. An alliance was formed between the Corporation and the Dublin Trades Council, and was led by councillors who became local Irish Party MPs on an avowedly 'Labour-Nationalist' ticket (the most vocal was William Field, a wealthy cattle trader, and the other figure of note was Joseph Nannetti, a skilled trade unionist and ex-President of the Trades Council). Dublin Corporation was by this point demanding the two housing powers most desired by British municipalities: increased borrowing limits for housing, and the right to build on suburban land outside the city area. In August 1899 the Corporation decided to call a housing conference, but was pre-empted by an ILGB inquiry into the city's health the following year. At the inquiry, Dublin Corporation declared that it wanted to borrow £500 000 to rehouse 10 000 of the poorest citizens at rents less than 3s per week, even if it meant incurring a housing rate charge of 6d in the £1. The Corporation also wanted powers to encourage speculative builders to provide suburban estates, or, if necessary, for it to build these itself.[110] Yet the Irish Party and Dublin Corporation were incensed when the Conservative Government refused to include Ireland in either the 1900 Housing Act (which gave suburban housing powers to local authorities) or the 1903 Housing Act (which removed the borrowing limit for municipal housing, and increased loan periods to up to 80 years). For the first time in 34 years, Ireland had been deliberately omitted from British *urban* housing legislation, and the divergence was soon to widen further.

The Irish Party, particularly William Field and Joseph Nannetti, demanded bitterly in the Imperial Parliament that Ireland be given comparable treatment at once.[111] To increase the pressure, the Corporation organised a special Housing Conference in September 1903 following a request by the Dublin Trades Council.[112] The conference was a one-sided Nationalist cabal, with no representatives from the Unionist suburbs, and not surprisingly the report simply reiterated the calls for the extension of the housing powers recently granted to British authorities. Of interest was the faith placed by the conference in the suburbanisation of the working class as the means to relieve overcrowding, and to provide lower rents by capitalising on cheaper land prices. Suburbanisation was envisaged as a combination of municipal activity and private speculation, the latter being encouraged by the offer of a ten-year rate remission on working-class dwellings (a similar incentive had been used by Belfast Corporation, and was recommended by British supporters of town extension planning such as Thomas Horsfall and John Nettlefold, the Chairman of Birmingham Corporation's Housing Committee).[113] Support for a policy of suburban housing was common within the Irish Party and included its leader, John Redmond.[114] But the most tireless advocate was a figure at the heart of Dublin Corporation's housing drive, Councillor Coughlan Briscoe. It was Briscoe who was the main mover in forming an effective national organisation known as the Town Tenants League in 1904, for which he acted as secretary. The role of the League was to continue and intensify the long-standing Nationalist campaign to win the same legal and rent protection against urban landlords as was enjoyed by rural labourers. The League therefore served an important function within the broad alliance that supported the cause of constitutional Nationalism. By taking up the grievances of the urban working class, it helped to ameliorate the friction that was inevitable in the unequal power relations between landlord and tenant. Playing the Nationalist card certainly seems to have kept these tensions at a much lower level than found in England or Scotland. But more significant here, the Town Tenants League also ensured that the issue of urban housing moved to the forefront of Irish Party policy.[115] William Field was appointed as the League's President; previously he had warned Parliament, using typically inflammatory language, that improved working-class housing:

> was a burning question in Dublin, and also in Cork, Limerick, Waterford, and other places . . . it is possible that our civilisation might be overturned; if it were, it would be by our slums—by the rebellion against the land system, the capitalist system, which condemned the workers to live in a state of barbarism.[116]

From 1904 the Town Tenants League provided a bridge for municipal housing agitation between constitutional Nationalists at local and national levels. There were parallels in Britain with the role of local Trades Councils and the Workingmen's National Housing Association, a combination which proved decisive on housing policy in towns like Sheffield or Coventry.[117] The key differences were that the British organisations represented only skilled workers desiring better quality housing, and they did not have a national political party solidly behind them. By contrast, the Town Tenants League was yet another outlet for the Irish Party. Thus in 1904 John Redmond threw his weight behind demands that the Conservative Government bring in new urban housing legislation for Ireland. At first, Chief Secretary Wyndham seemed willing to accede to this request. But, as was seen in the last chapter, in his dismal proposal for rural housing, the policy of 'constructive Unionism' was at this point being obstructed by those who were determined not to give increased spending powers to Nationalist municipalities. Wyndham incurred the wrath of the IPP by declaring that, due to a heavy legislative programme, action on Irish urban housing would have 'to await a more favourable time'.[118] As long as the Conservatives held power, there was little that the Irish Party could achieve.

Meanwhile, urban authorities in Ireland were experiencing severe difficulty in their determination to build dwellings for the poorest labourers at rents of no more than 3s per week. Evidence is sketchy, but figures given by a leading ILGB official in 1907 stated that the average municipal rent was 2s 4d, and that most Irish schemes incurred a loss to the rates.[119] The burden was less critical in smaller towns, since fewer houses were built and the availability of cheap land allowed the favoured option of 'Part 3' cottage schemes. Where site costs were higher, municipalities had to rely on a range of unsuccessful strategies. Dublin Corporation, for example, faced the most expensive sites in Ireland, and its financial problems were compounded by a rise in building costs in the early-1890s. Thus the Corporation pursued a complex and often vacillatory policy under the 1890 Housing Act, combining slum replacement schemes on central sites with suburban cottage estates at much lower densities.[120] Corporation slum-clearance during the 1890s ended in disaster in two tenement schemes early in the twentieth century. At Brides' Alley (1900–11) a total of 176 flats with two to three rooms were built in three- and four-storey blocks, with Dutch gables that echoed the adjacent Iveagh Trust housing (see Fig. 19). But due to exorbitant site costs (over £11 500 an acre) and expensive foundation works, rents were set at 3s 6d–6s 6d per week and Dublin Corporation decided to curtail the scheme. An even larger estate of austere five-storey tenements in the 'red-light' district of Foley Street was built in 1904–05 as a blatant attempt to house the very poor: 80 per cent of the 460 flats had only a single room plus scullery and WC. This scheme also backfired on Dublin Corporation when the estate earned such an unrivalled reputation for vice and squalor that loss-making rents, some as low as 1s per week, had to be set.[121] By 1913 these two schemes had between them lost over £70 000, amounting to half of the Corporation's housing deficit in the pre-war period.[122] Dublin Corporation tried the popular alternative of self-contained cottages for the first time in 1894–95, at St Joseph's Place (then White's Lane). Here 80 single-storey and three-room houses were laid out in terraces in the backlot of a Georgian street block. But the lower density of 160 persons per acre (far below the 400 plus in tenement blocks) meant rents of 4s to 6d per week that were beyond the reach of labourers. The cottage model became more widely used when a partial boundary extension in 1900 gave Dublin Corporation access to suburban land. Small schemes were built in Drumcondra (1903–04) and Clontarf (1904–05), but easily the largest was for 220 cottages at Inchicore from 1905 to 1910. The 13-acre site here cost only £320 per acre, around 5 per cent of the typical rate for central sites.[123] Yet again, a density of 138 persons (approximately 30 dwellings) to the acre, and the use of larger three- to four-room cottages, some with bathrooms, produced rents of 4s–7s 6d per week aimed explicitly at skilled artisans. Many Dublin councillors openly questioned the wisdom of suburban housing if housing was not being provided more cheaply, especially if tenants were going to have to pay transport costs on top. The *Freemans Journal* argued that 'the great cost of travel in Dublin makes it out of the question to house the worker at any distance from his work'.[124]

Cork Corporation tried a similar mixed policy of inner-city tenement blocks and cottage estates on green-field sites, but it too was unable under the 1890 Housing Act to set rents affordable to unskilled workers.[125] The authorities in Dublin's southern suburbs were faced by powerful ratepayers' associations opposed to any housing loss, and so tended to build only high-rent cottages. However, two competitions were also held to design cheap tenement schemes, the first by Rathmines UDC in 1900 and the other by Kingstown UDC in 1907. The latter was won by a London architect with a design for 134 flats with two rooms at only 2s per week, but it was so substandard that the ILGB insisted it be drastically altered.[126] No Irish municipality could find a satisfactory solution: tenement blocks for the very poor were unpopular and incurred heavy losses, whereas suburban cottage schemes resulted in expensive rents. In Britain, only Liverpool Corporation seriously tried to rehouse the very poor, and even with a loss on the rates, no more than half of its tenants were labourers. Every other pre-war municipality followed the lead of LCC (with its famous resolution in 1893 that rent income had to provide a minimum 3 per cent return on capital expenditure), and catered for the skilled artisan.[127] But while the rationale of high-rent cottages had some attraction in a British city with a large artisanal class, on the grounds that 'filtering-up' would help the poor, it had no validity in Irish towns where the overwhelming need was to rehouse casual labourers near to their workplace. By the mid-1900s it was obvious to most observers in Ireland—and particularly constitutional Nationalists—that urban housing subsidy was required. The prerequisite for this was sustained political agitation.

THE IRISH PARTY AND URBAN HOUSING AFTER 1906

The last chapter showed that the 1906 Labourers Act resulted from the need of the Irish Party, in collusion with the new Liberal Government, to offer social reform as a substitute for Home Rule. There were also great expectations for urban housing legislation amongst the party's supporters in Dublin Corporation. In January 1906 the incoming Lord Mayor, Joseph Nannetti, promised that it would be one of the first issues to be taken up, a message welcomed by the Irish TUC and the Dublin Trades Council.[128] The Town Tenants League mounted a sustained campaign calling for urban housing subsidy. The League even included housing provisions in its new draft Town Tenants Bill, but was persuaded to confine this measure simply to improving tenant rights.[129] Instead, the IPP leader, John Redmond, made it clear in September 1906 that urban subsidy would be his next goal, adding that 'no settlement of the labour question in Ireland can be complete or satisfactory which does not provide decent and cheap homes for the workers in the towns as well as in the country'.[130] A few months later his deputy, John Dillon, proclaimed that:

> the Irish Party have not the least idea of deserting THE CAUSE OF THE TOWN LABOURERS . . . We will take up their case now and press it with all our energy. Let me say this to the town labourers of Ireland . . . that if they want to get their cause brought on to a speedy success they ought to organise, and they ought to carry on this agitation in alliance with the Irish Party.[131]

There was, however, a difficulty for the Irish Party, which was that preparations for a new Housing Bill had already been set in motion by the President of the English Local Government Board, John Burns. The IPP was at first determined that Ireland would not be excluded again.[132] It was heartened when a Parliamentary Select Committee looked at the financial provisions of the Irish Labourers Acts, but then dismayed when the Chancellor of the Exchequer, H. H. Asquith, rejected outright any possibility of housing subsidy. Burns turned increasingly to the idea of town extension planning, as an alternative policy, during the lengthy and complicated manoeuvres that eventually resulted in the 1909 Housing and Town Planning Act in Britain.[133] To the IPP, ever dedicated to extracting subsidy from the Treasury as redress for what it saw as the economic exploitation of Ireland, this was a foolish diversion. One Irish Party MP summed up its approach when he declared that 'finance and finance alone was the means to remedy the grievance'.[134] By late-1906 the IPP had lost patience with Burns and was instead demanding separate legislation for Ireland. The problem, however, was that the two Irish Chief Secretaries concerned—first James Bryce, and then, from January 1907, Augustine Birrell—were both ideologically opposed to state subsidy, and did not want to prejudice any potential Government housing measure now that Burns had finally got round to addressing the issue directly.[135] The danger of stalling, however, stemmed from the fact that the 1907 parliamentary session was proving uneasy for the pact between the Liberal Cabinet and the Irish Party. The Castle Administration's attempt to push through a half-baked scheme of limited devolution had been sunk when the IPP withdrew support. By late-1907 the IPP's strategy of cooperation was being widely criticised in Ireland, and Redmond was not in a conciliatory mood.[136] In particular, there were two political threats facing the Irish Party. The first was a need to reassert its dominance over the Irish labour movement, following a new and sustained attempt from 1907 to organise unskilled labour in Dublin. This latest variant of 'new unionism' was led by Ireland's leading Marxist theorist, James Connolly, and the union boss *par excellence*, James Larkin. The medium was the renowned Irish Transport and General Workers Union (hereafter ITGWU), which in its goal to become 'one big Union' progressively absorbed virtually all labourers and transport workers, reaching a membership of 10 000 in 1913.[137] Larkin gradually won control of the Dublin Trades Council and Irish TUC, and pursued an effective combination of syndicalist strike action, socialist propaganda in the *Irish Worker*, and (from 1912) political action through the Irish Labour Party. The second threat to the IPP came from the minority separatist party, Sinn Fein. The two councillors from this party who now sat on Dublin Corporation, Thomas Kelly and William Cosgrave, argued for parsimony in municipal housing and rejected any policy dependent on legislation or subsidy from the Imperial Parliament. In late-1907 Sinn Fein also seriously worried the Irish Party by putting on an unexpectedly good show in a parliamentary by-election.[138]

Chief Secretary Birrell was aware that if constitutional Nationalism became perceived as a bankrupt policy, then the Liberal Government's strategy in Ireland would be in ruins. In October 1907 he warned Prime Minister Campbell-Bannerman that the Irish Party would have to be seen to win substantial concessions if it was to remain loyal. 'What are we going to offer Ireland this next Session?' the Chief Secretary asked.[139] Birrell's proposals were for the long-desired 'Catholic' University, which Redmond accepted, and a further land purchase measure, which was rejected. Instead, Redmond substituted the alternative of state subsidy for urban housing, which he knew would go down well with Nationalist municipalities and with the Town Tenants League. In late October 1907 Redmond chose a large rally in Sligo, a western port with many unskilled labourers and chronic slums, to announce the new policy. He pledged that on 'the housing of the working classes the Irish Party intend to make a proposal to the Government of a perfectly practical character, and to press it with all the power at their command'.[140] Urban housing reform was now the IPP's immediate top priority. The *Freemans Journal* loyally declared that the issue 'was second only to Home Rule . . . If an Irish Parliament was established tomorrow this is the very first problem with which it would be called upon to deal'.[141] Redmond handed the task of drafting the legislation to J. J. Clancy, an ex-councillor on Dublin Corporation and an IPP representative at the 1903 Housing Conference. Ten days after the Sligo speech, Clancy outlined a proposal based on urban subsidy and cheaper public loans. 'If we cannot carry it or some other equally large scheme, then one more irresistible argument will be furnished against foreign rule in this island', he warned the Cabinet.[142] Redmond declared that 'in the next Session of Parliament, the Irish Party and the Irish organisation will be directed with its full force to the consideration of this question'.[143] By late November the Chief Secretary had accepted the proposals, and publicly announced that an urban counterpart to the Labourers Acts would be rushed through Parliament. A temporary setback for the Irish Party arose when Dublin Corporation that same month rashly added some housing clauses into an Omnibus Bill that it was preparing, as part of a by now outdated pledge to implement the recommendations of the 1903 conference. Fortunately for the IPP, the Corporation's whole measure was sunk by ferocious opposition from Sinn Fein councillors, the Dublin Chamber of Commerce, and ratepayers' associations.[144]

The path was finally clear in February 1908 for the Irish Party to introduce their first measure of the new session, a private members Housing Bill.[145] It proposed, first, that a subsidised public loan fund be created by diverting £5 000 000 from the Irish Post Office Savings Bank to offer to urban authorities at the staggeringly low rate of 2.5 per cent interest (this was the same rate as paid to the bank's investors, and the Treasury was to underwrite the fund in case of a sudden rush of withdrawals). Repayment of interest was also to be deferred for the first two years of any loan. The IPP estimated that the fund would provide 25 000 houses based on an estimated cost of £200 each. The loan subsidy was insufficient to avoid a loss on the rates if rents were to be set at the desired level of 2s 6d per week, and so the Bill also proposed that a special Irish Housing Fund be set up to yield a direct annual subsidy of just under £40 000. Altogether it was a bold strategy, made even cleverer by the fact that the Irish Party could claim that it did not entail one single penny of money from British sources.[146] There was wide support for the Nationalists' Bill, even from Ulster Unionists who had been hitherto silent on the subject of urban housing subsidy, prompting one IPP member to say that he 'knew absolutely no question on which there was such unanimity of feeling in Ireland'.[147] Many Labour MPs and Liberal backbenchers were also behind the measure, as indeed were several Tories.

The critical test, however, was how the Liberal Government would respond. Chief Secretary Birrell struggled to find justifications for urban subsidy. He told Parliament that the alternative emphasis on town planning powers in Burns' forthcoming measure, 'while no doubt suitable to English industrial centres of population, would not meet the difficulties which present themselves in dealing with the housing problem in Ireland'.[148] Birrell tied himself in knots when arguing why a traditional Liberal like himself, who shared the Cabinet's disapproval of subsidy, might wish to reverse the Balfourian argument (that Irish urban conditions were no different to Britain) by now treating Irish towns as a special case. 'In Ireland wages are so low', he wrote, 'compared with England, that rents which would enable the houses to be built without heavy loss cannot be paid; and the high rates and indebtedness of most urban areas in Ireland preclude the local authorities from embarking on unremunerative schemes.'[149] Such subtleties were not to the taste of the Treasury, which had two objections to the subsidy proposals. The first was that the terms were so generous that there would be no charge to Irish authorities, and hence no check on municipal extravagance. But the more important objection stemmed from a crucial structural difference between Ireland and Britain. The principle of subsidy had already been conceded for Irish rural dwellings, which in 1908 constituted nearly 80 per cent of state housing there. By contrast, it has been estimated that 98 per cent of pre-war local authority housing in Britain was in urban areas.[150] Thus any concession on urban subsidy in Ireland, which in itself might not prove too onerous to the Exchequer, had a potentially devastating effect if the Treasury was forced to concede equal terms to British municipalities. At the same time, the Treasury realised that the Liberal Government could not sink outright a measure on which the Irish Party had set its stock, and which now had the backing of Ulster Unionists. Instead, the Treasury contented itself by emasculating the financial clauses. Chief Secretary Birrell had the embarrassing task of telling Parliament that the subsidy proposals, and indeed the whole principle of incurring no charge to the local rates, had been vetoed. Birrell then offered the Irish Party an olive branch. The Government was willing to take over the measure and pass it under its own steam, if only a compromise on state subsidy could be agreed whereby the 'deficit will have to be met in some way between the liability of the ratepayer and the willingness of the Exchequer to come to Ireland's assistance in this matter'.[151]

It was, of course, a fatal flaw in the strategy of constitutional Nationalism that if the Liberal Government ultimately refused to endorse a proposal, then there was nothing that the Irish Party could do without abandoning their whole *raison d'être*. Clancy was thus forced to work with Birrell and the Irish Lord Chancellor to find a reduced form of state subsidy.[152] The resulting Irish Housing Act, known as the Clancy Act, was passed in December 1908 as a pale imitation of the original. Many of the less important clauses were residues from the 1903 Housing Conference, such as that allowing municipalities to offer rate rebates to private builders (Irish Party MPs did not hide the fact that they expected this to have little effect).[153] And, to match British powers, the limit on municipal borrowing was finally lifted and loan periods were extended to a maximum of 80 years. Loan terms were slightly improved, but only to the lowest current rate available from the Local Loans Fund. There was to be a two-year moratorium before repayment began, and municipalities were able to borrow on the new terms to reschedule their housing debts. And when it came to the central issue of subsidy, the Clancy Act demonstrated the limitations of the Irish Party. True, the first direct subsidy for urban housing was created through an Irish Housing Fund, but the amount had been cut to just around £6000 per year. This sum was derived from the annual proceeds of investing £80 000 from the Suitors Fund, in the Irish Supreme Courts and £100 000 of consols from the Dormant Suitors Fund, enabling the Treasury to argue that it had not compromised its opposition to the principle of urban subsidy. 'There was no charge on the Exchequer', boasted the Chancellor, David Lloyd George, to the House of Commons.[154] Furthermore, the Treasury also extracted its pound of flesh by secretly blocking all attempts by Irish urban authorities to reschedule their debts, and by agreeing with the ILGB that 80-year loans would only be given to buy land, and never to build dwellings.[155] The result was continual animosity between the Irish Party and the Treasury, with the latter clearly resenting having to give improved financial terms to Nationalist authorities in Ireland.[156] The Liberal Government did, however, prove more resistant to attempts by the Conservative-dominated House of Lords to mutilate the measure. Anglo-Irish landowners, who had consistently opposed Dublin Corporation's boundary extension, were alarmed by the possibility of slum dwellers being rehoused *en masse* in Rathmines or Pembroke. 'I do not wish to say anything that may be in the back of the minds of the Nationalist Members of Parliament', declared the Earl of Mayo, 'but the real truth of the matter is that if that were allowed to take place it would alter the Parliamentary representation of the South Dublin constituency.'[157] In the end, the Clancy Act went through the Lords unloved but unchanged.

The Irish Party was dismayed by the dilution of the 1908 Housing Act. The Treasury was cast as villain, and the measure was instead portrayed as a crucial *first step* towards the solution of the urban problem. John Redmond declared triumphantly that urban subsidy was 'an entire innovation; there is nothing of the kind known in the legislation of England or of Scotland', and he later boasted that the IPP had 'set an example to Great Britain'.[158] This line was echoed by Clancy when he said that 'for the first time in the history of such legislation, cheap money and a free grant in aid would be afforded for the erection of houses for the workers in towns'.[159] In this manner, the 1908 Clancy Act joined the Labourers Acts in the party's litany of legislative achievements. The United Irish League called it 'one of the most beneficent measures ever secured by the Irish Party', and the *Freemans Journal* even described it as 'the greatest aid won for reform during the last twenty years'.[160] Praise was forthcoming from Catholic clergy, such as the Bishop of Galway, and the Irish Party carefully used the 1908 Act to legitimise its approach and to unite its rural and urban supporters. John Redmond told one meeting 'that what they have done for the farmers, and what they have done for the agricultural labourers, they have also done for the artisans of the towns'; he later added with satisfaction that now, 'with the great question of the Housing of the Working Classes practically settled, the decks are clear for Home Rule'.[161] Indeed, the principal aim of the IPP was to use the Clancy Act as tangible propaganda against the independent labour movement. Redmond noted:

> We have obtained for Ireland a measure which, in principle, is far ahead of anything proposed by John Burns in his Bill. That is a great achievement, and it is an indication that we are trustworthy representatives of the masses of people in the towns . . . we will in future, as in the past, endeavour to fulfil for Ireland in the fullest sense THE FUNCTIONS OF A LABOUR PARTY, believing that we are the Labour Party, as far as Ireland is concerned.[162]

The Irish TUC loyally agreed, and in 1911 declared that the IPP 'has been a Labour Party not only for Ireland, but for Great Britain, and the most effective that the masses could desire . . . The workers of England, Scotland, or Wales would be glad to have so potent a force at their command'.[163]

THE RESULTS OF THE 1908 IRISH HOUSING ACT

Although the Treasury had cut urban subsidy, the 1908 Clancy Act still had a great effect. It provided a further boost to a pre-war climate of opinion in Ireland that overwhelmingly favoured the municipalisation of working-class housing. Once again, only a few dared to express dissent.[164] By contrast, municipal representatives were totally enthusiastic. 'For twenty years', said one Wexford alderman, 'they had been trying to deal with the housing question, but until the Clancy Act came along they had been able to do little.'[165] Clancy boasted that municipalities were now only too keen to act due to the carrot of subsidy, rather than the stick of legal compulsion:

> In England they had to be coerced in this matter. The Irish public bodies did not require to be coerced. They would gladly enter into schemes if they had any reasonable hope that they would not have to burden the ratepayers to any considerable extent.[166]

The greater degree of municipalisation in Ireland was noted at the time by official departments such as the ILGB, and also by English housing experts interested in Irish rural and urban initiatives.[167] There were many Dublin Castle officials, notably the ILGB's Chief Engineering Inspector, Dr Peter Cowan, who personally favoured public utility companies and co-partnership housing societies, on the grounds that these promoted values of self-reliance and individualism.[168] But the reality in Ireland of a moribund private house-building industry, and then the collapse of semi-philanthropic activity, meant that there was little choice for the Castle Administration but to support municipalisation. In early-1909, the Irish Board of Works and the ILGB both predicted a surge of municipal housebuilding under the Clancy Act.[169] They were not to be disappointed. Two years after the measure was passed, a total of £150 000 had been advanced to 24 urban authorities and the ILGB was inspecting over 40 further proposals.[170] Allowing for a time-lag for schemes to be designed and approved, the surge induced by the 1908 Act was shown in 1911–13 by the first real peak in public loans for Irish urban housing (see Diagram D and Table 5). Average annual housing loans to urban authorities in the five-year period prior to 1908 had been £11 685; in the five years after the Clancy Act the figure soared to £80 550 per year. The zenith reached £230 000 in 1912–13, meaning that municipal housing accounted for nearly half of all the public loans in Ireland that year. By 1914, around 80 out of 125 urban authorities had taken out public advances for housing, to a combined total of around £950 000.[171] House completions boomed accordingly. The number of dwellings built by Irish urban authorities, which had been less than 80 per year immediately prior to the Clancy Act, rose steadily from 329 cottages in 1909–10, to 709 cottages in 1910–11, before dipping slightly to 665 the following year.[172] Official statistics vary slightly, but a reasonable assumption is that a cumulative total of 7600 dwellings had been built by Irish urban authorities by 1914.[173] This meant that Ireland, with a pre-war urban population only 5 per cent of that in Britain, had a municipal housing stock equal to nearly a third of the estimated 24 000 units in British urban areas.[174] In other words, Irish municipalities had built proportionately almost seven times as much per head of urban population.

The subsidy under the 1908 Clancy Act, however partial, was clearly the decisive factor. Municipalities found that the amount they received from the Irish Housing Fund was sufficient to cover the interest charge on public loans, and Clancy boasted that 'since 1908 not only has no expense whatsoever fallen on rates, but the various town authorities have had the rents of the houses built as pure profit'.[175] This was later echoed by Chief Secretary Birrell when he told the Treasury that 'the Clancy Act . . . enabled schemes to be started without loss, and led to a healthy rivalry among the different urban authorities'.[176] This rivalry was probably greatest amongst the middle-sized UDCs.[177] This category had by 1914 increased its share of Irish municipal housing to nearly 60 per cent. Urban councils in provincial centres took advantage of the Clancy Act to augment their stock prior to the First World War, including Galway (194 dwellings), Kilkenny (140 dwellings), Wexford (117 dwellings), and Drogheda (116 dwellings). Yet easily the most active were still in the southern suburbs of Dublin. Top came Kingstown UDC, with a total in 1914 of nearly 450 dwellings, followed by Pembroke UDC and Rathmines UDC with 354 dwellings apiece, and then Blackrock UDC with 205 units. These four Dublin suburbs had built 1360 dwellings, nearly 20 per cent of the total in Ireland. Given that their combined population was only around 95 000, they had therefore rehoused around 6.5 per cent of their inhabitants in municipal dwellings (over three times the Irish national average). The causes lay in the political composition of the southern Dublin suburbs, and particularly in the way in which supporters of the Irish Party used municipal housing to win working-class votes in their bid to overturn Unionist control. For instance, in 1911 a councillor in the smaller suburb of Dalkey reminded the voters that 'when the Nationalists assumed control of the administration of Dalkey they saw that magnificent, comfortable and sanitary dwellings were erected for the working classes . . . under the Clancy Act'.[178] Housing was also a key issue in adjacent Blackrock, not least because William Field was a councillor in one of the Nationalist wards. But perhaps the most political use of housing was in Pembroke, where Nationalists finally won control in January 1911 after campaigning on a ticket that derided the record of the previous Unionist council on the issue. A massive housing programme was duly inaugurated by the energetic new Chairman, Councillor Charles O'Neill, and became an important symbol of the success of the constitutional Nationalist approach at municipal level.[179] Of the South Dublin suburbs, only Rathmines UDC remained unique in continuing to be run by Unionists; yet it too realised the need to build, or else risk unflattering comparisons with its neighbours.

The converse of increased activity by the middle-sized UDCs was that the six large county boroughs saw their proportion of Irish municipal housing slide to only 38 per cent by 1914. These largest centres had by this point rehoused an average of just 1.3 per cent of their inhabitants. Dublin Corporation continued to be the largest single builder of dwellings, even if the losses on its tenement schemes and the ferocious opposition to its 1907 Omnibus Bill now made it painfully tentative in its housing aims.[180] An awkward working relationship grew between constitutional Nationalist councillors such as Coughlan Briscoe and Lorcan Sherlock (Lord Mayor from 1912 to 1914), and the Sinn Fein team of Thomas Kelly and William Cosgrave. Both groups believed that housing should be the top priority for Corporation expenditure, but beyond this there was much disagreement and obstructionism. The agreement reached in late-1911 to set up a Housing Committee was not implemented until February 1913.[181] Much internal debate arose from the fact that all but two of Dublin Corporation's pre-war schemes incurred substantial losses, with the result that its rent income of nearly £12 000 per year met only half the housing deficit and thus necessitated a charge to the rates of $2\frac{1}{2}$d in the £1. Yet the advent of subsidy was an undoubted help: a later estimate was that after the 1908 Clancy Act, Dublin Corporation received aid from the Exchequer equal to around 10 per cent of its expenditure.[182] Thus, by the outbreak of the First World War the total number of Corporation dwellings built stood at around 1450 units in a dozen or so schemes. This represented nearly 5 per cent of Dublin's housing stock, compared with an average provision by pre-war British municipalities of not more than 1 per cent of the stock.[183] Dublin Corporation chose another comparative statistic to show that it had built proportionately more housing than any other city in the United Kingdom. The Corporation claimed repeatedly that by 1914 it had rehoused 2.5 per cent of its population in municipal dwellings, and thereby exceeded the more famous programmes of Liverpool Corporation (2895 dwellings, but for only 1.7 per cent of the population) and the LCC (10 000 dwellings for only 1.2 per cent of the population; rising to 1.5 per cent if the 2500 units by lower tier London authorities are included).[184] It was an accurate claim, but what Dublin Corporation failed to mention was that, while in Britain the largest cities led the way, in Ireland the southern suburbs of Dublin such as Kingstown or Pembroke had provided many more dwellings per head of population than it had. Of the three other county boroughs in Southern Ireland, the most curious fact is that Cork Corporation carried out no schemes under the 1908 Irish Housing Act (in striking contrast to the 546 dwellings it had built up to 1906, which still meant that Cork was the second largest owner of municipal dwellings).[185] A possible reason for the hiatus after 1908 lay in the political structure of Cork, in which Independent Nationalists under

William O'Brien held much influence. The result was that there was not the decisive combination of active Irish Party MPs plus the Town Tenants League, that was to prove so effective in promoting the Clancy Act in other centres of nationalism (indeed in Sligo, the local IPP member even suggested that a branch of the League be formed just to coordinate the housing campaign). By the First World War, both Waterford and Limerick Corporations had each built over 250 dwellings, the latter providing most of its contribution in four pre-war estates under the impetus of the local Irish Party MP and councillor, Alderman Joyce, and a particularly energetic branch of the Town Tenants League that pressed vociferously for low-rent municipal cottages.[186]

The fact that Londonderry Corporation had still not built a single house by the First World War was more to be expected. Urban authorities of whatever size in Ulster were reluctant to engage in local expenditure, and defended their inaction with the Unionist argument that housing conditions were not nearly as bad as in Southern Ireland. It has been estimated that in Northern Ireland a total of only 634 houses were built by municipalities up to 1919.[187] And yet it was also Ulster that provided the clearest example of opportunism under the Clancy Act. Belfast Corporation decided in late-1909 to undertake a massive slum-clearance scheme to replace 700 dwellings in and around Hamill Street, which lay in the western industrial area that lay between the Falls Road and the Shankhill Road.[188] There were a number of reasons for this. The downturn in speculative housebuilding provoked calls for Unionist municipalisation in emulation of Liverpool Corporation, though always expressed in loyalist terms. 'It was from the urban classes that the Government got soldiers for its army and sailors for its fleet', Alderman Dr King Kerr proclaimed, 'and if the population declined in physique and numbers owing to bad housing conditions, it was obvious that that was a very serious consideration for the Government.'[189] But what finally spurred Belfast Corporation to act was the advent of subsidy, since it realised that it could silence its critics and yet ensure there would be no cost to the preciously guarded rates. The Imperial Treasury, alarmed by a request for a huge public loan of £108 000, wanted initially to tell Belfast Corporation to raise the sum by issuing municipal stock. However, the Treasury realised that it would be unable to refuse without a Unionist outcry of unequal treatment compared with Nationalist authorities.[190] Belfast Corporation duly got its loan and began an extensive clearance in 1912, only then to procrastinate (rebuilding was not finally started until 1917). The delay provoked a stinging attack in early-1914 by the ILGB's Chief Engineering Inspector, Dr Peter Cowan, on the grounds that the subsidy to the Corporation to clear the site had drained the Irish Housing Fund, and yet there were no houses to show for it. Even more serious were allegations by the Irish Party MP for West Belfast, Joseph Devlin, that the delay proved the Unionist Corporation had only cleared the area for the sectarian purpose of breaking up the Catholic vote in the local elections. This bitter controversy certainly did not help the rehousing work to start.[191] But the real reason for delay, as will be seen below, was the Corporation's inability to secure tenders low enough to convince the housebuilders' and ratepayers' lobbies that there would be no loss to the rates. The Nationalist accusations of housing sectarianism sprang from Belfast's social structure and the pre-war 'Ulster Crisis'. Since the most deprived slums were likely to be inhabited by poor Catholic labourers, as Hamill Street certainly was, then it was this group that was bound to be dispersed. In pre-war Liverpool, similar religious and political divides led to an identical accusation, but there too it was the product of wider ideological divisions rather than a conscious housing policy.[192] In Belfast it was particularly odd of Nationalists to accuse the Corporation of gerrymandering through slum clearance when, in marked contrast to Liverpool Corporation, it had not proposed a scheme until 1909!

HOUSING DESIGN IN PRE-WAR MUNICIPAL SCHEMES

The subsidy under the 1908 Irish Housing Act increased the pressure on municipalities to keep rents low. Clancy declared that 'a grant in aid out of public funds is necessary, if in the effort to house the POORER SECTIONS OF THE WORKERS in towns at rents which they can pay'.[193] The pre-war Mayor of Dublin concurred:

> We do not ask the assistance of the state to enable local authorities in Ireland to build houses for artisans . . . who, by virtue of their positions in life, are able to pay economic rents. I appeal for that mass of humanity existing in all cities on small wages and casual employment—the very poor who are unable to protect themselves.[194]

The target now commonly cited by Irish municipalities was a rent at only 10 per cent of the average labourer's wage, i.e. around 2s per week. The Clancy Act appears to have nearly achieved this ideal. An ILGB breakdown of municipal rents in late-1913 showed that well over half the dwellings were let at between 2s and 3s per week, and only the upper quarter had rents over 3s 9d per week.[195] And due to the subvention from the Irish Housing Fund, urban authorities also found they could avoid a loss to the rates. All this was in marked contrast to Britain, where the effect of the 1909 Housing and Town Planning Act was to further concentrate activity on higher-standard garden suburbs for skilled workers.[196] The policy in Ireland had a marked effect on design, for it meant a relatively greater cost-paring and utilitarianism in pre-war housing. One Irish municipality declared in 1913 that 'it is evident that the most we can expect to provide is a sanitary dwelling, without any of that ornamentation, and even luxury, which marks the houses at present being built in the garden cities of England and elsewhere'. The ILGB's chief housing expert agreed that there 'has been no extravagant expenditure on houses larger than are required by families of moderate size; on the contrary, the authorities have striven to build houses which could be let at economic rents within the means of the poorer classes'.[197]

The ILGB laid down no standard type-plans under the Clancy Act, as it had with full subsidy in the 1906 Labourers Act. Instead, it merely set out the first space requirements for urban dwellings: living rooms were to be a minimum of 1200 cubic feet (150 square feet); the main bedroom 960 cubic feet (120 square feet); and other bedrooms at least 640 cubic feet (80 square feet). These standards appear to have been rigorously enforced. The ILGB also made it clear that it regarded the self-contained two-storey cottage as the paradigm, and that it wanted to see larger schemes and lower densities than hitherto.[198] This championing of cottage estates was, however, rather superfluous in Ireland after the 1908 Act, since, given the disastrous precedent of Dublin Corporation's tenement schemes, it was the preferred model anyway. The United Irish League, for instance, called on municipalities in 1911 'to provide cottage homes, with a patch of garden and as much space as possible for play and recreation grounds'.[199] There was, however, little interest in design innovation. The typical Clancy Act design still conformed to the rigid layout and narrow-frontage terraced plan that had been used by bodies such as Cork Corporation from the 1880s. Pre-war examples of plain brick municipal terraces, with two or three bedrooms and frontages varying between 12 feet 6 inches and 16 feet 6 inches, were found in Waterford, Dundalk, and elsewhere: it was a conservative design approach that echoed the low-cost type officially recommended in 1913 by the English LGB.[200] The connection between minimal rents and unambitious design was particularly intense where land costs were high, again notably in Dublin. Steering a course between criticisms of tenement blocks and expensive suburban schemes, Dublin Corporation from 1908 tended to build self-contained cottages on cleared inner-city sites.[201] The dominant concern was that of Nationalist councillors, such as the pre-war Lord Mayor, Lorcan Sherlock, to see that the subsidy achieved by the Irish Party was made manifest by low rents. Sinn Fein members were also determined to restrict council expenditure, and the first woman councillor, Sarah Harrison, proved from 1913 to be a redoubtable champion of labourers' interests. In 1912 the Corporation agreed a resolution to let all new municipal dwellings at only 1s per room (this was a target that had been set by Liverpool Corporation in the 1880s but never achieved).[202] Yet at the same time, the Corporation responded to ILGB criticisms of its piecemeal strategy, by also deciding on a costly policy to build cottages to a higher space standard than officially required. All bedrooms were to be a minimum of 1000 cubic feet (125 square feet), and furthermore a small playground was included in every scheme. The outcome was that only two small Clancy Act schemes were actually completed by Dublin Corporation before the First World War, at Cook Street (1912–14) and Linenhall (1913–14). Together they contributed only 93 two-storey three-room cottages, at a density of around 40 dwellings per acre. In addition, there were in 1914 a number of similar slum-clearance schemes in the pipeline, such as Beresford Street/Church Street, Spitalfields, and Ormond Market (as well as two atypical proposals to build small flats for dock labourers in response to union demands for cheap housing). It would appear that the pre-war Dublin Corporation had only limited success in rehousing the poor: nearly 70 per cent of its dwellings in late-1913 were one- to three-room tenement flats at rents between 1s and 3s 6d per week, and just over 30 per cent were two- to four-room cottages at 2s 6d–7s 6d per week. While its cottage rents averaged only two-thirds of those paid by DADC tenants for a similar dwelling, the typical pre-war Dublin Corporation estate still contained probably around 25 per cent artisans. Daly has suggested that the Corporation catered for a sector that lay between the very poor in the tenements, and the working-class elite housed by the DADC.[203]

Limerick Corporation developed a slightly different house design, based on an Irish urban vernacular type used previously by municipalities in Waterford and elsewhere. The type used in Limerick was also terraced, yet had a very wide frontage of between 21 and 23 feet to allow a window to be placed on either side of the front door. Being double-fronted, it was hence nearly square on plan (see Fig. 24).[204] There were three variants: a single-storey three-room cottage; a two-storey four-room cottage with attic bedrooms and dormer windows upstairs; and a larger five-room type to provide either three bedrooms or two bedrooms plus parlour. The rear addition was eliminated entirely in the two smaller types by bringing the scullery, WC, and coal store into the main body of the house. One of the wide-frontage schemes by pre-war Limerick Corporation was built in the decayed central district of Pennywell, and included Mitchell Street and Grattan Street. Such radical planning, however, created problems. For instance, in the four-room house the WC was located directly off the scullery, and the coal store opened into the living room.

A few Irish municipalities sought to follow the previous lead of Rathmines and Kingstown, and hold design competitions. Nationalist examples include Waterford Corporation (1909), Athy UDC (1909), and Queenstown UDC (1910).[205] Yet the most important pre-war competition was that held by Belfast Corporation in 1912–13, in an attempt to reconcile conflicting pressures from the ILGB for a high standard of rehousing, and those from Unionist councillors determined to cut costs. The Belfast competition nearly resulted in a break from the normal terraced plan, since the winning practice from Cork, Chillingworth and Levie, proposed an ingenious solution for pairs of semi-detached, wide-fronted dwellings arranged either as single-storey bungalows or else as two-storey flats with a side entrance (see Fig. 25). Each type was compactly planned, with no rear projections, and had a WC, scullery, and one or two bedrooms opening off a main living room/kitchen. Elevations were in a simplified Neo-Georgian style, with well-proportioned sash windows and hipped roofs. The front facade of the semi-detached flats gave the impression of a substantial villa due to the absence of a front door or obvious internal subdivision. However, as soon as it was found that this design came over budget, Belfast Corporation reverted to a dull terraced plan (prepared by the Assistant City Surveyor) with only a 13 foot 6 inch frontage and an external WC in the rear yard.

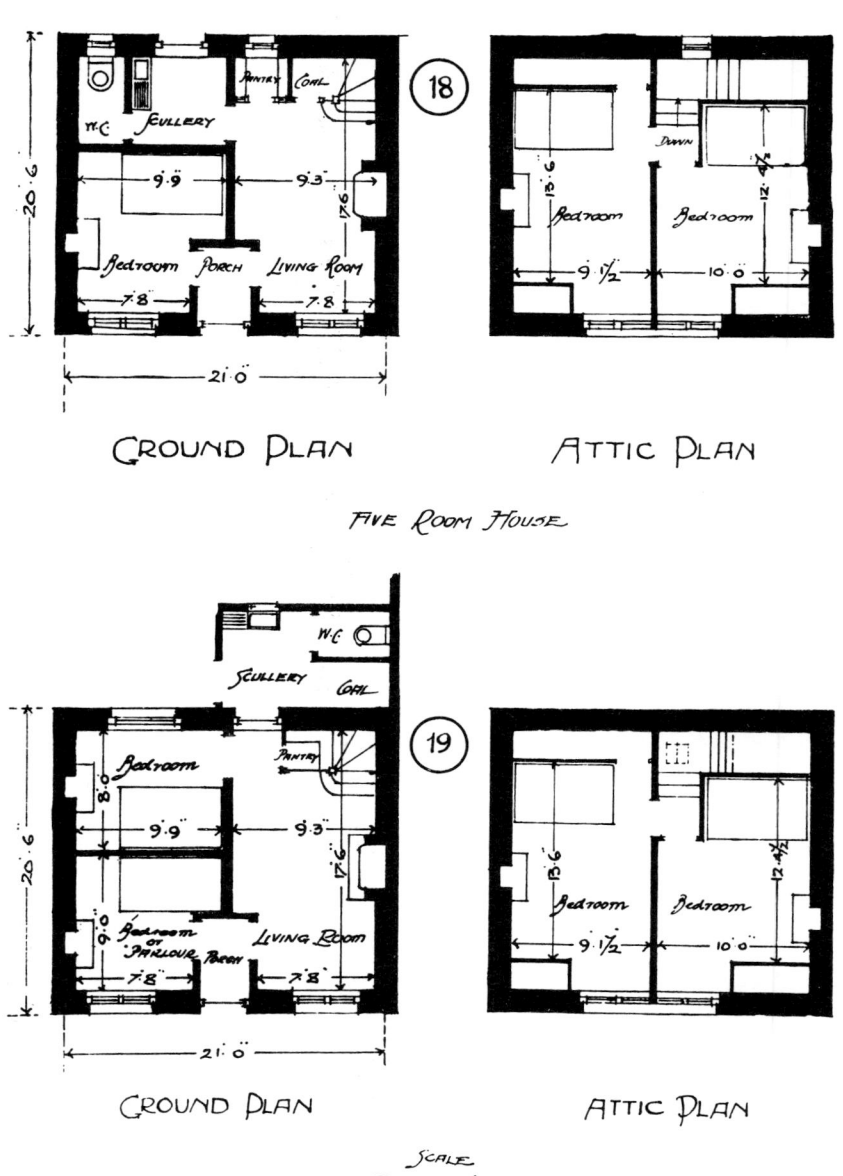

Fig 24. Limerick Corporation: wide-fronted terrace plans with front dormers (1912)

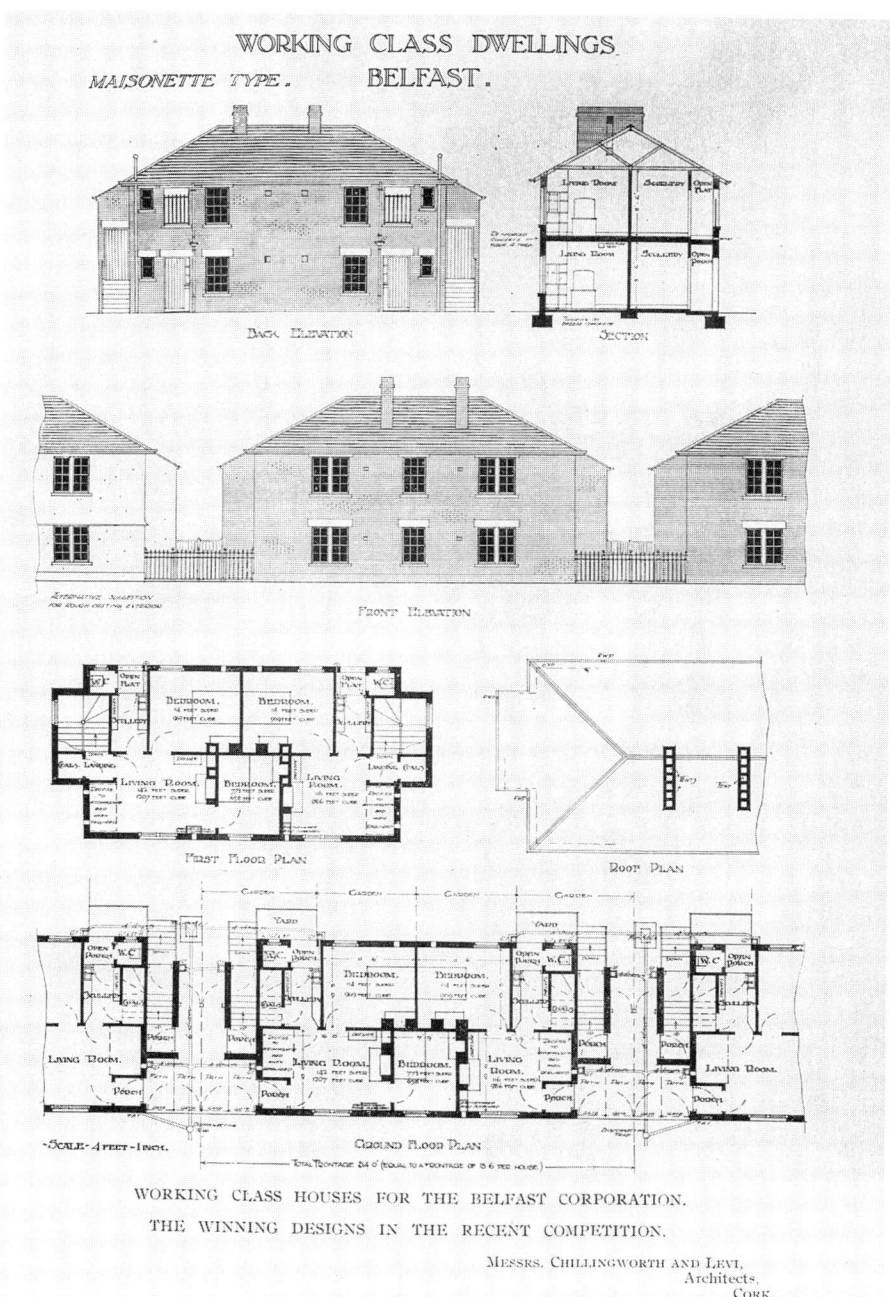

Fig 25. Chillingworth and Levie: winning entry for Belfast competition (1913)

This retrogressive decision prompted an already irate ILGB to accuse Belfast Corporation of having no real commitment to housing quality.[206] The result was a full-blooded row in early-1914 that disrupted any hope of progress in the City's rehousing work.

If competitions were unable to achieve better design within cost limits, then the only alternative option for municipalities was to pursue the English strategy of building large cottages at higher rents. But this was only feasible in the wealthier southern Dublin suburbs such as Pembroke and Dalkey, which contained a significant number of skilled artisans and lower-middle-class tenants. As the pre-war slump gradually eroded housing supply for this better-paid sector, so a few municipalities found themselves compelled to deviate from the general policy of rent-minimisation. The *Freemans Journal* defended the much-praised Nationalist Pembroke UDC on the grounds that the authority had to deal with an unfavourable combination of high land and building costs, plus a very low rate income.[207] However, the distinct policy in Dublin's southern suburbs did enable distinguished architects, such as Thomas Manly Deane for Dalkey UDC, and younger specialists, such as Edwin Bradbury for Pembroke UDC and J. L. Donnelly for Blackrock UDC, to design to a higher standard than found elsewhere under the Clancy Act.[208] The *Irish Builder* lauded the Pembroke scheme by Bradbury at Home Villas and St Broc's Villas in Auburn Avenue, Donnybrook (1911–12).[209] Here some 88 cottages were provided for a cost of £24 000, the majority in two-storey terraces with a 15 foot 6 inch frontage and containing a living room (135 square feet) and three bedrooms (120 square feet/90 square feet). There were also 11 smaller single-storey cottages with a 20 foot 3 inch frontage, comprising living room (149 square feet) and two bedrooms (106 square feet/69 square feet). The long brick elevations were punctuated by sash windows and a striking rhythm of partially-rendered gables. All dwellings had the luxury of a plumbed bath and sink in the scullery. The corollary was rents of 4s 9d per week for the single-storey units, and 7s for the larger four-room cottages. Another of the ambitious architects used by pre-war Pembroke UDC, George O'Connor, became (as will be seen in Chapter 4) one of the leading polemicists for innovative housing design. O'Connor declared in 1912, as incoming President of the Architectural Association of Ireland, that 'a hygienic and comfortable home, not unbeautiful in its external appearance, suitably planned to house the worker, was of really more importance to a nation than magnificent public buildings, and should not be beneath anyone's interest'.[210]

RESPONSES TO THE INADEQUACY OF THE IRISH HOUSING FUND

The Irish Housing Fund was a fixed, *ad hoc* subsidy unrelated to demand, and the sum of £6000 per year was soon exhausted by a rush of applications from Belfast Corporation and other bodies. Thus, while in 1911–12 the fund paid subventions to 34 urban authorities, sufficient to cover all their interest payments, by 1912–13 it could only meet 80 per cent of loan charges. The following year municipalities received 36 per cent of what they had to repay, and the momentum was such that, as an ILGB official noted, 'this percentage will gradually diminish as fresh borrowings are effected'.[211] From the outset, Clancy had pledged that 'it must be the business of the Irish Party to see to it that additions are made to this fund as opportunity offers'.[212] The IPP were provided with an immediate chance in June 1909, during the uproar over the attempt by the Conservative opposition and the House of Lords to defeat Lloyd George's so-called 'People's Budget'. The increases that the 1909 Budget imposed on whiskey were extremely unpopular in Ireland, and the IPP were not convinced by the controversial new taxes on the 'unearned' site-value of land. In Britain, Lloyd George had already promised disgruntled urban authorities half the proceeds of new land-tax revenue, to be used as supplemental rate relief from the Exchequer for education services.[213] Now the Irish Party began to demand, in return for supporting the Budget, that half of Ireland's share of the controversial land revenue be given to municipalities, not for education, but to subsidise urban housing. 'THE RESULT OF THIS LAND TAX', Redmond told his supporters, 'will be, most undoubtedly, that a considerable sum of money, and an increasing sum of money, will be available year by year to swell this Housing Fund in our Housing Bill.'[214] Amidst the escalating political crisis in June 1910, the IPP leader was still reminding Parliament 'that so far as Ireland is concerned we desired to have the half of the Land Taxes which were to go to local authorities, and that they should be reserved for the purpose of assisting our schemes for the housing of the working classes in the towns'.[215] But the demand for increased urban subsidy was halted, as in the last chapter, by the Irish Party's need to show unity with the Liberal Government during the constitutional storm of 1911 and the subsequent introduction of the third Home Rule Bill. Instead, the IPP could now only ask Nationalist municipalities to wait for Home Rule when a more sympathetic Irish Parliament could augment state subvention, and Chief Secretary Birrell brushed off attacks by arguing, against all the evidence, that the existing Irish Housing Fund was proving adequate.[216] A brief flurry of interest came in February 1912 when the Treasury quietly tried to top up the capital in the Irish Housing Fund, after the Irish Dormant Suitors Fund had become slightly over-stretched. Opposition MPs seized on the incident to embarrass the Liberal Government over the boast made in 1908 that no British tax revenue was going towards Irish urban housing.[217] But the sum involved was so minor, and clearly did no more than maintain the existing level of subsidy.

Against the background of a hamstrung Irish Party, the Association of Municipal Authorities of Ireland (hereafter AMAI) was formed in September 1912 after a conference organised by a town-planning pressure group (see Chapter 4). The role of the AMAI was to coordinate the campaign for increased urban housing subsidy. Soon it was demanding that municipalities receive public loans on Labourers Acts terms, and that the Irish Housing Fund be tripled to provide a subsidy of £20 000 per year.[218] The AMAI was therefore quite different from its counterpart in Britain (the Association for Municipal Corporations had been formed in 1872 and by the 1890s had become an effective mouthpiece of 'municipal socialism'), in that it was the specific product of the pre-war municipalisation of urban housing in Ireland. It was also avowedly non-partisan in its aims. The *Irish Times* observed that it had chosen the only pre-war issue which had 'the rare merit of being supported, in principle, by all Irish members of Parliament, without distinction of party'; and the AMAI's secretary noted 'that the exclusion of politics from the business of the association is one of its fundamental principles'.[219] Soon 62 Irish municipalities had joined, and within the climate of the 'Ulster Crisis' it had even received a letter of support from the Ulster Unionist leader, Sir Edward Carson. An active participant in the AMAI was Belfast Corporation's housing enthusiast, Dr King Kerr, who urged 'a great patriotic movement in which we can all take part, whether we come from the north or the south, whatever may be the particular shade of our party politics'.[220] Yet it was obvious that the majority of members were Nationalists, the most influential being Lorcan Sherlock (Lord Mayor of Dublin), Charles O'Neill (Chairman of Pembroke UDC), Thomas McGahon (Chairman of Dundalk UDC), and George Hadden (Alderman of Wexford UDC). Irish Party housing spokesmen such as Clancy and Field soon became closely involved, and this alliance was cemented in June 1913 when John Redmond received an AMAI deputation in London. The IPP then used the AMAI to distract attention from a campaign by Independent Nationalists which demanded that new funds earmarked for National Insurance in Ireland be given to urban housing subsidy instead.[221] Yet the dilemma remained that the Irish Party, which from the turn of the century had seized on urban housing as a key element of constitutional Nationalism, had by 1913 no real strategy to secure increased state subsidy. The absorption of the AMAI only reduced the effectiveness of the latter body in its campaign to convince the British Government.

THE 1913–14 DUBLIN LOCK-OUT AND THE HOUSING ISSUE

In mid-1913 the Liberal Government and the Irish Administration were confronted by a more urgent crisis in Dublin, namely the bitter industrial conflict provoked by the Irish Transport and General Workers Union as part of James Larkin's campaign to bring socialism to Ireland.[222] Larkin was by this point the virtual master of the Port of Dublin, but the ITGWU policy to incorporate all local unskilled labour ran into trouble when it targeted the employees of the Dublin United Tramway Company. This company was owned by one of Ireland's wealthiest railway capitalists, William Martin Murphy, who was also proprietor of the O'Brienite *Irish Independent* and a trenchant opponent of trade unions. Simmering industrial unrest escalated into a full-blooded confrontation when the ITGWU called a tram strike during the popular Dublin

Horse Show in late-August 1913. After a series of further provocations, Murphy galvanised the Dublin Employers' Federation into a 'lock-out' of all members of the ITGWU and sympathetic unions. Soon some 25 000 men were out of work in what was effectively an enforced general strike, and a total of around 100 000 members of Dublin's already long-suffering working classes were now without income. The United Kingdom's most titanic struggle to date in the battle between capital and labour resulted in Dublin being plunged into a state of disorder. James Larkin called it 'this grand class war', and his associate James Connolly wrote that 'Our enemy is the governing class; the political force of that enemy is the Liberal Government'.[223] Aided by the repressive elements of state, such as the Law Courts and the Dublin Metropolitan Police, and by conservative bodies such as the Roman Catholic Church, the employers inexorably wore down the ITGWU. But in doing so they lost much public support. Both Larkin and Connolly were temporarily jailed, causing widespread outcry. Police behaviour during the mass demonstration on 'Bloody Sunday' on 31 August 1913 was undoubtedly brutal, killing two demonstrators and injuring hundreds of others. Alarmed by the conditions in Dublin, Chief Secretary Birrell told the Cabinet that the city 'had been living in a state of terror under Larkin'.[224] The Castle Administration set up an inquiry into the dispute in September 1913, but the Dublin employers ignored its conciliatory report as well as appeals from a wide range of socialists and moderates including George Bernard Shaw and George ('A. E.') Russell. In November 1913 James Connolly defied the employers' hard-line stance by founding the Citizens Army to protect the ITGWU against potential attack. But in reality the ITGWU was by this point seriously depleted by a shortage of funds and by its failure to convince moderate British trade unions to support it. There was a gradual drift back to work until the dispute finally collapsed in February 1914. The glorious attempt to forge a socialist Ireland had ended in a defeat that was to retard the growth of trade unions and the nascent Irish Labour Party for several decades.[225]

One important by-product of economic turmoil was the establishment by the Castle Administration of the 1913–14 Dublin Housing Inquiry. The immediate impetus for the inquiry was the collapse on 2 September 1913 of two dilapidated tenement houses in Church Street, a particularly bad slum area which the Corporation had intended to clear. Seven people were killed. But, as was pointed out at the time, a fatal house collapse in itself was not enough to produce a major investigation: similar disasters had occurred previously in Dublin and other British cities, with no official response.[226] Far more important was the realisation by the Castle Administration and Dublin's middle classes that, at a time of bitter industrial upheaval (the city was still reeling from the 'Bloody Sunday' riot and the uproar over Larkin's imprisonment), the horrors of the slums constituted a damning social indictment. The ITGWU turned the 'housing issue' into an active element in class relations, and for explicitly political purposes. 'Labour advocates were not slow to see in this Church Street calamity a splendid object-lesson of the evils of Dublin capitalism', wrote a contemporary observer.[227] Housing conditions and tenement owners became the scapegoats for the failure of the economic system in Dublin.

James Larkin and the ITGWU had for several years been trying to seize the urban housing initiative away from moderate trade unions and the Irish Party. This was quite different from pre-war Britain, where skilled unions were most active in demanding municipal housing for their members, and where even in militant cities like Glasgow, unskilled labourers took no part in major rent strikes.[228] What was unique about Dublin in 1913 was that it was the underclass of casual labourers that was at the forefront of housing demands. James Connolly used the slums as a tangible and emotive illustration of his central Marxist argument that capitalism was an alien system introduced by British colonisers to exploit Irish labour and resources, and had brutally overthrown a pre-industrial Gaelic society that had more in common with socialism. The ITGWU tried to improve the life of its members by setting up a 'model' social and recreation centre (first at Liberty Hall and later at Croydon Park), and it used the *Irish Worker* to ally housing reform with socialism. Connolly wrote that by building up their union, 'the people will be given a better chance of living—they will be given better wages and better housing accommodation, instead of living in the slums'.[229] The ITGWU launched vitriolic attacks on its enemies in the Irish Party and Catholic Church, arguing that housing progress could only be achieved by electing genuine working-class municipal representatives to root out the interests of slum landlords. The Dublin Labour Party began its manifesto for Corporation elections in January 1914 with the slogan: 'VOTE FOR LABOUR and SWEEP AWAY THE SLUMS'.[230] It was not surprising, therefore, that during the 1913 Dublin Lock-out the ITGWU characterised the slums as the most visible product of the war that British and Irish capitalism waged on Irish labour. Larkin told the inquiry into labour unrest:

> What was the position of affairs in connection with industrial life in Ireland? . . . there are 21,000 families—four and a half persons to a family—living in single rooms. Who are responsible? The gentlemen opposite to him [Dublin employers] would have to accept the responsibility . . . They said they control the means of life; then the responsibility rests upon them. Twenty-one thousand people multiplied by five, over 100,000 people huddled together in the putrid slums of Dublin.[231]

A follower of Larkin told the same inquiry:

> The long period of stagnation in the labour ranks of Dublin was responsible for the growth in your midst of labour and housing conditions scarcely to be equalled outside Bombay or Constantinople. Now that the Irish Transport Union and its officials have set out to arouse the people; now that the fierce . . . fighting has inspired the suffering masses with a belief in their own ability to achieve some sort of emancipation; now, in short, that the luxury, comfort, and even the

security of the propertied classes are menaced, we see the quickening of a faint sense of social conscience in Dublin.²³²

And when it became clear that the strike was being lost, the IGTWU used the housing issue to draw attention away from its industrial defeat instead. Larkin proclaimed in January 1914:

> They, the workers, who produced all the wealth and built the houses of the rich, instead of living in the slums should be living in the fine mansions in Merrion Square and Mountjoy Square . . . the houses in which the workers lived were so bad that they should pay no rent for them. If the workers had the moral courage they would not pay a d**n cent of rent for the next twelve months. If that were done they would focus public attention on the question, and then the housing question in Dublin would solve itself.²³³

After defeat came, Connolly declared that increased concern about the slums 'was one of the fruits the strikers of Dublin had won through suffering, imprisonment, death and calumny that is crueller than death, in their historic conflict . . . Thus labour wins, even when it seems to have lost its all.'²³⁴ A resolution passed at the Irish TUC in June 1914 declared defiantly that 'labour unrest can only be ended by the abolition of the capitalist system of wealth-production, with its inherent injustice and poverty, and among the first steps to that end demands legislation to secure . . . the building of healthy homes for all'.²³⁵ It was an uncompromising message, repeated in the *Worker* (Connolly's short-lived successor to the *Irish Worker*) when it wrote:

> The houses of the poor of Dublin are altars, aye, altars to the worship of a Devil whose attendant ministers are the political and civic upholders of the capitalist system . . . Dublin slums, Dublin politics, Dublin misery are all but manifestations of the denial of that right for which we ask Dublin toilers to battle.²³⁶

But what was most remarkable about pre-war Dublin was that middle-class reformers responded so directly to attempts by the radical labour movement to turn the housing issue into a weapon of class warfare. Daly has recently suggested, following Stedman Jones' analysis of class relations in London during the 1880s, that it was the threat of socialism represented by the ITGWU lock-out that provoked widespread alarm about the slums.²³⁷ Crucial here was a growing belief in Ireland in the sociological theory of environmental determinism, which held that criminality and social unrest amongst the poor were not hereditary but were instead the product of bad living conditions. As one English observer wrote of the industrial unrest in the city:

> It is beyond doubt that the evil social conditions of Dublin were a cause, possibly the primary cause, of the Larkinite movement obtaining the hold it did. In the depressed and degraded population of the slums Mr

> Larkin found a double source of strength. . . . minds have been set actively at work to find a solution of the housing and other problems inherent in the present conditions of the city's life. If eventually out of the evil of labour strife good should come in the form of a reconstructed Dublin, the memory of Larkinism will be a less painful one; but nothing that may happen will deprive it of the reputation it has won as being the crudest and cruellest emanation of Labour belligerency that modern history takes count of.[238]

Similar views were voiced by Irish commentators. A leading Catholic social reformer, Dr John O'Connell, stated that 'at the bottom of all the trouble in Dublin for the past six months was the question of housing accommodation, and the lawlessness and discontent which occurred could never have manifested itself if the houses in which the working classes lived were satisfactory'.[239] Another housing reformer, E. A. Aston, wrote:

> The growth of Syndicalism, in the form of Larkin . . . cannot be accounted for by any natural tendency of the workman of Dublin. The heather of revolt against intolerable conditions of life has been dried in the one hundred thousand inhabitants of the twenty thousand single tenement rooms of Dublin. Syndicalism set the heather on fire, the conflagration extends, and even the conservative and restraining influence of the Catholic Church has failed to stay its progress.[240]

Alarmist warnings also came from academic observers, as part of a tendency of the Nationalist intelligentsia to temporarily blur labour issues into the general attack on British rule. The Professor of Architecture at UCD, William Scott, opined that 'many of the evils of the unrest are generated in the unsuitable, insanitary, uncongenial and unsympathetic dwellings and environment of the worker'.[241] Professor Kettle of the UCD Economics Department wrote of the syndicalist threat to Dublin:

> We must put before them [the working classes] a planned, systematic scheme for the extinction of the slums . . . and we have got to carry that scheme steadily through . . . We have got to go down to the workers, and we must not go with empty hands. And mark that a housing scheme of this character will probably involve the acceptance of a sacrifice in the shape of a new rate by the better streets of the city . . . It may be thought by men of little faith that it is impossible to find any mediating ground between the frenzy of Socialism and the obtuseness of Capitalism. If so, not only Dublin, but civilisation as we know it, approaches dissolution.[242]

Kettle formed a short-lived 'Peace Committee' of leading Dublin citizens to mediate in the labour dispute and to draw up a programme for social reconstruction. At its first meeting in October 1913, E. A. Aston called on both Larkin and Murphy to unite 'to carry out a high and holy war against the common enemy—the slum owner and the slum tenement in the City of Dublin. The combination of the force of the capitalist leader and the labour leader would produce the result they all longed for'.[243] Another source of concern over the link between the slums and the spread of labour militancy was voiced by the Roman Catholic Church. In February 1914 the Irish Hierarchy issued a pastoral calling for sweeping housing reform in Dublin, and elsewhere one Irish cardinal declared that 'social reform is what we want. We want something done for the workmen, something done for the poor in the way of housing . . . If that is done wonderful work will be done for social science, and social reform will kill socialism'.[244]

Yet it was the Press throughout the United Kingdom that stirred up the greatest fears over housing conditions in Dublin. Both the Unionist *Times* and the Liberal *Manchester Guardian* connected the slums to Larkinism.[245] In Ireland the most outspoken newspaper on the issue, the *Irish Times*, proclaimed that:

> the condition of the Dublin slums is responsible not only for disease and crime, but for much of our industrial unrest . . . The members of the ITGWU live for the most part in slums like Church Street. Their domestic conditions make them an easy prey to plausible agitators. We believe that, if every unskilled labourer in Dublin were the tenant of a decent cottage of three, or even two, rooms, the city would not be divided to-day into two hostile camps.[246]

The same point was echoed by the *Irish Builder* when it wrote:

> The terrible labour unrest . . . has been largely developed by reason of the bad condition of housing. It is safe to say that, had the labouring masses been better housed than they are . . . the agitators who now dominate the labour mind in the city would never have obtained such influence. Decently housed men would never have fallen such a complete prey to mob-oratory . . . the main factor that the citizens as a body are directly responsible for, and must grapple with and solve, is the housing problem.[247]

Politicians from all parties in Ireland and Britain reinforced the consensual view that Dublin's slums predicated labour unrest, and hence property owners became isolated as the scapegoat. The Irish Party pursued an ambivalent strategy of sympathising with the anger of the urban working class, but at the same time trying not to upset Nationalist petty-bourgeois interests by avoiding direct denunciations of slum landlordism. Yet many of the party's supporters did speak out. 'Bad housing and the evils that follow in its train', wrote the Chairman of Pembroke UDC, 'are . . . largely responsible for the discontent among the working classes.'[248] Sinn Fein members, notably Arthur Griffith and Patrick Pearse, used forthright condemnation of the slums during the 1913–14

Lock-out as part of its continuing campaign to win working-class support away from constitutional Nationalism, and over to their militant brand of anti-British sentiment.[249] In Westminster, concern was expressed by several Conservative members, and the rising Liberal MP, Christopher Addison, protested to the Chancellor of the Exchequer over Larkin's imprisonment by noting that 'the housing and wage conditions in Dublin are a disgrace to the community and I think he has done a good service in showing them up'. Lloyd George concurred, and much to the displeasure of Chief Secretary Birrell, helped to secure Larkin's release.[250] The sheer weight of the climate of opinion against property owners was such that only the belligerent leader of Dublin's employers, William Martin Murphy, dared to argue that the slums had little to do with industrial unrest. Murphy claimed that the issue was simply being exploited by the ITGWU in its struggle to overthrow the social order.[251] Yet his claim fell on deaf ears, and instead pressure mounted on the Castle Administration to mediate in the matter of Dublin's working-class housing.

THE 1913–14 DUBLIN HOUSING INQUIRY

In the wake of the Church Street collapse, the *Irish Times* called for an official inquiry into housing in Dublin.[252] Then in October 1913, Chief Secretary Birrell received three heavyweight deputations in quick succession. The first was from the Association of Municipal Authorities of Ireland, and was led by the Irish Party's housing spokesman, J. J. Clancy. The AMAI repeated its call for loans on Labourers Acts terms and an augmentation of the Irish Housing Fund to £20 000 per year. Clancy declared that 'in view of recent events, and what was going on at present, the State, in the interests of society at large, was bound to intervene'.[253] Birrell as usual prevaricated, stating that the Liberal Government was currently considering its housing policy and that Ireland would have to wait and see what was offered to the United Kingdom as a whole. A similarly vague reply was given by Birrell to demands for increased urban subsidy made by a deputation from the Women's National Health Association of Ireland.[254] What particularly incensed the Chief Secretary was that this deputation was led by Lady Aberdeen, and received by her husband in his role as Lord Lieutenant! Birrell at this time was privately telling Prime Minister Asquith that he regretted that he could do nothing to stop the Aberdeens from using their official influence in such matters.[255] The tension within the Castle Administration reached a head with a third deputation in late October 1913, again led by Lady Aberdeen, but this time from the Housing and Town Planning Association of Ireland (hereafter HTPAI). This garden suburb propaganda body, which will be discussed in detail in Chapter 4, sidestepped the issue of state subsidy and instead demanded that a Vice-Regal Commission be set up: a call supported by numerous memorials to Dublin Castle at the time.[256] In fact, the Chief Secretary had as early as mid-September also arrived at the conclusion that an official inquiry was needed, but because of pressing matters had not publicised his decision. In a letter to Asquith he declared regret at having to hold inquiries into police conduct and the causes of industrial unrest before investigating the Dublin slums, noting that it was 'rather dreadful to be wrangling about machinery in the midst of such squalor'.[257] Birrell knew that Irish public opinion would only be appeased by increased subsidy, and so therefore what was needed was accurate information to present to the Treasury about Dublin's housing problem and the financial implications of a proposed solution. However, he rejected outright the calls for an exhaustive Vice-Regal Commission, and argued instead that a departmental inquiry by the ILGB would be quicker, cheaper, and easier to organise. Many of those who had previously called for a Vice-Regal inquiry, such as Dublin Corporation, accepted his alternative offer. Not so the HTPAI and Lord Lieutenant Aberdeen, who believed that Birrell was trying to downgrade the importance of the inquiry so that the British Government could evade its financial responsibility. The HTPAI even went to the expense of sending three representatives to London in order to pressurise Birrell. This lobby was also intended to give backing to Lord Lieutenant Aberdeen, who was over in London at the same time for a meeting with Prime Minister Asquith. *The Times* alleged that Lord Aberdeen's aim was to overturn Birrell's decision to appoint a departmental inquiry.[258] If so, the plan failed and, in any case, distrust about Birrell's intentions was misplaced. The Chief Secretary appears to have been genuinely concerned about the danger of a lengthy inquiry (the Royal Commission into Working Class Housing in Scotland, for instance, was set up in 1913 and did not report until 1917). As he told the HTPAI deputation, 'quite frankly what I want is to have something in my hands by the time Parliament meets'.[259] Birrell readily agreed to hold the proceedings of the inquiry in public, and in his contemporary speeches he seized on the Castle Administration's role as mediator in housing reform to appeal for conciliation from the working classes, and to dispel criticism for having jailed Larkin.[260] Yet what is less clear is why the four ILGB officials appointed to the inquiry committee—that is, Charles O'Conor, J. F. MacCabe, A. P. Delany and S. Watt—did not include the department's housing expert, Dr Peter Cowan. This led to some criticism of the lack of experience within the investigatory committee, but the choice was probably intended to be diplomatically even-handed, given that Cowan was well known as a proponent of garden suburb design and a critic of Dublin Corporation's inner city schemes. Some sceptics doubted the commitment of the British Government given the imminence of Home Rule. But, in general, Nationalists and the AMAI believed that Birrell was acting in good faith, and that further urban housing subsidy would be forthcoming.[261]

The Dublin Housing Inquiry sat for 17 days in November and December 1913, and heard evidence from 76 witnesses from widely different social backgrounds.[262] It provided a unique analysis of contemporary attitudes to the issue of working-class housing. Around a quarter of witnesses were members of Dublin Corporation; another quarter were Corporation officials; a further quarter could be classed as social reformers or housing experts; while the remainder represented either private interests, various church bodies, or labour organisations. Not surprisingly—and as noted at the time by figures such as J. J. Clancy—the inquiry yielded little new information on the substandard nature of housing accommodation in the city, nor on the financial difficulties faced by semi-philanthropic bodies and Dublin Corporation in taking over responsibility from private housebuilders.[263] The horrors of the slums were luridly reported in newspapers such as the *Glasgow Herald* or as far afield as the *New York Times*.[264] Much of the inquiry's time was taken up by serious allegations of laxity in Dublin Corporation's public health enforcement, a deficiency that Daly has put down to the self-interest of some Nationalist councillors plus the lack of an effective political opposition within the Corporation.[265] The first criticism was that the Corporation's Sanitary Department was not closing down tenements when there was an obvious breach of by-law requirements (such as the failure to provide a water supply point on each floor, or a water closet for every 12 occupants). This was justified by the Chief Sanitary Officer, Sir Charles Cameron, on the grounds that an over-zealous closure policy would only increase overcrowding elsewhere. It was a commonly-held and pragmatic view, yet one that reduced the incentive to build better dwellings since equivalent profits could be made from slums without any capital investment. An even more serious allegation was that, in a few cases, members of Dublin Corporation who owned tenement property had received a rate rebate intended for landlords who carried out improvements, even though their properties did not meet the required standards. This was less a case of corruption within the Sanitary Department, than of the undue pressure that could be exercised by a few municipal slum landlords. The reality of Dublin Corporation's public health enforcement was not that it was corrupt but that it was largely irrelevant. The epitome of this irrelevance was a by-law which stated that every occupant of a tenement must have a minimum of 300 cubic feet of space. Because so many tenement rooms were in Georgian houses which had high ceilings, it meant that even patently overcrowded flats could still comply with the letter, but certainly not the spirit, of the regulation. Such disclosures, as revealed by the Housing Inquiry, were eagerly seized on by Unionists and the Larkinite labour movement in their attack on Dublin Corporation. In response, the Corporation pointed out that the inquiry was one-sided in that it did not look at the responsibility of the ILGB, nor did it subject other municipalities to similar scrutiny for comparison. The actual report of the ILGB Housing Inquiry tried to play down the more controversial revelations by praising the Corporation's housing record. One committee member, J. F. MacCabe, even appended a minority report which rejected all criticism of Dublin Corporation.

Instead, the ILGB Housing Inquiry was clearly more interested in putting forward proposals for a major housebuilding scheme in Dublin. The tone had been set by the Chairman in an opening statement that observed:

The financial difficulty had two sides. It had the difficulty of the Imperial Exchequer on the one hand, and on the other the burden cast on the citizens of Dublin for the proper housing of the poor. Both these questions were questions they would have to consider carefully . . . The more detailed information they could get the more accurately they could vouch on their account, as it were, to the Treasury, and the more likely they were to gain, what they desired to gain, the proper housing of the citizens of Dublin.[266]

Calls for generous Exchequer subsidy duly came from Nationalist members of Dublin Corporation, and from municipal officials. Much debate then revolved around whether inner-city schemes were best, as favoured by Sir Charles Cameron and the Town Clerk, Henry Campbell; or whether a mixed policy should be followed that included suburban estates for better-paid artisans, as argued by the City Architect, Charles MacCarthy, and the City Engineer's assistant, William Cranwill Wilson (the latter had been sent to England in 1911 to study Port Sunlight, Letchworth, and Hampstead Garden Suburb). Support for Unwinian garden suburbs also came from town planning enthusiasts who gave evidence to the inquiry, notably E. A. Aston and Patrick Geddes, the Scottish polymath biologist, sociologist, and geographer. Geddes was brought over by Lady Aberdeen and the Women's National Health Association (see Chapter 4), and expressed his belief that municipal activity and state aid should concentrate on rehousing the 'submerged' 10 per cent classed as very poor. A far broader view of state responsibility was put forward by Dublin labour representatives that attended. 'Every class of the community is assisted', noted Larkin's lieutenant and Vice-President of the Dublin Trades Council, William O'Brien, before going on to put the ITGWU case that subsidy be provided to enable suburban cottages to be built and let at a maximum of 10 per cent of labourers' wages, and, if necessary, built for free for those in desperate need.[267] The report of the Dublin Housing Inquiry did not go nearly as far as this, but was still notable for being the first official recommendation of state subsidy for a major programme of urban housing. Part 5 of the report began by asserting that the tenement system in Dublin must be broken up. This was to be achieved partly by the state providing 100 per cent loans to build 14 000 suburban cottages. At an estimated average cost of £250 per dwelling, this represented a total capital expenditure of £3 500 000. The report proposed that private enterprise should be encouraged through various incentives (such as tax relief and low-interest loans), but noted sharply 'that the provision of houses for the working classes through the medium of private enterprise under existing conditions can no longer be relied upon'.[268] Dublin Corporation, despite its shortcomings, was envisaged as the major housing agency. Next, the ILGB Report pointed out that the principle of substantial state aid had already been conceded for Irish rural housing in the Labourers Acts, and so it calculated the likely burden to the Exchequer of pursuing a similar policy for housing in

Dublin. Its estimate was that if the £3 500 000 required was borrowed at the current rate from the Local Loans Fund, then the 'economic rent' to cover the cost of new dwellings would have to be just under 5s 6d per week. This, the report argued, was beyond the means of those in need. Instead, it suggested a more reasonable target rent of only 3s 7d per week. This, however, would mean a shortfall of around 1s 11d per week on every cottage built, too heavy a burden on Dublin's already high rates. The ILGB Housing Report therefore looked at ways of reducing the loss, such as making repayments on the 'annuity' system and giving loans on Labourers Acts terms at 3.25 per cent interest over 68 years. Even so, the potential loss on each dwelling stood at just under 1s per week. Hence the report proposed that state subsidy should now contribute 16 per cent of the annual loan repayments. Realising that this proposal would alarm the Treasury, it suggested that if wages were to rise in the interim, then:

> The State might therefore hold that it should not be saddled with a fixed burden of 16% during the full period. We recommend, if our proposals are entertained, that the State should reserve to itself the right of revising its financial liability at the end of, say, each ten years.[269]

Importantly, the ILGB Housing Report envisaged that its recommendation of low-interest loans plus 16 per cent subsidy be extended to all Irish municipalities (an appendix duly gave summaries of the chronic housing conditions found in other urban centres). It even suggested that the existing Irish Housing Fund be reserved as a special additional aid to provincial towns with even worse financial problems than Dublin. The report contended that such extensive state investment would be recouped by improving the 'moral tone' of the Irish people, and through financial savings resulting from reduced crime and ill-health (such as by having to build fewer tuberculosis sanatoria). 'Both these considerations furnish, in our opinion, strong grounds for generous financial treatment', it concluded.[270] The Dublin Housing Report also made a host of other proposals. The 14 000 new units were to be self-contained three-bedroom suburban cottages. In addition, some 3803 of the best tenements could be remodelled to provide 13 000 modernised inner-city flats. The ILGB Report recommended that Dublin Corporation should analyse housing need and within two years put forward a complete scheme for the city, a point emphasised even more in MacCabe's minority report with its call for a civic survey and town plan in 'conformity with modern ideas'.[271]

The 1913–14 ILGB Dublin Housing Report was thus a significant document, and it was generally well received in Ireland. There was a minority of opposition to the subsidy proposals, mainly from the Sinn Fein Party with its implacable hostility to all British intervention in Ireland, and also from the residue of the voluntarist reform movement, such as the Statistical and Social Inquiry Society of Ireland.[272] The vast majority took a different view. For instance, the *Irish Times* described the ILGB Report as 'a document of almost

Urban State Housing before 1914   113

historic importance', and added that it 'has become obvious, as the report points out, that the ordinary laws of economics are not adequate to deal with the situation. We must have State action, whether we like it or not'.[273] The *Manchester Guardian* wrote that the report adopted 'the view that adherence to strict economic principles cannot be insisted upon in dealing with a grave social evil of this kind', and the ILGB reported to Parliament that because of the massive cost of the proposed scheme 'the Government might, therefore, consent to lend the money on Labourers Acts terms with a grant-in-aid'.[274] Interest groups as disparate as the Larkinite Dublin Trades Council and the Dublin Chamber of Commerce urged that the Inquiry's recommendations be implemented at once.[275] Dublin Corporation concentrated much of its effort in responding to Unionist attacks on its public health record, but not surprisingly welcomed the prospect of more housing subsidy from the Imperial Exchequer.[276] Therefore it is necessary to reject the recent interpretation that the ILGB Inquiry was a limited and conservative response to the city's housing problem, and instead to favour the view that the report 'had no hesitation . . . in placing a share of the responsibility for the solution of the housing problem at the door of the Treasury'.[277]

The ILGB Inquiry was thus a substantive contribution to the pre-war housing crisis in Dublin, and played its part in creating a near pathological fixation with the slum-lands that was vividly expressed by contemporary literary figures. Sean O'Casey was a labourer from the slums who became an admirer of Larkin and a short-term member of the Citizens Army, and he later used the atrocious housing system as a memorable locus for plays such as *The Shadow of a Gunman* (1923), *Juno and the Paycock* (1924), and *The Plough and the Stars* (1926), in which one character says of Nora Clitheroe:

> She's always grumblin' about havin' to live in a tenement house . . . 'I wouldn't like to spend me last hour in one, let alone live me life in a tenement,' says she. 'Vaults,' says she, 'that are hidin' th' dead, instead of homes that are shelterin' th' livin'.'

In his private correspondence, O'Casey called Dublin's slums 'the hidden Ireland', and in 1914 wrote that 'twenty thousand families are wriggling together like worms in a putrid mass in horror-filled one-room tenements'.[278] From a middle-class reformist perspective, Dr Oliver Gogarty in 1917 co-wrote a play called *Blight* which bitterly attacked slum landlords. Irish literary interest was echoed in Britain by the expatriate George Bernard Shaw, who joked blackly to a pro-Larkin meeting in the Albert Hall in November 1913, that he 'was extremely glad to hear it stated that 20 000 families in Dublin had one room apiece to live in. In his time . . . there was no such luxury; there were often two families in a room, and both families took in lodgers'.[279] The ILGB Report also evinced sympathy from many involved in social reform in Britain, including Patrick Geddes and the *Town Planning Review*.[280]

Within the Dublin Castle Administration, support was also readily forthcoming from the Lord Lieutenant, Lord Aberdeen, and his wife, Lady Ishbel Aberdeen. But they were both peripheral figures. More significantly, the Vice-President of the ILGB, Sir Henry Robinson, stood firmly behind the findings of his departmental committee, and appears to have been joined by the President of the Irish Board of Works, Sir George Stephenson.[281] A more unexpected source of support came from the Imperial Treasury's representative in Dublin Castle: the Treasury Remembrancer and staunch Unionist, Maurice Headlam. In an attempt, albeit unsuccessful, to secure extra payment for the ILGB committee members for working over Christmas, Headlam praised 'the unique character of the Enquiry, the excellent way in which it was conducted, and the great stress in getting it done quickly'.[282] However, the key link between the Castle Administration and the centre of power in Westminster was the Chief Secretary, Augustine Birrell. He continued to sit on the fence in an effort, on one hand, not to compromise his personal dislike of state subsidy, and on the other, to appear to go along with Irish demands to implement the proposals of the ILGB Housing Inquiry.[283]

Far more important for the fate of the ILGB Dublin Housing Report in early-1914 was the battle being played out in Westminster. Political backing for increased state subsidy was automatically guaranteed from the Irish Party, being part of its policy to build a broad urban base and to use social reform to prevent the growth of an independent labour party. As a result of the IPP's desire to negate any movement towards social radicalism, both urban housing policy and the municipalisation of working-class dwellings were far more developed in pre-war Ireland than in Britain (even if they lagged behind rural Ireland). This would support Lyons' view that the 1908 Clancy Act was one of a series of important measures that were 'very directly the outcome of the party's activity and could not be regarded merely as concessions devised by an English ministry for the purpose of conciliating the Irish members'.[284] It would conversely tend to dispel the view of other historians that the Irish Party, and supporting bodies like the Dublin Corporation, remained indifferent to the urban housing problem because of a combination of vested landlord interests and political apathy.[285] The role of slum-owners within Nationalist groups has been over-emphasised, especially given the links between the Irish Party and the Town Tenants League. The weakness of the constitutional Nationalist approach, however, was that it ultimately depended on support from Westminster. The reality of the problem had been shown by the Treasury's emasculation of the first-ever urban subsidy in the 1908 Clancy Housing Act. The use by the Liberal Government of the Balfourian argument that urban conditions in Ireland were no different from those on the mainland, did avoid setting too dramatic a precedent for urban subsidy at home. But in Ireland it had stalled the campaign to build the 25 000 town dwellings suggested by the Irish Party in 1908 as a solution to the problem (a provision, incidentally, that would have been proportionately greater than that built under the Labourers Acts in rural areas). British intransigence to urban subsidy became further entrenched once the Home Rule Bill was introduced, and so the structural housing crisis in Irish towns and cities worsened. Chronic poverty and the inertia of speculative housebuilding remained, with the latter even touching the hitherto complacent Belfast during the pre-war slump. Alarm about the threat to social stability posed by overcrowded slums became endemic in Dublin in the wake of the ITGWU's industrial unrest in 1913/14, and found clearest expression in the ILGB Housing Inquiry. It is now time to switch attention to see how the ILGB Report was received in Westminster. To understand this more fully, it is also necessary to look at the influence of the Labourers Acts programme on housing ideas in pre-war Britain.

Chapter 3

THE INFLUENCE OF EARLY IRISH STATE HOUSING ON BRITISH POLICY

This study is concerned with early state housing in Ireland not as a purely Irish affair, but as an element within colonial relations. Therefore, it is important to deal now with the other side of the colonial condition, and look at the reciprocal effect that Irish experience had on Britain. This chapter will focus first on British reactions to the rural Labourers Acts programme, so as to understand the extent of resistance in Westminster in early-1914 to an equally generous subsidy being granted for urban housing in Ireland.

An important general point to make is that British policy towards rural Ireland came to influence thinking on the mainland significantly. The need for concerted state intervention following the Famine ran against *laissez-faire* principles, and, coupled with the case put forward by Nationalists for the creation of a peasant proprietorship in Ireland, prompted writers such as John Stuart Mill in the late-1860s to begin to advocate policies of 'economic relativism'. This modified theory argued that the role of the state should be tailored to suit a country's specific circumstances rather than the abstracts of Classical political economy.[1] The 'Land War' and the subsequent policy of subsidised land redistribution in Ireland also helped to shape the numerous—if ultimately futile—theories of land reform put forward in late-nineteenth-century England, including Henry George's single-tax proposal and the 'Back to the Land' movement.[2] Interest was particularly keen due to the rapid economic decline of British agriculture following the 'great depression' of the 1880s, which had led to an almost total stagnation in private housebuilding by rural landowners in the period up to the First World War. The rural shortage came to be seen as the most intractable housing problem, and yet British housing legislation proved entirely ineffective in agricultural districts.[3] Only eight English rural authorities made use of the 1890 Housing Act. Its successor, the 1909 Housing and Town Planning Act, forced the closure of 13 000 cottages, but by 1914 had only provided loans to build a total of 470 rural dwellings throughout the country (and those that were built were let at punitively high rents of around 4s per week). Despite the protests of the English Local Government Board to the contrary, it was a pathetic total.

Irish Nationalists had no doubt that the solution to the rural housing impasse in Britain was to follow the precedent of the Labourers Acts. The Irish Party was especially keen to boast to British audiences about the unique successes it had won. The party's deputy leader told a meeting in Halifax in March 1911 that

Irish rural labourers 'were better housed and more independent than the labourers of Great Britain. Nearly forty thousand of them had got a nice, clean cottage and acre of land, for a shilling per week, and the employer could not turn them out. He wished that in the English counties the labourers had got the same terms'.[4] The *Irish Builder* noted of the repeated concern expressed over pre-war British rural housing:

> This is surely one of those things about which we are better off in Ireland, for we can boast of an enormous improvement in the housing of the rural labourer. The remedy for the unfortunate state of things in England is the application of the Irish Labourers Acts to England.[5]

Irish architects involved with the Labourers Acts believed that they had shown the way to a simplified design approach that was cheap but still attractive. They looked on with disdain at attempts on the mainland to design low-cost rural cottages, particularly when the competition held in Letchworth Garden City in 1905 failed to meet a target of £150 for building costs (a figure that was repeatedly achieved in Irish schemes).[6] Instead, the *Irish Builder* declared that the policy in Ireland of state subsidy and rationalised design 'may well, and probably will, serve as a model for other countries to follow, profiting by our experience and . . . mistakes'.[7] Thus, when reviewing a pre-war English rural scheme that consciously omitted unnecessary accommodation and fripperies, the same journal wrote that the design was 'very much on the lines of one of the standard plans of the Irish Local Government Board for labourers' cottages. It displays no point of novelty or ingenuity in planning.'[8]

PRE-WAR BRITISH REACTIONS TO THE IRISH LABOURERS ACTS

From as early as 1902, several British observers, notably those involved in the 'National Efficiency' movement, drew attention to the achievements of the Irish Labourers Acts and argued for the introduction of rural subsidy at home.[9] Amongst the press, the most influential advocate was Laurence Weaver, the conservative editor of *Country Life* and a rural housing campaigner. Weaver argued that if Irish precedent was transferred 'it should mean keeping on the land thousands of souls who are being driven by lack of good cottages into the towns or the Colonies'.[10] Even more important were British housing pressure groups and local authority associations, most of which enjoyed strong broad political support, and which also urged an emulation of the Irish Labourers Acts. These bodies included the Workingmen's National Housing Council, the Rural Co-partnership Housing Association, the National Land and Housing League, the County Councils Association, the Rural District Councils Association, and above all the National Housing Reform Council (subsequently renamed as the National Housing and Town Planning Reform Council).[11] The last-cited was led by the indefatigable Alderman William Thompson of Richmond District Council, who, as Sutcliffe has noted, 'was widely acknowledged as the leading housing reformer of his day'.[12] Thompson was a Progressive who advocated the municipalisation of suburban land, so as to prevent private owners from appropriating the profit (the 'unearned increment') that was created when sprawling urbanisation boosted land prices. Municipal town planning was to be used to improve working-class living standards, and significantly Thompson also became the pre-eminent British champion of what was then widely known as the 'Irish system' of state housing subsidy. Thus, the National Housing and Town Planning Council in 1912 demanded that the Liberal Government introduce rural subsidy, on the grounds 'that it is not consistent to deny such help to English labourers when an exactly similar class on the other side of the Irish Channel are benefitting enormously from this action'.[13] In September 1912, Thompson took a top-level delegation of his organisation across the Irish Sea to see the results at first hand. They were received by the ILGB and were shown the premier Labourers Acts schemes in Southern Ireland, including those in the Dublin region by Thomas Joseph Byrne and R. M. Butler. The report published by the Council stressed that subsidised rents had not held down rural wages in Ireland, and argued that only slight modifications were needed before applying the Labourers Acts in Britain. 'Our inquiries in Ireland', wrote the deputation, 'have deepened our conviction as to the wisdom and judgement of . . . the granting of some similar measure of State aid.'[14] The representatives were also impressed by the design of the post-1906 Act cottages, and the Council's secretary, Henry Aldridge, when later recommending garden suburb planning, noted that 'here, as in Ireland, the need for care in grouping will be recognised'.[15]

Conversely, there were lobbyists in pre-war Britain who were appalled by the 'Irish system' of state subsidy. Opponents included the Rural Housing and Sanitary Association, the *Municipal Journal* (mouthpiece of the British metropolitan authorities), and powerful individuals like John Nettlefold, Chairman of Birmingham Corporation's Housing Committee. Nettlefold was the most single-minded exponent of the policy of town-extension planning, and specifically recommended that municipal involvement be limited simply to the acquisition and layout of new suburbs. As in Germany, from where the model derived, he envisaged that private developers or housing companies were to provide the actual dwellings. Thus, in his influential book, *Practical Town Planning* (1914), Nettlefold denounced Irish rural subsidy as providing nothing other than debilitating 'charity-rents'.[16] In addition, there were a number of British architects who openly criticised the design of Labourers Acts cottages. The *Builder* wrote that the new dwellings, 'though a distinct advance in the interests of health and sanitation, are unfortunate from an aesthetic standpoint'.[17] Irish precedent therefore helped to polarise British attitudes to state housing subsidy in the period before the First World War, and nowhere was this disagreement more marked than between the two main political parties.

THE ATTITUDE OF THE CONSERVATIVE PARTY TO THE LABOURERS ACTS

The Conservative Party had shown since Disraeli that it would accept the idea of central government subsidy in specific cases where its own supporters benefited (for instance, the generous pay-off to Ascendancy landowners under the 1903 Irish Land Act). From the turn of the century, a powerful sector within the Tory Party promoted the creed of 'social imperialism', calling for a balance between the staunch defence of the British Empire abroad, and social reform at home which would improve 'national efficiency' and prevent the growth of socialism. Conservatives with backgrounds in Ireland, such as Lord Lansdowne and the ex-Chief Secretary, Sir Walter Long, came to the conclusion that the Irish policy of subsidising land redistribution to create a peasant proprietorship could now be used to build a bulwark of small property owners in Britain to protect landed wealth from working-class political demands.[18] It was a view that received much backing from the party leader, Arthur Bonar Law, and other senior figures such as Austen Chamberlain. It also greatly interested the 'Back to the Land' group within the Conservatives. The leading small-holdings campaigner, Jesse Collings, visited Ireland on behalf of the Rural League to examine the effects of state subsidy there.[19] Importantly, many Tory advocates of land redistribution in Britain also saw a concomitant need to subsidise rural housing. Walter Long declared:

> that of all the money which has been so well spent in the development of Ireland ... probably none of it has been spent with so much advantage to the community, as has been spent in the erection of labourers' cottages. If these results have followed from the application of those principles in Ireland, why should it be stated that similar results may not follow in this country?[20]

There were two main pillars within the pre-war Conservative Party which supported the calls for state housing subsidy by Long and Lansdowne. The first was constituted by reactionary editors of the Tory press who were directly involved in the design of improved rural housing, notably Laurence Weaver at *Country Life* and John St Loe Strachey of the *Spectator*.[21] The second lobby lay inside Westminster and was centred on the Unionist Social Reform Group. The leaders here were municipal Tories such as Sir Arthur Griffith-Boscawen, Chairman of the LCC's Housing Committee, and Colonel Kiffin-Taylor, his counterpart in Liverpool Corporation. This municipal lobby was convinced that it could exploit the inactivity of the Liberal Government over housing reform, and thereby appropriate the issue as its own. From 1912 to 1914 this group masterminded the introduction of no less than seven private Conservative Housing Bills that were based on the 'Irish system' of state subsidy.[22] None were successful, and indeed were fairly easily defeated as a result of the parliamentary influence of the President of the English Local Government Board, John

Burns, and his successor, Herbert Samuel. In many ways these defeats suited the Conservatives, for it is clear that the party as a whole had not reached agreement on housing policy. Many within the Tory Party were uncertain about state subsidy, and hence Walter Long was careful to reassure Bonar Law, when the first measure was being introduced, that 'of course it is a private members Bill and does not commit the party officially'.[23] Instead, the political purpose of the pre-war Conservative Housing Bills was to expose the Achilles' heel of a Liberal Government that had subsidised Irish rural housing but was now refusing demands to extend the policy to Britain. As one Tory supporter reminded Bonar Law, 'references to equality of treatment of the Irish Peasant and the English Labourer are well received'.[24] In bracing themselves for the Tory onslaught, an official in the English Local Government Board noted of state subsidy that 'It will be upon this point that the debate will centre and attention will again be drawn to what has been effected in Ireland by Imperial financial assistance'.[25]

Thus the private Rural Housing Bill introduced in 1912, and again in 1913, was explicitly modelled on the 1906 Irish Labourers Act. There were only a few minor alterations. The Tory MP who proposed the 1913 Bill said:

> The principle of the Bill is the same as in Ireland . . . I would urge upon the right honourable Gentleman [Burns] . . . to consider whether it is just or fair to English labourers to deny them the same facilities which we have given so generously and cheerfully to the labourers of Ireland.[26]

Some of the Opposition Housing Bills went one further, and proposed that Exchequer subsidy be granted to urban areas as well. This series of general Bills was drafted personally by Sir Arthur Griffith-Boscawen, and again they were justified by reference to Irish precedent. The proposer of the 1913 measure pointed out that 'this country has admitted in the case of Ireland the principle of assisting by State aid the building of cottages. If it is uneconomical to do it in Ireland it is equally uneconomical to do it in this country. If it is uneconomical in Ireland why did the house agree to it?'[27] Tory attacks on the hypocrisy of the Liberal Cabinet's double-standards towards housing in Ireland and Britain continued right up to the outbreak of the First World War.

The Conservative Party tried to broaden the attack on the Asquith Government by calling on other political parties to support housing subsidy for Britain. The Irish Party was put in an embarrassing position, since it had already publicly advocated the transference of its beloved Labourers Acts. But in the end, political reality made it impossible for it to side with an Opposition that was at that very time also voting against Home Rule.[28] The pre-war Labour Party was also somewhat compromised. The party was undecided on the issue of housing subsidy, yet several radical MPs were fervent advocates. Fred Jowett had in 1909 demanded the importation of the Labourers Acts, and now gleefully joined in the Tory assault. Jowett took relish in singling out John

Burns, the famous ex-union leader now seen by many in the labour movement as a 'class traitor':

> I believe that there is no possible solution of the housing question, either in rural districts or in urban areas, without the assistance of the State, and I cannot for the life of me understand the position of honourable Gentlemen who will with the utmost freedom vote for millions being loaned for Irish housing, for cheap loans and subsidies, and who will not, on principle, vote for a similar system for English housing . . . I am not sure that the President of the Local Government Board [Burns] approves of the Irish policy. But where is his consistency? If this policy of State subvention is wrong for England, it is wrong for Ireland, and the right honourable Gentleman ought to have opposed it.[29]

THE ATTITUDE OF THE LIBERAL PARTY TO THE LABOURERS ACTS

At one level, the debate over Irish housing precedent represented a game of political football between the main parties. However, it also went deeper than that. To Conservatives, Ireland was an integral part of the United Kingdom and not a separate nation. They believed, at least in theory, in the 'equalisation' of the legal and administrative systems.[30] Thus the Tory Party had no fundamental ideological difficulty in borrowing from Irish precedent, provided that the purpose ultimately reinforced the interests of wealthy landowners. The position of the Liberal Party was fundamentally different. Liberals saw Ireland as a distinct entity where conditions were not at all analogous, and therefore unusable as a model. It was a relativist or *sui generis* view that different systems were required in different countries. The Irish Party might have coerced housing subsidy out of the Liberal Government, but the latter was determined that the same policy would not be inflicted on Britain. The pre-war Cabinet appears to have had two principal objections to state subsidy. The first was that it interfered with the theory of political economy, by discouraging speculative housebuilding and holding down wages. Lloyd George told a deputation in May 1914 of his hatred for subsidy:

> Once that was done, no builder would enter the field. He was against that. He was in favour of giving the working-class a living wage. But he was against giving them charity rents . . . To give those necessaries at less than cost price would be the most degrading policy which they could embark upon, and no self-respecting workman would demand that commodities be given him under cost price. He hoped that men of all Parties would set their faces against it.[31]

The second objection was that subsidy destroyed the Gladstonian precept of state parsimony at national and local levels, by breaking the connection between rates and local expenditure. In addressing the Oxford Union in late-1913, Lloyd George warned of the potential costs involved:

> If you are going to make grants for the purpose of building houses, how are you going to stop in the rural districts? Are you going to tax the artisans in the towns for the purpose of paying the rent of the workmen in the villages? This is one of the most disastrous policies ever propounded in this country.[32]

The Cabinet figure who prided himself on being the most belligerent obstacle to state housing subsidy was John Burns at the English Local Government Board. The parliamentary committee set up in 1906 to consider the proposed Housing Bill had looked at whether the 'Irish system' should be applied to Britain. Subsidy was ruled out by the Liberal Government, and Burns had ensured that the 1909 Housing Act in Britain adopted instead the policy of town-extension planning.[33] He later took great pains to ensure that neither Lloyd George's 'Land Campaign', nor his successor from early-1914 at the Local Government Board, Herbert Samuel, gave any ground on the subsidy issue.[34] Burns argued trenchantly that Irish rural experience must not be taken as a precedent, since subsidy had only been condoned there because of the unique conditions of low wages and agricultural stagnation:

> You had in Ireland, as a result of political injustice, an economic depression, bad housing, and a condition of things that has not for centuries been equalled in any other part of Europe . . . the result was this exceptional and drastic remedy. You must take the Irish system with its advantages and its disadvantages, and . . . since subsidised cottages have been built in Ireland, no other cottages have been erected. I can conceive no greater condemnation of this system being adopted in this country.[35]

John Burns apparently interrupted one Cabinet discussion on the 'Land Campaign' in October 1913, and, in the words of Charles Hobhouse, 'gave us half an hour's lecture, from notes, against the Irish system of doles'.[36] It was a widespread view within the Liberal Party, and was lucidly expressed by the Parliamentary Secretary to the Local Government Board when he declared that:

> There are a good many violations of normal political economy in Ireland which have not yet crossed St George's Channel . . . we are giving a subsidy not merely to labourers, but generally to the rural areas of Ireland. I do not in the least degree object to such a thing, only . . . do not let us declare in light-hearted fashion that it is necessary for this House . . . to solve the problem by giving a subsidy to the farmers and landlords of the rural districts of England.[37]

The Irish Chief Secretary, Augustine Birrell, stated that the Labourers Acts were simply 'a necessary appendage of the great scheme of land purchase in Ireland', and another Liberal MP said that he did not think 'that because we have done something foolish in Ireland it is at all necessary that we should do foolish things in England'.[38]

A more constructive opposition to state subsidy within the pre-war Asquith Cabinet came from Lloyd George and his famous Land Enquiry Committee. This initiative was aimed at producing a radical land and housing policy, and was driven by the romantic nineteenth-century Liberal belief that there was an irreconcilable opposition between landed wealth and industrial capital, that could only be resolved by destroying the vested interests of landlordism.[39] The Land Enquiry Committee drew up two reports in 1913–14, both of which explicitly rejected the 'Irish system' of subsidies for land purchase and housing. Lloyd George denounced Tories such as Lord Lansdowne, who called for the creation of a peasant proprietorship, on the grounds that this policy had cost the Treasury a fortune in Ireland and was entirely inappropriate in an industrialised country like Britain.[40] Instead, the Land Enquiry Committee recommended that in rural areas a minimum wage be paid so that labourers would be able to afford unsubsidised speculative housing, with the burden of these higher wages falling on rural landowners. For urban areas, the Committee proposed that municipalities be given an increased Exchequer grant, and that the existing local taxation system financed by rates be augmented by a supplementary tax on site values, to be paid by ground landlords. By these means, both rural and urban Britain were to be rid of landlordism, but this time by taxing land values such that the profit margin on property was eroded.[41] In the event, Lloyd George's 'Land Campaign' came to little, hampered principally by utter confusion over its urban housing proposals. However, it did have substantial influence within the Liberal Government. For instance, the Board of Agriculture in Autumn 1913 decided on a programme to build farm labourers' cottages at strictly 'economic' rents, rejecting the idea of state subsidy in favour of the recommendation by the town planning expert, Raymond Unwin, that a better policy was to provide higher standard cottages designed on the garden suburb model.[42]

Indeed, the only member of the pre-war Asquith Government who dared to break ranks was the Paymaster-General, Lord Strachie (Sir Edward Strachey), and a look at what happened to him shows the Cabinet's tough stance. Strachie was a large Somerset landowner with links to Tory rural housing reformers through his more famous brother, John St Loe Strachey. From 1911, Lord Strachie was also President of the Rural District Council Association, and he used this position to advocate that the Labourers Acts system be introduced in Britain. He even organised a deputation to Chancellor Lloyd George in January 1913 to ask for a £5 000 000 loan on the Irish terms.[43] Conservatives tried to exploit this dissident opinion, so Prime Minister Asquith bluntly told Parliament that Lord Strachie did not represent the Cabinet in this matter. A letter was sent by Asquith to Strachie to insist that the latter stop bucking Government policy.[44]

THE REACTION IN WESTMINSTER TO THE DUBLIN HOUSING INQUIRY

It is important to bear in mind the depth of opposition of the Liberal Cabinet to the 'Irish system' of housing subsidy, when looking at the British response to the ILGB Dublin Housing Report. A copy of the document was laid before the Imperial Parliament in February 1914, and the appendix giving minutes of evidence was presented a month later. Immediately, politicians from a wide range of parties drew attention to the links with the recent industrial unrest, while Unionists and the Irish Party clashed over the public health record of Dublin Corporation.[45] The Asquith Government was clearly unwilling to allocate time to discuss the ILGB Housing Report, no doubt realising that Conservative demands for a debate would simply reopen the battle over the issue of state subsidy. Eventually a debate was only forced on 16 April 1914, when the Irish Party and Opposition MPs hijacked the parliamentary deliberations on the ILGB's financial vote for the next financial year. One of the IPP members for Dublin told the House of Commons unequivocally that what they wanted was increased urban subsidy:

> In my view, and I am fortified in that view by the [ILGB] Report which we have been considering, the problem can only be dealt with adequately on Imperial lines. Surely what has been done, and so successfully, for the Irish labourers ought to be done with equal success for the dwellers in our cities! It would be impossible to place the entire burden on the shoulders of the rate-paying community in Dublin, and it would be a good investment for the State, because it is only in the health and material well-being of the citizens, from the lowest to the highest, that true national prosperity can be secured.[46]

Tory Party support came from Sir Arthur Griffith-Boscawen when he observed that 'Just as we on this side have asked for State aid in this country for the purpose of rehousing people when turned out of the slums at a rent that they can afford to pay, so the [ILGB] Report asks for a similar condition of things to prevail in Ireland'.[47]

There is no record of a Cabinet decision on the matter, but Chief Secretary Birrell certainly toed the party line in abandoning his previously ambivalent stance. Birrell now told Parliament that the ILGB Housing Report was over-dramatic in its claims and far too sweeping in its conclusions. In typically elliptical prose, he rehashed the Liberal precept of state subsidy being the antithesis of free enterprise and self-reliance:

> Socialism may be a good thing or it may be a bad thing, but there is nothing worse than to try to combine Manchester principles with little

patches of philanthropic socialism. A large class of people living in an uneconomical way on 15s. or 16s. a week! And you will thereupon say that the public must supply the money to build nice, clean, charming residences, where they and their wives and their children can lead useful lives, and the rent may be provided for out of the pockets of other people. That is a rotten state of things.[48]

Birrell also rejected the recommendations of the ILGB Inquiry on the grounds that they would involve enormous expense to the Imperial Exchequer, justifying this by a resurrection of the Balfourian argument (which he had temporarily abandoned at the time of the 1908 Housing Act) that no real difference could be drawn between urban conditions in Ireland and Britain. He was now 'sure that no Chancellor of the Exchequer, to whatever side of politics he belongs, will be satisfied, or will be willing to make a grant to Ireland and refuse it to other places'.[49] Instead, the Chief Secretary merely offered some half-hearted alternatives to an increase in state housing subsidy, such as slightly improved terms for public loans and even a civic survey for Dublin.

The Irish Party was placed in a very awkward position, particularly since the imminent Home Rule Act made no explicit mention of financial provision for future housing reform. The IPP tried to reassure municipal representatives that any Exchequer subsidies that were introduced in Britain would still be paid to Ireland even under self-government. This it argued would not undermine their autonomy, but would simply be Ireland receiving redress from Imperial funds for social problems created by British rule. However, Unionists pointed out the obvious loophole that there would be no legal compunction on the British Government, since housing had not been proposed as a 'reserved service'. 'Irish housing', warned the *Irish Times*, '. . . will be brought to a standstill from the very moment when the Home Rule Bill reaches the Statute Book.'[50] From another direction, the O'Brienite Nationalists criticised the Irish Party for having failed to win more generous urban housing subsidy prior to Home Rule. As one Independent Nationalist MP put it, 'they cried "Freedom before Finance", as if finance is not the breath of freedom'.[51] Thus on the very eve of Home Rule, opponents turned the urban housing issue into a critical test of the validity of constitutional Nationalism. The IPP housing spokesman, J. J. Clancy, found himself unable to counter these attacks. Instead, the Irish Party sought to escape the predicament by pinning its hopes on securing a generous share of the housing and land reform initiatives widely expected in Lloyd George's forthcoming Budget.

THE 1914 BUDGET AND IRISH URBAN HOUSING SUBSIDY

It was the Asquith Government that had rejected the generous subsidy recommendations of the ILGB Housing Report, and so the Irish Party had no qualms in threatening a public row if Irish municipalities were left out of any improved housing terms that might be introduced in Britain. Hence, in early-April 1914 John Redmond wrote to Lloyd George, enclosing a hostile leader from the *Irish Times*:

> You will see from this article how vitally important this matter is to us, and how impossible our position would be with our own people if we did not get our proper equivalent grant . . . In your Budget Speech you must make some allusion to this matter. Otherwise, it will be raised by O'Brien or Healy [Independent Nationalists] . . . I would not bother you about this matter under present circumstances, were it not so very, very urgent.[52]

Chief Secretary Birrell confirmed to the Chancellor of the Exchequer that the issue could wreck the IPP's delicate position over the Home Rule Bill:

> They are undoubtedly in a *great fix* over your Budget. Never were they in a bigger . . . If it becomes *plain that but for 'my Bill'* . . . Ireland would get £400,000 a year *but now is to get nothing*—it is all up with Ireland as a Nation! . . . The *Irish press and the O'Brienites are on the watch* and I am speaking the *sober truth* when I say a *refusal* to let Ireland in, will ship enough water to sink the ship . . . On the other hand, if that *Windfall* tumbles in, just at *the right moment* to relieve the crazy finances of the Bill (*pace* Samuel) it will carry us through . . . Anyhow, take it from me—that it is a *Crisis*, big with fate.[53]

The pleas were heeded, and Ireland was fully incorporated in the Budget that was presented in early-May 1914. Lloyd George once again used his Budget as an instrument of social reform. This time he announced the introduction of Land Enquiry Committee proposals for a new local tax based on site values, plus increased rate-relief grants to local authorities to cover general public health matters. The additional Exchequer expenditure was to be met by raising the rate of income tax.[54] The Chancellor took care to stress that the £4 000 000 per annum of extra rate support would cover all of the United Kingdom, including Ireland. This was enthusiastically received by the Irish Party and its supporters, and after the Budget debate John Redmond told Lloyd George that it was the '*best* speech you ever made!'[55] Yet the boldness of the 1914 Budget belied the fact that the Cabinet had not been properly consulted about the cavalier new policy, and that the Treasury had grave reservations. The Budget speech by Lloyd George was full of the rhetorical bluff of the 'Land Campaign', and reads more as ideology in the absence of a considered land or housing strategy, and in preparation for a coming general election. Many who heard the speech were confused afterwards about what had actually been promised, and the feeling of unreality was confirmed by inter-party banter that followed. In the face of concerted attack from the Conservative Party, Lloyd George was unable to give firm details of how the scheme would work. One of the main areas of uncertainty, not surprisingly, was the relationship of the Budget to the Home Rule Bill. The Chancellor promised that Ireland's share of the new public health grants would be paid over to the Dublin Parliament to do as it wished, and an amendment to this effect was hurriedly inserted into the proposals for Home Rule finance.[56] This degree of autonomy, however, was contrary to the rest of the financial system on offer to Ireland, and this issue was fiercely debated by Tory MPs while the Budget controversy rolled on into June 1914. In the end, the Budget turned out to be a fiasco. First, Lloyd George fell foul of constitutional procedure when he tried to slip the rate reform clauses into the Finance Bill; and then the Cabinet jettisoned the local government proposals following a revolt by influential right-wing Liberals, who erroneously suspected the Budget of introducing a veiled state subsidy for housing and other matters. Thus, in the eventual 1914 Finance Act, tax reform was dropped and the additional Exchequer rate-relief grants were 'postponed'. Lloyd George continued to talk of the need for improved dwellings in both Britain and Ireland 'to increase the efficiency of the people, and to make a stronger and more enduring State'.[57] But in truth, all prospect of housing reform under the 1914 Budget had now evaporated.

The 'Land Campaign' lay irrevocably broken. As Swenarton has noted, it meant that there was no clear housing policy agreed by the Asquith Cabinet—let alone prepared for legislation—by the time that war broke out in August 1914.[58] The limitations of the Government's vision were shown by the feeble Housing Bill that was introduced in mid-1914. It was brought in as an interim measure, and pragmatically combined the need to build dwellings for employees at the Rosyth naval base and other military establishments (necessary due to the rapid European arms build-up), with a limited scheme to implement the Board of Agriculture's proposals for rural housing.[59] The 1914 Housing Bill stipulated that unsubsidised, 'economic' rents must be charged, and it saw public utility societies rather than local authorities as the main building agency. A fall-back clause permitted the Board of Agriculture to act in default if no housing society was set up in a particular rural district, but this provoked parliamentary outrage at the prospect of the state taking over the role of rehousing rural labourers. The Asquith Cabinet responded to this outcry by dropping the rural housing provisions entirely, making the 1914 Housing Act even narrower than originally intended. The measure was significant because it signalled official acceptance of the principles of garden suburb design, but in terms of finance or policy it was retrogressive. Indeed, when Opposition MPs such as Griffith-Boscawen called for the inclusion of state subsidy on the Irish model, they were unceremoniously dismissed.[60] It showed that right up to the First World War, the Liberal Government not only opposed state subsidy but also preferred private initiative to public intervention. Given the disparity with Irish demands, it was not surprising that 1914 proved to be a frustrating year for those involved in the housing movement in Ireland.

THE AFTERMATH OF THE REJECTION OF THE DUBLIN HOUSING INQUIRY

To conclude this chapter, it is worth looking at the results in Dublin in 1914 of the Liberal Government's failure to grant increased urban housing subsidy, or indeed to come up with any positive proposals for Ireland. Chief Secretary Birrell simply reiterated the Cabinet line that new housing legislation for all of the United Kingdom would be forthcoming, but not before the 1915 parliamentary session. It was a vague promise that failed to prevent a wave of Irish appeals for more urgent action.[61] Meanwhile, Irish municipalities were greatly stepping up their efforts. After a trough in 1913–14, when municipal housing loans fell by a third, there was a resurgence just before the First World War in loan applications by Nationalist authorities such as Dublin Corporation and Pembroke UDC (see Diagram D and Table 5).[62] But the reality was that the Irish Party and the Castle Administration were preoccupied with the 'Ulster Crisis' that was threatening Home Rule at the final moment of implementation. The IPP could no longer provide a lead on the urban housing issue, and the outcome was a stalemate leading to the fragmentation of the hitherto united Irish demand for greater state subsidy. The dissipation of efforts can be seen in two new initiatives in which the Larkinite labour movement played a key role: the Citizens Housing League, and the Irish Builders' Cooperative Society.

The Citizens Housing League (hereafter CHL) was formed in April 1914 after joint meetings between two social reform groups, the Civic League and the Irishwomen's Reform League, in conjunction with the Larkinite Dublin Trades Council.[63] The main organiser and honorary secretary of the CHL was E. A. Aston, a retired Unionist businessman and town planning advocate, who since the 1913 Lock-out had been trying to unite the opposing forces of capital and labour in Dublin around a campaign to remove the terrible slum tenements. In the CHL's own words, it was 'called into existence primarily to obtain immediate State assistance, and represents citizens of every class and political opinion in Dublin'.[64] In practice it incorporated the radical labour movement into the middle-class housing reform movement in Dublin. Hence the CHL included leading Unionist businessmen from the Dublin Chamber of Commerce, such as its Chairman James Shanks (an ex-Lord Mayor), as well as prominent socialists such as its Vice-Chairman, William O'Brien. This unlikely marriage of convenience was an extension of an 'Orange-Syndicalist' alliance first attempted during the Dublin Corporation elections in January 1914, when the Municipal Reform Party tried unsuccessfully to win municipal power on a programme that made extensive slum clearance its main priority.[65] The CHL sought to cement this temporary anti-Nationalist alliance around two specific aims. The first was to secure better financial terms to build the 14 000 new cottages recommended by the ILGB Housing Inquiry. It demanded that the Government provide a £3 500 000 loan at 3.5 per cent interest over 60 years, plus an Imperial Exchequer subsidy of £60 000 a year. Secondly, the CHL wanted to ensure that all future Dublin Corporation schemes conformed to the 'modern' town planning ideal of low-density suburban estates on Unwinian lines.[66] The initial prospects seemed good. The CHL's inaugural meeting was a massive demonstration on 12 May 1914 chaired by the Lord Mayor of Dublin, Lorcan Sherlock, and was addressed by numerous reformers and labour leaders. An overflow meeting was also held to hear the more radical speakers such as Larkin, Connolly, Countess Markiewicz, William O'Brien and Thomas Lawlor.[67] Further impetus was added by the débâcle over Lloyd George's much anticipated Budget, and the realisation that nothing was forthcoming to help housing in Dublin.

However, the CHL ran into serious problems when it openly criticised the inner-city schemes proposed by Dublin Corporation. The result was bitter clashes at ILGB inquiries into Corporation schemes in mid-1914, which, as will be seen in the next chapter, the CHL sought to overcome by supplying the services of Patrick Geddes and Raymond Unwin as advisers. But in doing so it made powerful enemies within the Irish Party, notably J. J. Clancy, and with the Sinn Fein members who dominated the Corporation's Housing Committee, Alderman Thomas Kelly and Councillor William Cosgrave. Opponents portrayed the CHL as an unelected pressure group trying to dictate municipal policy.[68] Another problem was that there was little love lost between the socialists and the middle-class reformers within the CHL, and significantly James Larkin (who was never himself a member) played a key part in undermining Aston's efforts to build a bridge to the ITGWU.[69] The CHL's façade finally disintegrated when it hatched a plan to send an umbrella housing deputation, led by Lord Mayor Sherlock, to Chancellor Lloyd George to demand that he provide a £60 000 annual subsidy to build cottages in Dublin. It was intended that the delegation go over to London in June 1914.[70] But Larkin launched a blistering attack on the CHL's policy, and steadfastly refused to go on the deputation or even give it his blessing. And many Nationalist and Sinn Fein members of Dublin Corporation, with again Alderman Thomas Kelly setting the lead, refused to join any coalition that included radical socialists. Instead, the Corporation voted decisively to send a separate deputation to the British Government.[71] The result was a bitter row between Aston and Kelly in June 1914, further fuelled when Larkin challenged the two disputants to an open debate on the housing question.[72] Even if the CHL had been able to organise a coordinated deputation it was unlikely to have achieved anything, since the embattled Lloyd George had decided that any Irish housing lobby should be referred instead to Chief Secretary Birrell.[73] The outbreak of war saw the fortunes of the CHL decline further, with Aston leaving to work first with the emergency Dublin Distress Committee and then with the Irish recruiting campaign.

The other factional housing initiative launched in Dublin in mid-1914 was the Irish Builders' Cooperative Society (hereafter IBCS), which arose from James Larkin's brief embrace of the linked ideals of cooperativism and guild socialism. The basic theory came from a group of British followers of John Ruskin and William Morris—notably A. R. Orage and S. G. Hobson in the *New Age*, and the Arts and Crafts architect, A. J. Penty—who argued that the conflict between capital and labour could only be overcome by organising industrial production into 'national guilds' run by the workers themselves.[74] For the beleaguered ITGWU at the end of the 1913–14 Dublin Lock-out, guild socialism offered an alternative means to by-pass and subvert Irish capitalism. Larkin thus began to work on a 'New Campaign' for a producers' cooperative which could incorporate all Irish labour in an organisation even more advanced than the model ITGWU.[75] A key element in the strategy was the IBCS, formed in February 1914 in conjunction with the agricultural cooperativist, George ('A. E.') Russell, and three leading socialists: Captain J. R. White (a retired British Army officer, and an organiser of Connolly's revitalised Citizens Army), Countess Constance Markiewicz (the renowned Anglo-Irish rebel, feminist, long-time worker with Dublin's poor, and member of the Citizens Army), and Councillor Richard O'Carroll (a Labour member of Dublin Corporation, and leader of the Dublin Labour Party). The *Irish Worker* declared that:

> one section of workers in Dublin have completed arrangements by which all the building operations in the new Dublin, about to be undertaken, may not only be affected but may be carried on by the workers themselves . . . The Irish Transport Union will appear in the future as a competitor with the bosses, and owing to the less need for private profit that exists in the case of the Union, the building boss bids fair to become a rapidly disappearing body.[76]

By killing off the private contractor, it was hoped that the IBCS would thus not only get rid of the Dublin slums but also improve the working conditions of building labourers. As early as January 1914 Larkin claimed to be preparing 'a scheme of model housing, which could be built by them, and they intended to show what could be done by organised and skilled labour in Dublin, independent of the politicians'; another supporter argued that when sufficient profits were accumulated from cooperativism, the ITGWU member 'might eventually decide to lay out a garden suburb for Dublin, and provide himself with a decent little house, large enough for privacy and comfort, and small enough to be homely'.[77] There is no evidence that an IBCS housing scheme was ever designed, but in mid-1914 James Larkin appears to have discussed the idea of a garden village for Dublin's dock labourers with Patrick Geddes (who, as will be seen in the next chapter, was over in connection with the 1914 Civic Exhibition and Summer School of Civics). The two had met in Edinburgh towards the end of the 1913–14 Lock-out, and Geddes was widely known to be a supporter of cooperativist ideas.[78] Larkin would also have heard about Geddes from his associate, William O'Brien, who was a key member of the CHL.

Meanwhile, the IBCS appointed a secretary, and in early-May 1914 an appeal was launched calling on Irish trade unionists to buy shares to provide a working capital of £1000.[79] A further boost was given when the first ever Irish meeting of the United Kingdom Cooperative Union was held in Dublin in early-June 1914. This was attended by William O'Brien, and he heard delegates extolling cooperativism as the only means to achieve labour and housing reforms in Ireland.[80] By this point Larkin had effectively crushed the CHL, and hence the IBCS had become the sole focus for the housing aims of the radical labour movement. At a public meeting in early-July 1914, chaired by Countess Markiewicz, leading labour representatives pledged their support. But despite subsequent appeals for more shares to be taken up, nothing was actually achieved.[81] Within a month war had broken out, and Larkin's cooperativist plans ended when he went to raise funds in the USA. The IBCS, however, did prefigure the post-war building guilds in Dublin, and certainly the radical ideas advocated by the ITGWU went far beyond those of the Glasgow Labour Party, which Englander has claimed were the most innovative of the pre-war period.[82] The ultimately futile efforts of the CHL and IBCS were symptomatic of a stalemate in the urban housing movement in pre-war Ireland, brought on by the paralysis of the Irish Party and the Asquith Cabinet's refusal to augment state subsidy. Another product of this unstable situation in 1914 was that the British town planning movement was able to step in and acquire an importance that had been previously denied it in Ireland. This will form the subject of the next chapter.

Chapter 4

HOME RULE AND GARDEN SUBURB IDEALS IN IRELAND BEFORE 1914

From 1911 to 1914 there was a determined attempt, involving many of the leading British exponents of town planning, to introduce garden suburb ideals to Ireland. The paradigm that was promoted was a combination of the social theory of Patrick Geddes and the low-density, picturesque model of suburban design pioneered by Raymond Unwin. The planning crusade in pre-war Ireland capitalised on the vacuum in urban housing reform that was caused by the preoccupation of the Irish Party with the Home Rule Bill and the 'Ulster Crisis'. Out of this crusade came a series of remarkable initiatives that included the 1914 Dublin Town Plan Competition, won by Patrick Abercrombie, and the housing report produced by Geddes and Unwin for Dublin Corporation at the outbreak of the First World War. And yet it is notable that, for all their efforts, Irish planning enthusiasts and their British mentors remained on the periphery of the housing issue. Recent accounts of this episode have not explained clearly why town planning failed to establish itself in pre-war Ireland.[1] This chapter will argue that marginalisation can only be explained by two factors: first, because town planning protagonists did not appreciate the ideological gap between their ideas and the preoccupation in Ireland with Home Rule; and second, because they did not take into account the relation of the Irish housing debate to that in Britain. In this sense, early garden suburb theory proved extremely limited when applied to a country like Ireland.

THE BEGINNINGS OF THE TOWN PLANNING MOVEMENT IN IRELAND

Until 1911 there had been no real Irish town planning movement, only a few isolated supporters.[2] This is not surprising, given that Ireland was hardly fertile ground for those advocating garden cities or garden suburbs. Ireland's slow industrial growth compared with Britain, and its predominantly agricultural economy, meant that it had neither the proliferation of ugly manufacturing towns nor the tradition of intellectual critiques of industrial urbanisation that had prompted the communitarian ideals of Ebeneezer Howard and Raymond Unwin. The few genuinely industrial towns that existed in Ulster prided themselves on being well housed, a complacent attitude best summed up in a lecture by a Belfast Corporation official in 1911 entitled 'How a Town

Succeeded without the Town-Planning Act'.³ Instead, the majority of Irish towns were seen as suffering from economic decay rather than the problems created by unregulated urban expansion, the slums of Dublin being the quintessential product. Hence the Irish Party's spokesman dismissed John Burns' 1909 Housing and Town Planning Act on the grounds that it was 'largely concerned with the planning of new towns, whereas our concern, unfortunately, is rather to do what we can to prevent old towns from becoming absolute ruins'.⁴ However, the certainty that British town planning had no relevance to Ireland became less convincing in the conditions of political uncertainty over Home Rule from 1911. Now that the planning movements in Britain and abroad were receiving greater official recognition through events such as the 1910 RIBA Town Planning Conference, they could no longer be so easily ignored. Even more important in Irish terms were the growing calls for the civic aggrandisement of Dublin, in the anticipation that it would soon become a real capital city once more.⁵

But if the focus for town planning in pre-war Ireland fell on Dublin, there is no doubt that the impetus derived from Britain (or more accurately, Scotland). The main protagonists were the Lord Lieutenant of Ireland, Lord Aberdeen, and his indefatigable wife, Lady Ishbel Aberdeen.⁶ Lord Aberdeen was a wealthy Northern Scottish landowner and a stalwart of the Liberal Party. He had served briefly as Irish Lord Lieutenant during the fiasco of the first Home Rule Bill in 1886, and was reappointed after the landslide election victory 20 years later. Both the Aberdeens were well known as Gladstonian Liberals and devout Christian social reformers, and Lady Aberdeen had won international recognition for her crusading work against tuberculosis in Ireland. They were concerned to find a way to heal the growing divisions in Irish society, which in the pre-war period were now appearing between capital and labour as well as between Nationalists and Unionists. In 1911 Lord and Lady Aberdeen visited Patrick Geddes' Cities and Town Planning Exhibition while it was in Edinburgh, and felt they had found the answer. Geddes, after all, claimed that his new discipline of 'Civics', and its physical application through town planning, represented the best means of ensuring the beneficial social evolution of mankind.⁷ He believed that by recapturing the lost values of citizenship, which he believed had existed in the pre-industrial city, there would be a regeneration of urban life which would sweep away the unhealthy industrial cities and the blind values of political nationalism. Meller has noted that Geddes' message of creating 'social peace' through civic reconstruction had a strong appeal for liberal administrators in troubled colonial provinces, such as Lord Aberdeen and his wife.⁸ In return, Geddes saw Ireland as an excellent testing ground for his theories precisely because of its complex social problems. He felt that political and economic factors had held back the evolutionary growth of cities such as Dublin, and that it would be his role to reveal this and to point the way towards harmony through civic endeavour.⁹ In this, Geddes saw himself following the example of Sir Horace Plunkett, who had long championed agricultural cooperativism in Ireland as a means of turning attention away from the Home Rule issue, and towards the goal of social and economic progress.

Town planning in Ireland received its first major impetus when, in 1911, Lord and Lady Aberdeen twice in the same year invited Geddes to bring his Cities and Town Planning Exhibition to Dublin.[10] The first opportunity was at the 'Ui Breasail' exhibition in late May and early June. Lord and Lady Aberdeen failed in their attempt to get John Burns to open the exhibition. Nevertheless a distinguished field of lecturers including Lord Leverhulme, Stanley Adshead and Henry Vivian came over to supplement talks given by Geddes and his assistant Frank Mears.[11] The exhibition went on briefly to Belfast, where it failed to make any real impression. In August 1911 it returned to Dublin for the Royal Institute of Public Health Congress, and once again British experts lectured in connection. By now Geddes had established himself as the dominant influence over the nascent Irish planning movement.

The main outcome of these two exhibitions was the formation in September 1911 of the Housing and Town Planning Association of Ireland (hereafter HTPAI).[12] The President of this body was Lady Aberdeen, and most of its membership comprised social reformers from the professional and business classes, such as E. A. Aston and D. A. Chart. Architects and engineers engaged in housing work were also well represented, including the Dublin City Architect, Charles MacCarthy, and the Chief Engineering Inspector of the Irish Local Government Board, Dr Peter Cowan. The message promoted by the HTPAI was that the way forward lay in a combination of Geddesian ideas about civic duty and the construction, not of garden cities, but of Unwinian garden suburbs to replace the chronic slums in Irish cities. The association campaigned for the extension of British town planning legislation to Ireland, and for a civic survey to be carried out in Dublin. Much of its time was spent in organising a series of exhibitions and conferences. The most important of these conferences was that on 'Housing and Town Development', held as part of the HTPAI's first annual meeting in October 1912. It was attended by many Irish municipal representatives, and resulted in a deputation being sent to Lord Lieutenant Aberdeen to demand that the subsidy terms under the Labourers Acts be given also to urban working-class housing. Out of this deputation, as was noted in Chapter 2, the Association of Municipal Authorities of Ireland was formed in December 1912 specifically to take over the agitation for urban housing subsidy, now that the Irish Party was no longer taking the lead. From this point on, the HTPAI virtually ignored the question of housing finance in order to concentrate itself fully on town planning propaganda. A look now at the reaction of Irish groups to garden suburb ideals will show that this division of responsibilities was to prove disastrous in practice.

REACTIONS TO TOWN PLANNING IDEALS IN PRE-WAR IRELAND

In Britain the claim of the garden city movement to be able to solve the problems of urban growth and housing conditions, while leaving the existing social system intact, meant that it managed to appeal to all political parties and to a wide spectrum of opinion ranging from wealthy industrialists such as Lever to socialists such as Unwin.[13] Clearly, figures such as Geddes felt that a similar message could potentially bring together otherwise antagonistic groups in Ireland.

However, the attitude of Irish groups towards garden suburb ideals proved to be more complicated. Unionists outside Ulster were open to ideas of social reform and indeed formed an important part of bodies such as the HTPAI. But much of their effectiveness depended on their alliance with Ulster Unionists, and it has already been noted that the latter had no real interest in housing matters, nor could they be convinced of the importance of town planning while the Home Rule controversy raged. While it is clear that the radical labour movement in pre-war Dublin favoured garden suburb housing, as was seen in the last two chapters, its leaders vilified the middle-class social reformers who they claimed had appropriated these ideals. Larkin and Connolly instead placed their hopes on achieving the election of labour municipal representatives, but this strategy was to have little success in breaking the IPP's hegemony over local politics.

It was the Irish Parliamentary Party that held the key to the fate of garden suburb ideals. As mentioned previously, the IPP had long tried to broaden its support amongst the urban working class by supporting bodies which took a leading role in the housing issue, notably the Town Tenants League. The main force within the League, Councillor Coughlan Briscoe of Dublin Corporation, became personally interested in town planning and visited many showpiece schemes in Britain and the Continent. After representing Dublin Corporation at the 1910 RIBA Town Planning Conference, on his return he recommended that the municipality should build a garden suburb at Marino.[14] A similar committment to town planning ideals was also shared by other individual representatives of nationalist municipalities, several of whom were members of the HTPAI. Leading examples were Councillor Lorcan Sherlock, the pre-war Lord Mayor of Dublin Corporation, and Councillor Charles O'Neill of Pembroke Council. However, despite this undoubted element of municipal support, the Irish town planning movement was unable to win over the Irish Party because it failed to deal directly with the key question of urban housing subsidy. Thus, while the IPP was ready to back the demands of the Association of Municipal Authorities for increased aid from the Imperial Treasury, it pointedly did not give any assistance to the HTPAI. 'Picturesque sites, artistic plans, and aesthetic disposition of the houses are desirable', wrote the nationalist *Freemans Journal*, 'but the main point is to secure that the houses will be let at rents within the means of the working classes.'[15] This line was taken even further by the IPP's main housing spokesman, J. J. Clancy. In 1913 he bluntly told Chief Secretary Birrell that what was wanted was 'not town-planning, or such ornamental development, but something that will house the people afresh in those localities in which now the conditions of life are abominable and intolerable'.[16] The accusation that town planning could offer nothing to solve the financial problem of housing meant that it was unable to overcome the indifference shown towards urban issues by large sections of the Irish Party's supporters, such as the Catholic Church.

It was also an argument that played straight into the hands of the Sinn Fein representatives on Dublin Corporation's Housing Committee, Alderman Thomas Kelly and Councillor William Cosgrave. Kelly in particular became the most trenchant opponent of town planning within the Corporation, arguing persuasively that because unskilled casual labour was predominant in Dublin, then the municipality must concentrate on providing cheap dwellings as close as possible to sources of work in the city centre. Due to the efforts of Kelly, above all, the plans for a garden suburb at Marino were frustrated, and town planning sympathisers remained a minority in the pre-war Dublin Corporation.[17]

THE INTENSIFICATION OF THE TOWN PLANNING CAMPAIGN IN 1913–14

The HTPAI had made little impact in Ireland during its first two years. It saw, however, a major opportunity for advancement as a result of the wave of housing concern during the 1913–14 Dublin Lock-out. As noted in Chapter 2, it was Lord and Lady Aberdeen, along with others in the HTPAI, who tried strenuously to have the official inquiry into the city's housing conditions turned into a Vice-Regal Commission. Their aim in doing so was to secure the appointment on to the inquiry team of a town planning expert.[18] When their strategy failed, Lady Aberdeen, acting through the agency of the Women's National Health Association, brought over Patrick Geddes to give evidence to the ILGB Housing Inquiry. Geddes and his devoted Irish follower, E. A. Aston, outlined to the inquiry the case for proper town planning, and both specifically urged the adoption of Unwinian garden suburbs. However, the final ILGB Housing Report concentrated on the issue of state subsidy and tended to play down town planning claims, save in a minority report appended by one of the inquiry team, J. F. MacCabe.[19]

Thus for the HTPAI, the 1913–14 Dublin Housing Inquiry represented a lost chance. In order to keep up the momentum, in January 1914 Lord and Lady Aberdeen launched two new initiatives that were both apparently suggested by Geddes. One was to hold the first Civic Exhibition in the United Kingdom, similar to that held in Ghent in 1913 and that scheduled for Lyons that year. The other initiative was the well-known 1914 Dublin Town Plan Competition.

There were two aims behind the Civic Exhibition. One was the Geddesian notion of focusing on 'Civics' and town planning as a means of overcoming the social divisions revealed by the Dublin strike. A brochure for the exhibition stated that it would 'not be by the exertions of the few but by the hearty cooperation of all classes that real progress will be made', and Geddes called on Ireland now to 'take a definite and historic place in this movement for citizenship which was now manifestly becoming a central movement throughout the world'.[20] A Civics Institute was formed to turn the exhibition into a permanent campaign, with Lord and Lady Aberdeen acting as its joint-presidents. Geddes also ran a Summer School which spelt out the need for a civic survey. The second aim of the 1914 Civic Exhibition was to address the thorny issue of Irish economic under-development. This it did by promoting the American theory that only town planning could ensure that cities would work as effective instruments of production and consumption. Several of the figures associated with what became called the 'City Functional' movement, and in particular the ambitious 'Boston-1915' campaign, were brought over to put across this viewpoint.[21] The leading US planner John Nolen, pointedly described as being of Irish-American descent, was employed as manager of the Civic Exhibition. He immediately began to stress economic factors. 'Unless there is some hard town-planning done', warned Nolen, '. . . Dublin will slip back.'[22] A brochure for the exhibition later claimed that it would 'show how Dublin can be made a better and more profitable place to do business in'.[23]

The Civic Exhibition opened on 15 July 1914 amidst much pomp. It contained a wide range of exhibits, but pride of place was given to the housing and town planning section. This showed many planning exemplars from the USA, Germany and elsewhere, and above all praised the British garden city tradition. Visitors were left in no doubt that, as the *Irish Architect* noted of the housing schemes on show, 'the Irish designs are not as a rule up to the standard of the English'.[24] The Civic Exhibition was held in the refurbished Linenhall Barracks, which Lord Aberdeen tried secretly to have given over permanently as a museum for the newly-founded Civics Institute. But despite his appeals to the Chancellor of the Exchequer, Lloyd George, the Treasury rejected this suggestion on the grounds that 'to give this away to even a much deserving enterprise would be tantamount to assisting it from public funds'.[25] Due to the outbreak of war in early-August 1914, the Civic Exhibition did not receive quite as many visitors as anticipated. However, its principal failing was that it patently failed to reconcile Irish factions as it had intended. Several Unionist municipalities, including Belfast Corporation, declined to attend in light of the rapidly escalating 'Ulster Crisis'. The exhibition also failed to attract Dublin's casual poor, partly because of the entrance charge, and partly because James Larkin called on his supporters to treat the exhibition with contempt.[26] Only on the last day was entrance made free, and the working classes responded by making off with much of the furniture and exhibits! Geddes in typical fashion tried to gloss over this episode, fantasising that 'each thief would now have a model of a little cottage on his mantelpiece, and that would show him the sort of place he should be living in, instead of the slums'.[27]

The second initiative launched in January 1914 was the Dublin Town Plan Competition. Lord Aberdeen offered a £500 prize, and Patrick Geddes and John Nolen were appointed as judges along with the Dublin City Architect. Since all agreed that a full civic survey was needed before any real plan could be decided on, the competition was always intended more to produce ideas and publicity. The key requirement of the competition brief was to provide the 14 000 new dwellings recommended by the Dublin Housing Inquiry. But, importantly, this was to be supplemented by a wholesale reorganisation of the transport system and land use in Dublin and its environs. Judgement of the eight submitted entries was delayed because of the First World War, and it was not until heated debate arose over the rebuilding of areas destroyed in the 1916 Easter Rising, that Lord Aberdeen and the Civics Institute were prompted into action. Patrick Abercrombie was now declared the winner. His entry was typical of the 'Liverpool School' approach, in that it combined a Geddesian theoretical framework with American 'Beaux Arts' monumental planning in central areas and Neo-Georgian housing estates in the suburbs (see Figs 26–28).[28] Abercrombie's grand public buildings were designed in a series of eclectic neo-historicist styles. At the core of his proposal lay a new 'traffic centre', just to the west of the existing heart of Dublin, to act as a fulcrum for new transport networks. A series of grand boulevards or 'parkways' were then to link the city core with a ring of garden suburbs, each suburb having its own axial and geometric layout, and comprising a distinct 'neighbourhood centre'. The housing types were all designed in a rationalised Neo-Georgian manner, and consisted of short terraces of two-storey cottages with wide frontages and a through-lit living room. Abercrombie repeatedly stressed his belief that housing and transport links had to be reformed together on a grand scale if Dublin was to be rescued from economic stagnation. But although Abercrombie's design was skilfully worked out, Geddes declared pointedly that its purpose was educative rather than proscriptive.[29] Geddes also took pains to state that the best written report had in fact accompanied the entry submitted by Charles Ashbee, the leading Arts and Crafts architect. This opinion is hardly surprising. Ashbee was a great admirer of Geddes, as shown by his subsequent book on town planning entitled *Where the Great City Stands: A Study in the New Civics* (1917). The problem for Ashbee, however, was that his design proposals for the Town Plan competition were extremely weak, and consisted mainly of two inconclusive birds-eye perspectives purporting to show what the 'new Dublin' might look like.[30]

Abercrombie's town plan for Dublin had little direct effect in Ireland until it resurfaced during the 1920s, when it was published by the Civics Institute as part of the campaign for town planning legislation in the new Irish Free State. In the short term, Abercrombie's design was more influential in Britain than in Ireland. It was described by H. V. Lanchester as 'the highest development that

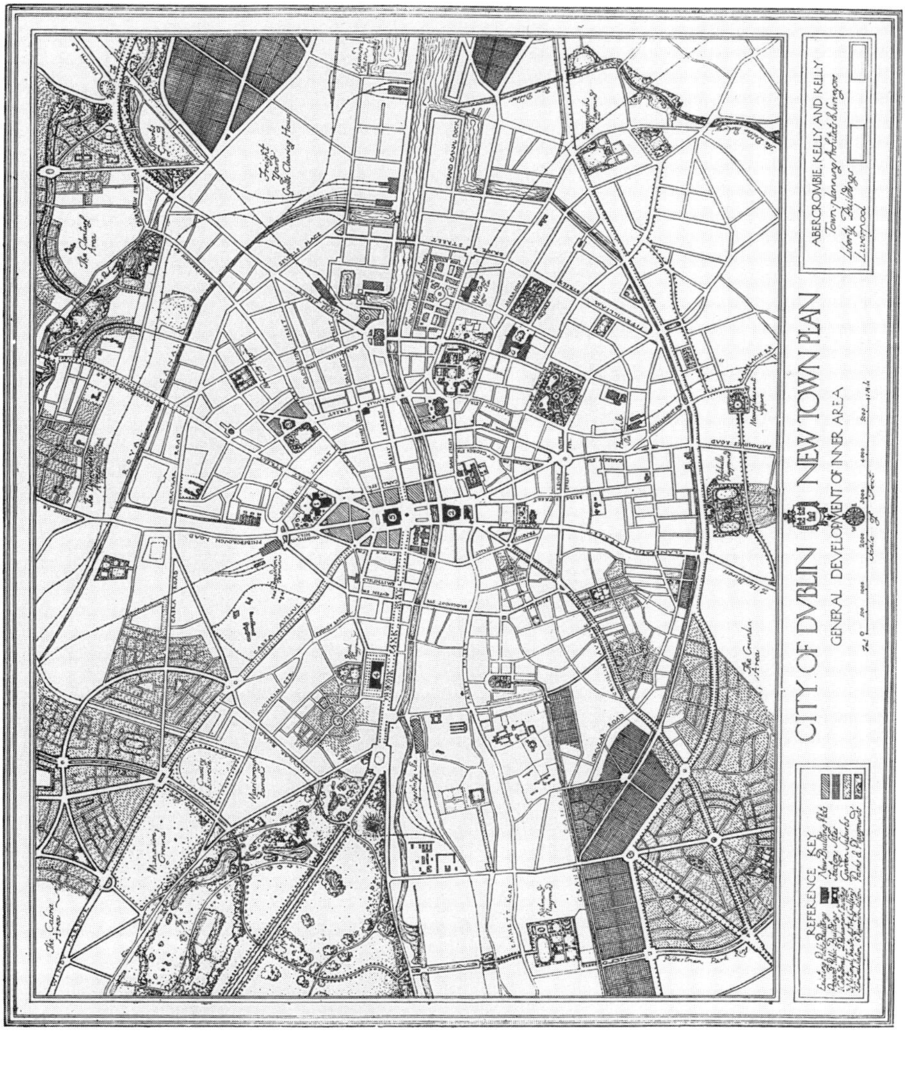

Fig 26. P. Abercrombie: winning entry in the 1914 Dublin Town Plan Competition

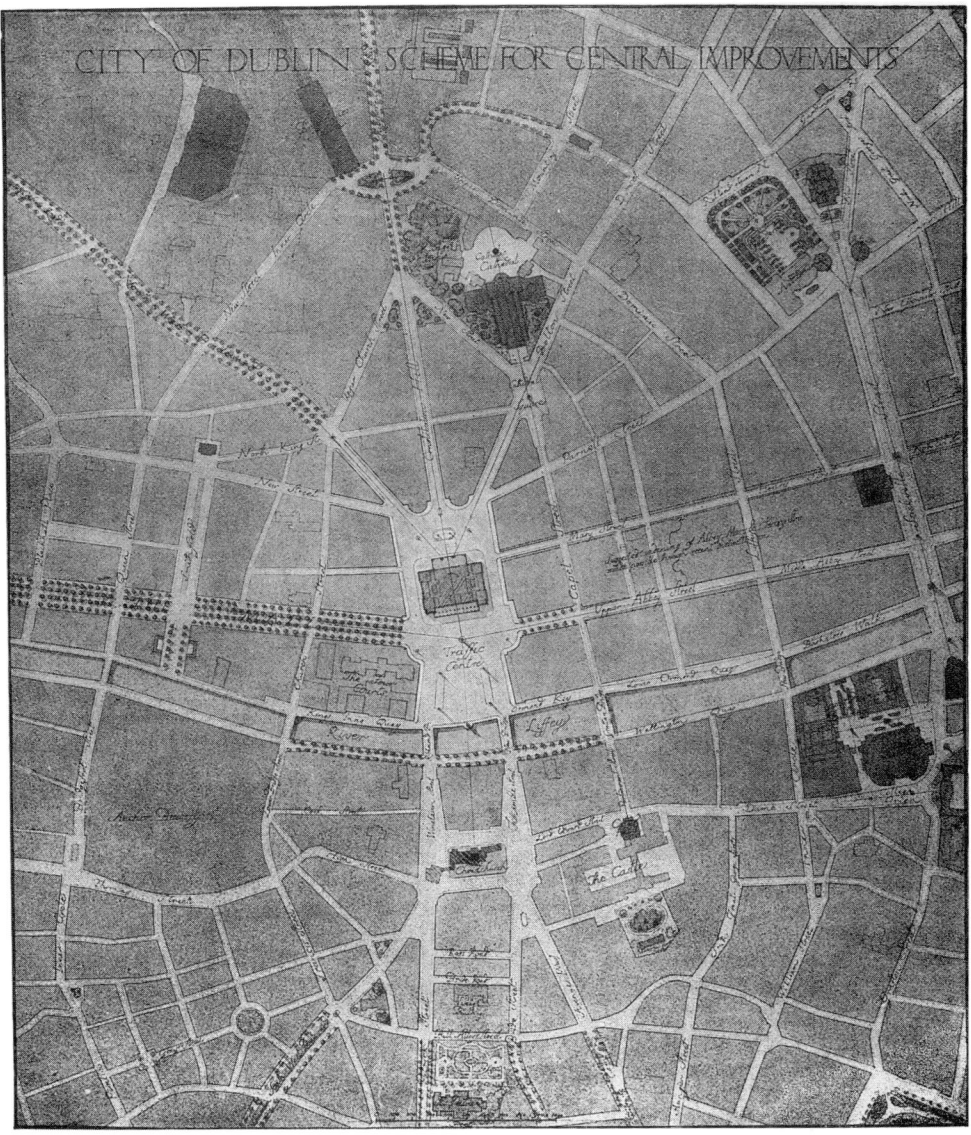

Fig 27. P. Abercrombie: proposal for civic improvements in central Dublin (1914)

had yet been reached in the matter of town planning in the United Kingdom', and Raymond Unwin recommended that it be studied 'by town planners all over the world, because it showed the state to which town planning was brought'.[31] Thomas Mawsom wrote in September 1916 that it was essential that the plan be implemented in the wake of the Easter Rising, because:

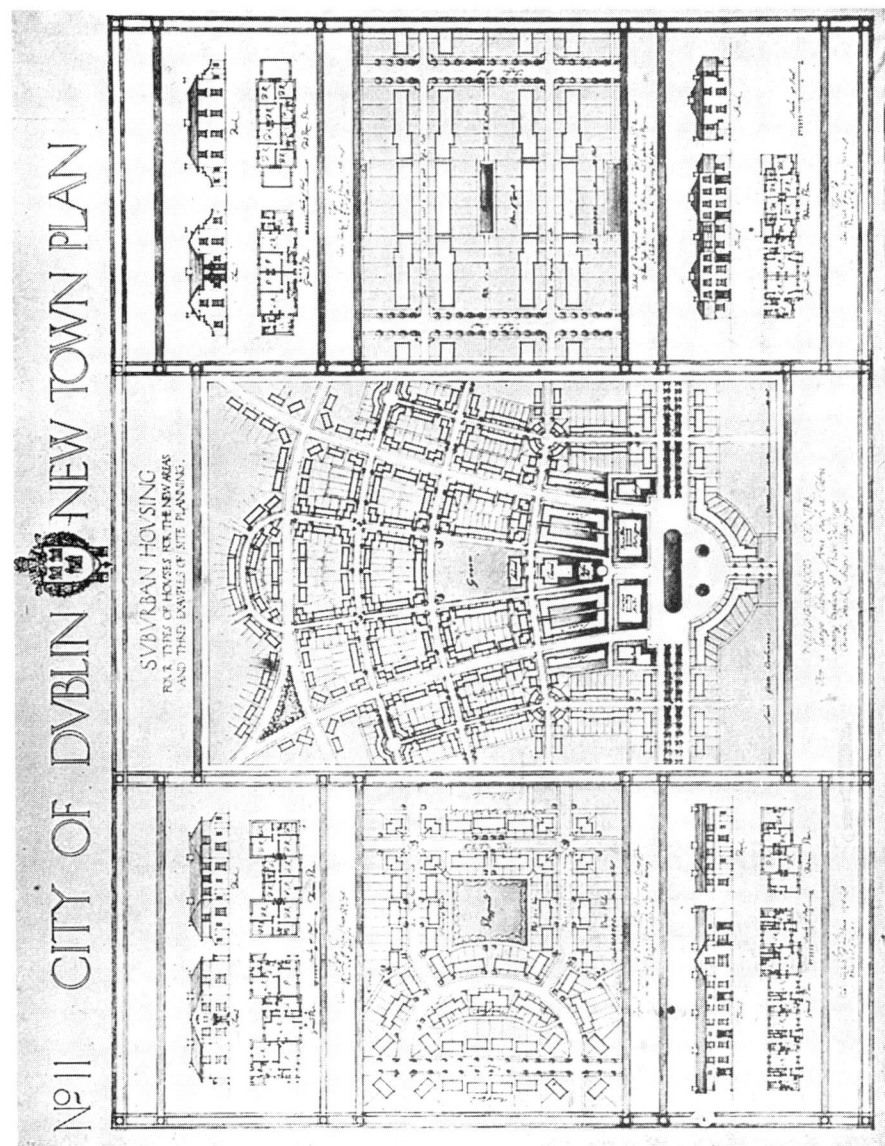

Fig 28. P. Abercrombie: proposal for Neo-Georgian suburban housing (1914)

142 *John Bull's Other Homes*

> the present occasion marks a crisis in the history of the town planning movement. On its results depends the place the art is to take in the future in this country for never before have such favourable conditions prevailed nor can we hope for another such opportunity.[32]

But given the extreme sensitivity of administrative policy in war-time Ireland, plus the controversy over the rebuilding of central Dublin (both of which will be seen in the next chapter), this statement reveals not an understanding of Irish conditions but rather an overriding concern for the furtherance of town planning theory and practice in Britain.

A similar blinkered attitude from British town planners can also be seen in the pre-war experience of the previously-mentioned Citizens Housing League. After clashing repeatedly with Dublin Corporation over the latter's continued preference for inner-city schemes, the League offered to supply the services of Geddes and Unwin as advisers to the Corporation's Housing Committee. Many councillors, especially Sinn Fein members, were totally opposed to the idea, but overall the Dublin Corporation voted to accept.[33] The actual report produced in September 1914 appears to have been written primarily by Unwin, and contained several specific housing suggestions. The most striking proposal was for a substantial and picturesque garden suburb on the Marino site, designed with help from Geddes' own assistant, Frank Mears (see Fig. 29).

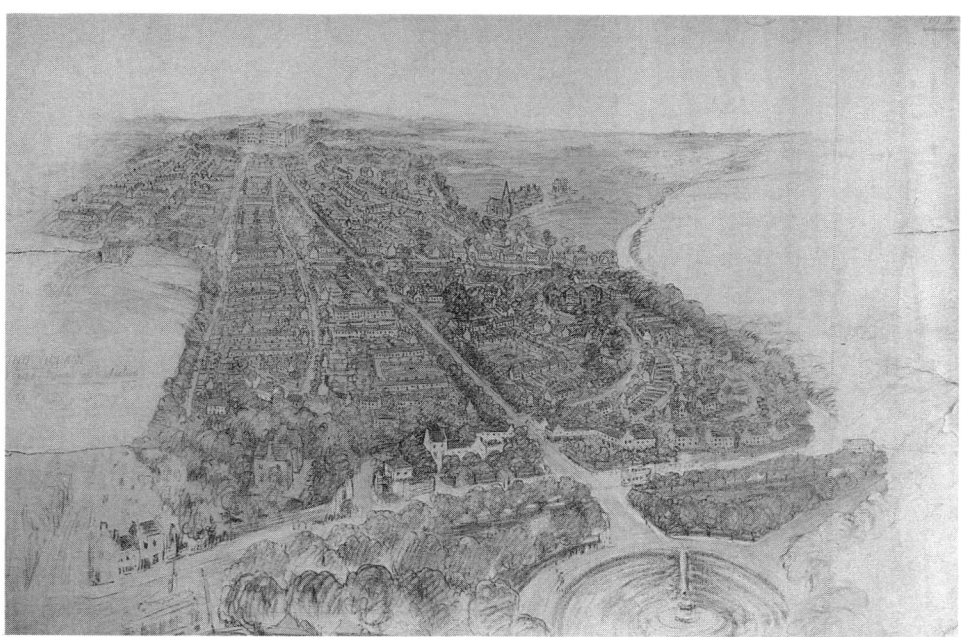

Fig 29. P. Geddes and R. Unwin: perspective of the proposal for the Marino Estate (1914)

However, any of the potential benefits from these suggestions were lost because the Geddes/Unwin Report consciously disregarded the central issue of state subsidy. The report stated that the housing question should not be mixed up with the general problem of poverty, which required other policies.[34] Instead it urged Dublin Corporation to build high-standard garden suburbs for those artisans who could pay higher rents, thereby allowing the very poor to 'filter up' into the dwellings which were vacated. This was a specifically British rationale, and one that had just been used for the acceptance of Unwinian design principles by the Land Enquiry Committee and the English Board of Agriculture. However, it clearly ran counter to the quasi-collectivist view in Ireland that state subsidy for the very poor was paramount. The outcome was that the Geddes/Unwin Report was easily denounced by Dublin Corporation as being based more on conditions to be found in an English manufacturing town, and of therefore having 'approached and reported on the subject from an exclusively Town Planning point of view'.[35]

THE OUTCOME OF THE PLANNING CRUSADE IN PRE-WAR IRELAND

What, then, had been achieved by the town planning movement in Ireland on the eve of the First World War? There were no significant private initiatives to speak of, nor had any co-partnership housing societies been set up. As was noted in the last chapter, in mid-1914 James Larkin hatched a scheme for a garden suburb to rehouse ITGWU members, using the profits of the new workers' building guild. But despite consultations with Patrick Geddes, nothing came of this plan. A tiny suburban estate along British Arts-and-Crafts lines was built in Pembroke in 1913–14, with advice from the HTPAI, to act as a memorial to the Earl of Pembroke.[36] It made little or no impact. In the case of private enterprise housing, one pre-war Belfast speculator advertised the building of a so-called 'garden suburb', but this referred merely to the provision of attractive housing for sale to the city's middle classes.[37] Municipalities were the main source of new working-class dwellings in pre-war Ireland, and in general, whether Nationalist or Unionist, their overriding preference was to build minimal cost inner-city schemes consisting of two-up-two-down terraced houses in high density arrangements. As was noted earlier in Chapter 2, only a few authorities in the wealthier southern suburbs of Dublin, where there was an atypically high proportion of skilled artisans who could afford more expensive rents, were even able to consider options such as the British strategy of garden suburb design. It is also significant that in all of these southern Dublin municipalities there were active members of the HTPAI or the Association of Municipal Authorities in important positions.

But even amongst the municipal bodies that were potentially sympathetic to town planning ideals in the pre-war era, only Pembroke UDC appears to have actually brought in the HTPAI to advise on the design of what it termed a 'garden suburb' in the Ringsend district.[38] This scheme, which was actually spread over several sites and was built between 1913 and 1916, received much praise from the Irish Local Government Board as a model for other municipalities to emulate. The architect was George O'Connor, an ambitious young member of the Irish town planning movement who had also designed the alterations for the 1914 Civic Exhibition. The largest site developed by Pembroke UDC was an estate of single-storey and two-storey terraces arranged on a gridded layout at Stella Gardens, just off the Irishtown Road. This design, however, represented not so much a genuine Unwinian garden suburb, but rather an improved municipal terraced scheme in the same sense as the pre-war estates built by the LCC. Higher space standards were provided, and the largest dwellings even had three bedrooms and a separate bathroom. Easily the most attractive of the Pembroke UDC designs was for two rows of terraced cottages in Harmony Avenue and Brookvale Avenue, in a quiet riverside site off Eglington Road (see Fig. 30). Here a subtle use of brickwork features such as a string-course and arched door openings, along with a rhythm of delicate gables above the main bedroom windows, served to blend in harmoniously with the leafy surroundings. But in the absence of increased state subsidy, the result was that Pembroke UDC was forced to charge substantial rents for its pre-war schemes, and it was for this very reason that other Irish authorities did not follow suit. 'So far the garden city epidemic has not visited Dublin', declared the *Irish Builder* in 1915, and this observation applied even more forcefully to the rest of Ireland.[39]

Fig 30. G. O'Connor/Pembroke UDC: Harmony Avenue, Donnybrook (1916)

Given this almost complete failure in practice, it would appear that ultimately the pre-war town planning movement in Ireland had more to do with British rather than Irish conditions. For British participants, the very attraction was the complexity of the political situation, and the hope that town planning and citizenship might be used to resolve the confrontation between Nationalism and Unionism and between capital and labour. Geddes felt that Ireland had a lesson for everywhere:

> Through such large civic endeavours as that of the town planning of Dublin, this correlation of Survey and Eutopia [sic] may be made plainer to other cities; and this is appealing to all parties, classes, occupations, and individuals. In such ways city surveys and exhibitions and plans are actually generating a new movement of education, that towards a School of Civics, as in Dublin, and soon in every city.[40]

Of course, nothing remotely like this happened in pre-war Dublin. Town planning failed to establish itself simply because it offered nothing to any of the groups who held power. It clearly could provide no solution to the opposition of Nationalists and Unionists over the question of Home Rule. Likewise, there was no real integration of radical labour groups into the town planning movement in Dublin, despite the efforts of bodies like the Citizens Housing League. Garden suburb ideals remained in general in the hands of a rather narrow clique of middle-class reformers. This explains why the Irish Administration and the British Government could remain so indifferent to demands for town planning in Ireland, since planning offered them little help in their delicate policy of balancing rival Irish groups. Garden suburb supporters such as Lord and Lady Aberdeen remained on the periphery of official British policy, and their involvement stemmed from their personal belief in the need to reform society. Thus, there was no sense in which town planning formed part of British policy in Ireland, as has been tentatively suggested.[41]

Instead, the propagation of garden suburb ideals should be seen as part of the wider attempt by many groups in Britain to deal with the problems engendered by potential self-government for Ireland. However, the failure of town planning advocates to adapt their precepts to suit pre-war Irish conditions meant that the movement tended to appear irrelevant in two ways. First, Geddes' attempt to remove the political dimension underestimated the need in Ireland, at such an uncertain juncture, to reinforce support either for or against Home Rule. For adherents of the Irish Party and other Nationalist groups, any attempt to turn away from the question of independence was seen ultimately as only playing into the hands of Unionists and the British Government. As has been observed of Sir Horace Plunkett, whom Geddes so much admired, the aim to bypass nationalism was perceived as simply another form of 'constructive Unionism'—that is, of promoting Irish social and economic reform to help divert from the demands for self-government.[42] Indeed, the ridiculous later contention by Geddes that the 1916 Easter Rising could have been averted if only money had been spent on housing and town planning reform, reads exactly like this.[43] The other way in which British town planners appeared to be irrelevant was that they simply did not appreciate the emphasis placed in Ireland on extracting more state subsidy for urban housing. Given the historical resentments that had built up against British rule, any solution that did not propose financial redistribution was seen again as only doing the Treasury's work for it. Both these omissions were to give the pre-war Irish town planning movement a definite air of unreality. Another aspect which many in Ireland found difficult to accept was the cultural imperialist assumption that English planning and housing design were inherently superior, and should be exported to dependent nations such as Ireland. This was clearly the view of Charles Ashbee, a strong admirer of Geddes and a commended entrant in the Dublin Town Plan Competition, and would appear to have been echoed in observations by Patrick Geddes.[44] Although Geddes was to take a different approach later in India, in his dealings with pre-war Dublin he saw the latter as a kind of laboratory in which to try out what Meller has described as a 'Geddesian social experiment'.[45] Therefore, what was being proposed for Ireland was not a neutral model of low-density suburban living that celebrated the values of the self-contained and single-family house. After all, any ideology which expressed such views would naturally have found favour with powerful groups in Ireland such as the Roman Catholic Church. Rather, what was being put forward was an intellectual structure that conceived the economic and social relations of housing design in explicitly British terms. It was this aspect that was found to be unpalatable in Ireland.

If the crusade to import British town planning values (i.e. Geddesian sociology and Unwinian garden suburb design) turned out to be a side issue in the pre-war urban housing debate in Ireland, it nevertheless offers an interesting case study in how ideas are transformed within colonial conditions. In Britain, town planning was a highly contentious subject. Garden suburb planning was promoted by many supporters, notably Lloyd George and the Land Enquiry Committee, as a political instrument to be used in the long-running battle between commercial and landed capital.[46] And, perhaps not surprisingly, opponents came to perceive town planning as a stalking-horse for land municipalisation, and thereby a threat to the potential profits that private landowners might earn from the expansion of industrial cities. No matter how much the issue was watered down to enable the 1909 Housing and Town Planning Act to be passed, these political tensions remained. Yet when British adherents of town planning came to campaign in Ireland, the emphasis was on portraying it instead as a consciously apolitical and technical issue. The emphasis on technocracy appears to have become even more marked in the later work of Patrick Geddes in further-flung colonies of the British Empire like India and Palestine.[47] Another undisputable intention of British participants in Ireland was to use that country's problems as an opportunity to publicise their views and make their names. 'The Irish experience was crucial in establishing

Home Rule and Garden Suburb Ideals before 1914   147

Geddes' position in the British town planning movement. Until Dublin he had been merely a propagandist', as Meller has written.[48] The young Edinburgh architect, Frank Mears, was the protégé of Geddes in the pre-war Dublin campaign, and in early-1915 he was still in Dublin trying to pick up the commission from the Corporation to design the Marino Estate and another nearby scheme.[49] And no-one benefited as much from the flurry of planning interest in Dublin as Patrick Abercrombie. Dix has observed that the 1914 Town Plan Competition 'drew national and international attention to Abercrombie and to his application of a Geddesian approach': he was thereby launched on a glittering career which made him the doyen of British planning from the time of the Doncaster Report (1922) through to his renowned plans for the County of London (1943) and Greater London (1944), and beyond.[50]

In concluding this chapter, it can also be observed that previous accounts of the pre-war movement in Ireland have followed the dominant mode of British planning historiography, wherein the 'development of planning has been to a large extent treated as a simple victory of professional aspiration in which the planner triumphs against the blind and wasteful operation of economic forces'.[51] The emphasis has been primarily on a narrative of events and an uncritical description of participants. The result has been the writing of history very much from the point of view of the early planning enthusiasts in Ireland. This has tended to distort the views of important groups in Irish society, and play down the extent of the forces that militated against the acceptance of garden suburb ideals. Another tendency has been to separate the planning debate from that of housing policy generally, thereby giving the early Irish town planning movement greater coherence than it actually had. Garden suburb ideals were but one aspect of a far broader and more politicised debate about urban housing, a debate that was to prove an influential factor within Irish society and in British policy towards Ireland. Indeed, it was to be as the result of housing policy during and after the First World War that garden suburb planning was eventually introduced to Ireland. The next chapter will now trace these war-time developments.

Chapter 5

WAR-TIME HOUSING AND RECONSTRUCTION AFTER THE 1916 EASTER RISING

This chapter, central in all senses, traces the way in which the pre-war stalemate between Ireland and Westminster over urban housing policy was transformed during the course of the First World War. At the outbreak of hostilities with Germany in August 1914, the main concerns of the British Government and the Dublin Castle Administration became the repression of anti-war propaganda and the promotion of the recruitment campaign. The Home Rule Act was passed but put on ice for the duration of the war, and the Irish Party showed its loyalty by advocating enlistment and support for the war effort. A policy of state retrenchment was introduced that severely restricted Irish rural and municipal housebuilding, and was to make new measures like the 1914 Housing (No. 2) Act irrelevant. However, the 1916 Easter Rising was to prove a decisive turning point. From this moment on, first the Castle Administration and then Westminster gradually took control of Irish state housing, and began to use the issue as a political tool in initiatives such as the 1917–18 Irish Convention. Ireland was thus the crucible in which Lloyd George's post-war policy of using housing for political ends was first expounded. While relatively few dwellings were actually built in war-time Ireland, the involvement of British officials reinforced a move towards garden suburb design in the schemes of Dublin Corporation. By the end of the First World War, the British Government had come to regard housing as an essential strategy in its search for a solution to the thorny question of Irish Home Rule.

WAR-TIME RETRENCHMENT IN IRISH URBAN HOUSING POLICY

The prospects for Irish urban housing at the start of the First World War were not promising. Two new initiatives emanating from Britain, the 1914 Housing (No. 2) Act and the housing programme of the Ministry of Munitions, made no impact on Ireland. The Housing (No. 2) Act was introduced in late-1914 by the British Government to meet parliamentary demands for a safeguard against potential unemployment in the building industry.[1] A sum of £4 000 000 was allocated to the English Local Government Board and the Board of Agriculture, to lend to local authorities or public utility societies for housing purposes up till 31 August 1915. The Chancellor of the Exchequer, Lloyd George, pledged that loans would receive a grant-in-aid from the Exchequer but only to meet war-time inflation in the cost of building materials. Duly he announced a 10 per cent free grant plus 90 per cent loan at 4.25 per cent interest over 60 years to local authorities, and a 10 per cent free grant plus 80 per cent loan at 5 per cent interest over 60 years to other agencies. The Treasury, however, strongly opposed the Housing (No. 2) Act, and in particular the prospect of state subsidy. Hence it issued a minute in December 1914 pointing out that the measure was specifically intended to relieve chronic unemployment rather than housing need, and that grants would therefore only be given in exceptional cases. This became a Treasury pretext to use the strict terms of eligibility, in having to prove 'exceptional and insistent distress' in an area due to lack of building employment, as the means to refuse all loan applications.[2] Since the anticipated war-time unemployment did not actually materialise, the 1914 Housing (No. 2) Act remained a dead letter.

A potential threat to the Treasury came from the determination of the Irish Party, backed by Dublin Corporation and the Association of Metropolitan Authorities of Ireland, to use the terms of the Housing (No. 2) Act as the long-desired augmentation of Irish urban subsidy. The IPP's spokesman, J. J. Clancy, told the Imperial Parliament that in Ireland 'the problem of increased unemployment is greater and the housing conditions worse than in Great Britain'.[3] Chief Secretary Birrell was pressured into securing an extending measure, known as the 1914 Housing No. 2 (Amendment) Act, to cover Ireland. There followed a dramatic rush in loan applications from Irish municipalities.[4] But when the Castle Administration applied in September 1914 for Ireland's share of the proposed loan fund, a sum estimated at around £350 000, the Treasury replied tartly that the measure 'is not intended as the foundation of a general housing scheme for which the present time is obviously most inopportune'.[5] Dismayed, Clancy wrote in blunt fashion to the Treasury on 7 October 1914:

> *I am writing now, at the instance and with the sanction of Mr John Redmond*, and I say that there really ought to be no higgling and haggling in this matter. The state of things here is too serious to be considered from the mere usual point of view, and the reasons for giving the grant to Ireland which is asked for are so plain that I need not refer to them. I believe that my views on that subject will be fully confirmed by the Local Government Board for Ireland . . . the seriousness of this matter from every point is so great that I hope that, in the public interest, no delay will be made in announcing a satisfactory answer from the Treasury.[6]

The Treasury reiterated that the Housing (No. 2) Act was purely a temporary relief measure, and that 'Ireland will be treated in no way differently from England, Scotland, or Wales'.[7] Several Irish municipalities then drew up detailed applications. The most authoritative came from Dublin Corporation in March 1915, and included testimonies from the Building Trades Employers' Association and the RIAI as to the likely unemployment in the local building trades during the forthcoming year.[8] Not surprisingly, the Treasury refused the claim, thereby causing the Sinn Fein Chairman of Dublin Corporation's Housing Committee, Alderman Thomas Kelly, to declare in exasperation 'that the Housing (No. 2) Act, 1914, about which there was such a great flourish of trumpets, was merely a make-believe and a sham'.[9] Much of the resultant Irish acrimony was directed towards the ILGB, but the real source of intransigence lay in the Treasury and therefore the British Government.

Ireland fared little better out of the major programme of state housing carried out by the Ministry of Munitions following its inception in June 1915. It was the cottages built by this department that received the first state subsidy in Britain, and which consolidated garden suburb design as the new orthodoxy.[10] In Ireland there was a shortage of facilities and resources suitable for munitions production, and political opposition to the war made it risky to produce armaments there. Even at the height of the First World War there were only around 14 500 munitions workers in Ireland (although many went to work in British factories), and hence the Irish branch of the Ministry of Munitions had little to do.[11] The only two sizeable centres of production were in the Belfast shipyards and the Kynochs Cordite Works at Arklow, Co. Wexford. Belfast was regarded as being a well-housed city, and so the only actual war-time munitions scheme built in Ireland appears to have been 112 cottages for explosives workers in Arklow. These dwellings in fact pre-dated the creation of the Ministry of Munitions, being erected by Arklow UDC using a £13 500 public loan in November 1914 after the Treasury had given up on its original insistence that only temporary dwellings be provided. The new municipal cottages were permitted in Arklow 'on the understanding that the buildings to be erected will not be in excess of the normal requirements of the District'.[12] Subsequently, however, the Treasury successfully fought off an attempt to revive a scheme for a 'garden village' at nearby Gorey to accommodate workers who commuted to Arklow. And when further housing need was identified in the locality in October 1915, the Castle Administration simply recommended to the Irish branch of the Ministry of Munitions that it lend £3 000 to the factory owners for a 300-bed temporary hostel.[13] It is not clear whether this hostel was ever built. Certainly nothing came of a later application by Arklow UDC to the Ministry of Munitions in February 1917, asking for a £20 000 grant for up to 200 permanent cottages.[14] By this point, in any case, the provision of munitions housing through the agency of local authorities had been abandoned in Britain.

Given retrenchment and the absence of positive housing initiatives from Westminster, state housing in Ireland dwindled with the onset of war. Despite a further grant of £1 000 000 under the 1914 Labourers Act, the rural programme was greatly curtailed. Only around 1100 rural cottages were built each year from 1914 to 1918, compared with an annual average of 3500 in the four preceding years (see Diagram A and Table 1).[15] Chief Secretary Birrell and the Castle Administration went along with a Treasury stipulation that only those rural schemes that had already received sanction should now be completed.[16]

The Treasury also announced in October 1914 that the limit for Irish public loans in the next financial year was to be cut to only £600 000, rather than the £700 000 previously envisaged. The President of the Irish Board of Works warned in reply that 'it would be extremely awkward if the smaller sum proved insufficient, and particularly if loans for Housing of the Working Classes (a burning question here) had to be refused or delayed'.[17] The Treasury thus reluctantly allowed loans for urban housing to continue to receive favoured status. Dublin Corporation was granted a sum of £43 500 in December 1914 to commence its three most advanced schemes, and the Irish Party leader, John Redmond, also secured a loan of £23 000 for Waterford Corporation to proceed with an estate of 38 single-storey cottages in Trinity Square, Ballybricken (1915–17). The latter loan, however, was only agreed by the Treasury on condition that Redmond used his influence over Nationalist municipalities to make them curb future urban housing applications.[18] Such voluntary restraint was not forthcoming. So when Dublin Corporation asked in April 1915 for a further £31 980 to build the scheme in Beresford Street/Church Street, the Treasury finally decided to extend to Ireland the moratorium on local authority expenditure that was already in operation in Britain. It called for Cabinet support on the matter:

> Our position in regard to Irish finance is stronger in so far as practically all the Irish authorities have recourse to the Local Loans Fund and do not (or cannot) borrow in the open market; it is weaker in so far as the Departments there are in alliance with the borrowers and hostile to economy. Our appeal to them to suspend current works (which cover a large proportion of the expenditure) would therefore be ineffective unless the decision was put to them as the decision of His Majesty's Government.[19]

The Treasury was duly empowered to send a directive to the Castle Administration on 21 April 1915, imposing a moratorium on all future public loans. This decision was notified to Irish local authorities through an ILGB Circular in early May.[20] Contrary to Treasury suspicions about the loyalty of Irish departments, the latter fully supported retrenchment once it was officially stated as British Government policy. The ILGB assiduously turned down all new applications for rural cottages under the Labourers Acts, and even sought to cancel existing contracts wherever possible. The Under Secretary for Ireland, Sir Matthew Nathan, pointed out the political sensitivity of pursuing a hard-line policy at a time of widespread anti-British sentiment, but on balance the Treasury doubted 'that a temporary suspension of new schemes would provoke a revolution'.[21] In terms of urban housing, the Vice-President of the ILGB, Sir Henry Robinson, observed that:

> As regards Public Health and Town Housing loans we have, to all intents and purposes, shut down inexorably on them, and are very glad

to do so, as Ireland hardly realizes the seriousness of the situation and the only way to put a stop to their anti-recruiting blackguardism . . . is to make the people over here feel the inconvenience and trial of the war.[22]

The ILGB's chief housing expert, Dr Peter Cowan, reminded Dublin Corporation at an inquiry in July 1915 that, because of the war, 'the claims on public resources for even so urgent a matter as the . . . housing of the working classes in Dublin should be subordinated to other claims of an unprecedented and dominating character on the energies and financial abilities of every part of the Empire'.[23] The outcome of the Treasury moratorium was a further decline in Labourers Acts schemes, and a dramatic fall in Irish municipal house building from mid-1915 (see Diagram D and Table 5).[24] The complacency of the Castle Administration about the urban housing issue was shown by its lack of interest in the discussions on the 1915 Rent Act (which prohibited war-time rent increases on dwellings with rateable values of up to £26, or £35 in London). The Under Secretary merely observed that rent control was not a burning issue in Ireland, since the departure of soldiers to the front and munitions workers to Britain meant that housing demand and thus pressure on rent levels was, if anything, on the wane.[25] And when an unnamed wealthy citizen offered to lend money to Dublin Corporation for housing purposes, Sir Matthew Nathan declared that such funds would be better diverted to the war effort.[26]

Yet the desire of the Castle Administration to impose thrift in Irish housing was simultaneously threatened by the British Government's need to retain the support of the Irish Party in the recruitment drive. This conflict came to a head when, after carefully preparing the ground, the ILGB informed John Redmond in August 1915 that the payment of the remaining £17 000 housing loan to Waterford Corporation would now be postponed until after the war. The ILGB requested of the Treasury 'that if John Redmond tackles your parliamentary chiefs you won't give way again', and the Treasury Remembrancer in Ireland declared that if the ILGB were to be overruled on this matter, then 'we shall be unable, I am afraid, to put the almost complete stopper on local loans which I had hoped for: because all the arguments in favour of Waterford apply—and in some cases with much greater force—to other places'.[27] John Redmond responded by privately threatening the Parliamentary Secretary to the Treasury, E. S. Montagu, that if 'the promise publicly given is broken, there will be very serious trouble in the City of Waterford, and I, personally, will be put into a position of extreme embarrassment'.[28] Montagu therefore agreed to a special loan of £5 000 to enable Waterford Corporation to continue its housing work, and Redmond tactfully asked local Nationalist councillors 'that no public splash be made about this at all'.[29] It was a political concession that greatly angered the Castle Administration, for it meant that the strategy of imposing a moratorium on urban housing loans was effectively sunk. Faced by a renewed wave of applications, the ILGB introduced another tactic in late-1915. It now told Dublin Corporation to borrow on the open market to fund future housing schemes, in the hope that inflated war-time interest rates would act as a deterrent to municipal building. The new policy was justified by the ILGB's Vice-President, Sir Henry Robinson, on the grounds that:

> many of these Boroughs are packed with Sinn Feiners who are openly anti-British and who declare that the war is no concern of theirs and that no Irishman has any interest or reason in fighting England's battles and should not be asked to enlist . . . It is a very good object lesson to these people to let them see how they are affected by the war.[30]

This latest attempt by the Castle Administration to turn off the tap of public funds provoked a predictably swift response in Ireland. An Irish Party deputation led by Redmond and Clancy met with the Chancellor of the Exchequer, Reginald McKenna, on 16 November 1915 to demand an urgent housing loan of £35 500 for Dublin Corporation. A plethora of documents were submitted in support of the application, including a pamphlet written by the Corporation which declared:

> Countless millions are being spent on the prosecution of a war to which Dublin alone has sent some 14,000 men to fight the Empire's battle . . . Are they to find the Empire's gratitude on their return represented in the refusal of the Government to allow the Corporation to lift their wives and children from the horrors of life in dilapidated tenement houses or cellar dwellings into the atmosphere of light and life in a sanitary, self-contained comfortable home?[31]

Unaware of the ILGB's ruling that housing loans should now be raised on the open market, the Chancellor of the Exchequer rashly approved a loan of £25 000 to Dublin Corporation to purchase sites at Ormond Market, Spitalfields and the McCaffrey Estate. The ILGB again complained bitterly that 'it is very hard for us to force the Treasury policy of retrenchment upon the local authorities when ministers make promises in individual cases without first hearing what we have to say in the matter'.[32] The Treasury, realising too late that the IPP deputation had been a 'try-on' which had successfully exploited the lack of communication between Dublin Castle and Westminster, resolved in future to always back the ILGB. They were compelled to give one further loan of £15 750 to Dublin Corporation to buy a site at Fairbrothers Fields, since this expenditure had already been sanctioned. But the Treasury made it clear that this was intended to be the last housing loan that would be made to Irish municipalities during the war. State expenditure and budgeting procedures in Ireland were now to be subject to the same level of Treasury control as operated in war-time Britain. Thus by March 1916, despite dire warnings of social unrest from the Irish Party, Dublin Trades Council, and journals such as the *Irish*

Builder, the Castle Administration and the British Government had together finally imposed strict retrenchment on urban housing.[33] The irony is that within a matter of weeks, the dramatic and unexpected events of Easter 1916 had altered once more the course of British housing policy in Ireland.

THE AFTERMATH OF THE 1916 EASTER RISING

The outbreak of rebellion in Dublin on Easter Monday 1916 came as a surprise to the Castle Administration, and highlighted its ineffectiveness in either controlling the supply of arms or in foreseeing the extent of anti-British opposition in Ireland.[34] The abortive uprising was led by a conjunction of hard-line Nationalists from the Irish Volunteers and the outlawed Irish Republican Brotherhood, along with socialists from James Connolly's Citizens Army. Although the insurgents made swift gains, the rebellion was forcefully crushed by the British Army within a week. The bombardment of the GPO building in Lower Sackville Street led to the surrender of the rebels' headquarters, and Ireland was immediately subjected to martial law under the firm hand of General Maxwell. The Easter Rising was in effect a futile 'blood sacrifice' which had little support at the time. Yet it proved significant for two reasons: first, because outrage against the Government's swift execution of the rebel leaders helped to drive many towards sympathy with Sinn Fein; and second, because the Rising foreshadowed the coalition of extreme Nationalists and labour elements in the post-war Nationalist movement. The participation of radical socialists was precipitated by a revulsion against imperial militarism, lucidly shown in their response to a British Army recruiting poster which proclaimed insensitively that 'The trenches are safer than the Dublin slums'. Connolly's retort was bitter: 'It is the idea of English wit . . . We may yet see the day that the trenches will be safer for those gentry than any part of Dublin'.[35]

The inevitable inquiry into the causes of the Easter Rising put the blame squarely on the Castle Administration for having been too soft on political opposition. However, a key question remained to be answered. Given that previous Irish agitation had been driven by rural discontent, why was this latest rebellion so obviously an urban phenomenon? A number of contributory factors were cited in the inquiry report, and, significantly, the pre-war concern about the link between social unrest and the extensive slum-lands in Dublin was now given official voice:

> Throughout the whole of this year Ireland was in a state of great prosperity so that Irish discontent could hardly be attributed to economic conditions, except that the housing conditions of the working classes in the City of Dublin might have accounted for an underlying sense of dissatisfaction with existing authority.[36]

General Maxwell told the Asquith Cabinet that urban housing conditions were one of the primary causes of the discontent that lay behind the rebellion, and a member of the Irish Army Command also observed that they 'must deal with the Slums in Cities like Dublin, Limerick, Cork, etc. which are very bad'.[37] The *Irish Builder* echoed the sentiments, yet the strongest attack on the Government came in the London-based *Architect* when it proclaimed that 'The Minister of Munitions has realised that he cannot keep his department going without building houses for workers, but the rest of the incompetents have not yet grasped the fact that squalid living is the finest of hotbeds for revolution and rebellion'.[38] And the link between poor housing and the Easter Rising was given a typically ironic twist by George Bernard Shaw:

> And why, oh why didn't the artillery knock down half Dublin while it had the chance? Think of the insanitary areas, the slums, the glorious chance of making a clean sweep of them! Only 179 houses [destroyed] and probably at least nine of them quite decent ones. I'd have laid at least 17,900 of them flat and made a decent town of it![39]

In the aftermath of martial law, the administration of Ireland was temporarily handed over to the Home Secretary, Herbert Samuel. Then in August 1916 a new Chief Secretary, H. E. Duke, was appointed not just to maintain control but also to explicitly address economic and social problems. He was a well-intentioned Unionist barrister who believed that a conciliatory policy was essential to keep Ireland a contented member of the British Empire.[40] Urban housing soon became one of Duke's main political concerns, but more immediately the Government and the Castle Administration had to deal with the rebuilding of the destroyed commercial areas in central Dublin. The general town-planning debate was reopened when, after prompting by the Civics Institute and the Town Planning Institute in London, the long-awaited judgement of the Dublin Town Plan Competition was brought forward (as seen in the last chapter).[41] More prosaically, the proposals for rebuilding soon polarised into a struggle over the cost and manner of reconstruction. On one hand Dublin Corporation, backed by some Irish Party MPs plus bodies such as the RIAI, wanted generous state finance and strong legislative powers (such as compulsory purchase and strict aesthetic controls) to impose a scheme for central Sackville Street in a grandiose 'commercial-Classical' style. In the other camp were the private property owners, represented by the Fire and Property Losses Association, who saw these proposals as needlessly expensive and an infringement of their right to rebuild as they chose. It was at this point that the British Government, initially through Prime Minister Asquith and Home Secretary Samuel, intervened to mediate in the dispute.[42] Legislation was drafted by Dublin Corporation in conjunction with the ILGB, and was promoted in Parliament by Chief Secretary Duke. When this proposal ran into difficulty, the Government agreed to a suggestion from Dublin Corporation (first proposed by the Civics Institute) that Raymond Unwin be seconded from the Ministry of Munitions to act as a negotiator.[43] There was some initial resentment over Unwin's involvement, but in general his contribution was positively received.

A compromise was reached in due course, and the Dublin Reconstruction Act passed into law on 20 December 1916. Under its terms, a low-interest public loan was to be provided after the war for Dublin Corporation to carry out street-widening, and to compensate private owners for any 'reasonable' aesthetic improvement to their design that might be suggested by the City Architect (a clause allowed for arbitration wherever an owner felt that the required alteration would be excessively costly). The 1916 Dublin Reconstruction Act constituted the first, tentative Irish planning legislation, and yet was never used: when Lower Sackville Street was reformed as O'Connell Street under a new regime in the 1920s, there was little cohesive urban vision.

Even more significant in the turmoil over the reconstruction proposals in mid-1916, was that the British Government used the issue of working-class housing in an attempt to pressure Dublin Corporation into scaling down its demands. When a deputation of Corporation councillors and Irish Party MPs met the Home Secretary in early June, Herbert Samuel declared:

> the greatness of Dublin depends not only on noble thoroughfares and palatial public buildings but also in no less degree on the provision of comfortable sanitary homes for the population, and so far as money is available I know that you have large schemes in prospect. You would not I am sure wish to spend great sums on too magnificent schemes of town planning while leaving this question of rebuilding slums in the background. It is of the first importance to provide for the health and comfort of the people; it is only a secondary object to make a noble and architecturally fine city.[44]

This was a naive tactical mistake, for the IPP members immediately demanded with alacrity that the Home Secretary should therefore support their appeals for an augmentation of the Irish Housing Fund. Samuel was forced to backtrack, and resort to the pre-war Liberal argument against the principle of housing subsidy:

> As to a grant, a gift of money for housing in Dublin, if that was given, what would all the towns in England say, many of which have got very bad housing conditions. In the House of Commons I have had to resist again and again very strong demands for gifts of money for housing purposes in England and Wales. I have always refused them. You in Ireland have been more fortunate because of the Labourers Acts, but so far as urban housing is concerned only loans may be given when money is available, but no subsidies.[45]

The overriding urgency of housing need in Dublin was also used by the Treasury when arguing against the state-financed town planning proposed in the Corporation's grand scheme for rebuilding. Unprompted, the Treasury in June 1916 estimated the likely cost of post-war housing provision:

> the Dublin Corporation ought not to be encouraged to embark upon grandiose schemes of beautification, which are of the nature of luxuries, at a time when they will have hard work to meet the requirements of public health [housing]; and further that, as the Government will presumably have to lend something approaching £500,000 for the latter purposes, the British taxpayer ought not to be asked to raise more money for Dublin by loan after the War.[46]

Such statements demonstrated a definite change in Westminster's attitude towards the issue of urban housing in Ireland. The belief in Britain, however misguided, was that the most effective way now to control Irish disaffection was to address urban grievances rather than rural issues. From this point on, the Castle Administration consciously employed housing as a political tool. Even before the new Chief Secretary had taken office, the Vice-President of the ILGB reported back to Duke that the seeds of the new policy had been sown amongst the Nationalist Dublin Corporation: 'I told the Lord Mayor that you wanted his confidential help and advice as to what you could do about Housing, whereat his "heart warmed to you", as he expressed it'.[47]

At his first public engagement in September 1916, which was to open the new Pembroke UDC estate at Stella Gardens, Chief Secretary Duke described Dublin's slums as 'a problem of as tremendous magnitude, probably as any problem, which in modern times can engage the attention of statesmen in connection with the well-being of the community of this Island and the Empire'.[48] Later the same month, the Lord Lieutenant, Lord Wimborne, told the annual meeting of the Association of Municipal Authorities of Ireland that 'there is no more important question before the Conference than the question of the better housing of the industrial and artisan classes'.[49] The central importance of housing to the Castle Administration's new strategy was also demonstrated by the active promotion of the matter in Westminster. A contemporary memorandum by the Attorney General for Ireland proposed that Home Rule should be granted at once, along with a generous financial settlement from Britain which included a housing grant of up to £4 000 000.[50] The Lord Lieutenant submitted his own personal plan for a conference to discuss Home Rule and conscription, and he added that it might also consider 'whether a substantial Treasury loan for the purpose of exterminating the urban slum evil would not go far to reconcile the labour dissatisfaction which was, and is, to a great extent, responsible for the Sinn Fein animus'.[51] And in September 1916, Chief Secretary Duke informed the Cabinet of the adverse results of war-time retrenchment in Ireland:

> Just as in Dublin, in the various provincial towns which I have visited, appalling conditions of housing exist, on a scale which affects an extraordinarily large proportion of the population. The suspension of works of social amelioration which are dependent upon governmental initiative or help, operating with the prevailing political discontents,

adds to the difficulties of administration. If local authorities could even be encouraged to provide for works to be done at the end of the war I think good would result.[52]

The new approach of the Castle Administration was widely welcomed in Ireland. As a direct result of Duke's speech at Pembroke, the Dublin Chamber of Commerce set up its own Housing Reform Committee. When the Under-Secretary deputised for Duke at a meeting of the Civics Institute in January 1917, one Irish Party MP remarked 'that the presence of a high Government official in the chair was an indication that the Government was at last beginning to recognise its duty in connection with the housing of Dublin'.[53] The Chief Secretary subsequently attended the 'Civic Week' exhibition, in which were displayed the entries for the 1914 Dublin Town Plan Competition. Following his visit, Duke restated the central message 'that town planning might be left over for happier times but [he] recognised that the housing of the poor was a matter of great urgency which would demand the united efforts and thought of all classes of citizens'.[54] The immediate problem for Chief Secretary Duke, however, was that Irish demands were focused on a resumption in public loans for urban housing. In November 1916, John Redmond was again able to use his personal influence to secure a further £5000 for Waterford Corporation, but the Treasury insisted that this was simply the fulfilment of an earlier promise. All other Irish municipalities were refused funds, and so Dublin Corporation began to look at the possibility of raising housing finance in the USA. Soon, interest centred on a proposed $2 000 000 (£419 000) loan from Messrs Lee, Higginson & Co. of Boston, but negotiations broke down when the Treasury refused to underwrite the deal and US interest rates rose.[55]

The collapse of Dublin Corporation's loan negotiations in early-1917 came at a difficult time for the Castle Administration. Around 1500 workers in Dublin had lost their jobs over the winter, and the total unemployed in the city was probably in the region of 7000 men. The issue of unemployment was especially contentious in Dublin because the British Government's recent anti-alcohol legislation threatened the important brewing industry which included the Guinness company. The Irish Party led a fierce opposition to the temperance measures, and did not shrink from emphasising the threat posed by political unrest. 'The Russian revolution has arisen in Petrograd from causes, in certain respects resembling past and prevailing conditions in Ireland's capital', warned one IPP member.[56] Thus the Chief Secretary, as part of a general strategy in early-1917 of public expenditure to encourage social peace, now urgently requested a £200 000 loan to restart housing work in Dublin. Duke asked the Chancellor of the Exchequer, Arthur Bonar Law, for an assurance that 'in the event of his being persuaded that employees of Guinness who lose their employment owing to the recent restrictions in the output of beer have a good prospect of being employed in the work of rehousing Dublin, the money will be forthcoming'.[57] At this point, as will be seen later, the Cabinet was embarking on a more consensual policy towards Ireland, and so was open to suggestions that would ameliorate social grievances. Hence in early-April 1917 the Chancellor, after consulting with the Prime Minister's secretariat, informed Duke that housing loans for Dublin housing were now available 'in respect of such schemes as ought in your opinion to be proceeded with'.[58] Armed with this pledge, the Lord Lieutenant and Chief Secretary returned to Dublin, and on 5 April 1917 told a Dublin Corporation deputation that housing schemes would now be resumed to relieve the problem of unemployment.[59] The ILGB now dropped its commitment to retrenchment, and helped the Chief Secretary to draft a plan for a war-time loan to Dublin Corporation of £100 000 a year. The aim was explicitly to reduce discontent and anti-war sentiment. The Vice-President of the ILGB, Sir Henry Robinson, noted that 'from our own point of view—that of relieving distress—the immediate commencement of the work at Spitalfields would remove a great deal of unrest in the city'.[60] But before looking at the resumption of housing work in Dublin in mid-1917, it is first necessary to look at the changes in housing design that took place in Ireland during the First World War.

WAR-TIME HOUSING DESIGN IN DUBLIN CORPORATION SCHEMES

The previous chapter showed that the principles of garden suburb design and higher-standard cottages exerted limited influence on state housing in Ireland prior to the First World War. This was in marked contrast to Britain, where Unwinian orthodoxy was officially accepted by the Board of Agriculture in 1913, and subsequently formed the basis for munitions housing.[61] The adoption of the garden suburb model in war-time Ireland took place more gradually, principally through two flagship projects of Dublin Corporation: first in the McCaffrey Estate, and then in the redesigned scheme for Fairbrothers Fields. Both of these projects were designed specifically to anticipate substantial subsidy from the British Government, and hence were kept distinct from the general slum clearance policy that continued to be favoured by the Corporation's Housing Committee.

Dublin Corporation signalled the first significant improvement in housing standards in early-1915 with the design of the McCaffrey Estate (later Ceannt Brown). This was partly in response to the repeated criticisms of high density inner-city schemes by the Geddes/Unwin Housing Report, and by bodies such as the Civics Institute and the Citizens Housing League. But the primary motive for the Corporation was that it hoped to secure subsidised funds under the 1914 Housing No. 2 (Amendment) Act, and it needed a centrepiece project to overcome any potential objections from the ILGB. The problem was that the City Architect, Charles MacCarthy, had no experience of designing garden suburbs, and so the Corporation brought in Thomas Joseph Byrne, architect for the highly-praised labourers' cottages in South Dublin RDC. Thus the design of the McCaffrey Estate represented the translation of the premier quasi-suburban Labourers Acts schemes into municipal housing. Byrne's distinctive Arts and Crafts approach can be seen at the McCaffrey Estate in the picturesque, Neo-Vernacular terraces built in yellow stock bricks, and adorned with complex, stepped rooflines punctuated by hips and gables. The elevational treatment was evocative of the 'street picture' diagrams in Unwin's *Town Planning in Practice* (1909), and hence followed both pre-war LCC estates and the picturesque strain of munitions housing epitomised by the Well Hall Estate in Woolwich (1915).[62] Equally important in the McCaffrey Estate was the overall site planning. The scheme as redesigned by Byrne cut the number of dwellings on the seven-acre site to 202 cottages, a density of 29 dwellings to the acre (see Fig. 31). This was substantially higher than the Unwinian stricture of 12 dwellings to the acre, but was well below the norm for Dublin Corporation schemes. The symmetrical, terraced layout also provided green spaces for two children's playgrounds. The other major innovation was to abandon a previous plan to provide mostly three-roomed houses. Instead, the scheme as built contained only four-roomed cottages with a parlour, living room, and two bedrooms, and let at a higher rent of 7s per week (see Figs 32 and 33). Two house-types were used: the majority (80 per cent of dwellings) had a 15 foot frontage and a typical terraced layout; yet there was also a new type (20 per cent of dwellings) with a wider 24 foot frontage, and a through living room (160 square feet) and a parlour on either side of a central staircase. Neither house-type had a separate bathroom, so, as in contemporary designs for the Ministry of Munitions, the bath was located in the scullery. Dublin Corporation

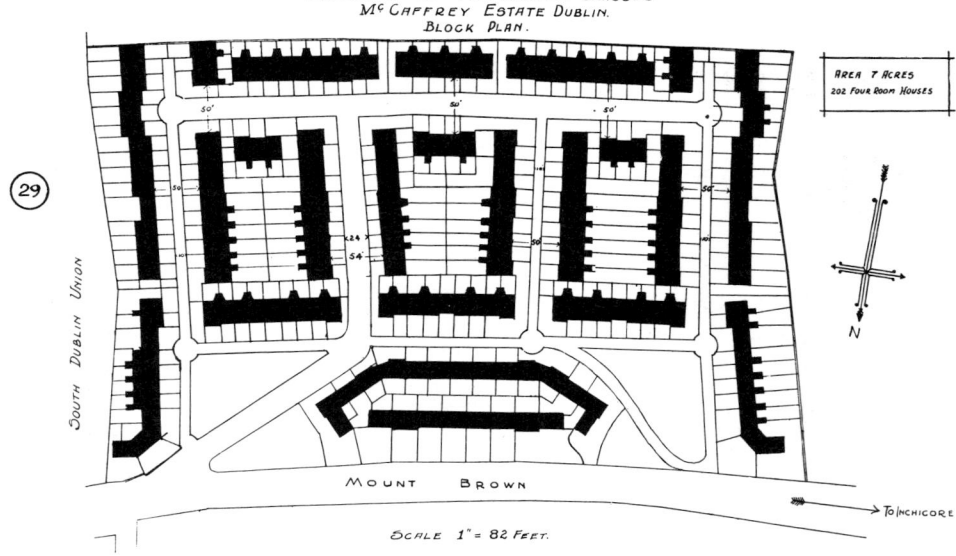

Fig 31. T. J. Byrne/Dublin Corporation: site plan of the McCaffrey Estate (1915)

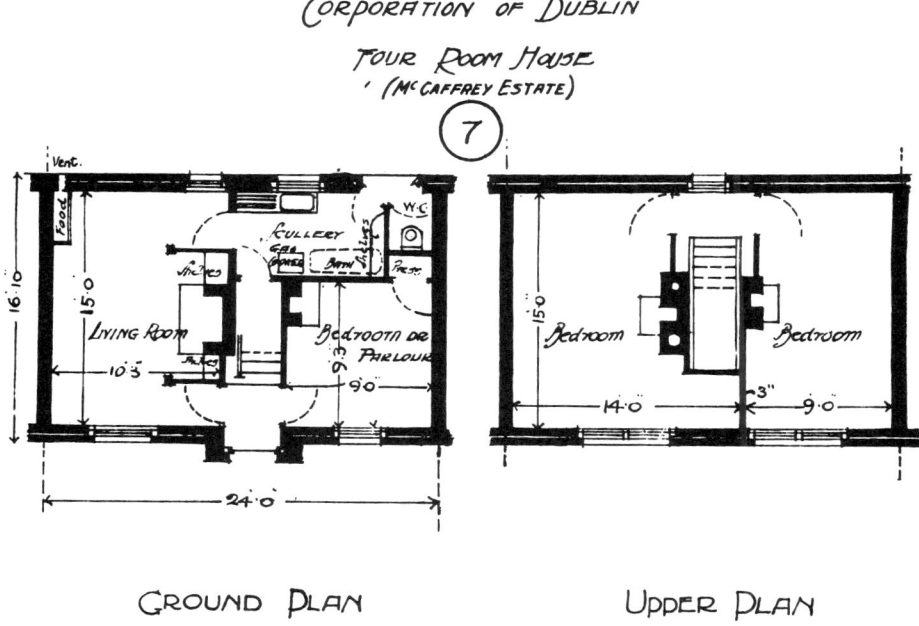

Fig 32. T. J. Byrne/Dublin Corporation: four-room type at the McCaffrey Estate

Fig 33. T. J. Byrne/Dublin Corporation: 'street picture' at the McCaffrey Estate

had never built to such a high standard before, and while the high rents were attacked by councillors who favoured housing for the very poor, the ILGB praised the new design for the McCaffrey Estate as 'admirable' and asked for only minor alterations.[63]

The McCaffrey Estate was, however, the exception within Dublin Corporation's housing strategy, and was intended to counter-balance the primary emphasis on providing cheap dwellings for unskilled labourers in central districts. The most cogent advocate for the latter policy was yet again Alderman Thomas Kelly, the Sinn Fein Chairman of the Corporation's Housing Committee. Kelly declared in October 1916 that until all the slums were cleared, 'there was no use talking of garden suburbs'.[64] Thus in other war-time housing schemes, the Corporation simply tended to refine the existing inner-city model. The design for the Ormond Market site contained three-roomed cottages and two-roomed flats in a high-density terraced layout around a central square. The other substantial slum-clearance schemes at the time were in Church Street/Beresford Street and in Spitalfields, where the only innovation was to add a greater variety of brickwork detailing to the elevations (see Fig. 34). These designs provoked bitter opposition from the Citizens Housing League and the newly-formed Dublin Tenants League, a working-class body set up by William Larkin (brother of James Larkin). Both bodies demanded vociferously that nothing but suburban housing should be built for the working classes. The Dublin Tenants League formed an unholy alliance with the Housing Reform Committee of the Dublin Chamber of Commerce, in an attempt to pressure the British Government into rejecting the Spitalfields scheme.[65] Events such as the 'Civic Week' held in Dublin in January 1917 were turned into polemical exercises for the promotion of garden suburb design. And when one of the Irish Party MPs for Dublin, Patrick Brady, suggested a broad-based conference to discuss post-war housing reconstruction, his altruistic proposal soon degenerated into a sectional attack by the Civics Institute and Dr Oliver Gogarty on Dublin Corporation's inner-city estates.[66] A more constructive approach during the war-time period came from the ILGB, whose Vice-President observed that his department had 'done [its] best to induce the Corporation to build houses on virgin soil on the outskirts of the City'.[67] Weight for this opinion was also provided by the Association of Municipal Authorities of Ireland, which wrote in late-1917:

> It is to be hoped that in the new schemes the system of building long rows of dreary-looking dwellings will not be tolerated, and that . . . an attempt will be made to provide gardens, open spaces, wide tree-shaded thoroughfares, and other modern town planning ideas.[68]

Dublin Corporation was not, however, unduly influenced by such opinions. When it attempted once more to set an even higher standard for Irish housing design—this time through the Fairbrothers Fields estate—the purpose was specifically to ensure that the scheme would receive subsidy from the British

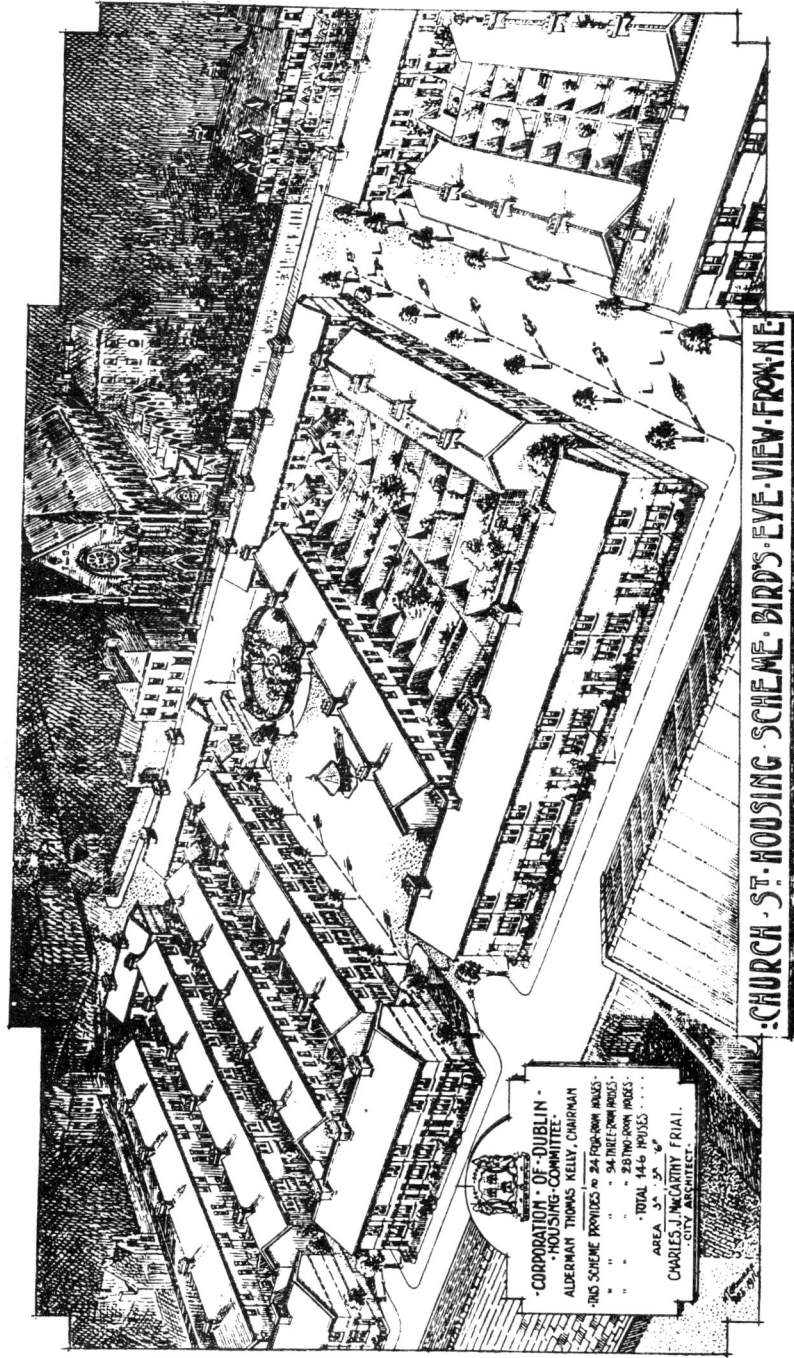

Fig 34. Dublin Corporation: perspective of the Church Street scheme (1916)

Government. The first redesign was commissioned in late-1916, when the Corporation was hoping to persuade the Treasury to contribute to the interest repayments on its abortive US loan. Now the City Architect, Charles MacCarthy, was called on 'to adopt a layout more nearly approaching the treatment recommended by the advocates of the Garden Suburb', although it is almost certain that his assistant, Horace O'Rourke (later City Architect from 1922 to 1945), was mainly responsible for recasting the Fairbrothers Fields design. His starting point was the suggestions contained in the 1914 Geddes/Unwin Housing Report.[69] Thus the density on the 22-acre site was lowered from 800 dwellings (36 per acre) to only 586 dwellings (26 per acre), and the street layout was realigned to form a strongly bi-axial plan. The new design represented the first use in Ireland of Unwinian set-backs and cul-de-sacs in order to break up the scale and monotony of the large site blocks. Even more striking was the decision to build enlarged three-room (44 per cent), four-room (38 per cent), and even five-room (18 per cent) cottages. The respective rents were set at levels of 6s, 8s, and 10s per week, easily the highest for any Corporation dwellings. The five-room cottages were also the first Dublin Corporation house-types to include separate bathrooms on the first floor, complete with hot and cold water supply. A setback came when the US loan fell through, but soon after the Castle Administration announced the new public loan from the Treasury in April 1917. Now the Corporation was even more determined to ensure that Fairbrothers Fields would qualify, even if retrospectively, for whatever post-war subsidy might be on offer.

The corollary of reliance on potential British Government subsidy was that the ILGB's Chief Engineering Inspector, Dr Peter Cowan, in turn expected a further increase in housing standards. He put this viewpoint forcefully at the ILGB inquiry held into the scheme in September 1917. Cowan wanted to reduce the site to only 16 acres, so that the remainder could be devoted to parks and allotments, and for the Corporation then to build larger cottages to a lower density.[70] The City Architect and the Corporation's Legal Officer were incensed by this unprecedented degree of interference from the ILGB, but the Housing Committee on balance decided to comply with the alterations rather than risk the loss of retrospective state subsidy. There followed numerous consultations with the ILGB in November and December 1917, with the City Architect noting ruefully at one point that 'I do not think that Mr Cowan will approve of any plans that do not fully comply with his suggestions'.[71] Cowan at this time was also preparing a report on post-war housing in Dublin for the Chief Secretary, as will be discussed later, and his plain intention in all this was to introduce British standards to Irish state housing.

Therefore it is no surprise that in the final version of the Fairbrothers Fields design, drawn up in March 1918, there were only 370 cottages on the 16-acre site. This represented a further reduction in density to 23 dwellings to the acre. And when the area given over to parks and allotments was included in the calculation, the overall density worked out at just 17 dwellings to the acre. The distribution of house-types was now 157 three-room (42 per cent), 128 four-room (35 per cent) and 85 five-room cottages (23 per cent), revealing a proportionate increase in the number of larger dwellings (see Figs 35 and 36). The three-room cottages had a 15 foot frontage, and were of two types: one with an external WC and a porch which opened directly into the living room; the other with a separate staircase lobby and internal lavatory. The four-room cottages now were given a wider 16 foot frontage, and had three variants: the first was for a non-parlour type with three bedrooms on the upper floor; the second type had a parlour and only two large bedrooms; and the third was a semi-detached version of the parlour-type, with a side entrance and a lavatory on the first floor. The five-room cottages had a generous 20 foot frontage and were also distinguished by having a first-floor bathroom. In all cases, the bedroom sizes were increased, particularly in the four-room cottages. Cottages were designed in blocks varying from semi-detached pairs to terraces of 12 units. Monotony in the elevations and rooflines was relieved only by the introduction of some very shallow gable-projections. Indeed, the use of a highly regularised rhythm of door and window openings, and the simplicity of the roof profile, demonstrated the clear influence of contemporary schemes for the Ministry of Munitions in Britain.[72] There were two particular groups of British architects now at the forefront of simplification and rationalisation in housing design. The first was Raymond Unwin's team at the Ministry of Munitions, who had moved away from the Neo-Vernacular intricacies of the pre-war period towards an increasingly rationalised approach in schemes such as Gretna. The other influence came from the Neo-Georgian preferences of the 'Liverpool School', which had been most clearly promoted in Ireland through Abercrombie's winning entry for the Dublin Town Plan Competition. The elevations for Fairbrothers Fields duly incorporated abstracted Neo-Classical details. A string-course was used to distinguish the fair-faced brick 'plinth' on the ground floor from the concrete-rendered upper storey, and the gables (particularly in the semi-detached five-room dwellings) were emphasised to give them a pedimented appearance. Roundels, as well as semi-circular arched panels with keystones in the gables, served to add yet further Neo-Classical references. All in all, the Fairbrothers Fields estate had been transformed into Dublin Corporation's most prestigious design to date. As the Chairman of the Housing Committee was to state later, 'the Corporation always regarded the Fairbrothers Fields scheme as their *magnus opus*'.[73] The revised scheme was published in the London-based *Architect*, the first Irish housing project to receive such an accolade, and the journal noted approvingly that the scheme was now 'laid out in a more pleasing manner, and it is proposed to plant all the main roads with trees, while the houses themselves will be spread out with a view to securing greater variety of effect'.[74] It is therefore right to describe the Fairbrothers Fields estate as the first genuine application of garden suburb design in Ireland.[75] It was produced by Dublin Corporation in accordance with

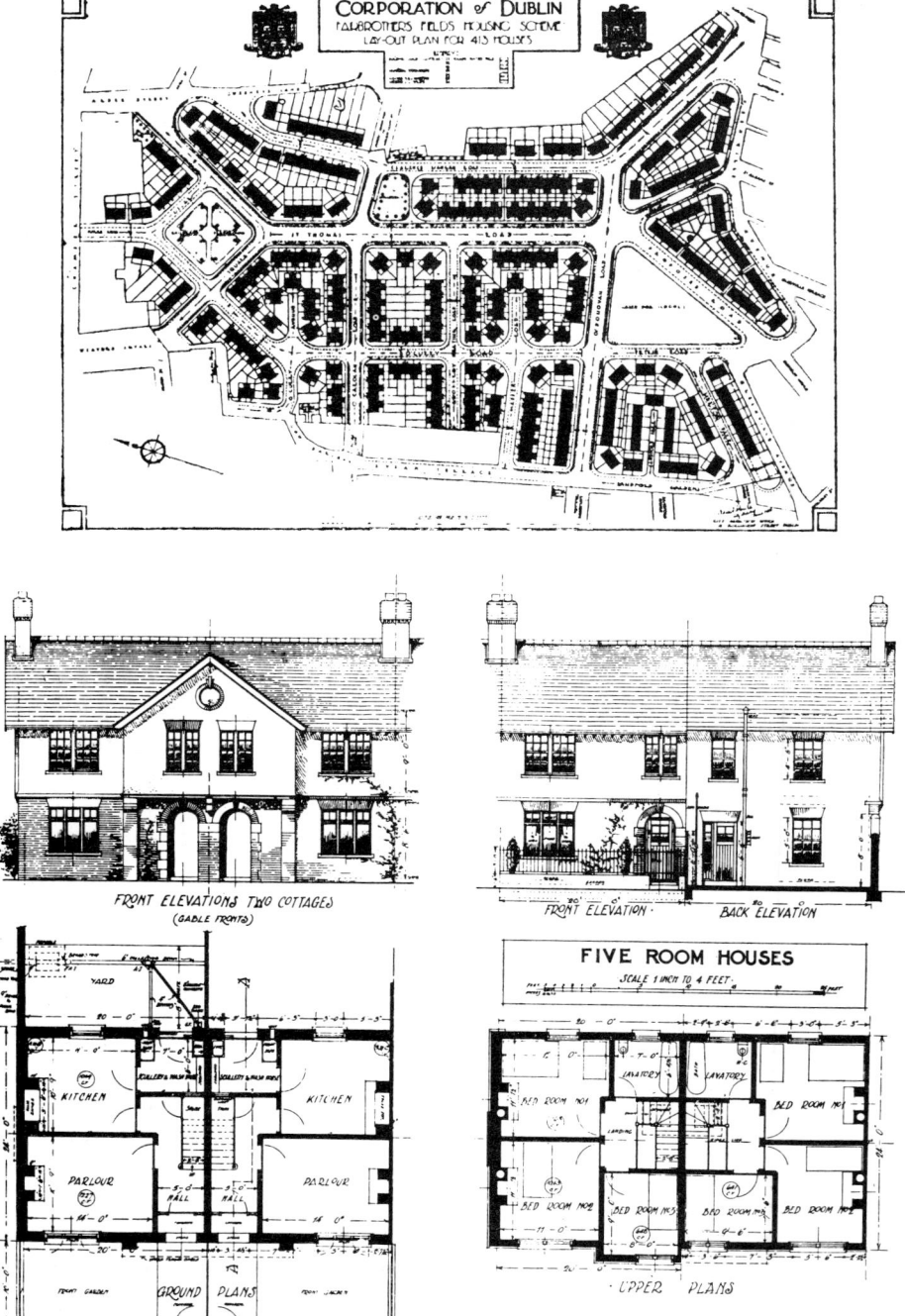

Fig 35. Dublin Corporation: site plan and five-room type at Fairbrothers Fields (1918)

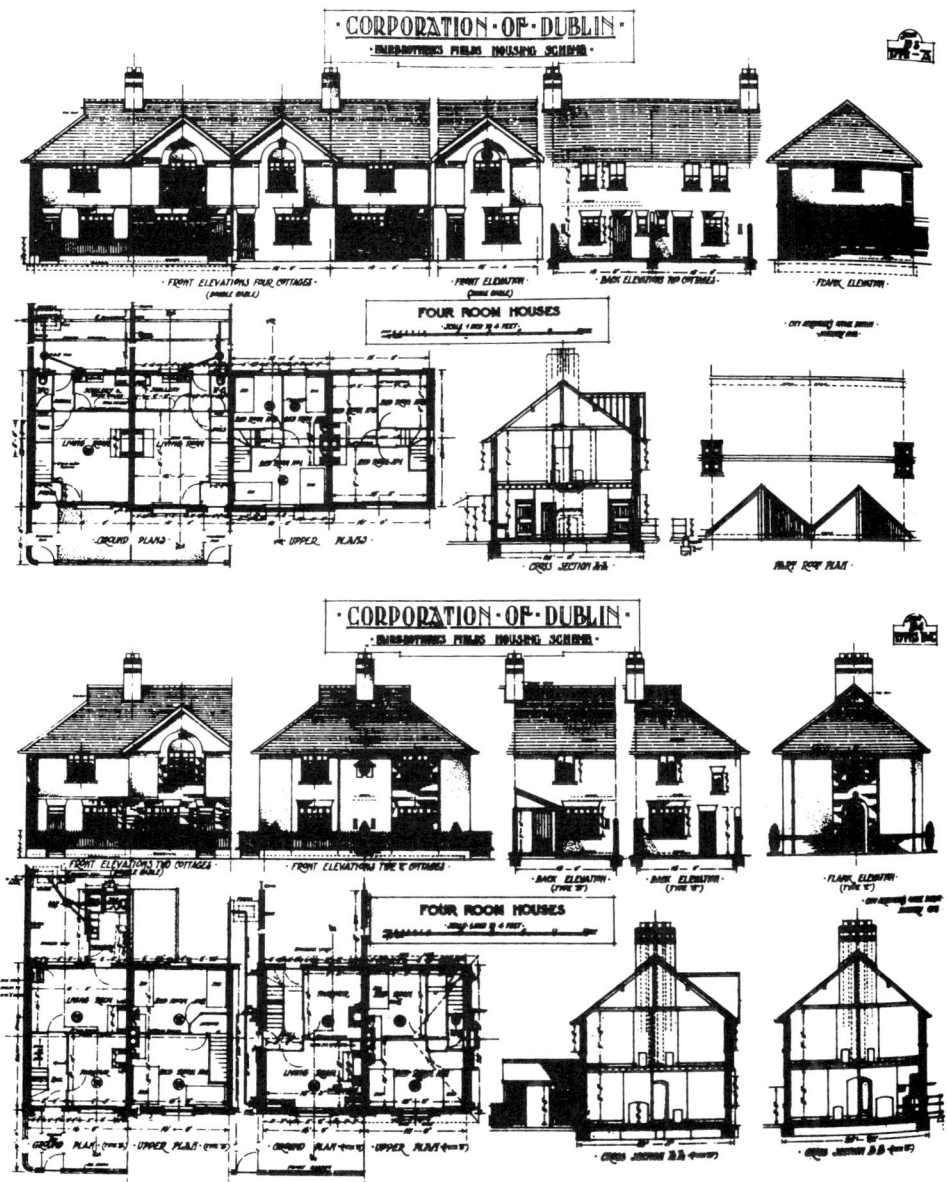

Fig 36. Dublin Corporation: various four-room types at Fairbrothers Fields

British housing expertise, with the specific aim of anticipating the post-war standards that might be set by Westminster.

In the negotiations with Chief Secretary Duke and the ILGB in April 1917 that led to agreement on an annual housing loan of £100 000 from the

Treasury, Dublin Corporation made clear its intention to continue with innercity schemes such as Spitalfields as well as the more prestigious suburban projects at the McCaffrey Estate and Fairbrothers Fields. An advance of £10 000 was granted to start building work at Spitalfields immediately. But by June 1917 the Corporation realised that it had under-estimated the financial effects of war-time inflation, and particularly of having to pay an interest rate of 5.5 per cent on the public loan. It therefore demanded from the ILGB a guarantee that whatever post-war housing subsidy might be decided would be given retrospectively to *all* schemes that might be built in the interim.[76] The ILGB recommended to the Treasury that this assurance be given, on the basis that the threat of social unrest in Dublin was so critical that housing employment was urgently required. The Treasury bluntly refused.[77] Dublin Corporation responded by taking a decision to proceed only with building work on the Spitalfields scheme. In the case of its other proposed housing schemes, the strategy was simply to finalise the purchase and clear the site. No more dwellings were to be provided until the Corporation could be absolutely sure of receiving state subsidy. This self-imposed stalemate, however, created its own dilemma. In May 1918, the Castle Administration reminded Dublin Corporation that only £44 000 of the first annual loan of £100 000 had been taken up. Given the strength of its previous rhetoric about housing need in Dublin, the Corporation was compelled, somewhat reluctantly, to start construction work on the McCaffrey Estate and at a small site in St James' Walk.

The key point to make is that, whereas housebuilding had all but ceased in British cities due to the First World War, it did continue on a reduced scale in Ireland principally as a result of municipal activity in Dublin. In early-1918 the *Architect* estimated that Irish annual house production stood at around a quarter of the level in 1909.[78] This was a notable achievement given the undoubted problems that hindered the war-time housing programme in Ireland. Dublin Corporation found that the Treasury continually tried to undermine and frustrate its plans. For instance, when the Corporation applied in Spring 1918 to clear a slum site at Boyne Street, the Treasury observed acidly:

> We should be especially careful as there appears to be a great deal of feeling in Dublin that the Corporation are wasting money in purchasing 'worthless rookeries' instead of building on the virgin soil of Fairbrothers Fields which scheme it is significant has not been started.[79]

This was somewhat rich, given that it was the Treasury's refusal to give an assurance on housing subsidy that had effectively turned the unique war-time housing loan to Dublin Corporation into a virtual dead-letter. In private, the Treasury noted with satisfaction that 'probably the Corporation will not proceed very actively with any building until they know what the Government intend to do for housing generally in Ireland'.[80] Thus, by May 1919, after two years there had only been a total of £85 000 advanced to the Corporation (and much of this was due to a recent loan of £24 930 to finally clear the site at

Fairbrothers Fields). Nor in the later stages of the First World War did anyone show much interest in the relative failure of the initiative. The emergency loan sought by Chief Secretary Duke in April 1917, while important at the time for revealing a novel use of state housing as a political tool, had simply become overshadowed by subsequent events. The preoccupation in Ireland was now the much larger issue of the British Government's plans for post-war reconstruction.

PLANS FOR IRISH RECONSTRUCTION AND HOUSING

A special committee had been set up by the Asquith Cabinet as early as March 1916 to start the preparations for reconstruction. This body acknowledged that some form of subsidised state housing programme would be needed after the war, to act as a temporary and transitional measure while the private house-building industry reconstituted itself.[81] The pre-war experience provided by the 'Irish system' of state subsidy was to prove invaluable in the consideration of possible housing strategies. 'Outside Ireland', the Treasury reminded the Reconstruction Committee in late-1916, 'the only case in which free grants have been given for housing is that of housing urgently needed for *war workers.*'[82] But given that munitions housing had been built under atypical circumstances, then Ireland alone offered a case-study of subsidised housing in peace-time conditions. However, progress on proposals for reconstruction remained painfully slow. No agreement was reached as to the nature of a post-war housing policy, nor were specific reconstruction plans for Ireland considered (indeed the issue of an Irish settlement was shelved after the collapse of Lloyd George's attempt to orchestrate an agreement in Summer 1916). Thus, when a new Coalition Government took power under the leadership of David Lloyd George in December 1916, a far more ambitious 'Second' Reconstruction Committee was launched. Radicals within the newly-formed Housing Panel, notably Seebohm Rowntree, called for a comprehensive post-war state housing campaign based on the model of munitions schemes. The whole issue of reconstruction was then brought to a head by a wave of strikes in May 1917 that imperilled the war effort. An Industrial Unrest Committee was appointed, and the resulting report—which effectively echoed the official reaction to the 1916 Easter Rising—declared that bad housing was a major contributory factor in labour unrest. The report recommended that the Government, while unable to embark on an immediate building programme during war-time, should nevertheless make a bold announcement about its future housing plans.[83] Hence in late-July 1917 the Lloyd George Cabinet authorised the English LGB to issue a circular to local authorities which promised as yet unspecified state assistance for post-war housing. Councils were also asked to measure and record the housing need in their area in preparation. There remained, however, substantial disagreement within the Government as to the scale and finances of the housing programme. On one side, the newly-created Ministry of

Reconstruction under the radical Liberal MP, Dr Christopher Addison, wanted a generous and wide-ranging strategy. A far more conservative and economical plan was promoted by the English LGB under its successive Presidents, Lord Rhondda and W. Hayes Fisher. The outcome was much inter-departmental friction, which enabled the Treasury to block all attempts to clarify the vague promise of subsidy contained in the English LGB circular of July 1917. Before looking at the outcome of this struggle in Whitehall, it is worth looking first at Irish reactions to these efforts by the British Government to defuse domestic labour problems by making announcements on housing policy.

In Ireland there were immediate calls for the ILGB to issue a similar circular on housing, and for the Government to put forward unequivocal subsidy proposals.[84] Particularly ominous for the Castle Administration in mid-1917 was the spread of industrial unrest in Ireland. One militant labour leader, invoking the Easter Rising and the contemporary political turmoil in Russia, told the Irish TUC in August 1917 that:

> if the state of things existing in Dublin with regard to housing were to continue much longer the delegates need not be astonished to hear of another rebellion. The workers would have to march out and seize the land available for buildings. Then they would seize the builuing yards, and . . . build there happy homes for the workers.[85]

The Irish TUC passed a militant resolution which demanded generous state aid for housing, and the labour threat was played up by both Irish Party MPs and the Association of Municipal Authorities of Ireland.[86] However, given the battle raging within the Cabinet itself, Chief Secretary Duke had little option but to stall. 'The housing of the working classes in the cities and towns of Ireland is a matter of urgent importance', he told Parliament, 'and will, I hope, be taken in hand as soon as possible after the War together with the housing proposals for Great Britain.'[87] Privately, Duke was worried as to whether Irish housing needs were in fact being taken into proper consideration by the Cabinet. In mid-August 1917 he wrote to the Chancellor of the Exchequer, Arthur Bonar Law, to reiterate the connection between urban slums and social discontent in Ireland. Duke also pointed out that the recent housing announcement in Britain had put intolerable political pressure on to the whole policy of the Castle Administration:

> I shall be obliged if you will let me know to what extent I may hold myself free to assure the representatives of public authorities in Ireland and other interested persons that equal generosity will be shown by the Chancellor of the Exchequer to the promoters of necessary works for the better housing of the poor whether this sphere of operations is in Ireland or in Great Britain. If you can give me this information before the adjournment of the Parliamentary Session it will put me in a position to avoid serious difficulties with which I must otherwise be

confronted while I am in Ireland, as I expect to be, during the Parliamentary Recess.[88]

The Treasury reply was that it could offer no firm guarantee until a general housing policy had been decided for Britain, nor until there was agreement on the larger question of how Irish Home Rule might be financed.[89] Duke tried to force the issue by inviting the Minister of Reconstruction to visit Dublin in November 1917 for a special housing conference. Realising that this would only raise Irish expectations, Addison tactfully declined.[90] Frustrated by what it saw as the ineffectuality of the Castle Administration, the Irish Party took their appeal directly to the President of the English Local Government Board. Yet although the IPP and the Association of Municipal Authorities of Ireland set up their own respective Housing Committees at the end of 1917, neither was able to extract any definite promises on the likely form of housing subsidy.[91] The simple truth was that the British Government was not in a position to make any details available.

Yet if the Castle Administration could not satisfy Irish demands on financial matters, it was able, as an alternative, to deal with the issue of the housing standards required for the post-war campaign. In mid-1917 an Irish Party member for Dublin, Patrick Brady, suggested to the Chief Secretary that a commission be asked to prepare a scheme for Dublin housing, adding that 'the setting up of such a Commission at this moment would do something to allay that spirit of unrest which unfortunately exists in Dublin as elsewhere'.[92] Duke realised that it would be impolitic to appoint a broad inquiry while the Cabinet was still formulating a policy. He took up instead a suggestion by the Vice-President of the ILGB that the department's chief housing expert, Dr Peter Cowan, be asked to report on the matter.[93] In late-July 1917, the Chief Secretary directed Cowan to prepare a confidential memorandum on how Dublin's housing needs could best be met. Cowan duly consulted with Dublin Corporation and a range of housing experts. The finished report was presented to Duke in January 1918, but was not shown to the Corporation until August, despite Irish demands for it to be published earlier.[94] It was a pragmatic report, intended principally to up-date and consolidate information already gathered by bodies such as the 1913–14 Dublin Housing Inquiry. Cowan's document was therefore far more limited in scope than its British counterpart, the Tudor Walters Report. The latter was drawn up by an influential committee appointed by the English LGB on 26 July 1917, and dealt in great detail with the design standard and economic implications of a variety of recommended house-types and construction methods. The remit of the Tudor Walters Committee was subsequently extended to include Scotland. But when Irish Party MPs tried to have the Tudor Walters Report further expanded to cover Ireland as well, Chief Secretary Duke replied that this was unnecessary since all of its recommendations would be incorporated as a matter of course into the post-war Irish programme.[95] There was a common link between the two reports in that the dominant architectural figure on the Tudor Walters Committee was Raymond Unwin, of whom Cowan had long been a dedicated supporter. However, it was the rather idiosyncratic approach of the Cowan Report, and particularly its view of the role of local authorities, that was to prove the most noticeable difference.

Cowan's central recommendation was that 16 500 cottages were now required in Dublin, and that these should be predominantly built on suburban sites in Clontarf, Drumcondra, Cabra and Crumlin (that is, in those areas already identified by the 1914 Town Plan Competition). In addition, 3800 existing tenement houses were to be renovated to provide a further 13 000 modern dwellings. The scale of the programme, estimated to cost £8 640 000, would obviously present problems:

> The task in Dublin is colossal, immensely greater proportionately than that of erecting 300,000 houses in England and Wales as soon as possible after the war, as the Government is now considering . . . It is evident, therefore, that measures which might suit England, where the work will be divided amongst a very great number of local authorities, are not likely to suffice in the case of Dublin.[96]

Cowan argued that Dublin Corporation was not fit to carry out the housing programme, not because it was especially inept or corrupt, but because he felt that it was a natural tendency for self-interested councillors to court working-class votes rather than pay proper attention to economy and efficiency. Instead he proposed that a Dublin Housing Board be set up from representatives of Government departments and local municipalities, and be given drastic powers to sweep away the social threat posed by the city's slums. State subsidy would be necessary but only as an unwelcome temporary feature:

> There is a great emergency now, and it must be met by emergency measures, but these should be so designed and limited so as to leave some prospect of arriving after a reasonable transitory period at a stage where healthy houses and healthy economic conditions may be found together . . . It may therefore be hoped that any period during which large numbers of the working classes in Dublin can be said to be in receipt of relief from the public purse in the matter of house accommodation will be short.[97]

In terms of housing standards, Cowan remarked that the designs for the McCaffrey Estate and Fairbrothers Fields were 'a great advance on earlier schemes in the City of Dublin'. Yet these too would now have to be exceeded:

> It is, however, quite clear that houses of ampler accommodation than have hitherto commonly been built for the working classes should be provided in any new housing schemes, even if our accustomed methods of construction have to be abandoned for a long period.[98]

The layout of housing estates from now was to be based on British garden suburb orthodoxy. There should be a maximum of 12 houses to the acre. Accommodation should be provided in large estates, each made up of around 400 dwellings. When it came to the question of individual house planning, Cowan's recommendations were much closer to the conservative ideals of the English LGB than the more generous standards now envisaged by, say, the Ministry of Reconstruction. The Cowan Report relied heavily on the findings of the long-running Royal Commission on Scottish Housing, which had finally been published in October 1917. Cowan thus recommended a minimum dwelling size of two bedrooms, living room and scullery, along with a larder, coal cellar and WC. There was to be the possibility of fitting a bath with hot water, but no need for a separate bathroom. As an overall proportion, there should be 60 per cent of the two-bedroom cottages; 35 per cent three-bedroom cottages; and only 5 per cent four-bedroom cottages. Some 40 per cent of the larger three-bedroom and four-bedroom houses (16 per cent of all dwellings) were to be provided with a parlour, allowing the living room to be made smaller. In terms of room sizes, Cowan took the standards set out in the 1917 RIBA Housing Competition. There should be a minimum area of 160 square feet for the living room; a minimum 160 square feet for the main bedroom; and 70 square feet for other bedrooms. Cowan's *Report on Dublin Housing* was the only official document on Irish housing produced during the war, and enjoyed a mainly favourable reception. Nationalists objected to the implicit attack on Irish municipalities, but the ex-Chief Secretary, H. E. Duke, called it 'a valuable contribution to a most serious subject'.[99] The *Architect* even went so far as to say that it was 'a masterpiece of clear and impartial reasoning and succinct expression . . . We doubt if a better report on any great subject has ever been written'.[100] Yet while the standards that Cowan took from Britain were higher than those obtaining in Ireland, they represented, as indeed did the memoranda of the English LGB in 1917, essentially the best of pre-war thinking. Thus the Cowan Report was to have little influence on the final standards introduced in post-war Ireland. The Tudor Walters Report, with its bolder vision and innovative recommended plan-types, made the greater impact.

By early-1918, Irish MPs were becoming noticeably more impatient with Chief Secretary Duke's bland reassurances that preparations for post-war housing in Ireland were being developed hand-in-hand with those for Britain.[101] For, in fact, the question of Irish housing was being virtually ignored in the Cabinet's deliberations. Partly this was due to the concern, as will be seen below, of the British Government to try once more to find a political settlement for Ireland. But it was even more to do with the fact that the Whitehall battle over post-war housing proposals had escalated in the wake of Lloyd George's 'war aims' speech of 5 January 1918. Now the Government was again offering housing promises, this time in an attempt to placate labour opposition to the proposal to divert manpower away from munitions work to military service.

This latest conscription plan was in breach of earlier promises, and provoked the threat of serious strike action.[102] Hence, in February 1918 the Cabinet saw a full-blooded confrontation between the Ministry of Reconstruction and the English LGB over the issue of specific pledges on housing subsidy. Christopher Addison proposed an extensive mandatory programme as part of a state-led transition from demobilisation to peace-time, with municipalities being subsidised for the whole of the excess cost of building after the war.[103] Addison envisaged 'a housing shortage of between 300,000 and 400,000 for England and Wales and 100,000 for Scotland and a substantial number for the urban districts of Ireland'.[104] In opposition, the President of the English LGB, Hayes Fisher, promoted the more tentative Treasury proposal to offer municipalities 75 per cent of the estimated annual loss for seven years, or a higher percentage if the total loss was likely to be greater than the produce of a local penny-rate (after seven years the state contribution was to be reassessed at 75 per cent of the local authority's loss over the recalculated value of the scheme). Despite strong objections from Addison, the less costly subsidy proposal from Hayes Fisher was incorporated into a further circular by the English LGB. During this heated Cabinet debate in February 1918, Chief Secretary Duke drew up a paper that stressed the appalling urban housing conditions in Ireland. He called for subsidised municipal housing for the desperately poor, and continued:

> The adoption of National Housing Proposals for England and Scotland will I think involve a similar proceeding with regard to Ireland. The uncertainty which exists as to the future of Irish Government will not relieve Parliament, as matters now stand, from the necessity of dealing with the housing problem. What is really to be decided seems to me to be the question of what is most prudent under the circumstances . . . After discussing the relative merits of the schemes proposed by the Minister of Reconstruction and the President of the Local Government Board, I have come to the conclusion that the latter is best adapted under existing circumstances to meet the cause of Ireland.[105]

Duke's support for the Hayes Fisher proposal demonstrated the rather limited approach towards state housing that still existed within Dublin Castle. It also reflected the dominant view in Westminster, where the urgency of issues such as housing and the 'manpower crisis' had been dramatically superseded by the German Army's massive offensive in Spring 1918. It was now not until after the Armistice, during preparations for the post-war election campaign, that Lloyd George and other British politicians were to return once more to making bold promises of 'homes fit for heroes'. Yet in Ireland, by contrast, the pressing question of self-government had led to the formation of a special Irish Convention in mid-1917, and this body was from February to April 1918 to temporarily take up the issue of a post-war Irish housing campaign.

THE 1917–18 IRISH CONVENTION AND STATE HOUSING PROPOSALS

There were two reasons why the Lloyd George Coalition Government was compelled to reopen the constitutional question of Irish self-government in April 1917. The first was that the Irish Party, fearing the growth of Sinn Fein if Home Rule was not achieved, had begun to use obstructive tactics in Parliament which posed a threat to the war administration.[106] Secondly, the Government was facing a growing shortage of military manpower. Ireland was an obvious source given that, as Conservatives and Unionists never failed to point out, it was the only part of the United Kingdom where conscription was not in force. But the Cabinet realised that to extend compulsory service to Ireland was politically impossible unless accompanied by a Home Rule Act. Irish strategy was at this point being principally drafted by Professor W. S. G. Adams, head of Lloyd George's own policy unit. Adams had worked in the Irish Department of Agriculture and Technical Instruction prior to becoming an Oxford don, and had subsequently served as a labour adviser in the Ministry of Munitions before his appointment to the Prime Minister's secretariat in 1916. Adams had now come to the conclusion that a consensual agreement on Home Rule could be achieved if the British Government was prepared also to make a generous financial settlement.[107]

Hence on 16 May 1917 the Prime Minister wrote to John Redmond offering the immediate introduction of Home Rule. This was to be modified by the temporary exclusion of the six North-Eastern Ulster counties, and the establishment of a council to legislate for all of Ireland on certain non-controversial matters. Significantly, the Government now proposed a substantial improvement in the financial deal for Ireland, with Lloyd George declaring in general terms that:

> the Government consider that the financial proposals of the Home Rule Act are unsatisfactory and ought to be reconsidered. There are a number of important objects, such as . . . the improvement of housing in the towns . . . which cannot, owing to changed conditions which have arisen since the war, be adequately dealt with under the powers of that Act, without imposing an undue burden on the Irish taxpayer.[108]

It was the first acknowledgement by Westminster that the post-war housing programme in Ireland would involve the Imperial Exchequer in shouldering the burden, and it also pre-dated the aforementioned public pledge given by the Government for Britain. However, the Prime Minister and Adams realised that the Nationalist Party would still probably reject any offer which proposed the exclusion of Ulster. Lloyd George therefore also suggested the alternative of organising a convention to devise a solution for self-government, on the sole condition that Ireland would remain within the British Empire. The second option was duly chosen, and so the Government began to recruit suitable representatives from the main Irish interest groups. The Irish Convention represented a final and ill-fated attempt by Westminster to reach an Irish settlement by consensus.[109] Its participants were not overly optimistic of success, and met intermittently under the chairmanship of Sir Horace Plunkett from July 1917 until April 1918. The entrenched opposition of Nationalist and Unionist opinions ensured that discussions became deadlocked over two contentious issues: whether Ulster should be excluded, and the degree of fiscal autonomy, particularly over customs and excise duties, that should be conceded to any new Irish Government. But the underlying failure of the Irish Convention was its continued inability to get Sinn Fein or the radical labour movement to participate.[110]

Irish Convention proceedings had clearly run into chronic difficulties by the end of 1917. The absence of agreement was a serious blow to the British Government in its attempts to clear the ground for the introduction of conscription in Ireland. Chief Secretary Duke was also worried that a 'revolutionary' party might sweep the country unless a settlement was reached quickly, and a sympathetic Irish Government installed.[111] So from December 1917 to February 1918 both Professor Adams and Sir Horace Plunkett 'orchestrated the government's policy towards the Convention in an attempt to prevent a collapse'.[112] Areas of common consent were sought to cement the fragile unity of the Irish Convention. A sub-committee on land purchase was set up in January 1918, and rapidly produced a report that recommended measures for the completion of the process of land transfer to tenants. Adams also suggested privately to Plunkett that it should be publicised that the Government was also prepared 'to treat as part of the plan of settlement substantial provision in connection with the vital problems of housing in Ireland'.[113] The Cabinet invited various municipal deputations over from Ireland, after which Lloyd George sent another letter to the Irish Convention on 25 February 1918 which declared that:

> The Government have also had submitted to them by the Labour Representatives in the Convention the need of provision for dealing with the urgent question of housing in Ireland, and on receiving recommendations from the Convention on the subject they would be prepared to consider the inclusion in the scheme of settlement of a substantial provision for immediately dealing with this vital problem.[114]

However, it would appear from accounts of the meetings in London that matters such as working-class housing were in fact of more urgency to the Government than to the 'labour' members of the Convention.[115] It was, of course, at this very point in February 1918 that Lloyd George was eager to make further housing promises to defuse labour unrest in Britain during the 'manpower crisis'. In Plunkett's report on the Irish Convention, he noted pointedly that on the issues of land purchase and urban housing, 'the Prime Minister had, it might almost be said, gone out of his way to be generous'.[116]

Thus, when the Convention resumed again in late February, the formation of a special Housing Committee was made the immediate priority. Plunkett reported secretly back to Adams:

> To-morrow we shall meet only in the morning and we are going to appoint a Housing Committee. That matter seems to interest the Convention immensely. Sundry County Councillors will try to get villages into the Town Housing problem, and very likely that harmless and futile effort will keep us off more dangerous topics.[117]

The Convention's Housing Committee had 15 members, and was presided over by the Lord Mayor of Dublin, Lawrence O'Neill. Plunkett noted with satisfaction that the Lord Mayor of Dublin was proving to be 'wholly friendly', and he continued to press home that generous subsidy from the Imperial Exchequer was now there for the asking.[118] Thus, although the Prime Minister's secretariat wanted it to appear that housing had been brought forward as an Irish demand, in reality the intention was to control the Housing Committee as part of Lloyd George's strategy of using housing as a political tool. This was clearly demonstrated by the fact that the Assistant Secretary appointed to the Convention, Roland Vernon, was entrusted with overseeing this crucial matter. Vernon was on secondment from a senior position in the Ministry of Munitions, where he was the civil servant in charge of the housing section.[119] Thus, when pressed for a rapid report in late-March 1918, Vernon was able to tell Adams that he would use his professional expertise:

> I am going to dictate tomorrow a memorandum which will, I hope, suffice as an outline of a report of the Housing Committee. It will of course be very sketchy. I will send you a copy of it. The Housing Committee is to meet on April 3rd to consider it. The Convention will meet on April 4th & 5th, and if all goes well we should be able to get through both the main Report and the Housing Report.[120]

Vernon subsequently sent the draft report to Adams for approval, adding:

> It has had to be prepared in great haste and with very little material. You will see that gaps are left for the figures which will of course be the pith of the Report. I originally put in 45 per cent as the degree of Government assistance which would be necessary but then decided that it would be better for me not to give the Committee a lead in the matter. I am inclined to think, however, that they will probably ask for something like this.[121]

Adams was concerned that the proposal appeared to require new housing legislation, and that this might delay the path of an urgent Home Rule Bill. However, Vernon gave a reassurance that all that was needed was 'only a grant of money!'[122] Using the draft produced by Vernon, the Convention's Housing

Committee met urgently on 3 April 1918 to discuss the issues of subsidy and housing standards, prior to finalising its recommendations.[123] The resulting report was accepted by the whole Irish Convention at its final session two days later. The principal demands were for a large post-war programme to build 67 500 houses in Ireland, and a fixed subsidy to municipalities of 50 per cent of capital expenditure incurred. At an estimated figure of £400 per dwelling, it was anticipated that the whole scheme would cost around £27 000 000. The Convention's Housing Committee took its cue on design standards from the Cowan Report and above all from Britain, drawing on advice from English LGB circulars and from Seebohm Rowntree's memorandum for the Ministry of Reconstruction's Housing Panel (which the committee was permitted to consult but in strict confidence).[124] Thus the report called for a maximum density of 12 houses to the acre, and the provision of mostly two- or three-bedroom cottages, albeit with some larger houses containing a parlour or fourth bedroom.

The Chairman of the Convention, Sir Horace Plunkett, used the report to praise the contribution of labour and municipal delegates to the search for an Irish settlement.[125] Chief Secretary Duke reported to the Cabinet that the housing recommendations 'will form part of the general plan of settlement', and he told the House of Commons in mid-April 1918 that:

> It will appear from the Report of the Irish Convention that His Majesty's Government is ready to recommend to Parliament the making of special provisions for the needs of urban localities in Ireland in connection with the measure for granting self-government to Ireland.[126]

In fact there was strong opposition within Westminster to a subsidy proposal that was obviously far more generous than anything which had been offered hitherto by the English LGB. Vernon tried to reassure the Government that the Convention's Housing Report was not 'really quite as alarming as it looks on the face of it', pointing out that it would take several years to climb to a maximum expenditure of £1 620 000 a year, and that the British contribution would even then only be half of this amount.[127] This did nothing to ease the alarm of the Treasury, which had just scored a success when the Cabinet accepted the subsidy terms of the English LGB rather than of Christopher Addison. The Treasury's main worry was that the more generous terms suggested by the Irish Convention's proposal would now be demanded by British municipalities. As one official noted, 'this may very easily upset our English scheme. Can it be camouflaged as part of a general Home Rule Settlement?'[128] The Treasury pointed out its fear to the Prime Minister:

> A free capital grant of 50 per cent far exceeds the modest proposals of 75 per cent of annual deficit on loan charges made for Great Britain. Even allowing for special circumstances in Ireland, a grant on so generous a basis will make it impossible to avoid something far more generous

than present proposals for Great Britain, at enormous cost to his Majesty's Government.[129]

However, the Treasury realised that Lloyd George was now politically committed to giving substantial Exchequer aid for Irish housing. Instead, it put forward an alternative proposal which accepted the principle of a 50 per cent capital subsidy, but suggested that the British contribution should be capped at a limit of £5 000 000 over a ten-year period, rather than the sum of £13 500 000 that was implied in the Irish Convention's estimates. A housing fund was to be created by allowing the new Irish Government to make a deduction from the annual revenue contribution that it would otherwise have to pay towards Imperial expenditure. This the Treasury argued would free Irish housing policy from interference from Westminster, and conversely 'being the scheme of the Irish Government would not react on Housing Policy in Great Britain in the same way as would a scheme devised for Ireland by the Imperial Government itself'. The point was emphasised by a senior Treasury official when he told Lloyd George:

> The last consideration is to my mind of very great importance, since the Scheme proposed by the Convention Committee (whether possible or not in Ireland) could not be copied in Great Britain without scrapping a scheme recently launched and completely 'socialising' not only all new building but the State System of working-class housing.[130]

In any event, the fundamental failure of the Irish Convention to reach a solution on self-government meant that the proposals of its Housing Committee were likewise lost. The British Government desperately tried to salvage what it could from the situation. A Cabinet Committee was set up in April 1918 under the staunch Unionist, Sir Walter Long, to draft a new Home Rule Bill. There was now to be in effect an imposed settlement, as an accompaniment to the introduction of conscription. Professor Adams was appointed as secretary to the Committee, although his personal influence was on the wane because of the failure of the Irish Convention.[131] The Cabinet Committee on Ireland drew up two alternative schemes in June 1918. One was based on the Convention's recommendation of dominion-style Home Rule ('Scheme A'), and the other was for a federal system which retained greater control for the Imperial Parliament ('Scheme B'). The latter was favoured by Sir Walter Long. Both alternatives contained a large-scale housing programme as an essential part of the settlement. Adams now accepted the Treasury's suggestion that the British contribution be offset from Ireland's payments towards Imperial expenditure, but he rejected outright any diminution of the Irish housing programme. Instead, Adams argued that the estimated Exchequer contribution of £13 500 000 towards the 67 500 cottages proposed by the Irish Convention should be deducted over a period of seven years. This worked out at around £1 930 000 per annum, which in subsequent calculations produced in mid-

1918 was rounded up to a figure of £2 000 000.[132] Hence, as the war drew to a close, the British Government was committed to financing a substantial housing campaign in Ireland as part of a Home Rule settlement. Irish housing policy was therefore now being decided entirely in Westminster. Significantly, Ireland was deliberately excluded from the unadventurous Housing Bill that was introduced by the President of the English LGB in October 1918 to demonstrate the Cabinet's commitment on housing, but then dropped when the General Election was called for that December.[133]

PREPARATIONS FOR THE POST-WAR IRISH HOUSING CAMPAIGN

Westminster's growing control over housing policy in Ireland was clearly shown by the weakened position of the Castle Administration and Irish political parties towards the end of the First World War. In May 1918 a new Executive was installed, comprising Lord French of Ypres as a powerful pro-consular Lord Lieutenant, and Edward Shortt as Chief Secretary. The main aims were now to escalate the recruiting programme, and to pursue a tougher policy of repression against Sinn Fein.[134] Despite the new broom, conditions in Ireland deteriorated when mass opposition was orchestrated in response to fears that conscription was finally about to be introduced. As a result of the bitter 'conscription crisis' in Ireland, by late-June 1918 the Government was forced to abandon all hopes of implementing compulsory military service balanced by Home Rule.[135] Dublin Castle instead attempted to deflect criticism by stressing important social issues such as urban housing, but on the issue the Castle Administration was still unable to offer any firm promises. When pressed further in August 1918, Chief Secretary Shortt replied weakly that 'I am going to consider the whole question during the Recess'.[136]

Irish political parties were far removed from the Cabinet debates on post-war reconstruction and housing, and their relative impotence was reflected in the rhetoric of the post-war election campaign. In the period before the First World War, the Irish Party had dominated politics outside Ulster, and had been closely involved in the development of housing policy. Yet by 1918 the IPP was in terminal decline (as shown by a series of disastrous by-election defeats) due to the inroads that Sinn Fein and its leader, Eamonn de Valera, had made by exploiting anti-British sentiment after the Easter Rising and during the 'conscription crisis'. An important element in Sinn Fein's success was the broad-fronted alliance it had managed to forge with the radical labour movement. Together they espoused abstentionism and republicanism, and bitterly attacked the policy of constitutional nationalism.[137] The problem for the labour movement was that, while Sinn Fein was eager to subsume the urban working classes into the separatist campaign, in reality the majority of extreme Nationalists had no real interest in social issues such as housing reform. The line taken by de Valera and Sinn Fein was expressed succinctly by one of their election candidates:

> There were no doubt many social and economic questions to be dealt with such as better housing for the people . . . but before these could be gone into they must first get at the foundation for all these, and by getting rid of the English connection with Ireland they secured this end.[138]

Nevertheless, for tactical reasons the Irish Labour Party gave its full support to the republican movement, and agreed not to contest the 1918 General Election. The way was now clear for Sinn Fein to sweep to power in Southern Ireland, and wipe out the old Irish Party. In a vain attempt to fight back, the IPP used housing as a crucial part of its political attack on Sinn Fein's abstentionist strategy of refusing to take up seats in the Imperial Parliament. The Irish Party argued that this would mean that Ireland would miss out on post-war housing subsidy, while at the same time continuing to contribute revenue towards the campaign in Britain. The IPP member for West Belfast, Joseph Devlin, exclaimed:

> Nearly a hundred million is going to be spent on housing in England. Am I to allow them to force us to pay our share for the housing of John Bull, while Paddy Murphy has to live in a slum? We are out for one thing, to improve and elevate the people, and are we going to allow the people to continue to live in slums, or are we going to Parliament to get our fair share of these funds for housing improvement?[139]

And one of the Irish Party members for Dublin launched a bitter attack on:

> the cruel and thoughtless absurdity of Sinn Fein. When the question of housing came to be dealt with the Irish Party would endeavour to force the Government to interpret the Cowan Report with regard to housing in Dublin in £.s.d., but if the Sinn Feiners were returned he would like to know who would be in Parliament to see that Ireland was not forgotten and would get her proper share of the millions that were to be spent on housing after the war?[140]

Another electoral tactic used by the IPP against Sinn Fein was to exploit fears of giving ground to the Ulster Unionists:

> Abstention from Parliament would certainly be the worst means for securing this. Portions of large grants that would be given in the future must be secured for Ireland. Must Carson secure all this for Ulster, if Carson alone would have representation in the House of Commons?[141]

Joseph Devlin tried to revive the spirit of the IPP's pre-war achievements, by pledging 'to use this great and efficient instrument which has been so splendidly successful to give our town dwellers the same decent housing accommodation and better than that which was given to labourers in agricultural

Ireland'.[142] Yet such sentiments were by now pure nostalgia, and only highlighted the fact that the illustrious days of the Irish Party were over.

In Ulster a remarkable transformation had taken place by the end of the First World War. The previously reactionary Sir Edward Carson and his Ulster Unionist Party had become fully committed to housing reform because of their growing fear of 'bolshevism'. In July 1918 the Ulster Unionist Labour Association was created, with Carson as its President, in an attempt to divert working-class support away from socialism and the Belfast Labour Party. From this point on, Ulster Unionists repeatedly warned of the need for state housing, particularly in Belfast, if the province was to avoid the social revolution that had occurred in Russia.[143] Concern was heightened by a wave of serious industrial unrest that shook the Ulster capital in the winter of 1918–19. Carson declared impatiently during the post-war election campaign:

> We are promised . . . by the Prime Minister, a great housing reform in England. We are not going to wait until he comes to terms with the Nationalists to have that reform for Ulster.[144]

There was undoubtedly a chronic housing need in Belfast, since the cessation of speculative housebuilding during the war had created an increasing shortage of accommodation. The Belfast Branch of the Auctioneers' and Estate Agents' Institute produced a widely circulated report in March 1918. This estimated that 5000 high standard cottages were required, and called for state subsidy to be given to private housebuilders to remedy the deficiency.[145] Soon after the Armistice, the *Irish Times* declared that there was not a single vacant house left in Belfast, and a general view was that at least 2000 new dwellings needed to be built at once.[146] In November 1918 both the Law Committee and the Improvements Committee of Belfast Corporation called for the stimulation of a large housing programme. The following month saw the creation of the city's first municipal committee to deal specifically with the housing issue. There was a strong division within the Housing Committee as to whether Belfast Corporation should become a major housebuilder itself, as many Unionist MPs now proposed, or whether it should rely on giving financial aid to private builders and public utility societies. The final decision, as reached in March 1919, was to stimulate private enterprise, but this only led the Corporation into renewed conflict with the Castle Administration in Dublin since it plainly contradicted the policy that was now emanating from Westminster.[147]

Demands on the British Government for action on post-war housing came not just from politicians in the Irish Party or Ulster Unionists, but also from a wide range of bodies such as Dublin Corporation, the Association of Municipal Authorities of Ireland, the Dublin Chamber of Commerce, Catholic reform societies, the RIAI, the Irish press, and professional journals such as the *Irish Builder*.[148] The pressure on the Castle Administration became intense when in November 1918 the English LGB wrote again to local authorities to ask that they start to prepare housing schemes. Chief Secretary Shortt denied Cabinet allegations made by Christopher Addison that Ireland was lagging behind in its housing plans, and instead assured Lloyd George:

> Moreover, the Committee of the Irish Convention have prepared an estimate of the total number of houses required for the whole of Ireland, and standard plans and specifications have been prepared by the Local Government Board so that there is really nothing lacking in the way of knowledge of Irish requirements which would delay the resumption of building schemes as soon as the financial aspect of the question is considered by the Government.[149]

The Chief Secretary's attitude was undoubtedly far too complacent, but it stemmed from a genuine structural problem in that the Irish housing programme was now entirely dependent on the decisions of the British Government. Professor Adams warned Lloyd George in late-December 1918 that a decision on subsidy was urgent:

> I need hardly emphasise the fact that a satisfactory announcement on these points would help to improve the situation in Ireland. The feeling in Ireland that Ireland is not in the great reconstruction proposals which are being discussed in Great Britain is undoubtedly increasing unrest and sense of grievance. The soonest, therefore, that definite proposals affecting reconstruction in Ireland can be announced the better.[150]

It was a point echoed by the Chief Secretary when he reported that a housing pledge might help to avert a dangerous political situation developing in Ireland:

> I can not get on because I can not get a definite statement as to the percentage of cost which will be borne by the Treasury. It is essential that we should get a definite statement at once. Do help me.[151]

Yet, despite Shortt's desperate pleading, all that the ILGB were able to send out to Irish local authorities in December 1918 was a general circular requesting that they follow their mainland counterparts, by making a start on housing proposals.[152] Thus, after the Easter Rising, official concern about the effects of slums on social unrest had led the Castle Administration to expound a policy of using housing for political ends. The results of this policy in war-time Dublin were minimal (save for encouraging the adoption of garden suburb design). Yet it did influence British Government strategy, as could be seen in the public announcements about the post-war housing campaign, and in the offer of Exchequer subsidy to the 1917–18 Irish Convention as an incentive to agree a Home Rule settlement. By the end of the First World War, Westminster had assumed full control of the Irish housing programme, and the manner in which proposals were subsequently formulated showed that British interests were paramount. No definite commitments on housing policy or finance had yet been authorised by the Lloyd George Cabinet, and the Treasury was especially determined to keep a tight control over any proposals for Ireland. The development of the post-war Irish housing campaign forms the subject of the next chapter.

Chapter 6

THE POST-WAR HOUSING CAMPAIGN IN IRELAND

In the wake of the General Election of December 1918, all aspects of Irish policy were being determined by the ideological divisions within the newly-elected Lloyd George Coalition Government. Home Rule was supported by Liberal ministers but was effectively stalled by influential Unionists inside the Cabinet, headed by the elder statesman of the Conservative Party, Sir Walter Long. The problems of the British Government were compounded by the fact that Sinn Fein had won the vast majority of Irish seats in the General Election, and duly proclaimed its own separatist republican Parliament, the Dáil Éireann. Meanwhile the policy for state housing in Ireland was still awaiting the outcome of the struggle between the English LGB and the Ministry of Reconstruction, over both the quality and quantity of the post-war campaign. It was the divisions in Westminster that were to ensure that the housing initiative devised for Ireland in 1919 was unique compared with that for the rest of the United Kingdom. Two characteristics of the Irish campaign stand out. First, the British Government's use of housing policy for political purposes explains its determination to see the programme through, even when opposition in Ireland was clearly making progress impossible. Second, once the Treasury and the Cabinet had decided that a distinct subsidy system was necessary in Ireland, the greatest obstacle to success became an obsessive attempt to ensure comparability between Britain and Ireland, so that neither was seen to be treated advantageously compared with the other. This chapter will look at the way in which post-war Irish housing policy was drawn up in Westminster, and at the reactions in Ireland to the new 1919 Irish Housing Act. It will then examine the design standards that were introduced in the post-war period, before discussing the reasons why the actual housing campaign in Ireland proved to be so ill-fated. A connected but distinct British initiative, specifically to rehouse Irish ex-servicemen returning from the front, will form the subject of the next chapter.

INITIAL BRITISH PROPOSALS FOR THE IRISH HOUSING CAMPAIGN

At the time of the Armistice, the British Government's policy in Ireland was in disarray. The offer of self-government that Lloyd George had made earlier in 1918, which included a sweetener for Ireland of £2 000 000 a year towards state housing, was a dead-letter. The Irish Convention had failed to achieve a settlement by consensus. Progress within the Cabinet Committee appointed to draft a new Home Rule Bill was being held up by opponents such as Sir Walter Long. The resultant stalemate had important political consequences for the British Government. It caused resentment in Irish communities abroad, especially in the USA, and it actively contributed to the wave of industrial unrest that was sweeping post-war Great Britain and threatening to shake the very foundations of the state. 'A satisfactory solution of the Irish question was most important from the point of view, not only as regards the industrial world, but also of our relations with the Dominions and the United States', the Prime Minister told the Cabinet.[1] The British Government thus realised that it had to portray itself as paying close attention to finding an Irish settlement, even if all it was actually doing was marking time. Hence in early-1919 the Cabinet devised a reconstruction policy for Ireland that would enable it to govern in the interim while political differences in Britain could hopefully be overcome.

An important consequence was that, as the Castle Administration had long urged, the post-war housing campaign in Ireland now came to be considered by the Cabinet alongside that for Britain. In December 1918 the Chancellor of the Exchequer, Austen Chamberlain, wrote to the Chief Secretary for Ireland, Edward Shortt, stating that he now 'thought it clear that housing terms given to the United Kingdom would have to be extended to Ireland'.[2] This decision coincided with a decisive change in the Government's attitude towards the housing campaign that has been comprehensively documented by Swenarton, and need only be summarised here.[3] Towards the end of the First World War, the question of housing had been reopened in Cabinet discussions, and during the post-war election Lloyd George had made much of a crusade to build 'homes fit for heroes'. Cabinet concern was fuelled by the serious wave of industrial unrest and by the concomitant fear that 'bolshevism' might sweep the country and overthrow the state, just as it had done in Russia (and to a lesser extent, in post-war Germany). The fear, although it might seem unfounded now, was made very tangible at the time by the demobilisation of five million militarily-trained servicemen, and the release from duty of a similar number of munitions workers. The British Government now promoted better housing as the main means of appeasing labour demands and convincing the working class that there was no reason to overthrow the existing social order. A belief that housing could avert unrest and provide legitimation for the state was not confined to the more radical members of the Government, but was also shared by Conservatives such as the Chancellor of the Exchequer, Austen Chamberlain. Consensus on issues like housing was essential to the post-war political coalition if it was to achieve a bourgeois realignment—a 'passive revolution' in Gramscian terms—that was based on a greater acceptance of state intervention. It signified the end of the *laissez-faire* 'liberal hegemony', which had collapsed in Britain due to the inroads made by working-class political organisation and the slow disintegration of the Imperial system.[4]

Thus by early-1919 housing had come to constitute, at least in the minds of the Cabinet, an 'insurance against revolution'. It was undoubtedly an alarmist view, but one that found ready support amongst all the political parties in Britain. However, what Swenarton has omitted from the account is the role of Ireland in helping to shape the Coalition Government's attitude towards housing. Lloyd George and others had come to realise by this point that the pre-war strategy of the 'Land Campaign' was moribund, and that another policy was urgently needed. The only alternative that was readily available and achievable was the policy of giving centralised state subsidy to local authorities. Would such a policy work in practice? The example of war-time munitions housing offered an obvious precedent, but one in which conditions had clearly been extraordinary. More relevant to these top-level deliberations was the successful case-study provided by the well-established 'Irish system' of subsidised housing. The British Government was fully aware of developments in state housing in Ireland. During the war, the Cabinet had authorised special housing funds for Dublin, to overcome political problems there, and Lloyd George had been willing to offer a generous level of housing subsidy as part of a Home Rule settlement. Now, after the Armistice, it was the example of land redistribution and subsidised labourers' cottages in Ireland that the Prime Minister used explicitly to justify his belief that social reform would be a successful antidote to insurrection. In his famous speech to the Cabinet on 3 March 1919, calling for a substantial programme of land settlement and housing to avert 'bolshevism', Lloyd George began with the declaration:

> The policy here advocated was the same as that put into effect by Mr Balfour [Chief Secretary from 1887 to 1891] in Ireland, although it was on a larger scale. In Ireland, Mr Balfour had found a condition of social disorder, chronic trouble, poverty, and misery, which he desired to ameliorate, and he had developed a large scheme for settling labourers on the land. It was not an economic scheme. It involved considerable grants from the State, certainly up to the beginning of the war, if not since. There was no doubt that Ireland had benefitted thereby. It was true she was not contented, but what would have happened in Ireland during the last five years if the same conditions had prevailed as before the Balfour schemes were put into operation? The same applied with regard to houses. About 50,000 had been built in Ireland, largely at the expense of the State. He had been told that they had transformed the whole country.[5]

Lloyd George's characterisation of subsidised Labourers Acts cottages as the product solely of Balfourist 'constructive Unionism' was not historically accurate (as was seen in Chapter 1), but it served the purpose of reminding Conservatives within the post-war Cabinet of their party's role in the policies of Irish land and housing reform.

The results of the major shift in Cabinet thinking towards housing was signalled by a memorandum drawn up in December 1918 by the new President of the English LGB, Sir Auckland Geddes.[6] This paper rejected the cautious line previously taken by this department, and instead supported the call by the Minister of Reconstruction, Christopher Addison, for a more radical post-war housing programme. It was now generally realised that the state would have to meet a more substantial portion of high post-war building costs, since it was politically necessary, to avoid labour agitation, that legal controls on working-class rents be continued for some time after the war (indeed, the 1919 and 1920 Rent Control Acts permitted maximum increases over pre-war levels of 10 per cent and 40 per cent respectively).[7] Geddes recommended the financial proposition that Addison had put forward in March 1918, namely that the state should for a period of seven years meet the excess cost of housing schemes above the produce of a penny-rate levied by the local authority. It constituted a great increase over the previous pledge by the English LGB to simply pay 75 per cent of the annual loan charges. The scheme was also designed to ensure that the smaller or more reluctant municipalities would act, if they knew that they had a fixed liability above which the Exchequer would meet all expenditure.

Various members of the Cabinet were again asked to comment on the latest proposal, and on 27 December 1918 Chief Secretary Shortt duly drew up a memorandum on Irish housing. The Chief Secretary was extremely alarmed at the consequence of offering a subsidy with no stipulated upper limit on state contribution, given that Irish authorities would undoubtedly be more than eager to build:

> I fear that none of the safeguards upon which Sir Auckland Geddes relies to secure the Exchequer against extravagance on the part of the local authorities would, in Ireland, offer adequate protection . . . To fix a border-line of one penny in the pound above which the ratepayers are not to be affected by any increase in the cost of their housing schemes would open up infinite possibilities of extravagance in Ireland, in the way of purchase of sites and the making of contracts . . . The views entertained by the rural district councils as to what should be regarded as 'economic rents' for labourers cottages, according to our experience convinces me that if the Treasury, alone, had to bear the losses involved by reductions of the rent, when the limit of one penny was exceeded, there might be very soon a strike against all rents, save those which were merely nominal and it would be very hard to induce the urban councils to dispossess the occupiers declining to pay.
>
> The only safe policy for this country, I am convinced, is to give a government grant in the shape of a fixed percentage of the annual charge for principal and interest. The percentage should be sufficient to enable the councils, if due economy and forethought are exercised, to build houses without appreciable loss, so that, on the one hand, if councils mismanage their funds, reduce their rents and build unproductive and extravagant houses, the ratepayers will share the burden

with the Exchequer; while on the other hand, if they decline to continue building houses, owing to the losses involved in their schemes, the terms will be sufficiently liberal to enable the Local Government Board to appoint an officer to exercise all their powers under the Housing Acts without undue loss.[8]

The Chief Secretary was thus arguing for the retention of the subsidy system previously devised by the English LGB, but mindful of the demands for greater state subsidy, he ventured that the fixed Exchequer contribution might be increased to 90 per cent of the annual loan charges. In conclusion, Shortt declared that if the Cabinet was to insist that an identical penny-rate subsidy system be given to Ireland, then the responsibility for building must be taken away from local authorities and given to a special Housing Commission.

The Cabinet did not have to respond to the sceptical views expressed by Shortt, for in January 1919 a new Chief Secretary for Ireland was appointed. The new incumbent, Ian Macpherson, was a Liberal Home Ruler, but one who believed that self-government could only be granted once law and order had been enforced, and Sinn Fein eradicated. In the interim, he was committed to a conciliatory policy to quell unrest and redress Irish grievances.[9] Macpherson was a politically significant appointment, for he had been a member of Lloyd George's pre-war Land Enquiry Committee and was versed in the issues of land and housing reform. It was no surprise, therefore, that the new Chief Secretary saw a bold housing initiative as the central and most urgent part of the reconstruction programme. Hitherto, the Cabinet had been wary about making decisions while the larger political issue of Home Rule lay unresolved, but in January 1919 the responsibility for Irish housing policy was handed over squarely to Macpherson. The Acting Cabinet Secretary ruled that it would 'not be necessary to raise the subject at the War Cabinet except in the case of disagreement' (even so, Lloyd George continued to monitor the discussions between the Chief Secretary and the Treasury).[10] On taking office, Macpherson told the Chancellor of the Exchequer, Austen Chamberlain:

> The situation in Ireland at the present time can hardly be exaggerated. Discontent is seething. Anything may happen at any moment, and both His Excellency [Lord Lieutenant French] and myself are strongly convinced that, while we must maintain law and order at all costs, we must at the same time meet the just demands of large public bodies like the Association of Municipal Authorities in Ireland who are clamouring for the fulfilment—long overdue—of a promise that a Scheme of Housing should be introduced and carried through . . . neither His Excellency or myself would seek to overstrain you at the present moment had it not been that our difficulties in Ireland are so stupendous.[11]

The Chief Secretary intended to make housing the centrepiece of his speech on his first visit to Ireland in February 1919, and so before setting off he pleaded with the Treasury Secretary, Stanley Baldwin:

> I need hardly tell you that in Ireland there is grave discontent because no announcement has been made with regard to this important problem, though in this country such an announcement has been made and a Bill even introduced. My predecessor drafted a Memorandum which was submitted in December to the War Cabinet, and about which I have been in communication with the Chancellor. In that Memorandum it is made quite clear that in the interests of the Imperial Exchequer it would not be advisable to have the penny rate . . . I have to go to Ireland towards the end of next week to meet Deputations from Municipal Authorities upon this question, and I would beg of you to place me in the position of being able to make a definite announcement. I do not like having to press in this way, but my position is almost intolerable unless I can make it clear that the interests of the country, which, through no wish of mine, I had been asked to look after, are not lost sight of.[12]

As soon as Macpherson landed in Dublin, he was told by one Castle official:

> I see by to-days Times that you have arrived and will be speaking on Monday about the housing problem. I want you to think over what I said to you about touring the country and devoting a little imagination and enterprise to propaganda. It is easy enough to organise opportunities for you to deliver speeches if you have in your mind a clear idea of a line of policy to counteract the Bolsheviks . . . Set this country talking about you and your schemes for a change.[13]

This was clearly the Chief Secretary's intention, for he immediately told a deputation from the Association of Municipal Authorities of Ireland that the issue 'which had caused more uneasiness in the minds of the public generally had been undoubtedly the housing problem . . . The cry now was for a land for heroes to dwell in. There could not be a better cry, nor could any State carry out a wiser or a better policy'.[14] Over the next few months both Lord Lieutenant French and the Chief Secretary continued to use state housing as a propaganda tool, with for instance Macpherson stating at an official dinner in Belfast that it 'was childish to talk of reform, of a betterment of the working classes if they did not, as a first measure in reform or reconstruction, provide the working classes of the people with better houses to live in. The home was the centre of all things'.[15] The new strand of Irish policy was also much publicised in Britain. In April 1919 the Chief Secretary told the Imperial Parliament of the paramount importance of the housing issue in Ireland:

> Indeed, it was the very first problem which occupied my thoughts when I took office in Ireland, and I set myself to see what could be done, and done quickly . . . On the urban side, the problem is urgent, and more urgent in certain parts of Ireland than in any other part of the United Kingdom. Report after report has disclosed the appalling conditions which, in my judgement, are a disgrace to civilisation . . . They are the allies of death and disease, of immorality and vice all over the world. But in Ireland they are that and something more. They are the allies of Bolshevism and Sinn Fein . . . The problem of housing is largely a problem of health in the family and in the State. A good house, with all the associations of a home, is the most effective weapon, in my judgement, to secure the sanest outlook on life, and is the best guarantee for the moral and physical well-being as well as for self-government.[16]

Yet the intention of the Castle Executive to use housing policy to fight against discontent and rebellion in Ireland—a threat that was, after all, far more real than any faced by the British Government at home—was compromised by the continuing determination of the Treasury to restrict Irish expenditure, and to ensure that British financial interests were paramount. In his initial pledges to Irish municipalities, Chief Secretary Macpherson had stressed that the housing campaign 'should be administered in Ireland and nowhere else, and by Irishmen and no one else'. The *Irish Times* warned prophetically:

> If, however, the Irish Government is to retain its authority for firm administration and is to be able to use to the full its present opportunities for social reform, it must have an absolutely free hand. Recent events suggest that its hands are now tied by influences in London . . . We cannot be sure that the promised blessings will ever reach us until we have definite knowledge that the Irish Government is to be its own master from the *Alpha* to the *Omega* of this great programme of reconstruction.[17]

In the event, Irish scepticism proved to be well founded. The Treasury was opposed to the penny-rate subsidy system in Britain, and so eagerly seized on the continuing doubts within the Castle Administration, repeated by Chief Secretary Macpherson, as to whether it would work in Ireland.[18] The poverty of Irish towns was, as the Attorney General for Ireland explained to Parliament, such that 'in a large number of cases where the conditions are worst and where it is most necessary to build, you would not get any substantial contribution from the community by a penny rate, and practically the whole of the cost would fall upon the State'.[19] Furthermore, there would be no safeguard to compel what were seen as traditionally extravagant Irish municipalities from charging anything but nominal rents, particularly (as was likely) if these bodies came to be controlled by Sinn Fein. The Chancellor of the Exchequer therefore accepted a Treasury note from Sir John Bradbury, in which the latter agreed 'with the Irish Government that the English Scheme (which I have all along regarded as a most dangerous one for Great Britain itself) will, if an attempt is made to apply it to Ireland, lead to wholesale scandal'.[20] However, once the penny-rate system was rejected, there remained for the Treasury and the Castle Administration the dilemma of what alternative might be used instead. In postwar Ireland there would clearly be the same structural problem as in Britain, whereby the continuation of rent control legislation meant that 'economic' rents could not be charged to cover the inflated costs of building new working-class dwellings. The problem then for the British Government was to find a different yet comparable subsidy system, while all the time working under the close scrutiny of interested parties in both Britain and Ireland.

Two other Irish subsidy proposals already lay on the table, but both were unceremoniously dismissed by the Treasury. The suggestion made by Chief Secretary Shortt, for a grant to meet 90 per cent of the annual loan charges, found initial support from his successor, Macpherson. It was rejected by the Treasury, however, on the grounds that it was even more extravagant than the terms it had been forced to concede in Britain. One official warned of 'the outcry it would immediately provoke from the Scotch and English Local Authorities who will have to put a 1d rate before they get anything at all from the Exchequer'.[21] The second alternative was the Irish Convention's proposal that the Exchequer give a free grant amounting to 50 per cent of the capital expenditure of building 67 500 new dwellings. A senior Treasury official noted loftily:

> In connection with the Irish Home Rule discussion last year it was contemplated that Ireland should get this £13,000,000, but that was of course as part of a settlement which would have precluded comparison of the treatment of Local Authorities in the United Kingdom and Ireland respectively by the British Government. For present purposes the incident may I think be disregarded.[22]

Instead, the Treasury devised a novel subsidy system for Ireland, in which the level of state contribution was conditional on the amount of rent that a municipality collected from the houses that it built. A fixed ratio of subsidy was to be set between the typical 'economic' rent necessary to cover building costs and maintenance, and the 'reasonable' rent that an authority could be expected to achieve. The Treasury argued that if an Irish local authority exercised due economy in erecting dwellings and in extracting rent income from new schemes, then in theory it could build with no loss at all to the rates (whereas in Britain every authority would have to bear a penny-rate charge). But the real purpose of the new subsidy proposal for Ireland was to ensure that if there were rent strikes, or if hostile municipalities set rents too low, then the amount of Exchequer subsidy would reduce accordingly. Hence the Treasury noted that its system 'would give the local authorities the strongest possible incentive to charging the highest rents possible and collecting them'.²³ The alternative subsidy proposal was readily accepted by Chief Secretary Macpherson and by Dublin Castle officials such as the Vice-President of the ILGB, Sir Henry Robinson, who also harboured a deep distrust of Irish local authorities. The Treasury Remembrancer pointed out a potential problem if the ILGB were made responsible for assessing the crucial ratio between 'reasonable' and 'economic' rents, adding that this was 'all right while Robinson is there, but if he died or retired, and was succeeded by a disloyalist, the Treasury would be terribly at his mercy'.²⁴ The Treasury gave full reassurance that it alone would fix the ratio of housing subsidy in Ireland.

Once the principle of the new system had been agreed, the Treasury, after further consultation with the ILGB, decided on the fixed subsidy ratio. For every £1 of rent collected, an Irish local authority was to receive £1 subsidy from the Imperial Exchequer. Robinson duly prepared the relevant notice, telling the Treasury that he had 'followed as closely as possible the Circular you approved for the English Local Government Board, and have merely departed from it where it was necessary to do so in order to meet the special arrangements for Ireland'.²⁵ The ILGB circular was issued to Irish municipalities on 31 March 1919. The period of subsidy was fixed at seven years, after which the whole system would be reviewed, especially in the case of local authorities which the ILGB regarded as not being economical or as charging too low rents. Schemes were to be submitted to the ILGB before 15 April 1920, and, as in Britain, were to be completed within three years of the date of enactment of the forthcoming Housing Bill. Robinson had argued that this would not give enough time to deal with housing needs in Ireland, but the Treasury insisted that a strict limit was necessary to ensure that local authorities got on with schemes immediately.²⁶ At the ILGB's instigation, it was agreed that the Exchequer should pay the interest on housing loans for the first year, while initial schemes were being built. This overcame an obvious flaw in the system, for otherwise authorities would not be eligible to receive subsidy until dwellings had been completed and let. In addition, the circular also gave the first notification that a design competition would be held by the RIAI and ILGB.

The constant problem for the Treasury was to convince both British and Irish local authorities that the unique terms being offered to Ireland were neither better nor worse than those for Great Britain. When the decision was made to offer £1 subsidy for every £1 of rent collected, one official was concerned 'that this gives better treatment than in England (or may be represented as so giving)'.²⁷ To stave off potential claims of unequal treatment, the Treasury Secretary, Stanley Baldwin, coined the phrase 'equivalence of subsidy' in a parliamentary reply in March 1919. This became the terminology subsequently used by the Castle Administration to defend the financial proposals.²⁸ It did not, however, stop the question of parity from taking up much of the Treasury's time. 'The joke is that the terms of the Irish Bill are exactly the same as the English Bill', exclaimed an official in exasperation, '. . . as a matter of fact probably a much more advantageous arrangement to a competent Local Authority than the English arrangement. Anyhow that is what the English Authorities think of it.'[29] Yet the truth was, as the Treasury privately admitted, that no-one could work out a proper basis to compare one subsidy system with the other. One official noted that it was 'impossible to get . . . an equation which we could successfully show to the English Authorities was no more favourable to the Irish than the English scheme, and to the Irish that it was no less favourable to them than the English scheme'.[30]

Another controversial issue arising from comparability of treatment with Britain, lay in the nature of housing loans to local authorities. Even though there was a concerted demand from Ireland that preferentially low rates of interest be given from the Local Loans Funds, since the rates for public loans had risen steeply due to post-war financial conditions, the Treasury had to refuse 'in order to prevent outcry from England and Scotland'.[31] There was also outrage in Ireland when Chief Secretary Macpherson initially stated that all Irish municipalities would have to borrow on the open market. This went against the proposal for Britain, where, to alleviate the financial worries of smaller local authorities, it had been agreed that towns with a rateable valuation under £200 000 should continue to qualify for loans from the public purse.[32] The Treasury pointed out that while this restriction excluded a large number of British towns (even those as small as Wrexham or Coatbridge), in Ireland it would mean that only Belfast and Dublin would be disqualified. But, after being reassured by the Castle Administration that it was precisely these two excluded authorities that were likely to provide the vast majority of post-war houses in Ireland, the Treasury reluctantly agreed to maintain parity on this issue. Public loans would therefore be available to every Irish municipality except Belfast and Dublin.[33] This Treasury concession did not, however, resolve the matter. It was clear that the problems faced by Dublin Corporation continued to make it a special hardship case. Rates in Dublin had soared to 17s in the £1 during the war, and political uncertainty about Home Rule meant that investors were extremely unwilling to lend money to Dublin Corporation or to buy its municipal stock. The Vice-President of the ILGB, Sir Henry Robinson, spoke for many Castle officials when he observed:

> The case of Dublin presents the only flaw in a really good scheme. The needs of the workers are so great, the rates are so high that, although the security is undoubted . . . nevertheless the temporary financial difficulties of the Corporation loom so large in the investor's eye and money in the open market would be so hard to get, that I fear the operations of the scheme will hang fire in the one city of the United Kingdom where the conditions of the working classes' houses is, admittedly, the most insanitary and deplorable.[34]

Even the parsimonious Treasury Remembrancer told his superiors:

> You will probably have to give way as to Dublin—it is the only place where housing is really required on a large scale except Belfast. And every Bank would have a profound distrust of the Dublin Corporation *administration*. Perhaps under a Corporation reformed by Proportional Representation (for which we are to have legislation at once) the Bank views might alter . . . But it is really politics: successive Chief Secretaries have talked so much about Dublin that they have to some extent already committed His Majesty's Government.[35]

Under pressure, the Treasury eventually conceded that in the last resort it would be prepared to make Dublin a special case, but only after Belfast Corporation had been forced to raise its housing loans on the private market. An official wrote:

> With regard to Dublin, we may have to let them in eventually, but we must present a stern front until Belfast have burnt their boats (which they are most anxious not to do); and even then I foresee considerable difficulty in establishing against other comers that Dublin is a very special case. Mr Macpherson quite agreed that Dublin may anyhow go through the performance of endeavouring to raise a loan and can only come to us *ex misericordia* when it can say that its efforts to raise money . . . are useless.[36]

The reason for the Treasury's deviousness was obvious. In order to sustain the argument that Dublin was a unique case, it was essential that Belfast Corporation was seen to be borrowing on the private market. Otherwise, it would appear that the whole of Ireland had been granted favoured terms for public housing loans, and there would be an enormous outcry from large British municipalities demanding equivalent treatment. Although the Castle Administration expected that Belfast would have no difficulty in borrowing on attractive terms, the issue continued to beleaguer the post-war housing campaign in Ireland. As redress for considering special treatment for Dublin Corporation, the Treasury insisted that none of the city's notorious slum landlords made a profit out of compulsory acquisition for post-war housing schemes. The Chief Secretary replied that since the ILGB would not sanction the purchase of expensive inner-city sites, where the slum landlords owned their property, then the situation was unlikely to arise.[37]

Given that post-war housing policy was being decided by the British Government with little or no discussion with Irish bodies, it is not surprising that in Ireland there was widespread concern that the country would not receive its fair share of funds for this important initiative.[38] This was of particular worry to Irish observers who shared Chief Secretary Macpherson's belief that a constructive housing policy was the most effective means to stifle unrest. The *Irish Times* wrote that:

> the alternative to social chaos must be found in something very like social revolution ... We have a right to know what Parliament will do to put our housing problem on the same plane of national importance and urgency to which the Government has lifted the problem in Great Britain ... It is very important that the Government should hasten to put a sound and generous programme of Irish legislation in contrast with *Sinn Fein's* barren policy of abstention.[39]

Underlying such statements was a fear about the possible growth of a militant labour movement in Ireland. In late-January 1919 an extraordinary debate on 'Socialism and the War' was held in the Unionist bastion of Trinity College Dublin. A line of heavyweight speakers, including the celebrated Nationalist poet William Butler Yeats, took turns to launch an attack on communism and urge instead the reform of the capitalist system through better working and housing conditions. In reply, the lone socialist and leader of the Irish Labour Party, Thomas Johnston, declared bluntly:

> That testing-time was coming for the Governments of Europe, and its results would prove whether the revolution would be a violent one or not. These revolutions could easily be avoided: cease the exploitation of labour, and there would be no revolution ... Those who did the work should control the work, and, if that idea took hold of the people in Belfast, it might spread through Ireland.[40]

Indeed it was the particular threat of trade union action in Belfast, spreading over from the militancy of 'Red Clyde', that provoked the greatest alarm. Housing was now widely regarded in Ulster as the crucial issue. The *Northern Whig* observed that 'the shortage of housing and the delay in the reduction of the cost of living have been very potent factors in creating and accentuating the prevailing labour unrest'.[41] And at a social reform meeting of the Presbyterian Church in Belfast, a speaker warned that if 'they did not produce some [housing] scheme tolerably soon the inevitable answer would be the rising up of what was called Bolshevism'.[42] The new-found interest of Ulster Unionist politicians was noted in the last chapter, and it grew apace after the Armistice. Sir Edward Carson declared in February 1919 that 'in Ireland, and especially the Constituency I now have the honour to represent [a working-class division of West Belfast], there is no more pressing question at the present moment than housing'.[43] A fellow Unionist MP told Parliament that:

> Not only is bad housing largely responsible for the drink evil, not only is it largely responsible for other evils of that character, but it is largely at the back of that greater evil, Bolshevism, and the extreme Socialism which is stalking through Europe to-day, and is causing so much difficulty, not only to the Government of this nation, but to the Governments of nearly every civilised nation of the world.[44]

The Ulster Unionist Labour Association, in conjunction with Belfast Corporation, sent a housing deputation to the ILGB in February 1919.[45] The key aims of the Ulster Unionists were to kill socialism at home, and also to have Ireland included in British social legislation, since it was believed that administrative integration with the mainland would militate against the introduction of Home Rule. But although the Ulster MPs managed to get Ireland added into Christopher Addison's new public health legislation in early-1919, they were notably less successful in the sphere of housing policy. All the Ulster Unionists could extract from the Castle Administration was a promise that a separate Irish Housing Bill would be passed at the same time as the corresponding measure for Britain.[46]

Nevertheless, from this point on it was the Ulster Unionists who were to lead Irish demands on the post-war housing campaign. This situation had come about for two reasons. Firstly, the Ulster Unionists were now the largest Irish political party in the Imperial Parliament. Thus in mid-1919 the Treasury Remembrancer, Maurice Headlam, warned the Treasury that 'a great opposition is being engineered against your scheme—and Ulster, which is of course strongest in the House of Commons, is I understand leading it'.[47] And, secondly, the housing issue in Southern Ireland was now completely clouded by the alliance between the radical labour movement and Sinn Fein. Two new parties formed in the South believed that they could seize on the housing campaign to win hearts and minds away from Sinn Fein: but neither the Unionist Anti-Partition League, led by Lord Midleton, nor the Irish Centre Party established by Sir Horace Plunkett (erstwhile Chairman of the Irish Convention), managed to establish any real political weight.[48] The rump of the Irish Party, which had been cut to only seven members in the post-war General Election, could do little by itself to influence British housing policy. The IPP's new leader in the House of Commons, Joseph Devlin (the MP for West Belfast), was humiliated into having to work alongside his previous enemies, the Ulster Unionists, in an attempt to secure a better deal for post-war housing in Ireland. Devlin weakly defended his strategy by declaring:

> Until we realise that we have fought for the right of small nations to fashion their own destinies—until that time comes—I am not going to allow my Constituents in Belfast to live under sordid conditions in squalid slums if I get the opportunity of giving them better homes.[49]

Of course, this degree of expediency and compromise only served as a reminder that the days of the old Irish Party were over. Political authority outside Ulster now lay with Sinn Fein, and more uneasily with the military wing of the republican movement, the Irish Republican Army. Sinn Fein won 73 seats in the post-war election, some three-quarters of the total representation for Ireland. Not a single one of these newly-elected members took up his seat in the Imperial Parliament in Westminster. Instead they unofficially constituted themselves as Dáil Éireann, the first republican Parliament.[50] The Dáil grew in strength, forming its own parallel executive government, administrative departments, and legal system. However, increasing harassment from the Castle Administration made it virtually impossible for Dáil Éireann and its unofficial departments to carry out their business. Eventually Sinn Fein was proscribed as illegal in most of Ireland in September 1919. The refusal of the democratic representatives of the majority of the Irish people to participate in post-war housing legislation might have been expected to produce a situation in which Sinn Fein would refuse to have anything to do with British housing proposals. But in fact the issue of urban housing was one on which the Dáil Éireann found it difficult to maintain a consistent position of opposition to British rule. Sinn Fein was essentially a conservative and lower-middle-class party, and it was always careful to distinguish itself from the social revolutionary uprisings elsewhere in Europe. Its leadership realised that any image of radicalism could alienate important sources of political and financial support, notably from the Roman Catholic hierarchy at home and from the Irish-American community in the United States. Yet, as has been noted previously, at the same time Sinn Fein was politically dependent on the radical labour movement in Southern Ireland. It therefore could not afford to stay silent about issues such as better working-class housing. The contradictory tendencies within Sinn Fein could be seen in the 'Democratic Programme' that was drawn up by the inaugural meeting of Dáil Éireann as a blueprint for the new republic. Many of the Sinn Fein political leaders were either imprisoned or abroad on diplomatic missions, and so the leader of the Irish Labour Party, Thomas Johnson, was able to insert a declaration which (although subsequently toned down) promised sweeping improvements in social welfare.[51] Yet clearly this document was intended merely as a temporary expedient to maintain republican unity, and did not correspond to any deep-seated commitment to social reform from Sinn Fein or its leader, Eamonn de Valera.[52] Sinn Fein's problems in balancing the demands of conservative Nationalists and labour representatives were eagerly exploited by political opponents. *The Times* argued that logically the Dáil should refuse British housing subsidy, but asked pointedly 'whether Sinn Fein will be foolish enough to hasten its own downfall by an unpopular movement of this kind, for the need for better housing in Ireland is widespread and acute'.[53] For the most part, the Dáil Éireann tried to avoid discussions on potentially divisive social issues. But the pressure from the labour movement could not be indefinitely postponed. On 17 June 1919 the Dáil was compelled to issue a decree which stated that 'the provision of suitable houses for the working classes is declared to be a matter of deep concern to the Nation and of urgent importance to the well-being of the people'.[54] A special Housing Committee was formed to look into the question, although, as will be seen again later, the attitude of Sinn Fein towards the Irish housing campaign was to remain ambivalent.

THE 1919 IRISH HOUSING ACT AND REACTIONS IN IRELAND

By mid-1919 both the British Government and the Castle Administration were well advanced with plans for the post-war housing campaign, and legislation was promised at once. The fundamental difference between the proposals for Ireland and those for mainland Britain was that in Ireland there was a far greater fragmentation of policy. One distinct initiative, as will be seen in the next chapter, was for the state to build cottages directly for returning ex-servicemen under the 1919 Irish Land (Provision for Soldiers and Sailors) Act. A further complication arose from the pre-war division between rural and urban housing programmes in Ireland. Rural housing was now universally acknowledged to be a residual issue, given the success of the Labourers Acts in providing nearly 48 000 cottages by the end of the First World War. Therefore, the Irish Labourers Act that was passed in late-1919 was a deliberately minor affair, serving only to widen eligibility to any rural worker who earned a wage, even if they were employed full-time in a craft or industry. No further money was allocated, since there still remained around £1 110 000 of unsanctioned funds available from pre-war legislation. And the Treasury, determined to ensure that the rural programme would proceed as slowly as possible, ruled against any increase on the pre-war level of subsidy paid for each dwelling, even when it was found that the average cost of the smallest house type had more than doubled to around £450.[55] The outcome was that, after the First World War, state housing in rural Ireland came to a virtual end (see Diagram B and Table 1). The priorities of the Castle Administration were now entirely different, as Chief Secretary Macpherson told Parliament in May 1919:

> The housing problem in Ireland was, in the past, largely a rural problem . . . Nothing has been so remarkable as the success of Irish rural housing . . . We are now faced with a more difficult problem—the housing problem as it affects Ireland in the cities.[56]

Hence the centrepiece of the post-war programme was to be the building of 50 000 urban cottages under the 1919 Housing (Ireland) Act. The Castle Administration repeatedly stressed that the target figure was proportionately far greater per head of urban population than the pledges that had been made for England and Wales, or Scotland. A separate legislative measure was deemed necessary for Ireland because of the unique subsidy system and the fact that rural areas had to be excluded. Otherwise, the Irish Housing Bill was closely modelled on that for England and Wales, and was introduced in early-April 1919, barely a fortnight after the latter.[57] Chief Secretary Macpherson hoped to reassure Irish MPs that progress in Ireland was viewed by the Government as just as vital as the mainstream 'homes for heroes' campaign in Britain, but his efforts proved unsuccessful. Acrimony marked the parliamentary debate on Irish housing legislation in the summer of 1919, in complete contrast to the virtual unanimity over the proposals for Britain. Irish protests were orchestrated by the Ulster Unionists, and focused on what was perceived as the unfairness of the subsidy system. A particular bone of contention was the potential consequences of forcing Belfast and Dublin Corporations to borrow on the open market, rather than providing them with low-interest public loans. A member of the Chief Secretary's staff pointed out to the Treasury that:

> owing to the difference between the British and Irish subsidy schemes, the consideration of the rate of interest at which it can borrow is not a matter of paramount importance to a British local authority, seeing that the burden of any excessive rate will be borne by the subsidy, whereas it is vital to an Irish local authority seeing that in their case the burden will fall on the local rates.[58]

The Treasury admitted that the problem was a genuine one, but was determined not to give way. As a result, the Chief Secretary was placed in an invidious position when dealing with Irish protests over the financial proposals. The Treasury Remembrancer reported that Macpherson had in private confided 'that he "could not justify" the differential treatment—and as the difference is due to the fact that Irish local authorities are not to be trusted, that is extremely likely'.[59] Calls for a fundamental rethinking of the subsidy system, and for the provision of public loans to Belfast Corporation, were raised by many Ulster Unionist and Irish Party MPs during the second reading on 13 May 1919. But, on balance, Irish MPs felt it better to downplay such criticisms rather than risk losing what was described by one Irish Party member as 'a great reform', and by an Ulster Unionist MP as 'one of the greatest Bills ever brought in for Ireland in our time'.[60]

However, the problems for Chief Secretary Macpherson flared up again when the financial estimates for the Irish Housing Bill were published in an extremely vague 'White Paper'. This document simply concluded that it was 'not practicable to do much more than guess at the ultimate annual charges, so uncertain are many of the factors'.[61] Since it was deemed impossible to say whether the average cost of a post-war dwelling might be £500 or £600 or £700 each, the estimated capital expenditure to build the target of 50 000 cottages was simply calculated as lying between £25 000 000 and £35 000 000. Then, assuming that expenditure would be spread over the three-year period proposed in the legislation, the total figure was crudely divided up such that the expenditure in 1919–20 was estimated as 20 per cent of the total; that for 1920–21 was assumed to be 40 per cent of the total; and that for 1921–22 the remaining 40 per cent. The 'White Paper' calculated that, given a subsidy ratio of £1 for every £1 of rent collected, and if average rents were set at just under 10s per week, then the Exchequer would have to provide £12 10s a year for every house that was built in Ireland. In this instance, the maximum subsidy contribution on the full 50 000 cottages would come to £625 000 per annum. However, if rents were fixed at just under 12s per week, then the state contribution would be £15 a year for every house and the maximum subsidy total would rise to £750 000 per annum. And if rents were just over 15s per week, then the figure would be £20 a year up to a limit of £1 000 000 per annum. This degree of financial vagueness was not unique to the Irish proposals. It was also a feature of the comparable calculations produced by the English LGB, but there it provoked little criticism.[62] In contrast, the woolly financial estimates for the Irish Housing Bill provoked an intense debate in the Imperial Parliament during the committee stage in late-June and early-July 1919. Conservative MPs were alarmed that there was no upper limit placed on the potential contribution from the Exchequer, but Irish members, after reminding Parliament that this was also a feature of the English subsidy system, counter-attacked by launching a concerted campaign to extract a better financial deal from the British Government.[63] For the next week there was deadlock over the financial proposals. On 2 July 1919, Chief Secretary Macpherson received a deputation of Irish municipal representatives, led by Belfast Corporation, and augmented by Ulster Unionist and Irish Party MPs. The deputation left him with a clear ultimatum that if the Irish housing campaign was to proceed at all, then more attractive subsidy terms would have to be provided.[64]

The Chief Secretary had staked his whole political future on the success of the Irish housing campaign, and so now, in desperation, he asked the Chancellor of the Exchequer and the Treasury for some urgent financial concessions. After dragging its heels, the Treasury agreed to a compromise formula whereby it would publicly announce that public loans could be given in the last resort to Belfast and Dublin Corporations, but only on the condition that it did not have to pledge that any housing advances to Ireland would be at preferentially low rates of interest.[65] More importantly, Chief Secretary Macpherson was also able to secure a slight improvement in the Irish subsidy terms. At first, the Chief Secretary attempted to placate the anger of Irish members by offering a special subsidy of 25s for every £1 of rent collected for those individual councils that the ILGB designated as 'exceptional cases'. When this partial gesture not surprisingly failed to satisfy his critics, Macpherson went back again to the Treasury to demand an across-the-board increase. Now he wanted a subsidy ratio of 25s for every £1 collected, rising to 27s 6d for authorities classified as having special difficulties. The Treasury at first refused on the grounds that any further financial concession would only incense British municipalities. But it was forced to relent when the Chancellor of the Exchequer, for purely political reasons, decided to support the Castle Administration. The Treasury notified the Irish Office:

> While we feel considerable hesitation in giving further increases to Ireland the Chancellor of the Exchequer is prepared to agree to this proposal on the understanding that it is accepted as a firm bargain in settlement of all claims, and that all other financial amendments will be dropped . . . The Chief Secretary will . . . realise we cannot have this

offer used as a jumping-off place for further demands . . . If you let the Irish members know that we have already agreed to it they will immediately think they can get something more by further pressure.[66]

English MPs were outraged by these secret negotiations. However, the Castle Administration was determined to use this hard-won Treasury concession to full advantage. On 8 July 1919, the Attorney General for Ireland triumphantly announced the new subsidy terms to the parliamentary committee. Subsequently, he reminded Irish members that Chief Secretary Macpherson had gone 'a long way in trying to get all the concessions that he could in reference to the finance of the Bill and other matters'.[67]

The 1919 Housing (Ireland) Act was passed on 15 August 1919. Compulsion was placed for the first time on Irish municipalities to meet the housing need in their area, and if they failed to do so, then the ILGB was given powers to carry out the function on their behalf. The procedure for acquiring housing sites was simplified, and local authorities were given greater power to obtain suburban land in order to build 'Part 3' schemes. Some weak town-planning clauses were also included, but these lagged far behind those in Britain; significantly, the Irish measure was not termed a 'Housing, Town Planning, etc., Act', like that for the mainland. The 1919 Irish Housing Act envisaged that municipalities would be the main vehicle for providing new urban housing, although a lesser subsidy was also offered to public utility societies and housing trusts (the terms were the same as for Britain, and consisted of a subsidy of 30 per cent on the annual charge for housing loans). To enable more private tenants to buy their homes, the limit on the market value of dwellings eligible for low-interest loans under the 1899 Small Dwellings Acquisition Act was raised from £400 to £800. Many Unionist and Irish Party MPs believed that home-ownership should also be increased by selling off even the new dwellings that were to be built by local authorities.[68] On 19 August 1919 the ILGB issued an explanatory circular, and gave official notice that Irish municipalities would in fact be entitled to 25s subsidy for every £1 of rent collected, in ordinary cases, and 27s 6d subsidy where financial circumstances were adjudged to be particularly adverse.

The manoeuvres of Chief Secretary Macpherson had finally succeeded in steering the 1919 Irish Housing Act through Parliament. It was no guarantee, however, that the measure would enjoy a good reception in Ireland. Only a very few commentators, such as the editor of the *Northern Whig*, were of the opinion that the Irish subsidy system was more generous than that for Britain.[69] Instead, from August 1919 a huge wave of opposition grew in Ireland that embraced the Ulster Unionists, the Unionist Anti-Partition League, the Irish Party, the Association of Municipal Authorities of Ireland, and newspapers such as the *Irish Times*.[70] The Housing Committee of the Dublin Chamber of Commerce even engaged a leading English housing and town planning expert, Henry Aldridge, to produce calculations to demonstrate that Irish urban authorities would be much worse off than their British counterparts. These findings were duly forwarded to the Castle Administration and the Treasury.[71] The Treasury Remembrancer observed that Chief Secretary Macpherson was 'evidently rather frightened' about the outcry against his housing scheme.[72] This simply reinforced the Treasury's determination that no further concessions be given.

A further twist to the problems faced by the Castle Administration arose from the need of the republican Dáil Éireann to commit itself to the housing programme, in order to sustain the alliance with the radical labour movement. The Irish Labour Party and Trade Union Congress passed a resolution in August 1919 which called for the creation of a special council of municipal and building union representatives, so as to press ahead with rehousing work irrespective of British Government proposals.[73] A further pressure on Sinn Fein came from its desire to extend political control over Southern Ireland by contesting the first post-war municipal elections, scheduled to be held in January 1920. The Irish Labour Party had declared its intention to stand in many of the municipal elections, and made it clear that it would be campaigning on radical labour issues such as state housing.[74] Thus in late-July and early-August 1919 the Housing Committee of the Dáil Éireann met three times under the chairmanship of William Cosgrave, the unofficial Minister of Local Government, and reported that:

> The Committee proceeded at once to deal with the ways and means of securing adequate housing accommodation for the working classes. The provisions in the Bill before the English Legislature were examined and the committee after due consideration of the facilities afforded by it, and the fact that there was at present no better machinery available; the present cost of buildings and building material which practically precludes private enterprises from undertaking the responsibilities of such a vast and costly scheme as is necessary; and the notoriously inadequate housing accommodation in Urban Districts which seriously reacts on the health and efficiency of the working population in these districts; unanimously decided to recommend that Local Authorities should proceed 'full steam ahead' to avail themselves of the facilities offered them in that Bill.[75]

In addition, the Housing Committee declared that 'as a well-informed and sympathetic public opinion was considered absolutely necessary, it was decided that a propaganda campaign be begun at once'.[76]. Members of the Dáil and all urban Sinn Fein branches were sent a number of papers 'outlining the principles of proper housing schemes' and explaining the terms of the 1919 Irish Housing Act. A series of local Housing Conferences were set up in 12 regional centres, each to be attended by a member of the Dáil's Housing Committee along with Sinn Fein municipal representatives.[77]

It was a remarkable state of affairs for the Dáil Éireann to be openly recommending that Irish municipalities should accept British housing legislation and British housing subsidy. However, it is equally apparent that Sinn Fein also realised that having to rely on Treasury loans would prove to be an administrative noose for republican councils. Already there were extensive fund-raising campaigns being organised by Irish republican groups in the USA. With the personal help of Eamonn de Valera in 1919–20, a total of around $6 000 000 was netted; of this, nearly three-quarters was actually spent in Ireland on the political and military campaign against British rule.[78] But while Dáil Éireann would never consider using essential funds for matters such as housing, the pattern was set for the most bizarre episode of the post-war Irish housing campaign. In late-August 1919, a previously unknown body called the National Development Company of Ireland announced that it would be prepared to grant housing loans at 5 per cent interest over 50 years. The money was apparently to come out of a staggering £150 000 000 fund.[79] The frontman for the shadowy organisation was J. J. Kelly, a Dublin businessman and alderman. He claimed that the money had been put up by a combination of Irish-American and Scottish trusts. Kelly persuaded the Sinn Fein Chairman of Dublin Corporation's Housing Committee, Alderman Thomas Kelly, that the Corporation should apply for a loan of £1 000 000. Soon a host of other Irish urban authorities were making inquiries, ranging from Cork Corporation to Belfast Corporation. These startling developments were followed with keen interest in Ireland and Britain, although no-one was ever quite sure whether the loan offer was genuine or not.[80] The Castle Administration regarded it as but another part of Dáil Éireann's propaganda campaign, and the Treasury Remembrancer reported back to his superiors in Whitehall:

> The Sinn Feiners are having great success with their loan in America, and they are proposing to lend the proceeds to the Dublin Corporation for Housing purposes. This will be the loan in the open market which you have been urging on Dublin—and Belfast—as opposed to the Government loan which was asked for. The result will be that the British Government will be practically guaranteeing the interest on the Sinn Fein loan.[81]

In reply, the Treasury stated that it did 'not see much harm in the Sinn Feiners' voting their money to the Dublin housing'.[82] But in the event, the National Development Company of Ireland turned out to be run by a dubious Irish-American financier, Patrick Kieran, as part of his multifarious attempts to make a fortune from post-war reconstruction projects. Alderman J. J. Kelly was an innocent whose involvement soon turned to nightmare when the scheme collapsed. Kelly tried to sue to recover the money that he had put into the project, and was attacked physically and lost his post as alderman on his return to Ireland.[83] Within a year, Kieran had been declared bankrupt, and the whole episode appears to have been a huge confidence trick that traded on the desperate housing needs of Irish municipalities.

The compromise that the Dáil Éireann was now being forced to make on the housing issue was most clearly revealed when the unofficial Minister of Local Government, William Cosgrave, attended a special conference organised by the Association of Municipal Authorities of Ireland on 22 October 1919. Cosgrave was nominally attending in the capacity as one of the delegates from Dublin Corporation (along with Alderman Thomas Kelly and Councillor Coughlan Briscoe). But his true role would have been known to everyone present. Cosgrave's presence therefore represented the first time that Sinn Fein had joined with its political opponents to denounce as inadequate the post-war housing plans of a Government that it refused to recognise! The conference was addressed by the ILGB's housing expert, Dr Peter Cowan. Yet despite his plea that local authorities now get on with their housing schemes, the Association of Municipal Authorities of Ireland resolved that it should first campaign for a further increase in Exchequer subsidy. Cosgrave in his report back to Dáil Éireann rejected the whole principle of the Treasury's rent-based subsidy system.[84] Instead he argued for a return to the subsidy system used in the Irish Labourers Acts, combined in the case of Dublin with a gradual increase in the local rates to create a special housing levy of 1s in the £1. The proposal was typical of Cosgrave's conservative attitude towards financial matters, and was undoubtedly conceived with the intention of minimising the subsidy commitment that might be expected from a future Sinn Fein Government. Nevertheless, the inherent implication of his report was that Sinn Fein, like all other political groups in Ireland, was committed in principle to an extensive programme of state housing.

EFFORTS TO IMPLEMENT THE POST-WAR IRISH HOUSING CAMPAIGN

At the end of 1919, the ground would therefore appear to have been prepared for the post-war housing campaign in Ireland. The survey returns prepared by local authorities under the 1919 Irish Housing Act revealed a total need of 61 648 dwellings, a higher figure than the Castle Administration's previous estimate of 50 000 houses.[85] Soon the great majority of municipalities had submitted proposed schemes comprising altogether nearly 42 000 urban dwellings.[86] However, at this same point the Irish housing campaign ran into a fundamental difficulty that stemmed from Britain. Swenarton has noted the unwillingness of the Lloyd George Coalition Government to impinge on the interests of the industrialists, businessmen, and City financiers, on whom it relied for power.[87] The Cabinet refused to bring in controls that would give housing schemes priority in the use of materials and labour, and its decision in December 1919 to prepare for a return to the pre-war 'Gold Standard' (as recommended by the Treasury and the City of London) meant that there was insufficient finance available for local authorities to borrow for housing schemes. As a result, the housing campaign throughout the United Kingdom was simply not receiving the allocation of resources that was required. The

Government was forced to announce two important expedients in November 1919. First, a Treasury Committee was set up to devise a new method for local authorities to raise housing loans on the open market, and thereby to head off the growing demands from the larger local authorities in Britain that they be provided with public funds. Since in Ireland this particular issue affected only Dublin and Belfast Corporations, and given that the Treasury had already secretly agreed to a concession in the case of Dublin, there was little for the Irish representative on the committee to do but go along with the recommendation that municipalities be permitted to issue special 'Local Housing Bonds'.[88] The Treasury hoped that this new initiative in Britain might also help to delay the point at which it might be forced to grant public loans to either Dublin or Belfast Corporations. An official noted that only when 'they have tried to raise stock or Local Bonds on reasonable terms and have failed, it will be time to consider whether special terms are required to get them out of their difficulty'.[89] In the event, the admittedly reluctant attempts of these two largest Irish authorities to raise funds through special 'Local Housing Bonds' was to achieve little.

The second innovation launched by the British Government in late-1919 was to offer state housing subsidy to private builders, as one strand of the miscellaneous provisions contained in the Housing (Additional Powers) Act.[90] The original draft of the new Housing Bill excluded Ireland and Scotland, and simply allocated a sum of £15 000 000 to subsidise a total of 100 000 dwellings to be built by private contractors in England and Wales. When the Minister of Health, Christopher Addison, introduced the new measure on 21 November 1919, he was forced to give a spirited defence against accusations that the housing campaign throughout the United Kingdom had all but collapsed. Irish MPs also used the debate to launch a bitter attack on the Castle Administration. One Ulster Unionist declared of the housing initiative that 'whether or not it has broken down in respect of England, Scotland, and Wales, it has undoubtedly broken down in respect of Ireland . . . We need the help of the Government more urgently in Ireland than in England or Scotland'.[91] Irish members demanded an immediate change in the system of municipal subsidy, as well as the extension to Ireland of the £150 grant now being proposed for private building contractors in Britain.

Chief Secretary Macpherson, who had not been consulted about the proposal to introduce private subsidy, stoutly denied that the Irish housing campaign was in trouble. He glossed over the fact that so far only two houses had been completed in Ireland. Instead, Macpherson pointed out that over 90 of the 127 Irish municipalities had submitted schemes to the ILGB, and that the latter had given approval for a total of 42 housing sites. He confidently proclaimed:

> With regard to the urban side, I say that the Irish Housing Act is a good one. I know that when I introduced a scheme entirely different, financially and otherwise, from the scheme which was introduced for

England and Scotland, I took my own political reputation in my hands, but the longer I live the more content I am to stand by that scheme . . . I am a great believer in the Irish scheme.[92]

The Chief Secretary gave a pledge to Parliament that he would urgently consider whether to introduce subsidy for private builders in Ireland. But in writing to the Chancellor of the Exchequer, Macpherson was decidedly lukewarm:

So far as I can see at present I am not altogether convinced of the necessity of extending this provision to Ireland, though if it is not granted we are certain to be strongly criticised. There is this much to be said for it, that if the provision of houses is left altogether in the hands of local authorities the contractors will form rings to force up the prices. If, however, we encourage private enterprise, as Addison proposes, the builders will make every effort to keep prices down.[93]

The Treasury was also less than enthusiastic about extending the new intiative, but saw one potential benefit were private subsidy to be granted to Ireland. As an official noted:

I am inclined to think that the £150 will be cheaper than the subsidy (in Ireland 25/- for every £ of rent collected) and may save us from giving improved subsidy terms to Ireland (of which premonitory rumblings are going on) . . . On the merits therefore I should be rather inclined to let Irish builders have the £150 . . . Moreover it will be difficult to refuse Ireland what is given to England and Scotland . . . I think the responsibility for deciding should be left with the Irish Government.[94]

Given the concerted demands from Ireland in favour of private subsidy, the Castle Administration duly wrote to the Minister of Health asking to be included in the new Housing Bill. On 3 December 1919 the Chancellor of the Exchequer, Austen Chamberlain, told the Housing Committee of the Cabinet 'that providing that the sum of £15,000,000 was not exceeded for the United Kingdom he had no objection to the number of houses being varied from the figure of 100,000 originally proposed'.[95] To provide more cottages would have meant dropping the subsidy for each house below the £150 level, which was seen as making the offer unattractive to private builders. So instead, the target ceiling of 100 000 dwellings was retained, but now the figure was to be shared out across the United Kingdom. Provisional agreement was reached that the subsidy under the 1919 Housing (Additional Powers) Act should be allocated in the following proportions: £12 000 000 for England and Wales; £1 650 000 for Scotland; and £1 350 000 for Ireland. The share for Ireland was estimated as sufficient to subsidise 9000 privately-built dwellings.[96] The new Housing Act received Royal Assent in late-December 1919, and was also notable for being the only piece of post-war British housing legislation—and indeed the first measure for nearly 30 years—to directly include Ireland in its provisions.

In drafting a circular to notify Irish builders about the terms for private grants, the Treasury insisted that the ILGB inserted a clause which, unlike in Britain, limited the application of the 1919 Housing (Additional Powers) Act to only the urban areas covered by the main Irish Housing Act.[97] The ILGB circular was finally issued to all Irish local authorities on 23 April 1920, and followed the English precedent in that it now offered a variable subsidy that depended on the size of the house that was built. Private builders were entitled to a £160 grant for a five- or six-roomed parlour house, provided that the total floor area was a minimum of 920 square feet; a £140 grant for a four-roomed non-parlour house if the total floor area was a minimum of 780 square feet; or a grant of £130 for a three-roomed non-parlour house of at least 700 square feet. No house over 1400 square feet was eligible for subsidy, thereby ruling out larger middle-class dwellings. All dwellings had to be started after 23 December 1919 and be completed by 23 December 1920. The continued dominance of British interests in this matter was shown by the fact that, only a month after the ILGB circular was issued, the Minister of Health, without consulting the Irish Administration, decided to increase the level of private subsidy by £100 in each of the three size categories.[98] The obvious consequence of raising the subsidy to £230–260, was to reduce significantly the number of dwellings that could be built out of Ireland's share of the overall grant. If Irish contractors were to decide to provide only the largest type of dwellings, for instance, then the potential total might be as low as 5200 cottages.

Nevertheless, by the end of 1919 Ireland had a legislative programme that was broadly analogous to that in Britain. Both possessed a main Housing Act now augmented by a supplementary measure which, amongst other things, widened the subsidy to private speculators. Swenarton has noted that in England the effect of the post-war campaign was to switch the primary responsibility for state housing from local authorities to central government.[99] The process of centralisation in Ireland was both more marked and more complex, since the unique conditions of colonial rule meant the involvement also of an intermediary administrative tier in Dublin Castle. The Castle Administration had to implement a housing policy which had been decided in Westminster, and in many instances its officials resentfully felt that they were being kept in the dark. In February 1919 the ILGB wrote to the Under Secretary for Ireland that:

> in view of the statements appearing in the Press as to the intentions of the Government with respect to the financing of housing schemes in England, Scotland and Wales, it would be desirable that the Board [ILGB] should be furnished as soon as possible with information as to what arrangements are contemplated in this respect as regards housing in Ireland in order that they may be in a position to dispel the

uncertainty and misconception on this head at present prevailing throughout the country.[100]

The greatest contribution made by the ILGB was to sort out problems created by ill-considered decisions made in Westminster. It was the ILGB's Vice-President, Sir Henry Robinson, who pointed out to the Treasury that the state would need to pay the initial interest on loans while dwellings were being built. He also suggested that if a local authority decided to charge deliberately high rents in order to receive more subsidy, and thereby make a profit, then the state contribution should be reduced accordingly.[101] In reward for this help, the Treasury ruled that the Irish housing campaign should be overseen by the ILGB, and not by an independent Housing Commission as recommended by many Irish MPs.[102] In England and Wales, the responsibility for the housing campaign was transferred to the newly-created Ministry of Health, which sat at the head of a three-tier hierarchy in which regional housing commissions acted as mediators between local authorities and central government.[103] In Ireland, the intermediary role was fulfilled by a hand-picked advisory Housing Committee, set up in May 1919 as a nominally independent body.[104] In reality, the Housing Committee was simply another arm of the ILGB. The chairman was the ILGB's Chief Engineering Inspector and housing expert, Dr Peter Cowan. Two other members were Louis Deane, the ILGB's Chief Architect, and Charles O'Connor, who had presided over the 1913–14 ILGB Dublin Housing Inquiry prior to becoming Chairman of the Agricultural Wages Board. The predominance of ILGB officials was widely criticised by municipalities in Ulster and Southern Ireland. So, to present at least an image of impartiality, the final place on the Housing Committee was given to Hugh Law, a Unionist barrister. But as Sir Henry Robinson later explained to the Treasury:

> I succeeded in persuading Macpherson that it [the English system] was unnecessarily extravagant, and he got over it by promising a Housing Committee with outsiders represented thereon. He was asked if the Committee he proposed to set up would be independent of the Local Government Board, and he erroneously replied—'Yes, certainly', but as a matter of fact, the Committee, its finance and policy, is rigidly controlled by the Local Government Board . . . However, Macpherson's assurance was accepted, and the only claim which our Housing Committee has to be regarded as a departure from the old system and a fulfilment of the Chief Secretary's promise, is the presence of Law as one of its members.[105]

The primary concern of the Housing Committee was to provide a general stimulus for the housing programme, and it met regularly to advise on design and to discuss a wide range of financial and procedural issues.[106]

The actual Housing Department within the ILGB, like its counterpart in the Ministry of Health on the mainland, continued to direct overall policy and to approve or reject individual housing schemes submitted by Irish municipalities. The permanent ILGB Housing Inspector was the recently demobilised Colonel J. F. MacCabe, who had also sat on the 1913–14 Dublin Housing Inquiry. Under him were between three and five 'temporary' housing inspectors, most of whom were architects. The most respected and longest serving inspector was Thomas Joseph Byrne, who had of course come to note by designing labourers' cottages for South Dublin RDC and the war-time McCaffrey Estate for Dublin Corporation. The *Irish Builder* wrote of Byrne that 'it is no reflection on other Irish architects to say that he is by far the best authority on housing in Ireland', and undoubtedly his appointment to an important position in the ILGB helped to establish Unwinian garden suburb design as official policy.[107] Other inspectors included Thomas Strahan (later to become the Chief Housing Inspector for the new Ministry of Local Government after independence, and a founder member in 1923 of the Dublin Civic Survey Committee), and yet another architect, Frank Aylward.[108] The staff of both the Housing Committee and the ILGB's Housing Department were of the highest calibre available in Ireland. But despite this undisputed eminence, as soon as it became likely that there might be no real progress under the Irish housing campaign, the administrative mechanism that had been carefully set up by the ILGB was continually weakened by threats of retrenchment emanating from the Treasury in Whitehall.

An example of the ILGB's relative impotence was its inability to secure a sufficient and cheap supply of building materials, and particularly bricks, for the post-war Irish housing campaign. In England and Wales the Cabinet had authorised the Ministry of Munitions (and subsequently the Ministry of Health) to buy housing materials in bulk, as a less contentious alternative to prioritising the whole supply of materials through building controls.[109] The ILGB's Housing Department estimated that post-war materials costs in Ireland were now 300–400 per cent above pre-war levels, and therefore that the potential savings offered by mass purchasing were substantial. But although the Treasury agreed to incorporate Scotland into the policy of bulk purchasing, it refused to do the same for Ireland despite repeated pressure from the Castle Administration from May 1919 onwards.[110] It was another example of the Treasury's overriding concern to protect British interests at the expense of attempts to stimulate the flagging Irish housing drive.

DESIGN STANDARDS FOR THE IRISH HOUSING CAMPAIGN

A central concern of the Irish Administration, and particularly the ILGB, was to ensure that post-war state housing would be built to a higher standard than hitherto seen in Ireland. By early-1919 the basis for design standards was no longer Dr Peter Cowan's *Report on Dublin Housing* of the previous year, but the far more generous recommendations of the Tudor Walters Report. It signalled an almost universal acceptance in Ireland that the undoubted source of 'modern' housing design was Britain. Swenarton has argued that the Lloyd George Cabinet believed that the quality of post-war dwellings was equally as important as the quantitative aspect of the housing campaign. In other words, architectural design was seen as a central part of the policy of using state housing as tangible proof of the irrelevance of revolution.[111] In Ireland, a similar climate of opinion led to calls for demonstrably better houses for the working class, and was expressed in the views of politicians, the press, and professional bodies such as the RIAI. The *Irish Times* stated that 'the type of house now demanded is more spacious, and contains many more conveniences than the house which was regarded a few years ago as an ideal "workman's dwelling"'.[112] The editor of the *Irish Builder* wrote of the threat posed by bad housing:

> If we are to avoid a spirit of social revolt, leading perhaps to anarchy, the problem must be dealt with in a wide and statesmanlike way, and the houses made comfortable, convenient and attractive, a system in which garden plots must be an essential feature, as well as abundant open spaces.[113]

It was therefore with considerable conviction that Chief Secretary Macpherson declared that new dwellings must be built as what he described as 'happier homes'.[114] The new leader of the Irish Party, Joseph Devlin, echoed the sentiment:

> I think also there ought to be . . . greater attention paid to the character of these houses . . . This ought to be a Bill not only to rush people into rooms where they can live and sleep, but it should be one for the purpose of making the whole surroundings a thing of beauty, an attraction, a fascination, something which will make those who live in the houses believe that, after all, we are not engaged in camouflage when, in Parliament or outside, we say to the people that we want to make these Islands lands fit for heroes to live in.[115]

Improvements in housing design were to be achieved in a number of ways. In terms of layout, it was believed that the healthier atmosphere and recreational benefits of suburban estates would create a better standard of living. Hence the Ulster Unionist leader, Sir Edward Carson, stated that he would 'like to see these houses extend more and more out into the country'.[116] Aesthetically, there were calls for a more careful consideration of the 'architectural qualities', or in other words the exterior design, of suburban cottages.[117] Another concern was to increase internal space provision through the provision of a parlour where possible, and by requiring a minimum of three bedrooms. The justification for the latter provision was to allow gender separation in children's sleeping arrangements. As one Irish MP observed, this would 'make the life of the people sweeter and better, and . . . more Christian'.[118] Domestic arrangements were also to be raised by providing improved services such as electricity or a hot water supply. Chief Secretary Macpherson opined that he was 'glad to think that every house will provide for a bathroom and a wash-house'.[119] The corollary of higher standards was an unprecedented consensus in Ireland that felt that only trained architects were qualified to design post-war housing schemes. 'The actual planning, the architectural side of the work, is very difficult', noted one Ulster Unionist MP, 'calling for special experience and qualifications in those who are responsible for it, if full advantage is to be taken of the site.'[120] It was a view that was fully supported by the Castle Administration, with the ILGB notifying municipalities that 'the assistance of competent Architects is indispensable'.[121]

The RIAI tried to capitalise on the new mood in its continuing battle to strengthen the architectural profession in Ireland. Its model as always was the Royal Institute of British Architects, which was closely involved in housing preparations on the mainland, and in 1919 had confidently raised the recommended fee-scale for architects from 5 to 6 per cent to cover post-war inflation. In Ireland, the RIAI and its Honorary Secretary, Harry Alberry, made housing its primary interest from early-1919. A Housing Committee was formed to consider issues such as materials shortages, fee-scales for housing work, and the need for a housing design competition.[122] The RIAI's motivation was partly that of self-interest, for it saw an opportunity to expand the workload of its members, and thereby to attract more recruits. It expanded noticeably in the post-war period, with the *Irish Builder* writing in January 1920 that the RIAI 'has had a busy year, notably in questions associated with housing, and has this year taken the step of throwing open its membership to a much wider circle than was previously eligible'.[123] However, there was also a deep belief amongst Irish architects that their involvement would lead to cost-effectiveness in housing design. Only this way could the state provide dwellings with the maximum accommodation at the minimum expense. As the editor of the *Irish Builder*, R. M. Butler, later put it: 'Good planning—that is to say, the scientific and skilful disposition of the several items of accommodation—is of the first importance, for good planning means economical building, and bad building means waste'.[124]

The target set by the RIAI was to have included in the 1919 Irish Housing Bill a clause stipulating the mandatory employment of architects (a raw nerve ever since the Castle Administration had refused to do so in connection with the 1906 Labourers Act). The RIAI claimed 'that the result will not only prove of ultimate benefit to the whole Architecture profession in Ireland irrespective of Membership of this Institute, but will also tend to safeguard the industrial classes against the evils arising from badly designed and ill-constructed houses'.[125] There was strong sympathy for this demand from the Under Secretary, James McMahon, and ILGB officials such as Peter Cowan.[126] Although Chief Secretary Macpherson finally accepted this viewpoint, he still rejected the notion that it needed to be made legally compulsory to employ architects for post-war housing work. Instead, the ILGB and the RIAI were asked to set up a joint committee to draw up an approved list of designers, which might possibly include non-registered architects or engineers if they could prove that they had the appropriate experience. Nevertheless, the likelihood was that most housing schemes in Ireland would from now be designed by qualified architects, and that, as in Britain, engineers and surveyors would be displaced from a field that they had previously dominated.[127]

The RIAI had even greater success in their demand that a housing design competition be held along the lines of those organised by the Royal Institute of British Architects for England and Wales (1917), and by the Royal Incorporation of Architects of Scotland and the Scottish LGB (1918). Backing for the RIAI came from the ILGB and Lord Lieutenant French. At first, the Treasury argued that Ireland could simply make use of the designs secured by the British competitions.[128] Then, under pressure from Chief Secretary Macpherson, the Treasury finally relented in early-April 1919 on condition that it retained final approval over the terms of the competition.[129] A sum of £650 was granted to the RIAI and the ILGB to cover organisational costs. Disregarding appeals from the Ulster Society of Architects that it be allowed to hold a separate event, by mid-1919 a competition had been arranged in Ireland 'for the purpose of securing the best designs for suitable and economical types of houses'.[130] The central part of the competition asked for cottage designs for three typical suburban sites, although there was also a subsidiary section dealing with tenement rehabilitation. A total of £500 in prize money was offered. Three architects were appointed as judges: William Kaye Parry, President of the RIAI; Henry Seaver, an eminent Belfast architect; and Thomas Joseph Byrne, soon to be appointed as a 'temporary' housing inspector by the ILGB. In addition, the assessors received help from two members of the Dublin Trades Council in making their awards.[131]

The requirements set out by the ILGB and RIAI for the housing competition were essentially British standards.[132] Entrants all received a copy of the 1917 Royal Commission on Scottish Housing; the 1918 Report of the Women's Committee to the Ministry of Reconstruction; the winning designs from the 1917 RIBA Housing Competition; and, above all, the influential Tudor Walters Report of November 1918. Three general conditions of the Irish Housing Competition also ensured that it kept in line with developments in Britain. The first was the proviso that competitors did not necessarily have to comply with every current building by-law: a waiver first pioneered by Raymond Unwin in *Town Planning in Practice* (1909) and at Hampstead Garden Suburb, in order that savings on road construction could be made by introducing innovative site-planning features such as cul-de-sacs and access-only routes. The second stipulation was that entrants adhere to the simplification and standardisation of house design that had been introduced by Unwin and by the 'Liverpool School' in war-time schemes for the Ministry of Munitions. Thus the conditions of the 1919 Irish Housing Competition noted: 'In all new houses, return buildings are to be avoided, as far as possible. Simplicity in form of roofs and avoidance of unnecessary breaks in walls are most desirable in the interest of economy'.[133]

The third area of British influence was in housing standards. Main bedrooms were to be a minimum of 160 square feet and other bedrooms at least 80 square feet (although the latter could be reduced if they were designated as 'sleeping cubicles'). Parlours, where provided, were to be a minimum of 110 square feet, and in cases when they were omitted, a corresponding increase was to be made in the size of living rooms. Ceilings were to be at least eight feet high. And importantly, every dwelling was to have a separate bathroom with hot-and-cold water supply. Altogether, the competition represented a marked increase in standards from Dr Peter Cowan's *Report on Dublin Housing* (1918). This was clearly seen in the relative proportions of house-types. Now some 61 per cent of cottages were to have three bedrooms and 39 per cent were to have two bedrooms, compared with figures of 35 per cent and 60 per cent respectively in the Cowan Report. The 1919 Irish Housing Competition also asked for parlours in 26 per cent of all dwellings, compared with only 16 per cent as recommended by Cowan.

Competitors were asked to provide designs for four types of two-storey cottage dwellings. Type 1 was to be a three-roomed non-parlour house containing two bedrooms; Type 2 was a four-roomed non-parlour house with three bedrooms; Type 3 was a five-roomed parlour house with three bedrooms. For each of these three different house types, alternative plans were also requested for end-of-terrace cottages, narrow fronted mid-terrace cottages, and wide fronted mid-terrace cottages with a through living room. The fourth dwelling type stipulated by the competition was for two-bedroom flats arranged in a group of four within a two-storey block (with the requirement that any two flats on a floor should be convertible to create a large three-bedroom unit and a smaller one-bedroom unit). This fourth type was similar to the winning design by Chillingworth and Levie for Belfast Corporation's pre-war housing competition. However, it was taken even more directly from a proposal for semi-detached 'cottage-flats' by the idiosyncratic English architect, Robert Thompson, which Cowan had previously included in his *Report on Dublin Housing*. The basic motivation for Thompson was continually to provide alternatives that challenged the dominant orthodoxy of Unwinian house-types, which he openly criticised. To this effect, Thompson had obtained useful publicity in Britain during the war through being championed by the National Workingmen's Housing Council and its organ, the *Housing Journal*.[134] The results of Thompson's success in selling himself to the ILGB will be noted again later. In addition to the general requirements of the Irish Housing Competition, entrants also had to design three regional permutations to take account of differing social conditions. The first was for industrial towns in Ulster, where estates were to be comprised of 20 per cent three-roomed houses; 30 per cent four-roomed houses; 40 per cent five-roomed parlour houses; and only 10 per cent two-bedroom flats. The second variant was for large towns in the rest of

Ireland, which were to have 35 per cent three-roomed houses; 35 per cent four-roomed houses; only 18 per cent five-roomed parlour houses; and 12 per cent two-bedroom flats. The final permutation was for smaller Irish towns, and asked for 40 per cent three-roomed houses; 40 per cent four-roomed houses; 20 per cent five-roomed parlour houses; and no flats. The principle of regional design variations was not novel (having been included in the 1917 RIBA Housing Competition), and indeed the only real concession to Irish conditions in the RIAI/ILGB competition was a minor section for the conversion of four tenement houses into modern three- or four-roomed flats, each with a separate bathroom.

In the event, the 1919 Irish Housing Competition proved to be of little benefit except to publicise the new standard of housing that would be required for the post-war campaign. Only 22 architects entered the competition, submitting an average of two schemes each.[135] Of the 11 prize-winners, all but two came from Dublin or its suburbs, and most were leading Irish practices with previous experience in housing design. The competition entries reflected the strong influence of British garden suburb principles, with estates being laid out around central greens, and using cul-de-sacs and set-backs in the building line to break up what was otherwise a pattern of large site blocks (see Fig. 37). The ILGB did not publish the winning designs until the end of 1919, and when it did, it subjected each entry to meticulous scrutiny. Designs were criticised for providing too little public space, and in particular for proposing unsatisfactory house plans that were poorly arranged, failed to take proper account of aspect, and give insufficient access to back gardens. 'Generally the Competition has indicated that the ability to lay-out a site suitably does not necessarily accompany the faculty of sound and economical house planning', the ILGB wrote dismissively.[136] Because the ILGB thought that the competition designs were too close to the picturesque model of pre-war garden suburbs in Britain, it attached some 'corrective' plans. One exemplar that was now included was a copyrighted design for an economical two-storey two-bedroom cottage by Robert Thompson (the ILGB noted that Thompson was willing to grant licences to Irish local authorities, demonstrating that it was again willing to promote British housing designs even from non-official architects).[137] The other guidance offered by the ILGB came from a set of preferred type-plans that had been designed by its in-house architects, and which had previously been sent out to all Irish municipalities in a circular in September 1919.

It is now worth looking at the two circulars on housing design issued by the ILGB in 1919, since these formed the main route by which the Castle Administration instilled the Unwinian principles of rationalised cottage plans and garden suburb planning. The first ILGB design circular was issued on 5 May 1919, and covered the requirements for the selection of sites, the layout of estates, house-types, internal planning, space requirements, and the provision of services. It was taken directly from similar memoranda issued in Britain, principally the English LGB's *Manual on the Preparation of State-aided Housing*

216 John Bull's Other Homes

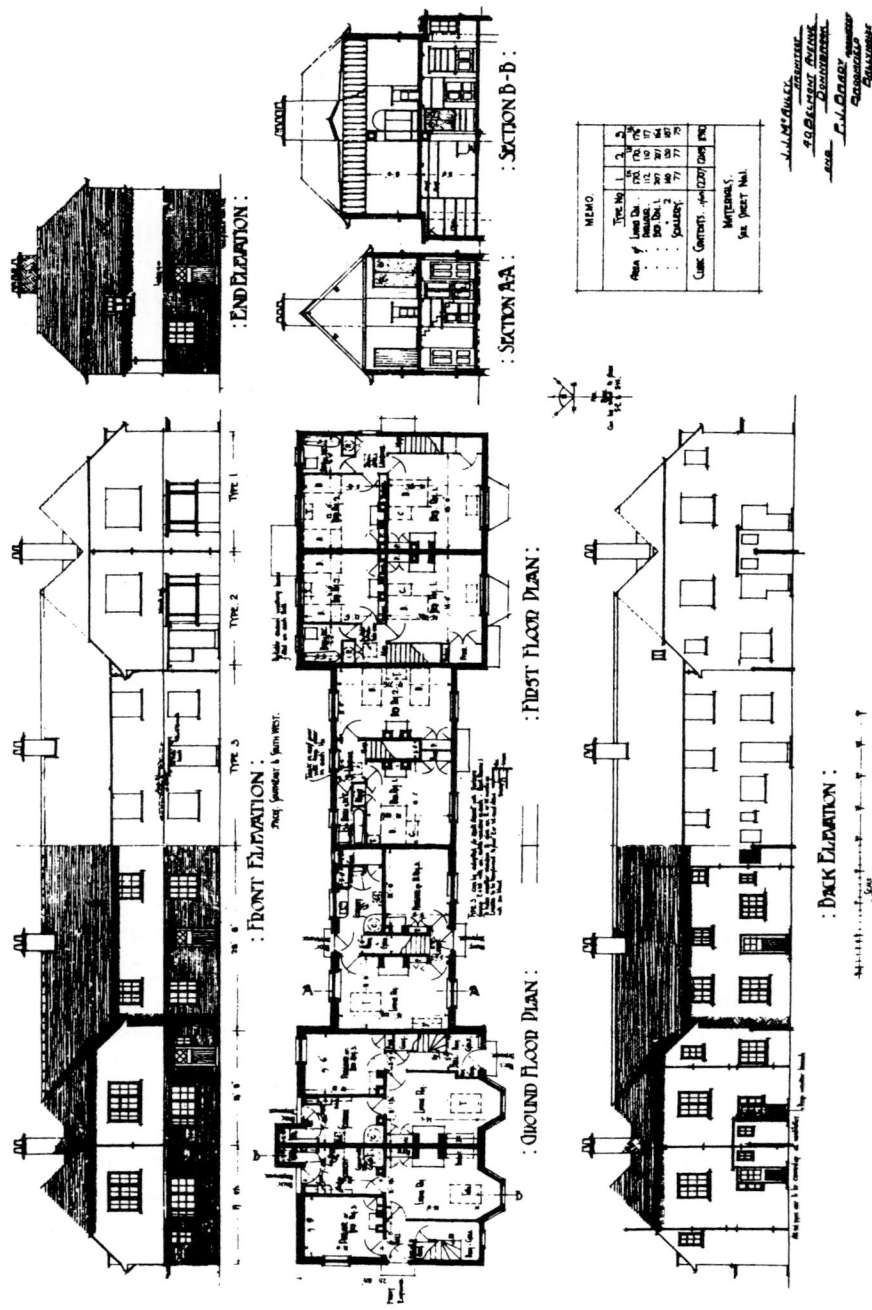

Fig 37. Typical competition entry from the 1919 RIAI/ILGB Housing Competition

Schemes published the previous month.[138] The ILGB circular of May 1919 called for the careful selection of large suburban sites, and strongly recommended the employment of qualified architects. The average housing density across the site was not allowed to exceed 12 dwellings to the acre, and there was to be a maximum figure of 20 cottages on any single acre. Good sized gardens had to be provided, along with areas for public parks and gardening allotments. Semi-detached cottages were deemed to be the most desirable form of housing, although it was recognised that it might be necessary to build terraces of up to eight dwellings wherever savings needed to be achieved. In terms of elevational design, the ILGB paraphrased the Unwinian precepts contained in the Tudor Walters Report:

> A good architectural effect can be most satisfactorily secured, not by expensive ornamental treatment or great variations in the design of the houses, but by grouping them skilfully so as to avoid the monotony of long, unbroken lines. Corner sites should be treated with special care so that blank gable walls may not be prominent features.[139]

A similar rationalisation in design was also to be applied to the internal planning and orientation of cottage plans:

> It is desirable that the plan of a house should be nearly square, but rooms of oblong shape are most advantageous . . . Return buildings should be avoided as far as possible, and for simplicity and economy there should be no unnecessary breaks in roof or walls . . . It is most important that the internal plan of *each* house should be carefully adapted to its site. The living room and principal bedrooms should have the sunniest aspect, and to secure that, in all houses, different plans should be used for the two sides of the road, or a long-fronted type of house with a through living room lighted at both ends.[140]

The ILGB circular of 5 May 1919 also confirmed the new standard for house-types and internal space provision that had been set out in the 1919 Irish Housing Competition. Space requirements were generally the same. Main bedrooms were to be a minimum of 160 square feet, other bedrooms were to be at least 80 square feet (except where provided as 'cubicles'), and parlours at least 110 square feet. All dwellings were to have separate WC and a hot-and-cold water supply, with space for a bath. There was also to be a fireplace in every room, proper provision for coal storage, a decent larder, and space to store a pram and bicycle. Furthermore, in certain ways the ILGB circular advanced a slightly higher standard than the Irish Housing Competition. Living rooms in parlour houses were now to be a minimum of 160 square feet and 180 square feet in non-parlour houses. Sculleries were to be at least 80 square feet if there was no separate bathroom, and 60 square feet if a bathroom was provided. In terms of house size, parlour houses were now to constitute 40 per cent of all dwellings, and in larger schemes even substantial four-bedroom houses would be allowed.

The second design circular issued by the ILGB on 11 September 1919 contained sample type-plans for dwellings.[141] The suggested plans were clearly influenced by the British trend towards standardisation and simplification, but significantly they did not correspond directly to the contemporary house-types provided for British municipalities by the Ministry of Health. Instead, the ILGB's architects produced variations on the design by the British architect, Robert Thompson, for a semi-detached two-storey cottage with side entrance (which, as noted above, was also appended to the booklet on the Irish Housing Competition). In the ILGB circular of September 1919, Thompson's own copyrighted plan was recommended only as a possible layout for the very smallest type of three-roomed dwelling ('Type A'). What the ILGB's architects then did was to take the basic semi-detached layout, and adapt it for the design of larger houses. The semi-detached plan configuration was one that overcame the criticisms made by the ILGB of entries for the Irish Housing Competition, since it provided an economical box-like shape with maximum daylight and ventilation in every room, and also allowed direct access to all rear gardens.

The ILGB circular showed six types of semi-detached cottages, of differing sizes. There was a minor variant included for one of the house-types, and in addition, for the smaller house-types there was also an alternative layout to show how the plans might be rearranged as flats if required (see Figs 38–41). 'Type A' was for a small three-roomed cottage, with a living room (180 square feet), main bedroom (180 square feet), and second bedroom (120 square feet). 'Type B' was a four-roomed parlour version, with a living room (160 square feet), parlour (110 square feet), main bedroom (190 square feet), and second bedroom (80 square feet). 'Type C' was a four-roomed non-parlour cottage, with a living room (193 square feet), main bedroom (160 square feet), second bedroom (120 square feet), and third bedroom (80 square feet). The ILGB noted that this was probably the most economical house to erect in large numbers.[142] There was also a variant of this type which had an even larger living room (210 square feet) that could be divided up to create a study room. The remaining three house-types were intended for larger families. 'Type D' was for a five-roomed parlour cottage, containing a living room (160 square feet), parlour (110 square feet), main bedroom (190 square feet), second bedroom (130 square feet), and third bedroom (80 square feet). 'Type E' was a five-roomed non-parlour version, with a living room (180 square feet), main bedroom (190 square feet), second bedroom (130 square feet), third bedroom (90 square feet), and fourth bedroom (80 square feet). 'Type F' was for a rather large six-roomed parlour cottage, with a living room (180 square feet), parlour (120 square feet), main bedroom (160 square feet), second bedroom (121 square feet), third bedroom (121 square feet), and fourth bedroom (80 square feet). The ILGB recommended that the last type should only ever be used when municipalities were certain that sufficiently high rents could be charged. The

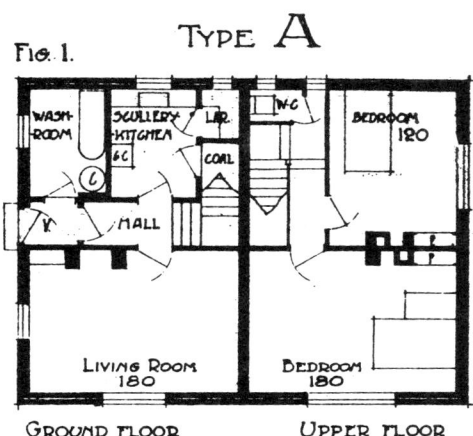
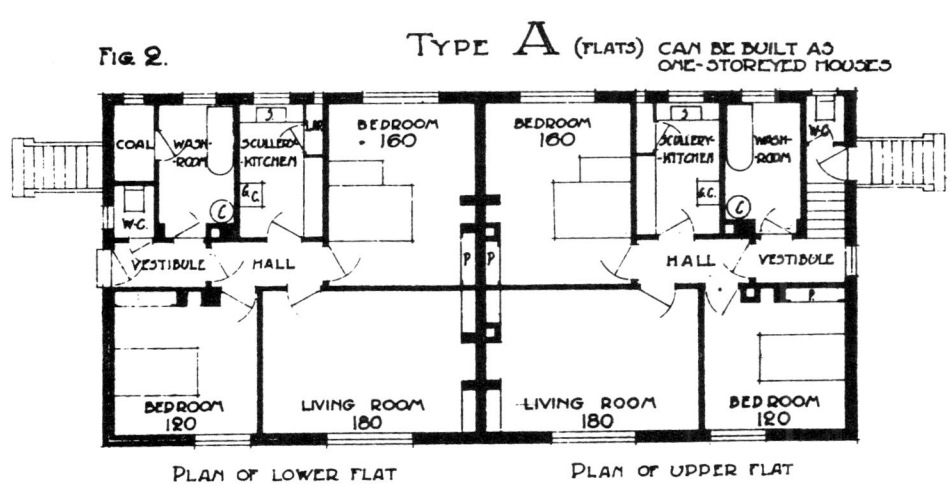

Fig 38. ILGB: recommended 'Type A' four-room plan from the 1919 circular

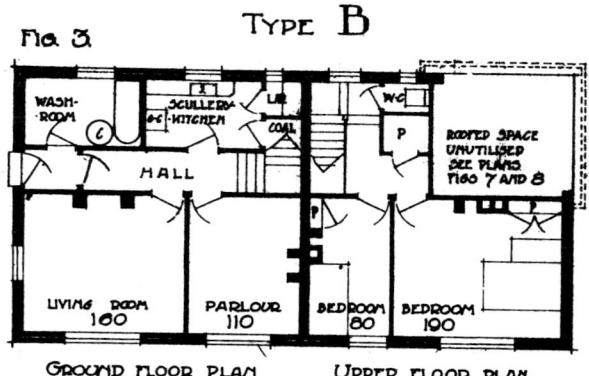

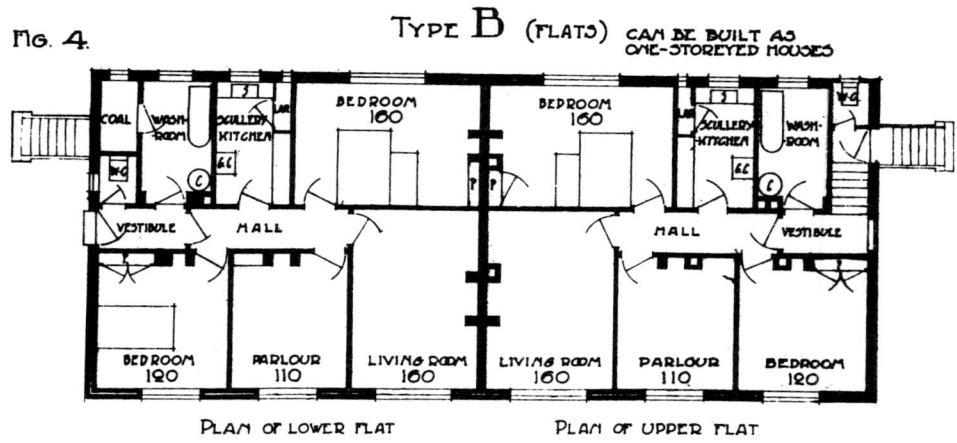

Fig 39. ILGB: recommended 'Type B' four-room plan from the 1919 circular

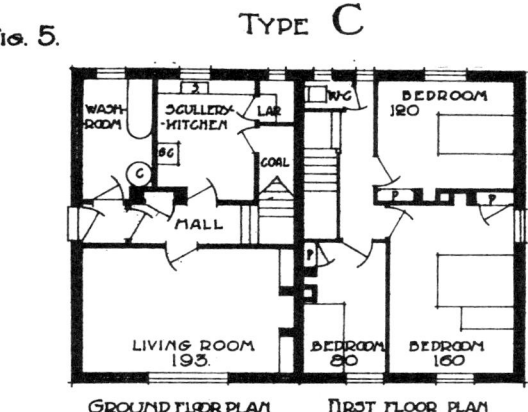

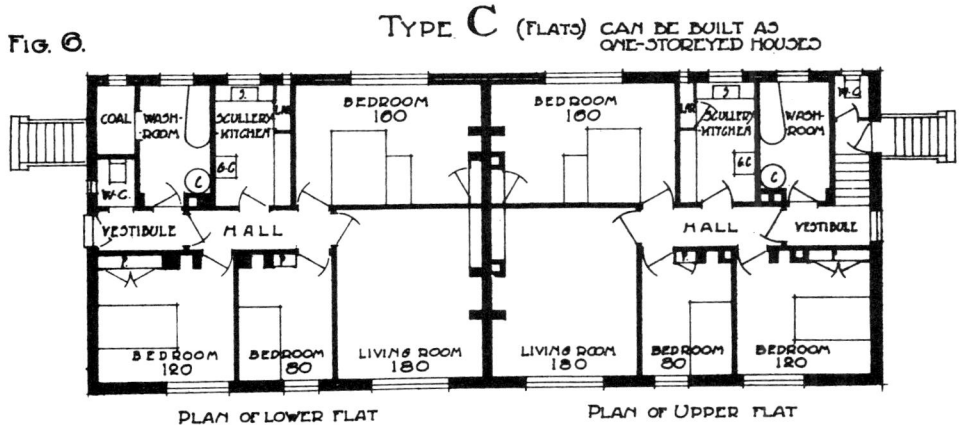

Fig 40. ILGB: recommended 'Type C' five-room plan from the 1919 circular

222 John Bull's Other Homes

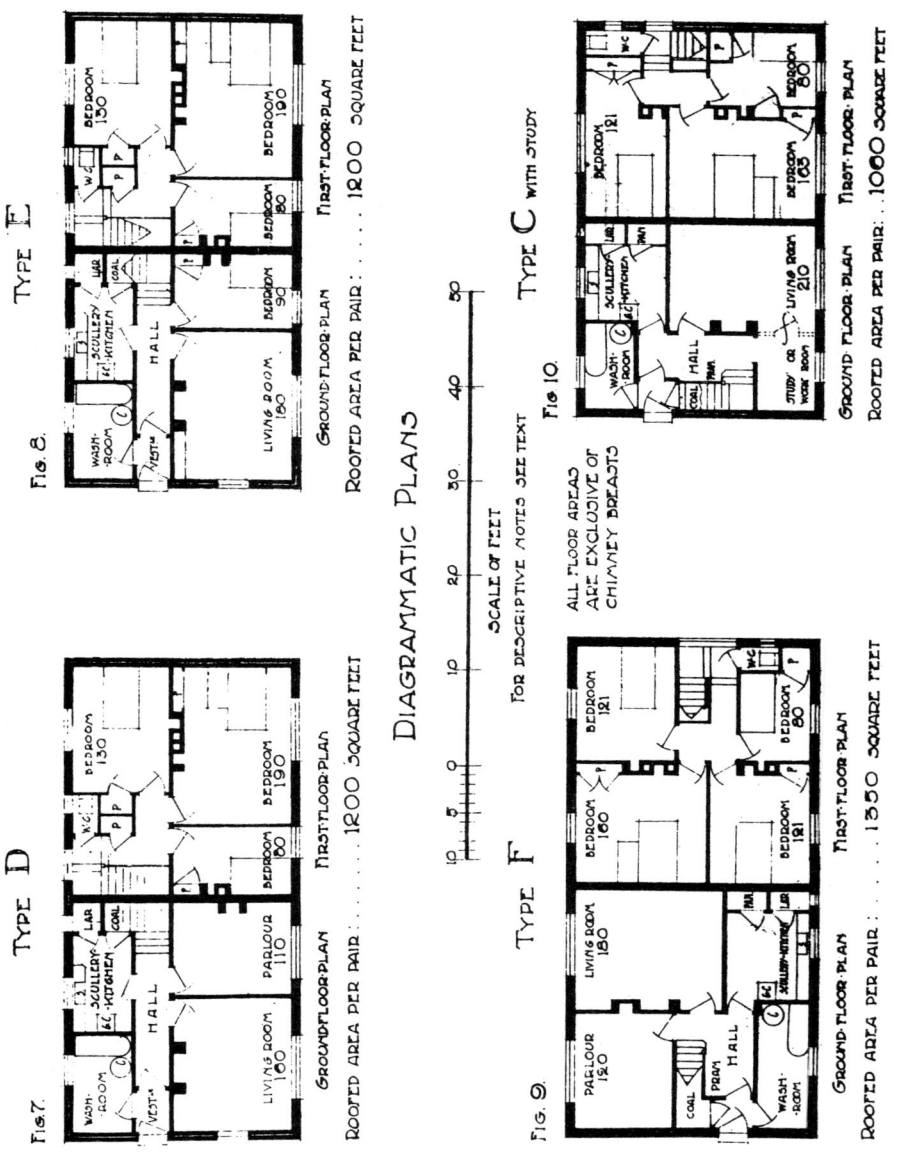

Fig 41. ILGB: recommended 'Type C/D/E/F' plans from the 1919 circular

designs contained in the ILGB circular of September 1919, and particularly the 'Type E' and 'Type F' cottages, clearly represented an unprecedented standard of working-class housing in Ireland. The sizes of individual rooms were well above the minimums laid down in the circular of May 1919, with, for instance, an average living room area of 176 square feet (compared with the 160 square feet minimum), and an average main bedroom of 178 square feet (compared with the 160 square feet minimum). All the ILGB's house plans contained a kitchen, large larder, coal store, and an upstairs WC. Each also had a ground floor bathroom directly off the front entrance lobby, avoiding the need for an expensive circulating system to pump hot water to the upper floor.

The ILGB does not appear to have provided sections or elevations to accompany the suggested cottage types, although the symmetrical disposition of door and window openings indicated on the plans seems to imply an acceptance of the rationalised Neo-Georgian manner adopted for the post-war campaign in Britain. It was the ILGB's stated intention, following the line taken by the Tudor Walters Report, that it should not be seen as providing comprehensive, finalised designs for housing schemes. Rather, it was to be left to Irish municipalities to employ architects who could apply their own design ability and knowledge to meet the general standards set out by the ILGB circulars.[143]

A crucial test for the Irish housing campaign was how the promotion by the ILGB of higher design standards from Britain would be received in Ireland. Here it appears that a continuing dependence on British architectural ideas meant an almost complete absence of ideological opposition. Several of the key figures involved were already well known as garden suburb enthusiasts. The role of Thomas Byrne within the ILGB has been noted, and his brother-in-law, Professor William Scott, was consultant architect to Enniskillen UDC until his early death in 1921. The RIAI kept in close contact with the Royal Institute of British Architects over housing issues. Most importantly, Unwinian orthodoxy was regarded in Ireland as embodying the best of contemporary practice. Therefore, to adopt rationalised garden suburb design was represented as the 'modernisation' and not the 'anglicisation' of Irish state housing. The *Irish Builder* wrote of the ILGB circular of May 1919 that it 'inculcates the elementary principles of modern practice in these matters. It is a very great step forward in this country, and the first of its kind'.[144] The same journal later added of the municipal schemes produced along the lines promoted by the ILGB: 'In other words, an entirely new standard has been set. Unfortunately these houses exist only on paper. They, however, form the sole development of architectural design that we have witnessed in Ireland for quite forty years'.[145] The Housing Committee of Dublin Corporation, despite its general hostility to British rule, admitted in September 1919 that the Tudor Walters Report 'is now regarded as a work of reference on housing questions', and it gave a copy of the report to all the consultant architects that it employed.[146] Quite simply, there was a general belief in Ireland that to follow British precedents in housing design was inevitable. A social reformer in Dublin even asked in desperation at one point, 'is there no Irish Mr Raymond Unwin . . . ?'[147]

Widespread acceptance in Ireland of the need to introduce British housing principles also enabled the ILGB to fight off the attempts by some municipalities, notably Belfast Corporation, to cut standards. Demands for cost-paring stemmed from the fact that inflated post-war construction costs threatened to make state housing schemes hopelessly uneconomic. The estimate of £400–600 per cottage that had been used by Chief Secretary Macpherson at the outset was to prove hopelessly wrong. For example, in Belfast a typical pre-war building cost of around £250 per dwelling had by 1919–20 soared to an average tender price of £900–1000 for non-parlour cottages, and up to £1200–1300 for the largest parlour dwellings.[148] Irish municipalities realised that they still stood to make a loss even if they were to set rents at an exorbitant level of 15s per week. One solution to the problem was obviously an increase in Exchequer subsidy. Another was to permit local authorities to reduce the standard of provision in order to cut building costs. A general resolution to this effect was passed by the Association of Municipal Authorities of Ireland in September 1919.[149] Belfast Corporation was the prime instigator behind the move, since its primary and obsessive concern was to ensure that there would be no charge at all to the rates as a result of its housing activities (see Chapter 8). At the ILGB inquiries into the housing proposals for Belfast that were held in the city in October 1919 and in May 1920, the Corporation insisted that it be allowed to abandon the semi-detached layout promoted by the ILGB's design circulars. Instead, it proposed to build short blocks of smaller and cheaper non-parlour dwellings. 'Belfast people did not want big semi-detached houses . . . They wanted good terraced houses', declared the Chairman of Belfast Corporation's Housing Committee. 'What they wanted to do was to get the Local Government Board to reduce its standard.'[150] This led to an extremely acrimonious clash with the ILGB inspector, Dr Peter Cowan. In the ensuing row, Cowan described the Corporation's designs as being 'very amateurish', and he admonished the municipality for being 'content now to lag in the rear and to forget that the housing standard of a past generation was not a good modern standard'.[151] Considerable pressure was also exerted on the Chief Secretary by Ulster Unionists in the Imperial Parliament. In November 1919 one Unionist MP drew the 'attention of the Government to the danger of putting forward too high a type of house'.[152] In Britain, the outcome of similar demands to cut costs was that the Ministry of Health responded in May 1920 by introducing a range of modified type-plans with more flexible accommodation.[153] Yet in Ireland, the ILGB steadfastly refused to reduce standards or even to suggest alternative layout types, despite an almost constant barrage of hostility from Unionist municipalities such as Belfast Corporation.[154] By remaining firm, the ILGB won itself much praise from other groups, such as Irish Party MPs. The *Irish Builder* observed that it was 'gratifying that the Local Government Board is maintaining a firm stand in the matter of insisting upon modern principles being followed in the planning and laying out of the houses. This has several times brought them into conflict with local authorities'.[155]

THE COLLAPSE OF THE POST-WAR IRISH HOUSING CAMPAIGN

In late-September 1919, the ILGB wrote to municipalities to set out the timetable for implementing the 1919 Irish Housing Act. The surveys of local housing need were required to be returned by November 1919. Design proposals for housing schemes were then to be submitted by April 1920, and all dwellings had to be completed by 15 August 1922 unless an extension of time was specifically authorised.[156] There was undoubtedly a strong commitment to the Irish housing campaign within the British Government and Dublin Castle, as could be seen by the speedy incorporation of Ireland into the 1919 Housing (Additional Powers) Act. Furthermore, a broad political consensus in Ireland was in favour of the initiative. Thus in November 1919, *The Times* reasoned that 'the new housing scheme can easily be made a success, and, if the local authorities approach their task in a business-like, disinterested, and efficient manner, there is no reason why Ireland's formidable problem should not be solved to the satisfaction of everybody'.[157] In the early months of 1920, it was still possible to portray the Irish housing campaign in a positive light. Chief Secretary Macpherson announced to Parliament in February 1920 that some 97 out of 127 Irish municipalities had submitted outline housing schemes. Of these, 74 had also included detailed plans. The ILGB had held inquiries into schemes that covered a total of 640 houses. Although only 25 houses had actually been completed, the Castle Administration claimed that a further 243 dwellings were at an advanced stage of construction. Therefore, on the surface at least, progress was not proportionately far behind that in England and Wales, where by the same date only around 1250 houses had been built.[158] By the deadline date for the submission of Irish housing proposals in April 1920, a total of 85 municipalities had provided detailed design proposals and a further 24 had given at least outline information.[159]

However, at this same point the wider problems of British rule in Ireland were becoming all too apparent. The operations of the Castle Administration outside Ulster had run into chronic difficulty, due to escalating political opposition from Sinn Fein and military action by the Irish Republican Army. The response of the British Government remained undefined, but the knee-jerk reaction advocated by Conservative Unionists in the Cabinet was to repress dissent. Sinn Fein had been proscribed as illegal in most of Ireland in September 1919. A further crisis was precipitated by the first post-war municipal elections in January 1920. Despite the introduction of proportional representation by the British Government, Sinn Fein still won overall control of 72 out of the 127 municipalities in Ireland, and shared power with the Irish Labour Party in another 26 councils (the hegemony of Sinn Fein in rural areas was to prove even greater, taking over 28 out of 33 county councils and 182 out of 206 RDCs in elections held in mid-1920).[160] The consequences for the main urban housing campaign in Ireland were stark. If the initiative was now to proceed, then in most cases the necessary loans and subsidies from the Imperial Exchequer would have to be granted to die-hard separatists. There were also complex administrative repercussions. When the Chairman of Dublin Corporation's Housing Committee, Lord Mayor Thomas Kelly, was deported to England in March 1920 (along with Councillor William Cosgrave), his deputy wrote to Lloyd George to point out provocatively that the Government's action had 'undoubtedly held up Corporation work—housing, planning, etc.—in which you have always taken such a lively interest'.[161]

And yet, as McColgan has pointed out, the paralysis in British rule inflicted by Sinn Fein at the same time prompted the British Government and the Castle Administration into attempting sweeping policy changes to regain the initiative.[162] This was only possible because there remained among some groups a strong commitment to the maintenance of British rule in Ireland. Perseverance could be seen, for instance, in the efforts of the ILGB to revive the housing campaign when it became apparent that only Ulster—and hence effectively Belfast Corporation—was likely to press ahead with schemes. In February 1920 the ILGB's Vice-President, Sir Henry Robinson, went back to the Treasury to seek approval for further financial concessions.[163] Robinson suggested that the Exchequer should now pay the loan interest charges for the first two years of any housing scheme, in order to allow more time for building. He also asked that the Treasury drop its ruling that subsidy levels would be recalculated after a period of seven years. Robinson felt that instead they should make a longer-term commitment to Irish municipalities. Furthermore, the ILGB recommended that the Irish subsidy system should be improved by linking the Exchequer contribution to an agreed 'economic rent', and not to the actual amount of rent collected. This refinement would mean that municipalities would not be financially crippled in the event of a rent strike, when otherwise they stood to lose both rent income *and* subsidy. The Treasury was totally against any amendment that in its view removed the incentive for Irish municipalities to maximise rent collection. As to the argument that the current subsidy system was particularly unfair if tenants refused to pay, one official wrote that 'as the temptation to strike for no-rents will probably make more appeal to the Irish mind, it is perhaps appropriate that the punishment should be a double one'.[164] The bottom-line concern of the Treasury was that any improvements made in the Irish system might provoke resentment in Britain. So the Treasury took pains to consult with other British departments, asking whether the Ministry of Health 'would be embarrassed if we met them [ILGB] on one or two points'; it was informed in no uncertain terms that any substantial concession to Ireland was likely to lead to spiralling demands from hard-pressed British municipalities.[165] Therefore, the Treasury told the ILGB that it could only accept one minor suggestion put forward by Robinson, which was to lengthen the period over which interest payments on loans would be met. For the moment, the attempt by the Castle Administration to rescue the Irish housing campaign was frustrated.

The only source of political power that could resolve the problems of Irish state housing lay higher up in Westminster. In September 1919, a new Cabinet Committee had been set up under Sir Walter Long to consider the question of Irish self-government. There followed an obvious narrowing of the ideological divisions within the Lloyd George Government, once Unionist ministers had come to realise that a purely coercive Irish policy would not suffice. Some instrument of redress was also required.[166] The Cabinet Committee produced a draft plan for Irish self-rule in early-1920, although continuing disagreements meant that the new Government of Ireland Act was not eventually passed until the end of the year. The essence of the 1920 Government of Ireland Act was that Ulster must not be coerced into a united Ireland—which was in effect to formalise partition—and that Ireland as a whole must be kept within the Empire. Lloyd George reminded the Cabinet that he was 'still a Gladstonian Home Ruler, and he wished to keep Ireland as an integral part of the United Kingdom'.[167] British supremacy was to be upheld in matters of defence and commerce. In other words, there was to be limited devolution to two new federal-style Irish administrations. Ireland was to make an annual 'Imperial Contribution' of £18 000 000 towards expenditure on reserved matters such as the army, police, land purchase, and taxation. A few minor matters were entrusted to a joint 'Council of Ireland', consisting of representatives from both new Irish administrations, but in general the 1920 Government of Ireland Act meant the partition of virtually all transferred services.[168]

Professor W. S. G. Adams was appointed as secretary to the Cabinet Committee, and in the various draft proposals it was still clearly envisaged that the British Government would continue to finance Irish state housing after the transfer of power. The Cabinet was told on 3 December 1919 that to help the new administrations, 'from a financial point of view, it was of the greatest importance that the cost of the local services should not be increased by any additions such as . . . Housing'.[169] The amount of Exchequer contribution was pencilled in at £2 000 000 per annum, the figure proposed by the 1917–18 Irish Convention. This sum was to be paid for the first seven years following devolution.[170] The Treasury was still of the opinion that the estimate was too high. It received influential support from the Chancellor of the Exchequer, Austen Chamberlain, who by late-1919 was beginning to advocate cut-backs in the British housing campaign as well. Hence the Cabinet Committee on Ireland now stepped in to impose a much tougher line on Adams' financial proposals:

> There is also the question of a grant of £2,000,000 for housing. No promise of this kind has been made, though the Prime Minister undertook to give a grant for housing as part of the Home Rule scheme offered in 1917, which was rejected by Mr Redmond when he accepted the Irish Convention instead. On the other hand, an Irish Housing Act,

involving an expenditure out of taxes of 5/4th of the rents charged and collected has already been passed. This may mean an annual expenditure of £100,000 a year, rising by, say, £100,000 to a million a year.[171]

In the 'White Paper' on expenditure under the Government of Ireland Bill that was published in May 1920, the subject of Irish state housing was not itemised as such. However, it would appear from the calculations that there was now only to be around £1 000 000 per annum granted under this heading, to cover both Ulster and the rest of Ireland.[172] In terms of strategy, Austen Chamberlain declared that it would be simpler to repeal the 1919 Irish Housing Act, and hand a free grant over to the Northern and Southern Governments to frame their own housing policies. The majority of the Cabinet Committee disagreed. Instead, the 1920 Government of Ireland Act reverted to the formula first proposed by the Treasury to Adams back in the summer of 1918. An annual payment towards Irish housing was to be provided by making the appropriate deduction from Ireland's overall contribution to Imperial expenditure.[173] At first, the Cabinet Committee decided that administrative control over state housing should be temporarily reserved by Britain for the first year, and then handed over as a non-partitioned matter to be overseen by the 'Council of Ireland'. However, skilful manoeuvring by Ulster Unionists, whose aim was to minimise the chances for future Irish unity, meant that in the final draft it was assumed that the administrative responsibility for state housing would be partitioned and handed over immediately.[174]

The 1920 Government of Ireland Act showed that Westminster had still not relinquished its intention to finance Irish housing. But of more significance for the post-war campaign was the Cabinet's realisation that a thorough reform of Dublin Castle was essential if there was ever to be a successful implementation of self-government. It was necessary to remove senior Unionist officials who were known to be hostile to a transfer of power. The administrative machinery also had to be in good working order to ensure an efficient handover. Therefore, in April 1920 a new Chief Secretary, Sir Hamar Greenwood, was appointed to give greater support to Lord Lieutenant French. The next month the Treasury Secretary, Sir Warren Fisher, conducted an inquiry which concluded that the chaotic Castle Administration 'does not administer'.[175] The British Army in Ireland was duly strengthened to demonstrate the resolve against lawlessness, and a new breed of progressive thinking and politically neutral officials were appointed to powerful positions within Dublin Castle. Staff councils were set up to improve labour relations with senior officials, as an extension of the 'Whitley' scheme of civil service reform introduced in Britain. The system of controlling Irish finances was also streamlined by removing the post of Treasury Remembrancer. Instead, the incoming Joint Under Secretary, Sir John Anderson, was given a second role as head of the newly-created Irish Treasury. As McColgan has observed, the arrangement meant that Sir John Anderson now had:

the same financial powers in Ireland as those of the Secretary to the Treasury in Britain. Combining both the administrative and financial function of the Irish administration under one person—though at times producing the odd spectre of Anderson requesting funds in one capacity and refusing himself in another—was an extraordinary step and underscores how serious British officials regarded the administrative emergency in Ireland.[176]

The reformed Castle Administration from May 1920 faced the task of preparing for the implementation of the forthcoming Government of Ireland Act. A further Joint Under Secretary, Sir Ernest Clark, was appointed in September 1920 following strong pressure from Ulster Unionists. Clark began at once to quietly and assiduously build the foundations for a separate Northern Irish Government. Within the space of a year, an effective administrative mechanism had been set up in Ulster well in advance of preparations in the South.[177] In Southern Ireland progress was being hindered by the open hostility between the Castle Administration and Sinn Fein. Dublin Castle stepped up military repression in an effort to clamp down on unrest and guerrilla activity. In reprisal, Sinn Fein called for industrial strikes and a complete boycott of Government institutions to frustrate British rule. Housing policy was caught up in the battle. In May 1920, Chief Secretary Greenwood stalled a demand from the Association of Municipal Authorities of Ireland for increased housing subsidy.[178] For at this point, the Cabinet was more concerned with ensuring that whenever property damage or personal injury occurred in Ireland, then local people should bear the burden. Approval was given in late May to a Coercion Bill which stipulated that compensation payments would automatically be deducted from state subsidies to the local authority for that area.[179] It was a provocative gesture that dealt a severe blow to local government activities in general, and the housing campaign in particular. The consequences were devastating. Sinn Fein municipalities—which were now the vast majority outside Ulster—would simply be unable to predict what housing subsidy they might be likely to receive, since obviously they could not guarantee that there would be no military action in their district.

The Dáil Éireann was forced to respond to the Cabinet's concerted attack on its hold over Irish local government. From May 1920, the unofficial Ministry of Local Government held a series of meetings to consider what strategy might be recommended to local authorities under its control. Because of the continual desire to avoid a split in the alliance with the radical labour movement, it was decided that Sinn Fein must not be seen to take precipitate action that might terminate popular initiatives such as the housing campaign. Instead, the British Government should be forced into making the first move. As the deputy Minister of Local Government, Kevin O'Higgins, told the Dáil Éireann:

> If we are not prepared, of our own initiative, to cut adrift from the Local Government Board I see no sufficient reason why we should burden

ourselves with a self-denying ordinance against making full use of them in the matter of Housing Loans, drainage, etc. Housing is a matter of absolutely paramount importance and if the word went out that our Councils were absolutely debarred from taking any steps in this matter the political effect would be distinctly bad . . . If we refuse to forward minutes to [the] English Local Government Board, to accept their audit and otherwise to conform to existing regulations we cannot consistently apply for inquiries under their auspices to obtain sanction for loans from [the] Board of Works or from the British Treasury . . . Therefore Housing, Drainage, and all similar activities of public bodies would be at a standstill. What the effect of this would be in Labour circles it is easy to conceive.[180]

A special Dáil conference on 29 June 1920 agreed that Irish municipalities should simply be requested to pass resolutions which repudiated the authority of the ILGB and swore sole allegiance to Dáil Éireann. The ILGB chose not to respond to this tactic, and decided instead to play a waiting game in the expectation that Irish local authorities would soon change their tune when they needed state funds for housing and other matters.[181] However, the provocative taunts from Sinn Fein councils outraged Ulster Unionists and leading Conservatives. The Cabinet angrily proclaimed that no Exchequer loans or subsidies would be given to any local authority that refused to recognise the Castle Administration. A warning letter to this effect was sent out by the ILGB in late July. Then on 4 August 1920 an official directive was sent to all Irish authorities stating that they would not receive public loans unless they pledged to submit their accounts for annual audit. At the same time, the British Government passed the 1920 Coercion Act, finally providing Dáil Éireann with the ideal opportunity to act. The Dáil issued a decree in mid-August which instructed sympathetic local authorities to sever relations with the ILGB and pursue a policy of total non-cooperation.[182] Within a few months, an ILGB official noted that Ireland was 'in a parlous state, and the work of the Local Government Board is at a standstill in all branches except old age pensions'.[183]

If the Dáil Éireann now expected municipalities to refuse to accept housing loans from the British Government, Sinn Fein politicians were careful not to state this as official policy and run the risk of irritating municipal and labour representatives.[184] But neither could any alternatives be offered to Irish local authorities as long as British rule lasted. Dáil Éireann had decided that the priority for Sinn Fein funds must be the immediate political and military struggle. Expensive policies such as municipal housing could not be supported, especially if there was now little hope of British subsidy. Hence, in refusing an application for a housing loan from one municipality, the Dáil stated that the unofficial Ministry of Local Government 'are alive to the urgency of the Housing problem and they hope that at a later stage it may be found possible to make provision for affording financial assistance to local bodies in dealing with it'.¹⁸⁵ Another body was told:

> There are no funds earmarked for Irish housing . . . Local authorities must bear in mind the abnormal conditions of affairs prevailing, and endeavour in local matters to shoulder their own burden until the main cause of the abnormal condition of affairs, viz. foreign domination, is finally removed.¹⁸⁶

Dáil Éireann's refusal of loans provoked the protest from some municipalities that, since the housing campaign was of vital urgency, they should be given special permission to extract the necessary finance from the British Government. The issue threatened to wreck the annual conference in September 1920 of the Association of Municipal Authorities of Ireland, an organisation now dominated by Sinn Fein. Unity was only maintained through a compromise resolution which agreed to 'go fully into the housing problem, not with a view to obtaining a subsidy from the Government, but with a view to carrying out housing schemes from a national point of view'.¹⁸⁷ It was, however, a meaningless formula given that there was virtually no alternative capital available in Ireland to devote to state housing. The extent of the problem was revealed by the difficulties faced by Dublin Corporation in trying to complete its war-time schemes. By August 1920 the Corporation owed £160 000 to the contractor for the McCaffrey Estate and St James' Walk schemes. Now that the ILGB was withholding public loans, it needed urgently to find another source of funds. The matter was complicated by the fact that William Cosgrave was both the unofficial Minister of Local Government *and* Chairman of Dublin Corporation's Finance Committee. Cosgrave told the unofficial Finance Minister about the Corporation's predicament:

> We are in immediate danger of bankruptcy, in the sense that we have undertaken Capital expenditure but so far have not been able to secure a loan . . . The matter is so serious that if we don't get the money, the only solution would be for me to retire altogether from public life, as it would not be in the interest of the Republic that such a failure in the Corporation could continue as head of the Local Government Department.¹⁸⁸

Despite Cosgrave's resignation threat, which if carried out might have denied the future Irish Free State its first-ever President, the unofficial Ministry of Finance was reluctant to help. Dublin Corporation was only eventually able to cover its debt by selling stock to the Bank of Ireland. It was also forced to suspend all further housing work.¹⁸⁹

The inability of Dáil Éireann to provide funds for municipalities was an obvious weakness in the strategy of non-cooperation. The Castle Administration realised that if it now offered increased state subsidy to revive the Irish housing campaign, then not only would it be seen to be dealing with a chronic social problem, but it could also help to isolate Sinn Fein. In July 1920 the ILGB Housing Committee recommended that the present subsidy system be scrapped, in favour of a suggestion by the Association of Municipal Authorities of Ireland that the Exchequer pay 5.25 per cent of the annual capital expenditure (rising to 6 per cent for atypical slum-clearance projects). However, the ILGB's Vice-President, Sir Henry Robinson, argued that this would be disastrous given the rebelliousness of Sinn Fein authorities:

> It is impossible to ignore the political situation . . . The Municipal Authorities are now asking for loans on favourable terms and for largely increased grants from the Government which they decline to recognize and which they pledge themselves to do all in their power to resist . . . the difficulty is in applying to Parliament for an amended Act, or for sanction to amended Regulations, by which largely increased grants will be given for distribution to disloyal bodies. One brief example of the irony of the situation can be gathered from to-day's paper, from which it appears that an Urban Council having ordered the water supply to be cut off from the military and police barracks, then proceeded with the consideration of an application to the Government for a large loan for housing purposes for the benefit of their District! . . . The grounds for this [rent-based subsidy] were clearly explained to the Irish Government at the time, and the case is probably stronger now that the new Councils are composed largely of men elected because they possess no means and would not be a mark for costs.[190]

By early-November 1920 the Joint Under Secretary, Sir John Anderson, stated in an internal memo that it was now 'urgent' that permission to introduce new housing solutions be sought from the Chancellor of the Exchequer.[191] It showed that within Dublin Castle there was a political imperative attached to state housing that was by now in marked contrast to developments in England and Wales, where even the Minister of Health, Christopher Addison, had conceded in face of widespread criticism that sights needed to be lowered.[192] The Castle Administration sought to resurrect the Irish housing programme through three initiatives: by increasing the level of state subsidy to municipalities; by bulk purchasing building materials; and by improving the subsidy on offer to private building contractors. The first was easily the most important, and was suggested by Sir Henry Robinson (and accepted by Chief Secretary Greenwood) as an alternative to changing the basis of the Irish subsidy system. The pretext given to Parliament was that extra assistance was necessary to cover the inflation in Irish building costs—estimated at around 34 per cent—since the housing campaign started in mid-1919.[193] Yet this escalation in post-war construction costs was hardly new information. What was different was the revival in political commitment to Irish state housing. After discussions with the ILGB and the Housing Committee, the Chief Secretary's Office advocated that the ordinary level of subsidy should be increased to 35s for every £1 rent collected (a ratio of 7:4 compared with 5:4 previously). Furthermore, the state would now give 40s for every £1 of rent (a ratio of 2:1 compared with 11:8 previously) for special cases, where the ILGB decided that local economic circumstances were so harsh that only low rents could ever be charged.[194]

What was also new was the manner in which the recommendation of higher subsidy was received. Contrary to the hostility and parsimony shown previously by his departmental counterparts in Westminster, Sir John Anderson declared in reply that the Irish Treasury:

> recognize that there has been an appreciable increase in the cost of building since the rates of subsidy at present embodied in the regulations were fixed, and . . . are prepared to admit that some increase of subsidy is now necessary. On the other hand, the steady and appreciable rises of wages which have taken place in most employments since July 1919 justify the expectation of rents higher than those contemplated at that time.[195]

In return for conceding a subsidy increase, the Irish Treasury stipulated that the higher band of subsidy should only be granted in a few exceptional areas of economic hardship. Anderson also ruled that there now needed to be a mandatory review of municipal subsidy after a period of only four years, on 31 March 1925, to check that local authorities were charging appropriately high rents.[196] The latter decision was criticised by the Chairman of the Housing Committee, Dr Peter Cowan, on the grounds that it:

> appears to strike at the basis of the Irish system of subsidy, by giving an undetermined rate of subsidy for the major period of the loan periods instead of a rate which an honest and efficient Local Authority can regard as certain . . . It should not be forgotten that the difficulties in framing and carrying out building schemes are at present so great, on account of the scarcity of skilled labour and the scarcity and high cost of materials, that no very large number of houses could be built in Ireland within four years, even if political conditions were normal . . . It would seem to be not only unnecessary but most impolitic to add to the restrictions inherent in the Irish form of subsidy the safeguarding provisions required in Great Britain. The only certain effect of doing so would be to increase the hesitancy of Irish Local Authorities in embarking on housing schemes.[197]

Despite the expression of similar sentiments by Sir Henry Robinson, the Irish Treasury saw no reason to change its mind about the mandatory four-year review.[198] The second method by which the Castle Administration tried to stimulate the housing programme was in the matter of building materials supply. When the ILGB applied in November 1920 for a reduced sum of £250 000 to buy materials for the year 1921–22 (of which £187 500 would be recovered by the resale to municipalities), it received a favourable response from the Chief Secretary and the Irish Treasury. The only condition imposed was that building materials should never be given to local authorities that refused to present their accounts for audit.[199] And the third strategy was to increase the scope of private subsidy under the 1919 Housing (Additional Powers) Act. Only 342 dwellings had been completed under this measure in Ireland by late-1920, although the total was predicted to climb to nearly 1000 cottages by the deadline on 23 April 1921. At the suggestion of the ILGB and Ulster Unionists, the Irish Treasury now agreed to extend the date of eligibility and also to allow semi-rural dwellings to receive the subsidy.[200] Thus the 1921 Housing Act, which extended private subsidy throughout the United Kingdom to houses completed by 23 June 1922 (or by 23 October 1922 with special permission), also contained a specific clause for Ireland permitting the inclusion of houses built within a 1.5 mile radius of urban districts.

Despite the new housing initiatives brought in by the reformed Castle Administration, it is not surprising that they produced little on the ground. By April 1921, some 372 local authorities (72 per cent) out of a total of 516 Irish urban and rural councils either refused to recognise the ILGB, or were at least markedly ambivalent about British rule.[201] Chief Secretary Greenwood told Parliament that 'there is a campaign extending . . . to the whole administration of the Local Government Board in Ireland, and it is bringing Ireland to chaos and misery'.[202] Most municipalities, particularly in Southern Ireland, had for political reasons given up all hopes of receiving housing subsidy from the Imperial Exchequer. Sir Henry Robinson declared privately that 'the local authorities would have been content to go on with their schemes while negotiations [for higher subsidy] were proceeding . . . had it not been that they were ordered by Dáil Éireann to hold no communication whatsoever with the Local Government Board'.[203] Thus, in Southern Ireland by April 1921 the ILGB had sanctioned only a paltry £58 000 of public loans out of total figure of £2 180 000 for municipal housing applications. Only two small schemes totalling 30 dwellings were ever built in the South under the 1919 Irish Housing Act. Dalkey UDC borrowed £20 786 to build 22 dwellings (1921–22), and in north Co. Dublin, the Balbriggan Town Commissioners provided a mere 8 cottages.[204] The lack of progress was particularly poignant when bearing in mind that nearly 80 per cent of the dwellings that were required in post-war Ireland were needed in Southern towns and cities. The dilemma of the slums in Dublin was frequently used by political opponents to deride Sinn Fein's rejection of British housing funds after August 1920. 'What political object can such a sacrifice achieve?' asked the *Irish Times*. 'Even if *Dáil Éireann* should win its Republic, would it wish to find its capital in the last stages of municipal decay?'[205]

However, as many participants pointed out at the time, the failure of the Irish housing campaign could not simply be attributed to political abstentionism by Sinn Fein. The example of loyalist Ulster shows that the unique and unfavourable rent-based subsidy system designed by the Treasury was also a major cause. By April 1921, Northern municipalities had applied for £2 250 000 of public loans under the 1919 Irish Housing Act. Of this total, loans for nearly £706 000 had already been sanctioned.[206] Yet in Northern Ireland by mid-1921 there were still only some 90 dwellings completed by just three councils: Portadown UDC, Tanderagee UDC, and Belfast Corporation. In addition Belfast Corporation had just embarked on a programme, as will be seen in Chapter 8, that was to bring the eventual total built in Ulster under the 1919 Irish Housing Act to just over 530 houses.[207] The slow rate of completion by Belfast Corporation was partly due to an obsessive desire to avoid a loss to the rates. This meant that the Corporation diverted much of its energy in early-1921 into demands for more state subsidy and a cut in standards.[208] But it also had to be admitted that Belfast Corporation had a legitimate right to be worried about a system of state subsidy that provided neither a ceiling on the municipal contribution, nor a constant contribution from the Exchequer. 'Belfast is the only place in Ireland where the Government's housing scheme has had a chance of success', adjudged the *Irish Times*, 'but the result of the Corporation's effort to put it into operation has not been very encouraging.'[209]

Bitter experience in Ulster and in the South of Ireland led, therefore, to widespread disillusionment about the Irish housing campaign by early-1921. At the same time in Britain, the Cabinet and the Ministry of Health were encouraging various *ad hoc* expedients to accelerate housebuilding, while still avoiding antagonising powerful financial and industrial interests.[210] But while these British experiments were yet again studied in Ireland, their actual implementation was limited. The few Irish expedients that were attempted were, significantly, private initiatives to solve the economic and political problems of housing independently of the Castle Administration. For example, there was in Ireland no scientific investigation of new building methods to overcome shortages of materials and skilled labour. There was no comparable body to the Building Materials Research Committee, formed in Britain in 1917 at the suggestion of Raymond Unwin. Knowledge in Ireland of non-traditional construction remained vague, and the nearest thing to an Irish building system was the little-used 'Orion' walling block marketed by the Ryan Manufacturing and Construction Company. Limited efforts to use the 'Orion' system for ex-servicemen's housing at Killester will be discussed in the next chapter.[211] A second expedient used in Britain was to encourage alternative housing agencies and financial sources. In Ireland this was confined to a handful of public utility societies with specific ideological intentions behind their actions. The most publicised was the St Barnabas Public Utility Society in north-east Dublin, which sought to revive Unionist voluntarist philanthropy. By the mid-1920s the society had only built in the region of 175 cottages.[212] A third initiative stemming from Britain was the attempt to modify the building process in such a way as to eliminate the profit paid to private contractors, and by doing so to reduce construction costs. As will be noted in Chapter 8, Belfast Corporation failed to reach an agreement with the local builders' federation on tender prices, and reluctantly turned to using its own direct labour force on some schemes. It was a move urged by local building unions and the Belfast Labour Party, and was copied from the pioneering British scheme at Newbury in late-1919 and subsequently adopted in Liverpool, Glasgow, and other cities.[213] Another example was the creation of the Dublin Building Trades' Guild. As will also be seen in Chapter 8, this socialist guild had been given its first contract by Dublin Corporation to help build some dwellings at Fairbrothers Fields. The explicit model was the post-war guild movement of Northern England that had begun in Manchester. And the aim, as an Irish labour leader told Sinn Fein, was to show 'that the workers were capable of building houses cheaper and better than they could be built by the capitalists of Dublin or any other city'.[214] The Dublin Building Trades' Guild was a product of the post-war alliance between the labour movement and republican separatists, and hence it received support from Sinn Fein members of Dublin Corporation such as William Cosgrave. Yet in Ireland the use of direct labour or guilds did not prove to be noticeably cheaper than tenders from private contractors, and such experiments withered under sustained ideological opposition from conservative vested interests.

HOUSING POLICY AT THE END OF BRITISH RULE IN IRELAND

The attempts by the Castle Administration and other groups to inject life into the post-war housing campaign were by mid-1921 totally overshadowed by political events in Ireland. General Elections were held in both Northern and Southern Ireland in May 1921 to form the new Parliaments under the 1920 Government of Ireland Act.[215] The election outcomes were entirely predictable. In the North, the Ulster Unionists won 40 out of 52 seats. On 7 June 1921 the new Government led by Sir James Craig was sworn in, and preparations began for the formal transfer of power to Ulster. In Southern Ireland, despite increased repression by the British Army, Sinn Fein appropriated the election to select members for what it called the Second Dáil Éireann. By this point, even the hardliners within the Cabinet realised that they could not introduce the Government of Ireland Act in the South without an unacceptable degree of military force. After secret and mostly unproductive peace negotiations, the Lloyd George Government used King George VI's inaugural speech to the Northern Parliament in June 1921 to offer an olive branch to Sinn Fein. A 'Truce' was declared in mid-July by Lloyd George and the Sinn Fein leader, Eamonn de Valera. There followed complex negotiations over a formula for self-government that would also be acceptable to Northern Ireland. A 'Treaty' was finally signed in late-December 1921, although bitter division within the republican movement over the terms of settlement was to lead to bloody conflict in the South following independence.

As well as the wider political uncertainties created by the ending of British rule, Irish state housing was also conditioned by the imposition of a moratorium on the mainland housing campaign in mid-1921. The latter move had been on the cards for some time. Treasury proposals to restrict the housing programme began in late-1920, and intensified when Christopher Addison was replaced by Sir Alfred Mond as Minister of Health the following March.[216] Designs for smaller and narrow-fronted house-types were issued by the Ministry of Health, and the process culminated in a Cabinet decision to impose a complete moratorium on housing expenditure. The announcement was made by Sir Alfred Mond in the House of Commons on 14 July 1921. Now only those schemes already contractually committed were allowed to proceed. The result was that only 176 000 houses, instead of the 500 000 dwellings originally envisaged, were built in England and Wales under the 1919 Housing Act. Subsidy for private housebuilding was likewise curtailed. Retrenchment came ironically at a time when, due to the fact that the post-war inflationary boom was starting to evaporate, local authorities were at last able to overcome their financial and administrative problems. By mid-1921, tender prices had fallen to an average of around £800, and the rate of house completions had risen sharply. Swenarton has therefore argued that the termination of the housing campaign in Britain was just as politically motivated as its conception had been. Economic boom had turned to slump in the winter of 1920–21. The 'insurance against revolution' was no longer needed, given that wages were falling and the threat from militant labour power had all but collapsed.[217] The decline in labour power was graphically shown by the British Government's decisive victory over the miners' union, once the general strike threatened by the 'Triple Alliance' (i.e. the miners, railwaymen, and transport workers) had failed to materialise in April 1921. This interpretation has, however, been disputed by Daunton, who has in turn suggested that the moratorium on the Addison housing programme derived more from the long-standing aim of the Coalition Government to deflate the economy in preparation for a return to the 'Gold Standard' system of currency regulation.[218]

In Ireland it was undoubtedly political factors that determined the reaction of the Castle Administration to the announcement that the British housing campaign had been ended. Both the ILGB and its Housing Committee immediately began to argue against the extension of the Treasury's moratorium to Ireland. In a memorandum written on 16 July 1921, the Housing Committee pointed out that, due to political crisis and an unfavourable subsidy system, to date there had only been built around 300 of the 50 000 dwellings that had been planned under the 1919 Irish Housing Act. Were a stop to be imposed now, then 'the municipal housing scheme for Ireland will be paralysed and it would be some time before the new Governments in this Country could frame a new policy and revive the former activities of the local authorities'.[219] The Housing Committee suggested two lesser restrictions that might be placed on the Irish campaign. Either a new target figure of 25 000 dwellings could be set, or else subsidy might now be confined to municipalities that started schemes before 15 August 1922 and completed them within two years.[220] Senior officials within Dublin Castle were fully alert to the political dangers of imposing a moratorium, at a time when the British Government was engaged in sensitive discussions with Ulster Unionists and Sinn Fein about the transfer of power. The Joint Under Secretary and head of the Irish Treasury, Sir John Anderson, told the Chief Secretary:

> Owing to the disturbed state of the country and the attitude taken up by local authorities but little progress has been made. Conditions may improve but at best the commitments entered into by the time these matters pass out of the hands of the United Kingdom Government are practically certain to fall far short of the equivalent of the provision already secured in both England and Scotland . . . In the circumstances I do not think there is any need to impose special limitations upon the development of the scheme. As a matter of precaution however I would give the Local Government Board an administrative direction—which need not be made public—that they are not to enter into commitments representing more than 15,000 houses—without further authority. The point is never likely to arise.[221]

Anderson also suggested that the previous decision to raise Irish housing subsidy to 35s for every £1 of rent collected in ordinary cases, and 40s for special cases, should immediately be made public. In late-August 1921, the Chief Secretary let out news of the subsidy increase in a letter to Councillor T. E. McConnell, Vice-Chairman of Belfast Corporation's Housing Committee, and an Ulster Unionist MP for the city.[222]

Yet if the Castle Administration wished to give the public appearance that Ireland was the only part of the United Kingdom in mid-1921 that was actually receiving *improved* financial terms for state housing, behind the scenes there was a rather different strategy in operation. The Irish Treasury was determined to take measures to minimise the burden that would fall on the Imperial Exchequer when housing responsibilities were handed over to the new Irish Governments. Thus, although an Irish housing moratorium was never announced, a *de facto* ceiling on potential housebuilding was imposed by a ruling that the ILGB must restrict building work to schemes that had already been sanctioned and committed.[223] The Irish Treasury also effectively pruned back the subsidy to private builders. It stated that grants would now only be paid for dwellings that had been begun before 1 July 1921, or for cases where a contract had been agreed before 14 July 1921 and work started on-site by 25 August 1921.[224] By September 1921, only about 400 dwellings had been built with private subsidy and another 450 cottages were in the pipeline. It was a total that fell well short of the original promise for Ireland under the 1919 Housing (Additional Powers) Act.[225] Another avenue of retrenchment explored by the Irish Treasury in late-1921 was to close down the ILGB's Housing Department and associated Housing Committee.[226] The ILGB successfully fended off this cut-back, by arguing that decisions about housing administration were no longer a responsibility for the British Government alone. By

January 1922, some ILGB officials were about to be transferred to Ulster, and it was pointed out:

> The Board [ILGB] are not aware of the policy of the new Government in Southern Ireland and it appears to them that the continuance, abolition, or reduction of the Housing Branch of this Office is a matter to be left for decision to the Provisional Government who will deal with it in accordance with the views they may adopt in regard to this important section of the Board's work.[227]

The position of the Castle Administration on state housing had become virtually impossible by the winter of 1921–22. The underlying desire to minimise housing expenditure was compromised by the need for it to appear that the new Northern and Southern Governments were about to be handed unconditional responsibility for policy. The outcome was much confusion and recrimination, particularly in Ulster. For example, as will be discussed in Chapter 8, Belfast Corporation was incensed when the Irish Treasury declared that it would provide no extra funds to pay for the recently announced increase in housing subsidy. The Corporation's outrage was complete when the nascent Ministry of Home Affairs of the Northern Government also refused to honour the deal.[228] But before looking at the difficult consequences of independence and partition from 1922, the next chapter will examine the other key strand of the British Government's post-war campaign in Ireland, which involved the building of cottages for Irish ex-servicemen.

Chapter 7

POST-WAR HOUSING FOR IRISH EX-SERVICEMEN

Previous chapters have described a series of unique housing policies that resulted from the complex inter-relationship of Ireland and Britain. No episode was more curious than the scheme to provide cottages plus landholdings for returning servicemen under the 1919 Irish Land (Provision for Sailors and Soldiers) Act. Through this code, the British Government itself undertook to build housing in Ireland and it did so for a definite political purpose. By the end of the First World War, it had become increasingly clear to Westminster and the Castle Administration that separatists united under the Sinn Fein banner were likely to win control of national and local politics, with the exception of Ulster. In that eventuality, the majority of Irish local authorities could not be trusted to rehouse what were seen as the most deserving cases: namely, the sailors and soldiers who had enlisted voluntarily and were now returning home from battle. As one Castle official noted later, a scheme was deemed to be essential for Irish ex-servicemen 'owing to the fact that in this country they were likely to be placed at a disadvantage in the allocation of houses under the Local Authorities' Housing schemes'.[1] Furthermore, there was in Ireland a definite ideological purpose for the Government to build cottages to an unprecedentedly high standard on superior garden suburb principles. If trained fighting men were to be prevented from being recruited into Sinn Fein and its military wing, the Irish Republican Army, then some tangible gesture was needed to remind them that their best prospects lay with the country for which they had fought in the war. An ideal opportunity was presented to the Castle Administration by the virtual eclipse of the pre-war Labourers Acts programme. The housing for ex-servicemen could therefore be framed as a specialised rural counterpart to the more urgent campaign proposed under the main Irish Housing Act. All these factors ensured that post-war conditions in Ireland were not at all analogous to those on the mainland. In Britain the plan to resettle 100 000 demobilised soldiers and sailors on the land had the broad support of the populace, even if the final achievement of only around 23 000 holdings was far less than intended. Building work in England and Wales was carried out primarily by local authorities (indeed the post-war Office of Works was only pressed into contributing directly when it was realised that the main Addison Act was failing). North of the border, the programme was orchestrated by the Scottish Board of Agriculture and a specially appointed Director of Land Settlement. Conflict did erupt in western Scotland between militant ex-servicemen and wealthy landowners who resented being forced to give up land, although this was merely the continuation into the post-war era of a long-standing pattern of land agitation in the Highlands and Islands. This chapter, by contrast, will show that the way in which Government policy was framed and implemented in Ireland was radically different. It is therefore incorrect to regard the 1919 Irish Land Act as being 'in tune' with the post-war programme to resettle veterans in Britain, as Aalen has suggested recently.[2] Instead, the closest parallel to the post-war cottages for Irish ex-servicemen were those which had been paid for and constructed in Britain by the Ministry of Munitions. As essentially 'war-time' housing carried out in a state of civil unrest in Ireland, the cottages finally built under the Irish Land Act were quite unlike any other social housing initiative in post-war Europe.

PREPARATIONS FOR THE 1919 IRISH LAND ACT

The impetus behind the ex-servicemen's housing programme came from a decisive change in British policy towards Ireland in the last months of the First World War. As noted in Chapter 5, the manpower shortage following the massive German offensive in Spring 1918 had forced the Cabinet to intimate that conscription would soon have to be introduced in Ireland. The British Government searched once more for a formula for Irish self-government, and a tough new Lord Lieutenant, Field Marshal Lord French, was appointed in May 1918 as the proconsular head of what was now in effect a quasi-military administration in Dublin Castle. French was appointed to the Cabinet, and the new Chief Secretary, Edward Shortt, was given a subordinate role in charge of administration.[3] Despite a more coercive policy, the British Government found that again it had to postpone conscription when confronted by ferocious Irish opposition. Instead, French decided to escalate the recruiting campaign to attract 50 000 more volunteers. The Lord Lieutenant believed that, in Ireland, the Cabinet had to go beyond the vague post-war pledges that had already been made to servicemen. It must now give a definite promise of a plot of land for everyone who enlisted. In late-May 1918, Lord French told the Prime Minister, Lloyd George, that he was 'very anxious to get the Congested Districts Board and the Estates Commissioners to entertain the idea of making small grants of land to Irish soldiers returning from the front'.[4] This hastily conceived gesture was turned into an abortive 1918 Irish (Soldiers and Sailors) Land Bill, through which the Castle Administration intended to give ex-servicemen special status by allowing the Irish Land Commission to grant them subsidised small-holdings (or even sizeable farms), on the same terms as existing land redistribution legislation.[5] Not surprisingly, the offer was bitterly attacked by Nationalists as being a flagrant bribe. The proposal also came under heavy ridicule from all the Irish political parties in the House of Commons. It was also potentially divisive to offer land in order to encourage Irish recruits, without giving equal treatment to anyone who might enlist in Britain. Faced with a serious political embarrassment, the Government simply dropped the measure.

With the war drawing to a close, the issue of post-war reconstruction became an ever more pressing concern of the Cabinet. Lord Lieutenant French also realised the importance of the matter. In October 1918 he set up a small private Advisory Council, consisting mainly of compliant Unionists, to discuss post-war proposals for Ireland. Soon the council was recommending that £2 000 000 be given to rebuild Irish agriculture and industry, and that this should be entrusted to an Irish equivalent of the Ministry of Reconstruction.[6] The clear motive of the Castle Administration was to stop the growth of separatist Nationalism. As Chief Secretary Shortt told the Cabinet in December 1918:

> In Ireland political conditions are of a much greater importance and are much more far reaching than they are in Great Britain. In the present state of unrest it would be highly dangerous to have a large number of men standing about idle, however generous are the unemployment grants; and for that reason it is essential that work of some kind should be found for them without delay. It is an undoubted fact that returned soldiers and sailors will not receive the patriotic welcome in Ireland which they will receive in England and Scotland and Wales, and it is of the highest importance that everything should be done to let it be known that those who have done their duty are receiving proper assistance.[7]

The Cabinet was unwilling to hand over sweeping powers to a separate Irish department. Then a bitter internal clash between Lord French and his Chief Secretary, over who should be in control of Irish industrial reconstruction, served to sink the proposal. Nevertheless, the issue of post-war reconstruction remained paramount. There were something like 80 000 Irish servicemen about to return to their country.[8] Against the background of Sinn Fein's sweeping General Election victory in Southern Ireland in December 1918, Lord French urgently decided on what appeared to be a more pragmatic and achievable policy. The Lord Lieutenant demanded a Treasury grant of £250 000 in order to convert the Irish Recruiting Council into a post-war Demobilisation Committee, so that it could carry out public works with the specific intention of employing ex-servicemen. It was envisaged that relief projects would be predominantly rural in nature, such as land drainage or building country roads. The plan was similar to proposals in Britain, but to the Castle Administration there was an added imperative. The belief was, in the Treasury's words, 'that most of these men *could* be saved from absorption into the ranks of militant Sinn Fein so long as they were employed and in receipt of regular wages'.[9] Lord French warned that 'if this money is not forthcoming all our efforts will be frustrated and we may find the Sinn Fein organisation . . . strengthened by a powerful and numerous body of soldiers fresh from service in the field'.[10] The new Chief Secretary appointed in January 1919, Ian Macpherson, was a keen advocate of conciliatory policies such as state housing, and his desire to stop the deterioration of law and order made him a reliable supporter of Lord French's efforts to strangle Sinn Fein. Macpherson told the Treasury:

> The question of ensuring employment for demobilised soldiers and sailors who are returning to Ireland has been causing the greatest anxiety to the Irish Government . . . in Ireland there is unfortunately clear evidence of hostility or reluctance to engage returned soldiers and sailors. It has happened that other workers have objected to work with ex-service men, and this symptom, if allowed to develop, will add to the grave industrial unrest existing in the country. The Sinn Fein organisation is furthermore openly hostile to those men who have served, and the Irish Government, accordingly feel it imperative not only in the interests of the men themselves, but in the interests of the peace of Ireland itself, that the returning soldiers and sailors must be placed in the way of obtaining employment.[11]

There was active support within the Castle Administration for French's employment scheme, notably from stalwart Unionists such as the Vice-President of the ILGB, Sir Henry Robinson. However, the most active figure proved to be a defeated Irish Party MP, Captain Stephen Gwynn. Appointed as propaganda agent for the Demobilisation Committee, Gwynn warned the British Cabinet about returning Irish servicemen:

> Their resentment against Government may easily ally them even with those who are the occasion of their trouble. Other influences may draw them in the same direction, and Sinn Fein may gain several thousand adherents who are accustomed to throwing Mills bombs . . . It follows that the problem for Ireland concerns not merely the interests of the discharged men, nor the industrial welfare of the country, but firstly and chiefly public order and safety.[12]

In Britain, the principal champion of Lord French's new strategy was the Unionist Colonial Secretary, Sir Walter Long. It was Long who had, above all, persuaded the Cabinet to maintain a hard-line towards dissent in Ireland. 'It was a fair and square fight between the Irish Government and Sinn Fein as to who is going to govern the country', he told his colleagues in December 1918.[13] Sir Walter Long was also, as a result of his experience in the Irish Administration, a vocal advocate in Cabinet of policies to finance the resettlement of ex-servicemen. He believed that only this could avert social revolution. Long therefore informed the Chancellor of the Exchequer, Austen Chamberlain, of the Castle Administration's view 'that if they could only get the money they could get on and keep the soldiers out of Sinn Fein and Bolshevism, but if they are paralysed by lack of funds they can do nothing and will have to sit down and see the best of the Irishmen drawn into the Sinn Fein vortex'.[14] Long was an unrepentant alarmist. When it was pointed out to him that Sinn Fein were far from being 'bolshevists', he retorted that 'I don't trouble my head about these niceties: I know they are all rebels, and I don't mean them to succeed.'[15]

The *Irish Times* offered support for the hard-line Unionist view, stating that French and Macpherson's policy 'will hasten *Sinn Fein*'s collapse in no way more surely and quickly than by meeting its policy of economic destruction with a policy of economic construction'.[16] The stumbling block for the Castle Administration remained, as ever, the Treasury. In Dublin the Treasury Remembrancer, Maurice Headlam, was opposed to giving funds to any Irish body given the usual problems of ensuring strict financial control. Headlam also pointed out a key weakness in the proposal to finance relief works, which was 'that the bulk of the Irish Recruits came from the towns; and would not be willing to go into wild places, and risk attacks—except with adequate housing and high wages'.[17] It was indeed a serious objection, and one that needed to be overcome if the employment relief scheme for ex-servicemen was ever to succeed. The Castle Administration now realised that it needed at the same time to build dwellings and provide landholdings for veterans in rural areas. The consequence of this, however, was that from March 1919 the plans advanced by Lord French became completely enmeshed in the Cabinet debate about legislation to provide land and housing for British ex-servicemen. Bills for England and Wales and Scotland had already been drafted, but were much contested. The Treasury objected to the inclusion of building powers in the Land Settlement Bills for Britain, both on the grounds of expense, and because it would duplicate the work of the Addison Housing Act. In contrast, Lloyd George and the majority of Cabinet members saw the legislation as a political necessity, and so ruled that dwellings should also be provided.[18] While this was the decision that the Irish Administration wanted, the political disagreements in Westminster led to a substantial delay. In May 1919, Lord French had asked Sir Walter Long to put the Castle Administration's case to the Treasury. In a public speech a few weeks later, the Lord Lieutenant gave notice of his plan 'to establish small colonies of discharged soldiers living close to one another, each one possessing some personal interest in the soil, and a loyal attachment to it'.[19] However, it was not until late September that the Cabinet finally got around to authorising the Irish Land (Soldiers and Sailors) Bill, and only then after French had warned ominously that it was on such measures that the 'future pacification of the country largely depends'.[20]

The Irish Land (Provision for Sailors and Soldiers) Bill, as introduced to Parliament in November, therefore allowed that new cottages could be built to accompany grants of land. But the measure differed from the corresponding British legislation in two main ways. Firstly, in Britain it had—to the horror of the Treasury—been agreed that while veterans should be given priority, land settlement terms were to be open to civilians as well.[21] In the case of Ireland, the British Government ensured that the legislation applied only to the loyal citizens who had served during the war. 'The one test in this Bill', declared the

Chief Secretary, 'is the test of service.'[22] The other difference was that in Britain the responsibility for allocating land and new housing was given to local authorities, while in Ireland this was seen as politically unacceptable. The Castle Administration was constantly aware that, however long it might delay local elections after the Armistice, sooner or later the majority of councils would be controlled by separatist Nationalists (as was noted in the last chapter, Sinn Fein was indeed to establish a hegemony outside Ulster by mid-1920). Chief Secretary Macpherson therefore stated:

> The second important point is that there is a direct transaction by the ex-Service man, not with the local council, district or otherwise, but with the Government, or a Department of the Government . . . I hope the House will agree that this plan is much better, much safer, and much more valuable than one under which the ex-Service men would be at the beck and call of or under the influence of local councils.[23]

Hence the Irish Land Bill passed responsibility to Government agencies in Ireland. For ex-servicemen who wanted substantial holdings of 10–12 acres in order to become full-time farmers, the Bill allowed (as had its predecessor) for the Irish Land Commission or the Congested Districts Board to provide land on the financial terms of the Land Purchase Acts. However, it was recognised that the majority of potential applicants would not wish to earn their living solely through agriculture. So for those who were engaged in some other trade, but wanted to live in a small-holding near to a town to supplement their income, the Bill offered plots of up to two acres. This was intended as a deliberate increase on the maximum plot allowed under the Labourers Acts, as, in the Chief Secretary's words, because 'of the special circumstances of these cases, and of the meritorious service which these men have rendered to their country and to the Empire, extension of another acre as the full limit is quite a proper extension . . . The Government desires to be very generous in its assistance to these men'.[24] A further clause in the Irish Land Bill permitted the ILGB, for a period of two years after the war, to build dwellings on the site of new small-holdings. As the Treasury noted:

> The object is . . . to provide for men who may not be fitted to become small farmers. It is proposed to provide them with a cottage and a plot not exceeding two acres. Rural District Councils have power to do this (up to one acre) for labourers and are subsidised for the purpose under the Labourers Acts. In present Irish conditions such Councils would not do anything for ex-soldiers and it is proposed therefore to give the Local Government Board the powers of a Rural District Council for the purpose, financing them out of Votes.[25]

The Irish Land Bill proposed a significant degree of social engineering. Cottage building was to be based not on the existing housing need in an area, as under the Labourers Acts, but on a desire to form distinct communities of loyal ex-servicemen. As Macpherson declared:

> I look forward myself to seeing large colonies of these soldiers scattered all over Ireland . . . Whatever our feelings may be about Ireland, it is true that these men have had since their return in many parts of the country a very difficult time. Their association together in a colony of this kind will not only be of material value to them, but will afford them a great amount of coherent sympathy and protection.[26]

The policy of creating loyalist 'colonies' appealed especially to Ulster Unionist MPs. They asked for the time-scale of the scheme to be extended, and for the ILGB to be actually compelled to build cottages. Sir Edward Carson described the powers to build dwellings for non-agricultural workers as 'probably the most important part of the Bill', particularly in Ulster, where he predicted a great demand amongst the industrial population.[27] Given the anti-democratic political slant of the Bill, it is not surprising that Nationalists of all persuasions were almost unanimously hostile. There was little distinction between the statements of Sinn Fein separatists and the MPs who constituted the rump of the old Irish Parliamentary Party. Both groups emotively characterised the Castle Administration's strategy as a new 'Plantation', and both echoed the view of the *Irish Bulletin* that Irish ex-servicemen should simply ignore what was patently 'a bribe to divide them from their fellow country-men'.[28] Sinn Fein were able to remain uncompromised on the issue, since they had refused to take their seats in the Imperial Parliament. For the few Irish Party MPs left, it was simply one more humiliation when they realised that all that they could do was boycott the parliamentary debate.

The Irish Land (Provision for Soldiers and Sailors) Act received Royal Assent on 23 December 1919. The ease of its passage through Parliament belied several onerous restrictions which the Treasury had imposed behind the scenes. At first, the Irish Administration had estimated that 7600 cottages would be built at an average cost of £600 including land (obviously the cost would be higher for larger holdings). Since the programme was to be built entirely by the Irish Administration, then the full cost was to fall on the British Government. The total cost to the Exchequer was therefore expected to be in the region of £4 560 000. An alarmed Treasury wished to reject the proposal outright. But since it had already been forced to accept similar proposals for Britain, the Chancellor of the Exchequer conceded that: 'I do not think that in face of what is being done for the English ex-serviceman we can dispute the policy of the Irish Government as to cottages with land attached'.[29] Instead the Treasury sought to reduce the housing proposals, by proposing an alternative target figure of around 2000 dwellings and a total expenditure of only £1 000 000. It had notable success in trimming the time-span for building cottages down to two years, rather than the five-year period favoured by the Irish Administration. The Treasury insisted that the 'spendthrift' ILGB should not be allowed to carry out the actual building work. An unwieldy compromise was duly reached whereby the ILGB was made responsible for overall administration and site acquisition, but it was the Irish Board of Works that was to design and erect all dwellings.[30] The Treasury also attempted to restrict the maximum amount of land that could be given with a cottage to only one acre, but was forced to back down on the issue after strong opposition from Dublin Castle. The Vice-President of the ILGB, Sir Henry Robinson, argued:

> In any district in the north . . . where there was a steady demand for labour and the returned soldiers would be under no boycott of any kind, we should not dream of giving two acres with the cottage . . . But in the south and west, where there is a set against the soldiers, or where land is scarce, many a soldier would have grave difficulty in making both ends meet by what he would earn and the extra acre for additional crops or for a cow would be of inestimable benefit in such cases. Moreover, it would be a good object-lesson for the disloyal people of these districts to note that the Government had not forgotten the patriotic Irishmen who stood by the Empire in times of stress.[31]

THE IMPLEMENTATION OF THE 1919 IRISH LAND ACT

Nationalist politicians of all descriptions unequivocally rejected the scheme to rehouse Irish ex-servicemen, and called on would-be recipients to do the same. This clearly carried little weight with those who saw a chance to secure a better dwelling for themselves. Demand for cottages under the Irish Land Act proved to be far greater than the Castle Administration expected. In late-November 1919, the Attorney General for Ireland had predicted a total of around 3000 beneficiaries. Yet within a few months there were already around 5700 applications.[32] The Chief Secretary claimed in March 1920 that four cottage schemes would soon be started in Ulster, and by this date the ILGB had secured 10 sites on which to build a total of 222 cottages.[33] It was seen as essential by the Castle Administration that the design of cottages should be of a demonstrably higher standard than pre-war dwellings. Thus the ILGB noted that, in consultation with the Irish Board of Works, it had 'adopted three types of cottages in all of which accommodation of a somewhat superior character to that obtaining in the cases of cottages built by Rural District Councils under the Labourers Acts will be provided'.[34] It meant that the homes produced for Irish ex-servicemen would be equivalent to the innovative, 'modern' standards adopted by the ILGB for the main Irish Housing Act of 1919.

The optimistic start to the ex-servicemen's housing campaign was, however, short-lived. There was at the time a chronic lack of direction in Castle Administration policy, prompted by its failure to control the steadily deteriorating political and military situation in Ireland. One British official who visited in late-1919 found that many Irish departments were barely on speaking terms.[35]

As was noted in the last chapter, it was precisely this problem that prompted a major reorganisation of Dublin Castle in Spring 1920 under a new Chief Secretary, Sir Hamar Greenwood. A fresh approach was taken to all aspects of Irish policy. Hence, in May 1920 several Castle officials (most notably the powerful Joint Under Secretary and head of the Irish Treasury, Sir John Anderson) stepped in to intervene in a bitter inter-departmental wrangle between the ILGB and the Irish Board of Works. The cause of the row was the complicated division of responsibilities imposed by the Irish Land Act, and the actual dispute centred on two issues.[36] The first was the problematic issue of eligibility. At the outset, both the Castle Administration and the British Government had intended the Irish Land Act as a rural measure to complement the main Housing Act. Since then, there had been sustained pressure from the British Legion and other groups to extend the terms to urban areas. The ILGB had opposed any dilution, whereas the Irish Board of Works was more favourable. After further heated exchanges, the Castle Administration in August 1920 reluctantly decided on balance to also allow ex-servicemen who lived in towns and cities to be rehoused. 'This new decision of the Government letting in urban cases throws thousands more of applicants on us', moaned the ILGB's Sir Henry Robinson, 'and as land near Towns is so expensive I am much troubled by it.'[37] Another instance of the dispute between the ILGB and the Irish Board of Works over the terms of eligibility was whether housing could be built at the privately owned Wolfhill and Castlecomer Collieries, if the owners promised to employ ex-soldiers and sailors as miners. Sir Henry Robinson was fully in support of these schemes, warning that 'any action in the way of blocking or delaying the Schemes and thereby keeping the men out of employment in Districts where high wages are offered, will be regarded as a breach of faith and might tend to drive these loyal men in despair into the ranks of Sinn Fein'.[38] However, the Irish Board of Works was successful in blocking the ILGB proposals. In the end, the Irish Treasury imposed such strenuous financial restrictions on the colliery owners that only some very basic temporary huts were ever built.

The other issue for inter-departmental dispute arose from financial considerations. Post-war inflation, plus the decision to build to an unprecedentedly high standard, meant that in mid-1920 the Board of Works found itself unable to obtain tenders from contractors for less than £1200 per cottage.[39] It was, of course, the same problem as was being experienced at the time by local authorities in Ireland and Britain under the main Housing Acts. But in the case of Irish ex-servicemen's cottages it provoked another furious row between the Irish Board of Works and the ILGB. The former felt that costs should be kept down by restricting the number of applicants and by building on cheaper rural sites. In contrast, the ILGB solution (as voiced by Sir Henry Robinson and Dr Peter Cowan, Chairman of the Housing Committee) was to achieve savings through the use of shorter-term, 'semi-permanent' construction for as long as post-war inflation persisted. The Irish Treasury instinctively sided with the

ILGB, and was particularly persuaded by the associated argument that if non-traditional building methods were used, then it was possible to stipulate that a certain proportion of unskilled ex-servicemen *had* to be employed by the building contractor.[40] Thus it was the potential to provide employment as well as tangible housing results that created a new impetus for the programme. As the Irish Treasury noted:

> Moreover these cottages are intended for an emergency. It is far more important to get a cottage of *some* sort for the ex-serviceman, than to give him nothing at all, because for our credit we will not build for less than 100 years, and that costs more than we can afford to spend! On political grounds the answer is quite clear.[41]

In December 1920, the deadlock on the issue was finally broken when the Irish Treasury notified the Irish Board of Works that it had 'come to the conclusion that the Government must definitely abandon the standard . . . of the Labourers Cottages Acts, and must be content with a type of cottage which can be erected more cheaply, and, if possible, more quickly, even though this saving may be obtained by a sacrifice of durability and economy of maintenance'.[42]

The Vice-President of the ILGB, Sir Henry Robinson, took advantage of this decision to embark on a housing estate for ex-servicemen on a 40-acre site at Killester, in the north-eastern suburbs of Dublin. Killester was the only scheme to be built directly by the ILGB, and it was specifically intended to represent a paradigm of the post-war policies promoted by Lord French and the Castle Unionists. In the Killester Estate, the British ideological conjunction of loyalty to Empire, favouritism towards Irish ex-servicemen, technical standardisation, and garden suburb planning, all reached their apotheosis. The site had been bought in 1916 by Sir Henry McLaughlin, a wealthy Unionist building contractor and head of the Irish Recruiting Council. At first, the property was entrusted to a Local Relief Committee (indeed a tentative plan was hatched by Robinson in 1917 to turn it into a model farm to provide work). After the war it was first offered to Dublin Corporation for housing purposes. When this plan fell through, McLaughlin, who was by now head of Lord French's Demobilisation Committee, made a free gift of the land to the ILGB.[43] Sir Henry Robinson immediately started to ask for funds, so that the ILGB could employ a team of ex-servicemen to clear the site over the forthcoming winter, as a special relief scheme. In late-October 1920 he wrote:

> There is every indication that we may be faced with severe difficulties during the Winter months owing to unemployment and depression in trade, especially in urban areas. On similar occasions in the past, the centre of disturbance has always been Dublin . . . It would be a most grievous thing and a triumph for the disloyal if they [ex-servicemen]

were driven to make demonstrations of their want in the streets of Dublin.⁴⁴

Indeed, it was an increasingly tense time in Southern Ireland. Only three weeks after Robinson's letter, a particularly grisly day in Dublin saw the IRA shoot 11 Englishmen accused of being spies, and then the notorious 'Black-and-Tans' retaliate by opening fire on a crowd at a Gaelic football match, resulting in the death of 12 people and the injuring of 60 more. Martial law was declared in County Cork in December 1920, soon to be followed by most of Munster. The Castle Administration was now particularly worried that the evident collapse of the post-war economic boom in late-1920 might lead to even more disaffected ex-soldiers joining the ranks of Sinn Fein. As Sir John Anderson told a senior Treasury official in Whitehall:

> Ex-soldiers as a class in Ireland can be a great political asset or the reverse. They are just the sort of people the rebels would like to entice into the ranks of the Irish Republican Army. The tendency a few months ago was all in this direction. The rot has been stopped: we don't want it to start again as the result of unemployment.⁴⁵

It was this concern that prompted the approval in December 1920 for a grant from the Reconstruction Fund to clear and prepare the Killester housing site. 'The Board of Works do not object', noted Anderson, '. . . and in the circumstances I have told Sir Henry Robinson that he can count on £10,000. It is very important to keep the Dublin ex-service men in good heart.'⁴⁶ A team of around 180 veterans, under the direction of an ILGB official and ex-Royal Engineer, Colonel MacCabe, began to build roads on the site. But Robinson's intention was, of course, to create something that was far more than just a temporary relief scheme. By late-February 1921, the ILGB team was laying foundations and drains. Robinson declared that the Killester project 'will be the means, not only of affording much-needed employment at present, but of allaying a good deal of discontent amongst ex-service men on the housing question'.⁴⁷ Robinson and the ILGB also intended to use the scheme to showcase a particular 'semi-permanent' method of construction, the 'Orion' system. This system was marketed by an Irish company, Ryan Ltd, amongst whose directors were two leading lights of the war-time recruiting campaign. One was Sir Henry McLaughlin, whose role at Killester was mentioned above, and the other was E. A. Aston, who had been a noted town planning enthusiast since the pre-war era. Ryan Ltd had already built a few exhibition dwellings at Victoria Road, Clontarf (near to the Killester site), and these had been visited in July 1920 by Sir Henry Robinson and an official from the Irish Treasury.⁴⁸ In September, the ILGB signed a contract with Ryan Ltd to build a further 38 semi-permanent cottages on the Clontarf estate. This small scheme was then taken over for veterans' housing on its completion in mid-1921.⁴⁹ The patented 'Orion' dwellings were designed by George O'Connor, the much-praised architect for Pembroke UDC's war-time estates, and set an uncompromisingly high standard for ex-servicemen's dwellings. The standard plans offered two alternative types of semi-detached cottages. The first was for a four-room bungalow with two bedrooms, a bathroom, and a frontage of 30 feet (a total area of 765 square feet). The second was for an extremely substantial seven-room dwelling on two storeys (over 1050 square feet), and contained a parlour, living room, four bedrooms, and a separate bathroom.

The Irish Board of Works, however, continued to raise objections to the use of 'Orion' dwellings. The nature of the system indeed sounded dubious. It basically consisted of laying lightweight walling blocks made out of gypsum plaster mixed with sawdust. These were then coated with vulcanite to form a damp-proof barrier, before being finished externally with cement render on metal lathing. The building blocks had no real strength, so in the case of the two-storey dwellings a concealed structural steel frame had to be provided. When the Irish Treasury was forced to consult the English Ministry of Health about the suitability of the 'Orion' construction method, even sending some sample blocks over for inspection, the latter appears to have sided with the Irish Board of Works.[50] But what finally killed off the ILGB's plan to use 'semi-permanent' construction was that in the event they could not obtain tenders for much less than £1000 per dwelling. The system was thus unlikely to prove any cheaper than traditional construction. So in late-1920 the Irish Board of Works and the ILGB started to negotiate again over the design of ex-servicemen's cottages. A compromise was reached in which concrete blocks were to be used instead of brick, and asbestos-cement or cheap clay tiles were to replace slate roofs. The Irish Board of Works took pains to point out that the 'alterations made in the plans have not involved any material decrease in the accommodation provided', and that the new construction method would still have a long-term life.[51] Tenders were soon being received at £900 per dwelling and it was expected that building costs would fall further as the recession deepened. Given this climate, the intention to use Ryan Ltd's experimental 'Orion' system at Killester was quietly dropped in favour of rendered concrete blockwork.

The omission of 'semi-permanent' construction was only a minor blow to those promoting the Killester project. Sir Henry Robinson and his allies clearly had larger issues in mind for the 247 dwellings that were to make up the estate. As Sir Henry McLaughlin declared, Killester was to be 'the first considerable instalment of housing for ex-Service men . . . [and] a model for similar schemes throughout the country'.[52] The scheme was intended to epitomise the best of British garden suburb design. To this end, Robinson was presented with a free site layout by a small clique of town planning enthusiasts headed by the well-to-do Dublin philanthropist, Frederick Purser Griffith. The latter had succeeded E. A. Aston as the main protagonist in the Citizens Housing League, and was also connected to the Killester scheme by his close associations with Aston and Colonel MacCabe. In keeping with the precedent set by the pre-war town planning campaign in Dublin, it was to Edinburgh and the Geddesian connection that this clique turned for help. Frank Mears, the son-in-law of Patrick Geddes and the latter's assistant on the 1914 Dublin Housing Report, was invited over in late-1920 to design the layout plan for Killester and a few other possible sites (Mears also designed in the same period an unrealised project for a public utility society set up by Aston in Killester, and was the following year involved with Aston and Griffith in drawing up town planning proposals for central Dublin).[53] The outcome was that the design for the Killester Estate received wide praise. Patrick Abercrombie was reportedly 'delighted with it', and even the Irish Treasury, while regretting the expense of a garden suburb arrangement, admitted that Killester was 'quite a successful attempt at lay out which has been generally admired by independent persons'.[54]

The Killester design therefore had most of the hallmarks of the layout of a typical post-war suburban scheme in Britain (see Fig. 42). Many existing site features such as roads and trees were retained, and the new insertions were arranged in a winding yet carefully contrived manner to exploit the changing aspects, or 'street pictures', seen by observers as they walked around the scheme. Dwellings were set well back from the road, and were arranged in large blocks of land broken up by cul-de-sacs and by communal recreation facilities located in the centre of the blocks. Yet the Killester design also varied slightly from British practice in two aspects, both of which stemmed from the desire of Robinson and the Castle Administration to produce a quality of design appropriate for ex-army officers (be they commissioned or non-commissioned). The first variant was that Killester had an exceedingly low and semi-rural density of only four cottages to the acre. Second, in keeping with the quasi-rural ambience and the general cultural preference in Ireland for bungalows, all the dwellings were single-storey. There were three standard house-types repeated throughout the estate, the majority being built to a size and standard that was noticeably higher even than the dwellings designed elsewhere for ex-servicemen by the Irish Board of Works.[55] The best type at Killester was represented by 32 very large detached bungalows with five rooms (a total area of 1007 square feet), comprising a parlour (121 square feet), living room (162 square feet), three bedrooms (80–160 square feet), a large kitchen/scullery (89 square feet), and bathroom. These detached cottages were concentrated in the southern part known as 'The Demesne', and were aimed squarely at commissioned officers. The other bungalows at Killester were all laid out in semi-detached pairs. The vast majority were simply four-room non-parlour versions (841 square feet) of the above type. There were, however, also some 38 dwellings aimed at the ordinary soldier, and containing only three rooms (675 square feet). The Killester elevations were very plain, being rendered externally with pre-cast concrete surrounds to doors and windows. Since the cottages were single-storey there was in fact little elevation to be seen, and contemporary photographs show a streetscape dominated by a forest of powerful, vertical chimneys which pierce the diagonal pattern of asbestos-cement tiles that were used to cover the large, hipped roofs (see Figs 43–44).

Post-war Housing for Irish Ex-servicemen 253

Fig 42. F. Mears/ILGB: site plan of the Killester Estate (1920–22)

Fig 43. F. Mears/ILGB: photograph of the Killester Estate in the late-1920s

Fig 44. F. Mears/ILGB: photograph of the Killester Estate now

Although the dwelling types at the Killester Estate were obviously designed to a very high standard, Robinson still anticipated tenders of £700 for the semi-detached cottages and £900 for the detached dwellings. He even appears to have volunteered to meet any excess costs above these levels from his own funding sources.[56] In the event, the high standard of design, and the use of an inefficient direct labour force of unskilled ex-servicemen to build the infrastructure, meant that the average cost worked out at nearly £1500 per dwelling. As a consequence, rents at Killester were staggeringly high, set at a punitive 12s 6d–20s per week depending on the type of dwellings (as will be seen, this was to provoke rent strikes that reduced this figure). 'The Killester houses are, after all, exceptional', as one official was later to justify.[57] By 1922 the Irish Treasury was being openly critical of Sir Henry Robinson, accusing him of 'lamentable extravagance' at Killester and asking that he make good his promise to contribute towards the excess cost.[58] The existing programme with the contractor at Killester was abruptly cut short, and the remainder of the scheme was re-tendered, but this time under the control of the Irish Board of Works. The original design for 247 cottages was finally completed in August 1923, and the estate was extended by another 42 dwellings later in the decade.

If the ILGB's unique initiative at Killester represented the *crème de la crème* of post-war housing for ex-servicemen, how then did the typical schemes built by the Irish Board of Works compare? Altogether nearly 1400 cottages were built to the latter department's designs in Southern Ireland, along with another 390 units in Ulster.[59] Since the 1919 Irish Land Act was originally intended as a rural measure, it is not surprising that many of the ex-servicemen's cottages tended to be grouped in isolated clusters of between two and ten dwellings. But alongside this stood the desire of the Castle Administration to create larger and more visible 'colonies' for veterans. The decision in late-1920 to include schemes for urban and suburban areas resulted in a number of higher-density developments which contained between 30 and 60 homes. Some of these early schemes subsequently grew to become substantial estates, such as the 146 cottages built at Cregagh near Belfast, although none was ever to match Killester in size. The Irish Board of Works designed a wide variety of dwelling types, all of which clearly exceeded the standard found in pre-war Labourers Acts housing. The types were always in the form of two-storey cottages, sometimes detached but mostly in semi-detached pairs. Deliberate variety in the elevations was combined with a uniformity in house size. 'In no two schemes are the designs alike', observed the *Irish Times* in 1922, 'although most of the houses are four-roomed with sculleries and out-houses, and bathrooms in urban districts.'[60] In not one version of the cottages built by the Irish Board of Works was there a parlour. The most common type for rural districts was a small four-room semi-detached cottage with a frontage of 22 feet (Type 2 and 2^A; total floor area of 720 square feet—see Fig. 45). The plan had a side entrance leading through a hall to a large living room (176 square feet) and a ground floor bedroom (92 square feet). The other two bedrooms were upstairs (92–176

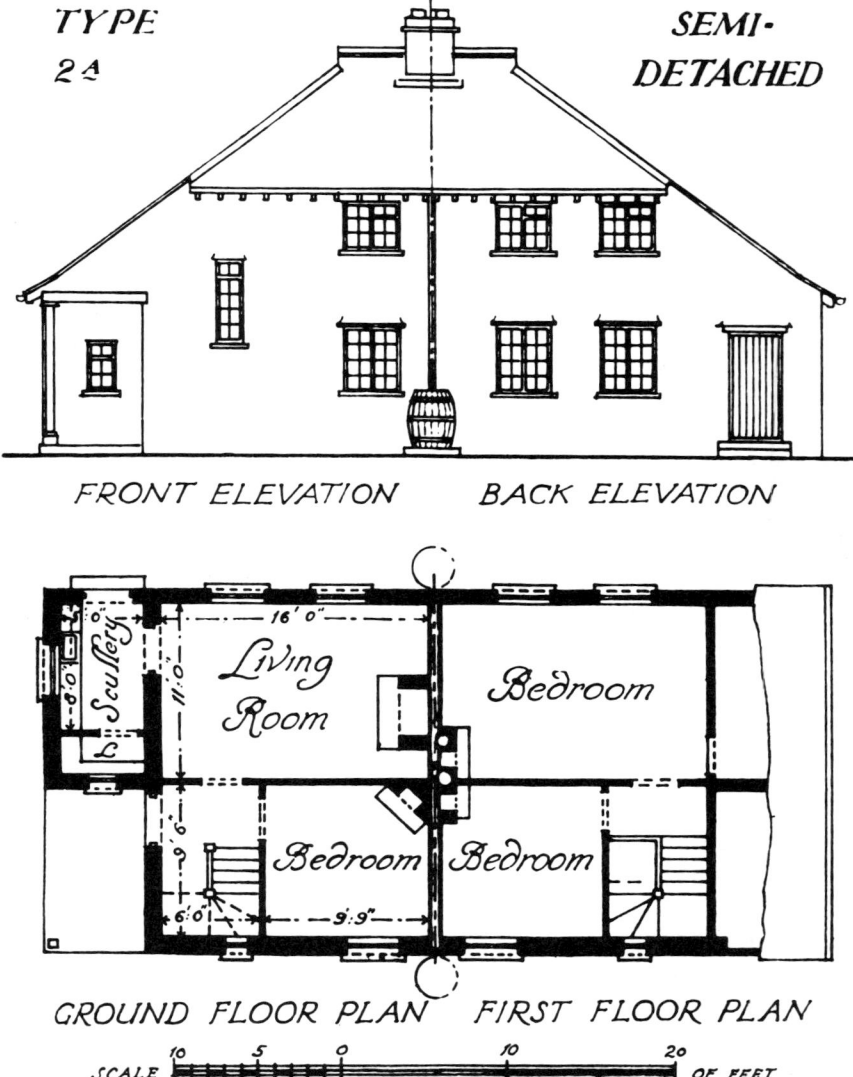

Fig 45. Irish Board of Works: 'Type 2^A' four-room cottage for ex-servicemen

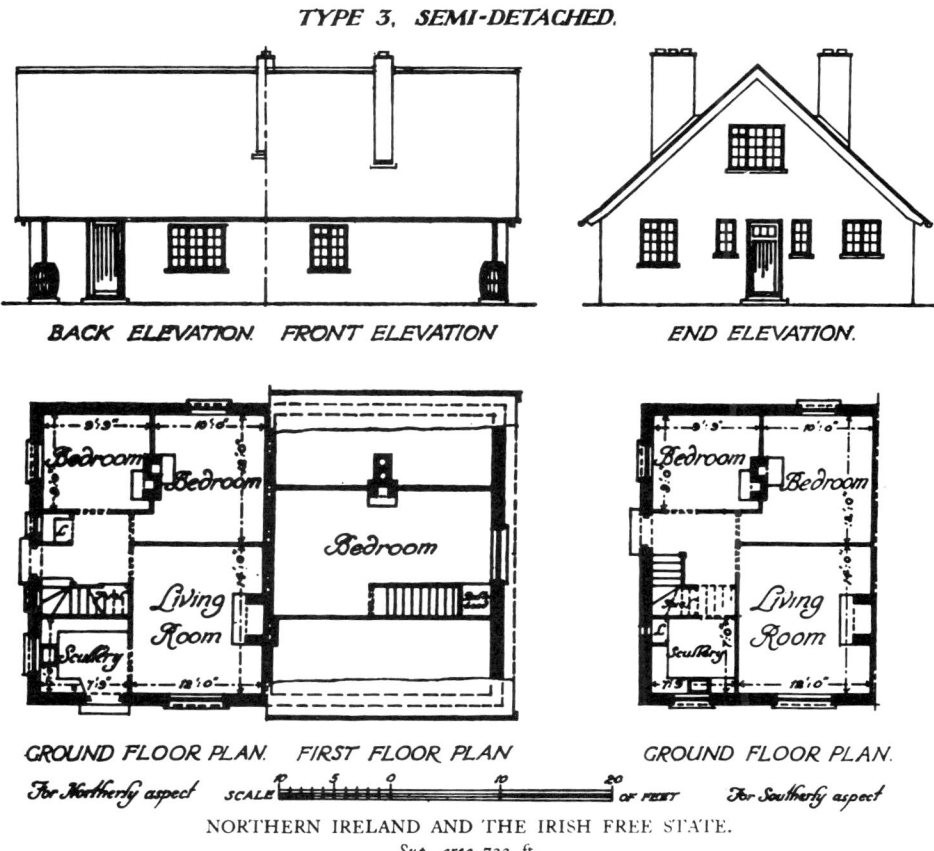

Fig 46. Irish Board of Works: 'Type 3' four-room cottage for ex-servicemen

square feet). Due to the lack of a water supply and drainage system in rural areas, this version was basic in terms of services provision. There was no bathroom, but simply an external earth closet, and the scullery was located in a small side projection opening off the main living room. The compactness and austerity of the plan and volume were reminiscent of the plain 'boxes-with-lids-on' found in British post-war housing, and typified the approach used by the Irish Board of Works. The other alternative type-plans for rural areas all had the same basic four-room plan arrangement, and either offered a through living room (Types 1 and 6) or were laid out as essentially a single-storey plan with only an attic bedroom upstairs (Type 3) (see Fig. 46). For some of the rural variants there was an attempt to counter monotony by introducing more picturesque elements such as hipped roofs, projecting eaves, and a front porch. In the house-types for urban and suburban areas, the Irish Board of Works also retained the format of a four-room semi-detached cottage, but increased the standard by making the dwelling larger in size (750–900 square feet) and by including a ground floor bathroom and WC. The kitchen/scullery was also substantially larger than in rural cottages, and created in effect a five-room cottage. Therefore, the semi-detached urban dwellings provided for ex-servicemen by the Irish Board of Works corresponded to the medium-sized cottage layouts recommended by the ILGB for the main Irish Housing Act. The construction of the Irish Board of Works dwellings, as has already been noted, was generally in rendered concrete blockwork to reduce cost. In one slightly later scheme in Kingstown, the design emulated a precedent first set by Liverpool Corporation, by using patterns of coloured fair-faced blockwork to decorate the elevations.[61]

EX-SERVICEMEN'S HOUSING AND THE TRANSFER OF POWER IN IRELAND

Despite the administrative reform launched within Dublin Castle in May 1920, there was still very little actual progress under the Irish Land Act. By the spring of 1921, only 134 ex-servicemen had been given farm holdings.[62] In terms of cottage-building the figures were just as bad. The Castle Administration noted that 'owing to labour troubles and the general state of unrest in Ireland progress has not been as expeditious as could be desired'.[63] Hence by August 1921 a grand total of only 15 dwellings had been completed, although another 926 cottages were at some stage of construction. It was a paltry achievement when compared with the fact that the ILGB had by this point received 14 000 applications for cottages, and had given approval for schemes totalling 1670 cottages.[64] Dublin Castle departments declared optimistically that many more dwellings for ex-servicemen would be commenced in the near future. It was hoped that progress would be hastened by a predicted downward trend in building costs, and by finance that was now available from a £1 250 000 emergency fund recently approved by the Irish Treasury and Whitehall.[65]

Although the determination of the Castle Administration had removed most of the financial and administrative restrictions by mid-1921, nevertheless the campaign to build ex-servicemen's housing continued to be hampered by wider political factors. An immediate blow was the imposition by the Cabinet in July 1921 of the moratorium on post-war housing expenditure. In Britain, the announcement had the effect of finally killing off the already moribund initiative to resettle ex-servicemen on the land.[66] As was noted in the last chapter, the Castle Administration and Westminster decided for political reasons not to publicly declare a moratorium in Ireland. The safeguard was that there was unlikely to be much Irish state housing built in the interim before responsibilities were handed over to the new Governments in Northern and Southern Ireland. However, the campaign to build cottages for ex-servicemen was obviously a separate and very special case. The basis of the scheme was that it was funded entirely by the Imperial Exchequer, and was only intended for a specific loyal minority who had served Britain during the war. Since it was therefore likely to remain a permanent 'reserved service' even after the transfer of power, the British Government was forced to treat this particular aspect of Irish housing policy as an initiative affected by the recently imposed moratorium. Within the Castle Administration there was already a growing dispute between the ILGB and the Irish Treasury. The latter was determined to do something about the high tenders still being received for dwellings under the Irish Land Act. Therefore the Irish Treasury had summarily halved the financial allocation for Irish ex-servicemen's housing in 1921–22 to only £1 500 000. Relations between the two departments only worsened in June 1921 when the ILGB was instructed to stop buying expensive urban sites.[67] With the advent of a full-scale housing moratorium in Westminster in early July, the balance of power shifted decisively in favour of the Irish Treasury. Supporters of the ex-servicemen's housing campaign tried to fight back by reviving the old alarmist scares. The ILGB argued that any retrenchment 'would probably have very serious consequences throughout the country . . . The almost inevitable result of such action, if persisted in, will be to drive the ex-service men into the ranks of those who are the disturbing element in the country.'[68] And the Unionist *Irish Times* launched a savage attack on the Irish Treasury, declaring that:

> to allow these men to become Bolsheviks (and what else can they become?) in order that the Treasury . . . may save a few thousand pounds . . . is a crime against civilization, as well as a betrayal of the men who saved the Empire by their courage and tenacity.[69]

But by this date, with the Lloyd George Government now making overtures to Sinn Fein, such warnings carried little weight inside Dublin Castle. The Chief Secretary, Sir Hamar Greenwood, and the Joint Under Secretary, Sir John Anderson, began to wield the knife during the autumn of 1921. To conciliate Sir Henry Robinson at the ILGB, they agreed that there would be no staff cut-backs in the section dealing with ex-servicemen's housing, and that, in order 'to avoid a breach of faith' by the Government, those urban schemes that had already been approved could still be completed (thereby saving the later stages of the Killester Estate).[70] Chief Secretary Greenwood and Sir John Anderson, however, completely rejected the ILGB's suggestion that the target figure for the ex-servicemen's campaign should remain in the region of 4500–6000 dwellings to ensure that Northern Ireland, where little had been built, would receive its fair share.[71] They replied that any imbalance between Northern and Southern Ireland could be remedied instead by simply dropping some of the schemes for the latter region. Thus, in early-November 1921 the Irish Treasury was authorised to rule that, with regard to the ex-servicemen's housing programme in Ireland,'no new commitments in either Southern or Northern Ireland should be entered into, either in Urban or Rural Districts'.[72] This meant that there was now a complete moratorium on new schemes. The next issue to decide was just how many of the current commitments should be honoured. After much haggling, it was agreed that the final total under the campaign should be fixed at 3672 dwellings. This, in turn, was subdivided into a ratio of 2626 cottages for Southern Ireland and 1046 cottages for Ulster. The revised total was only half of the figure that the ILGB had up to this point hoped might still be provided. But now the Castle Administration had made it clear that the reduced programme would represent the final obligation of the British Government towards the housing of ex-soldiers and sailors in Ireland.

A genuine problem for the Castle Administration in the winter of 1921–22 was how to proceed with a scaled-down campaign to rehouse ex-servicemen at a time of sensitive political negotiations over the transfer of power. By this point, the Northern Ireland Government was already *de facto* in existence. In the South, a Provisional Government was set up in January 1922 to take over administration gradually while preparations were completed for a hand-over to the new Irish Free State. The British Government saw the housing programme for veterans as a means to help both new Irish administrations. A Cabinet sub-committee noted in March 1922 that 'the settlement of between 3000 and 4000 men with suitable houses and allotments will prove a national asset of the first value'.[73] At first, the Irish Treasury proposed that responsibility for the completion of the 3672 cottages should be given over at once to both Irish Governments. Under this plan, the Imperial Exchequer was to pay for the entire cost of building in Ulster in exchange for receiving the entire rent income after completion. In the case of the Southern Government, which the Treasury did not trust to ensure proper economy in construction, it was envisaged that the Exchequer would contribute only 50 per cent of the capital costs and receive only half of the rent income.[74] Not surprisingly, the Northern Ireland Administration was amenable to the offer of preferential financial treatment. But at the same time, it was also determined to fight for a larger share of ex-servicemen's dwellings; the grounds were that since over half of the 145 000 recruits in Ireland had come from Ulster, then the province should receive at least 1400 cottages (40 per cent of the total). In March 1922, only 73 dwellings had as yet been built in Ulster, with another 540 units in the pipeline. However, the Treasury realised that there would be a political outcry in the Irish Free State were there to be any suggestion of readjusting the housing allocation under the Irish Land Act. Instead, it counter-attacked by openly accusing the Northern Government of trying to evade its housing responsibilities. If anything, the mood in the Treasury was to cut the provision for Ulster in order to make further savings.[75]

The disagreements between Whitehall and the Northern Government were eclipsed by those between the Irish Treasury in Dublin Castle and the new Provisional Government for Southern Ireland. Sinn Fein had from the start been ferociously opposed to the campaign to build dwellings for ex-servicemen. Its strategy of calling on veterans to boycott the Irish Land Act was sufficient for as long as nothing, or next to nothing, was being built. But when the programme finally began to take off in mid-1921, just as peace negotiations were beginning between the Government and Sinn Fein, the whole issue became extremely sensitive. Republicans now accused the Castle Administration of taking advantage of the ceasefire to push through what they considered to be a highly provocative policy. Discussions were held within Sinn Fein to decide what form of political or military resistance was appropriate. The hardline position was represented by Dáil Éireann's unofficial Minister for Agriculture, A. O. Concubair. He believed that, although many ex-servicemen had indeed served Sinn Fein well, 'there are others who are so much out of sympathy with the desires and aspirations of the majority of our people that their settlement either individually or in Colonies—the latter being in the nature of a new "Plantation"—in parts of the country would be a menace that under no circumstances should be tolerated'.[76] Concubair went on to state in November 1921 that:

> I am of opinion that the attempt to settle Ex-soldiers on our lands is an invasion of our Sovereign Rights which should be resisted by every means at our disposal right up to the use of force. I believe that the parties concerned in the country so regard it as a hostile act that in places it may lead to a breach of the Truce if persisted in.[77]

A belligerent reaction such as this would obviously have had serious repercussions for the delicate peace process. So the Dáil Éireann decided merely to declare once more its opposition to the principle of the scheme, and to warn the British Government that the continuation of building work was not conducive to a political settlement. Continued bad feeling over the ex-servicemen's housing programme resurfaced in early-1922. At this point, the new Provisional Government was wrestling to assert its authority over the administrative departments that had been inherited. A member of the new Ministry of Local Government told the Dáil Cabinet that the ILGB was being deliberately obstructive:

> Another instance of the undesirable activities of the other Department [ILGB] is the working of the Soldiers' and Sailors' Provision of Land Schemes. It is our policy to temporarily suspend these, as there is a grave danger of serious trouble in rural areas over this matter. A most undesirable class of ex-soldiers are getting those lands, while I.R.A. Soldiers are walking about unemployed . . . We believe that those orders are being deliberately issued to prejudice us, as the Act has been practically moribund for two years. There is a large sum of money, we believe, about £600,000 ear-marked for this Scheme, and it may be undesirable to lose it, but, it is most necessary that during the transition period we should suspend the operation of those acts under a Dáil Department.[78]

The Provisional Government of the Irish Free State was placed in a tricky position by the fact that the British Government wanted to continue with the veterans' housing campaign. The Irish economy had entered a serious downturn in the period from 1921 to 1923 and unemployment was escalating.[79] The financial problems being experienced in Southern Ireland severely limited the capacity of the Provisional Government to deal with the housing issue. Another source of finance would have been welcome. Yet, on the other hand, the fact that Westminster was asking the South to contribute towards the cost of rehousing ex-servicemen made it politically impossible for the Provisional Government to accept (particularly at a time when the acrimonious debate over the terms of the 'Treaty' was set to plunge Southern Ireland into civil war). An Irish Treasury official in Dublin Castle reported that the private views of William Cosgrave, Minister of Local Government (and soon to become President of the Free State), were as follows:

> Cosgrave, while admitting frankly our argument that the money spent brought solid material advantages to the Irish people and Government as a whole, said that . . . it was simply impossible for the Irish Government to ask the Free State Parliament to vote money expressly for the benefit of men who had fought for the British Government in the European War. The answer would be at once: What are you doing for *our* ex-service (I.R.A.) men? and as he intended to do nothing, outside the general housing scheme, and the Ministry of Finance had no money to spare . . . he would certainly be defeated on the motion for the Vote.[80]

Cosgrave was particularly annoyed at being asked to help finance the completion of the notoriously expensive scheme at Killester, associated as it was with the arch-Unionist faction led by Sir Henry Robinson. But even though the Treasury offered to finish the Killester Estate at its own expense, as part of a package of financial incentives, the Provisional Government held firm in its refusal to take over responsibility for the ex-servicemen's campaign.[81]

THE CREATION OF THE IRISH SAILORS' AND SOLDIERS' LAND TRUST

The campaign to build cottages for ex-servicemen in Ireland was an unusual initiative to begin with, and as a result of the transfer of power to both North and South it became even more so. When the proposal to involve the Provisional Government of the Irish Free State was turned down by the latter in late-April 1922, William Cosgrave suggested an ingenious alternative. His proposal was that a special housing trust be set up for the whole of Ireland to complete the building works and manage the estates.[82] The Treasury was initially lukewarm about the idea, but came to see certain advantages. An independent trust could be relied on to be more zealous in collecting rents, and if it agreed to the proposal then the Free State Government might be persuaded to contribute to the cost (the Treasury was again to be disappointed on this score). Therefore, as a result of unique legislation passed in Westminster and in both Irish Parliaments during the winter of 1922–23, a body known as the Irish Soldiers' and Sailors' Land Trust (hereafter ISSLT) was created in January 1924. Its prime task was to complete the target figure of 3672 dwellings in accordance with the ratio that had been agreed several years before (i.e. 2626 units in the South and 1046 units in Ulster). By the start of 1924, nearly 1500 cottages had been built already for ex-servicemen in Ireland, the vast majority being located in Leinster and Munster. The ISSLT therefore needed to supply a balance of just over 2000 dwellings, and it had to pay much more attention to the demands of Ulster. A capital expenditure of £1 500 000 was allowed for under the legislation.[83] A board of four trustees was appointed to oversee the programme, while the actual building of the cottages continued to be carried out by the same departmental sections that had stepped into the breach in 1922. In the case of Northern Ireland, the task fell to a branch of the Ministry of Finance. The counterpart for the Irish Free State was a special Dublin section of the British Government's Colonial Office (until the function was subsequently taken over by the ISSLT itself in April 1925). The creation of a single trust to cover the whole of Ireland was unusual at a time when the two new Irish Governments were effectively refusing to acknowledge each other's existence. One housing expert observed optimistically that the ISSLT offered 'one of the very few points of direct contact between the two areas into which the island has unhappily been divided'.[84]

In reality, the ISSLT could not avoid the implications of partition. The four trustees were all ex-army officers, two from Southern Ireland and two from Ulster. Both pairs of trustees tended to champion the cause of their respective part of Ireland. This sectionalism suited the Imperial Treasury perfectly, given the latter's determination to maintain a strict control over the ex-servicemen's housing campaign. The only real issue for the Treasury was who was going to be Chairman of the ISSLT, and to this post it purposely appointed an Englishman, George Duckworth. Although it was the case that Duckworth had a long track record as a housing reformer (he was a supporter of Octavia Hill and had worked for ten years as a researcher on Charles Booth's mammoth social survey of London), it was two particular qualities that recommended him to the Treasury. 'During the War', wrote one official, 'Mr Duckworth was engaged in the Housing Department of the Ministry of Munitions, and the experience he then acquired is of special value for the Trust work.'[85] He had in fact for 18 months been an effective administrative head for the whole munitions housing programme. Duckworth brought this attitude of national loyalty to his new role, by declaring that the purpose of the ISSLT was foremost to build 'practical' as well as symbolic war memorials. He confided privately that he regarded:

> the provision of houses and land under the Act out of Imperial Funds as a continuing Imperial service forming a war memorial which should be maintained not merely for the life of the ex-service man, but should be

carried on . . . in favour of his children. In this way our little settlements all over Ireland would become living, visible and more or less abiding monuments of England's gratitude to the Irishmen who fought for her in the Great War.[86]

The other attraction for the Treasury was that Duckworth would only take the post on condition that he was based in London. Indeed, the Treasury Secretary stated that the department saw 'the London Headquarters, with Duckworth or some other impartial Englishman as Chairman, as a necessary condition of handing over to an otherwise irresponsible body such a large capital sum'.[87] Duckworth served as Chairman of the ISSLT until mid-1927. During this time, he acted essentially as a Treasury puppet in the continual struggle to restrict what was seen as would-be extravagance by the Irish trustees. A British official noted:

> During 1924 strong differences of opinion developed between Mr Duckworth, the Chairman of the Trust, whose main concern was that the Trust should operate efficiently and that the rents to be charged for the houses should be set at such a figure as would ensure the proper maintenance of the Trust's property out of their income, and the other four members, some of whom showed a tendency either to seek popularity among ex-service men by fixing rents at such a figure as would necessitate drawing upon capital for maintenance or to consider themselves as the servants of the Irish Governments rather than of the British Government.[88]

The primary cause of dispute with the trustees was the Treasury's determination to achieve a reduction in the overall expenditure limit of £1 500 000. The Treasury secretly consulted the housing departments set up by the new Governments in the Irish Free State and Northern Ireland, to see if there was any way in which they could use prevailing Irish standards as a basis to cut the ISSLT's building costs. Even in these secretive consultations, the Treasury showed a clear bias towards the Unionist Administration in Ulster. 'I have no doubt that in Belfast we should be bound to provide baths because the standard of civilisation there presumably requires it', noted one Treasury official, 'But I am by no means certain that this is necessary in the South even in the towns.'[89] At the end of 1924, the Treasury duly notified the ISSLT that it was now imposing a maximum 'all-in' cost limit of only £500 per dwelling. The trustees saw this as an outrageously low figure, and bitterly accused the British Government of wanting to build 'dog kennels' rather than houses for ex-servicemen. However, the tactic proved merely to be the Treasury's opening gambit. The Treasury loftily offered to remove the cost ceiling for each dwelling, and to waive all restrictions over the number of cottages to be built, if only the ISSLT would agree to accept a reduced lump sum as a final settlement from Westminster. After much acrimonious bargaining, a compromise total of

£1 300 000 was agreed. The deal did not, however, give the ISSLT any real autonomy. The Treasury insisted on three restrictive safeguards: the headquarters had to remain in London; the British Government was still to appoint the chairman; and the Treasury was to continue to stipulate minimum rent levels. Duckworth could not have been surprised to receive a resentful note from his colleagues which observed that 'the Treasury have issued Regulations which render the Irish Trustees largely without power or authority'.[90] Nor were the trustees able to apply to a higher authority for help. The truth of the matter was that by the mid-1920s, the British Government was only interested in finishing the programme at the minimum cost. In 1926 the Chancellor of the Exchequer, Winston Churchill, refused to grant any further funds. Churchill justified the decision on the grounds that the £3 000 000 that had been spent already 'was on a far more generous scale than anything which it was found possible to do in the way of providing houses or land holdings for ex-service men in this country'.[91]

Cost cutting was clearly what was expected from the ISSLT. In mid-1924, Duckworth asked that the trustees should in future only approve cottages that were '*smaller* and rather more suitably planned than those built hitherto'.[92] What his directive in fact meant was that the ISSLT was now required to abandon the exceptionally high standards deemed necessary for ideological reasons under the 1919 Irish Land Act, and instead look to methods of economy used by British local authorities to face the realities of the mid-1920s. Duckworth consulted Raymond Unwin, Chief Architect at the Ministry of Health, over the possible use of prefabricated concrete construction, although nothing came of this initiative. More productive was a series of visits by Duckworth to study the latest municipal schemes in Britain. Following these investigations, he declared that the new house-types to be provided by the ISSLT 'will, on an average, be smaller than those built [previously] by the Irish Local Government Board and will be grouped, where it is possible to do so, into pleasant "garden-suburbs" '.[93] In terms of layout, this meant that the density of ISSLT schemes was to be *increased* to the British garden suburb standard of between 8 and 12 houses per acre, rather than the semi-rural density of only 4 and 6 dwellings per acre that had been used to create what were termed 'garden villages' at Killester and in the early schemes of the Irish Board of Works. Duckworth's ruling on site density had important design implications. Garden plots would now obviously have to be smaller, and there would be less land for communal amenities. Increased density also required the introduction of short terraces of four cottages alongside the more dispersed semi-detached types designed hitherto under the Irish Land Act. And it also meant a concentration on building a few larger schemes on what were increasingly suburban sites, rather than providing small rural clusters. For the ISSLT, the building of smaller dwellings posed many problems. An experimental scheme of eight tiny three-room dwellings was built at Sallynoggin. The design was indeed novel (Type A; total area of only 550 square feet), consisting of a terrace of single-storey cottages, each with a cruciform plan. Two small bedrooms opened directly off a central cooking and living space, and there was not even a scullery, let alone a bathroom. However, the ISSLT did not find the building costs to be sufficiently low to compensate for the drastic drop of standards involved. No further examples of these dwellings were built. Instead, the ISSLT decided to make savings by trimming its general standards, and by building almost entirely four-room dwellings. For future schemes, the proportion of five-room houses was now not allowed to exceed 10 per cent of the total units provided.

The pruning of standards was not applied uniformly across Ireland. As a result, there was a noticeable difference between the houses provided by the ISSLT in Northern Ireland and in the Irish Free State following the financial cut-backs in 1924. The houses built in the former tended to be larger (712–859 square feet), and usually contained a bathroom. Schemes in Ulster were now almost always located in large suburban sites. Layouts tended to be strongly axial and symmetrical, and contained a mixture of short terraces and semi-detached dwellings. The largest development was the 146-cottage estate at Cregagh near Belfast, but probably the most attractive design was at Shantallow, near Londonderry. In the latter scheme, a total of 57 Neo-Georgian houses were built to a wide-fronted plan type (Type Z.1: 804 square feet), each cottage having a 26 foot frontage and a generous internal arrangement (see Figs 47–48). A large front hall gave access to a bathroom and, on the other side, a large through living room (187 square feet). There were three sizeable bedrooms (64–163 square feet) on the first floor. Although the ISSLT's schemes in Southern Ireland were also usually built in groups of 30–80 dwellings on the outskirts of towns such as Dublin and Cork, the actual quality of the house designs was significantly lower. The overall space provision (600–780 square feet) was smaller than in the cottages in Ulster, and furthermore, as the Treasury had demanded, nearly 60 per cent of dwellings had no bathroom. Even types which were clearly based on designs produced for Northern Ireland were built to a lower standard south of the border. Type D was a version of the above-mentioned type at Shantallow, with a through living room and ground floor bathroom, but in the South it was given a slightly narrower (24 foot 8 inch) frontage and smaller rooms (see Fig. 49). This type was also built in terraces of four dwellings, complete with attractive hipped gables over the end-returns, rather than in semi-detached pairs as in Ulster.

All the ISSLT trustees within a relatively short period of time came to accept that the cheaper and smaller dwellings urged by Duckworth and the Treasury had the merit of enabling rents to be set at levels more affordable to ex-servicemen. There were nevertheless plenty of other instances of conflict with the Treasury. One battle which the trustees lost was over their plan to sell off ISSLT cottages to tenants at a much reduced cost. This was blocked by both Duckworth and the Treasury on the grounds that the British Government wanted the houses to be maintained by the ISSLT as permanent

Fig 47. ISSLT: photograph of the Shantallow Estate, Co. Londonderry

war memorials. Where the trustees did have success was in preventing a Treasury move to increase rents in order to create a surplus that could be used as a contingency fund. This went against the feelings of ISSLT tenants, who, looking enviously at Labourers Acts cottages which were let at only 1s 6d–2s per week, became increasingly belligerent in their demand that their rents should be lowered. Tenant militancy began, not surprisingly, on the Killester housing estate. With soaring unemployment in Dublin in the winter of 1923–24, the Killester tenants went on a rent strike which finally won them a 4s-per-week reduction on all rents on the estate. This victory only encouraged other ISSLT tenants to try the same tactic. A wave of rent strikes broke out. Average arrears in the Irish Free State soared to around 12 per cent by late-1925. Soon afterwards, the Killester tenants embarked on another campaign which managed to secure a further reduction of 4s per week. Tenant militancy, which was backed wholeheartedly by the Southern trustees and the British Legion, produced a definite downward trend in rent levels. The average rent in 1926 fell to just over 6s per week (although this varied from 3s in very rural areas, to a maximum figure now of 12s 6d for the largest cottages at Killester). Organised rent strikes only worsened relations with the Treasury, which characterised events as 'the old battle between English economy, represented by Duckworth and the headquarters of the Trust in London, and Irish wastefulness'.[94]

Controversy over rents and the determination to reduce building costs undoubtedly resulted in a hiatus in the preparation of housing schemes for ex-servicemen. Thus, while £520 000 had been spent and 2425 dwellings

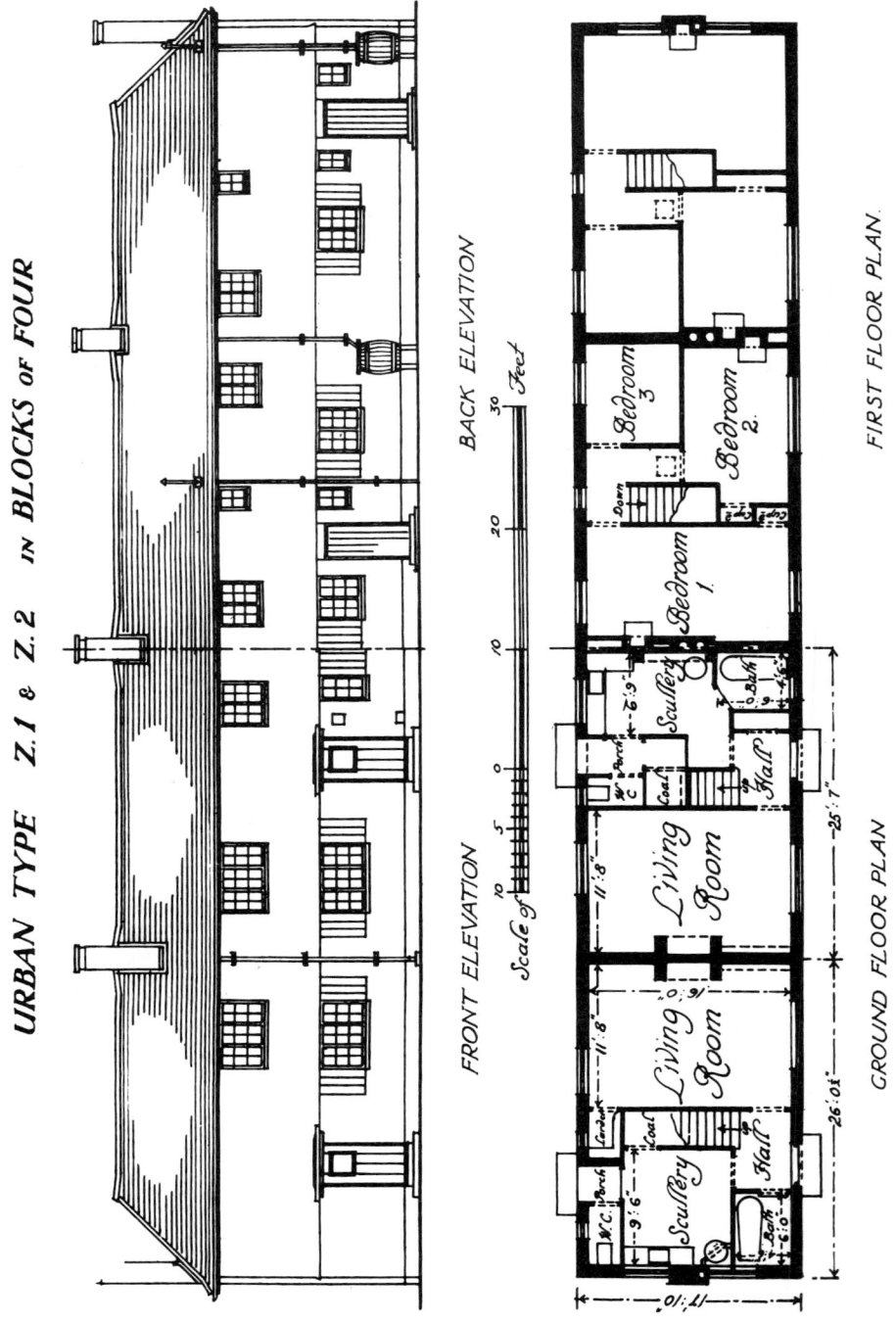

Fig 48. ISSLT: 'Type Z.1' two-storey five-room cottage as used at Shantallow

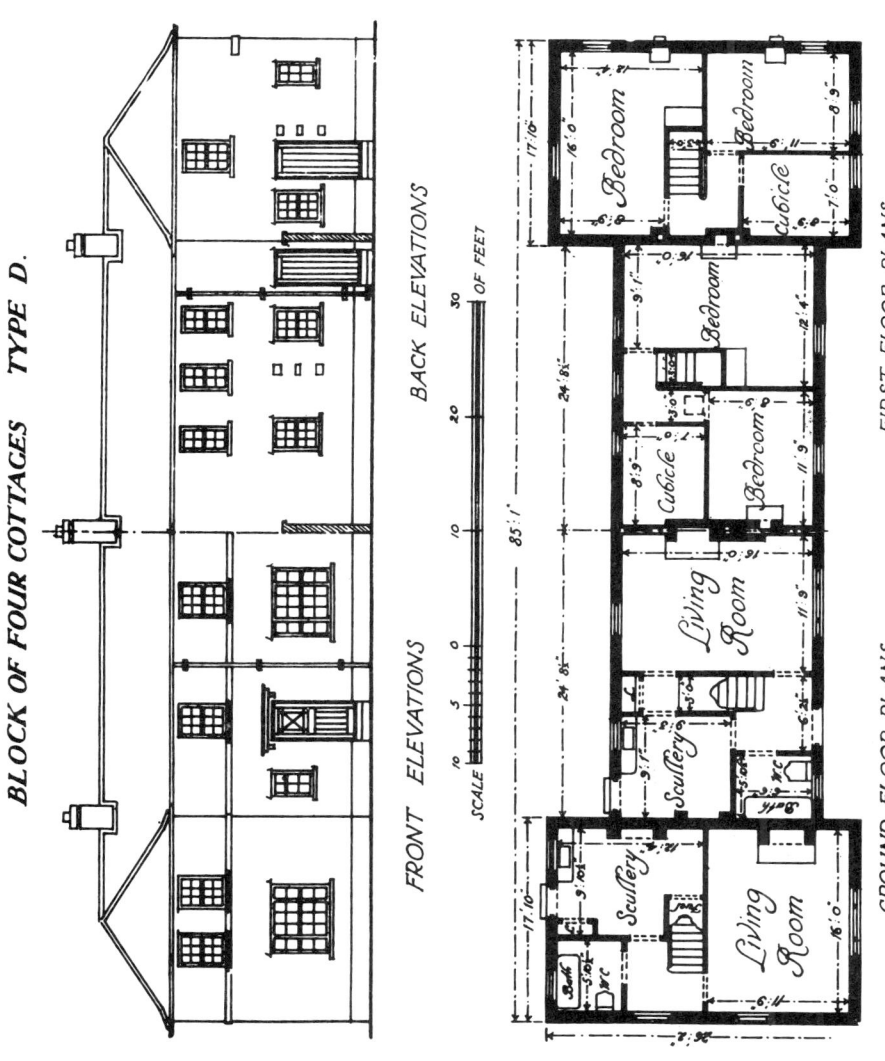

Fig 49. ISSLT: 'Type D' two-storey four-room cottage as used in the Irish Free State

completed by mid-1926 (1692 in Southern Ireland and 733 in Ulster), most of the houses had been built in projects inherited by the ISSLT. There were very few new schemes in construction at this date, prompting the British Legion and the *Irish Times* to launch a high profile attack on the ISSLT's inertia.[95] Tenant dissatisfaction in the Irish Free State was so strong that the Government there was forced reluctantly to act. Up to this point President Cosgrave and other officials had been determined not to interfere in the matter. The Irish Governor-General, Tim Healy, although he felt that the ISSLT headquarters ought to be moved to Ireland, was otherwise reported by Duckworth as having said 'that he swelled with pride and satisfaction at the Trust's houses whenever he drove past our Killester Scheme'.[96] However, with the new crescendo of protests about the ISSLT, the Free State Government was pressurised in 1927 into appointing a special inquiry (the Lavery Commission). The Imperial Treasury was incensed by this development, and its annoyance only grew when the resulting critical report called for further rent reductions and an increase in the number of ex-servicemen's dwellings to be built.[97]

Duckworth had attempted to resign as Chairman of the ISSLT in April 1927, but it was some months before he was eventually replaced by Sir James Brunyate. Under a new head, the ISSLT was determined to confront the stinging criticisms being made of it. The Southern trustees now called for even lower standard cottages containing only three rooms. The justification was that, as the director of the Dublin office put it, 'the Trust have catered primarily for the middle or lower middle class, and . . . the requirements of the labouring man have not, perhaps, been sufficiently considered'.[98] Brunyate was opposed to the principle, but conceded that in new schemes up to 25 per cent of dwellings could be provided as three-room cottages. In March 1930, the ISSLT even considered the building of cheap flats, but found that the terms of its charter forbade this. Instead, it further increased the density on new estates up to 15 houses per acre. As well as cutting building costs, the ISSLT received a financial boost in mid-1927 when, after sustained lobbying by the Northern trustees, it was finally made eligible for subsidy from the Northern Ireland Government. The ISSLT now received £80 for every cottage that it built in Ulster, and financial assistance was extended in 1929 by the creation of a subsidy fund amounting to £35 000. This prompted the Free State Government to belatedly offer the ISSLT a subsidy of £45 per cottage under its 1930 Housing Act, and then to increase the grant under new legislation two years later. However, in actuality, building progress continued to be painfully slow. Only 2897 dwellings were completed by March 1929. Of these, 2018 cottages were in Southern Ireland and 879 cottages were in Ulster. Tardiness led to renewed protests from the British Legion on behalf of Irish ex-servicemen.[99] It took the ISSLT until March 1933 to eventually meet its original target, which had been to ensure that just under 3700 dwellings were available for veterans throughout Ireland.

Even though the housebuilding efforts of the ISSLT were widely criticised,

Post-war Housing for Irish Ex-servicemen 271

the trustees sought to win favour in other ways. In spite of severe restrictions imposed by the Treasury, a scheme was finally started to sell off dwellings to tenants at 50 per cent of the replacement cost in rural areas, and 66 per cent in urban districts. As a consequence, the ISSLT's housing stock was gradually wound down, and a financial surplus was produced for re-investment.[100] The ISSLT also continued the process of cutting rents. By 1929, the average rent had fallen to only 5s 2d per week, and within five years the figure stood at around 3s 9d per week. But neither policy endeared the ISSLT to its tenants, and a catalogue of rent disputes persisted. In the Free State, tenant conflict culminated in 1932 when the Supreme Court ruled that the ISSLT had no legal powers to charge any rent at all. The result was that all building work promptly stopped in Southern Ireland. Similar legal action in Ulster failed, allowing the programme there to limp along such that the final total of dwellings built for ex-servicemen approached nearly 4000 units. However, the ISSLT suffered from being a complete anachronism, best summed up when an official in the British Ministry of Health exclaimed in late-1931 that 'I can only be thankful that there is nothing of this kind in England and Wales'.[101] The ISSLT survived, barely, until Westminster legislation in 1987 finally dissolved the agency and redistributed its surplus capital. This most curious of episodes was finally over. At its genesis, the Irish Land Act had demonstrated lucidly the degree to which housing policy in Ireland prior to 1922 was dictated by the political structure of British rule. Furthermore, the residual British influence in Ireland even after independence and partition was seen by the fact that financial support was provided for ex-servicemen's housing (however grudgingly) by Westminster, even after a point when surely any possible political benefits had passed.

Chapter 8

STATE HOUSING IN NORTHERN IRELAND AND THE IRISH FREE STATE

In the history of Ireland 1922 was a seminal year. It marked the transfer of power to the new Governments in Northern Ireland and the Irish Free State. Yet independence and partition had another consequence: state housing ceased at a stroke to be an important political issue in Ireland. There was a striking similarity in the way in which state housing effectively dropped out of the story in both parts of the country during the 1920s. The governments of both the North and the South provided an initial and short-term injection of funds for working-class housing, in an attempt to legitimise their new-found position and to deal urgently with chronic unemployment problems. But within a year or so, each of the administrations had drastically scaled down its ambitions. Housing policy in Northern Ireland was to lay moribund until after the Second World War. The lull in the Irish Free State was followed by a revival of state housing in the early-1930s. This chapter is therefore intended as an epilogue and a counterpoint to the preceding analysis. It will briefly outline the consequences of the ending of British rule for housing design and policy on both sides of the Irish border, and will discuss the schemes that resulted from post-war initiatives in the respective capitals of Belfast and Dublin.

POST-DEVOLUTION HOUSING POLICY IN NORTHERN IRELAND

Looking first at Northern Ireland, it is important to remember that the 1920 Government of Ireland Act had envisaged the temporary partition of the six counties of North-East Ulster. The opportunity was seized upon by Unionists determined to lose no time in setting up a new Government for the province. Preparations effectively began in September 1920, with the appointment of Sir Ernest Clark to Dublin Castle to oversee the transfer of power. In the event, the formal handover had to be delayed to coincide with the creation of the Irish Free State two years later.[1] In the meantime, the housing situation in Ulster was deteriorating badly. By October 1921, the province had seen very little activity under the 1919 Irish Housing Act. Only 95 cottages were built and another 219 started, and of these new dwellings nearly 80 per cent were concentrated in Belfast. Hence it was Ulster Unionist members who led Irish demands in the House of Commons for an increase in housing subsidy. What was needed, they argued, was a subsidy of 35s for every £1 of rent collected in ordinary cases, and 40s where exceptional hardship was diagnosed. As was noted at the end of

Chapter 6, the agreement of the Irish Treasury and Westminster to the subsidy increase in November 1921 proved to be a purely cosmetic gesture. The new Ministry of Home Affairs in Belfast was told at the same time that there would be no corresponding augmentation of the housing funds to be transferred over to Northern Ireland.[2] This was to be typical of the parsimony shown by the Imperial Treasury towards Ulster. It provoked a belligerent but fruitless attempt by the Northern Government to improve the subsidy deal. What did result in 1922 was some rather ill-tempered haggling about the North's share of residual housing funds from sources as diverse as the ex-servicemen's programme and the now insignificant remains of the Irish Labourers Acts and 1908 Housing Act.[3]

Westminster's lack of commitment to the province helped to shape the two fundamental structural problems that beset Northern Ireland in the inter-war period, and which militated against initiatives such as state housing.[4] The first problem was financial, and arose from the continual shortfall and uncertainty that the Northern Government faced in terms of public revenue. During the 1920s, the Imperial Treasury in Whitehall was primarily concerned with enforcing retrenchment in public spending in order to achieve a return to the 'Gold Standard' system. One consequence was that, by the early-1930s, the vital 'Imperial contribution' from Britain to Northern Ireland had fallen to only 5 per cent of the figure that had been envisaged at the outset of the new state ten years before. This was particularly damaging given that a sharp downturn in the two traditional industries of North-East Ulster, linen and shipbuilding, was creating a deep economic depression. Ulster's mean unemployment rate stood at 19 per cent during the 1920s, and rose to an even more crippling level of 27 per cent in the following decade. Wages in Northern Ireland were on average at least 10 per cent lower than in Britain. Social conditions were clearly much worse than those on the mainland, and yet the lack of public revenue meant that there was proportionately less finance available for services such as housing. The second structural problem in Ulster was a political stultification that arose from being, in effect, an impregnable one-party state run by Unionists at both central and local levels. Protestant 'siege mentality' was best symbolised by the imposing solidity and grandeur of the Stormont Parliament House (1927–32), wherein ruled the party led by Sir James Craig (later Lord Craigavon) from the inception of the new state until his death in office in 1940. Yet, despite the obvious absence of any effective opposition, there was little check placed on Unionist hegemony by Westminster.[5] Any potential challenge from the province's Labour Party tended to be fractured and nullified by bitter sectarian divisions. North-East Ulster was the only economically modernised region of Ireland, but still there was no strong working-class organisation able to press for state intervention in housing.

Housing policy in inter-war Northern Ireland therefore rarely progressed beyond the level of rhetoric. The bold initial pledge from Sir James Craig and his ministers was that the population could expect the same standard of social provision as in the rest of Britain.[6] And, initially, the province saw a spate of working-class housing funded by the residue of funds under the 1919 Irish Housing Act, and by the Northern Government's own contribution through the 1922 Housing (Unemployment Relief) Scheme. The latter represented an attempt to relieve some of the social unrest created by widespread unemployment, and generously committed the state to pay 80 per cent of the labour costs on approved housing schemes. Yet the flurry of activity it produced was short-lived. When retrenchment from Britain began to bite, the Unionist Government fell back on the more favoured policy of non-intervention. As in other fields of Ulster's social policy, the 1923 Northern Ireland Housing Act and successive measures for urban housing were all based explicitly on precedents set by the Conservative Party in Britain.[7] Hence, in Northern Ireland the task of rehousing the working class was also regarded once more as being primarily the responsibility of private housebuilders. Local authorities were to play only a secondary, supporting role. Subsidy terms were less favourable than in Britain. The system used in Northern Ireland involved a single lump-sum payment rather than an annual contribution from the state, and resulted in a lower overall contribution per dwelling. There was also far more volatility in the way in which subsidy levels were fixed. Under the 1923 Housing Act, the Northern Government provided £60 per dwelling, and local authorities were then permitted to offer a further £40 subsidy plus the possibility of an interest-free loan of up to £100 on each house. Centralised state subsidy in Ulster rose slowly to a peak of £100 per dwelling in 1927, but then fell progressively in the 1930s before eventually being phased out in 1937.[8] Furthermore, in Northern Ireland there was a far sharper decline in the standard of housing that was provided. The 1923 Housing Act allowed subsidy to be given to new dwellings of between 600 and 950 square feet in area. Yet by 1927, the Minister of Home Affairs was openly declaring 'that the greater need was now for smaller houses'.[9] The undisguised intention of the Northern Government was to cut costs. Hence by 1928 the maximum house size that was eligible for subsidy was fixed at only 650 square feet, and preference was being given to three-room 'kitchen' cottages without parlours. Rural dwellings were even permitted to be as small as 500 square feet. In 1933, with central subsidy plummeting, the latter figure became the maximum size for any subsidised dwelling.

All in all, it was an unambitious housing policy that was carried out by the Craig Government. This was also shown by the fact that, to deal with rural housing, there was a revival in 1923 of the subsidy terms and powers of the pre-war Labourers Acts (this code continued, albeit with a temporary suspension from 1931 to 1935). Social conservatism did not just permeate central government. It was also a fundamental creed of Unionist local authorities that the rates should be burdened as little as possible. Given that most councils in Ulster suffered anyway from very low rateable incomes, the result was that they were rendered largely inactive. Therefore, despite the initial Unionist pledge to match 'step-by-step' the level of social progress on the mainland, the actual achievements of inter-war Ulster were paltry. Only a total of 50 000 new dwellings were built from all sources in Northern Ireland between 1919 and 1939. In comparison, Britain had built 80 times more dwellings in the same period even though the population on the mainland was only 30 times greater. Scotland alone, with a populace four times that of Ulster, produced a total of 311 500 units in the inter-war era.[10] The specific performance of local authorities in Northern Ireland was proportionately even worse. In all, a total of nearly 7500 council dwellings were built in Ulster between 1919 and 1939, of which approximately half were in urban areas and half were in rural districts. Yet council dwellings constituted only 15 per cent of the total housing output in the province, a proportion that fell well below the corresponding figure of around 25 per cent in Britain (from 1919 to 1934 the level of state provision was a staggering 61 per cent in Scotland). It was not until after the Second World War, with the need to rebuild the destroyed areas of Belfast and the advent at last of an adequate contribution from Westminster towards social expenditure, that the Northern Government was seriously to make working-class housing a public responsibility. In 1944, a distinct Ministry of Housing and Local Government was formed. The 1945 Northern Ireland Housing Act introduced generous subsidies to help create the 200 000 dwellings that were estimated to be needed to make up the housing shortage and remove the slums. By 1963, nearly 112 383 houses had been built. Of these, 37 per cent were provided by local authorities and a further 24 per cent by the special agency of the Northern Ireland Housing Trust.[11]

MUNICIPAL HOUSING IN BELFAST FROM 1919

Belfast Corporation was the dominant influence on Ulster attitudes towards state housing both before and after devolution. Indeed, a look at the Corporation and its activities from 1919 crystallises the problems of inter-war Northern Ireland.[12] It remained a solidly Unionist body, particularly once the post-war expedient of proportional representation in local elections was scrapped by the new regime in 1922. In 1928, only 5 per cent of Corporation employees were Catholics.[13] As with everything else in Belfast Corporation, housing policy was determined by a small clique of Unionist councillors. Sir Crawford McCullagh presided unchallenged over the Housing Committee that had been set up at the end of the First World War. McCullagh was loyally supported by his Vice-Chairman, T. E. McConnell, who was a leading estate agent in the city. From 1919, these two councillors were at the forefront in promoting Belfast Corporation's policy on the housing issue: the ideal was that private enterprise should build working-class dwellings, but given the short-term political and economic necessities, then the Corporation would also have to act. The Housing Committee was alarmed by the impact of post-war inflation on building costs, and so (as noted in Chapter 6) engaged on a double-edged strategy. On one hand the Corporation campaigned for an increase in Exchequer subsidy under the

1919 Irish Housing Act, and on the other demanded that the ILGB reduce design standards to pre-war levels. Sir Crawford McCullagh and his colleagues made no secret of their intention to defy the principle of shared financial responsibility set out by the Lloyd George Cabinet. Instead, the only goal of the Housing Committee was to ensure that municipal housebuilding did not result in any charge at all to the local rates. 'Belfast Corporation was the only authority dealing with housing in Great Britain that had not spent a penny on it', boasted one councillor in late-1923.[14] It was a stance that was presented locally as being sound Unionist 'business-sense', but it made a mockery of Belfast Corporation's initial appeal for a massive £2 000 000 loan under the 1919 Irish Housing Act. The outcome in the immediate post-war years was that, despite an estimated need of between 5000 and 8000 dwellings in the city, only a few schemes of demonstration houses were actually built.

With the drive towards devolution in full swing in mid-1921, Belfast Corporation finally secured a not-insubstantial £500 000 public loan under the terms of the 1919 Act. The actual overseeing of the building programme was entrusted to the incoming Northern Ireland Government. Housebuilding in Belfast thus finally got under way, and the £227 500 subsidy that the Corporation received to erect 459 cottages in the early-1920s made it the only major Irish municipality to use the measure.[15] Most of the dwellings built in Belfast under the 1919 Irish Housing Act were substantial parlour cottages, due to the ILGB's refusal to allow the Corporation to deviate from post-war design guidelines. The result was that rents were set at levels of up to 18s per week, or 22s including rates. By far the largest and most prestigious estate under the 1919 Act was of 224 dwellings on the Wandsworth Road, built from 1922 to 1924. Imposing rendered cottages were grouped in short terraces, and were given carefully modulated elevations broken up by shallow bay windows aligned with the roof gables above (see Fig. 50). In parallel, Belfast Corporation also seized on the Northern Ireland Government's interim Unemployment Relief Scheme to provide a further 1102 dwellings in the period from 1922 to 1925. The prime example in this instance was the Woodvale Estate, and here the 355 cottages provided were typical of the slightly lower standards that now prevailed. A high proportion of non-parlour 'kitchen' houses were now included, at rents of only 11s per week (13s 6d with rates). Furthermore, parlour dwellings were reduced in size so that the maximum rent level on the estate could be kept down to 13s per week (16s with rates). Elevationally there was also a move towards the use of a simpler roof line, and a reliance on cheaper concrete rendering on the upper storey of cottages to provide visual variety.[16] The designs for housing schemes under both measures were provided by a local 'Panel of Architects', and in terms of planning consciously followed the low-density layouts and house-types recommended in the Tudor Walters Report. A Belfast Corporation deputation even went over to England in 1922 to examine post-war schemes there. The overall outcome was that, despite the Corporation's protests, the post-war municipal housing in Belfast was built to a

Fig 50. Belfast Corporation: parlour houses on the Wandsworth Road Estate (1922–24)

higher standard than hitherto found in Ulster. All cottages now had three bedrooms plus a scullery and bathroom, and around 60 per cent of dwellings also had a separate parlour. Methods of constructional economy were sought in an effort to reduce costs to the range of £500–800 per dwelling. Belfast Corporation took up a suggestion by local labour organisations that it should set up its own direct labour force, rather than rely on the exorbitant tenders being submitted by private contractors. Half of the Corporation's dwellings built in the early-1920s were put up using direct labour. It also experimented with a concrete block system devised initially for municipal housing in Liverpool. Furthermore, in late-1923 Belfast Corporation initiated a policy to sell the cottages that it had built under the 1919 Irish Housing Act to tenants for around £310–550 each. The aim was to ensure that if state subsidy were to be terminated, then the Corporation would still incur no loss to the rates.[17]

As noted earlier, the 1923 Northern Ireland Housing Act marked both a decisive move by the Craig Government towards retrenchment and a policy switch in favour of private enterprise. Belfast Corporation now saw itself as fulfilling the residual role of housing the very poor, and, not surprisingly, was extremely critical of the low level of subsidy on offer. The simple solution of the Corporation was to cut design standards to pre-war levels. This time, however, it was done with the blessing of the Ministry of Home Affairs and the Prime

Minister, Sir James Craig. Bathrooms were omitted and only two-bedroom non-parlour house-types were used. Traditional long terraces with narrower frontages of only 15 feet made a reappearance. A typical housing scheme from this phase was the 209 dwellings built in Donegall Avenue at an average cost of only £370 per unit.[18] In keeping with its much reduced housing role in the mid-1920s, the ambition of Belfast Corporation was now to build merely a further 630 dwellings. Yet even this limited programme was plunged into disarray when in 1925–26 a judicial report (the Megaw Commission) revealed that corruption was rife in the city's housing contracts.[19] The report was the pretext for a savage pruning and reorganisation of the Corporation's general powers, and it dealt a body blow to the municipal housing initiative. Belfast Corporation had by this point built a combined total of 2188 post-war houses, and while it limped on to provide another 464 dwellings (mostly on the Seaview Estate from 1927), the situation prior to the Second World War was one of paralysis. The Corporation provided less than 10 per cent of the inter-war housing in the city, a contribution that was nearly as hesitant as the single slum-clearance scheme undertaken before 1914. Social conditions in the city meanwhile worsened. Brett has observed that in terms of both local authority and private housebuilding, no other inter-war city in Britain had a poorer record than did Belfast.[20]

POST-INDEPENDENCE HOUSING POLICY IN THE IRISH FREE STATE

The initial pattern in the Irish Free State from 1922 was in many ways similar to Northern Ireland. Under the dominion-type status that was offered by Lloyd George in the negotiations that led to the 'Treaty' in December 1921, the new Southern administration was promised 'uncontrolled authority over . . . the health and homes of her people'.[21] Yet despite the grand hopes of visionary republicans and labour representatives in the Dáil Éireann, it soon became apparent that the newly-elected Cumann na nGaedheal Government under William Cosgrave, which held power for a decade, was not committed to radical social improvement. 'We were probably the most conservative minded revolutionaries that ever pushed through a successful revolution', boasted a leading member of the new Free State Government.[22] The lack of social ambition has generally been attributed to two factors.[23] The first was an obsessive desire by the Cosgrave Government to be seen to govern efficiently in the face of enormous difficulties. There was open militancy from republicans, such as Eamonn de Valera, who saw the 'Treaty' as a betrayal of the demand for complete independence from the British Crown. Conflict spilled over into bloody civil war in 1922–23. Furthermore, the economy in the South had entered a severe economic slump. Agricultural prices, which had boomed during the First World War, fell by almost 45 per cent in the period from 1920 to 1924. The Free State Government was determined to follow the British deflationary policy of returning to the pre-war 'Gold Standard'. This required fiscal restriction and state retrenchment. Between 1924 and 1927, public spending in Southern Ireland was slashed by over 40 per cent in order to balance the budget. The second problem in the Irish Free State was that, irrespective of the state of the economy, there was an entrenched ideology of social and cultural conservatism amongst the groups that now constituted the ruling alliance. These included the petty-bourgeois commercial class, the Catholic Church, and, above all, farming interests (agriculture still accounted for just over half the workforce, and by now virtually every farm was owner-occupied). State action was frowned upon and there was little or no interest in the redistribution of wealth. Social conservatism was also undoubtedly helped by the continuing structural weakness of the organised labour movement in both urban and rural areas. The 1920s in the Free State witnessed the marginalisation of the Irish Labour Party and the Irish TUC, and hence their calls for an ambitious housing programme, to be carried out by a special national agency, fell on deaf ears.[24]

What was also remarkable was the degree to which social inertia was underpinned by the very structure and administrative apparatus of government. A modernised civil service had been inherited from British rule with virtually no interruption to business, creating a climate which favoured a conservative adaptation of British precedents in spheres such as social policy.[25] The reality of entrenched colonial influence could be seen in the continued economic dependence on Britain. In the mid-1920s, nearly 98 per cent of exports from Southern Ireland still went to the United Kingdom (including Ulster), and just over 75 per cent of the Free State's imports flowed in the other direction. McDonagh has observed that the Irish Free State 'remained effectively a provincial segment of a mature economy in the British Isles . . . a pocket of under-development in an advanced region'.[26] Economic dependence only began to decline in the mid-1930s following an acrimonious trade war with Britain. Even then, change was gradual. Thus, despite the public rhetoric of the Cosgrave Government after 1922, and the much vaunted campaign to promote Irish-speaking in schools, in general the tendency was to imitate British policies with only slight amendments to suit conditions in the Free State. Self-government brought not cultural independence or a policy of 'de-anglicisation', but rather a continuing British hegemony.[27]

The gap between the rhetoric of the Cosgrave Government and the low priority given to social policy was nowhere more evident that in the field of state housing.[28] From early in 1922 the Provisional Government had been openly challenged to address the urban housing problem that Nationalists had made so much of in the days of British rule. 'None of the many problems which await solution by the Irish Free State is of more vital importance than the question of housing', declared the *Irish Times* in February 1922.[29] It was also clearly a political issue that could not simply be ignored, without running the risk of losing support to the Irish Labour Party. 'The housing problem was, perhaps, the greatest problem they had to tackle', as President Cosgrave boldly told the Dáil Éireann.[30] Thus the Provisional Government in March 1922 announced a brief injection of funds to act as a transitional unemployment relief measure. The policy became popularly known as the 'Million Pound Scheme'.[31] The target was for municipalities to build 2150 new urban houses, at an average cost of £750 apiece, and then let them at rents of 10s 6d per week. To this purpose, local authorities in total were asked to raise £125 000 by charging a local housing-rate equivalent to 1s in the £1, and a further £375 000 by taking out short-term loans on the open market. When this had been done, then the Free State Government promised to provide a matching amount of £500 000 from central funds. Altogether the scheme produced a total of 2000 houses between 1922 and 1924. The new dwellings were built by 20 local authorities, mainly in Dublin and the surrounding townships. Since the 1919 Irish Housing Act had been virtually unused in Southern Ireland, these were effectively the first post-war municipal dwellings south of the border. And as such, they made concrete the long-awaited increase in design standards. All of the cottages built under the 'Million Pound Scheme' were given three bedrooms, and 40 per cent also contained a parlour. The housing initiative was used as a major campaigning point by Cosgrave in the 1923 General Election. The clear aim, which proved successful, was to win votes away from the Irish Labour Party and to deride the ineffectiveness of the anti-'Treaty' faction.[32] Yet having won the election, the housing commitment of the Cosgrave Government promptly evaporated in favour of financial retrenchment. Instead, there ensued a dull imitation of British housing policy, in which the latter, while obviously no longer having the status of a controlling or determining force, was nevertheless still regarded as the accepted source for ideas. 'Britain's progress should excite emulation rather than envy', wrote the *Irish Times*, 'and the Irish Free State should go about its [housing] task in the same enterprising way as its neighbour.'[33] British values were supported by the official expert on Free State housing policy, Thomas Joseph Byrne, who had moved from his post-war position as a 'temporary' ILGB inspector, to an important new role from 1923 as Principal Architect at the Irish Board of Public Works.[34] During the 1920s, there was also a repeated consultation and exchange of information between Irish civil servants involved in housing matters, and their counterparts in London (a connection that has been noted elsewhere between officials in the Free State's Ministry of Finance and the Imperial Treasury).[35]

Thus, from 1924 the Cosgrave Government abandoned any pretence that it was trying to solve the housing problem. Instead, it offered a somewhat limited subsidy to private builders. There was also an explicit orientation towards the provision of larger dwellings for better-paid workers and the lower middle classes, on the grounds that the Free State simply could not afford to build for the very poor.[36] The 1924 Housing (Building Facilities) Act provided a grant of £250 000 to subsidise the building of 3000 new dwellings, plus another £50 000 for the rehabilitation of existing houses. Urban subsidy was available for new dwellings of between three and five rooms, and was set out on a scale of £20 for each room provided (rural subsidy was slightly lower in each case). Houses had to be between 520 and 1000 square feet in area to qualify for subsidy, although it was permitted that the maximum limit could be increased to 1500 square feet if the house was built for a civil servant! Local authorities were initially confined to simply offering rate rebates or cheap sites to encourage developers, but an amending Housing Act in December 1924 extended state subsidy to municipalities. Subsequent legislation along similar lines gave local authorities a marginally higher subsidy than private builders, but in practice did little to stimulate activity.[37] In the ten years from 1922 to 1932 under the Cosgrave Government, slightly fewer than 10 000 subsidised dwellings were built by local authorities and another 16 500 were provided by private builders (the latter mostly in rural areas). It was not an impressive total, and barely equalled the number of cottages that had been built by local authorities alone in the ten years prior to 1914.[38] A tendency towards conservatism was also shown in the policy of selling dwellings to tenants to cover expenditure. 'The purchase scheme induces thrift and the tenant ownership adds pro tanto to the sense of civic responsibility', noted an official in the Ministry of Local Government and Public Health.[39] It was a strategy that was to be widely applied by Dublin Corporation and other authorities, and which pre-dated the Thatcherite 'right-to-buy' policy in Britain by half a century.

Housing design in the 1920s Irish Free State, whether under the 'Million Pound Scheme' or subsequent legislation, was clearly derived from the low-density garden suburb model urged by the Tudor Walters Report and the 1919 circulars of the ILGB. British influence was acknowledged by the *Irish Builder* in the mid-1920s when it wrote that 'the illustration of many of the most admirable housing schemes in England in the building papers, has also helped to improve taste, and the result is seen in some of the houses about Dublin built under housing grants'.[40] The Dublin City Architect, Horace O'Rourke, declared that 'England . . . has been able to show all civilisation the way to plan ideal houses for all classes of the people'.[41] In the Irish Free State, as in Northern Ireland, there was a noticeable reduction in standards after 1924 to help cut average costs down to £600 per dwelling, or even lower if possible. The maximum permissible size for local authority dwellings was dropped to 820 square feet (although private builders could still build up to 1250 square feet), and parlours were generally omitted. Dwellings in rural districts could be as small as 500 square feet in area. In one recommended type-plan for a single-storey four-room rural house, the bathroom and even the internal WC were omitted.[42] Yet despite the tendency to prune standards, the Unwinian model of suburban estates came to dot most Southern cities from the mid-1920s. Examples include McSwineys and MacCurtains Villas in Cork, the Kileely area of Limerick, and, as will be seen below, the outskirts of Dublin.

There were few new avenues of thinking about architectural design in the post-independence Irish Free State. Calls for the creation of an 'Irish' style were discounted by architects, and nothing came of the vague suggestion by William

Butler Yeats that the blend of tradition and innovation to be found in Swedish Romantic Neo-Classicism offered a possible model to follow.[43] A certain sense of *déjà vu* was also provided by the revival in 1922 of town planning proposals for Dublin. That tireless campaigner, E. A. Aston, founded the Greater Dublin Reconstruction Movement. The object was to prepare a plan for the rebuilding of areas destroyed in 1916 and during the early-1920s, and for the relocation of the important public buildings that were needed to aggrandise Dublin now that it was a true capital once more. Frank Mears, who as noted in the last chapter had been brought over to design the ex-servicemen's estate at Killester, was engaged as the main architect and planner.[44] The activities of the Greater Dublin Reconstruction Movement, however, provoked a temporary split in the planning movement. Both Aston and Mears now argued that the 1914 Dublin Town Plan by Patrick Abercrombie was too costly and grandiose, and had to be replaced by a more realistic proposal if they were ever to win favour with the parsimonious Cosgrave Government. Mears told his father-in-law, Patrick Geddes, that Abercrombie's plan 'cannot be worked, and least of all in a now impoverished country'; more scurrilously, Mears added that 'Abercrombie is a very fine chap for the commercial industrial midlands of England but doesn't understand Dublin a little bit'.[45] Mears called on Geddes to use his influence to discredit the 1914 Town Plan. Geddes duly had a private, and highly discouraging, conversation with Abercrombie. Meanwhile, the patrons of the Abercrombie plan, Lady Aberdeen and the Civics Institute, retaliated by claiming that the design proposed by Aston and Mears was equally premature according to the Geddesian principles of analysis. The Civics Institute therefore set up the Dublin Civic Survey Committee in 1923–24, and published the committee's findings in 1925. Meanwhile, the Civics Institute had also published Abercrombie's plan in 1923. The following year, it brought him over to press his services on to those responsible for the future development of Dublin.[46] Town planning ideals were likewise promoted in a civic survey carried out in 1922 by a local association in Cork, again with Patrick Abercrombie as adviser.[47] Interest in town planning was also shown by the Greater Dublin Commission, which had been asked to investigate the administration and possible future development of the Irish capital and its environs. In the early-1930s, a campaign led by Manning Robertson secured the first genuine planning legislation in the Free State, which was modelled closely on English precedent. It was to prove highly ineffectual, and of little relevance to the issue of state housing.

A more significant housing development occurred in 1931 when the Cosgrave Government, in emulation of the policy switch heralded by the 1930 Greenwood Housing Act in Britain, introduced legislation that for the first time offered a special subsidy for slum clearance by municipalities. Thus, in urban areas the replacement of insanitary stock was now to be given preference over the provision of additional new dwellings.[48] The 1931 measure had little chance to take effect, for in the next year the Cosgrave Government fell from office. The dominant group was now the Fianna Fáil Party led by Eamonn de

Valera. Policy centred on the promise of trade protectionism and economic self-sufficiency for Ireland. For a brief period after the 1932 General Election, the Irish Labour Party held the balance of power. It used this position to ensure that the new de Valera Government kept to a commitment to raise income tax in order to pay for increased activity on social issues such as housing.[49] Thus, the 1932 Housing (Financial and Miscellaneous Provisions) Act provided yet more generous terms. Now the state contribution for slum clearance was equal to 66 per cent of the annual loan charges (a higher figure than for rural dwellings, and twice the amount available to build additional houses in the suburbs). It has been estimated that subsidy under the 1932 Act was effectively double that which had been on offer to municipalities in the Irish Free State in the 1920s.[50] The design standard of local authority housing in the 1930s was raised slightly, with some 80 per cent of new houses having three bedrooms even if no parlour. This, however, was offset by a fall in building costs. A dwelling of around 700 square feet could now be provided for only £350. The overall result was an impressive campaign that in the ten years from 1932 to 1942 saw some 47 900 dwellings built by local authorities, of which nearly 60 per cent were in urban areas and 40 per cent in rural districts. Along with a further 32 700 houses built by private enterprise, it made up a total approaching 81 000 units in the period.[51] Of the municipal dwellings, by the early-1940s over 10 000 dwellings had been built in Dublin. A quarter of the new units in the capital were in blocks of flats. When taken in conjunction with the previous decade, it meant that some 41 per cent of the total inter-war dwellings in the Irish Free State were built by local authorities: a proportion that was higher than in Northern Ireland (15 per cent), or England and Wales (25 per cent), and was only surpassed by Scotland.[52] And yet the transformation wrought by the Fianna Fáil housing campaign should not be over-stated. In the 1930s Free State, the prevailing ethos remained one of social conservatism in close alliance with the Catholic Church. Thus, de Valera's housing campaign stemmed from a realisation of the pragmatic benefits of state intervention rather than a radical attempt to meet working-class needs. The aim was populism, not socialism. Hence the 1939–43 Dublin Housing Inquiry found that 23 000 dwellings were still wanted in the Irish capital and that overcrowded slums and ill-health remained chronic. Abercombie was brought back in the late-1930s to produce another plan for Dublin, published in 1941. In 1948, the total requirement for post-war housing in what was now the Irish Republic was estimated at 61 000 working-class dwellings, of which nearly 45 000 were in urban areas (the response was the first genuine 'welfare state' housing policy in the South, even if this was to prove short-lived).[53]

MUNICIPAL HOUSING IN DUBLIN FROM 1919

The case of Dublin Corporation best illustrates the course of housing policy in the Irish Free State.[54] By early-1920, the Corporation had drawn up proposals to address an estimated need of 21 780 dwellings.⁵⁵ No real start was possible for a republican authority under British rule, yet neither did the euphoria of independence last long for Dublin Corporation. The Cosgrave Government soon embarked on a 'centralising' policy to improve local administration and stifle political opposition, and this was largely achieved by disbanding the elected councils in most cities in the Free State. From 1924 to 1930, Dublin Corporation was dissolved and its powers handed over to appointed City Commissioners. The suspension of local democracy, however, did not greatly alter the outline of a housing policy that was already geared to the building of suburban cottage estates. Indeed, the two prestigious 'model' schemes conceived by Dublin Corporation, at Fairbrothers Fields and the Marino Estate, were subsequently completed by the City Commissioners.

Dublin Corporation had tried during the First World War to begin work at the Fairbrothers Fields scheme, as was seen in Chapter 6. The scheme that was redesigned to suit the ILGB in 1917–18 was along the garden suburb lines recommended by Geddes and Unwin, and now comprised 370 dwellings with four or five rooms laid out in streets around a diamond-shaped central green.⁵⁶ Site clearance was commenced with the housing loan arranged by Chief Secretary Duke in 1917, but progress had then been halted when the Treasury refused to confirm that the scheme would be eligible for retrospective post-war subsidy. Work at Fairbrothers Fields was restarted in 1921 using a short-term Corporation loan, but the estate was eventually to be built under the Free State Government's 'Million Pound Scheme'. The scheme was completed by 1927 in three stages, and consisted of 334 five-roomed cottages with parlours (at a cost of around £955 each) plus another 82 four-roomed non-parlour houses (mostly built in the last phase, and costing £677 each). It set an unprecedented standard of housing, and this was reflected in the quality with which the brickwork and rendered details were brought together in the elevations (see Fig. 51). As well as being the first thorough-going design in Ireland along British garden suburb principles, Fairbrothers Fields was also notable for being built partly by the Dublin Building Trades Guild. This body, as mentioned in Chapter 6, was formed along the lines of post-war guilds in Britain. It represented, however, a manifestation of the republican coalition between the Irish Labour Party and Sinn Fein. Dublin Corporation awarded a series of contracts to the Dublin Building Trades Guild between 1921 and 1924, for a total of 129 houses in all.⁵⁷ In reality, the use of guild labour proved to be more expensive than anticipated, and the body withered along with the Irish labour movement in general. Once the Dublin City Commissioners took over housing responsibility for the city in 1924, cost-cutting became the prime target. Fairbrothers Fields was used as a pilot scheme in which new houses were sold off to tenants by charging a weekly 'pay-back' system instead of rent. Over the next decade or so, all of the council's inter-war suburban cottages were sold to tenants. This represented a total of 4248 dwellings, equivalent to just over a quarter of the municipal housing stock (during the 1920s, only a few small

Fig 51. Dublin Corporation: the Fairbrothers Fields Estate as completed (1921–27)

blocks of municipal flats were built to actually supplement the existing rented accommodation).[58]

The 'jewel in the crown' of Dublin Corporation's suburban estates of the 1920s, and indeed the most important inter-war estate in the whole of Ireland, was located in the northern suburb of Marino.[59] This was the site that Geddes and Unwin had paid special attention to in 1914, and it was then given to the Assistant City Architect, Horace O'Rourke, to draw up a detailed proposal in 1918–19. O'Rourke's more immediate guide was the Tudor Walters Report, and his new design for Marino showed the post-war tendency towards a more symmetrical and axial Neo-Georgian layout for garden suburbs (see Figs 52 and 53). There were now to be 550 dwellings with frontages of between 18 and 31 feet, at a density of 11 houses to the acre. Houses were to have between three and five rooms, but the majority were to be four-room houses with separate bathrooms and let at 8s per week rent. Political events prevented the building of O'Rourke's design. When Dublin Corporation's Housing Committee finally came to reconsider the Marino Estate in 1922, as part of its contribution to the 'Million Pound Scheme', the site was enlarged to 126 acres. The design was also now handed over to F. G. Hicks, an English-born Arts and Crafts architect who had lived in Dublin since the 1890s and had designed the Irish section of the 1904 St Louis Fair.[60] The choice of Hicks as architect served as a perfect symbol of the Anglo-Irish nature of the Marino Estate. The new scheme that was designed by Hicks, and built in two phases from 1923 to 1927, had a layout that imposed an even more rigid geometry. The foci were now two circular greens, both of differing sizes, with roads and T-shaped cul-de-sacs radiating like spokes off a central wheel (see Fig. 54). In total there were 1262 municipal dwellings built at Marino at a density of 12 houses to the acre. Virtually all were

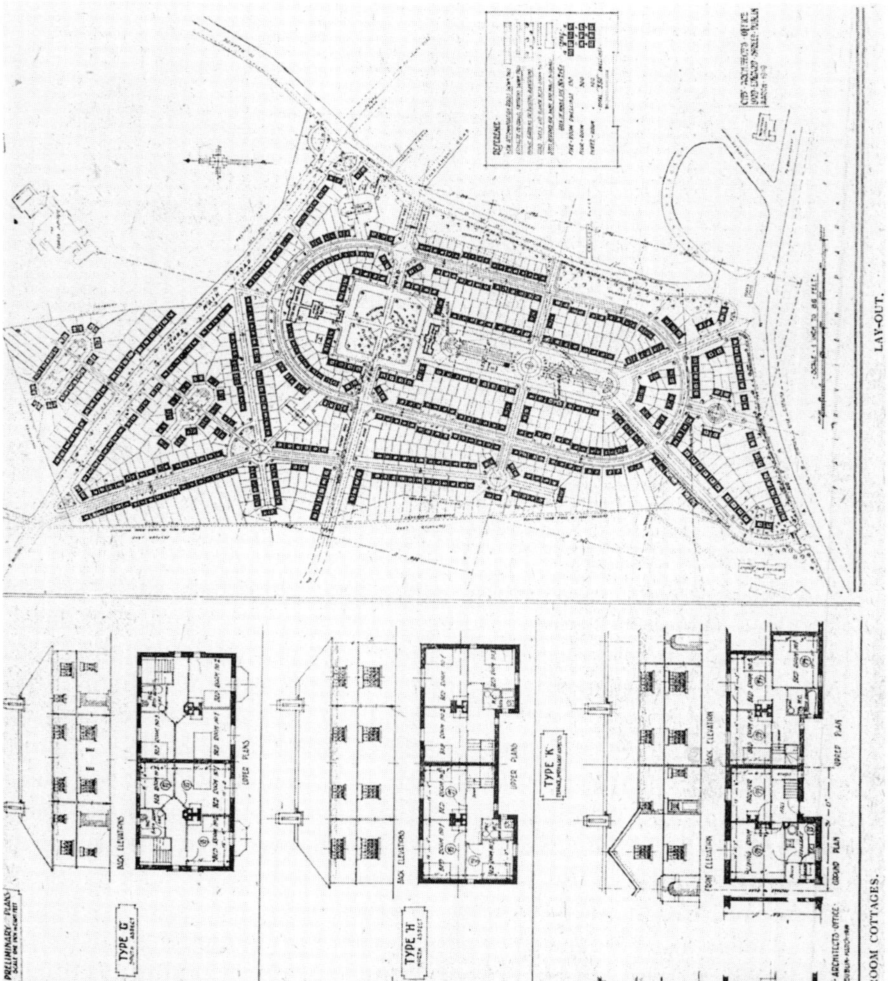

Fig 52. H. T. O'Rourke/Dublin Corporation: first design for Marino Estate (1920)

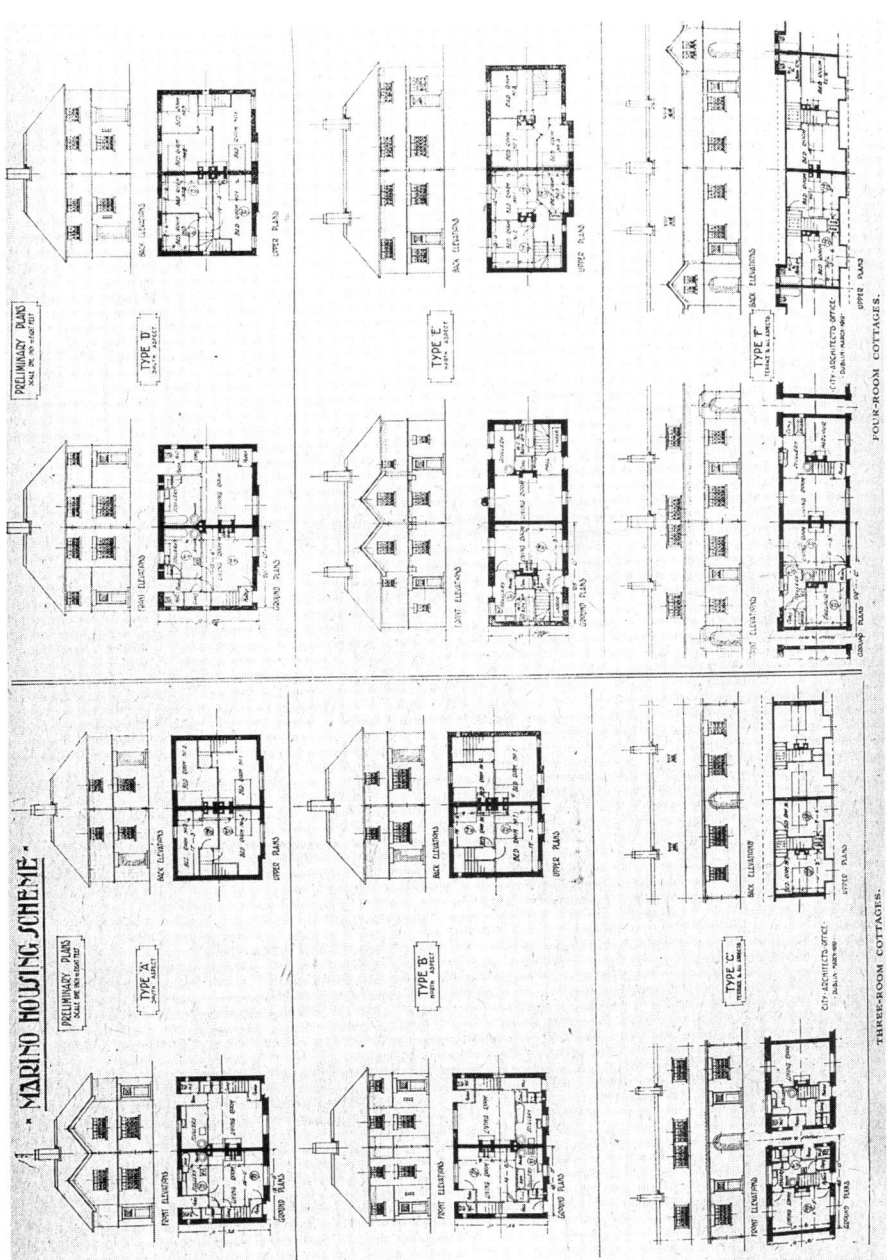

Fig 53. H. T. O'Rourke/Dublin Corporation: first house-types for the Marino Estate

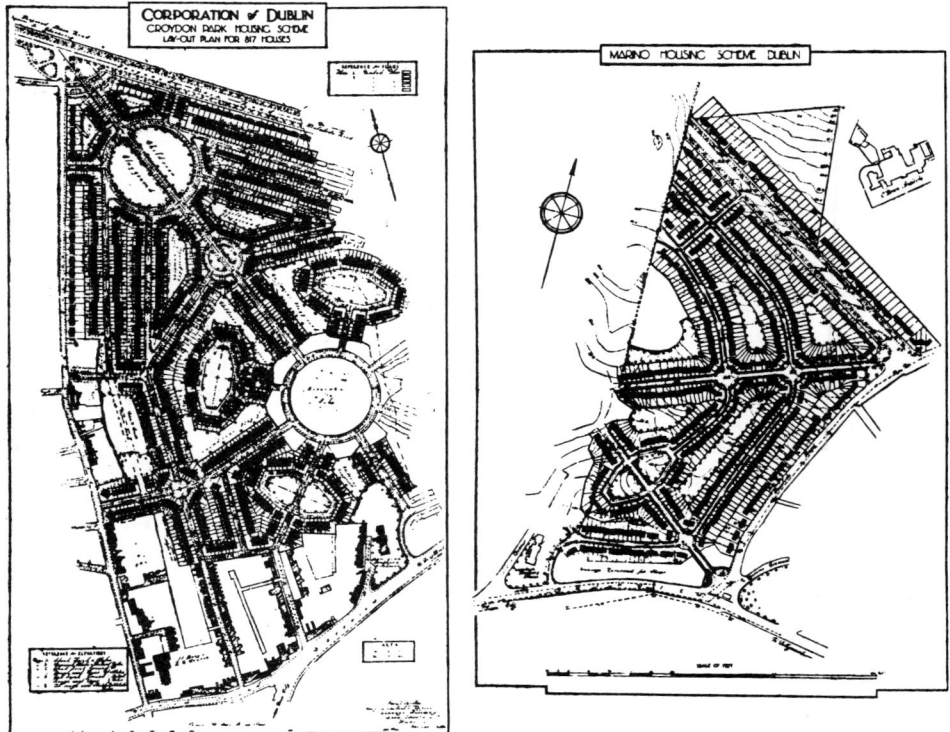

Fig 54. F. G. Hicks/Dublin Corporation: final site plan of Marino Estate (1923–27)

substantial five-room parlour cottages with separate bathrooms. Eight plan-types were used in all, but there were two principal forms of house on the estate. One was a Neo-Georgian two-storey cottage laid out in semi-detached pairs or in short terraces, while the other type was built in longer terraces with a mansard roof to give the ostensible appearance of being a single-storey block. The effort that went into making Marino the most prestigious estate was also seen in the variety of materials that were introduced to overcome visual monotony (see Fig. 55). Throughout the scheme, the integration of brick, blockwork, rendering, slates and clay tiles was skilfully handled. There was also a high standard of space provision on the estate in terms of private gardens and playgrounds, although like most suburban schemes of the period there was a noticeable shortage of shops and other services. Another intriguing element of the Marino Estate came out of the determination of the City Commissioners to reduce costs on the second section of the scheme. Officials were sent to look at new building techniques on the Continent, and particularly concrete construction in Rotterdam and Amsterdam. In due course a Bremen firm, Kossel Construction, was awarded a contract to use a proprietary eight inch in-situ concrete-wall system for a phase involving 230 houses. The *Irish Times* noted

Fig 55. F. G. Hicks/Dublin Corporation: the Marino Estate as completed

that 'it will be the first time that a big housing contract in the British Isles has gone to a German concern'.[61] In the event, the first contract was blocked by the Ministry of Local Government and Public Health, on the grounds that the concrete system was untested, but in 1926 a later contract for 104 dwellings was given to the same firm. Yet the Marino Estate was very far from being a Frankfurt-style modernist *siedlung*! 'Little of continental European thought or experience was directly tapped or assimilated by the Irish', as Chubb has observed of post-independence Southern Ireland.[62] Far more of an influence on Marino and its ilk were the municipal garden suburbs of England. In 1923, Dublin Corporation sent officials to visit the premier LCC estate at Roehampton, and they came back very much impressed.[63]

Indeed, the Roehampton Estate provides the most useful parallel for the Marino scheme.[64] Both schemes set the standard for their respective countries, and the variety of materials and forms at Marino, including the use of mansard-roof terraces, appear to derive directly from the LCC's designs. Yet it must also be pointed out that the almost universal provision of five-room parlour dwellings on the Marino Estate far exceeds the proportion of similar-sized dwellings (just under 50 per cent) in the London precedent. Thus Marino was not merely a second-string application of Unwinian garden suburb design, visually indistinguishable from hundreds of schemes in Britain, but was in fact superior certainly in terms of housing standards. The reason for the higher standard is that Dublin Corporation in the early days of the Irish Free State had rejected any pretence of even trying to provide homes for the poorer working class. Thus the Corporation's Housing Committee had decided in 1922 to build only five-room houses for better-paid workers, on the basis that poor slum dwellers might then occupy the vacated dwellings. It was the well-worn argument of 'filtering-up' that had first been voiced in Britain, but now Dublin Corporation was pursuing the stance more wholeheartedly than, say, the LCC. The results were plain to see. As the *Irish Times* noted in June 1925, the new Marino tenants 'are among the aristocracy of labour in Dublin . . . The housing problem is being solved—how slowly!—by a process of "moving up" '.[65] It was, after all, part of an attitude adopted by the City Commissioners whereby new cottage estates were to be built explicitly for sale to tenants. Yet by the mid-1920s, however, the contradictions of this 'elitist' approach were also becoming obvious. Despite falling building costs in the mid-1920s (the cost of a five-room cottage at Marino dropped from £805 to £680 by 1927), the use of expensive house-types at a time of strict public retrenchment meant of course that fewer dwellings could actually be built. 'Capital Expenditure involved in a very early solution of the Housing Problem on the basis of the present costs of building is entirely beyond the financial resources of the city', observed an official report on unemployment relief in 1927.[66] The Ministry of Local Government and Public Health was also strongly advocating that Dublin Corporation should now build smaller houses, and so in the mid-1920s the City Commissioners gradually moved over to this alternative policy. Hence, in subsequent suburban estates the standard was reduced: first to a mixture of four-room non-parlour dwellings and five-room parlour dwellings, such as at Drumcondra (535 houses; completed by 1928) and Emmet Road (702 houses; 1929); and then to a total reliance on four-room non-parlour cottages at Donnycarney (421 houses; 1930) and Cabra (641 houses; 1931).

The reinstatement of an elected Dublin Corporation in 1931 came at the end of the Cosgrave administration. Progress under the housing legislation of the 1920s had been muted, and as a result the municipality had only built around 5000 dwellings in the decade after independence. With the advent of the Fianna Fáil campaign in the early-1930s, there was a stepping up of the Corporation's completion rate. Dwellings were now no longer built for sale. By 1939 a further 7650 dwellings had been added under the 1932 Housing Act, making a total of nearly 12 650 inter-war dwellings built by the Corporation. The attention given to slum clearance in the 1930s saw a greater provision of blocks of flats containing smaller two- or three-room units. Flats formed 22 per cent of the Dublin Corporation dwellings between 1932 and 1939, compared with only 8 per cent in the previous decade (making an overall average of 17 per cent in the inter-war period). The use of flats was widely criticised, with, for example, the 1939–43 Dublin Housing Inquiry accusing this form of housing of being more expensive and socially undesirable than suburban cottages.[67] Rothery has suggested that the design of many of the Corporation flat blocks, such as those at Townshend Street (1934–36), was influenced by the 'Amsterdam School' of Michel de Klerk and his followers. Such a link, however, is not proven, and a more likely source of inspiration was the contemporary inner-city schemes built by the LCC and other British municipalities.[68] Dublin Corporation meanwhile continued apace. By 1947, around 14 400 dwellings had been provided under the 1932 Act alone, and the Corporation had built to date nearly 24 000 homes.[69] Yet again, this far from effected a radical change in the circumstances of the poorer citizens. The 1939–43 Dublin Housing Inquiry showed that things had barely improved since the similar official investigation just before the First World War. Some 28 679 families (24 per cent of the population) still lived in 6307 tenement houses. Nearly 70 per cent of families lived in one room, and 13 000 people lived in dwellings unfit for human habitation. The estimate was that 21 000 houses were required, plus around another 1500 units per annum to keep pace with new demand.[70] A similar story of increased municipal activity failing to improve housing conditions was found in Cork, where the need for a further 3500 dwellings still existed in 1939.[71] All in all it was a unhappy state of affairs, especially given the fact that the urban housing issue had up to 1922 played an important role in the relationship between Ireland and Britain. In conclusion, it is now necessary to draw the underlying themes of this study together.

CONCLUSION

If, then, the issue of Irish state housing lost its urgency in the cold reality of independence and devolution, what does this tell us about developments up to 1922? The fundamental point to make is that state housing had been significant as an aspect of the relationship of Ireland with the United Kingdom. The result was that Ireland, prior to 1914, was the first, and apparently the only, country to have a national policy of state housing based on centrally subsidised municipal dwellings and recommended design types. There was by no means a completely uniform policy. For instance, the structure was more fully developed for Irish rural housing, and notably less so for urban areas. Nevertheless, within the context of Europe and America before 1914, it is clear that Ireland had by far the most socialised system of working-class housebuilding. A recent cross-cultural comparison has suggested that Ireland was atypical in that it tended to be led by rural developments, in contrast to other countries, where urban concerns were the prompt for pre-war housing initiatives.[1] This might well be expected of an agricultural and relatively non-industrialised nation. But while Irish rural agitation was undoubtedly decisive, it is also important to stress that even in terms of *urban* housing the impetus towards state subsidy in Ireland before the First World War was noticeably more advanced than elsewhere. Political factors were paramount, and these affected Irish towns and cities just as much as the countryside.

The process by which state housing policy was determined in Ireland before the First World War was *ad hoc* and reactive. It involved a crucial tripartite mediation between Irish Nationalists, the British Government, and the Castle Administration which oversaw British policy (there was in addition a lesser influence from groups such as opposition parties in Westminster, the Irish labour movement, and town planning advocates). Useful in this context is the Gramscian concept of a continual and unstable 'hegemonic struggle' for the control of housing ideas and policies, particularly during the period prior to 1914 in which the economic and political uncertainties of the Imperial system made the 'Irish Question' a key factor in the crisis of British liberalism. In the sphere of state housing policy, the force of Irish Nationalism was represented almost entirely by the constitutional approach of the Irish Party. The IPP had proved extremely adept at exploiting the desire of Westminster to maintain constitutional stability at critical moments. 'Native political success in claiming some voice in decision-making during the nineteenth century', Lee has written, 'was not won by rejecting the rules of the English political game, but largely by mastering them, and playing effectively within English terms of reference.'[2] The primary tactic of the Irish Party from the 1880s was to use the issue of land redistribution as the 'engine' that would pull Home Rule in its train. Connected to this within the IPP's umbrella of social reform was the demand for state housing subsidy. The latter policy arose for two distinct reasons. Firstly, the campaign for rural and then urban housing reform served to overcome ideological and class tensions created by the emphasis on helping tenant farmers through land purchase, and thereby enabled constitutional Nationalism to build a broad support base which prevented the growth of an independent labour party in town or country. Secondly, the Irish Party desired economic redress for the disadvantages that agricultural Ireland suffered in comparison with a rapidly modernising Britain. Thus the achievement of housing subsidy under the 1906 Labourers Act, and partially under the 1908 Clancy Housing Act, was seen as clawing back financial benefits from an exploitative Imperial system. By obtaining uniquely favourable housing terms for Ireland (at a time when the country was receiving merely equal treatment in, for instance, old age pensions or National Insurance), enabled the IPP to portray the pre-war Irish housing legislation as the crowning glory of constitutional Nationalism in the sphere of working-class interests. 'THE IRISH PARTY HAS BEEN THE LABOUR PARTY IN PARLIAMENT FOR THE PAST THIRTY YEARS', declared John Redmond in 1909.[3]

The overriding concern of the British Government and its representatives in the Dublin Castle Administration was always to maintain political peace in Ireland, in order to protect the Imperial economic system from external threat. In practice, the distinction between Conservative and Liberal social policy in Ireland was never that substantial, even if the two British parties differed in their specific intentions and ideological viewpoints. These differences meant that there was never a fixed or consistent policy on state housing. The Conservative policy of 'constructive Unionism' was predicated on the belief that social order was the product of economic progress, and that therefore Irish discontent could be defused by addressing rural poverty.[4] The attempt to bypass Nationalist demands was demonstrated by the introduction of the first element of rural housing subsidy by Chief Secretary Balfour under the 1891 Land Act, and by George Wyndham's interest in 1903 in a new Labourers Bill. Yet 'constructive Unionism' was doomed by an inherent limitation. In the final analysis, staunch Unionists would not accept so much financial and political power being given over to Nationalist bodies in Ireland. What was to prove more productive in terms of Irish state housing was the need of the Liberal Party from 1906 to accept unpalatable policy innovations proposed by the Irish Party *in lieu* of Home Rule legislation. Interpreted in Gramscian terms, this represented an attempt to reconstruct the faltering Liberal hegemony by absorbing and thereby 'transforming' the demands of Irish Nationalism.[5]

It was the larger political divisions engendered by Home Rule and the pre-war 'Ulster Crisis' that led to the paralysis of the Irish Party on the issue of state housing. Responsibility at first devolved to the Castle Administration: initially through the 1913–14 Dublin Housing Inquiry (a conciliatory device to absorb the demands of radical labour and town planning adherents), and then, following the débâcle of the 1916 Easter Rising, to the first concerted adoption of state housing as a tool of government policy. 'The general problem of the housing of the working classes in Dublin is one of the most pressing problems that are engaging the attention of the Government in Irish affairs', Chief Secretary Duke told the Imperial Parliament in 1917.[6] The special war-time housing loan to Dublin Corporation was intended to reduce political opposition in Ireland during a critical period of the war, and thereby to help pave the way for the introduction of conscription. Yet the problem now for the Liberal Government was that with the decline of the Irish Party, there was no longer a clear avenue of support on state housing policy. Instead, the issue became subsumed into what has been described as the war-time Government's attempt to establish a middle-ground, 'coalitionist' compromise with the Conservative Party.[7] Thus, in 1917–18 Lloyd George and his advisers offered substantial housing subsidy as an enticement to those taking part in the ill-fated Irish Convention. Coalition in British politics was, of course, achieved by the post-war Lloyd George Government, and was echoed in the sphere of Irish state housing by the fact that for the first time Ulster Unionists became actively involved. Worries in Ulster and in Dublin Castle derived from the absorption of the radical Irish labour movement into the separatist republicanism of Sinn Fein, and from the fear of trained demobilised soldiers swelling the ranks of the Irish Republican Army. The outcome in post-war Ireland was an autocratic housing policy that emanated from Westminster, via the Castle Administration, as a grotesque relative of the Addison campaign on the mainland. Typical was the unfavourable subsidy system under the 1919 Irish Housing Act, based on the amount of rents collected, and above all the unique programme to build directly houses for ex-servicemen. The degree of separation from actual Irish demands was but a portent of the collapse of British rule by 1921, and the handing over of housing policy the following year to both parts of Ireland.

These *ad hoc* and reactive swings in Irish housing policy, however, always took place within a structural condition in which every initiative was distorted by—or at least contingent upon—what MacDonagh has termed 'British states of mind'.[8] There was a continuing inability to see Irish problems in anything other than British terms, and the resulting restrictions were four-fold. First, all housing initiatives were ultimately subject to Imperial veto in Westminster, depending on whether it was believed that they would support political and economic stability in Ireland (and thereby sustain British rule). Second, no policy was ever introduced if it was likely to cause too much friction with interest groups in Britain. Substantial rural housing subsidy could therefore be condoned on the grounds that Irish agriculture was a special case, as Chief Secretary Balfour had argued in 1891. Yet the Irish Party's pre-war proposals for an equivalent urban treatment were emasculated by the Liberal

Government for fear of provoking an unstoppable momentum of demand from British municipalities. The generous subsidy proposal of the Irish Convention in early-1918 sent panic through the Treasury. The result was an obsession with the idea of 'equivalence' in post-war efforts to devise a separate subsidy system for Ireland that could not be construed as being either less or more favourable than that for the mainland. Third, the Imperial Treasury always insisted on strict controls over what it saw as the profligacy of Government departments and local authorities in Ireland, in reciprocation for any concessions it was forced to make. For the Treasury knew full well that the goal of constitutional Nationalists was always to extract as much money as possible from the Imperial Exchequer. Thus, for instance, the granting of full rural subsidy under the 1906 Labourers Act was offset by the publication of the first ever recommended type-plans for state housing (the aim being both to provide models of economic design, and to save on architects' design fees). The fourth point to make is that there was a continual, virtually unchallenged assumption that British models of housing design were inherently better. On the part of Irish architects and housing campaigners, this was due to what Lee has described elsewhere as 'the dependency syndrome that has wormed its way into the Irish psyche during the long centuries of foreign dominance'.[9] The outcome was a tendency by journals such as the *Irish Builder* to repeatedly compare Irish achievements unfavourably with those in its larger, industrial neighbour.

However, cultural inferiority was ultimately the product of a British Imperialist ideology that denigrated the values of rural Ireland, and categorised 'primitive Celtic' alongside the native cultures of remoter outposts of the Empire. The most visible manifestations of British condescension were the fake Irish villages designed for the international exhibitions of the late-nineteenth and early-twentieth centuries.[10] It must, however, also be stressed that there was a socially-progressive side to the efforts to draw a distinction between 'advanced' Britain and 'uncivilised' Ireland. For the concern of British imperialists in the late-nineteenth century involved not just a mission of territorial acquisition and moral 'improvement' in regions such as Africa, but also a consolidation of the existing parts of the Empire. This ideological mind-set believed that underdeveloped countries such as Ireland, if they were to survive in a rapidly modernising world characterised by aggressive colonial expansionism, had to be shown how to integrate into the dominant value-system of the British Empire. It was in effect a 'social Darwinism' that sprang from the same source as the 'national efficiency' campaign launched after the Boer War débâcle, and which lay at the base of the generalised policy known as 'social imperialism'.[11] Hence the emphasis on social efficiency, and the attendant desire to eliminate Irish Nationalist dissent, that can be seen in the writings of Sir Horace Plunkett and Patrick Geddes. An unquestioning acceptance of the benefits of the anglo-centric colonial 'mission' was not surprising given the extent to which it infused British cultural attitudes. John Ruskin, the founding father of the tradition of romantic social critique in nineteenth-century art and architecture, was a supporter of imperialist values. In his inaugural lecture as Slade Professor of Art at Oxford University in 1870, Ruskin had said of Britain's historical role:

> There is a destiny now possible to us—the highest ever set before a nation to be accepted or refused. We are still undegenerate in race; a race mingled of the best northern blood. We are not yet dissolute in temper, but still have the firmness to govern, and the grace to obey. And we are rich in an inheritance of honour, bequeathed to us through a thousand years of noble history, which it should be our daily thirst to increase with splendid avarice, so that Englishmen, if it be a sin to covet honour, should be the most offending souls alive. Within the last few years we have had the laws of natural science opened to us with a rapidity which has been blinding by its brightness; and means of transit and communication given to us, which have made but one kingdom of the habitable globe. One kingdom;—but who is to be its king? . . .
>
> . . . But it must be—it *is* with us, now, 'Reign or Die'. And it shall be said of this country, 'Fece per viltate, il gran rifiuto', that refusal of the crown will be, of all yet recorded in history, the shamefullest and most untimely. And this is what she [England] must either do, or perish: she must found colonies as fast and far as she is able, formed of her most energetic and worthiest men;—seizing every piece of fruitful waste ground she can set her foot on, and there teaching these colonists that their chief virtue is to be fidelity to their country, and that their first aim is to be to advance the power of England by land and sea . . . But that they may be able to do this, she must make her own majesty stainless; she must give them thoughts of their home of which they can be proud. The England who is to be mistress of half the earth, cannot remain herself a heap of cinders, trampled by contending and miserable crowds; she must yet again become the England she was once, and in all beautiful ways.[12]

From such sentiments it was an easy step to the declaration in 1907 by the journal *Garden City* that what was needed was 'not only England but all parts of the Empire to be covered with Garden Cities'.[13] The result was that the early town planning enthusiasts such as Geddes, Unwin, Adshead, or Abercrombie, acted as unwitting agents for the imposition of a professional ideology that served to incorporate and control the colonial cities of the British Empire.[14] Certainly one notable admirer of Geddes was the socialist Arts and Crafts architect, Charles Ashbee, an entrant in the 1914 Dublin Town Plan Competition, and (according to his biographer) 'a cultural imperialist' in attitude.[15] A similar propensity to condition Ireland ideologically to the realities of British rule was also present in the recommendation of garden suburb housing by Geddes and Unwin in the pre-war era.

Thus the other side of the same anglo-centric coin was that Irish state housing design was undoubtedly modernised by the assimilation of the latest models from Britain. In terms of rural dwellings, this came less from the recommended cottage designs of the Irish Board of Works in 1869, or those later of the Congested Districts Board, than through the larger two-storey types produced by the ILGB for the 1906 Labourers Act to augment the traditional single-storey vernacular. Unwinian suburban housing was promoted by town planning enthusiasts, but before the First World War had made limited impact save for a few small schemes by South Dublin RDC and some designs by Pembroke UDC. Yet by the end of the First World War, the new orthodoxy was accepted in the Fairbrothers Fields scheme of Dublin Corporation, and in the reports of the Irish Convention's Housing Committee and of the ILGB's Dr Peter Cowan. The institutionalised framework for garden suburb design was created by the circulars of the ILGB in May and September 1919. An adherence to British housing design was to continue after 1922 in both Northern Ireland and the Irish Free State, the declared intention of 'de-anglicisation' in the latter notwithstanding. It was one part of a bland, consensual continuum almost untouched by independence. 'No architectural splendours can be pointed to as expressions of a confident, assertive . . . society', is the judgement that Brown has made of an Irish Free State that remained obsessed by the mythology of the remote and beautiful rural districts of Western Ireland.[16]

The structural restrictions of British rule aside, the paradox remains that, due to political pressures, what appears to have been the most advanced housing policy in the United Kingdom before 1914 came about in the least developed nation. Both the main political parties in Britain accepted a greater socialisation of state housing in Ireland than was permitted elsewhere. It was a situation that prompted Liberals and Conservatives to define their ideological beliefs more carefully. 'Ireland forces upon us these great social and great religious questions—God grant that we may have courage to look them in the face, and to work through them', Gladstone had written way back in 1845.[17] In order to reconcile Irish political demands with the desire to safeguard British rule, the pre-war Liberal Cabinet found itself having to reluctantly *absorb* what ministers such as John Burns derided as the 'Irish system' of subsidised municipal housing. Yet the Liberal Government, with the sole exception of Lord Strachie, was still determined that there would be no transference of the policy to mainland Britain. Ireland remained, in Liberal eyes, sui generis. By contrast, many influential figures within the pre-war Conservative Party were now calling for the introduction of state housing subsidy on the Irish model. Chief amongst them were figures such as Sir Walter Long who argued that Balfourian 'constructive Unionism' had killed off socialism in Ireland. The belief was that similar socio-economic intervention would head off working-class disaffection in Britain, and would also reaffirm the integrity of the United Kingdom. Several Labour MPs capitalised on Irish experience to attack the precept that state subsidy held down wages, and as a result they found themselves rallying around the Opposition Conservative Housing Bills that were introduced between 1912 and 1914. The ideological division over Irish housing precedent was not confined to politicians, but also affected well-known housing reformers. William Thompson, for example, became a champion of the 'Irish system', whereas John Nettlefold of Birmingham Corporation remained implacably opposed. By the end of the First World War, the previous ideological divisions had been blurred. The new coalitionist alliance formed by Lloyd George with the Conservative Party and Ulster Unionists entirely accepted Irish precedent in principle, if not in actual detail. 'The policy here advocated was the same as that put into effect by Mr Balfour in Ireland', Lloyd George told the Coalition Cabinet in March 1919; '. . . About 50,000 [houses] had been built in Ireland, largely at the expense of the State. He had been told that they had transformed the whole country.'[18] The somewhat inaccurate description of subsidised housing as a 'Balfourist' strategy served to bind Conservatives to a policy aimed at neutralising social democratic demands. State housing thereby had a key role in effecting a 'passive revolution' in the reconstructed post-war bourgeois hegemony. The pre-war experience of Ireland thus helped to shape, even if it did not determine, the framework for housing policy in Britain in 1919.

It is clear that the analysis of early Irish state housing substantially modifies the current interpretations of the origins of state housing policy in Britain that were mentioned at the outset.[19] The first stage of state intervention in Ireland was to provide dwellings for farm labourers, yet this policy began at a time when the rural proletariat was already declining sharply as a consequence of land redistribution, and their standard of housing was, if anything, improving. Therefore, any theory that takes as its basis the notion of a perceived housing need cannot apply to Ireland. In terms of Offer's explanation, certainly the pre-war slump of 1906-12 eroded the speculative building of working-class dwellings in Belfast. There was still, however, relatively little pressure in Ulster for state action. By comparison, in cities such as Dublin the link between chronic poverty and appalling housing had been noted by Engels as early as the mid-1840s, and by this century had become a commonplace remark. One prewar Sinn Fein councillor stated that 'the main cause of the social evils of Dublin is the dire poverty of the major portion of the working classes, which is the greatest barrier to social progress. If work and wages were plentiful and ample, the solution of the housing problem would be simple'.[20] The inherent contradictions within profit-based housebuilding had long been apparent, and there was in the extensive slums of Dublin (if the phrase is to mean anything) a genuine crisis for the 'reproduction of labour power'. Yet in this most desperate case of housing need and class conflict, the Liberal Government resisted the demands for increased urban subsidy voiced by the 1914 Dublin Housing Inquiry. Nor is there any real evidence in Ireland for the emphasis placed by Englander on tenant militancy as the force that broke the dominance of housing capitalists. The Irish Party took up the running—first on rural housing, and then on the urban issue through the Town Tenants League—precisely to stop the growth of working-class political agitation. It was an avowedly non-radical strategy that aimed to counterbalance the influence of petty-bourgeois urban landlords. And even the radical labour movement during the Dublin industrial upheaval of 1913–14 was less concerned with the housing problem *per se*, than in using it emotively as part of a Marxist argument for fundamental social revolution against British capitalism. When comprehensive state subsidy for urban housing in Ireland came to be introduced by the British Government in 1919, it was at a time when the Irish labour movement had become increasingly marginalised in both North and South.

Instead, the analysis of early state housing in Ireland shows that the issue was less and less to do with the reality of working-class demands, and more and more to do with its function as an instrument of political ideology. This accords most closely with the theory of an 'insurance against revolution' advanced by Swenarton. Yet the Swenarton thesis needs to be modified in two key aspects in light of Irish experience. Firstly, the advent of rural subsidy and partial urban subsidy in pre-war Ireland did not result from a condition in which the British Government could determine housing policy centrally or in isolation. Rather, the pattern of imposing policy 'from above' only began once Westminster and the Castle Administration took the upper hand following the 1916 Easter Rising. The trend was consolidated as a response to alarmist post-war fears about the threat to Imperial stability posed by an alliance of 'bolshevism' and republicanism. Secondly, the state subsidy introduced by the 1919 Addison Housing Act in Britain was not a novel or untried solution. It was instead the transfer and adaptation of the hitherto rejected 'Irish system', now seen by the Lloyd George Government as a means to maintain political peace. This second modification, however, also serves to reinforce the Swenarton thesis, since it counters the criticism made by Daunton and others that state housing was too cumbersome and uncertain to be used as a primary tool of social legitimation.[21] The view expressed within the Cabinet in 1919, however erroneous it might have been, was that subsidised state housing had been directly effective in mitigating unrest in rural Ireland.

This study of one particular social aspect of British rule in Ireland obviously cannot be used to construct a comprehensive theory, but it can shed some light on the general workings of colonialism. A tendency in recent writings on imperialism has been to discount unitary or generalised theories about the process of colonisation. Imperialism is instead usually described as a complex phenomenon with interrelated political, psychological, economic, and social dimensions.[22] Circumstances vary considerably depending on which country is being analysed. The case of Ireland presents particular difficulties: first, because British domination pre-dated the phase of 'classical imperialism' pursued by European countries from the 1880s up to 1914; and second, because there was a far greater degree of economic and social integration between Ireland and Britain than was found in more distant colonies. It is, however, the greater degree of interconnection that makes Ireland such an important subject for the study of political and cultural influences. Ireland by no means formed a 'social laboratory' for the British Government. Nor could it ever do, as long as a situation existed wherein no single group could devise, control, or monitor any would-be policy experiments. And yet it proved to be the case that Irish experience constituted one of the crucial pressures that was to cause Britain after the First World War to move away from *laissez-faire* liberalism and towards a more collectivist society.[23]

State housing subsidy in Ireland represented a mediation of Nationalist demands for redress given the unequal industrialisation, and hence uneven economic modernisation, of the United Kingdom. It represented at most an *indirect consequence* of the economic modernisation of Britain, and yet nevertheless the outcome was that one aspect of social provision in Ireland was to a large extent modernised along the lines of the most advanced policy available at the time. Irish demands on the issue of state housing were essentially economic, and the strategy for achieving financial redistribution was played out in the political sphere. The corollary on the cultural level was that little interest was shown by the Irish Party or other groups in finding sources of housing design that might provide alternatives to British models. Nationalists offered little resistance to the widespread perception that the advanced model of Unwinian garden suburbs should be adopted as the physical form of modernisation. And yet at the same time, the debate about housing developments in Ireland were fed back into the 'hegemonic struggle' over ideas about state housing in Britain. Thus there was a definite influence on British ways of thinking—what might be termed an 'inverse-diffusion' of cultural values from 'periphery' to 'core'—but an influence that was heavily filtered and transformed by the structural realities of Imperial domination. However, it meant that the development of a modernised social housing policy in Britain after the First World War was the result not just of the political and economic pressures deriving from widespread industrialisation on the mainland, but was also conditioned by realities created by the unequal modernisation of the United Kingdom as a whole.

Thus, in the final analysis it is the importance of the interrelationship between state housing policy in Ireland and in Britain before 1922 that forms the underlying thread of the study. Developments in the different parts of the United Kingdom were by no means stereotyped, but neither can they be studied independently. This observation is part of a phenomenon that has been noted by many Irish historians, and of which Oliver MacDonagh has written:

> British values and criteria would sooner or later be imposed on Ireland, and sooner or later would be themselves profoundly influenced by Irish experience . . . Ireland showed in microcosm some of the forces making for collectivism everywhere . . . Ireland's needs differed in intensity and form of manifestation rather than in type from those of

the other island. No departure in Ireland was ultimately irrelevant to Britain.[24]

Specific studies of the effect of colonial interrelationships on the production of the built environment have, however, remained relatively few. One notable exception has been the work of Anthony King, in which it is convincingly argued that the bungalow house-type, to take one specific Anglo-Indian example, and indeed the overall form of the modern city, have been 'globally produced'.[25]

On an even wider level, this present study offers a testimony to the incisive analysis put forward by the distinguished cultural theorist and literary critic, Edward Said.[26] At the heart of Said's writings lies the belief that Western imperialism, and the nationalist resistance and opposition that it spawned, has been the most important conditioning factor on cultural development over the last two centuries. For Said, the response of the contemporary intellectual should not be to apportion blame or to vainly attempt to overturn the consequences of colonialism in a given country. It is far more essential to reveal, carefully and systematically, that all cultures, and particularly those of oppressor and oppressed, are by their very nature interdependent. The primary role of investigation is therefore to demolish the 'ideology of separation' that was promoted by imperial nations in order to 'divide-and-rule'. The goal, in other words, is a post-colonialist dismantling of the orthodox intellectual structures—culture, history, geography, and the rest—which were used to create an imperialist hegemony predicated on illusions of national separateness and racial purity. As Said has noted:

> One of imperialism's achievements was to bring the world closer together and, although in the process the separation between Europeans and natives was an insidious and fundamentally unjust one, most of us should now regard the historical experience of empire as a common one.[27]

All cultures are seen by this analysis as 'hybrids' which fundamentally affect each other, albeit under conditions that are crucially determined by the all-too-real structures of political and economic power which form the framework of colonial interrelationships. Said has written: 'Partly because of empire, all cultures are involved in one another; none is single and pure, all are hybrid, heterogeneous, extraordinarily differentiated, and unmonolithic'.[28] This has important consequences for our understanding of relations between Ireland and Britain, especially given the latter country's continuing tendency to refuse to acknowledge cultural influences from elsewhere. In the field of Irish literature, it was William Butler Yeats who most notably created a shining model of 'colonial' expression from out of the search for a national signature that was opposed to British rule. And yet at the same time, Yeats was also indebted to the sense of 'Englishness' that pervaded Irish culture. On a more prosaic and tangible level, the preceding analysis of Irish state housing suggests a sphere in which a close connection developed between otherwise politically and culturally divided nations. The pattern in general seems to have been that policy innovations originated in Ireland, whereas Britain remained the primary source for ideas about architectural design. Early state housing in Ireland was a profoundly Anglo-Irish creation.

DIAGRAMS AND TABLES

Diagram A ANNUAL TOTAL OF LABOURERS ACTS LOANS
[Source: ILGB/IBoW/Irish Land Commission Annual Reports]

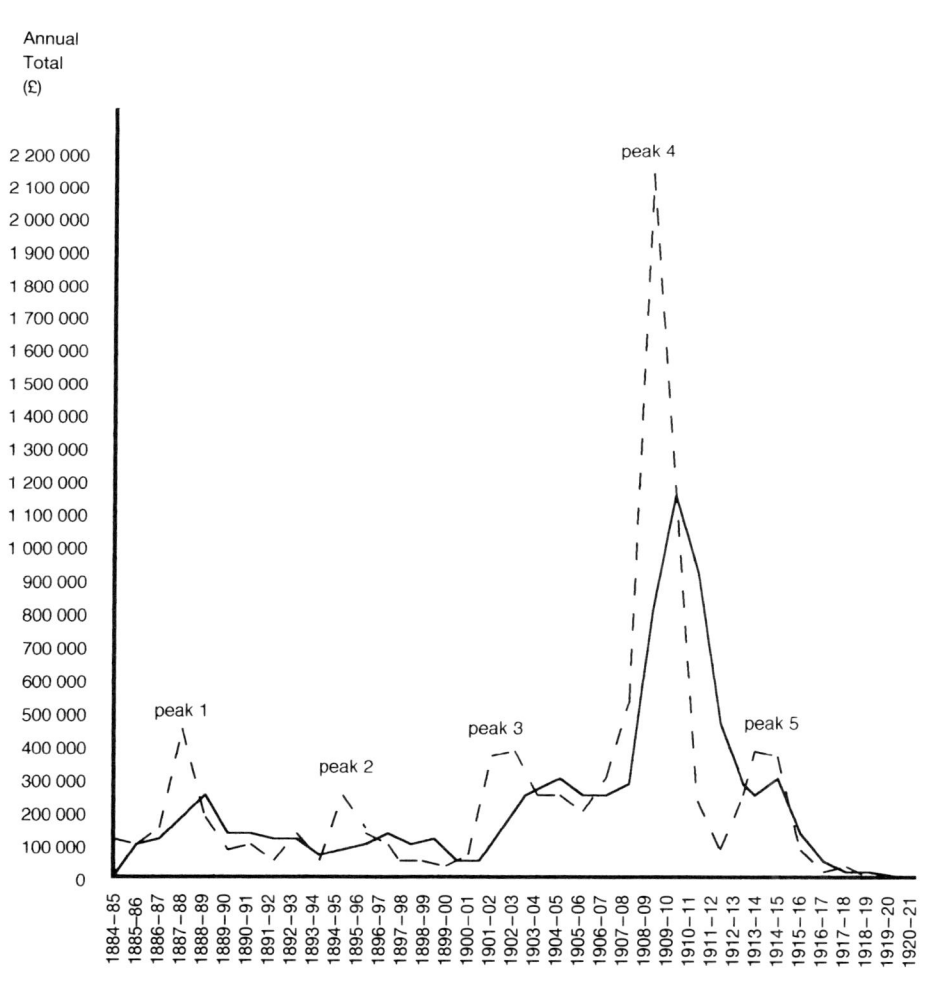

Diagram B ANNUAL TOTAL OF LABOURERS ACTS HOUSES BUILT
[Source: Irish Local Government Board Annual Reports]

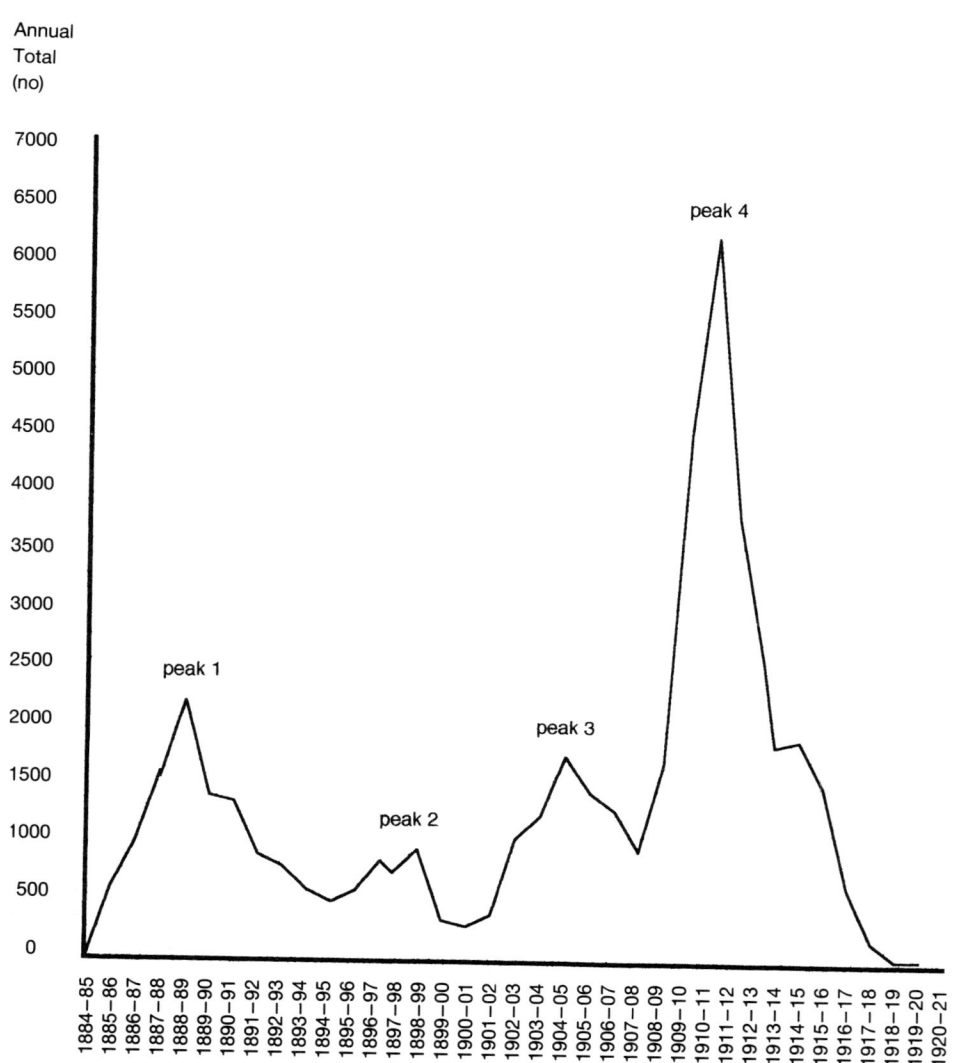

Diagrams and Tables 305

Diagram C CUMULATE TOTAL OF LABOURERS ACTS LOANS
[Source: ILGB/IBoW/Irish Land Commission Annual Reports]

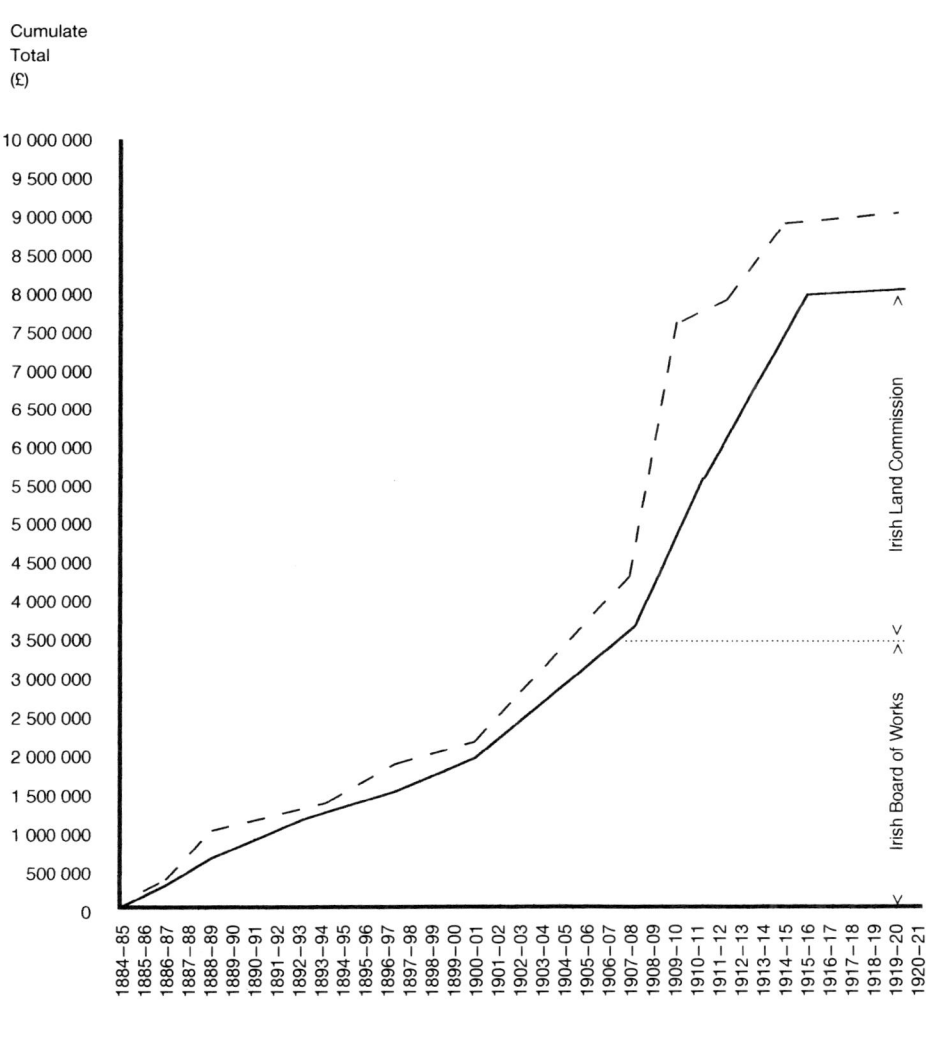

Diagram D ANNUAL TOTAL OF IRISH URBAN HOUSING LOANS
[Source: Irish Board of Works Annual Reports]

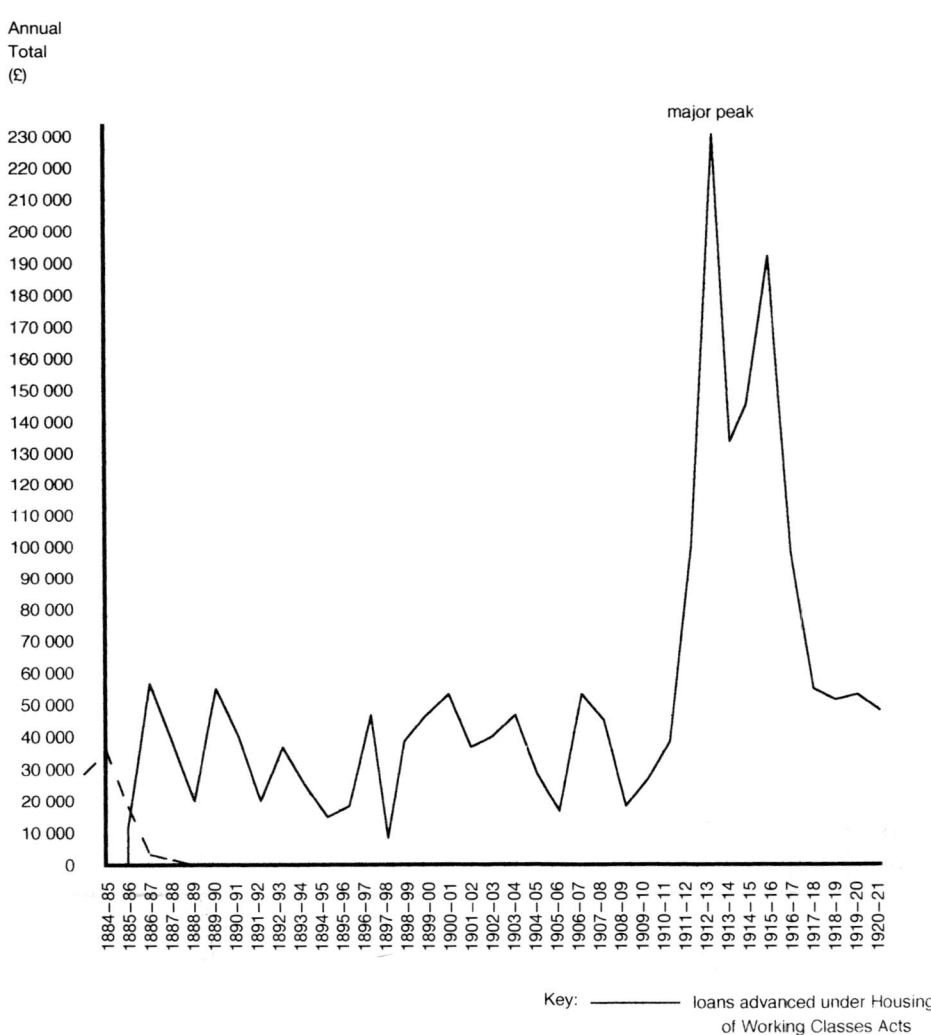

Diagram E CUMULATE TOTAL OF LOANS ADVANCED UNDER THE HOUSING OF THE WORKING CLASSES (IRELAND) ACTS
[Source: Irish Board of Works Annual Reports]

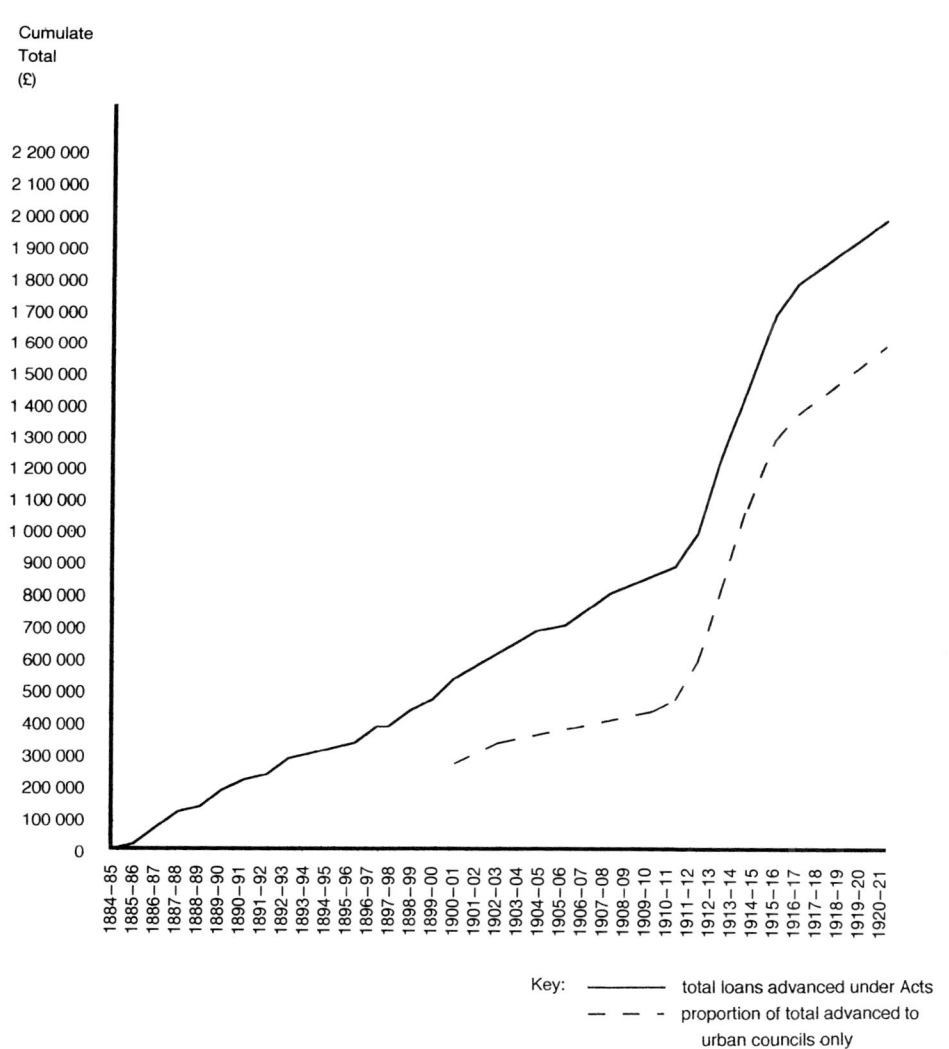

Table 1 ABSTRACT OF LOANS SANCTIONED AND HOUSES BUILT UNDER THE 1883–1919 LABOURERS ACTS, FROM 1884/85
[Source: Irish Local Government Board Annual Reports]

	Total of loans santioned		Number of houses approved		Number of houses built	
	annual total £	cumulate total £	annual total no	cumulate total no	annual total no	cumulate total no
1884–85	118 454		3022			
1885–86	102 173	220 627	379	3401	610	
1886–87	139 394	360 021	4151	7552	1023	1633
1887–88	460 977	820 998	2000	9552	1539	3172
1888–89	188 742	1 009 740	617	10 169	2188	5360
1889–90	89 032	1 098 772	468	10 637	1382	6742
1890–91	107 077	1 205 849	873	11 510	1341	8083
1891–92	48 626	1 254 475	361	11 871	872	8955
1892–93	123 573	1 378 048	491	12 362	798	9753
1893–94	43 916	1 421 964	575	12 937	599	10 352
1894–95	241 374	1 619 421	1126	14 063	496	10 848
1895–96	132 608	1 752 029	768	14 831	621	11 469
1896–97	105 030	1 857 059	713	15 544	871	12 340
1897–98	52 252	1 909 311	204	15 748	761	13 101
1898–99	49 370	1 958 681	308	16 056	933	14 034
1899–00	29 816	1 988 497	247	16 303	351	14 385
1900–01	62 877	2 051 374	863	17 166	304	14 689
1901–02	358 748	2 410 122	2375	19 541	401	15 090
1902–03	388 827	2 798 949	1734	21 575	1069	16 159
1903–04	248 755	3 047 704	1040	22 315	1252	17 411
1904–05	241 125	3 288 829	1025	23 340	1750	19 161
1905–06	198 009	3 486 838	976	24 316	1473	20 634
1906–07	297 972	3 784 810	1894	26 210	1314	21 948
1907–08	529 539	4 314 349	5931	32 141	973	22 921
1908–09	2 137 539	6 451 888	13147	45 288	1726	24 647
1909–10	1 185 504	7 637 393	2375	47 663	4539	29 186
1910–11	236 188	7 873 581	712	48 375	6223	35 409
1911–12	77 936	7 951 517	400	48 775	3832	39 241
1912–13	254 933	8 206 450	1577	50 352	2611	41 852
1913–14	374 394	8 580 844	1925	52 277	1850	43 702
1914–15	99 275	8 950 119	1591	53 868	1890	45 592
1915–16	87 011	9 037 130			1482	47 044
1916–17	20 329	9 057 459			641	47 685
1917–18	30 815	9 088 274			183	47 868
1918–19	8354	9 096 628			47	47 915
1919–20					51	47 966
1920–21						
1921–22						

Table 2 ABSTRACT OF LOANS ADVANCED FOR RURAL HOUSING UNDER THE LABOURERS ACTS, FROM 1885/86
[Source: Irish Board of Works Annual Reports/Irish Land Commission Annual Reports (from 1906)]

	Loans from Irish Board of works		Loans from Irish Land Commission		Total	
	annual total £	*cumulate total £*	annual total no	*cumulate total no*	annual total no	*cumulate total no*
1885–86	106 115				106 115	
1886–87	116 288	*222 403*			116 288	*222 403*
1887–88	194 439	*416 842*			194 439	*416 842*
1888–89	242 597	*659 439*			242 597	*659 439*
1889–90	139 450	*798 890*			139 450	*798 890*
1890–91	139 135	*938 025*			139 135	*938 025*
1891–92	115 133	*1 053 158*			115 133	*1 053 158*
1892–93	111 498	*1 164 655*			111 498	*1 164 655*
1893–94	71 627	*1 236 283*			71 627	*1 236 283*
1894–95	89 875	*1 326 158*			89 875	*1 326 158*
1895–96	100 060	*1 426 218*			100 060	*1 426 218*
1896–97	139 005	*1 565 223*			139 005	*1 565 223*
1897–98	107 750	*1 672 973*			107 750	*1 672 973*
1898–99	110 013	*1 782 986*			110 013	*1 782 986*
1899–00	47 203	*1 830 189*			47 203	*1 830 189*
1900–01	54 746	*1 884 934*			54 746	*1 884 934*
1901–02	157 890	*2 042 744*			157 890	*2 042 744*
1902–03	251 368	*2 294 112*			251 368	*2 294 112*
1903–04	287 764	*2 581 876*			287 764	*2 581 876*
1904–05	300 642	*2 882 518*			300 642	*2 882 518*
1905–06	255 816	*3 138 333*			255 816	*3 138 333*
1906–07	219 017	*3 357 351*	40 990		260 007	*3 398 340*
1907–08	80 583	*3 437 934*	206 845	*247 835*	287 428	*3 685 768*
1908–09	18 661	*3 456 595*	794 760	*1 042 595*	813 421	*4 499 189*
1909–10	3962	*3 460 557*	1 158 745	*2 201 340*	1 162 707	*5 661 896*
1910–11	3938	*3 464 495*	910 746	*3 111 816*	914 684	*6 576 580*
1911–12	2253	*3 466 748*	477 013	*3 588 829*	479 266	*7 055 846*
1912–13	4867	*3 471 615*	283 202	*3 872 031*	288 069	*7 343 915*
1913–14	1489	*3 473 104*	242 167	*4 114 198*	243 656	*7 587 571*
1914–15	300	*3 473 404*	301 060	*4 415 258*	301 360	*7 888 931*
1915–16	125	*3 473 529*	126 821	*4 542 079*	126 946	*8 015 877*
1916–17			44 742	*4 586 821*	44 742	*8 060 619*
1917–18			14 660	*4 601 481*	14 660	*8 075 279*
1918–19			4675	*4 606 156*	4675	*8 079 954*
1919–20			2975	*4 609 131*	2975	*8 082 929*
1920–21						
1921–22						

TABLE 3 ABSTRACT OF REGIONAL DIFFERENCES UNDER THE 1883–1919 LABOURERS ACTS

a) Cumulate proportion of loans sanctioned, by province—to be read in conjunction with Table 1
[Source: Irish Board of Works Annual Reports]

	Munster		Leinster		Connaught		Ulster	
	cumulate total £	[% of total]	cumulate total £	[% of total]	cumulate total £	[% of total]	cumulate total £	[% of total]
1888–89	615 626	[61]	383 627	[38]	6904		3583	
1892–93	804 573	[59]	550 496	[40]	8359		10 845	
1898–99	1 068 311	[54]	832 082	[42]	14 913	[1]	47 067	[2]
1903–04	1 558 426	[51]	1 208 805	[40]	58 374	[2]	220 462	[7]
1906–07 (part)	1 714 361	[47]	1 370 892	[38]	85 212	[2]	456 028	[13]

b) Cumulate proportion of houses built, by province—to be read in conjunction with Table 1
[Source: Irish Local Government Board Annual Reports]

	Munster		Leinster		Connaught		Ulster	
	cumulate total no	[% of total]	cumulate total no	[% of total]	cumulate total no	[% of total]	cumulate total no	[% of total]
1888–89	3525	[66]	1788	[33]	46		1	
1893–94	6232	[60]	3961	[38]	75		84	
1898–99	7952	[57]	5738	[41]	111		233	
1903–04	9254	[53]	7005	[40]	247	[1]	905	[5]
1908–09	11 727	[48]	9532	[39]	547	[2]	2841	[11]
1913–14	17 988	[41]	15 959	[37]	2165	[5]	7590	[17]
1918–19	19 090	[40]	17 335	[36]	2459	[5]	9031	[19]

Table 4 ABSTRACT OF LOANS ADVANCED UNDER ALL URBAN HOUSING CODES IN IRELAND, FROM 1882/83

[Source: Irish Board of Works Annual Reports]

	1866 Labourers Dwellings Act		1875 Artisans Dwellings Act		1885–1919 Housing Acts		Total	
	annual total £	cumulate total £	annual total £	cumulate total £	annual total £	cumulate total £	annual total £	cumulate total £
1882–83	10 908	118 421		64 000			10 908	182 461
1883–84	19 695	138 116	10 300	74 300			29 995	212 416
1884–85	29 476	167 593	6700	81 000			36 176	248 592
1885–86	19 154	186 746			12 400		31 554	280 146
1886–87	3016	189 762			56 873	69 272	59 888	340 034
1887–88	100	189 862			38 544	108 816	38 644	378 678
1888–89					19 803	127 619	19 803	398 481
1889–90					54 224	181 843	54 224	452 705
1890–91					39 070	220 913	39 070	491 775
1891–92					19 692	240 605	19 692	511 467
1892–93					37 401	278 006	37 401	548 868
1893–94					24 116	302 122	24 116	572 984
1894–95					14 264	316 385	14 264	587 248
1895–96					17 750	334 135	17 750	604 998
1896–97					46 187	380 322	46 187	651 185
1897–98					8260	388 582	8260	659 445
1898–99					38 576	427 158	38 576	698 021
1899–00					47 560	474 718	47 560	745 581
1900–01					53 360	528 078	53 360	798 941
1901–02					36 824	564 902	36 824	835 765
1902–03					40 559	605 461	40 559	876 324
1903–04					46 014	651 475	46 014	922 338
1904–05					27 841	679 316	27 841	950 179
1905–06					16 465	695 781	16 465	966 644
1906–07					53 504	749 285	53 504	1 020 148
1907–08					45 264	794 549	45 264	1 065 412
1908–09					17 607	812 156	17 607	1 083 019
1909–10					26 950	839 106	26 950	1 109 969
1910–11					38 700	877 806	38 700	1 148 669
1911–12					102 280	980 086	102 280	1 250 949
1912–13					229 589	1 209 675	229 589	1 480 538
1913–14					132 653	1 342 328	132 653	1 613 191
1914–15					144 690	1 487 018	144 690	1 757 881
1915–16					191 253	1 678 271	191 253	1 949 134
1916–17					97 907	1 776 178	97 907	2 047 041
1917–18					55 369	1 831 547	55 369	2 102 410
1918–19					52 771	1 884 318	52 771	2 155 181
1919–20					53 099	1 937 417	53 099	2 208 280
1920–21					48 239	1 985 656	48 239	2 256 519
1921–22								

Table 5 ABSTRACT OF LOANS ADVANCED UNDER THE 1885–1919 HOUSING OF THE WORKING CLASSES (IRELAND) ACTS, FROM 1885/86
[Source: Irish Board of Works Annual Reports]

	Loans advanced to urban councils				Loans advanced to private builders		Total	
	annual total £	[% of total]	cumulate total £	[% of total]	annual total £	cumulate total £	annual total £	cumulate total £
1885–86							12 400	
1886–87							56 872	69 272
1887–88							38 544	108 816
1888–89							19 803	127 619
1889–90							54 224	181 843
1890–91							39 070	220 913
1891–92							19 692	240 605
1892–93							37 401	278 006
1893–94							24 116	302 122
1894–95							14 264	316 385
1895–96							17 750	334 135
1896–97							46 187	380 322
1897–98							8260	388 582
1898–99							38 576	427 158
1899–00							47 560	474 718
1900–01			266 287	[50]		261 791	53 360	528 078
1901–02	35 490	[96]	301 777	[53]	1 334	263 125	36 824	564 902
1902–03	39 930	[98]	341 707	[56]	629	263 754	40 559	605 461
1903–04	13 304	[29]	355 011	[54]	32 710	296 464	46 014	651 475
1904–05	9838	[35]	364 849	[53]	18 003	314 467	27 841	679 316
1905–06	4540	[28]	369 389	[53]	11 925	326 392	16 465	695 781
1906–07	12 654	[24]	382 043	[51]	40 850	367 242	53 504	749 285
1907–08	18 090	[40]	400 133	[50]	27 174	394 416	45 264	794 549
1908–09	13 607	[77]	413 741	[51]	4000	398 416	17 607	812 156
1909–10	23 050	[86]	436 791	[52]	3900	402 316	26 950	839 106
1910–11	38 050	[98]	474 841	[54]	650	402 966	38 700	877 806
1911–12	98 437	[96]	573 278	[58]	3843	406 809	102 280	980 086
1912–13	229 589		802 867	[66]			229 589	1 209 675
1913–14	132 653		935 520	[70]			132 653	1 342 328
1914–15	144 690		1 080 210	[73]			144 690	1 487 018
1915–16	191 253		1 271 463	[76]			191 253	1 678 271
1916–17	97 907		1 369 370	[77]			97 907	1 776 178
1917–18	55 369		1 424 739	[78]			55 369	1 831 547
1918–19	52 771		1 477 510	[78]			52 771	1 884 318
1919–20	53 099		1 530 609	[79]			53 099	1 937 417
1920–21	48 239		1 578 848	[80]			48 239	1 985 656
1921–22								

Table 6 PROPORTIONS OF RURAL AND URBAN HOUSING LOANS IN RELATION TO TOTAL PUBLIC LOANS ADVANCED IN IRELAND, FROM 1903/04
[Source: Irish Board of Works Annual Reports]

	Total public works loans issued	Loans for Labourers Acts		Loans for Housing of Working Classes Acts	
	annual total £	annual total £	[% of total]	annual total £	[% of total]
1903–04	774 593	287 764	[36]	46 013	[6]
1904–05					
1905–06	600 542	255 815	[43]	16 465	[3]
1906–07					
1907–08	434 796	80 583*	[19]*	45 264	[10]
1908–09					
1909–10	293 233	3962*	[1]*	26 950	[9]
1910–11					
1911–12	409 312	2253*		102 280	[25]
1912–13	529 567	4867*	[1]*	229 589	[43]
1913–14	402 224	1489*		132 653	[33]
1914–15	488 973	300*		144 690	[30]
1915–16	414 821	125*		191 253	[46]
1916–17	148 197			97 907	[66]
1917–18	172 370			55 368	[32]
1918–19	72 459			52 771	[73]
1919–20	62 340			53 099	[85]
1920–21	87 351			48 329	[55]
1921–22					

* Residue only (after 1906 Act public loans came from Irish Land Commission for this purpose)

REFERENCES

STANDARD ABBREVIATIONS

AMAI	Association of Municipal Authorities of Ireland
BL ADD MSS	British Library Additional Manuscripts
HC DEB	House of Commons Debates
HLL	House of Lords Library
HTPAI	Housing and Town Planning Association of Ireland
ILGB	Irish Local Government Board
IWM	Imperial War Museum
JSSISI	Journal of the Statistical and Social Inquiry Society of Ireland
NLI MSS	National Library of Ireland Manuscripts
NLS MSS	National Library of Scotland Manuscripts
PP	Parliamentary Papers
PRO	Public Records Office (Kew)
RIAI	Royal Institute of Architects of Ireland
RPDCD	Reports and Printed Documents of the Corporation of Dublin
SPO	State Paper Office (Dublin)
TCD	Trinity College Dublin
UCD	University College Dublin
WRO	Wiltshire Record Office

INTRODUCTION (1–20)

1. The classic study is still: E. J. Hobsbawm, *Industry and Empire*, 1968.
2. The general historical outline that follows is derived from: L. M. Cullen, *The Emergence of Modern Ireland 1600–1900*, 1981: R. F. Foster, *Modern Ireland 1600–1972*, 1988: J. Lee, *The Modernisation of Irish Society 1848–1918*, 1973: F. S. L. Lyons, *Ireland Since the Famine*, 1971: O. MacDonagh, *Ireland: The Union and its Aftermath*, 1967/77: M. A. G. O'Tuathaigh, 'Ireland and Britain under the Union, 1800–1921: an overview', in P. J. Drudy (ed.), *Ireland and Britain since 1922 (Irish Studies 5)*, 1986, pp. 1–20: B. Chubb, *The Government and Politics of Ireland*, 1970/82.
3. M. A. G. O'Tuathaigh, op. cit., p. 13: see also: R. F. Foster, op. cit., pp. 200–03.
4. D. McAleese, 'Anglo-Irish economic interdependence: from excessive intimacy to a wider embrace', in P. J. Drudy (ed.), *Ireland and Britain since 1922 (Irish Studies 5)*, 1986, p. 87: see also: L. M. Cullen, *An Economic History of Ireland since 1660*, 1972, pp. 97–99, 103–07, 125–29.
5. B. Chubb, op. cit., p. 8: M. Hechter, *Internal Colonialism: The Celtic Fringe in British National Development, 1536–1966*, 1975, pp. 264–73.
6. M. Hechter, op. cit., pp. 76–77, 184–85, 267–70.

7. O. MacDonagh, *States of Mind: A Study of Anglo-Irish Conflict 1780–1950*, 1983, p. 54: see also: O. MacDonagh, op. cit., p. 33.
8. D. Fraser, *The Evolution of the Welfare State*, 1973/84, pp. 99–176: E. J. Hobsbawm, op. cit., pp. 225–44: an important study of this phenomenon in relation to the prewar attitude to unemployment is given in: J. Harris, *Unemployment and Politics: A Study in English Social Policy 1886–1914*, 1972.
9. M. A. G. O'Tuathaigh, op. cit., p. 7: see also for instance: B. Chubb, 'Britain and Irish constitutional development', in P. J. Drudy (ed.), *Ireland and Britain since 1922 (Irish Studies 5)*, 1986, p. 24: F. S. L. Lyons, op. cit., pp. 71–103: O. MacDonagh, op. cit. (1967/77), pp. 33–51: R. McDowell, *The Irish Administration 1801–1914*, 1964, pp. vii, 27, 194–229.
10. W. L. Burn, 'Free trade in land: an aspect of the Irish question', *Transactions of the Royal Historical Society*, 4th Series, vol. 31: F. S. L. Lyons, op. cit., pp. 74, 76, 98: O. MacDonagh, op. cit. (1967/77), pp. 33–52.
11. J. Lee, op. cit., pp. 26–27, 34–35: O. MacDonagh, op. cit. (1967/77), pp. 34, 42.
12. C. Townshend, 'Modernisation and nationalism: perspectives in recent Irish history', *History*, vol. 66, 1981, p. 234.
13. For studies of Irish cultural and political reaction, see: R. F. Foster, op. cit., pp. 431–33: F. S. L. Lyons, *Culture and Anarchy in Ireland 1890–1939*, 1979: O. MacDonagh, op. cit. (1967/77), pp. 72–101.
14. C. Townshend, op. cit., pp. 233–43: the first real analysis of the subject was in: J. Lee, op. cit..
15. For a succinct analysis of Weber's thought, see: C. Antoni, *From History to Sociology: The Transition in German Historical Thinking*, 1940/1959, p. 135: for recent studies on imperialism, see: W. Baumgart, *Imperialism: The Idea and Reality of British and French Colonial Expansion, 1880–1914*, 1982: W. J. Mommsen, *Theories of Imperialism*, 1980.
16. See, for instance: M. Hechter, op. cit., pp. 59–64: I. Lustick, *State-Building Failure in British Ireland and French Algeria*, 1985, pp. 1–5.
17. D. G. Boyce, *Nationalism in Ireland*, 1982, pp. 375–79: R. F. Foster, op. cit., p. 569.
18. C. Townshend, op. cit., p. 241.
19. The basic Gramsci texts in English are: A. Gramsci, *Selections from the Prison Notebooks*, 1971: A. Gramsci, *Selections from Political Writings (1910–1920)*, 1977: A. Gramsci, *Selections from Political Writings (1921–1926)*, 1978: A. Gramsci, *Selections from Cultural Writings*, 1985: for the development of Gramscian ideas, see for instance: C. Buci-Glucksmann, *Gramsci and the State*, 1980: T. Bennett, 'Introduction', and C. McArthur, 'The dialectic of national identity: the Glasgow Empire Exhibition of 1938', in T. Bennett, C. Mercer and J. Woollacott (eds), *Popular Culture and Social Relations*, 1986, pp. xiv–xv, 117–34: S. Hall and B. Schwarz, 'State and society, 1880–1930', and R. Wilson, 'Imperialism in crisis: "the Irish dimension" ', in M. Langan and B. Schwarz (eds), *Crises in the British State 1880–1930*, 1985, pp. 7–32, 151–78.
20. See, for the example of Belfast: H. Dixon, *Ulster Architecture*, 1972, pp. 5–7.
21. S. Rothery, *Ireland and the New Architecture 1900–1940*, 1991, pp. 56–58, 90–100.
22. *Irish Builder*, 1 September 1878, p. 247: also 15 June 1879, p. 184; 15 November 1880, p. 313; 1 December 1881, p. 344.
23. RIAI, *Reports of Council and of Annual General Meeting*, 1907–08, and *Journal of the RIAI*, 1909–14.

24. *Irish Builder*, 15 December 1898, p. 183: also 15 December 1891, p. 279; 1 January 1899, pp. 5–6.
25. *Irish Builder*, 28 November 1908, p. 730; 12 December 1908, p. 800; 6 February 1909, p. 68–69; 22 January 1910, p. 50; 23 July 1910, pp. 466–69; 12 November 1910, pp. 696–99; 26 October 1912, pp. 602–03, 606; 24 February 1925, p. 127; 16 May 1925, pp. 385–89; 22 August 1925, p. 675: *Irish Architect and Building Trades Journal*, 26 October 1912, pp. 1137–42: S. Rothery, op. cit., pp. 62–66.
26. *Irish Builder*, 25 December 1909, p. 815: see also, for example: 11 July 1908, p. 430.
27. *Irish Builder*, 25 February 1922, p. 114: also 27 June 1925, p. 521.
28. For background data on white-collar professions, see for instance: M. Daly, *Dublin, the Deposed Capital: A Social and Economic History, 1860–1914*, 1984, pp. 124–33, 145–51: Daly's statistics, though not specifically mentioning architects, show that Protestants/Presbyterians formed only 18 per cent of Dublin's population and yet nearly 48 per cent of the professional class in 1871; that this fell only slightly to 14 per cent of the population and nearly 38 per cent of professionals by 1911; and surrounding townships contained many Protestant professionals who commuted.
29. *Irish Builder*, 15 December 1900, p. 580: see also: RIAI, *Journal of the RIAI 1913*, 1913, p. 2.
30. Quoted in: J. Sheehy, *The Rediscovery of Ireland's Past: the Celtic Revival 1830–1930*, 1980, p. 116.
31. *Irish Builder*, 14 June 1924, pp. 515–16.
32. *Irish Builder*, 15 January 1874, p. 26.
33. M. Brown, *The Politics of Irish Literature: From Thomas Davis to W. B. Yeats*, 1972: R. F. Foster, op. cit., pp. 450–53: F. S. L. Lyons, op. cit. (1979): J. Sheehy, op. cit., pp. 95–106.
34. *Irish Builder*, 19 November 1921, p. 741.
35. F. S. L. Lyons, op. cit. (1979), p. 64: for more background to the literary debate, see also: F. S. L. Lyons, op. cit. (1971), pp. 224–46.
36. This tendency has been admirably covered in: J. Sheehy, op. cit.
37. See, for instance: *Irish Builder*, 27 May 1911, p. 346; 2 March 1912, p. 124: *Irish Architect and Building Trades Journal*, 14 March 1914, pp. 715–16: *Irish Times*, 26 August 1926, p. 6: M. Craig, *The Architecture of Ireland: From the Earliest Times to 1880*, 1982, pp. 293–94.
38. *Irish Builder*, 24 October 1907, p. 582: J. Sheehy, op. cit., pp. 134–42.
39. *Irish Builder*, 25 February 1922, p. 114.
40. J. Sheehy, op. cit., p. 145: also pp. 9, 188, 193.
41. R. Caulfield Orpen, 'Architecture in Ireland', in *Manchester Guardian Commercial*, 26 July 1923, Section 3 'European Reconstruction Series: Ireland', p. 48: see also: *Irish Builder*, 8 April 1922, p. 226; 6 May 1922, p. 310.
42. *Irish Times*, 9 February 1922, p. 4.
43. Hence there is no real basis for the American influence argued in S. Rothery, op. cit., pp. 5–20, 68–74, 155–67. While Rothery contends that there were some general links with US architecture in Irish buildings, the case remains unproven and he can only produce two instances of actual American design: the work of the Irish-American sculptor Augustus Saint-Gaudens for the Parnell Monument in Dublin (1909–11), and then Barry Byrne's Church of Christ the King in Cork (1927–31).

44. Following Yeats' fulsome praise of Ragnar Ostberg's Stockholm Town Hall (1909–23), the Swedish architect was brought over to Dublin in 1926 after collecting the RIBA Gold Medal in London: S. Rothery, op. cit., pp. 98, 140–41.
45. A different view, which minimises the British connection, is given in: S. Rothery, op. cit., pp. 196–229: for a detailed critique of this book, see review by M. Fraser in *AA Files*, no. 24, Autumn 1992, pp. 96–98.
46. *Irish Builder*, 15 December 1891, p. 278; 26 November 1910, pp. 726–28; 25 March 1922, p. 186; 29 July 1922, p. 514; 2 June 1923, p. 401; 20 October 1923, p. 794; 19 September 1925, p. 772.
47. *Irish Builder*, 20 October 1906, p. 834: see also: S. Rothery, *Ireland and the New Architecture 1900–1940*, 1991, pp. 23–55.
48. For Kilkenny 'Garden Village' see: *Irish Builder*, 30 November 1907, pp. 818–19; 21 December 1912, p. 718: *Irish Times*, 16 July 1914, p. 9: HTPAI, *Housing and Town Improvement*, 1912, p. 21: J. Sheehy, op. cit., p. 139.
49. *Irish Builder*, 5 June 1920, p. 378; also 20 March 1926, pp. 205–10.
50. *Irish Builder*, 2 November 1907, pp. 746–53; 25 February 1922, p. 114: 19 September 1925, p. 772: for a critique of this received view, and an analysis of British Government involvement in the development of Georgian Dublin, see M. Fraser, 'Public building and colonial policy in Dublin, 1760–1800', *Architectural History*, vol. 28, 1985, pp. 102–22.
51. *Irish Builder*, 19 November 1921, p. 741: also 18 March 1911, p. 173; 25 November 1911, p. 781; 13 April 1912, pp. 220–22; 20 July 1912, pp. 419–20; 25 February 1922, p. 117; 6 May 1922, p. 313; 17 June 1923, p. 423; 9 February 1924, pp. 101–02; 29 November 1924, p. 1021; 23 January 1926, pp. 58–61: *Irish Times*, 9 October 1925, p. 6: see also: S. Rothery, op. cit., pp. 74–82, 90–103.
52. *Irish Builder*, 28 November 1908, pp. 722–30; 19 September 1925, p. 770 : see also, for instance, *Irish Architect and Building Trades' Journal*, 14 March 1914, pp. 715–16; 21 March 1914, p. 730: *Irish Times*, 28 October 1926, p. 8.
53. The main studies within this traditional approach are: M. Bowley, *Housing and the State 1919–1944*, 1945: J. Burnett, *A Social History of Housing 1815–1970*, 1978: E. Gauldie, *Cruel Habitations: A History of Working Class Housing 1780–1918*, 1974: J. N. Tarn, *Working-Class Housing in Nineteenth-Century Britain*, 1971: J. N. Tarn, *Five Per Cent Philanthropy: An Account of Housing in Urban Areas between 1840 and 1914*, 1973: A. S. Wohl, *The Eternal Slum: Housing and Social Policy in Victorian London*, 1977.
54. D. Fraser, op. cit., pp. xxi–xxxi.
55. J. Dyos, *Victorian Suburb: A Study of the Growth of Camberwell*, 1961: G. Stedman Jones, *Outcast London: A Study in the Relationship between Classes in Victorian Society*, 1971.
56. M. Daunton, *House and Home in the Victorian City*, 1983, p. 3.
57. S. Merrett, *State Housing in Britain*, 1979, p. 21.
58. C. J. Pooley, 'Housing for the poorest poor: slum-clearance and rehousing in Liverpool, 1890–1918', *Journal of Historical Geography*, vol. 11, no. 1, 1985, pp. 71, 84–85.
59. M. J. Daunton, op. cit., pp. 203–16: D. Englander, *Landlord and Tenant in Urban Britain 1838–1918*, 1983, p. 53: A. Offer, *Property and Politics 1870–1914: Landowner-ship, Law, Ideology, and Urban Development in England*, 1981, pp. 282–93.
60. See, for example: S. Webb, 'Social movements', in A. W. Ward, G. W. Prothero and

S. Leathes (eds), *The Cambridge Modern History: Vol. XII. The Latest Age*, 1910, pp. 730–65.
61. A. Offer, op. cit.: F. Engels, 'The housing question', in K. Marx and F. Engels, *Collected Works: Volume 23 (1871–74)*, 1988, pp. 317–19, 338, 355.
62. However, claims that the Liberal Government in Britain had come round to an acceptance of subsidy by 1914 are based on some scanty and doubtful evidence in P. Wilding, 'Towards Exchequer subsidies for housing 1906–14', *Social and Economic Administration*, vol. 6, no. 1, January 1972, pp. 15–18: for the counter view, see: M. Swenarton, *Homes Fit for Heroes: The Politics and Architecture of Early State Housing in Britain*, 1981, pp. 44–46: also Chapters 3 and 5 below.
63. M. Castells, *The Urban Question: A Marxist Approach*, 1972/76: S. Merrett, op. cit., pp. 19, 29–30: for a critique of this position, see M. J. Daunton, *A Property Owning Democracy: Housing in Britain*, 1987, pp. 110–13: M. Swenarton, op. cit., p. 194–95.
64. D. Fraser, op. cit., pp. xxi–xxxi.
65. D. Englander, op. cit.
66. D. Fraser, op. cit., pp. xxi–xxxi.
67. M. Swenarton, op. cit.
68. D. Fraser, op. cit., pp. xxi–xxxi.
69. M. J. Daunton, op. cit. (1983), pp. 297–98: M. J. Daunton (ed.), *Councillors and Tenants: Local Authority Housing in English Cities, 1919–1939*, 1984, pp. 10–11: M. J. Daunton, op. cit. (1987), pp. 91–92, 237–38: M. J. Daunton, 'Housing', in F. M. L. Thompson (ed.), *The Cambridge Social History of Britain 1750–1950: Vol. 2. People and their Environment*, 1990a, pp. 234–42: M. J. Daunton (ed.), *Housing the Workers, 1850–1914: A Comparative Perspective*, 1990b.
70. M. J. Daunton, op. cit. (1983), p. 194.
71. M. J. Daunton (ed.), op. cit. (1990b).
72. M. J. Daunton (ed.), op. cit. (1984), pp. 8–14: M. J. Daunton, op. cit. (1987), p. 250.
73. F. H. A. Aalen, *Man and the Landscape in Ireland*, 1978: F. H. A. Aalen, 'Approaches to the working-class housing problem in late Victorian Dublin: the Dublin Artisans Dwellings Company and the Guinness (later Iveagh) Trust', in R. J. Bender (ed.), *New Research on the Social Geography of Ireland*, 1984, pp. 161–90: F. H. A. Aalen, 'The working-class housing movement in Dublin, 1850–1920', in M. J. Bannon (ed.), *The Emergence of Irish Planning 1880–1920*, 1985, pp. 131–88: F. H. A. Aalen, 'The rehousing of rural labourers in Ireland under the Labourers (Ireland) Acts, 1883–1919', *Journal of Historical Geography*, vol. 12, no. 3, 1986, pp. 287–306: F. H. A. Aalen, 'Public housing in Ireland, 1880–1921', *Planning Perspectives*, vol. 2, 1987, pp. 175–93: F. H. A. Aalen, 'Homes for Irish heroes: housing under the Irish Land (Provision for Soldiers and Sailors) Act 1919, and the Irish Sailors' and Soldiers' Land Trust', *Town Planning Review*, vol. 59, no. 3, 1988, pp. 305–23: F. H. A. Aalen, *The Iveagh Trust*, 1990: F. H. A. Aalen, 'Health and housing in Dublin c. 1850 to 1921', in F. H. A. Aalen and K. Whelan (eds), *Dublin City and County: From Prehistory to Present*, 1990: F. H. A. Aalen, 'Ireland', in C. G. Pooley (ed.), *Housing Strategies in Europe 1880–1930*, 1992: F. H. A. Aalen, 'Constructive Unionism and the shaping of rural Ireland, c. 1880–1921', *Rural History*, vol. 4, no. 2, pp. 137–64.
74. Vernacular studies include: A. Gailey, *Rural Houses of the North of Ireland*, 1984, pp. 4, 203–05: P. Shaffrey, *Irish Countryside Buildings*, 1985, pp. 60–62: urban studies of Belfast include: C. E. B. Brett, *Housing a Divided Community*, 1986: W. D.

Birrell, P. A. R. Hillyard, A. Murie and B. J. D. Roche, *Housing in Northern Ireland*, 1971, pp. 49–80.
75. For Northern Ireland, see: P. J. Buckland, *The Factory of Grievances: Devolved Government in Northern Ireland 1921–39*, 1979: R. J. Lawrence, *The Government of Northern Ireland: Public Finances and Public Services 1921–1964*, 1965, pp. 147–52: for the Republic of Ireland, see: P. Meighen, *Housing in Ireland*, 1965: D. Roche/Institute of Public Administration, *Local Government in Ireland*, 1980, pp. 220–43.
76. J. V. O'Brien, *Dear Dirty Dublin: A City in Distress, 1899–1916*, 1982: M. Daly, 'Late nineteenth- and early twentieth-century Dublin', in D. Harkness and M. O'Dowd (eds), *The Town in Ireland*, 1981, pp. 221–52: M. Daly, *Dublin, The Deposed Capital. A Social and Economic History, 1860–1914*, 1984: see also some minor theses by history students at UCD, mostly on issues raised by Daly.
77. M. J. Bannon (ed.), *The Emergence of Irish Planning 1880–1920*, 1985: M. J. Bannon (ed.), *Planning: The Irish Experience 1920–1988*, 1989.
78. P. Harbison, H. Potterton and J. Sheehy, *Irish Art and Architecture: From Prehistory to the Present*, 1978, pp. 187–264: J. Sheehy, op. cit.: S. Rothery, op. cit.
79. As well as the book by Swenarton cited above, see also: M. Swenarton, *Architects and Artisans: The Ruskinian Tradition in Architectural Thought*, 1989: A. Forty, *Objects of Desire: Design and Society 1750–1980*, 1986: B. Finnimore, *Houses from the Factory: System Building and the Welfare State*, 1989.

1. RURAL HOUSING AND THE STATE IN IRELAND BEFORE THE FIRST WORLD WAR (21–60)

1. L. M. Cullen, *An Economic History of Ireland Since 1660*, 1972, pp. 118, 134–35: B. Chubb, *The Government and Politics of Ireland*, 1970/82, appendix A, Table A. 1, p. 341.
2. Account here based on: R. F. Foster, *Modern Ireland, 1600–1972*, 1988, pp. 318–25, 331–37, 378–79: F. S. L. Lyons, *Ireland Since the Famine*, 1971, pp. 15–16, 26, 34–54: L. M. Cullen, op. cit., pp. 109–18, 134–40, 160–62: J. Lee, *The Modernisation of Irish Society 1848–1918*, 1973, pp. 1–11: K. T. Hoppen, *Elections, Politics, and Society in Ireland 1832–1885*, 1984, pp. 94–106: L. Kennedy, 'The rural economy, 1820–1914', in L. Kennedy and P. Ollerenshaw, *An Economic History of Ulster, 1820–1940*, 1985, pp. 1–61.
3. D. L. Armstrong, *An Economic History of Agriculture in Northern Ireland, 1850–1900*, 1989, pp. 93–101: L. Kennedy, op. cit., pp. 1–61.
4. B. L. Solow, *The Land Question and the Irish Economy, 1870–1903*, 1971, pp. 90–120: S. Clark, *The Social Origins of the Irish Land War*, 1979, pp. 111–20: R. F. Foster, op. cit., p. 375.
5. *Irish Builder*, 1 November 1871, pp. 280–81: also 15 November 1871, pp. 297–99; 1 March 1872, pp. 72–73; 15 December 1874, p. 343; 15 November 1875, p. 318; 15 July 1876, p. 204; 15 July 1977, p. 211; 1 June 1883, p. 178; 1 September 1883, p. 270; 1 December 1885, pp. 316, 320–24: D. B. King, *The Irish Question*, 1882, p. 270: J. S. Donnelly Jr, *The Land and the People of Nineteenth Century Cork*, 1975, pp. 66–68: F. H. A. Aalen, 'The rehousing of rural labourers in Ireland under the Labourers (Ireland) Acts, 1883–1919', *Journal of Historical Geography*, vol. 12, no. 3, 1986, p. 290.

6. P. Bew, *Land and the National Question in Ireland 1858–82*, 1978, p. 2.
7. A. R. G. Griffiths, *The Irish Board of Works, 1831–1878*, 1987, pp. 148–54.
8. R. E. Matheson, 'The housing of the people of Ireland during the period 1841–1901', *JSSISI*, 56th Session, vol. 11, no. 4, November 1903, pp. 196–212: see also K. Danaher, *Ireland's Vernacular Architecture*, 1975/78, p. 30: the squalor of the pre-Famine dwellings later became the emotive stuff of historical novels, such as L. O'Flaherty, *Famine*, 1937, pp. 9–10, 16–17, 121–22.
9. J. S. Donnelly Jr, op. cit., pp. 23–25.
10. Cited in PP 1906 Cd.3202 li, 'Report of the Vice-Regal Commission on poor law reform in Ireland: Volume 1', ff. 361, 364.
11. F. Engels, *The Condition of the Working Class in England*, 1845/1958, pp. 306–07.
12. J. S. Donnelly Jr, op. cit., pp. 165–69: A. Gailey, 'Changes in Irish rural housing, 1600–1900', in P. O'Flanagan, P. Ferguson and K. Whelan (eds), *Rural Ireland 1600–1900: Modernisation and Change*, 1987, pp. 100–03.
13. Board of Public Works, Ireland, *Land Improvement: Instructions with the Rules and Conditions under which Loans are Made; and Addenda, Containing Specimen Plans, Specifications, etc*... 1869.
14. For an account of vernacular rural housing in Ireland, see F. H. A. Aalen, 'Evolution of the Traditional House in Western Ireland', *RSAI Journal*, 1966: K. Danaher, op. cit., pp. 5–14: A. Gailey, *Rural Houses of the North of Ireland*, 1984: A. Gailey, op. cit. (1987), pp. 86–103: P. and M. Shaffrey, *Irish Countryside Buildings*, 1985, pp. 54–60: in general, the typical medieval cottage in Ireland had been single-storey, usually detached, and built in timber frame and thatch. In plan, it was almost always only one room deep, no matter how many rooms were added along the length, and access was of the 'direct-entry' type so that livestock could be brought into the main living room. From the seventeenth century, two main innovations occurred, which Gailey has convincingly argued were English features brought over during the Ulster Plantation. These were the introduction of the 'hearth-lobby' plan, whereby an internal lobby prevented cattle from entering, and the use of stone or brick chimneys to remove smoke and thus enable the addition of a second storey. The former soon became an accepted variation within the rural Irish vernacular, but the reaction to the latter was mixed. Chimneys did indeed become more common, with the usual location of the hearth remaining in the centre of the dwelling (only in North-West Ulster, and the western seaboard, where they were generally placed on the gable-end wall). But historical custom militated against a departure from the single-storey dwelling. In terms of vernacular building materials, the spate of new cottages built in late-eighteenth-century Ireland to meet the rural population growth coincided with one significant development: namely the more frequent use of mass random-stone walling, usually mud-rendered and whitewashed, to replace timber construction. Otherwise, the rate of technology change was exceedingly slow. Roofs continued to be built of basic cruck frames with sod grass or thatched coverings. The introduction of brick walls and slate roofs in rural areas did not really begin until the mid-nineteenth century, and even after then, both materials remained relatively rare outside Ulster.
15. Examples of Neo-Gothic and Neo-Vernacular model estate cottages in England can be found in: S. Martin Gaskell, *Model Housing: from the Great Exhibition to the*

Festival of Britain, 1987, pp. 24–29, 39–46: this mode was typical of the architectural output of the Irish Board of Works, as can be seen in: C. O'Connor and J. O'Regan (Architectural Association of Ireland), *Public Works: The Architecture of the Office of Public Works 1831–1987*, 1987, pp. 10–26.
16. P. Harbison, H. Potterton and J. Sheehy, *Irish Art and Architecture: From Prehistory to the Present*, 1978, p. 208: P. and M. Shaffrey, op. cit., p. 60: this strain of romanticised and anachronistic medievalism was later to reach its apogee in the design by the dilettante English architect, Clough Williams-Ellis, for a square of picturesque two-storey cottages at Cushenden, Co. Antrim (1912/1925): see S. Rothery, *Ireland and the New Architecture 1900–1940*, 1991, pp. 40, 43.
17. *Irish Builder*, 15 September 1875, p. 253.
18. PRO/RECO.1/485 (report by Gollancz on the Labourers [Ireland] Acts 1883–1914, undated but probably 1916): *Irish Builder*, 15 August 1877, p. 243: see also J. Lee, op. cit., pp. 36–39: D. Roche, *Local Government in Ireland*, 1982, p. 221: D. L. Armstrong, op. cit., pp. 212–15, 251: by 1885 only around £310 000 had been advanced (an average of around £12 000 a year), and after yet another 25 years this had edged slowly up to just over £400 000 (average of £8000 a year): PP 1886 Cd.4774 xix, '54th Annual Report of the Commissioners of Public Works in Ireland for year ended 31 March 1886', ff. 703–76; PP 1911 Cd.5845 xl, '79th Annual Report of the Commissioners of Public Works in Ireland for year ended 31 March 1911', ff. 131–223.
19. B. L. Solow, op. cit., p. 87: R. F. Foster, op. cit., pp. 395–97: J. Lee, op. cit., pp. 60–61.
20. L. M. Cullen, op. cit., pp. 148–50: B. L. Solow, op. cit. (1971), p. 123: F. S. L. Lyons, op. cit., pp. 164–65.
21. B. L. Solow, op. cit. (1971), pp. 130–45: S. Clark, op. cit., pp. 225–314: R. F. Foster, op. cit., pp. 400–15: F. S. L. Lyons, op. cit., pp. 160–77: J. Lee, op. cit., pp. 65–105.
22. B. L. Solow, op. cit., pp. 169–85: R. F. Foster, op. cit., pp. 413–14.
23. 283 HC DEB, 17 August 1883, col. 1486 (Salisbury).
24. Nearly 20 years later, only some £14 000 had been advanced for rural housing under the Irish Land Act clauses: PP 1898 Cd.9029 xx, '66th Annual Report of the Commissioners of Public Works in Ireland for the year ending 31 March 1898', ff. 505–89: G. Slater, 'Rural housing—A lesson from Ireland', *Contemporary Review*, vol. 82, September 1902, p. 405.
25. D. Fitzpatrick, 'The disappearance of the Irish agricultural labourer, 1841–1912', *Irish Economic and Social History*, vol. vii, 1980, pp. 66–92: S. Clark, op. cit., pp. 113–17, 248–49: J. W. Boyle, 'A marginal figure: The Irish rural labourer', in S. Clark and J. S. Donnelly (eds), *Irish Peasants: Violence and Political Unrest, 1780–1914*, 1983, p. 334: L. Kennedy, op. cit., pp. 44–48: by 1930 there were only 160 000 labourers.
26. S. Clark, op. cit., pp. 113–14: a contrary view is given in D. Fitzpatrick, op. cit., pp. 76–80.
27. J. Lee, op. cit., pp. 92–93: P. Bew, op. cit., pp. 142–43, 174–75, 185–90.
28. Quoted in D. B. King, op. cit., p. 275: see also F. S. L. Lyons, *Charles Stewart Parnell*, 1977, pp. 263, 280: it was the case that Parnell, a middle-ranking Protestant landowner in Co. Wexford, had engaged on benevolent improvements on his

estate, including some cottages for agricultural labourers: R. F. Foster, *Charles Stewart Parnell: The Man and his Family*, 1976, pp. 168, 370.
29. J. S. Donnelly Jr, op. cit., pp. 238–40: J. W. Boyle, op. cit., p. 327: R. F. Foster, op. cit. (1988), p. 411.
30. P. Bew, op. cit., p. 185.
31. D. Roche, op. cit., p. 221.
32. *Irish Builder*, 15 December 1871, p. 328; 1 July 1872, p. 179; 15 April 1874, p. 107; 15 May 1874, p. 135; 1 September 1874, p. 235; 1 August 1875, p. 203; 15 November 1878, pp. 323–24; 1 October 1883, pp. 301–02; 1 June 1884, pp. 155–56; 1 November 1900, p. 523.
33. D. B. King, op. cit., p. 20.
34. 278 HC DEB, 13 April 1883, col. 169 (Dunraven): also cols 180 (Carlingford), 182 (Fortesque): 279 HC DEB, 30 May 1883, cols 1240 (O'Connor), 1243 (King-Harman).
35. J. Burnett, *A Social History of Housing 1815–1870*, 1978, pp. 119–35: E. Gauldie, *Cruel Habitations: A History of Working Class Housing 1780–1918*, 1974, pp. 21–69.
36. PRO/RECO.1/485 (report by Gollancz on the Labourers [Ireland] Acts).
37. D. D. Sheehan, *Ireland since Parnell*, 1921, p. 177.
38. For an overview of the Irish Labourers Acts, see F. H. A. Aalen, op. cit. (1986), pp. 287–306: F. H. A. Aalen, 'Public housing in Ireland, 1880–1921', *Planning Perspectives*, vol. 2, 1987, pp. 176–79.
39. 279 HC DEB, 30 May 1883, cols 1240 (O'Connor), 1248 (Parnell): PP 1884–5 Cd.4547 xxxi, '3rd Report of Her Majesty's Commissioners for inquiring into the Housing of the Working Classes', ff. 190–91: PP 1906 Cd.376 ix, 'Report and Special Report from the Select Committee on the Housing of the Working Classes Acts Amendment Act', ff. 355, 363.
40. 279 HC DEB, 30 May 1883, col. 1252 (Trevelyan).
41. 283 HC DEB, 17 August 1883, col. 928 (Wemyss).
42. Ibid., col. 929 (Argyll).
43. PP 1884 Cd.317 viii, 'Report from the Select Committee on Agricultural Labourers (Ireland): together with the Proceedings of the Committee, Minutes of Evidence, and Appendix', ff. 245–401: PP 1884–85 Cd.32 vii, 'Report from the Select Committee on Agricultural Labourers (Ireland): together with the Proceedings of the Committee, and Minutes of Evidence', ff. 559–677.
44. L. P. Curtis Jr, *Coercion and Conciliation in Ireland 1880–1892*, 1963, p. 46.
45. Previously, public loans for Irish rural housing had been given at 4 per cent interest (5.35 per cent including principal) over a 35-year period: from 1885 there was a choice of loans at 3.25 per cent (4.5 per cent including principal) over 35 years, 3.5 per cent for a 40-year loan, and 3.75 per cent for 50 years.
46. P. Bew, op. cit., pp. 188–90: K. T. Hoppen, op. cit., p. 478.
47. PP 1886 Cd.4774 xix, '54th Annual Report of the Commissioners of Public Works in Ireland for the year ended 31 March 1886', ff. 703–76; PP 1886 Cd.4728 xxxii, '14th Annual Report of the ILGB for the year ended 31 March 1886', ff. 15–23: PP 1889 Cd.5769 xxxvi, '17th Annual Report of the ILGB for the year ended 31 March 1889', ff. 132–39: G. Slater, op. cit., p. 406.
48. PP 1894 Cd.7450 xxvii, '62nd Annual Report of the Commissioners of Public Works in Ireland for the year ended 31 March 1894', ff. 373–452.

49. J. W. Boyle, op. cit., p. 333: for an anecdotal example that supports this view, see Sir H. Robinson, *Further Memories of Irish Life*, 1924, pp. 205–10.
50. PP 1884 Cd.317 viii, 'Report from the Select Committee on Agricultural Labourers (Ireland)', ff. 260–61: G. Slater, op. cit., p. 406: H. A. Law, 'Irish Housing in Town and Country', Section 3, *Manchester Guardian Commercial*, 26 July 1923, p. 39.
51. D. L. Armstrong, op. cit., p. 254: A. Gailey, op. cit. (1984), p. 203.
52. A. L. H. Gailey, *Ireland and the Death of Kindness: The Experience of Constructive Unionism 1890–1905*, 1987, pp. 1–7, 310–11: E. O'Halpin, *The Decline of the Union: British Government in Ireland 1892–1920*, 1987, pp. 2, 11–51, 215: see also F. H. A. Aalen, 'Constructive Unionism and the shaping of rural Ireland, c. 1880–1921', *Rural History*, vol. 4, no. 2, 1993, pp. 137–64: F. S. L. Lyons, op. cit. (1971), pp. 203–23.
53. F. H. A. Aalen, op. cit. (1993): L. P. Curtis Jr, op. cit., pp. 355–62: W. L. Micks, *History of the Congested Districts Board*, 1925.
54. J. Lee, op. cit., pp. 123–25.
55. F. H. A. Aalen, op. cit. (1987), pp. 179–83.
56. 113 HC DEB, 6 March 1919, col. 591–92 (Macpherson): F. H. A. Aalen, op. cit., pp. 181–82: by 1919 the total investment of the Congested Districts Board in housing was near to £750 000, including grants for minor repairs to another 3000 houses: in addition, small sums had also been given to cottiers, usually for outbuildings for livestock.
57. PP 1906 Cd.3202 li, 'Report of the Vice-Regal Commission on Poor Law Reform in Ireland: Volume 1', ff. 430–31, 437.
58. F. H. A. Aalen, op. cit. (1987), pp. 182–83: Congested Districts Board of Ireland, *Plans for Houses*, 1914.
59. L. Weaver, *The 'Country Life' Book of Cottages*, 1913, p. 6.
60. *Irish Builder*, 22 April 1916, p. 177: also 4 January 1913, p. 19.
61. J. Lee, op. cit., p. 103: P. Bew, *Conflict and Conciliation in Ireland 1890–1910*, 1987, pp. 97–102.
62. B. L. Solow, op. cit., pp. 186–94: S. Clark, op. cit., pp. 347–48.
63. BL ADD MSS, Balfour Papers, Ms. 49804 (note on 'A general sketch of Irish policy', unsigned but probably Wyndham, 28 September 1903).
64. For an analysis of the Irish agricultural slump in the late-1880s, see: L. M. Geary, *The Plan of Campaign 1886–1891*, 1986: P. Bew, op. cit. (1987), p. 77.
65. 343 HC DEB, 1 May 1890, cols 1862–63 (Balfour): also 342 HC DEB, 24 March 1890, cols 1708–14 (Balfour).
66. 344 HC DEB, 14 May 1890, col. 878 (Fox): also col. 880–81 (O'Connor).
67. 352 HC DEB, 20 April 1891, cols 962–86 (Sexton, Healy, Balfour); 24 April 1891, cols 1335–61 (Sexton, Balfour): 354 HC DEB, 12 June 1891, col. 296 (Parnell, Jackson); 19 June 1891, col. 905 (Parnell, Madden); 29 June 1891, cols 1727–28 (Parnell, Balfour): PP 1890–91 Cd.6439 xxxv, '19th Annual Report of the ILGB for the year ended 31 March 1891', ff. 136–45: PP 1895 Cd.7818 liii, '23rd Annual Report of the ILGB for the year ended 31 March 1895', ff. 54–63: PP 1897 Cd.8599 xxxvii, '25th Annual Report of the ILGB for the year ending 31 March 1897', ff. 456–65: PP 1898 Cd.8958 xli, '26th Annual Report for the ILGB for the year ended 31 March 1898', ff. 156–81, 195: PP 1906 Cd.376 ix, 'Report and Special Report

from the Select Committee on the Housing of the Working Classes Acts Amendment Bill', ff. 355–56: G. Slater, op. cit., pp. 406–07.
68. PP 1896 Cd.8239 xxiv, '64th Annual Report of the Commissioners of Public Works in Ireland for the year ended 31 March 1896', ff. 508: PP 1898 Cd.9029 xx, '66th Annual Report of the Commissioners of Public Works in Ireland for the year ended 31 March 1898', ff. 505–89: PP 1905 Cd.2657 xxii, '73rd Annual Report of the Commissioners of Public Works in Ireland for the year ended 31 March 1905', ff. 359–477: legislation in 1891 allowed loans for up to 50 years, and in September 1895 the Treasury reduced the rate of interest on a 30-year loan to 3.25 per cent, on a 40-year loan to 3.375 per cent and a 50-year loan to 3 per cent: 2 years later, interest was reduced further to 2.75 per cent, 3 per cent, and 3.25 per cent respectively: in 1904, however, the rate was raised again to 3.75 per cent for a 30-year loan, and 4.25 per cent for a 50-year loan.
69. PP 1895 Cd.7818 liii, '23rd Annual Report of the ILGB for the year ending 31 March 1895', ff. 44, 141–47: in the few cases where this power was used, such as in Strabane, there was little reward.
70. PP 1902 Cd.1259 xxxvii, '29th Annual Report of the ILGB for the year ended 31 March 1901', f. 45: G. Slater, op. cit., p. 404: J. W. Boyle, op. cit., p. 333: J. Lee, op. cit., p. 128: E. O'Halpin, op. cit., pp. 16–17: B. Chubb, op. cit., pp. 292–93.
71. PP 1905 Cd.2655 xxxiii, '33rd Annual Report of the ILGB for the year ended 31 March 1905', ff. xliii–xliv.
72. G. Slater, op. cit., p. 405.
73. BL ADD MSS, Balfour Papers, Ms. 49804 (note on 'A general sketch of Irish policy', unsigned but probably Wyndham, 28 September 1903): 'Land Conference Report, 3 January 1903', reprinted in W. O'Brien, *An Olive Branch in Ireland and its History*, 1910, p. 478.
74. BL ADD MSS, Balfour Papers, Ms. 49804 (note on 'A general sketch of Irish policy'): the 'National Efficiency' argument was common at the time, and was used by several ILGB officials involved in the Labourers Acts campaign, such as Richard Smith O'Brien and Peter Cowan: *Irish Builder*, 14 July 1906, p. 564; 13 July 1907, p. 496; 30 January 1915, p. 48: for British views, see G. Slater, op. cit., pp. 409–10.
75. BL ADD MSS, Balfour Papers, Ms. 49804 (Wyndham to Balfour, 5 March 1904).
76. 162 HC DEB, 27 July 1906, col. 35 (Denham): NLI MSS, Ms. 15176 (draft letter from Clancy, 1 August 1904: D. Gwynn, *The Life of John Redmond*, 1932, p. 133.
77. M. Davitt, *The Fall of Feudalism in Ireland: or The Story of the Land League Revolution*, 1904, p. xi.
78. *Municipal Journal*, vol. 21, no. 1031, 1 November 1912, p. i (supplement on the visit of the National Housing and Town Planning Council deputation): PRO/RECO.1/485 (report by Gollancz on the Labourers [Ireland] Acts).
79. PP 1884 Cd.317 viii, 'Report from the Select Committee on Agricultural Labourers (Ireland)', ff. 256: J. Lee, op. cit., p. 8.
80. D. L. Armstrong, op. cit., p. 242: D. Fitzpatrick, op. cit., p. 81 and table iv: L. Kennedy, op. cit., p. 47: for English statistics, see W. G. Savage, *Rural Housing*, 1915, p. 156: F. E. Green, *A History of the English Agricultural Labourer, 1870–1920*, 1920, pp. 336–37.
81. PP 1906 Cd.376 ix, 'Report and Special Report from the Select Committee on the

References (Chapter 1) 325

Housing of the Working Classes Acts Amendment Bill', f. 291–96, 349–50, 352–54, 361–62: J. W. Boyle, op. cit., p. 334: L. M. Cullen, op. cit., p. 156: F. S. L. Lyons, op. cit. (1971), pp. 53–54: J. Lee, op. cit., p. 8: D. L. Armstrong, op. cit., pp. 228–55: J. S. Donnelly, op. cit., pp. 242–44: again, a somewhat contrary conclusion in reached in D. Fitzpatrick, op. cit., pp. 80–82.

82. *Irish Builder*, 2 June 1906, p. 446: under the Labourers Acts, rural authorities could levy a housing rate of up to 1s in the £1, and in special cases the ILGB had powers to increase this to 1s 3d.
83. PP 1884 Cd.4051 xxxviii, '12th Annual Report of the ILGB for the year ended 31st March 1884', f. 81: PP 1884–85 Cd.32 vii, 'Report from the Select Committee on Agricultural Labourers (Ireland)', f. 640: M. O'Sullivan, *A Key to the Labourers (Ireland) Acts, 1883 to 1896*, 1902, p. 207.
84. PP 1884 Cd.317 viii, 'Report from the Select Committee on Agricultural Labourers (Ireland)', ff. 253, 262, 268–69.
85. PP 1884 Cd.4051 xxxviii, '12th Annual Report of the ILGB for the year ended 31st March 1884', f. 82.
86. See, for instance: PRO/RECO.1/485 (report by Gollancz on the Labourers [Ireland] Acts).
87. F. H. A. Aalen, op. cit. (1986), pp. 287–306: F. H. A. Aalen, op. cit. (1987), pp. 179–80: A. Gailey, op. cit. (1984), pp. 4–7, 203–05: P. and M. Shaffrey, op. cit., pp. 60–62.
88. W. Thompson, *The Housing Handbook*, 1903, p. 138.
89. F. H. A. Aalen, op. cit. (1987), pp. 179–80: T. C. Griffiths, 'Local Authority rural housing: a case study of the Tallaght Area' (TCD Dept of Geography BA Thesis, 1986).
90. *Irish Builder*, 20 April 1907, p. 273: also 22 November 1913, p. 729.
91. *Irish Builder*, 1 May 1884, p. 136.
92. PP 1884–85 Cd.32 vii, 'Report from the Select Committee on Agricultural Labourers (Ireland)', f. 640: also J. W. Boyle, op. cit., p. 333.
93. *Irish Builder*, 20 June 1901, p. 773: also 1 May 1884, p. 136; 15 May 1895, p. 123; 27 January 1906, pp. 64–66.
94. P. Jalland, *The Liberals and Ireland: The Ulster Question in British Politics to 1914*, 1980, pp. 16, 24–25: R. Wilson, 'Imperialism in crisis: the "Irish dimension" ', in M. Langan and B. Schwarz (eds), *Crises in the British State 1880–1930*, 1985, pp. 153–55.
95. F. S. L. Lyons, *The Irish Parliamentary Party 1890–1910*, 1951, pp. 244, 253–54: F. S. L. Lyons, op. cit. (1971), pp. 265–66.
96. Letter from Dillon to Redmond, 7 February 1906, as quoted in D. Gwynn, *The Life of John Redmond*, 1932, p. 121.
97. *Freemans Journal*, 23 April 1906, p. 8: also 8 January 1906, p. 8; 17 January 1906, p. 9; 31 January 1906, pp. 5–6; 6 March 1906, p. 9.
98. BL ADD MSS, Campbell-Bannerman Mss, Ms. 41211 (letter from Bryce to Campbell-Bannerman, 26 April 1906).
99. BL ADD MSS, Campbell-Bannerman Mss, Ms. 43542 (letter from Bryce to Lord Ripon, 22 July 1906: D. Gwynn, op. cit., p. 133.
100. R. E. Matheson, op. cit., pp. 201, 204.
101. PP 1907 Cd.3682 xxviii, '35th Annual Report of the ILGB for the year ended 31

March 1907', ff. xxxvii–xxxix, 337–84: of the 36 per cent state subsidy, 20 per cent came from Imperial Exchequer grant (*c.* £28 000 a year) and 16 per cent from Irish sources (*c.* £22 000 a year).
102. 158 HC DEB, 28 May 1906, col. 111 (Bryce).
103. 161 HC DEB, 23 July 1906, col. 873 (Asquith).
104. 158 HC DEB, 13 June 1906, cols 998 (Dillon), 974 (Redmond), 1016–19 (Craig): also 18 HC DEB, 7 July 1910, cols 1798–99 (Clancy), 1811–12 (Redmond): *The Times*, 15 June 1906, p. 9, c–d; 28 August 1906, p. 4, c: F. S. L. Lyons, op. cit. (1951), p. 244.
105. 158 HC DEB, 13 June 1906, col. 1021 (Corbett).
106. 51 HC DEB, 7 April 1913, col. 828 (McKinnon Wood): *Glasgow Herald*, 1 November 1912, p. 11, h: *Municipal Journal*, vol. 21, no. 1031, 1 November 1912, p. i.
107. *Freemans Journal*, 10 February 1912, p. 6: *Official Catalogue of the Civic Exhibition, Ireland, 1914*, 1914, p. 85: HTPAI, *Housing and Town Improvement*, 1912, pp. 43–48.
108. *Irish Builder*, 4 January 1913, p. 19.
109. PP 1911 Cd.5847 xxxiii, '39th Annual Report of the ILGB for the year ended 31 March 1911', ff. 54–56: PP 1914 Cd.7561 xxxix, '42nd Annual Report of the ILGB for the year ended 31 March 1914', ff. 646–48.
110. 18 HC DEB, 4 July 1910, cols 1471–72 (Birrell); 7 July 1910, cols 1797–1801 (Clancy), 1811–12 (Redmond), 1812–18 (Clancy).
111. *Limerick Echo*, 7 January 1913, p. 3.
112. See, for example: PRO/RECO.1/485 (report by Gollancz on the Labourers [Ireland] Acts).
113. N. Synnott, *The Housing of the Rural Population in Ireland: A Review of the Labourers' Acts*, 1904: N. Synnott, *Proposals for a New Labourers' Bill*, 1906: *Freemans Journal*, 3 March 1906, p. 8.
114. *Irish Builder*, 27 January 1906, p. 61; 20 August 1910, p. 524.
115. *Freemans Journal*, 23 February 1914, p. 8: J. R. O'Connell, 'The Catholic Church and the problem of the housing of the poor' (article from *Rosary*, October 1911), in *The Problem of the Dublin Slums*, 1913, p. 15.
116. P. Bew, op. cit. (1987), pp. 76–77: J. S. Donnelly Jr, op. cit., p. 242.
117. 29 HC DEB, 11 August 1911, col. 1504 (Sheehan): also 38 HC DEB, 6 May 1912, col. 107 (Devlin).
118. *Irish Builder*, 27 January 1906, p. 61: also 29 August 1914, p. 509: *Freemans Journal*, 6 September 1909, p. 9; 18 September 1909, p. 10; 31 December 1914, p. 6.
119. L. M. Cullen, op. cit., pp. 134–35: R. F. Foster, op. cit. (1988), pp. 353–54: F. S. L. Lyons, op. cit. (1971), pp. 45, 53–54: J. Lee, op. cit., pp. 8–9.
120. *Freemans Journal*, 8 February 1912, p. 8.
121. 55 HC DEB, 21 July 1913, col. 1739 (Redmond); also 18 HC DEB, 7 July 1910, col. 1811 (Redmond); 26 HC DEB, 31 May 1911, col. 1174 (Dillon): *Freemans Journal*, 29 May 1906, p. 4; 16 August 1906, p. 8; 24 September 1906, p. 8; 14 October 1906, p. 5; 30 July 1907, p. 7; 19 October 1908, p. 8; 5 January 1910, p. 6; 30 November 1910, p. 9; 4 June 1912, p. 8; 27 July 1915, p. 8; 4 August 1915, pp. 6–7: J. Clancy, *The Housing Problem: How to Solve It*, 1908, p. 6.
122. 18 HC·DEB, 7 July 1910, cols 1801 (Clancy), 1803 (Joyce).

References (Chapter 1) 327

123. *Freemans Journal*, 23 April 1906, p. 8; 24 April 1906, p. 9: also 29 April 1909, p. 8; 23 October 1911, p. 8.
124. *Freemans Journal*, 26 July 1907, p. 5; 9 December 1907, p. 8; 23 May 1910, p. 9; 28 March 1913, p. 6.
125. 18 HC DEB, 7 July 1910, col. 1814 (Birrell): also *Freemans Journal*, 23 November 1907, p. 8: BODLEIAN MSS, Birrell Mss, Dep. C. 302 (memo by Birrell on 'Irish land purchase', 14 July 1913).
126. *Irish Times*, 28 March 1913, p. 6; 14 January 1914, p. 4: *Glasgow Herald*, 17 October 1912, p. 8, d.
127. W. O'Brien, op. cit., pp. 388–93: D. D. Sheehan, op. cit., pp. 180–86: P. Bew, op. cit. (1987), pp. 221–22.
128. W. O'Brien, op. cit., p. 388: 50 HC DEB, 27 March 1913, cols 1872, 1873 (O'Brien).
129. 158 HC DEB, 13 June 1906, col. 1019 (Craig): PP 1907 Cd.3682 xxviii, '35th Annual Report of the ILGB for the year ended 31st March 1907', f. 342: W. Barrett and H. J. McCann, *The Law of the Labourers and the Labourers Question*, 1906, p. 185.
130. 158 HC DEB, 28 May 1906, col. 108 (Bryce): *Irish Builder*, 2 June 1906, p. 440: *Freemans Journal*, 15 June 1906, p. 6.
131. *Freemans Journal*, 25 July 1906, p. 6.
132. RIAI, *Report of the Council for 1906, and of Annual General Meeting*, 1907, p. 13.
133. 161 HC DEB, 23 July 1906, col. 835 (Bryce), 837 (Corbett); 162 HC DEB, 27 July 1906, col. 37 (Denham): PP 1907 Cd.3682 xxviii, '35th Annual Report of the ILGB for the year ended 31 March 1907', f. 342: Local Government Board for Ireland, *Labourers (Ireland) Acts, 1883 to 1906: General Form of Specification for the Erection of Labourers Cottages*, 1907, p. 3.
134. *Irish Builder*, 29 December 1906, p. 1043: also 28 July 1906, p. 600; 11 August 1906, p. 654; 22 September 1906, pp. 763–64; 4 May 1907, p. 309.
135. Letter from Birrell to RIAI, 27 May 1907, quoted in *Irish Architect and Craftsman*, 1 June 1912, p. 888.
136. *Irish Builder*, 23 March 1907, p. 197; 28 December 1907, p. 890; 26 December 1908, p. 800; 20 March 1909, p. 161; 8 January 1910, p. 17; 20 August 1910, p. 527; 6 January 1912, p. 12.
137. PRO/RECO.1/485 (report by Gollancz on the Labourers [Ireland] Acts): also *Irish Builder*, 1 July 1887, pp. 190–91; 8 September 1906, p. 724; 29 April 1911, pp. 282–83; 3 February 1912, p. 76; 8 June 1912, pp. 341, 344–47; 24 May 1913, p. 333; 5 July 1913, p. 430; 18 July 1914, p. 443.
138. Local Government Board for England and Wales, *The Housing of the Working Classes Acts, 1890–1909: Memorandum with Respect to the Provision and Arrangement of Houses for the Working Classes*, 1913: this document has been wrongly acclaimed as the first official housing design guide in S. Martin Gaskell, op. cit., p. 148.
139. The ILGB sent one of its inspectors, J. F. MacCabe, over to Letchworth, and his unflattering report echoed the general view of the British press that the cottages were conceived more as weekend homes for the middle classes than for agricultural labourers: PP 1906 Cd.3012 xxxvi, '34th Annual Report of the ILGB for the year ended 31 March 1906', ff. 818–20: see also J. McGahey, ' "Bolt-holes for weekenders": the press and the Cheap Cottages Exhibition, Letchworth Garden City 1905', *Planning History*, vol. 12, no. 2, 1990, pp. 17–18.

140. *Irish Builder*, 17 November 1906, p. 943; 1 December 1906, pp. 960–63; 26 January 1907, pp. 44–45, 59, 69–70; 23 March 1907, pp. 214–22.
141. A. Gailey, op. cit. (1984), p. 4: A. Gailey, 'Traditional buildings in the landscape: conservation and preservation', in F. H. A. Aalen (ed.), *The Future of the Irish Rural Landscape*, 1985, p. 30.
142. RIAI, *Report of Council for 1907, and of Annual General Meeting*, 1908, pp. 5–6: *Irish Builder*, 26 January 1907, p. 45; 9 March 1907, p. 157; 23 March 1907, p. 214; 20 April 1907, pp. 273, 286, 301; 4 May 1907, p. 333; 24 August 1907, pp. 589–90: F. J. Biggar, *Labourers' Cottages for Ireland*, 1907, pp. 5, 9: R. Brown, 'The housing of the Irish artizan', in Irish International Exhibition (1907), *Irish Rural Life and Industry, With Suggestions for the Future*, 1907, pp. 295–303: A. Gailey, op. cit. (1984), pp. 203–04: C. E. B. Brett, *Housing a Divided Community*, 1986, p. 23.
143. Local Government Board for Ireland, *Labourers (Ireland) Acts, 1883–1906: Model Plans of Labourers' Cottages*, 1907: PP 1908 Cd.4243 xxxi, '36th Annual Report of the the ILGB for the year ended 31 March 1908', ff. 60–61, 338–41.
144. PP 1906 Cd.3012 xxxvi, '34th Annual Report of the ILGB for the year ended 31 March 1906', f. 820.
145. Irish International Exhibition (1907), op. cit., pp. 281–94: *Irish Builder*, 29 June 1907, p. 453; 13 July 1907, p. 497.
146. *Irish Builder*, 7 January 1911, p. 23: A. Gailey, op. cit. (1984), pp. 204–05, fig. 221: F. H. A. Aalen, op. cit. (1986), p. 298.
147. H. R. Aldridge, *The Case for Town Planning*, 1915, p. 454.
148. *Municipal Journal*, vol. 21, no. 1031, 1 November 1912, p. i.
149. HTPAI, op. cit., p. 48 and photographs.
150. *Irish Builder*, 20 August 1910, p. 527: also 4 January 1913, p. 6; 22 November 1913, p. 7: *Freemans Journal*, 26 May 1911, p. 5: *Irish Times*, 1 May 1913, p. 4; 16 July 1914, p. 9.
151. 9 HC DEB, 26 August 1909, col. 2447 (Devlin): also 26 HC DEB, 31 May 1911, cols 1176–77 (O'Neill).
152. 18 HC DEB, 7 July 1910, col. 1813 (Birrell): also 26 HC DEB, 31 May 1911, col. 1168 (Birrell): 55 HC DEB, 21 July 1913, col. 1724 (Birrell).
153. 26 HC DEB, 31 May 1911, col. 1182 (Redmond).
154. W. O'Brien, op. cit., p. 393.
155. *Irish Builder*, 29 July 1905, p. 522; 27 January 1906, p. 62: also 13 February 1904, p. 84; 30 October 1909, p. 693; 20 August 1910, pp. 527, 532–33; 6 December 1913, p. 775.
156. M. Swenarton, *Homes Fit For Heroes: the Politics and Architecture of Early State Housing in Britain*, 1981, pp. 24–26: C. R. Ashbee, *A Book of Cottages and Little Houses*, 1906, p. 37: A. Crawford, *Charles Robert Ashbee: Architect and Romantic Socialist*, 1985, pp. 268–72.
157. *Irish Builder*, 22 February 1919, p. 33: also 1 November 1900, p. 523; 12 January 1906, p. 5; 21 September 1907, p. 645; 2 May 1908, pp. 286–87; 11 July 1908, p. 443; 12 September 1914, p. 529; 27 February 1915, p. 93.
158. C. O'Connor and J. O'Regan (Architectural Association of Ireland), op. cit., pp. 31–32: for Byrne's housing and planning ideas, see: *Irish Builder*, 10 June 1911, p. 406: *Freemans Journal*, 26 May 1911, p. 5: PRO/RECO.1/485 (paper read

by Byrne to 5th Annual Conference of the AMAI on 26–27 September 1916, p. 101, as quoted in report by Gollancz on the Labourers [Ireland] Acts).
159. *Irish Builder*, 15 January 1916, pp. 26–28: see also T. C. Griffiths, op. cit.: S. Rothery, op. cit., pp. 50, 54.
160. *Irish Builder*, 15 January 1916, p. 28.
161. *Irish Builder*, 27 February 1915, p. 93; 18 December 1915, p. 537: also 20 August 1910, pp. 527, 532–33; 17 September 1910, p. 584; 10 June 1911, p. 393; 22 May 1915, p. 233; 31 May 1919, p. 26; 5 May 1923, p. 317; 19 May 1923, p. 373: *Freemans Journal*, 26 May 1911, p. 5: PRO/RECO.1/485 (report by Gollancz on the Labourers [Ireland] Acts).
162. *Municipal Journal*, vol. 21, no. 1031, 1 November 1912, p. i: *Irish Builder*, 10 June 1911, p. 377; 27 September 1913, p. 609; 16 January 1915, p. 40; 31 July 1915, p. 338: *Irish Architect and Craftsman*, 22 June 1912, p. 919; 5 July 1913, p. 29: the scheme for Gorey Garden Village began as a private initiative in 1908, but was taken up by the local Irish Party MP, Sir Thomas Esmonde, to emulate the improved estate villages that he had seen in Newfoundland—in 1914 approval was obtained to build 72 cottages with one acre attached, but only 12 cottages were started before war intervened. Esmonde was unsuccessful in his efforts in 1915 to link the scheme to housing need for the nearby Arklow munitions factory: PRO/T.1/11683/23569 no. 23569 (Esmonde to Birrell, 2 July 1915; Harmsworth, Treasury to Montagu, 15 July 1915; Esmonde to McKenna, 22 July 1915): *Freemans Journal*, 3 July 1915, p. 4; 30 August 1915, p. 4: *Irish Builder*, 11 September 1915, p. 406.
163. O. MacDonagh, *Ireland: the Union and its Aftermath*, 1967/1977, p. 67: P. Jalland, op. cit., pp. 27–48.
164. NLI MSS, Miscellaneous Papers, Ms. 26, 173 (draft public notification of functions assigned to various Irish Departments, undated but probably late-1914): E. O'Halpin, op. cit., pp. 97–98.
165. P. Jalland, op. cit., pp. 265, 267–68.
166. HLL, Lloyd George Papers, C/2/4/20 (Carter to Lloyd George, 28 May 1914): also C/2/4/27 (Storey to Lloyd George, 29 May 1914): R. Douglas, 'God gave the land to the people', in A. J. A. Morris (ed.), *Edwardian Radicalism*, 1974, p. 159.
167. HLL, Lloyd George Papers, C/36/2/12 (speech by Lloyd George at Huddersfield on 21 March 1914, reported in *Huddersfield Daily Examiner*, 23 March 1914).
168. D. Grigg, *Lloyd George: From Peace to War 1912–1916*, 1985, pp. 38–39, 91–104.
169. 50 HC DEB, 12 March 1913, col. 242 (Birrell); 27 March 1913, cols 1860–67 (Sheehan), 1872–73 (O'Brien): 51 HC DEB, 10 April 1913, cols 1340–41 (Sheehan, Birrell): 52 HC DEB, 24 April 1913, cols 511–12 (Ginnell, Sheehan, Birrell): 29 April 1913, cols 1004–05 (Sheehan, Birrell): 30 April 1913, col. 1180 (Ginnell, Lloyd George): 6 May 1913, cols 1867–68 (Ginnell, Sheehan, Birrell): May 1913, col. 2042 (Ginnell, Lloyd George): 8 May 1913, col. 2206 (Sheehan, Gulland): 53 HC DEB, 29 May 1913, col. 300 (Ginnell, Russell): 54 HC DEB, 16 June 1913, col. 43 (Ginnell, Birrell): 56 HC DEB, 31 July 1913, col. 706–07 (Sheehan, Birrell).
170. PP 1914–16 Cd.8042 xxiv, 'Annual Report of the Irish Land Commissioners for the year ended 31 March 1915', f. 238.
171. PRO/T.143/1 (Headlam to Treasury, 7 December 1911, ff. 188–89; Headlam to

Treasury, 6 December 1912, ff. 427–29): PRO/T.143/2 (Headlam to Treasury, 23 June 1913, f. 144; Headlam to Treasury, 27 November 1913, ff. 307–08).
172. PRO/T.1/11808/17813 (internal Treasury note, unsigned and undated but probably late-1914).
173. In the early-1960s, two-thirds of the rural housing stock dated from before the First World War, though this has now dropped to around 40 per cent: T. J. Baker and L. M. O'Brien, *The Irish Housing System: A Critical Overview*, 1979, p. 2 (Table 1.1): J. M. Blackwell and E. Brangan, *Survey of the Housing Stock—1980: A Summary Report*, 1984, pp. 9, 31 (Table 1).

2. URBAN STATE HOUSING IN IRELAND BEFORE 1914 (61–115)

1. L. M. Cullen, *An Economic History of Ireland since 1660*, 1972, pp. 167–70: J. Lee, *The Modernisation of Irish Society 1848–1918*, 1973, pp. 9–20, 35: F. S. L. Lyons, *Ireland since the Famine*, 1971, pp. 54–70: R. F. Foster, *Modern Ireland 1600–1972*, 1988, pp. 321–22, 342.
2. H. Mayhew, *London Labour and the London Poor*, 1849–52/1985, pp. 56–60, 142–45, 155–59, 260–63, 415–17: J. A. Jackson, *The Irish in Great Britain*, 1963: E. Hobsbawm, *Industry and Empire*, 1968, pp. 309–12: R. Swift and S. Gilley (eds), *The Irish in the Victorian City*, 1985: R. Swift and S. Gilley, *The Irish in Britain 1815–1939*, 1989: J. Burnett, *A Social History of Housing 1815–1970*, 1978/85, pp. 9, 58–59, 66: P. J. Waller, *Democracy and Sectarianism: A Political and Social History of Liverpool 1868–1939*, 1981, pp. 1–12: G. F. A. Best, 'Another part of the island', in H. J. Dyos and M. Wolff, *The Victorian City: Images and Realities, Vol. 2*, 1973, p. 399: R. F. Foster, op. cit., pp. 345, 362–69.
3. B. Chubb, *The Government and Politics of Ireland*, 1970/82, pp. 3, 343 (Table A.4): E. Hobsbawm, op. cit., diag. 13.
4. L. M. Cullen, op. cit., pp. 158–62: F. S. L. Lyons, op. cit., pp. 27, 60–67: P. Ollerenshaw, 'Industry, 1820–1914', in L. Kennedy and P. Ollerenshaw (eds), *An Economic History of Ulster, 1820–1940*, 1985, pp. 62–108.
5. S. Gribbon, 'An Irish city: Belfast 1911', in D. Harkness and M. O'Dowd (eds), *The Town in Ireland*, 1981, pp. 203–20: C. O'Leary, 'Belfast urban government in the age of reform', in D. Harkness and M. O'Dowd, op. cit., pp. 194, 201–02.
6. PRO/T.1/11271/4624 (internal Treasury note by 'O. G. N.' 24 October 1910): the Treasury estimated that on the old valuation, the rates in Belfast would have been around 10s in the £1.
7. PP 1900 Cd.243/244 xxxix, 'Report of Committee appointed by ILGB to inquire into the Public Health of the City of Dublin', f. 867: PP 1908 Cd.4128 xxxi, 'Report of Belfast Health Commission to ILGB', f. 710: *Irish Builder*, 30 March 1918, pp. 171–72.
8. A typical design for a brick Belfast terraced house is described in H. Dixon, *Ulster Architecture 1800–1900*, 1972, p. 15: for a British precedent, see: J. Burnett, op. cit., pp. 154–63: M. Swenarton, *Homes Fit for Heroes: The Politics and Architecture of Early State Housing in Britain*, 1981, pp. 12–14: M. J. Daunton, *House and Home in the Victorian City*, 1983, pp. 11–60: S. Martin Gaskell, *Model Housing: from the Great Exhibition to the Festival of Britain*, 1987, pp. 50–53.
9. *Irish Builder*, 8 November 1913, p. 711: also 28 March 1914, p. 181; 30 March 1918,

pp. 171–72: PP 1884–85 xxxi Cd.4547, '3rd Report of Her Majesty's Commissioners for inquiring into the Housing of the Working Classes (Ireland)', f. 194: PP 1884–85 xxxi Cd.4547–1, 'Minutes of evidence, etc. . . of the 3rd Report of Her Majesty's Commissioners for inquiring into the Housing of the Working Classes (Ireland)', ff. 260–63: PP 1900 Cd.243/244 xxxix, 'Report of Committee appointed by ILGB to inquire into the Public Health of the City of Dublin', f. 867: PP 1908 Cd.4128 xxxi, 'Report of Belfast Health Commission to ILGB', ff. 707, 778, 789: T. W. Grimshaw, *The House Accommodation of the Artisan and Labouring Classes in Ireland, with Special Reference to Dublin and Other Large Towns*, 1885, p. 10: I. Budge and C. O'Leary, *Belfast: Approach to Crisis. A Study of Belfast Politics 1613–1970*, 1973, pp. 108–09: E. Jones, 'Late Victorian Belfast: 1850–1900', in J. C. Beckett and R. E. Glasscock, *Belfast: The Origin and Growth of an Industrial City*, 1967, pp. 111–12: J. Gray, *City in Revolt: James Larkin and the Belfast Dock Strike of 1907*, 1985, p. 11: C. E. B. Brett, *Housing a Divided Community*, 1986, pp. 16–18, 20: F. H. A Aalen, 'Public housing in Ireland, 1880–1921', *Planning Perspectives*, Vol. 2, 1987, p. 189.

10. *Freemans Journal*, 30 January 1909, p. 8: for Unionist views, see: 186 HC DEB, 20 March 1908, col. 949 (Lonsdale): 38 HC DEB, 8 May 1912, col. 460 (Larner): 61 HC DEB, 16 April 1914, col. 359 (Griffith-Boscawen): *Irish Times*, 26 April 1913, p. 6: *Irish Architect and Craftsman*, 5 August 1911, p. 393.

11. PP 1884–85 xxxi Cd.4547, '3rd Report of Her Majesty's Commissioners for inquiring into the Housing of the Working Classes (Ireland)', f. 196: PP 1902 Cd.1260 xxxvii, 'Supplement to 29th Annual Report of ILGB—Reports on the Sanitary Circumstances and Administration of Cities and Towns in Ireland', f. 482: *Freemans Journal*, 11 October 1913, p. 6; 21 October 1913, p. 4: *Irish Builder*, 1 February 1896, p. 25: L. M. Cullen, op. cit., p. 160: F. S. L. Lyons, op. cit., pp. 63–64: C. E. B Brett, op. cit., p. 23.

12. K. T. Hoppen, *Elections, Politics, and Society in Ireland 1832–1885*, 1984, pp. 436–40: L. M. Cullen, op. cit., pp. 140–44, 156, 162: J. Lee, op. cit., pp. 97–99.

13. The account here based on: J. V. O'Brien, *Dear Dirty Dublin: A City in Distress, 1899–1916*, 1982: M. Daly, *Dublin, the Deposed Capital: A Social and Economic History, 1860–1914*, 1984.

14. *Freemans Journal*, 24 September 1913, p. 5.

15. F. S. L. Lyons, op. cit., p. 278: J. V. O'Brien, op. cit., p. 200: M. Daly, op. cit., pp. 5–6, 15–17, 64–67, 124–25, 138–40.

16. E. Larkin, *James Larkin: Irish Labour Leader, 1876–1947*, 1965, pp. 43–45: M. Daly, op. cit., pp. 77–116.

17. F. S. L. Lyons, op. cit., p. 68: M. Daly, op. cit., pp. 67–76, 110–12.

18. F. Engels, *The Condition of the Working Class in England*, 1845/1958, p. 40: J. D. Clarkson, *Labour and Nationalism in Ireland*, 1925, pp. 119–21.

19. *Irish Builder*, 25 October 1913, p. 678: three areas stood out as being the lowest of the low, i.e. the area around the Coombe and Francis Street in the industrial south-west, between St Patrick's Cathedral and the Guinness brewery; from Capel Street to Smithfield on the north bank of the Liffey, to the west of the city centre and behind the magnificent Four Courts building; and to the east of the centre, from Marlborough Street to Amiens (now Connolly) Station, bounded to the north by Mountjoy Square and containing the notorious brothel district around

332   John Bull's Other Homes

Foley Street: see for example: *Freemans Journal*, 12 April 1913, p. 8: RPDCD, 1916 (Vol. 1), no. 35, p. 340.
20. *The Times*, 4 September 1913, p. 6, d; 22 October 1913, p. 9, d: also 18 October 1913, p. 5, e; 1 December 1913, p. 69, c–d: *Freemans Journal*, 24 September 1913, p. 5; 15 October 1913, p. 8; 12 November 1913, p. 5; 9 December 1913, p. 8: *Builder*, 11 May 1878, p. 479; 18 May 1878, p. 479; 24 April 1914, p. 489.
21. 118 HC DEB, 18 February 1903, col. 191 (Field): also 186 HC DEB, 20 March 1908, cols 930 (Clancy), 946–66 (Nannetti).
22. *The Times*, 1 December 1913, p. 64, a: also 186 HC DEB, 20 March 1908, col. 976 (Birrell): for Labour Party views, see 186 HC DEB, 20 March 1908, col. 988 (Duncan): 46 HC DEB, 15 January 1913, col. 2143 (Outhwaite): 58 HC DEB, 18 February 1914, cols 976 (Barnes), 1015–17 (Roberts).
23. 61 HC DEB, 16 April 1914, col. 371 (Cecil): also 76 HC DEB, 9 December 1915, cols 1700–01 (Long).
24. A. Wright, *Disturbed Dublin*, 1914, p. 29: *Freemans Journal*, 23 May 1914, p. 4: also 30 May 1911, p. 6; 13 August 1912, p. 6; 4 January 1913, p. 6; 12 April 1913, p. 8.
25. PP 1884–85 xxxi Cd.4547, '3rd Report of Her Majesty's Commissioners for inquiring into the Housing of the Working Classes (Ireland)', f. 193: PP 1902 xxxvii Cd.1260, 'Supplement to 29th Annual Report of ILGB–Reports on the Sanitary Circumstances and Administration of Cities and Towns in Ireland', ff. 444–45: for developments in Britain, see: J. Burnett, op. cit., p. 93: D. Fraser, *The Evolution of the British Welfare State*, 1973/84, p. 136: E. Gauldie, *Cruel Habitations: A History of Working Class Housing 1780–1918*, 1974, pp. 145–84: A. S. Wohl, *The Eternal Slum: Housing and Social Policy in Victorian London*, 1977, pp. 21–72: D Englander, *Landlord and Tenant in Urban Britain 1838–1918*, 1983, p. xi.
26. *Freemans Journal*, 4 January 1913, p. 6: RPDCD, 1914 (Vol. 2), no. 120, p. 179: also pp. 164, 181.
27. M. Daly, op. cit., pp. 117–239.
28. *Irish Builder*, 20 June 1914, p. 384: also 27 October 1913, p. 678; 28 March 1914, pp. 181–82: RPDCD, 1914 (Vol. 2), no. 120, p. 158: H. T. O'Rourke and The Dublin Civic Survey Committee, *The Dublin Civic Survey Report*, 1925, p. 13: L. M. Cullen, op. cit., p. 166: boundary extension had been recommended in a number of official reports from 1879, but even when achieved in 1900, the House of Lords emasculated the measure so that it included only the less wealthy northern/western suburbs such as Clontarf, Drumcondra, and Kilmainham: this was offset only partly by the 1901 Rate Equalisation Act, under which for the first time Rathmines and Pembroke contributed towards the city resources.
29. PP 1880 xxx Cd.2605, 'Report of the Royal Commissioners appointed to inquire into the Sewerage and Drainage of the City of Dublin, and other matters connected therewith, together with Minutes of Evidence, Appendix, Index, etc.', ff. 20–23, 28–29, 60–68, 90–91, 120–24, 197–99, 205–09: PP 1884–85 xxxi Cd.4547, '3rd Report of Her Majesty's Commissioners for inquiring into the Housing of the Working Classes (Ireland)', ff. 192–93: PP 1914 Cd.7273 xix, 'Report of the Departmental Committee appointed by the ILGB to inquire into the Housing Conditions of the Working Classes in the City of Dublin', ff. 66–70: RPDCD, 1903 (Vol. 3), no. 176, pp. 390–91: (IFS) Department of Local Government and Public Health, *Report of Inquiry into the Housing of the Working Classes of the*

City of Dublin 1939/43, 1944, pp. 15–23: J. V. O'Brien, op. cit., pp. 101–09, 126–58: M. Daly, op. cit., pp. 277–319: F. H. A. Aalen, 'The working-class housing movement in Dublin, 1850–1920', in M. J. Bannon (ed.), *The Emergence of Irish Planning 1880–1920*, 1985, pp. 131–88.
30. RPDCD, 1914 (Vol. 2), no. 120, p. 167: 1920 (Vol. 2), no. 110, p. 424: 61 HC DEB, 16 April 1914, col. 348 (Clancy).
31. *Irish Builder*, 1 July 1872, p. 179; 15 May 1874, p. 135: also 1 November 1880, pp. 297–98.
32. PP 1884–85 Cd.4547–1 xxxi, 'Minutes of evidence, etc. . . of the 3rd Report of Her Majesty's Commissioners for inquiring into the Housing of the Working Classes (Ireland)', f. 304: the same situation was described 30 years later in: PRO/T.1/11782/5824 (Williams, Office of Public Works, Ireland to Treasury, 13 April 1914): also RPDCD, 1914 (Vol. 2), no. 120, pp. 158, 179–80: H. T. O'Rourke et al, op. cit., pp. 60–61.
33. PP 1913 Cd.6955 lxvi, 'Report of an Enquiry by the Board of Trade into Working Class Rents and Retail Prices together with the rates of Wages in Certain Occupations in Industrial Towns of the UK in 1912', f. 752: G. F. A Best, op. cit., pp. 401–04.
34. A. Roche, 'The housing of the working classes', *Tracts on Social and Industrial Questions, 1896–1905*, no. 7, 1905, pp. 3–5: 61 HC DEB, 16 April 1914, cols 344–45 (Clancy).
35. *The Times*, 20 September 1913, p. 3, f.
36. PP 1913 Cd.6955 lxvi, 'Report of an Enquiry by the Board of Trade into Working Class Rents and Retail Prices together with the rates of Wages in Certain Occupations in Industrial Towns of the UK in 1912', f. 752: *Freemans Journal*, 11 October 1913, p. 6.
37. M. Daly, op. cit., p. 111–12: E. Gauldie, op. cit., p. 168: J. Burnett, op. cit., pp. 145–49.
38. *The Times*, 22 October 1913, p. 9, d: see also: *Irish Worker*, 10 June 1911, p. 1; 29 July 1911, p. 1; 27 September 1913, p. 1; 27 December 1913, pp. 1, 2: *Glasgow Herald*, 21 February 1914, p. 8, f; 17 April 1914, p. 8, d: M. Daly, op. cit., pp. 283–89: R. F. Foster, op. cit., p. 437.
39. PP 1880 xxx Cd.2605, 'Report of the Royal Commissioners appointed to inquire into the Sewerage and Drainage of the City of Dublin, and other matters connected therewith, together with Minutes of Evidence, Appendix, Index, etc.', ff. 20–23, 28 - 29: *Irish Builder*, 1 October 1879, p. 311; 15 October 1879, pp. 324–26; 15 July 1880, p. 205; 15 October 1880, p. 291; 15 December 1880, pp. 347–48: PP 1902 Cd.1260 xxxvii, 'Supplement to 29th Annual report of ILGB—Reports on the Sanitary Circumstances and Administration of Cities and Towns in Ireland', ff. 444–52: PP 1914 Cd.7273 xix, 'Report of the Departmental Committee appointed by the ILGB to inquire into the Housing Conditions of the Working Classes in the City of Dublin', f. 69: *Freemans Journal*, 16 February 1907, p. 7.
40. PP 1884–85 xxxi Cd.4547, '3rd Report of Her Majesty's Commissioners for inquiring into the Housing of the Working Classes (Ireland)', ff. 194–96: PP 1884–85 xxxi Cd.4547–1, 'Minutes of evidence, etc. . . of the 3rd Report of Her Majesty's Commissioners for inquiring into the Housing of the Working Classes (Ireland)', ff. 268–90: PP 1902 Cd. 1260 xxxvii, 'Supplement to 29th Annual

Report of ILGB—Reports on the Sanitary Circumstances and Administration of Cities and Towns in Ireland', ff. 460–715: PP 1904 Cd.2012 xxvii, '31st Annual Report of ILGB for year ending 31 March 1903', ff. 156–64: PP 1913 Cd.6955 lxvi, 'Report of an Enquiry by the Board of Trade into Working Class Rents and Retail Prices together with the rates of Wages in Certain Occupations in Industrial Towns of the UK in 1912', ff. 750–54: PP 1914 Cd.7317 xix, 'Appendix to the Report of the Departmental Committee appointed by the ILGB to inquire into the Housing Conditions of the Working Classes in the City of Dublin: Minutes of Evidence, with appendices', ff. 382–93 (Appendix xxxvii): *Freemans Journal*, 18 March 1907, p. 6; 26 March 1907, p. 6; 5 August 1909, p. 9; 23 December 1910, p. 10; 4 June 1914, p. 7: *Irish Worker*, 29 July 1911, p. 1; 18 November 1911, p. 1; 26 September 1914, p. 3: *Cork Weekly Examiner*, 15 November 1913, p. 6: *Irish Builder*, 15 January 1878, p. 18; 14 October 1885, pp. 287–88; 1 February 1893, p. 32; 15 February 1894, p. 44; 15 March 1894, p. 71; 15 September 1898, p. 142; 26 March 1903, p. 1651; 11 December 1909, pp. 780, 782; 25 June 1910, p. 396; 12 November 1910, p. 685; 2 March 1918, pp. 109–10: *Irish Architect and Craftsman*, 8 June 1912, pp. 899–900, 903; 2 November 1912, pp. 1151–52; 28 February 1914, p. 693: A. M. MacSweeney, 'A study of poverty in Cork City', *Studies*, vol. 4, 1915, pp. 93–104: A. J. Rahilly, 'The social problem in Cork', *Studies*, vol. 6, 1917, pp. 177–88: Dr E. D. Mapother, *Lectures on Public Health*, 1867, pp. 298–302, 367–91: T. W. Grimshaw, op. cit., pp. 9–10: HTPAI, *Housing and Town Improvement*, 1912, pp. 14, 49: Cork Town Planning Association, *Cork: A Civic Survey*, 1926, pp. vi, 14–15: M. Gough, 'Socio-economic conditions and the genesis of planning in Cork', in M. J. Bannon (ed.), *The Emergence of Irish Planning 1880– 1920*, 1985, pp. 307–15: F. H. A. Aalen, op. cit. (1987), p. 190: a typical nineteenth-century single-storey terrace of decaying cottages is shown in K. Danaher, *Ireland's Vernacular Architecture*, 1975/78, p. 29.
41. R. E. Matheson, 'The housing of the people of Ireland during the period 1841–1901', *JSSISI*, 56th Session, vol. 11, no. 4, November 1903, pp. 208–10: *Freemans Journal*, 11 October 1913, p. 6: *Limerick Echo*, 6 September 1913, p. 3: the process of economic and housing decay is described in J. Hill, *The Building of Limerick*, 1991, pp. 149–50.
42. PRO/T.1/11271/4624 no. 18711 (Sharrah, Irish Board of Works to Treasury, 15 October 1910); *Irish Builder*, 18 March 1911, p. 173: also 24 October 1914, p. 589; 8 November 1911, p. 711: *Freemans Journal*, 17 September 1906, p. 5; 5 August 1909, p. 9: *Irish Architect and Craftsman*, 4 March 1911, p. 73: *Irish Worker*, 9 March 1912, p. 1: PRO/T.1/11282/6065 no. 4958 (Irish Board of Works to Treasury, 13 March 1911).
43. 61 HC DEB, 16 April 1914, col. 351 (Clancy).
44. For semi-philanthropy in England, see: J. N. Tarn, *Five Per Cent Philanthropy*, 1973: E. Gauldie, op. cit., pp. 73–141, 221–35: A. S. Wohl, op. cit., pp. 11–21, 141–78: S. Martin Gaskell, op. cit., pp. 19–23, 30–34, 46–49: for Scotland, see: G. F. A. Best, op. cit., p. 393.
45. *Builder*, 18 May 1878, p. 506.
46. M. Daly, op. cit., pp. 114–16, 272–76.
47. PP 1880 xxx Cd.2605, 'Report of the Royal Commissioners appointed to inquire into the Sewerage and Drainage of the City of Dublin, and other matters

connected therewith, together with Minutes of Evidence, Appendix, Index, etc.', f. 91.
48. Dr A. G. Malcolm, *The Sanitary State of Belfast, with Suggestions for its Improvement*, 1852: P. Froggatt, 'Industrialisation and health in Belfast', in D. Harkness and M. O'Dowd, *The Town in Ireland*, 1981, pp. 166–67, 171–75: PP 1880 xxx Cd.2605, 'Report of the Royal Commissioners appointed to inquire into the Sewerage and Drainage of the City of Dublin, and other matters connected therewith, together with Minutes of Evidence, Appendix, Index, etc.', f. 191.
49. PP 1884–85 xxxi Cd.4547–1, 'Minutes of evidence, etc. . . of the 3rd Report of Her Majesty's Commissioners for inquiring into the Housing of the Working Classes (Ireland)', ff. 223.
50. C. Brady, *The Practicability of Improving the Dwellings of the Labouring Classes*, 1854: R. D. Urlin, 'On the dwellings of working men in cities, and the efforts that have been made to improve them', *JSSISI*, 18th Session Part 29, January 1865, pp. 158–64.
51. PP 1884–85 xxxi Cd.4547–1, 'Minutes of evidence, etc. . . of the 3rd Report of Her Majesty's Commissioners for inquiring into the Housing of the Working Classes (Ireland)', f. 247.
52. The account here based on: J. V. O'Brien, op. cit., pp. 126–29: M. Daly, op. cit., pp. 55–56, 295–301: F. H. A. Aalen, op. cit. (1985), pp. 141–62.
53. N. Robinson, *The Conditions of the Dwellings of the Poor in Dublin, with a Glance at the Model Lodging Houses*, 1862: N. Robinson, *Homes for the Working Poor*, 1862: Dr E. D. Mapother, 'The sanitary state of Dublin', *JSSISI*, 17th Session Part 27, May 1864, pp. 62–76; 'The Unhealthiness of Irish towns, and the want of sanitary legislation', *JSSISI*, 19th Session Part 31, January 1866, pp. 250–75: Dr E. D. Mapother, op. cit. (1867), pp. 297–326, 367–91, 440–90, 581–600.
54. M. Daly, op. cit., pp. 257–64, 271–72.
55. A. R. G. Griffiths, *The Irish Board of Works, 1831–1878*, 1987, pp. 154–55 (the Treasury, however, stipulated a maximum loan of £60 per dwelling): for the comparative development of British legislation, see E. Gauldie, op. cit., pp. 239–81: A. S. Wohl, op. cit., pp. 73–108.
56. PP 1890–91 Cd.6480 xxv, '59th Annual Report of Commissioners of Public Works in Ireland for year ending 31 March 1891', ff. 587–665: *Builder*, 3 August 1878, p. 799: A. R. G. Griffiths, op. cit., pp. 155–57.
57. *Irish Builder*, 15 February 1871, p. 52.
58. *Irish Builder*, 15 August 1871, p. 207; 1 April 1872, p. 101; 15 August 1872, pp. 224–25; 15 November 1873, p. 307; 15 May 1874, p. 135; 1 February 1876, pp. 40–41; 15 February 1876, p. 51; 1 March 1876, pp. 68–69; 15 January 1877, p. 25; 1 May 1879, p. 137; 15 September 1879, pp. 277–78; 1 January 1881, pp. 10–11; 15 May 1882, pp. 140–141; 1 July 1882, p. 186; 1 January 1887, p. 1; 15 December 1889, p. 301: C. Dawson, *Improved Dwellings for the Working Classes*, 1876: PP 1880 xxx Cd.2605, 'Report of the Royal Commissioners appointed to inquire into the Sewerage and Drainage of the City of Dublin, and other matters connected therewith, together with Minutes of Evidence, Appendix, Index, etc.', ff. 197–99.
59. *Irish Builder*, 1 December 1871, pp. 310–11; 15 December 1870, p. 332: Dublin Sanitary Association, *Report of the Executive Committee of the Dublin Sanitary Association for the year ending 31st December 1885*, 1886, pp. 15–37: PP 1880 xxx

Cd.2605, 'Report of the Royal Commissioners appointed to inquire into the Sewerage and Drainage of the City of Dublin, and other matters connected therewith, together with Minutes of Evidence, Appendix, Index, etc.', ff. 120–22.
60. 223 HC DEB, 18 March 1875, col. 45 (Gibson): *Irish Builder*, 1 April 1875, p. 91; 1 September 1875, p. 243: Dublin Sanitary Association, op. cit., pp. 27–29: G. Stedman Jones, *Outcast London*, 1971, pp. 197–99: this measure was in itself the product of pressure from the Charity Organisation Society in England.
61. 223 HC DEB, 18 March 1875, col. 59 (Cross), cols 60–62 (Mundella, Nolan, O'Gorman, O'Conor Don): *Irish Builder*, 1 April 1875, p. 91.
62. PP 1884–85 xxxi Cd.4547–1, 'Minutes of evidence, etc. . . of the 3rd Report of Her Majesty's Commissioners for inquiring into the Housing of the Working Classes (Ireland)', ff. 240–245: PP 1914 Cd.7273 xix, 'Report of the Departmental Committee appointed by the ILGB to inquire into the Housing Conditions of the Working Classes in the City of Dublin', ff. 81–82: PP 1914 Cd.7317 xix, 'Appendix to the Report of the Departmental Committee appointed by the ILGB to inquire into the Housing Conditions of the Working Classes in the City of Dublin: Minutes of Evidence, with appendices', ff. 292–96, 462–65 (App. xxvii, xxviii, xxix): *Irish Builder*, 15 July 1874, p. 202; 1 May 1876, pp. 117–18; et seq.
63. *Irish Builder*, 15 January 1878, p. 19; 1 June 1886, p. 138.
64. S. Harty, 'Some considerations on the working of the Artisans' Dwellings Acts, as illustrated in the case of the Coombe Area, Dublin', *JSSISI*, 37th Session Part 62, July 1884, pp. 508–22: *Irish Builder*, 15 April 1877, p. 117; 1 November 1877, p. 325: this was also the case for similar semi-philanthropic companies in Britain: A. S. Wohl, op. cit., pp. 141–47: S. Merrett, *State Housing in Britain*, 1979, p. 21.
65. PP 1884–85 xxxi Cd.4547, '3rd Report of Her Majesty's Commissioners for inquiring into the Housing of the Working Classes (Ireland)', ff. 191–92: PP 1914 Cd.7317 xix, 'Appendix to the Report of the Departmental Committee appointed by the ILGB to inquire into the Housing Conditions of the Working Classes in the City of Dublin: Minutes of Evidence, with appendices', Appendix X, ff. 444–50.
66. *Irish Builder*, 1 August 1876, pp. 219–20; 15 August 1876, p. 246; 15 December 1876, pp. 359–63, 367; 1 March 1877, p. 70; 15 April 1877, p. 117; 1 December 1886, p. 315.
67. *Irish Builder*, 1 June 1879, p. 159; 15 September 1880, pp. 254–55; 15 August 1881, p. 247.
68. *Irish Builder*, 15 April 1877, p. 117: also 23 March 1907, p. 202.
69. *Irish Builder*, 15 October 1881, p. 308; 1 October 1884, pp. 285–86; 15 June 1897, p. 124: for Britain, see: S. Merrett, op. cit., p. 23: J. Burnett, op. cit., pp. 64, 83–85, 173–75.
70. The other semi-philanthropic company of note in the capital was the Dublin and Suburban Workmen's Dwelling Company, which built a mere 288 dwellings: otherwise there was only the Cork Improved Dwellings Company (420 dwellings), and the Thomond Artisans Dwelling Company in Limerick.
71. A sum of £200 000 was provided at the same time for housing reform in London: A. S. Wohl, op. cit., pp. 153–64, 171–72: PP 1914 xix Cd.7273, 'Report of the Departmental Committee appointed by the ILGB to inquire into the Housing Conditions of the Working Classes in the City of Dublin', f. 82: *Irish Builder*, 1 June

1894, p. 131; 20 June 1901, p. 767: J. V. O'Brien, op. cit., pp. 128–29: F. H. A. Aalen, op. cit. (1985), pp. 153–59.
72. The others were promoted by the Church of Ireland, and were linked respectively to the two bastions of Unionist higher education in Dublin, Trinity College and Alexandra College: PP 1900 xxxix Cd.243/244, 'Report of Committee appointed by ILGB to inquire into the Public Health in the City of Dublin', ff. 737–38, 899–902: PP 1914 xix Cd.7317, 'Appendix to the Report of the Departmental Committee appointed by the ILGB to inquire into the Housing Conditions of the Working Classes in the City of Dublin: Minutes of Evidence, with appendices', ff. 72–75, 186–89, 190–91: *Irish Builder*, 1 May 1876, p. 118, 15 June 1897, pp. 124–25; 15 December 1898, pp. 181–82; 7 May 1903, p. 1734: W. Lawson, 'Remedies for overcrowding in the City of Dublin', *JSSISI*, Vol. 12, Part 89, January 1909, pp. 237–48: M. Daly, op. cit., pp. 299–301: F. H. A. Aalen, op. cit. (1985), pp. 159–61: for an account of Octavia Hill's work see: O. Hill, *The Homes of the London Poor*, 1875: G. Stedman Jones, op. cit., pp. 193–96: E. Gauldie, op. cit., pp. 213–20: A. S. Wohl, op. cit., 1977, pp. 169–70, 179–99: G. Darley, *Octavia Hill*, 1990.
73. PRO/T.1/10994/5264 (Irish Board of Works to Treasury, 8 March 1909).
74. PP 1914 xix Cd.7273, 'Report of the Departmental Committee appointed by the ILGB to inquire into the Housing Conditions of the Working Classes in the City of Dublin', ff. 17–19: M. Daly, op. cit., p. 318.
75. *The Times*, 22 October 1913, p. 9, e.
76. PP 1884–85 Cd.4475 xx, '53rd Annual Report of Commissioners of Public Works in Ireland for year ended 31 March 1885', ff. 671–79: PP 1883 Cd.3581 xxix, '11th Annual Report of the ILGB for year ending 31 March 1883', ff. 27–28: PP 1887 Cd.5124 xxxvii, '15th Annual Report of ILGB for year ending 31 March 1887', f. 50: in Britain, only 12 municipalities appear to have applied for loans under the Cross Act, and the schemes carried out in London only worsened housing conditions for the poor: E. Gauldie, op. cit., pp. 265–81: G. Stedman Jones, op. cit., pp. 200–07, 213–14: the most detailed study of the failure of this legislation in the capital is given in: J. A. Yelling, *Slums and Slum Clearance in Victorian London*, 1986.
77. *Waterford News and General Advertiser*, 5 July 1878, p. 3; 9 August 1878, p. 3; 4 October 1878, p. 3; 7 February 1879, p. 3; 21 February 1879, p. 3; 6 February 1880, p. 3; 4 June 1880, p. 3: PP 1884–85 xxxi Cd.4547–1, 'Minutes of evidence, etc. . . of the 3rd Report of Her Majesty's Commissioners for inquiring into the Housing of the Working Classes (Ireland)', ff. 279–80, 290: PP 1914 Cd.7317 xix, 'Appendix to the Report of the Departmental Committee appointed by the ILGB to inquire into the Housing Conditions of the Working Classes in the City of Dublin: Minutes of Evidence, with appendices', ff. 492–93 (Appendix xxxvii): this means that an erroneous date of 1889 is given for the first Waterford Corporation dwellings, actually the second scheme in Green Street in: E. Gribbin and P. Braniff, *Urban Housing Waterford: A Case Study of Two Areas*, 1979, pp. 25, 38–39.
78. The Irish economic depression is discussed in: L. M. Cullen, op. cit., pp. 146–48: M. Daly, op. cit., pp. 57–62: the classic study of housing concern in 1880s Britain is still: G. Stedman Jones, op. cit. : see also: D. Fraser, op. cit., pp. 122–23.
79. *Irish Builder*, 1 November 1883, p. 336: also 1 May 1883, p. 131; 1 December 1883, pp. 367–68.
80. Dublin Sanitary Association, op. cit., p. 37: also T. W. Grimshaw, op. cit.

81. PP 1884–85 xxxi Cd.4547, '3rd Report of Her Majesty's Commissioners for inquiring into the Housing of the Working Classes (Ireland)', ff. 187–203: *Irish Builder*, 1 June 1884, pp. 155–56; 1 July 1885, pp. 185–86: for analysis of Royal Commission in England, see: G. Stedman Jones, op. cit., pp. 223–24, 229–30: A. S. Wohl, op. cit., pp. 221–49.
82. NLI MSS, Ms. 22, 978 (Davitt to Smith, 15 March 1886).
83. 310 HC DEB, 28 January 1887, col. 160, index: E. Gauldie, op. cit., p. 291.
84. PP 1880 xxx Cd.2605, 'Report of the Royal Commissioners appointed to inquire into the Sewerage and Drainage of the City of Dublin, and other matters connected therewith, together with Minutes of Evidence, Appendix, Index, etc.', f. 90: *Irish Builder*, 1 August 1881, p. 231; 15 October 1881, p. 275; 15 October 1881, pp. 308–309; 15 November 1881, p. 340; 15 May 1882, pp. 140–42.
85. *Irish Builder*, 1 August 1882, pp. 216–17; 1 June 1883, p. 164; 1 December 1883, p. 369; 15 February 1884, p. 49; 1 September 1884, p. 254.
86. PP 1884–85 xxxi Cd.4547–1, 'Minutes of evidence, etc. . . of the 3rd Report of Her Majesty's Commissioners for inquiring into the Housing of the Working Classes (Ireland)', f. 228 (Beveridge): also ff. 216–17, 221–23: *Irish Builder*, 1 March 1886, p. 73; 1 June 1886, pp. 167–68: M. Daly, op. cit., pp. 301–02: F. H. A. Aalen, op. cit. (1985), pp. 162–66.
87. PP 1914 Cd.7317 xix, 'Appendix to the Report of the Departmental Committee appointed by the ILGB to inquire into the Housing Conditions of the Working Classes in the City of Dublin: Minutes of Evidence, with appendices', ff. 118–35.
88. They were: Dublin Corporation, 230; Cork Corporation, 90; Waterford Corporation, 42; Kilkenny UDC, 37; Sligo UDC, 28; Wexford UDC, 26; New Ross TC, 26; Limerick Corporation, 24; Cavan UDC, 20; Mullingar UDC, 16; Kinsale TC, 13; Enniskillen UDC, 12; Trim TC, 3: for evidence, see: PP 1884–85 xxxi Cd.4547–1, 'Minutes of evidence, etc. . . of the 3rd Report of Her Majesty's Commissioners for inquiring into the Housing of the Working Classes (Ireland)', ff. 279–80, 290: PP 1889 Cd.5769 xxxvi, '17th Annual Report of ILGB for year ending 31 March 1889', f. 140 : PP 1890 Cd.6094 xxxiv, '18th Annual Report of ILGB for year ending 31 March 1890', f. 413: PP 1906 xcvii Cd.337, 'Housing of the Working Classes Acts: A Return showing Particulars as to the action of Local Authorities in Ireland under the Acts, compiled to the 31st day of March, 1906', ff. 843–73: PP 1914 Cd.7317 xix, 'Appendix to the Report of the Departmental Committee appointed by the ILGB to inquire into the Housing Conditions of the Working Classes in the City of Dublin: Minutes of Evidence, with appendices', ff. 492–503 (Appendix xxxvii): SPO/CSO.RP (1914)/13552, ('Loans for Housing Purposes (Ireland)', HMSO, 1914): Irish Government White Paper, *Housing—Progress and Prospects*, 1964, p. 35 (Appendix 1. 1).
89. P. C. Cowan, *Report on Dublin Housing*, 1918, plan 12: M. Gough, op. cit., pp. 309–11.
90. PP 1886 Cd.4728 xxxii, '14th Annual Report of ILGB for year ending 31 March 1886', f. 24: PP 1888 Cd.5465 xxxiii, '56th Annual Report of Commissioners of Public Works in Ireland for year ending 31 March 1888', f. 479.
91. The municipalities were Devonport, Liverpool, Nottingham, Glasgow and Edinburgh, the latter two through the agency of special housing trusts: S. Merrett, op. cit., pp. 20, 26–27: see also: P. J. Waller, op. cit., pp. 87–90, 163–64: B. Edwards,

'The Glasgow Improvement Scheme as a model of urban renewal', *Planning History*, Vol. 12, No. 3, 1990, pp. 7–14: P. J. Smith, 'Planning as environmental improvement: slum clearance in Victorian Edinburgh', in A. Sutcliffe (ed.), *The Rise of Modern Urban Planning, 1800–1914*, 1980, pp. 99–133.

92. 345 HC DEB, 24 June 1890, cols 1850–52 (Chance), 1859 (Kenny).
93. PP 1902 Cd.1260 xxxvii, 'Supplement to 29th Annual Report of ILGB—Reports on the Sanitary Circumstances and Administration of Cities and Towns in Ireland', pp. 433–715: PP 1914 Cd.7317 xix, 'Appendix to the Report of the Departmental Committee appointed by the ILGB to inquire into the Housing Conditions of the Working Classes in the City of Dublin: Minutes of Evidence, with appendices', ff. 492–503 (Appendix xxxvii): SPO/CSO.RP (1913)/21697 (memo by Bourke, ILGB, 8 October 1913): SPO/CSO.RP (1914)/13552, ('Loans for Housing Purposes [Ireland]', HMSO, 1914): Irish Government White Paper, op. cit., p. 35 (Appendix 1. 1): J. J. Clancy, *The Housing Problem: How to Solve It*, 1907/08, p. 4: *Irish Builder*, 13 July 1907, p. 497.
94. Statistics here taken from: PP 1906 xcvii Cd.337, 'Housing of the Working Classes Acts: A return showing particulars as to the action of Local Authorities in Ireland under the Acts, compiled to the 31st day of March, 1906', ff. 843–73: PP 1914 Cd.7317 xix, 'Appendix to the Report of the Departmental Committee appointed by the ILGB to inquire into the Housing Conditions of the Working Classes in the City of Dublin: Minutes of Evidence, with appendices', ff. 118–35, 492–503: SPO/CSO.RP (1914)/13552, ('Loans for Housing Purposes [Ireland]', HMSO, 1914).
95. M. Daly, op. cit., pp. 152–65, 175–202.
96. M. Swenarton, op. cit., p. 30.
97. L. M. Cullen, op. cit., pp. 165–66: M. Daly, op. cit., pp. 55, 62–64, 102–13: *Irish Builder*, 23 March 1907, p. 197; 26 December 1908, p. 800; 8 January 1910, p. 17; 6 January 1912, p. 12: for British slump, see: A. Offer, *Property and Politics 1870–1914: Landownership, Law, Ideology and Urban Development in England*, 1981, pp. 254–312: J. Burnett, op. cit., pp. 139–41, 217.
98. PP 1908 Cd.4128 xxxi, 'Report of Belfast Health Commission to ILGB', f. 710: *Irish Builder*, 30 March 1918, pp. 171–72.
99. PP 1893–94 Cd.7073 xliv, '21st Annual Report of ILGB for year ending 31 March 1893', ff. 49–50: PP 1894 Cd.7454 xli, '22nd Annual Report of ILGB for year ending 31 March 1894', f. 50: PP 1900 Cd.243/244 xxxix, 'Report of Committee appointed to inquire into the Public Health of the City of Dublin', ff. 867–72: PP 1900 Cd.338 xxxv, '28th Annual Report of ILGB for year ending 31 March 1900', f. lxv–lxvi: *Irish Builder*, 1 April 1900, p. 327: W. Thompson, *Housing Up-to-date*, 1907, pp. 96–97.
100. PP 1901 Cd.724 xvii, '69th Annual Report of the Commissioners of Public Works in Ireland for year ending 31 March 1901', f. 547.
101. J. Lee, op. cit., pp. 107–08: K. T. Hoppen, op. cit., pp. 437–40: M. Daly, op. cit., pp. 204–07: M. Murphy, 'The economic and social structure of nineteenth century Cork', in D. Harkness and M. O'Dowd (eds), *The Town in Ireland*, 1981, pp. 126–27, 141–42: B. J. Graham and S. Hood, 'Town tenant protest in late nineteenth- and early twentieth-century Ireland', *Irish Economic and Social History*, vol. 21, 1994, pp. 39–57.
102. J. D. Clarkson, op. cit., pp. 251–53: A. Mitchell, *Labour in Irish Politics 1890–1930*,

1974, pp. 15–24: B. McDonnell, 'The Dublin Labour Movement, 1894–1907' (UCD PhD thesis 1979), pp. xxi-xxix, xliv–lvii, 205–307, 343–46: E. Larkin, op. cit., pp. 48–49: P. Lynch, 'The social revolution that never was', in T. D. Williams (ed.), *The Irish Struggle 1916–1926*, 1966, pp. 41–42: E. O'Halpin, *The Decline of the Union: British Government in Ireland 1892–1920*, 1987, pp. 16–17: F. S. L. Lyons, op. cit., p. 275: M. Daly, op. cit., pp. 216–19.

103. The best accounts of the Irish labour movement are in: J. D. Clarkson, op. cit.: A. Mitchell, op. cit.: F. S. L. Lyons, op. cit., pp. 270–86: A. Boyd, *The Rise of the Irish Trade Unions*, 1972/85.
104. J. Gray, op. cit., pp. 26–43: E. Larkin, op. cit., pp. 26–40, 48–49: R. Foster, op. cit., pp. 439–41.
105. B. McDonnell, op. cit., pp. xxx–xlviii, 76–144: M. Daly, op. cit., p. 70: M. Murphy, op. cit., pp. 151–54.
106. F. S. L. Lyons, *The Fall of Parnell 1890–91*, 1960, pp. 257–60: J. Lee, op. cit., pp. 117–22: B. McDonnell, op. cit., pp. xlix–lvii.
107. 352 HC DEB, 28 April 1891, col. 1621 (Parnell).
108. 352 HC DEB, 28 April 1891, cols 1626, 1633 (Balfour): for Gladstone's use of this argument to dismiss calls for legislation on behalf of Irish urban tenants, see: B. J. Graham and S. Hood, op. cit., p. 47.
109. A second private members' Irish Housing Bill in February 1892 sank without trace: 1. 1 HC DEB, 10 February 1892, col. 162.
110. PP 1900 Cd.243/244 xxxix, 'Report of Committee appointed by ILGB to inquire into the Public Health of the City of Dublin', ff. 681–701, 737–38, 919–24, 950–55: PP 1902 Cd.1260 xxxviii, 'Supplement to 29th Annual Report of ILGB—Reports on the Sanitary Circumstances and Administration of Cities and Towns in Ireland', ff. 448, 452: *Irish Builder*, 15 November 1900, pp. 544–45; 1 December 1900, p. 564.
111. 84 HC DEB, 25 June 1900, col. 978 (Chaplin): 101 HC DEB, 17 January 1902, cols 218–21 (Field), 233–36 (Nannetti).
112. RPDCD, 1903 (Vol. 3), no. 176, pp. 381–96: A. Roche, op. cit., pp. 7–8.
113. *Irish Builder*, 15 October 1884, pp. 302–03; 15 February 1890, p. 51: *Freemans Journal*, 20 December 1907, p. 10; 30 December 1907, p. 2: M. Daly, op. cit., pp. 169, 309: for British advocates, see: A. Sutcliffe, *Towards the Planned City*, 1981, pp. 67–71.
114. *Freemans Journal*, 8 May 1906, p. 11; 29 October 1907, p. 8.
115. *Freemans Journal*, 22 February 1907, p. 9: 20 December 1907, p. 10: 17 February 1908, p. 8; 17 October 1910, p. 8; 20 October 1910, p. 9; 3 November 1910, p. 5: *Irish Builder*, 26 November 1910, p. 732; 18 February 1911, p. 100: for a broader picture of the role of the Town Tenants League, see: B. J. Graham and S. Hood, op. cit., pp. 50–53.
116. 118 HC DEB, 18 February 1903, cols 191–93 (Field).
117. S. Merrett, op. cit., pp. 24–25: M. J. Daunton, *A Property-Owning Democracy?*, 1987, pp. 56–59: D. Englander, op. cit., pp. xii, 102, 162–87: M. Swenarton, op. cit., p. 29: A. S. Wohl, op. cit., pp. 317–30: R. Hebblethwaite, 'The municipal housing programme in Sheffield before 1914', *Architectural History*, Vol. 30, 1987, pp. 145–46.
118. 133 HC DEB, 25 April 1904, col. 1055 (Wyndham): 130 HC DEB, 25 February

1904, col. 955 (Nannetti, Wyndham): 131 HC DEB, 14 March 1904, col. 987 (Redmond, Wyndham): 134 HC DEB, 2 May 1904, cols 120–21 (Nannetti, Wyndham): BL ADD MSS, Balfour Papers, Ms. 49804, ff. 188–90 (note entitled 'A general sketch of Irish policy', unsigned but probably Wyndham, 28 September 1903): *Freemans Journal*, 8 January 1906, p. 8; 29 October 1907, p. 8.
119. *Irish Builder*, 13 July 1907, p. 497.
120. PP 1914 Cd.7317 xix, 'Appendix to the Report of the Departmental Committee appointed by the ILGB to inquire into the Housing Conditions of the Working Classes in the City of Dublin: Minutes of Evidence, with appendices', ff. 118–35: M. Daly, op. cit., pp. 302–08: F. H. A. Aalen, op. cit. (1985), pp. 166–72.
121. *Irish Worker*, 27 December 1913, p. 1: J. V. O'Brien, op. cit., p. 143.
122. PP 1914 Cd.7317 xix, 'Appendix to the Report of the Departmental Committee appointed by the ILGB to inquire into the Housing Conditions of the Working Classes in the City of Dublin: Minutes of Evidence, with appendices', ff. 139–46, 444–50 (Appendix X): *Irish Builder*, 4 December 1902, p. 1504; 3 December 1904, pp. 804–06; 22 September 1906, p. 767.
123. P. C. Cowan, op. cit., pp. 9–12.
124. *Freemans Journal*, 11 October 1913, p. 6: also 5 October 1906, p. 7: *Irish Builder*, 16 July 1903, p. 1880; 10 April 1915, p. 175: RPDCD, 1915 (Vol. 1), no. 78, p. 753: M. Daly, op. cit., pp. 173–74: there was not the same structure of cheap workmen's fares on Dublin's public transport as in British cities, and the tram company was owned by William Martin Murphy, a supporter of the Independent Nationalists and hostile towards Dublin Corporation.
125. M. Gough, op. cit., pp. 311–14.
126. *Freemans Journal*, 5 April 1907, p. 10; 7 February 1908, p. 6; 18 February 1908, p. 2: *Irish Builder*, 15 July 1890, p. 167; 15 June 1900, p. 387; 18 November 1905, p. 830; 6 April 1907, pp. 234–41; 14 December 1907, p. 845; 3 October 1908, p. 608; 20 February 1909, p. 113.
127. For Liverpool Corporation, see: P. J. Waller, op. cit., pp. 88, 163–64: C. J. Pooley, 'Housing for the poorest poor: slum-clearance and rehousing in Liverpool, 1890–1918', *Journal of Historical Geography*, vol. 11, no. 1, 1985, pp. 71, 82–86: J. Burnett, op. cit., pp. 181–82: for other British municipalities, see: M. Swenarton, op. cit., pp. 34–35: S. Beattie, *A Revolution in London Housing*, 1980: I. G. Gibbon and R. W. Bell, *The History of the London County Council, 1889–1939*, 1939, pp. 369–75: A. S. Wohl, op. cit., pp. 250–84: P. J. Smith, op. cit., pp. 112–13: R. Hebblethwaite, op. cit., pp. 143–61.
128. *Freemans Journal*, 8 January 1906, p. 8: also 24 February 1906, p. 5; 12 November 1906, p. 9.
129. *Freemans Journal*, 8 October 1907, p. 5: also 29 January 1906, p. 5; 6 March 1906, pp. 6–7, 9; 13 March 1906, p. 7; 6 April 1906, p. 7; 5 June 1906, p. 3; 31 August 1906, pp. 4–5; 13 October 1906, p. 4; 1 November 1906, p. 10; 26 March 1907, p. 8; 9 April 1907, p. 8; 19 April 1907, p. 10; 20 May 1907, p. 10; 21 May 1907, p. 6; 13 July 1907, p. 10; 3 August 1907, p. 9; 30 October 1907, p. 2; 12 December 1907, p. 4; 20 December 1907, p. 10; 27 January 1908, p. 8.
130. *Freemans Journal*, 24 September 1906, p. 8.
131. *Freemans Journal*, 21 January 1907, p. 8: also 14 October 1906, p. 5; 5 November 1906, p. 8; 22 October 1907, p. 8.

132. *Freemans Journal*, 8 May 1906, p. 11: J. J. Clancy, op. cit., p. 7.
133. The most detailed analysis of the build-up to Burns' 1909 Act is given in A. Sutcliffe, 'Britain's first town planning act: a review of the 1909 achievement', *Town Planning Review*, vol. 59, no. 3, 1988, pp. 289–303: see also: M. Swenarton, op. cit., pp. 31–33: A. Sutcliffe, op. cit. (1981), pp. 72–85: P. Wilding, 'Towards Exchequer subsidies for housing 1906–1914', *Social and Economic Administration*, vol. 6, no. 1, January 1972, pp. 3–8: A. Offer, op. cit., pp. 363–87, 392–98.
134. 186 HC DEB, 20 March 1908, col. 966 (Nannetti).
135. 158 HC DEB, 28 May 1906, col. 1009–10 (Bryce), 1013 (Redmond): 159 HC DEB, 19 June 1906, cols 46–47 (Redmond, Bryce); 26 June 1906, cols 782–83 (Redmond, Cherry): 169 HC DEB, 26 February 1907, col. 1447 (Joyce, Birrell): 177 HC DEB, 1 July 1907, col. 341 (Ginnell, Birrell); 3 July 1907, cols 700–01 (O'Shaugnessy, Birrell); 10 July 1907, cols 1616–17 (O'Shaugnessy, Cherry): 181 HC DEB, 22 August 1907, col. 1100 (McHugh, Birrell).
136. F. S. L. Lyons, *The Irish Parliamentary Party 1890–1910*, 1951, pp. 246–48: P. Rowland, *The Last Liberal Governments: The Promised Land, 1905–1910*, 1969, pp. 139–40.
137. E. Larkin, op. cit.: A. Mitchell, op. cit., pp. 25–46: F. S. L. Lyons, op. cit. (1971), pp. 270–86: J. V. O'Brien, op. cit., pp. 199–240: B. McDonnell, op. cit., pp. 300–06.
138. *Freemans Journal*, 14 April 1908, p. 6; 28 August 1908, p. 10; 1 December 1909, p. 5; 24 February 1910, p. 5: J. V. O'Brien, op. cit., pp. 89–91: F. S. L. Lyons, op. cit. (1971), pp. 247–59.
139. BL ADD MSS, Campbell-Bannerman Papers, Ms. 41240, f. 127 (Birrell to Campbell-Bannerman, 30 October 1907): L. O'Broin, *The Chief Secretary: Augustine Birrell in Ireland*, 1969, pp. 15–18.
140. *Freemans Journal*, 29 October 1907, p. 8.
141. *Freemans Journal*, 7 November 1907, p. 7.
142. *Freemans Journal*, 7 November 1907, p. 5: J. J. Clancy, op. cit., p. 9.
143. *Freemans Journal*, 18 November 1907, p. 8: also 23 November 1907, pp. 6–8; 25 November 1907, pp. 7–9; 28 November 1907, pp. 7–8.
144. *Irish Builder*, 13 January 1906, p. 30: *Freemans Journal*, 5 November 1907, p. 5; 29 November 1907, p. 8; 20 December 1907, p. 10; 30 December 1907, p. 2; 31 December 1907, p. 5; 20 February 1908, p. 5; 2 March 1908, pp. 4, 10; 6 March 1908, p. 4; 13 March 1908, p. 6; 16 March 1908, p. 9: J. V. O'Brien, op. cit., pp. 144–45: M. Daly, op. cit., pp. 309–10.
145. PP 1908 Bills 6/268/389, 'Housing of the Working Classes (Ireland) Bill, 1908, and various amendments': *Freemans Journal*, 3 March 1908, pp. 7–9; 4 March 1908, p. 6.
146. 183 HC DEB, 3 February 1908, col. 541 (Hogan, etc.): 186 HC DEB, 20 March 1908, cols 928–37 (Hogan, Clancy): the Irish Housing Fund was to be achieved by investing £370 000 from the dormant portion of the Irish Suitors Fund and then using the proceeds, and by appropriating £25 000 each year from the Irish Crown and Quit Rents income.
147. 186 HC DEB, 20 March 1908, col. 968 (Redmond): also col. 949–53 (Lonsdale), 956–60 (Barrie), 969–70 (Sloan).

References (Chapter 2) 343

148. 185 HC DEB, 9 March 1908, col. 1086 (Birrell); 11 March 1908, col. 1494 (Sheehan, Burns).
149. PRO/T.1/11668/18955 (Birrell to Montagu, 22 September 1914).
150. S. Merrett, op. cit., pp. 26–27.
151. 186 HC DEB, 20 March 1908, col. 982 (Birrell).
152. SPO/CSO.RP (1913)/21697 (speeches by Clancy and Birrell at AMAI deputation to Chief Secretary Birrell on 17 October 1913).
153. 186 HC DEB, 20 March 1908, col. 933 (Clancy): 192 HC DEB, 10 July 1908, col. 304 (Clancy, Nannetti).
154. 189 HC DEB, 27 May 1908, col. 1040 (Lloyd George).
155. PRO/T.1/11022/10318 (Treasury minute, 14 May 1909, regarding letter from Finlay Heron, Blackrock UDC to Treasury, 23 July 1910): PRO/T.1/11271/4624 (internal Treasury note by 'A. W. H.', 24 October 1910): *Freemans Journal*, 15 April 1913, p. 6.
156. PRO/T.1/11198/6970 (draft note on letter by 'S. A. S.' to Irish Board of Works, 13 April 1910): PRO/T.1/11271/4624 no. 18711 (Sharrah, Irish Board of Works to Treasury, 15 October 1910: internal Treasury notes by 'A. W. H.' and 'O. G. N.', 24 October 1910; Treasury to Irish Board of Works, 29 October 1910).
157. 192 HC DEB, 21 July 1908, col. 1675 (Mayo): also cols 1677–79 (Ashbourne, Lansdowne): 194 HC DEB, 22 October 1908, cols 1295–1301 (Mayo, Pembroke, Lansdowne): 195 HC DEB, 27 October 1908, cols 26–42: 196 HC DEB, 18 November 1908, cols 1192–96; 19 November 1908, cols 1353–59: *Freemans Journal*, 2 September 1908, p. 8; 12 October 1908, p. 6; 24 October 1908, p. 6.
158. *Freemans Journal*, 2 September 1908, p. 8; 5 January 1910, p. 7: also 19 June 1908, p. 6; 6 July 1908, p. 10; 23 October 1908, p. 8; 24 May 1910, p. 8: 192 HC DEB, 10 July 1908, col. 277 (Redmond).
159. *Freemans Journal*, 8 March 1909, p. 8: also 3 June 1908, p. 6; 15 June 1908, p. 6; 11 July 1908, p. 7; 20 August 1908, p. 8; 8 January 1909, p. 8; 29 September 1911, p. 4: *Irish Builder*, 6 February 1909, p. 69: 61 HC DEB, 16 April 1914, cols 352–53 (Clancy).
160. *Freemans Journal*, 11 February 1910, p. 7; 12 April 1911, p. 6: also 21 February 1910, p. 7; 8 February 1912, p. 8; 15 April 1913, p. 6: F. S. L. Lyons, op. cit. (1951), pp. 248, 253–54.
161. *Freemans Journal*, 2 September 1908, p. 8: 29 March 1909, p. 8: see also: letter from Redmond to O'Mara quoted in D. Gwynn, *The Life of John Redmond*, 1932, p. 155.
162. *Freemans Journal*, 15 February 1909, p. 8.
163. *Freemans Journal*, 8 June 1911, p. 6.
164. N. J. Synnott, *The Housing Question in Irish Towns*, 1908: *Freemans Journal*, 5 September 1908, p. 8.
165. SPO/CSO.RP (1913)/21697 (speech by Hadden at AMAI deputation to Chief Secretary Birrell, 17 October 1913).
166. SPO/CSO.RP (1913)/21697 (speech by Clancy at AMAI deputation to Chief Secretary Birrell, 17 October 1913).
167. PP 1906 Cd.3012 xxvi, '34th Annual Report of ILGB for year ending 31 March 1906', f. 818 (report by Nolan on 1905 Liège International Housing Congress, 19

344   *John Bull's Other Homes*

August 1905): M. Kaufman, *The Housing of the Working Classes and of the Poor*, 1907, pp. 111–14: W. Thompson, op. cit., pp. 96–97, 259.

168. *Irish Builder*, 13 July 1907, p. 498; 2 September 1911, p. 584; 3 August 1912, p. 448: *Irish Architect and Craftsman*, 19 August 1911, pp. 414–16: P. C. Cowan, op. cit., pp. 14–15, 31: this paralleled the pre-war preference of the English Local Government Board for a pluralist strategy that did not give too much power to municipalities: C. Bellamy, *Administering Central–Local Relations, 1871–1919: The Local Government Board and its Fiscal and Cultural Context*, 1988, pp. 11–15, 96–97, 245–50.

169. PP 1909 Cd.4941 xlvi, '77th Annual Report of the Commissioners of Public Works in Ireland for year ending 31 March 1909', ff. 231–32: PP 1909 Cd.4810 xxx, '37th Annual Report of ILGB for year ending 31 March 1909', f. 46.

170. PRO/T.1/11009/8105 (Irish Board of Works to Treasury, 13 April 1909): SPO/CSO.RP (1913)/22106/(1910: 24849) (memo on 1908 Housing Act, undated but probably June 1910): 20 HC DEB, 22 November 1910, cols 283–84 (Ginnell, Birrell): PP 1911 Cd.5847 xxxiii, '39th Annual Report of ILGB for year ending 31 March 1911', ff. 56–57: the first Clancy Act schemes were completed in the financial year 1910–11, with municipalities such as Kingstown UDC being the first to receive subsidy payments from the Irish Housing Fund.

171. SPO/CSO.RP (1914)/13552 ('Loans for Housing Purposes [Ireland]', HMSO, 1914).

172. 52 HC DEB, 21 April 1913, cols 50–51: a slightly different spread, but the same total, is given in: Irish Government White Paper, op. cit., p. 35 (Appendix 1. 1).

173. An ILGB housing official stated in mid-1911 that around 6000 working-class dwellings had been built in urban areas by that date, and a memo by the same department in late-1913 puts the number of completions at nearly 7400 units: both these would support a much later official figure of 7600 urban dwellings built by pre-war Irish municipalities: *Irish Architect and Craftsman*, 19 August 1911, pp. 414–16: SPO/CSO.RP (1913)/21697 (memo by Bourke, 8 October 1913): Irish Government White Paper, op. cit., p. 35 (Appendix 1. 1): see also: PP 1914 Cd.7317 xix, 'Appendix to the Report of the Departmental Committee appointed by the ILGB to inquire into the Housing of the Working Classes in the City of Dublin: Minutes of Evidence, with appendices', ff. 478–503 (Appendices xxxvi–xxxvii): an estimate of 8700 dwellings in 1919, i.e. including war-time building, is given in A. McCashin and M. Morrissey, 'Housing policy: north and south', *Administration*, vol. 33, no. 3, 1985, p. 298.

174. British local authority expenditure on housing by 1914 has been put at only £1 000 000 per year, and municipal dwellings formed less than 5 per cent of new houses in Britain between 1890 and 1914: S. Merrett, op. cit., pp. 26–27: E. Hobsbawm, op. cit., p. 166: J. Burnett, op. cit., p. 181: M. J. Daunton, op. cit. (1983), p. 194.

175. *Freemans Journal*, 5 March 1913, p. 8: also SPO/CSO.RP (1913)/21697 (speech by Clancy at AMAI deputation to Chief Secretary Birrell on 17 October 1913).

176. PRO/T.1/11668/18955 (Birrell to Montagu, 22 September 1914).

177. Statistics here taken from: PP 1914 Cd.7317 xix, 'Appendix to the Report of the Departmental Committee appointed by the ILGB to inquire into the Housing of

the Working Classes in the City of Dublin: Minutes of Evidence, with appendices', ff. 478–503 (Appendices xxxvi–xxxvii).
178. *Freemans Journal*, 12 January 1911, p. 10.
179. *Freemans Journal*, 9 January 1911, p. 8; 24 January 1911, p. 5; 20 February 1911, p. 10; 30 March 1911, p. 9; 14 October 1911, p. 6; 26 October 1911, p. 5; 14 November 1911, p. 8; 12 August 1912, p. 4; 24 September 1912, pp. 4, 6; 12 November 1912, p. 9; 29 November 1912, p. 10; 17 December 1912, pp. 4, 6; 10 April 1913, p. 6; 13 September 1913, p. 5; 7 January 1914, p. 6: *Irish Builder*, 4 February 1911, p. 83; 1 April 1911, p. 209; 10 June 1911, p. 377; 28 October 1911, p. 709.
180. PP 1914 Cd.7273 xix, 'Report of the Departmental Committee appointed by the ILGB to inquire into the Housing Conditions of the Working Classes in the City of Dublin', ff. 78–80: PP 1914 Cd.7317 xix, 'Appendix to the Report of the Departmental Committee appointed by the ILGB to inquire into the Housing Conditions of the Working Classes in the City of Dublin: Minutes of Evidence, with appendices', ff. 112–52, 372, 435–51 (Appendices iii–xii): J. V. O'Brien, op. cit., pp. 99, 146–48.
181. *Freemans Journal*, 25 February 1913, p. 8; 4 April 1913, p. 9; 11 November 1913, p. 8; 24 January 1914, p. 7.
182. Department of Local Government and Public Health, op. cit., pp. 205–10.
183. M. Daly, op. cit., p. 318: for Britain, see: S. Merrett, op. cit., p. 26: M. J. Daunton, op. cit. (1983), p. 194.
184. PP 1914 Cd.7273 xix, 'Report of the Departmental Committee appointed by the ILGB to inquire into the Housing Conditions of the Working Classes in the City of Dublin', f. 78: PP 1914 Cd.7317 xix, 'Appendix to the Report of the Departmental Committee appointed by the ILGB to inquire into the Housing Conditions of the Working Classes in the City of Dublin: Minutes of Evidence, with appendices', ff. 122: *The Times*, 9 December 1913, p. 12, e: W. G. Fallon, 'The municipal problem of Dublin', *Studies*, vol. 4, 1915, pp. 615–16: the proportion of the population of Liverpool living in municipal housing in 1914 has recently been put at 1.3 per cent in M. J. Daunton, op. cit. (1983), p. 31: see also P. J. Waller, op. cit., pp. 163–64: C. J. Pooley, op. cit., pp. 70, 85: I. G. Gibbon and R. W. Bell, op. cit., pp. 367, 369–75: A. S. Wohl, op. cit., pp. xii, 282, 362–67 (Appendix 4): municipal rehousing in most English cities appears to have been minimal, as the examples of Sheffield, Leeds and Bristol demonstrate in R. Hebblethwaite, op. cit., pp. 143–61: M. J. Daunton (ed.), *Councillors and Tenants: Local Authority Housing in English Cities, 1919–1939*, 1984, pp. 103–04, 155–58.
185. M. Gough, op. cit., p. 314.
186. *Freemans Journal*, 23 January 1909, p. 2; 17 February 1909, p. 10; 28 July 1909, p. 10; 5 August 1909, p. 9; 7 August 1909, p. 8: 13 September 1909, p. 5; 12 October 1909, p. 4; 10 December 1909, pp. 7–8; 13 July 1910, p. 10; 15 March 1911, p. 9; 5 April 1911, p. 8; 31 May 1911, p. 4; 27 May 1912, pp. 5–6: *Irish Builder*, 6 March 1909, p. 145; 17 April 1909, p. 241; 7 August 1909, p. 501; 18 March 1911, p. 173: *Limerick Echo*, 15 November 1913, p. 4; 20 December 1913, p. 3; 23 December 1913, p. 4: *Limerick Chronicle*, 3 January 1914, p. 6; 4 June 1914, p. 2.
187. W. D. Birrell, P. A. R. Hillyard, A. Murie and D. J. D. Roche, *Housing in Northern*

Ireland, 1971, p. 49: A. McCashin and M. Morrissey, op. cit., p. 292: see also F. H. A. Aalen, op. cit. (1987), pp. 189–90.
188. *Irish Builder*, 30 October 1909, p. 693; 25 December 1909, p. 817; 14 May 1910, p. 317: *Irish Architect and Craftsman*, 16 September 1911, p. 473; 23 December 1911, p. 633; 16 November 1912, p. 1178: C. E. Brett, op. cit., pp. 20–21: F. H. A. Aalen, op. cit. (1987), p. 189: S. Gribbon, op. cit., pp. 206, 214: S. Gribbon, *Edwardian Belfast: A Social Profile*, 1982, p. 40.
189. SPO/CSO.RP (1913)/21697 (speech by Kerr, from memo on AMAI deputation to Chief Secretary Birrell on 17 October 1913): also *Irish Architect and Craftsman*, 9 November 1912, p. 1164.
190. PRO/T.1/11918/6970 (Irish Board of Works to Treasury, 8 April 1910; internal Treasury notes by 'S. A. S.', 13 April 1910; draft reply by 'S. A. S.', Treasury to Irish Board of Works, 13 April 1910; notes by 'C. W. W.', Treasury on proof of 1910/11 Report of Public Works Loan Commission, 25 April 1910; Treasury to Irish Board of Works, 7 May 1910).
191. *Freemans Journal*, 30 January 1911, p. 8; 14 July 1915, p. 6: *Irish Builder*, 20 December 1913; 28 February 1914, p. 118; 11 April 1914, p. 238: I. Budge and C. O'Leary, op. cit., p. 127: C. E. B. Brett, op. cit., p. 21: S. Gribbon, op. cit. (1982), p. 30.
192. P. J. Waller, op. cit., pp. 151, 259.
193. *Freemans Journal*, 20 August 1908, pp. 7–8: also 8 January 1909, p. 7.
194. SPO/CSO.RP (1913)/21697 (speech by Sherlock at AMAI deputation to Chief Secretary Birrell, 17 October 1913).
195. AMAI, *Report of Conference held in City Hall Dublin on 11th and 12th December 1912*, 1913, p. 71: SPO/CSO.RP (1913)/21697 (memo by Bourke, 8 October 1913).
196. The Housing of the Working Classes Acts, 1890 to 1909, *Memorandum with respect to the Provision and Arrangements of Houses for the Working Classes*, HMSO, 1913, p. 3: M. Swenarton, op. cit., pp. 40–41: A. Sutcliffe, op. cit. (1981), pp. 57, 67–72, 81–86.
197. PP 1914 Cd.7317 xix, 'Appendix to the Report of the Departmental Committee appointed by the ILGB to inquire into the Housing Conditions of the Working Classes in the City of Dublin: Minutes of Evidence, with appendices', f. 496 (Appendix xxxvii): P. C. Cowan, op. cit., pp. 41–42.
198. PP 1906 Cd.3102 xxvi, '34th Annual Report of ILGB for year ending 31 March 1906', f. 815: *Irish Builder*, 1 May 1909, pp. 272–74: RPDCD, 1913 (Vol. 2), no. 176, p. 636.
199. *Freemans Journal*, 19 January 1911, p. 9.
200. P. C. Cowan, op. cit., plans 15, 16, 22, 23, 24, 25: for pre-war English municipal housing, see: *The Housing of the Working Classes Acts, 1890 to 1909*, op. cit., plan type A: M. Swenarton, op. cit., pp. 38–39.
201. PP 1914 Cd.7317 xix, 'Appendix to the Report of the Departmental Committee appointed by the ILGB to inquire into the Housing Conditions of the Working Classes in the City of Dublin: Minutes of Evidence, with appendices', ff. 128–35: *Irish Builder*, 18 September 1909, p. 597; 25 December 1909, p. 801; 8 January 1910, p. 5; 25 June 1910, pp. 410–13; 17 September 1910, p. 587; 30 September 1911, p. 662; 17 August 1912, p. 484; 14 September 1912, p. 521; 4 January

1913, p. 23; 21 June 1913, p. 415; 27 September 1913, p. 617; 9 May 1914, pp. 284–87: F. H. A. Aalen, op. cit. (1985), pp. 169–72.
202. *Irish Builder*, 10 July 1909, p. 427: RPDCD, 1913 (Vol. 1), no. 83, pp. 976–78; 1913 (Vol. 3), no. 208, p. 281: *Freemans Journal*, 24 February 1912, p. 10; 7 May 1912, p. 5; 4 January 1913, p. 6; 6 January 1913, p. 4; 11 November 1913, p. 10: P. J. Waller, op. cit., p. 88.
203. M. Daly, op. cit., p. 308.
204. P. C. Cowan, op. cit., plans 17–19: *Irish Builder*, 24 October 1914, p. 589.
205. *Irish Builder*, 15 June 1900, p. 387; 31 December 1903, p. 3055; 14 December 1907, p. 845; 15 May 1909, p. 309; 26 June 1909, p. 389; 10 July 1909, p. 437; 24 July 1909, p. 469; 6 August 1910, p. 504; 14 August 1915, p. 357; 28 August 1915, pp. 377, 386: it should be noted that Irish architects deplored the accompanying practice of fee-tendering to cut design costs.
206. *Freemans Journal*, 22 February 1913, p. 4: *Irish Builder*, 15 February 1913, p. 99; 1 March 1913, pp. 130, 134–36; 12 April 1913, p. 249; 6 December 1913, p. 775; 17 January 1914, p. 47; 28 February 1914, p. 118; 28 March 1914, pp. 181–82, 199; 11 April 1914, p. 236: *Irish Architect and Building Trades Journal*, 9 November 1912, pp. 1163–64; 16 November 1912, p. 1178; 4 January 1913, p. 1261; 22 March 1913, pp. 103–05: P. C. Cowan, op. cit., plans 9–11.
207. *Freemans Journal*, 13 November 1912, p. 6; 2 December 1912, p. 6; 11 February 1913, p. 9: also *Irish Builder*, 28 October 1911, p. 709; 28 September 1912, p. 549; 7 December 1912, pp. 684–86.
208. *Irish Builder*, 3 June 1905, p. 386; 22 September 1906, p. 768–70; 6 April 1907, pp. 234–41; 14 December 1907, p. 861.
209. *Irish Builder*, 7 December 1912, pp. 684–86 and photo.
210. *Irish Builder*, 26 October 1912, p. 619: also 21 November 1914, pp. 637–38; 20 November 1915, p. 498.
211. SPO/CSO.RP (1913)/21697 (Bourke, ILGB to Le Fanu, CSO, 8 October 1913); (1913)/22106 (1912: 23553) (memo on parliamentary question by Clancy, 18 June 1912): 61 HC DEB, 16 April 1914, col. 352 (Clancy): 62 HC DEB, 21 May 1914, col. 2114–15 (Birrell).
212. *Freemans Journal*, 20 August 1908, p. 8: also 19 February 1909, p. 10: *Irish Builder*, 6 February 1909, p. 69.
213. A. Offer, op. cit., pp. 384–85: for Irish opposition to the Budget, see: F. S. L. Lyons, op. cit. (1971), pp. 266–67.
214. *Freemans Journal*, 5 January 1910, p. 7: also 26 June 1909, pp. 6, 9; 29 June 1909, p. 6; 5 July 1909, p. 8; 28 July 1909, p. 10; 13 August 1909, p. 8: 16 November 1909, pp. 7–8; 18 November 1909, p. 8; 24 May 1910, p. 8.
215. 18 HC DEB, 30 June 1910, col. 1155 (Redmond): *Freemans Journal*, 1 July 1910, p. 8.
216. *Freemans Journal*, 9 December 1910, p. 6; 29 September 1911, p. 4; 7 January 1913, p. 6: SPO/CSO.RP (1913)/(1911: 24381) (memo on parliamentary question by Ffrench, 23 March 1911): 21 HC DEB, 21 February 1911, cols 1870–71 (Doris, Birrell): 23 HC DEB, 23 March 1911, col. 593 (Ffrench, Birrell); 30 March 1911, cols 1512–13 (Sheehan, Birrell).
217. 34 HC DEB, 27 February 1912, cols 1205–31 (Birrell, Banbury, Clancy, Mitchell-Thompson, Castlereagh, Craig, Birrell).

218. AMAI, op. cit.: *The Times*, 16 October 1913, p. 15, f; 16 October 1913, p. 10, d: 17 October 1913, p. 5, e: *Freemans Journal*, 25 October 1912, p. 4; 25 February 1913, pp. 8, 10; 17 April 1913, pp. 6, 8; 23 April 1913, p. 4; 12 June 1913, p. 6; 21 August 1913, p. 9; 16 October 1913, p. 10; 18 October 1913, pp. 5, 7; 12 November 1913, p. 5; 12 May 1914, p. 8; 15 July 1914, p. 5: *Irish Times*, 3 February 1913, p. 6; 10 March 1913, p. 5; 16 October 1913, pp. 4, 7: *Dundalk Democrat*, 14 June 1913, p. 4: *Irish Architect and Building Trades Journal*, 14 December 1912, p. 1219; 21 December 1912, pp. 1237–39; 8 March 1913, pp. 77–78, 80–81; 22 November 1913, p. 527: SPO/CSO.RP (1913)/21697 (Heron, AMAI to Le Fanu, CSO, 16 October 1913: much of the AMAI's effectiveness was due to its diligent secretary, R. Finlay Heron, Clerk to Blackrock UDC).
219. *Irish Times*, 11 March 1913, p. 6: *Freemans Journal*, 21 August 1913, p. 9.
220. *Irish Architect and Building Trades Journal*, 16 November 1912, p. 1178: also *Freemans Journal*, 23 April 1913, p. 4: SPO/CSO.RP (1913)/21697 (speech by Kerr at AMAI deputation to Chief Secretary Birrell on 17 October 1913).
221. *Freemans Journal*, 5 March 1913, p. 8; 8 March 1913, p. 6; 28 March 1913, p. 6: *Irish Times*, 11 March 1913, p. 6: *Irish Weekly Independent*, 22 February 1913, p. 4: *Cork Weekly Examiner*, 1 February 1913, p. 12: 50 HC DEB, 10 March 1913, col. 54 (O'Brien); 17 March 1913, col. 704 (O'Brien).
222. The account here based on: E. Larkin, op. cit.: A. Boyd, op. cit., pp. 87–97: F. S. L. Lyons, op. cit. (1971), pp. 281–86: L. O'Broin, op. cit., pp. 71–72.
223. *Irish Worker*, 1 November 1913, pp. 1–2.
224. PRO/CAB.41/34 (sovereign letter, 12 November 1913): E. David (ed.), *Inside Asquith's Cabinet: From the Diaries of Charles Hobhouse*, 1977, p. 148.
225. E. Larkin, 'Socialism and Catholicism in Ireland', *Church History*, vol. 30, 1964, pp. 462–82: E. Rumpf and D. Hepburn, *Nationalism and Socialism in Twentieth Century Ireland*, 1977, pp. 15–16: James Larkin turned briefly to guild cooperativism before going to the USA in late-1914. There he was jailed during the infamous 1919 'Red Scare', before returning to Ireland in April 1923 to deepen the split within the Irish labour movement through a bitter struggle for control of the ITGWU against the more moderate William O'Brien. James Connolly stayed in Dublin to inherit the leadership of the battered ITGWU, before embarking on his tragic plan for a military insurrection by the Citizens Army which was to result in martyrdom in the 1916 Easter Rising.
226. *Freemans Journal*, 3 September 1913, p. 6.
227. A. Wright, op. cit., p. 151.
228. M. Swenarton, op. cit., p. 29: D. Englander, op. cit., pp. xiv, 113–89.
229. *Irish Worker*, 17 July 1911, p. 2: also 5 August 1911, p. 4; 10 June 1911, p. 1; 29 July 1911, p. 1; 21 October 1911, p. 1; 18 November 1911, p. 1; 20 January 1912, p. 2; 9 March 1912, p. 1; 1 June 1912, p. 4; 31 August 1912, p. 3; 7 September 1912, p. 4; 20 September 1913, p. 11; 27 September 1913, p. 1; 8 October 1913, p. 4; 8 November 1913, p. 1; 15 November 1913, p. 1; 6 December 1913, p. 2; 27 December 1913, p. 1; 8 February 1914, p. 2; 14 February 1914, p. 2; 26 September 1914, p. 3: D. J. O'Neill, 'Explaining Irish underdevelopment: Plunkett and Connolly prior to 1916', *Eire-Ireland*, vol. 22, no. 4, Winter 1987, p. 61.
230. *Irish Worker*, 3 January 1914, p. 1: also 14 February 1914, p. 2.
231. *Freemans Journal*, 6 October 1913, p. 7: also 7 October 1913, p. 7; 6 November

References (Chapter 2) 349

1913, p. 10; 17 November 1913, p. 9; 24 November 1913, p. 7; 26 November 1913, p. 7: E. Larkin, op. cit. (1965), pp. 126, 134, 141.
232. *Freemans Journal*, 6 October 1913, p. 9.
233. *Freemans Journal*, 13 January 1914, p. 10.
234. *Irish Worker*, 16 May 1914, p. 2.
235. *Freemans Journal*, 20 May 1914, p. 4.
236. *Worker*, 26 December 1914, p. 2.
237. M. Daly, op. cit., p. 319.
238. A. Wright, op. cit., pp. 256, 265.
239. *Freemans Journal*, 3 March 1914, p. 4: also *Irish Architect and Building Trades Journal*, 22 November 1913, pp. 524–26: J. R O'Connell, *The Problem of the Dublin Slums*, 1913, pp. 9, 25–26.
240. *Freemans Journal*, 4 September 1913, p. 9: also 3 September 1913, p. 8: *Irish Times*, 5 September 1913, p. 8.
241. *Irish Builder*, 8 November 1913, pp. 700–01: for the reaction of the intelligentsia, see: R. Foster, op. cit., pp. 444–45.
242. *Freemans Journal*, 30 September 1913, p. 5.
243. *Freemans Journal*, 8 October 1913, p. 8: also 28 October 1913, p. 8; 10 November 1913, p. 8.
244. *Freemans Journal*, 1 June 1914, p. 3: also 1 January 1914, p. 8; 20 February 1914, p. 5; 23 February 1914, pp. 7–8: *Irish Worker*, 18 April 1914, p. 4; 23 May 1914, p. 1.
245. *The Times*, 20 September 1913, p. 3, f; 1 December 1913, p. 69, c/d: *Manchester Guardian*, reprinted in *Irish Worker*, 22 November 1913, p. 2.
246. *Irish Times*, 4 September 1913, p. 6: also 1 November 1913, p. 6; 13 January 1914, p. 4; 3 February 1914, p. 4; 23 February 1914, p. 4.
247. *Irish Builder*, 25 October 1913, p. 678: also 8 November 1913, p. 708; 14 February 1914, pp. 96–98; 25 September 1915, p. 420: see also *Irish Architect and Building Trades Journal*, 18 October 1913, p. 461; 8 November 1913, pp. 497–98; 21 February 1914, p. 677.
248. *Freemans Journal*, 13 September 1913, p. 5: the same view was later expressed by the IPP MP, William Field, and the Dublin Trades Council: *Irish Builder*, 3 February 1917, p. 52: PRO/T.1/ 11914/7107 no. 10641 (memorandum from Dublin Trades Council, attached to letter from Henry, Dublin Corporation to Montagu, Treasury, 13 November 1915).
249. J. D. Clarkson, op. cit., pp. 259–63, 276–77, 285–86: A. Mitchell, op. cit., pp. 56–67: F. S. L. Lyons, op. cit. (1971), pp. 333–34.
250. HLL, Lloyd George Papers, C/10/2/24a (Addison to Lloyd George, 10 November 1913); C/10/2/24b (Lloyd George to Addison, 11 November 1913).
251. *Freemans Journal*, 17 November 1913, p. 8.
252. *Irish Times*, 17 September 1913, p. 4.
253. SPO/CSO.RP (1913)/21697 (note on AMAI deputation to Birrell, 17 October 1913).
254. SPO/CSO.RP (1913)/21697 (note on WNHAI deputation to Birrell, 29 October 1913): *Irish Times*, 18 October 1913, p. 6; 21 October 1913, p. 6; 30 October 1913, p. 6.

255. BODLEIAN MSS, Ms. Asquith. 38, f. 236 (Birrell to Asquith, 16 October 1913, f. 236): L. O'Broin, op. cit., pp. 126–27.
256. SPO/CSO.RP (1913)/21697 (note on HTPAI deputation to Birrell, 31 October 1913).
257. BODLEIAN MSS, Ms. Asquith. 38, f. 197 (Birrell to Asquith, 20 September 1913): L. O'Broin, op. cit., pp. 74, 78.
258. *The Times*, 7 November 1913, p. 6, b; 8 November p. 8, c: for HTPAI manoeuvres, see: SPO/CSO.RP (1913)/21697 (Irish Office to Griffiths, HTPAI, 7 November 1913; Griffiths, HTPAI, to Birrell, 12 November 1913; note by Robinson, ILGB, 17 November 1913).
259. SPO/CSO.RP (1913)/21697 (note on arguments against a Vice-Regal Commission, unsigned and undated, but probably by CSO in October 1913): *Freemans Journal*, 1 November 1913, pp. 7–8.
260. *The Times*, 26 November 1913, p. 8, a/b: *Freemans Journal*, 24 November 1913, p. 7; 26 November 1913, p. 7: thus there seems no basis for the recent claim that the Castle Administration was reluctant to undertake an inquiry, in J. V. O'Brien, op. cit., p. 150.
261. *Freemans Journal*, 11 November 1913, p. 8, 10; 26 November 1913, p. 6; 8 January 1914, p. 6; 10 January 1914, p. 6; 13 January 1914, pp. 6–7; 9 March 1914, p. 6; 15 January 1914, p. 9.
262. PP 1914 Cd.7273 xix, 'Report of the Departmental Committee appointed by the Local Government Board for Ireland to inquire into the Housing Conditions of the Working Classes in the City of Dublin': PP 1914 Cd.7317 xix, 'Appendix to the Report of the Departmental Committee appointed by the Local Government Board for Ireland to inquire into the Housing Conditions of the Working Classes in the City of Dublin: Minutes of Evidence, with appendices'.
263. 61 HC DEB, 16 April 1914, cols 344–45 (Clancy): *Irish Builder*, 3 January 1914, p. 13; 14 February 1914, pp. 96–98: see also *Freemans Journal*, 15 October 1913, p. 6: F. H. A. Aalen, op. cit. (1985), p. 177.
264. *Glasgow Herald*, 21 February 1914, p. 8: *New York Times*, 15 March 1914, p. 4.
265. M. Daly, op. cit., pp. 217, 270–72, 287–90, 315–16, 318: for a defence of Dublin Corporation's sanitary policy, see: Sir Charles Cameron, *Brief History of Municipal Health Administration in Dublin*, 1914: *Irish Times*, 11 June 1914, p. 6: *Irish Worker*, 13 June 1914, p. 1.
266. *Freemans Journal*, 19 November 1913, p. 11.
267. PP 1914 Cd.7317 xix, 'Appendix to the Report of the Departmental Committee appointed by the Local Government Board for Ireland to inquire into the Housing Conditions of the Working Classes in the City of Dublin: Minutes of Evidence, with appendices', f. 195: see also: *Irish Worker*, 8 November 1913, p. 2.
268. PP 1914 Cd.7273 xix, 'Report of the Departmental Committee appointed by the Local Government Board for Ireland to inquire into the Housing Conditions of the Working Classes in the City of Dublin', f. 79, 85: J. V. O'Brien, op. cit., p. 154.
269. PP 1914 Cd.7273 xix, 'Report of the Departmental Committee appointed by the Local Government Board for Ireland to inquire into the Housing Conditions of the Working Classes in the City of Dublin', f. 88.
270. Ibid., f. 89.
271. Ibid., f. 94.

272. *Freemans Journal*, 20 February 1914, p. 10: *Irish Times*, 28 March 1914, p. 8: *Irish Architect and Building Trades Journal*, 2 April 1914, pp. 758–60; 18 June 1914, pp. 925–26: Sir C. Cameron, op. cit.
273. *Irish Times*, 18 February 1914, p. 6; 20 February 1914, p. 6; also 17 September 1913, p. 4; 16 October 1913, p. 4; 17 October 1913, p. 4; 19 November 1913, p. 6; 20 February 1914, p. 6; 24 April 1914, p. 6; 19 May 1914, p. 6: for similar press response, see: *Freemans Journal*, 18 February 1914, p. 6; 24 February 1914, pp. 4–5; 23 May 1914, p. 4: *Dublin Evening Herald*, 28 February 1914; *Irish Builder*, 28 February 1914, pp. 128–32: *Irish Architect and Building Trades Journal*, 21 February 1914, p. 677.
274. Quoted in *Freemans Journal*, 9 April 1914, p. 9: PP 1914 (Cd.7561) xxxix. 595, '42nd Annual Report of ILGB for year ending 31 March 1914', f. 639.
275. *Irish Worker*, 28 March 1914, p. 4: *Freemans Journal*, 5 March 1914, p. 5.
276. RPDCD vol. 2, no. 120 (1914), pp. 155–87; vol. 1, no. 35 (1916), pp. 337–57.
277. M. Daly, op. cit., pp. 314–16: C. Lincoln, 'Working class housing' (UCD MA Thesis 1979), pp. 1–16: a contrary interpretation comes from J. V. O'Brien, op. cit., p. 154.
278. S. O'Casey, *Autobiography Volume 4: Inishfallen, Fare Thee Well*, 1949/72, p. 118: D. Krause (ed.), *The Letters of Sean O'Casey 1910–41: Volume 1*, 1975, p. 41: S. O'Casey, *Three Plays*, 1968.
279. *The Times*, 3 November 1913, p. 5, d.
280. P. Geddes, *Cities in Evolution*, 1915, pp. 243–44: *Town Planning Review*, vol. 7, 1916–18, p. 270.
281. SPO/CSO.RP (1913)/24059 (Barlas to Under Secretary, 26 November 1913): SPO/CSO.RP (1914)/5006, (Robinson to Treasury, 24 February 1914): PRO/T.1/11782/5824 no. 7882 (Williams to Treasury, 13 April 1914): PRO/T.1/11914/7107 no. 10069 (Williams to Treasury, 13 May 1914).
282. PRO/T.143/1, f. 162 (Headlam to Treasury, 7 March 1914): also PRO/T.143/1, ff. 329–30 (Headlam to Treasury, 3 December 1913): SPO/CSO.RP (1913)/24059 (Heath to Under Secretary, 10 December 1913): CSO/RP (1914)/5006 (Robinson to Treasury, 24 February 1914; Heath to Under Secretary, 21 March 1914).
283. *Freemans Journal*, 24 November 1913, p. 7; 26 November 1913, pp. 6–7; 10 January 1914, p. 6; 24 February 1914, p. 5: 50 HC DEB, 12 March 1913, col. 243 (Birrell).
284. F. S. L. Lyons, op. cit. (1951), p. 248: also F. S. L. Lyons, op. cit. (1971), pp. 260, 265–66.
285. A. Mitchell, op. cit., pp. 15–16: M. Daly, op. cit., pp. 315, 318–22: R. Foster, op. cit., pp. 436–38.

3. THE INFLUENCE OF EARLY IRISH STATE HOUSING ON BRITISH POLICY (116–131)

1. J. S. Mill, *England and Ireland*, 1868: O. MacDonagh, *Ireland: The Union and its Aftermath*, 1967/1977, pp. 46–47: O. MacDonagh, *States of Mind: A Study of Anglo-Irish Conflict 1780–1950*, 1983, p. 47: J. Lee, *The Modernisation of Irish Society, 1848–1918*, 1973, p. 26.
2. A. Offer, *Property and Politics 1870–1914: Landownership, Law, Ideology and Urban*

Development in England, 1981, pp. 36, 150–56, 184, 332–84: F. A. Aalen, 'Ebeneezer Howard's Garden City: the rural context *c.* 1880–1920', paper to 1989 International Planning History Group Conference: J. P. Dunbabin, *Rural Discontent in Nineteenth Century Britain*, 1974, p. 173.

3. PRO/HLG.29/106 (memo by Local Government Board on rural housing, February 1912): F. E. Green, *The Tyranny of the Countryside*, 1913, p. 24: J. Burnett, *A Social History of Housing 1815–1970*, 1978/85, pp. 135–37: E. Gauldie, *Cruel Habitations: A History of Working Class Housing 1780–1918*, 1974, p. 69: S. Merrett, *State Housing in Britain*, 1979, pp. 26–27: M. Swenarton, *Homes Fit for Heroes: The Politics and Architecture of Early State Housing in Britain*, 1981, p. 31.
4. *Freemans Journal*, 20 March 1911, p. 8.
5. *Irish Builder*, 3 June 1905, p. 378: also 21 May 1903, p. 1755; 19 November 1904, p. 778; 27 January 1906, p. 62; 13 May 1911, p. 318; 12 April 1913, p. 244: HTPAI, *Housing and Town Improvement*, 1912, p. 15.
6. *Irish Builder*, 29 July 1905, pp. 520–22; 23 September 1905, p. 649; 10 February 1906, pp. 107–08; 8 September 1906, p. 709: PP 1906 Cd.3012 xxxvi, '34th Annual Report of the ILGB for the year ended 31 March 1906', ff. 818–20: J. Cornes, *Modern Housing in Town and Country*, 1905, pp. 127–96.
7. *Irish Builder*, 4 January 1913, p. 19.
8. *Irish Builder*, 1 August 1914, p. 471; also 6 December 1913, p. 757.
9. G. Slater, 'Rural housing—a lesson from Ireland', *Contemporary Review*, vol. 82, September 1902, pp. 401–02: M. Kaufman, *The Housing of the Working Classes and of the Poor*, 1907, pp. 64, 111–15: F. E. Green, 'The problem of providing cottages for rural labourers', in L. Weaver, *The 'Country Life' Book of Cottages, Costing from £150 to £600*, 1913, pp. 6–11: W. G. Savage, *Rural Housing*, 1915, pp. 289–91.
10. L. Weaver, op. cit., p. 15: also pp. 12–17.
11. PP 1906 Cd.376 ix, 'Report and Special Report of the Select Committee on the Housing of the Working Classes Acts Amendment Bill', f. 182, 316: *The Times*, 19 June 1906, p. 4, e; 3 April 1908, p. 9, e; 15 December 1911, p. 14, f; 17 May 1912, p. 7, a; 22 May 1912, p. 13, d; 1 November 1912, p. 4, d; 11 January 1913, p. 8, c: *Municipal Journal*, vol. 21, no. 1018, 3 August 1912, pp. 951–52: report of deputation of National Housing Reform Council to Prime Minister Campbell-Bannerman and Minister of Local Government Burns in November 1906, reprinted in H. R. Aldridge, *The Case for Town Planning*, 1915, appendix 1, pp. 163, 167–68.
12. A. Sutcliffe, 'Britain's first town planning act: a review of the 1909 achievement', *Town Planning Review*, vol. 59, no. 3, 1988, p. 292: see also J. A. Yelling, *Slums and Slum Clearance in Victorian London*, 1986, pp. 64–66.
13. PRO/HLG.29/106 (memo from National Housing and Town Planning Council, 15 June 1912): see also: W. Thompson, *The Housing Handbook*, 1903, pp. 138–40: W. Thompson, *Housing Up-to-date (Companion Volume to the Housing Handbook)*, 1907, pp. 136–40, 259: W. Thompson, *The Housing Problem—Paper Presented to 1908 Pan-Anglican Congress*, 1908, p. 7: BL ADD MSS, Burns Papers, Ms. 46302 (Lord Crewe to Burns, 14 March 1912): *Municipal Journal*, vol. 22, no. 1049, 7 March 1913, p. 321.
14. *Municipal Journal*, vol. 21, no. 1031, 1 November 1912, p. iii: also pp. i–iv (supplement on the visit of the National Housing and Town Planning Council deputation):

Garden Cities and Town Planning, vol. 11, no. 11, November 1912, pp. 250–51: *The Times*, 1 November 1912, p. 4, d.

15. H. R. Aldridge, op. cit., p. 454: *Irish Builder*, 28 September 1912, p. 550; 4 January 1913, p. 19: *The Times*, 21 September 1912, p. 8, d.
16. J. S. Nettlefold, *Practical Town Planning: A Land and Housing Policy*, 1914, pp. 137, 192–93, 480–82: *Municipal Journal*, vol. 22, no. 1054, 11 April 1913, p. 463: *The Times*, 10 December 1912, p. 6, b: A. Sutcliffe, *Towards the Planned City*, 1981, pp. 71–72: J. A. Yelling, op. cit., p. 68.
17. *Builder*, 5 January 1917, p. 4: see also: J. G. Allen, *The Cheap Cottage and Small Home*, 1912, preface.
18. A. Offer, op. cit., pp. 150–56: S. Hall and B. Schwarz, 'State and society, 1880–1930', in M. Langan and B. Schwarz (eds), *Crises in the British State 1880–1930*, 1985, p. 21: WRO, Walter Long Papers, 947/438 (Long to Bluminfeld, mid-August 1910; Long to Collings, 15 September 1910): BL ADD MSS, Ms. 49777 (Long to Balfour, 3 October 1910): *The Times*, 25 July 1912, p. 7, f, 8, a, b: Sir C. Petrie, *Walter Long and his Times*, 1936, p. 144.
19. *The Times*, 13 September 1909, p. 2, f; 19 September 1911, p. 5, f; 22 February 1912, p. 6, a; 29 July 1912, p. 7, f, 8, a; 16 November 1912, p. 6, d: BL ADD MSS, Balfour Mss, Ms. 49736 (Chamberlain to Balfour, 24 October 1907; Chamberlain to Balfour, 23 September 1910): WRO, Walter Long Papers, 947/438 (Collings to Long, 2 April 1910; undated memorandum on Unionist Land Policy meeting; Collings to Balfour, 1 April 1910; Long to Collings, 15 September 1910): J. Collings, *The Colonisation of Rural Britain*, 1914.
20. 51 HC DEB, 18 April 1913, col. 2299 (Long).
21. BL ADD MSS, Walter Long Papers, Ms. 62403 (Long to Landsdowne, 27 June 1914); Ms. 62404 (Long to Bonar Law, 27 June 1913?): HLL, Bonar Law Papers, 26/3/28 (Collings to Law, 17 May 1912); 29/4/5 (Strachey to Law, 5 May 1913); 29/4/8 (Strachey to Law, 13 May 1913); 29/5/8 (Strachey to Law, 3 June 1914): *The Times*, 28 July 1913, p. 11, f: C. Williams-Ellis, *Cottage Building in Cob, Pise, Chalk and Clay: A Renaissance*, 1919, p. 13: L. Weaver, op. cit.: Strachey had organised the 1905 Letchworth Cheap Cottages Competition, and had built on his estate near Guildford several cheap model cottages based on the use of innovative techniques such as timber framing and pise-de-terre, to designs by Clough Williams-Ellis and himself.
22. National Unionist Association of Conservative and Liberal Unionist Associations, *The History of Housing Reform*, 1913, and *The Campaign Guide: A Handbook for Unionist Speakers*, 1914, pp. 556–70: HLL, Bonar Law Papers, 26/3/28 (Collings to Law, 17 May 1912); 29/4/5 (Strachey to Law, 5 May 1913); 29/4/8 (Strachey to Law, 13 May 1913); 29/5/8 (Strachey to Law, 3 June 1913); 32/2/5 (Flannery to Law, 2 April 1914): WRO, Walter Long Papers, 947/441 (Fisher to Long, 9 January 1914): BL ADD MSS, Burns Mss, Ms. 46335 (diary entry for 4 April 1913, f. 77); Walter Long Papers, Ms. 62403 (Long to Lansdowne, 27 June 1914); Ms. 62404 (Long to Bonar Law, 27 June 1913): *The Times*, 2 July 1912, p. 7, a; 9 October 1912, p. 11, d; 12 December 1912, p. 4, c: the Irish precedent for these pre-war Conservative Bills has been overlooked in: P. Wilding, 'Towards housing subsidies for housing', *Social and Economic Administration*, vol. 6, no. 1, January 1972, pp. 8–12: A. Offer, op. cit., pp. 361–62, 405: M. J. Daunton, *A Property-Owning Democracy*, 1987, pp. 55–58.

23. HLL, Bonar Law Papers, 24/2/164 (Long to Bonar Law, 29 December 1911).
24. HLL, Bonar Law Papers, 32/2/5 (Flannery to Bonar Law, 2 April 1914).
25. PRO/HLG.29/106 (memo by Kershaw on 'The Housing of the Working Classes Bill 1912', 12 March 1912).
26. 51 HC DEB, 4 April 1913, cols 714 (Fletcher), 736–44 (Stanier), 745–50 (Atherley-Jones): also *The Times*, 21 January 1913, p. 10, f; 28 July 1913, p. 11, a–c.
27. 51 HC DEB, 18 April 1913, cols 2240–41 (Baker), 2281 (Cavendish-Bentinck), 2298–99 (Long): 35 HC DEB, 15 March 1912, cols 1424 (Griffith-Boscawen), 1433–34 (Bathurst), 1461 (Guinness), 1465–66 (Sutton): 65 HC DEB, 24 July 1914, col. 854 (Griffith-Boscawen): National Unionist Association of Conservative and Liberal Unionist Associations, op. cit. (1914), p. 563.
28. 18 HC DEB, 7 July 1910, cols 1822–23 (Jardine), 1823–24; 51 HC DEB, 4 April 1913, col. 717 (Fletcher): 61 HC DEB, 16 April 1914, cols 361–62 (Griffith-Boscawen), 362 (Brady).
29. 51 HC DEB, 4 April 1913, cols 754–55 (Jowett): also 18 April 1913, col. 2277 (Roberts): 188 HC DEB, 12 May 1908, col. 983 (Jowett): 3 HC DEB, 5 April 1909, cols 774 (Jowett), 869 (Brodie): 35 HC DEB, 11 March 1912, cols 833–34 (Jowett): J. S. Nettlefold, *Practical Town Planning: A Land and Housing Policy*, 1914, p. 137: M. J. Daunton, op. cit., p. 59.
30. A. L. H. Gailey, *Ireland and the Death of Kindness: The Experience of Constructive Unionism 1890–1905*, 1987, p. 47.
31. HLL, Lloyd George Papers, C/36/2/19 (deputation of Welsh slate producers to Lloyd George on 30 May 1914, from *Manchester Guardian*, 1 June 1914): M. J. Daunton, op. cit., pp. 53–54.
32. HLL, Lloyd George Papers, C/36/1/24 (speech by Lloyd George at Oxford Union debate on 21 November 1913, reported in *Oxford Chronicle*, 28 November 1913): also C/12/2/17 (memorandum by Lloyd George for Cabinet, 19 October 1913); C/15/2/3 (memorandum by Lloyd George for Cabinet, June 1914): E. David (ed.), *Inside Asquith's Cabinet: From the Diaries of Charles Hobhouse*, 1977, p. 147: C. Bellamy, *Administering Central-Local Relations, 1871–1919: the Local Government Board and its Fiscal and Cultural Context*, 1988, p. 24.
33. PP 1906 Cd.376 ix, 'Report and Special Report of the Select Committee on the Housing of the Working Classes Acts Amendments Bill', f. 352; also ff. 182, 291, 296, 301–02, 316, 349–50, 352–64, 526–31: A. Sutcliffe, 'Britain's first town planning act: a review of the 1909 achievement', *Town Planning Review*, vol. 59, no. 3, 1988, pp. 289–303.
34. BL ADD MSS, Burns Mss, Ms. 46335 (diary entries for 3 April 1913, f. 77; 4 April 1913, f. 77; 18 April 1913, f. 83; 19 April 1913, f. 84; 10 October 1913, f. 170; 17 October 1913, f. 173; 24 October 1913, f. 177; 6 November 1913, f. 183; 7 November 1913, f. 184; 2 December 1913, f. 196; 4 December 1913, f. 197); Ms. 46336 (diary entry for 29 January 1914, f. 39): HLL, Lloyd George Papers, C/3/9/1 (Burns to Lloyd George, 9 October 1913): K. B. Brown, *John Burns*, 1977, p. 172: E. David (ed.), op. cit., pp. 147–48: P. Wilding, op. cit., pp. 4–12: C. Bellamy, op. cit., pp. 96–97.
35. 51 HC DEB, 4 April 1913, col. 774 (Burns).
36. E. David (ed.), op. cit., p. 148.
37. 188 HC DEB, 12 May 1908, col. 1047 (Masterman).

38. 61 HC DEB, 16 April 1914, col. 393 (Birrell): 51 HC DEB, 4 April 1913, col. 756 (Banbury): also 18 April 1913, col. 2284 (Verney), 2312–13 (Burns): 35 HC DEB, 15 March 1912, cols 1483–91 (Burns): *The Times*, 4 July 1912, p. 10, b.
39. A. Offer, op. cit., pp. 363–84.
40. Land Enquiry Committee, *The Land: The Report of the Land Enquiry Committee—Vol. 1, Rural*, 1913, pp. 329–32: Land Enquiry Committee, *The Land: The Report of the Land Enquiry Committee—Vol. 2, Urban*, 1914, p. 178: HLL, Lloyd George Papers, C/2/1 to C/2/4; C/15/1/3 (speech by Lloyd George at Queens Hall, 23 March 1910); C/36/1/10 (speech by Lloyd George in London on 6 July 1913, reported in *Manchester Guardian*, 7 July 1913): 35 HC DEB, 15 March 1912, col. 1491 (Burns).
41. A. Offer, op. cit., pp. 389–96: R. Douglas, 'God gave the land to the people', in A. S. A. Morris (ed.), *Edwardian Radicalism 1900–1914*, 1974, pp. 148–61.
42. M. Swenarton, op. cit., pp. 41–44.
43. *The Times*, 3 July 1912, p. 6, d; 11 January 1913, p. 10, f; 22 January 1913, p. 7, e; 28 July 1913, p. 11, f: L. Weaver, op. cit., pp. 12–15.
44. 41 HC DEB, 30 July 1912, col. 1833 (Bathurst, Asquith): 42 HC DEB, 10 October 1912, cols 519–20 (Griffith-Boscawen, Asquith); 22 October 1912, col. 1909 (Griffith-Boscawen, Asquith).
45. 58 HC DEB, 16 February 1914, col. 547; 18 February 1914, cols 976 (Barnes), 994 (Brady), 1015–1017 (Roberts): 59 HC DEB, 5 March 1914, cols 584 (Boscawen), 629 (Cooper); 12 March 1914, cols 1530–32 (Griffith-Boscawen), 1536 (Birrell): 60 HC DEB, 24 March 1914, col. 201 (Brady, Birrell); 30 March 1914, col. 797: *Freemans Journal*, 27 October 1913, p. 7; et seq.
46. 61 HC DEB, 16 April 1914, col. 371 (Brady).
47. Ibid., col. 361 (Griffith-Boscawen).
48. Ibid., cols 392–93 (Birrell).
49. Ibid., col. 394 (Birrell).
50. *Irish Times*, 17 April 1914, p. 6: also 14 January 1914, p. 4: *Freemans Journal*, 13 January 1914, pp. 6–9: *Glasgow Herald*, 17 April 1914, p. 8.
51. 62 HC DEB, 20 May 1914, col. 2008 (Healy).
52. HLL, Lloyd George Papers, C/7/3/8 (Redmond to Lloyd George, 7 April 1914).
53. HLL, Lloyd George Papers, C/3/8/3 (Birrell to Lloyd George, Easter Monday [13 April] 1914).
54. D. Grigg, *Lloyd George: From Peace to War 1912–1916*, 1985, pp. 104–07: A. Offer, op. cit., pp. 396–98.
55. HLL, Lloyd George Papers, C/13/1/18 (note from Redmond to Lloyd George, 11 May 1914): 62 HC DEB, 4 May 1914, cols 76–78 (Lloyd George): *Freemans Journal*, 7 May 1914, p. 9; 12 May 1914, p. 8: *Irish Builder*, 23 May 1914, p. 314.
56. 62 HC DEB, 14 May 1914, col. 1283 (Lloyd George); 18 May 1914, cols 1598 (Lloyd George), 1739 (Samuel); 19 May 1914, col. 1758 (Lloyd George); 20 May 1914, cols 1954 (Lloyd George), 1975–76 (Samuel).
57. 63 HC DEB, 24 June 1914, col. 1882 (Lloyd George): also 62 HC DEB, 7 May 1914, col. 541 (Newman): 63 HC DEB, 25 June 1914, col. 2024, et seq.
58. M. Swenarton, op. cit., p. 34: it is therefore necessary, as Swenarton argues, to discount the misreading of the pre-war situation that states that the Government had decided on a subsidised housing policy by mid-1914, as is erroneously given in: P. Wilding, op. cit., pp. 15–16: the lack of a cohesive Cabinet policy on housing

comes as no surprise when it is considered that similar inconsistency existed in relation to an issue that the Cabinet had placed higher up its agenda, namely unemployment relief: J. Harris, *Unemployment and Politics: A Study in English Social Policy 1886–1914*, 1972, p. 352.
59. M. Swenarton, op. cit., pp. 44–47: a total of £5 000 000 of public loans were to be made available under the 1914 Housing Act (40 per cent for military bases, 60 per cent for rural labourers) to build in all around 25 000 dwellings—the Treasury was to increase the proportion of low-interest loans to public utility societies from 66 per cent to 90 per cent of capital expenditure.
60. 65 HC DEB, 24 July 1914, col. 809 (Runciman), 853–54 (Griffith-Boscawen).
61. 65 HC DEB, 21 July 1914, col. 266 (Birrell); 24 July 1914, col. 809 (Runciman): SPO/CSO.RP(1914)/4932, (resolution from Irishwomen's Reform League, 20 March 1914): SPO/CSO.RP (1914)/5234 (resolution from Dublin Trades Council, March 1914): SPO/CSO.RP (1914)/8305 (resolution from Citizens Housing League, 20 May 1914).
62. PP 1914–16 (Cd.8119) xxxiv. 117, '83rd Annual Report of Commissioners of Public Works in Ireland for year ending 31 March 1915', f. 137: PRO/T.1/11668/18955 (Birrell to Montagu, 22 September 1914; Clancy to Montagu, 19 October 1914): PRO/T.1/11914/7107 no. 28987 (Williams to Treasury, 23 November 1914; Montagu to Redmond, 25 November 1914): *Irish Builder*, 15 August 1914, p. 496; 12 September 1914, p. 534: RPDCD 1915 (Vol. 3), no. 240, p. 115.
63. *Freemans Journal*, 9 April 1914, p. 9; 11 April 1914, p. 4: *Irish Worker*, 25 April 1914, p. 2.
64. Citizens Housing League, *Dublin: Its Slums and Death Rate*, 1914: also *Irish Times*, 13 May 1914, p. 6: *Freemans Journal*, 19 May 1914, p. 10.
65. *Freemans Journal*, 1 January 1914, p. 6; 7 January 1914, p. 6; 1 July 1914, p. 4; 2 July 1914, p. 4; 7 July 1914, p. 5; 15 December 1914, p. 3: *Irish Times*, 31 December 1913, p. 4; 7 January 1914, p. 6; 13 January 1914, p. 4.
66. Citizens Housing League, op. cit.: *Freemans Journal*, 24 April 1914, p. 8; 13 May 1914, p. 9; 19 May 1914, p. 10: *Irish Builder*, 23 May 1914, p. 309.
67. *Freemans Journal*, 13 May 1914, p. 9: *Irish Times*, 6 May 1914, p. 8; 19 May 1914, pp. 6, 8; 20 May 1914, p. 8: *Irish Worker*, 9 May 1914, p. 2: Citizens Housing League, op. cit.
68. *Freemans Journal*, 19 May 1914, p. 5; 22 June 1914, p. 10; 23 June 1914, p. 4; 30 June 1914, p. 4; 1 July 1914, p. 4; 2 July 1914, p. 4; 6 July 1914, p. 4; 7 July 1914, p. 5; 8 July 1914, p. 4; 17 September 1914, p. 3.
69. *Irish Worker*, 20 June 1914, p. 2; 27 June 1914, p. 2; 4 July 1914, p. 1: N. O'Flanagan, 'Dublin City in an age of war and revolution, 1914–1924', (University College Dublin MA thesis, 1985), p. 124.
70. *Freemans Journal*, 19 May 1914, p. 5: *Irish Times*, 30 May 1914, p. 9: Dublin Corporation Council Minutes, 18 May 1914, min. 378b: PRO/T.1/11914/7107 no. 1064 (Sherlock to Lloyd George, 10 July 1914).
71. SPO/CSO.RP (1914)/9641 (note by Magill to Under Secretary, 11 June 1914): *Freemans Journal*, 15 July 1914, p. 5; *Irish Times*, 20 June 1914, p. 6: Dublin Corporation Council Minutes, 19 June 1914, min. 470.
72. *Freemans Journal*, 22 June 1914, p. 10; 23 June 1914, p. 4; 24 June 1914, p. 7: *Irish Times*, 24 June 1913, p. 9: *Irish Worker*, 27 June 1914, p. 2.

73. PRO/T.1/11914/7107 no. 1064 (note by 'J. P. H.', 19 August 1914, on letter from Sherlock to Lloyd George, 10 July 1914).
74. M. Swenarton, *Artisans and Architects: The Ruskinian Tradition in Architectural Thought*, 1989, pp. 167–88.
75. *Irish Worker*, 27 December 1913, p. 3, 14 February 1914: A. Wright, *Disturbed Dublin: The Story of the Great Strike of 1913–14*, 1914, pp. 259–64: E. Larkin, *James Larkin: Irish Labour Leader, 1876–1947*, 1965, pp. 168–69: E. O'Connor, *Syndicalism in Ireland 1917–1923*, 1988, pp. 46–51.
76. *Irish Worker*, 21 March 1914, p. 1.
77. *Freemans Journal*, 8 January 1914, p. 10; *Irish Builder*, 2 May 1914, p. 1: also 28 March 1914, p. 181.
78. P. Kitchen, *A Most Unsettling Person: An Introduction to the Ideas and Life of Patrick Geddes*, 1975, pp. 248–50: H. E. Meller, *Patrick Geddes: Social Evolutionist and City Planner*, 1990, p. 187.
79. *Irish Worker*, 2 May 1914, p. 4; 6 June 1914, p. 1.
80. *Freemans Journal*, 1 June 1914, p. 3; 2 June 1914, p. 2; 3 June 1914, p. 8: *Irish Worker*, 20 June 1914, p. 2.
81. *Irish Worker*, 11 July 1914, p. 2; 18 July 1914, p. 2.
82. D. Englander, *Landlord and Tenant in Urban Britain 1838–1918*, 1983, pp. 162–66.

4. HOME RULE AND GARDEN SUBURB IDEALS IN IRELAND BEFORE 1914 (132–147)

1. F. H. A. Aalen, 'The working-class housing movement in Dublin, 1850–1920', in M. J. Bannon (ed.), *The Emergence of Irish Planning 1880–1920*, 1985, pp. 174–80: M. J. Bannon, 'The genesis of modern Irish planning', in M. J. Bannon (ed.), op. cit., pp. 189–243: M. Miller, 'Raymond Unwin and the planning of Dublin', in M. J. Bannon (ed.), op. cit., pp. 263–82: H. E. Meller, *Patrick Geddes: Social Evolutionist and City Planner*, 1990, pp. 182–89: M. Miller, *Raymond Unwin: Garden Cities and Town Planning*, 1992, pp. 151–53.
2. E. P. Alabaster, *New Dublin*, 1905: Miss Rooney, 'Some remedies for overcrowded city districts', *JSSISI*, vol. 12, part 87, December 1906, pp. 52–61: however, it was left to the *Irish Builder* to show the greatest interest in championing British town planning: *Irish Builder*, 29 July 1905, pp. 520–22; 10 February 1906, pp. 107–08; 5 May 1906, pp. 360–63; 18 September 1909, p. 594; 16 October 1909, pp. 654–57; 11 December 1909, pp. 780–82; 5 February 1910, pp. 78–81; 23 July 1910, pp. 469–70; 6 August 1910, pp. 489, 510; 29 October 1910, pp. 664–67; 26 November 1910, pp. 728, 732; 27 May 1911, p. 354; 17 August 1912, p. 469; 31 August 1912, pp. 504–06.
3. *Irish Architect and Craftsman*, 5 August 1911, p. 393.
4. *Freemans Journal*, 8 January 1909, p. 7.
5. RPDCD, 1911, vol. 1, no. 54, p. 568: *Irish Architect and Craftsman*, 8 April 1911, p. 151; 5 April 1913, pp. 126–29: *Irish Builder*, 24 May 1913, p. 344: *Freemans Journal*, 12 April 1913, p. 8; 19 September 1913, p. 5.
6. Lord and Lady Aberdeen, *We Twa (2 Vols)*, 1925, pp. 187–91.
7. H. E. Meller, 'Patrick Geddes 1854–1932', in G. E. Cherry (ed.), *Pioneers in British Planning*, 1981, pp. 46–71: H. E. Meller, op. cit. (1990), pp. 142–46.

8. H. E. Meller, 'Cities and evolution: Patrick Geddes as an international prophet of town planning before 1914', in A. Sutcliffe (ed.), *The Rise of Modern Urban Planning, 1800–1914*, 1980, pp. 214–16.
9. P. Geddes, *Cities in Evolution*, 1915, pp. 2, 102, 228–29, 243–44, 258, 294, 296, 366, 378: NLS MSS, Geddes Papers, Ms. 10514 (Geddes to Biggar, 9 December 1913).
10. The course of events can be followed in: *Irish Builder*, 29 April 1911, p. 265; 27 May 1911, p. 358; 10 June 1911, pp. 377, 393, 406; 24 June 1911, pp. 422–25; 8 July 1911, pp. 445, 457, 469; 5 August 1911, pp. 513–14, 517; 19 August 1911, p. 557; 2 September 1911, pp. 578–85.
11. BL ADD MSS, Burns Mss, Ms. 46282, ff. 122–23 (Violet Asquith to Burns, 4 May 1911).
12. *Irish Builder*, 28 October 1911, p. 734; 9 December 1911, p. 821; 20 January 1912, pp. 44–45; 13 April 1912, p. 213.
13. M. Swenarton, *Homes Fit for Heroes: The Politics and Architecture of Early State Housing in Britain*, 1981, pp. 6–7.
14. *Irish Builder*, 26 November 1910, pp. 728, 732; 18 February 1911, p. 100; 20 January 1912, p. 51: the Corporation sent the City Engineer's Assistant, William Cranwill Wilson, over to see Port Sunlight, Letchworth and Hampstead Garden Suburb, and on his return he produced a report and began to design a garden suburb on the Marino site: PP 1914 Cd.7317 xix, 'Appendix to the Report of the Departmental Commissioners appointed by the Local Government Board for Ireland to Inquire into the Housing Conditions of the Working Classes of Dublin: Minutes of Evidence, with appendices', ff. 130–33: see also M. J. Bannon, op. cit., pp. 194–95.
15. *Freemans Journal*, 17 December 1912, p. 6.
16. SPO/CSO.RP (1913)/21697 (report of AMAI deputation to Chief Secretary Birrell, 17 October 1913): see also *Freemans Journal*, 30 June 1914; 6 July 1914, p. 4; 9 July 1915, p. 8.
17. *Irish Builder*, 26 November 1910, p. 732: *Freemans Journal*, 14 January 1914, p. 9; 22 June 1914, p. 10, 23 June 1914, p. 4; 29 June 1914, p. 4; 2 July 1914, p. 4: RPDCD 1913 (Vol. 2), no. 176, p. 652; 1914 (Vol. 2), no. 183, p. 489: Dublin Corporation Minutes, 20 April 1914, min. 260, p. 178; 4 May 1914, pp. 225–26.
18. SPO/CSO.RP (1913)/21697 (Griffiths to Birrell, 12 November 1913; Robinson to Birrell, 17 November 1913).
19. PP 1914 Cd.7273 xix, 'Report of the Departmental Committee appointed by the Local Government Board for Ireland to Inquire into the Housing Conditions of the Working Classes in the City of Dublin', ff. 25, 26, 30.
20. SPO/CSO.RP (1914)/6087 (brochure for Civic Exhibition, 25 February 1914): *Freemans Journal*, 12 March 1914, p. 8; also 8 January 1914, p. 9; 26 January 1914, p. 4; 14 July 1914, p. 8; 25 July 1914, p. 8: for a description of the Exhibition, see: *Official Catalogue of the Civic Exhibition, Ireland, 1914*, 1914.
21. *Freemans Journal*, 10 February 1914, p. 9; 27 April 1914, p. 9; 30 April 1914, pp. 6, 9: M. C. Boyer, *Dreaming the Rational City: The Myth of American Town Planning*, 1983, pp. 59–136: M. Scott, *American City Planning since 1890*, 1969, pp. 110–82.
22. *Freemans Journal*, 19 March 1914, p, 9: also 10 February 1914, p. 9; 4 March 1914, p. 6; 7 March 1914, pp. 7–8; 12 March 1914, pp. 7–8: *Irish Times*, 4 March 1914,

p. 4: *Irish Builder*, 14 March 1914, pp. 156, 171: RIAI, *Journal of the RIAI*, 1914, p. 23: Lord and Lady Aberdeen, op. cit., p. 190.
23. PRO/T.1/11782/5824 no. 3016 (brochure entitled 'The Civic Exhibition: what it will do', undated): also (official brochure on Civic Exhibition, 1914, p. 17).
24. *Irish Architect and Craftsman*, 30 July 1914, p. 1021: also *Irish Builder*, 14 March 1914, pp. 149, 156: *Builder*, 24 July 1914, p. 96.
25. PRO/T.1/11782/5824 no. 14928 (note by 'F. L. R.', 3 August 1914): (also O'Connell and Son to Irish Board of Works, 3 July 1914; Sharrah to Treasury, 20 July 1914; Williams to Treasury, 22 August 1914); no. 3016 (note by Whitehouse, 8 May 1914; Lloyd George to Aberdeen, 8 May 1914; Aberdeen to Whitehouse, 12 May 1914; note by 'F. L. H.', 16 May 1914; Aberdeen to Whitehouse, 19 May 1914; Brady to Montagu, 24 August 1914; MacFadyean to Brady, 25 August 1914; Brady to MacFadyean, 28 August 1914; Stevenson to Heath, 2 September 1914; MacFadyean to Brady, 4 September 1914; Aberdeen to Lloyd George, early-February 1915; etc.); no. 7882 (Williams to Treasury, 13 April 1914; Heath to Irish Board of Works, 18 April 1914; Stevenson to Heath, 29 April 1914); no. 17511 (O'Connell and Son to Irish Board of Works, 18 August 1914; Treasury to Irish Board of Works, 28 August 1914).
26. *Irish Worker*, 13 June 1914, p. 1; 4 July 1914, p. 1; 18 July 1914, pp. 2, 3.
27. P. Mairet, *Pioneer of Sociology: Patrick Geddes*, 1952, pp. 149–50: J. V. O'Brien, *Dear Dirty Dublin: A City in Distress, 1899–1916*, 1982, p. 69.
28. P. Abercrombie, S. Kelly and A. Kelly, *Dublin of the Future: The New Town Plan*, 1923: *Town Planning Review*, vol. 6, no. 3, January 1916, pp. 171–90; vol. 7, 1916–18, pp. 78–79, 104–23: J. Nolen, 'Greater Dublin: competitive designs for the Town Plan of Dublin Ireland', *Landscape Architecture*, vol. 7, October 1916–July 1917, pp. 73–77: *Freemans Journal*, 18 November 1916; 21 November 1916, p. 6; 6 January 1917, p. 7; 23 January 1917, p. 6; 26 January 1917, p. 4: *Irish Builder*, 25 November 1916, pp. 573, 581; 3 February 1917, pp. 51–52: M. J. Bannon, op. cit., pp. 232–41: G. Dix, 'Patrick Abercrombie 1897–1957', in G. E. Cherry (ed.), op. cit., pp. 105–06: S. Pepper and M. Swenarton, 'Neo-Georgian Maison-Type', *Architectural Review*, vol. 168, no. 1002, August 1980, pp. 87–92.
29. H. E. Meller, op. cit. (1980), pp. 216, 223: the criticism by Geddes must, however, be seen as part of an internecine dispute in the Irish planning movement in the mid-1920s, as discussed briefly in Chapter 8.
30. *Architectural Record*, vol. 41, May 1917, pp. 403–22: *Builder*, 5 January 1917, pp. 14, 16: *Town Planning Review*, vol. 7, 1916–18, pp. 111, 121, 123: C. R. Ashbee, *Where the Great City Stands: A Study in the New Civics*, 1917, pp. 37–38, 76, 151.
31. *Freemans Journal*, 6 January 1917, p. 7; 18 November 1916, p. 6: also *Architect*, 29 September 1916, pp. 188–89; 24 November 1916, p. 313; 26 January 1917, pp. 55–58; 8 June 1917, p. 237: *Architectural Review*, vol. 41, January 1917, pp. 21–22: *Builder*, 5 January 1917, pp. 14–16, 30; 12 January 1917, pp. 35–36, 40.
32. *The Times*, 9 September 1916, p. 5, d.
33. *Freemans Journal*, 27 June 1914, p. 8; 29 June 1914, p. 4; 30 June 1914, p. 4; 1 July 1914, p. 4; 2 July 1914, p. 4; 4 July 1914, p. 8; 6 July 1914, p. 4; 7 July 1914, pp. 5, 6: *Irish Times*, 1 July 1914, p. 6; 7 July 1914, p. 6: RPDCD 1914 (Vol. 2), no. 164, p. 392: Dublin Corporation Minutes, 10 August 1914, min. 606, pp. 370–72; 5 October 1914, min. 737, pp. 432–33; 2 November 1914, min. 780, p. 453.

34. RPDCD 1915 (Vol. 1), no. 78, pp. 715–22: see also M. Miller, op. cit., pp. 267–79.
35. RPDCD 1915 (Vol. 1), no. 78, p. 752: for the British rationale for Unwinian garden suburbs, see: M. Swenarton, op. cit., pp. 40–47.
36. M. J. Bannon, op. cit., p. 204: *Irish Builder*, 23 May 1914, p. 324.
37. *Irish Builder*, 15 July 1905, pp. 486–87; 5 May 1906, pp. 360–63; 10 August 1907, pp. 546–49.
38. *Irish Builder*, 10 June 1911, p. 377; 28 October 1911, p. 709; 28 September 1912, p. 549; 15 February 1913, p. 97; 1 March 1913, p. 129; 7 June 1913, p. 365; 16 August 1913, p. 549; 17 January 1914, p. 47; 12 September 1914, pp. 533, 534; 26 September 1914, p. 558; 24 October 1914, p. 602; 30 January 1915, p. 57; 30 September 1916, p. 477.
39. *Irish Builder*, 10 April 1915, p. 168: also *Freemans Journal*, 23 September 1915, p. 6: *Dundalk Democrat*, 18 July 1914, p. 4: Lord and Lady Aberdeen, op. cit., pp. 187–88.
40. P. Geddes, op. cit., p. 366.
41. M. Miller, op. cit., pp. 195–96: instead, for an analysis of the antagonism shown by the Castle Administration hierarchy to the 'interference' of Lord and Lady Aberdeen in matters such as housing and town planning, see: BL ADD MSS, Long Papers, Ms. 62418 (Robinson to Long, 12 October 1914): BODLEIAN MSS, Ms. Asquith 38, ff. 235–36 (Birrell to Asquith, 16 October 1913); Nathan Ms. 449, ff. 123–24 (Birrell to Nathan, 14 February 1915): Sir H. Robinson, *Memories: Wise and Otherwise*, 1923, pp. 199–200, 224, 228: P. Jalland, 'A Liberal Chief Secretary and the Irish Question: Augustine Birrell, 1907–1914', *Historical Journal*, vol. 19, no. 2, 1976, p. 422: L. O'Broin, *The Chief Secretary: Augustine Birrell in Ireland*, 1969, pp. 126–27: L. O'Broin, *Dublin Castle and the 1916 Rising*, 1971, p. 22.
42. D. J. O'Neill, 'Explaining Irish underdevelopment: Plunkett and Connolly prior to 1916', *Eire-Ireland*, vol. 22, no. 4, Winter 1987, pp. 58, 68.
43. A. Defries, *The Interpreter Geddes: The Man and His Gospel*, 1927, p. 181.
44. A. Crawford, *C. R. Ashbee: Architect, Designer, and Romantic Socialist*, 1985, p. 53, 118–19, 155–58, 160, 167–68, 251, 259: P. Geddes, op. cit., p. 223: *Irish Architect and Craftsman*, 22 April 1911, p. 182.
45. H. E. Meller, op. cit. (1981), p. 58.
46. The demands for land municipalisation and the neutralisation of the 1909 Act to appease landowners is described in: A. Sutcliffe, 'Britain's first town planning act: a review of the 1909 achievement', *Town Planning Review*, vol. 59, no. 3, 1988, pp. 289–303: the general political battle between commercial/industrial wealth and landed property is given in: A. Offer, *Property and Politics 1870–1914: Landowner-ship, Law, Ideology and Urban Development in England*, 1981.
47. H. E. Meller, 1990, pp. 201–88.
48. Ibid., p. 189.
49. NLS MSS, Ms. 10514 (Geddes to Bernington, 1 September 1914); Ms. 10573 (Mears to Geddes, 20 December 1914; Mears to Geddes, 25 February 1915): Mears maintained his Dublin connections, and actually secured some work after the First World War, as will be seen in Chapter 8.
50. G. Dix, op. cit., p. 106.
51. M. J. Daunton, *House and Home in the Victorian City*, 1983, p. 5: examples of this tendency in Irish planning history are: M. J. Bannon, op. cit.: M. Miller, op. cit.: and in Britain: M. Miller, *Raymond Unwin: Garden Cities and Town Planning*, 1992.

5. WAR-TIME HOUSING AND RECONSTRUCTION AFTER THE 1916 EASTER RISING (148–184)

1. M. Swenarton, *Homes Fit for Heroes: The Politics and Architecture of Early State Housing in Britain*, 1981, pp. 48–49.
2. PRO/T.1/11677/21753 (Montagu to MacFadyean, 30 September 1914): PRO/T.1/11813/19421 no. 19421 ('M. G. H.' to Bradbury, 31 March 1915); no. 27579 (Bradbury to Montagu, 8 December 1914).
3. 65 HC Deb, 10 August 1914, col. 2249 (Clancy).
4. PRO/T.1/11914/7107 no. 28987 (Montagu to Redmond, 25 November 1914): PP 1914–16 (Cd.8119) xxxiv, '83rd Annual Report of Commissioners of Public Works for Ireland for year ending 31 March 1915', f. 137.
5. PRO/T.1/11668/18955 (Ramsay to ILGB, 30 September 1914): also (Montagu to Birrell, 29 September 1914).
6. PRO/T.1/11668/18955 (Clancy to Montagu, 7 October 1914): also (Clancy to Montagu, 19 October 1914; internal Treasury note by MacFadyean, 26 October 1914; internal Treasury note by Niemeyer, 26 October 1914; Clancy to Montagu, 25 November 1914; Montagu to Clancy, 27 November 1914).
7. PRO/T.1/11668/18955 (Montagu to Clancy, 15 October 1914).
8. RPDCD vol. 2, no. 128 (1915), pp. 133–46: there was also a claim from a Londonderry public utility company: 68 HC Deb, 16 November 1914, cols 247–48 (Birrell): PRO/T.1/11712/28946 (Barlas, ILGB to Treasury, 21 December 1914; internal Treasury note by 'F. L. R.', 11 January 1915; memorial from P. Campbell, Londonderry Artisans Dwellings Company Ltd, 7 January 1915).
9. RPDCD vol. 3, no. 240 (1915), p. 109: *Freemans Journal*, 20 October 1915, p. 6.
10. M. Swenarton, op. cit., pp. 49–66: S. Pepper and M. Swenarton, 'Home front: garden suburbs for munitions workers 1915 to 1918', *Architectural Review*, vol. 68, no. 976, June 1978, pp. 366–75.
11. R. B. McDowell, *The Irish Administration 1801–1914*, 1964, p. 292.
12. PRO/T.1/11683/23569 no. 23569 (Heath to Office of Public Works, 2 November 1914).
13. BODLEIAN MSS, Ms. Nathan 465, f. 63 (Nathan to Robinson, 18 October 1915); ff. 78–80 (Nathan to Kelly, 20 October 1915).
14. *Irish Builder*, 3 March 1917, p. 111: PRO/T.143/5 (Headlam to Leith Ross, 31 May 1917; Headlam to Leith Ross, 2 June 1917).
15. PP 1916 (Cd.8365) xiii, '44th Annual Report of ILGB for year ending 31 March 1916', f. 250: PP 1917–18 (Cd.8765) xvi, '45th Annual Report of ILGB for year ending 31 March 1917', ff. 314–15: Irish Government White Paper, *Housing—Progress and Prospects*, 1964, Appendix 1, p. 35.
16. BODLEIAN MSS, Ms. Nathan 449, ff. 50–55 (Birrell to Nathan, 14 December 1914); ff. 56–57 (Birrell to Nathan, 11 December 1914); Ms. Nathan 462, ff. 316–17 (Nathan to Birrell, 1 January 1915): PRO/T.143/3 (Headlam to Leith Ross, July 1915; Headlam to Treasury, 26 October 1915: PRO/T.143/4 (Headlam to Treasury, 30 November 1916).
17. PRO/T.1/11914/7107 no. 28987 (Stevenson to Ramsay, 29 July 1914); no. 21956.
18. PRO/T.1/11914/7107 no. 28987 (Montagu to Redmond, 25 November 1914).
19. PRO/T.1/11914/7107 no. 7856 (note by Leith Ross, 8 April 1915).

20. RPDCD vol. 3, no. 240 (1915), pp. 119–20.
21. PRO/T.1/11808/17813 (memo by Leith-Ross, 17 July 1915).
22. PRO/T.1/11808/17813 (Robinson to Heath, 22 July 1915): also PRO/T.1/11914/7107 no. 2501 (Robinson to Blackett, 22 March 1915).
23. *Freemans Journal*, 8 July 1915, p. 8.
24. PP 1916 (Cd.8414) xv, '84th Annual Report of Commissioners of Public Works for Ireland for year ending 31 March 1916', f. 279.
25. BODLEIAN MSS, Dep. c. 299, f. 215 (Nathan to Birrell, 14 November 1915): Ms. Nathan 465, f. 150 (Nathan to Magill, 28 October 1915); f. 306 (Nathan to Robinson, 14 November 1915): for the British background to the 1915 Rent Act, see: D. Englander, *Landlord and Tenant in Urban Britain 1838–1918*, 1983, pp. 193–243.
26. BODLEIAN MSS, Ms. Nathan 460, ff. 206–07 (Robinson to Nathan, 19 November 1915); Ms. Nathan 465, f. 341 (Nathan to Robinson, 18 November 1915), f. 348 (Nathan to Fingall, 18 November 1915) and f. 358 (Nathan to Fingall, 19 November 1915).
27. PRO/T.1/11808/17813 (Robinson to Heath, 22 July 1915); PRO/T.1/11914/7107 no. 28987 (Headlam to MacFadyean, 12 August 1915; see also Robinson to Redmond, 10 August 1915).
28. PRO/T.1/11914/7107 no. 28987 (Redmond to Montagu, 2 September 1915).
29. NLI MSS, Redmond Papers, Ms. 15261 (Redmond to Mayor of Waterford, 18 September 1915).
30. PRO/T.1/11914/7107 no. 10641 (Robinson to Hewby, 8 December 1915).
31. RPDCD vol. 1, no. 35 (1916), pp. 337–52: see also: PRO/T.1/11914/7107 no. 10641: *Freemans Journal*, 13 November 1915, p. 4.
32. PRO/T.1/ 11914/7107 no. 10641 (Robinson to Hewby, 8 December 1915).
33. 76 HC DEB, 9 December 1915, cols 1697–1701 (Clancy): W. Field, *Housing Homily*, 1916: *Irish Builder*, 25 September 1915, p. 420.
34. F. S. L. Lyons, *Ireland since the Famine*, 1971, pp. 329–80: R. Foster, *Modern Ireland 1600–1972*, 1988, pp. 477–86: L. O'Broin, *Dublin Castle and the 1916 Rising*, 1971.
35. Quoted in: M. Hechter, *Internal Colonialism: The Celtic Fringe in British National Development, 1536–1966*, 1975, p. 290.
36. PP 1916 Cd.8279 xi, 'Report of Royal Commission on the Rebellion in Ireland', p. 7.
37. BODLEIAN MSS, Ms. Asquith 37, f. 10 (Hutchinson to Bonham-Carter, 25 May 1916): G. Dangerfield, *The Damnable Question*, 1976, pp. 246–47: J. V. O'Brien, *Dear Dirty Dublin: A City in Distress, 1899–1916*, 1982, p. 268.
38. *Architect*, 5 May 1916, p. 320: also *Irish Builder*, 13 May 1916, pp. 213–14; 24 June 1916, p. 273; 22 July 1916, p. 338.
39. Quoted in L. O'Broin, op. cit., p. 166.
40. E. O'Halpin, *The Decline of the Union: British Government in Ireland 1892–1920*, 1987, pp. 118–56: see also D. G. Boyce and C. Hazlehurst, 'The unknown chief secretary; H. E. Duke and Ireland, 1916–18', *Irish Historical Studies*, no. 79, March 1977.
41. *Freemans Journal*, 17 June 1916, p. 4; 6 July 1916, p. 4; 18 July 1916, p. 4; 25 July 1916, p. 2: *The Times*, 20 June 1916, p. 9, e: *Irish Builder*, 8 July 1916, p. 301: *Architects and Builders Journal*, 26 July 1916, p. 44.

42. BODLEIAN MSS, Ms. Asquith 37, f. 34 (Samuel to Asquith ?, 2 June 1916), ff. 37–38 (Chalmers to Bonham-Carter, 5 June 1916); Ms Asquith 44, f. 70 (deputation to Samuel, 5 June 1916): PRO/T.1/12038/8599 no. 20595 (Stevenson to Heath, 18 June 1916).
43. M. Miller, 'Raymond Unwin and the planning of Dublin', in M. J. Bannon (ed.), *The Emergence of Irish Planning 1880–1920*, 1985, pp. 282–96: M. Miller, *Raymond Unwin: Garden Cities and Town Planning*, 1992, pp. 153–54: S. Rothery, *Ireland and the New Architecture 1900–1940*, 1991, pp. 82–85: N. O'Flanagan, 'Dublin City in an age of war and revolution, 1914–24' (UCD MA Thesis, 1985), pp. 128–32: 88 HC DEB, 4 December 1916, cols 743–72 (Duke).
44. BODLEIAN MSS, Ms. Asquith 44, f. 72 (deputation to Samuel, 5 June 1916).
45. Ibid., f. 74.
46. PRO/T.1/12038/8599 no. 20595 (Heath to Hamilton, 21 June 1916).
47. BODLEIAN MSS, Dep. c. 714, f. 81 (Robinson to Duke, 21 August 1916).
48. *Freemans Journal*, 15 September 1916, p. 2.
49. *Freemans Journal*, 27 September 1916, p. 6: also 10 October 1916, p. 5.
50. BODLEIAN MSS, Dep. c. 714, ff. 154–60 (memorandum by O'Connor, 29 September 1916).
51. BODLEIAN MSS, Ms. Asquith 44, f. 32 (memo attached to letter from Wimborne to Asquith, 25 October 1916).
52. HLL Lloyd George Papers E/9/4/3 (memo by Duke, 26 September 1916): also 86 HC DEB, 26 October 1916, col. 1360 (Duke): *Freemans Journal*, 15 September 1916, p. 4.
53. *Freemans Journal*, 25 January 1917, p. 68.
54. *Freemans Journal*, 26 January 1917, p. 4.
55. PRO/T.1/12034/6607 no. 34332 (Higginson and Co. to Bradbury, 31 January 1917): PRO/T.1/12396/44750 no. 30212 (Guinness, Mahon and Co. to Dublin Corporation, 18 October 1916): SPO/CSO.RP (1920)/2381 no. 2824 (Dublin Corporation to Clancy, 17 January 1917; Magill to Clancy, 1 February 1917); no. 24572 (Redmond to Duke, 2 December 1916): RPDCD vol. 2, no. 103 (1917), pp. 172–74: *The Times*, 21 October 1916, p. 9, c.
56. *Freemans Journal*, 21 March 1917, p. 8: for the background to the unrest in Dublin, see: N. Flanagan, op. cit., pp. 14–16, 19–20, 48.
57. PRO/T.1/12396/44750 no. 13447 (JCD to Hamilton, 30 March 1917): also *Freemans Journal*, 31 March 1917, p. 4: Duke also obtained approval for a plan to build Ford's first European tractor plant near Cork, and to create a special fund (which was never used) to finance development schemes: PRO/CAB/23/1 (Cabinet Meeting, 14 February 1917, item 15): PRO/CAB/23/4 (Cabinet Meeting, 6 November 1917, item 9): E. O'Halpin, op. cit., pp. 151–54.
58. PRO/T.1/12396/44750 no. 13447 (Bonar Law to Duke, 3 April 1917): also HLL Lloyd George Papers F/30/2/15 (Hamilton to Davies, 3 April 1917).
59. *The Times*, 5 April 1917, p. 7, c: *Daily Express*, 6 April 1917.
60. PRO/T.1/12396/44750 no. 13347 (Robinson to Duke, 17 April 1917): SPO/CSO.RP (1920)/2381, no. 10763 (Treasury to Byrne, 3 May 1917).
61. M. Swenarton, op. cit., pp. 41–44, 48–66.
62. Ibid., pp. 35–38, 53–58.
63. *Freemans Journal*, 10 July 1915, p. 8: *Architect*, 12 September 1917, p. 122.

64. *Freemans Journal*, 10 October 1916, p. 2: also 9 June 1915, p. 8; 9 July 1915, p. 8; 23 September 1915, p. 6; 6 October 1915, p. 9; 2 January 1917, pp. 5–6; 31 July 1917, p. 3; 4 January 1918, p. 5.
65. PRO/T.1/11914/7107 no. 7107 (Dublin Tenants League to McKenna, 25 January 1916): PRO/T.1/12396/44750 no. 21000 (Dublin Chamber of Commerce to Treasury, 26 June 1917): *Irish Builder*, 29 September 1917, p. 485: N. Flanagan, op. cit., p. 82.
66. *Irish Builder*, 3 February 1917, pp. 51–52; 23 June 1917, pp. 310–13: *Freemans Journal*, 1 January 1917, p. 3; 4 January 1917, p. 2; 21 July 1917, pp. 362–67; 23 June 1917, p. 310.
67. PRO/T.1/11914/7107 no. 7107 (Robinson to Hamilton, 16 February 1916).
68. *Freemans Journal*, 2 November 1917, p. 4.
69. RPDCD vol. 2, no. 109 (1917), p. 287.
70. *Freemans Journal*, 15 September 1917, p. 6.
71. RPDCD vol. 3, no. 221 (1918), p. 412: see also p. 420.
72. M. Swenarton, op. cit., pp. 49–66.
73. *Freemans Journal*, 17 August 1918, p. 6.
74. *Architect*, 29 November 1918, p. 299.
75. As pointed out in: F. H. A. Aalen, 'The working class housing movement in Dublin, 1850–1920', in M. J. Bannon (ed.), *The Emergence of Irish Planning 1880–1920*, 1985, p. 176.
76. PRO/T.1/12396/44750 no. 24506 (Eyre to Robinson, 18 June 1917).
77. SPO/CSO.RP (1920)/2381, no. 16993 (Barlas to Byrne, 10 July 1917); no. 19550 (Treasury to Byrne, 8 August 1917).
78. *Builder*, 15 June 1917, p. 379: *Architect*, 25 January 1918, p. 56.
79. PRO/T.1/12396/44750 no. 18470 (note by 'C. B.', 11 May 1918).
80. PRO/T.1/12396/44750 no. 18470 (note by 'J. M.', 11 May 1918); no. 37382 (note by Gilbert, 31 January 1919).
81. P. B. Johnson, *Land Fit for Heroes: The Planning of British Reconstruction 1916–1919*, 1968, pp. 19–21, 36–67: M. Swenarton, op. cit., 1981, pp. 67–70: D. Hardy, 'War, planning and social change', *Planning Perspectives*, vol. 4, 1989, pp. 191–94.
82. PRO/T.1/12303/13599 no. 28612 (memo by 'G. N.', undated but probably November 1916).
83. M. Swenarton, op. cit., pp. 70–72.
84. *Freemans Journal*, 30 July 1917, pp. 2–3: *Architect*, 15 August 1917, p. 75.
85. *Freemans Journal*, 8 August 1917, p. 4.
86. *Freemans Journal*, 17 September 1917, p. 4; 19 November 1917, p. 4.
87. 96 HC DEB, 3 August 1917, col. 2504 (Duke): also 97 HC DEB, 16 August 1917, col. 1575 (Duke).
88. PRO/T.1/12303/13599 no. 26388 (Duke to Bonar Law, 11 August 1917).
89. PRO/T.1/12303/13599 no. 26388 (L. J. H. to Heath, 15 August 1917).
90. PRO/RECO.1/481 (Carter to Addison, 13 November 1917; Addison to Nash, 15 November 1917; Nash to Addison, 26 November 1917).
91. *Freemans Journal*, 24 August 1917, p. 3; 27 October 1917, p. 4.
92. SPO/CSO.RP (1920)/2381, no. 18530 (Brady to Duke, 13 July 1917): *Irish Builder*, 18 August 1917, p. 416.
93. SPO/CSO.RP (1920)/2381, no. 18350 (Robinson to Magill, 16 July 1917).

References (Chapter 5) 365

94. P. C. Cowan, *Report on Dublin Housing*, 1918: SPO/CSO.RP (1920)/2381, nos 11455 and 12343.
95. 96 HC DEB, 3 August 1917, col. 2504 (Duke): 97 HC DEB, 6 August 1917, col. 34 (Duke).
96. P. C. Cowan, op. cit., pp. 12–13.
97. Ibid., p. 7.
98. Ibid., p. 42.
99. BODLEIAN MSS, Ms. Eng. Lett. c. 213, f. 164 (Duke to Magill, 19 August 1918).
100. *Architect*, 27 December 1918, p. 350: there was more restrained praise in: *Builder*, 10 January 1919, pp. 53–54: *Freemans Journal*, 14 August 1918, p. 2.
101. 99 HC DEB, 23 November 1917, col. 1538–40 (Duke, Scanlan): 103 HC DEB, 14 February 1918, cols 244–46 (Duke): 104 HC DEB, 12 March 1918, cols 271–84 (Sheehan, Duke).
102. M. Swenarton, op. cit., pp. 72–77.
103. In early 1918, the Ministry of Reconstruction looked into the possibility of using the pre-war subsidy terms of the Irish Labourers Acts, but decided that this would be too costly to implement: PRO/RECO.1/485 (memo by Wallace on report by Gollancz, 7 January 1918; memo by Reiss to Carter, 7 January 1918).
104. PRO/CAB 24/44 GT. 3877: a similar vagueness by Addison on Irish housing needs can also be seen in: PRO/T.1/12303/13599 no. 1549 (memo by Addison, undated).
105. PRO/CAB 24/42 GT. 3682.
106. J. Turner, *Lloyd George's Secretariat*, 1980, p. 84.
107. HLL Lloyd George Papers F/63/1/7 (Adams to Lloyd George, 13 May 1917).
108. PP 1917/18 Cd.8573 xxxviii.
109. R. B. McDowell, *The Irish Convention 1917–18*, 1970, p. vii.
110. J. Turner, op. cit., p. 112.
111. BODLEIAN MSS, Dep. c. 717, f. 82 (memo by Duke, 19 February 1918).
112. J. Turner, op. cit., p. 85: also R. B. McDowell, op. cit., p. 147.
113. HLL, Lloyd George Papers F/66/5/11 (memo by Adams, undated).
114. PP 1918 Cd.9019 x, 'Report of the Proceedings of Irish Convention', p. 22.
115. R. B. McDowell, op. cit., p. 160.
116. Sir H. Plunkett, *The Irish Convention. Confidential Report to His Majesty the King*, 1918, p. 88.
117. HLL, Lloyd George Papers F/64/7/2 (Plunkett to Adams, 27 February 1918).
118. BODLEIAN MSS, Dep. c. 716, ff. 112–13 (Plunkett to Irish Convention, 9 March 1918).
119. D. Englander, op. cit., p. 199.
120. HLL, Lloyd George Papers F/65/3/16 (Vernon to Adams, 22 March 1918).
121. HLL, Lloyd George Papers F/65/3/17 (Vernon to Adams, 25 March 1918).
122. HLL, Lloyd George Papers F/65/3/19 (Vernon to Adams, 28 March 1918).
123. Sir H. Plunkett, op. cit., p. 119: PRO/RECO.1/602 ('Summary of the Report of the Housing Committee appointed by the Irish Convention', p. 136).
124. PP 1918 Cd.9019 x, 'Report of the Proceedings of Irish Convention', ff. 833–35.
125. Sir H. Plunkett, op. cit., pp. 88, 119.
126. BODLEIAN MSS, Dep. c. 716, f. 174 (Duke to Cabinet, 6 April 1918); 104 HC DEB, 11 April 1918, col. 1614 (Duke).

127. HLL, Lloyd George Papers F/65/3/20 (Vernon to Adams, 5 April 1918).
128. HLL, Lloyd George Papers F/67/2 (memo by Ramsay, 20 April 1918).
129. HLL, Lloyd George Papers F/67/2 (memo by Niemeyer, 22 April 1918).
130. HLL, Lloyd George Papers F/67/2 (Bradbury to Adams, 22 April 1918).
131. J. Turner, op. cit., pp. 112–17.
132. HLL, Lloyd George Papers F/67/2 (memo by Adams, 30 April 1918): PRO/CAB 27/69, C. I. 9.
133. The aim of the 1918 Housing Bill was simply to allow county councils to build if local authorities failed to, and to tempt authorities by extending the loan period and offering Treasury subsidy of 75 per cent of loan charges: the Castle Administration argued that the provisions were unnecessary in Ireland: 110 HC DEB, 28 October 1918, cols 1203–04 (Samuels).
134. E. O'Halpin, op. cit., pp. 157–79.
135. R. B. McDowell, op. cit., p. 191: R. Foster, op. cit., pp. 489–90.
136. 109 HC DEB, 7 August 1918, col. 1361 (Shortt): see also *Freemans Journal*, 30 October 1918, p. 3.
137. J. D. Clarkson, *Labour and Nationalism in Ireland*, 1925, pp. 325–434: R. Foster, op. cit., pp. 488–93: F. S. L. Lyons, op. cit., pp. 381–99: A. Mitchell, *Labour in Irish Politics 1890–1930*, 1974, pp. 67–103: E. Rumpf and A. C. Hepburn, *Nationalism and Socialism in Twentieth-Century Ireland*, 1977, pp. 19–25.
138. *Freemans Journal*, 25 November 1918, p. 7.
139. *Freemans Journal*, 9 December 1918, p. 2: also 21 March 1918, p. 4; 1 April 1918, p. 3; 2 April 1918, p. 3; 17 June 1918, pp. 3–4; 16 August 1918, p. 5; 9 October 1918, pp. 3–4; 22 November 1918, p. 4; 23 November 1918, p. 6; 5 December 1918, p. 4.
140. *Freemans Journal*, 23 November 1918, p. 6.
141. *Freemans Journal*, 2 December 1918, p. 6: also 22 November 1918, p. 4; 7 December 1918, p. 6.
142. *Freemans Journal*, 21 March 1918, p. 4: also 30 November 1918, p. 6.
143. *Northern Whig*, 15 July 1918, pp. 2, 3; 9 November 1918, p. 6; 16 November 1918, pp. 3–4; 27 November 1918, p. 4; 29 November 1918, p. 4; 4 December 1918, p. 2; 7 December 1918, p. 6; 12 December 1918, p. 6; 14 December 1918, p. 8: 108 HC DEB, 22 July 1918, col. 1457 (Carson); 109 HC DEB, 7 August 1918, col. 1360 (Carson): R. B. McDowell, op. cit., p. 192: H. Patterson, *Class Conflict and Sectarianism: The Protestant Working Class and the Belfast Labour Movement 1868–1920*, 1980, pp. 97–100, 124–30, 134–42: R. Wilson, 'Imperialism in crisis: the "Irish dimension" ', in M. Langan and B. Schwarz (eds), *Crises in the British State 1880–1930*, 1985, pp. 168–69.
144. *Freemans Journal*, 16 November 1918, pp. 5–6.
145. *Northern Whig*, 8 March 1918, p. 5; 20 January 1919, p. 4: *Irish Builder*, 30 March 1918, pp. 171–72.
146. *Irish Times*, 3 January 1919, p. 2; 26 February 1919, p. 4: *Northern Whig*, 24 January 1918, pp. 4, 6; 19 March 1918, p. 2; 2 October 1918, p. 4; 3 January 1919, p. 3: *Freemans Journal*, 27 September 1916, p. 6; 19 November 1917, pp. 3–4; 27 December 1917, p. 4; 30 November 1918, p. 6: *Irish Builder*, 16 February 1918, p. 94; 2 March 1918, p. 120.
147. *Irish Times*, 24 January 1919, p. 4: *Northern Whig*, 2 January 1919, p. 4; 7 January

1919, p. 4; 17 January 1919, p. 7; 18 January 1919, p. 3; 24 January 1919, pp. 3, 6; 3 March 1919, p. 2; 26 March 1919, pp. 4, 6; etc.: *Irish Builder*, 9 November 1918, p. 482; 14 December 1918, p. 534; 11 January 1919, p. 23; 8 March 1919, p. 105.
148. For the latter, see: *Irish Builder*, 19 January 1918, p. 40; 2 March 1918, p. 117; 12 October 1918, p. 381; 9 November 1918, p. 485; 11 January 1919, pp. 13–15; 5 April 1919, p. 150: *Architect*, 29 November 1918, p. 296: *Architects and Builders Journal*, 25 September 1918, p. 150.
149. HLL, Lloyd George Papers F/69/4 (Shortt to Lloyd George, 3 December 1918): for Addison's strong attack, see: PRO/RECO.1/529 (Addison to Shortt, 19 November 1918; Shortt to Addison, 20 November 1918).
150. HLL, Lloyd George Papers F/69/4 (Adams to Lloyd George, 12 December 1918).
151. HLL, Lloyd George Papers F/45/6/14 (Shortt to Lloyd George, 16 December 1918).
152. RPDCD vol. 1, no. 18 (1919), pp. 129–30.

6. THE POST-WAR HOUSING CAMPAIGN IN IRELAND (185–239)

1. PRO/CAB.23/15 (Cabinet Meeting, 5 August 1919).
2. PRO/T.1/12469/4046 no. 16386 (Chamberlain to Shortt, 20 December 1918).
3. M. Swenarton, *Homes Fit for Heroes: The Politics and Architecture of Early State Housing in Britain*, 1981, pp. 77–87.
4. S. Hall and B. Schwarz, 'State and society, 1880–1930', in M. Langan and B. Schwarz (eds), *Crises in the British State 1880–1930*, 1985, pp. 7–32: R. Wilson, 'Imperialism in crisis: the "Irish dimension" ', in M. Langan and B. Schwarz (eds), *Crises in the British State 1880–1930*, 1985, pp. 151–78.
5. PRO/CAB.23/9 (Cabinet Meeting, 3 March 1919, Item 2): see also: P. B. Johnson, *Land Fit for Heroes: The Planning of British Reconstruction 1916–1919*, 1968, pp. 345–51: P. Rowland, *Lloyd George*, 1975, p. 508.
6. M. Swenarton, op. cit., pp. 79–80.
7. D. Englander, *Landlord and Tenant in Urban Britain 1838–1918*, 1983, pp. 263–97.
8. PRO/CAB.24/72 (G. T. 6559; memo by Shortt entitled 'Housing of the working classes', 27 December 1918).
9. HLL, Lloyd George Papers F/46/1/2 (Macpherson to Lloyd George, 14 April 1919): C. Townshend, *The British Campaign in Ireland 1919–1921: The Development of Political and Military Policies*, 1975, p. 21: E. O'Halpin, *The Decline of the Union: British Government in Ireland 1892–1920*, 1987, pp. 180–81, 186–87.
10. PRO/T.1/12469/4046 no. 16386 (Jones to Macpherson, 21 January 1919; also Macpherson to Chamberlain, 27 January 1919): HLL Lloyd George Papers F/46/1/1 (Lloyd George to Macpherson, 14 February 1919).
11. PRO/T.1/12469/4046 no. 16386 (Macpherson to Chamberlain, 27 January 1919).
12. PRO/T.1/12469/4046 no. 16386 (Macpherson to Baldwin, 14 February 1919).
13. BODLEIAN MSS, Ms. Eng. Hist. C. 490, f. 89 (Sullivan to Macpherson, 22 February 1919).
14. *Irish Times*, 25 February 1919, p. 5.
15. *Irish Times*, 30 April 1919, p. 5: also 16 April 1919, p. 4.
16. 114 HC DEB, 3 April 1919, cols 1537–38 (Macpherson).
17. *Irish Times*, 25 February 1919, p. 4.

18. PRO/T.1/12469/4046 no. 16386 (Macpherson to Chamberlain, 19 February 1919): for Treasury opposition to British proposals, see: M. Swenarton, op. cit., pp. 80–81.
19. 117 HC DEB, 26 June 1919, cols 494–96 (Samuels).
20. PRO/T.1/12469/4046 no. 16386 (note by Bradbury, 13 February 1919; Chamberlain to Macpherson, 15 February 1919).
21. PRO/T.1/12469/4046 no. 16386 (Chamberlain to Macpherson, 15 February 1919).
22. PRO/T.1/12469/4046 no. 16386 (note by Niemeyer, undated but probably February 1919).
23. PRO/T.1/12469/4046 no. 16386 (note by Bradbury, 13 February 1919).
24. PRO/T.1/12469/4046 no. 16368 (Headlam to Niemeyer, 28 February 1919; also Macpherson to Chamberlain, 19 February 1919; Robinson to Macpherson, 4 March 1919).
25. PRO/T.1/12469/4046 no. 16386 (Robinson to Niemeyer, 21 March 1919; also Niemeyer to Robinson, 8 March 1919): PP 1920 Cd.578 xxi, 'Annual Report of the LGB for year ended 31 March 1919', f. 55.
26. PRO/T.1/12469/4046 no. 16386 (Niemeyer to Robinson, 13 March 1919).
27. PRO/T.1/12469/4046 no. 16386 (Niemeyer to Bradbury, 7 March 1919).
28. 113 HC DEB, 3 March 1919, cols 4–5 (Lloyd-Greene, Baldwin); 6 March 1919, col. 593 (Macpherson): 114 HC DEB, 3 April 1919, cols 1538–39 (Macpherson).
29. PRO/T.1/12469/4046 no. 16387 (Niemeyer to Headlam, 17 April 1919).
30. PRO/T.1/12469/4046 no. 16386 (note by Niemeyer, undated but probably February 1919).
31. PRO/T.1/12469/4046 no. 16386 (note by Niemeyer, 22 February 1919).
32. 114 HC DEB, 3 April 1919, cols 1539–40 (Macpherson); *Irish Times*, 25 February 1919, pp. 5–6.
33. PRO/T.1/12469/4046 no. 16387 (Stevenson to Niemeyer, 10 April 1919).
34. PRO/T.1/12469/4046 no. 16386 (Robinson to Macpherson, 4 March 1919; also Stephenson to Niemeyer, 24 February 1919).
35. PRO/T.1/12469/4046 no. 16386 (Headlam to Niemeyer, 4 March 1919).
36. PRO/T.1/12469/4046 no. 16386 (Niemeyer to Bradbury, 7 March 1919).
37. PRO/T.1/12469/4046 no. 16386 (memo by Chamberlain, 13 February 1919: Macpherson to Chamberlain, 19 February 1919; Robinson to Macpherson, 4 March 1919: Niemeyer to Robinson, 8 March 1919).
38. 112 HC DEB, 13 February 1919, col. 264 (Devlin, Law, Guinness); 17 February 1919, cols 524–25 (O'Neill, Redmond, Devlin, Samuels, Law); 26 February 1919, col. 1767 (Devlin, Samuels).
39. *Irish Times*, 12 February 1919, p. 4: also 10 March 1919, p. 6; 4 April 1919, p. 4; 10 April 1919, p. 4; 19 April 1919, p. 6: *The Statist*, 19 October 1918, p. 595: *Irish Builder*, 11 January 1919, p. 15.
40. *Irish Times*, 30 January 1919, p. 6.
41. *Northern Whig*, 26 March 1919, p. 4: also 14 May 1919, p. 4.
42. *Northern Whig*, 20 March 1919, p. 6.
43. 112 HC DEB, 26 February 1919, col. 1850 (Carson): also 114 HC DEB, 3 April 1919, col. 1482 (Carson): H. Patterson, *Class Conflict and Sectarianism: The Protestant Working Class and the Belfast Labour Movement 1868–1920*, 1980, pp. 120–21.

References (Chapter 6)   369

44. 115 HC DEB, 13 May 1919, col. 1489 (O'Neill): also col. 1500 (Dixon).
45. PP 1920 Cd.578 xxi, 'Annual Report of the ILGB for year ended 31 March 1919', f. 66: *Northern Whig*, 26 February 1919, p. 4.
46. 114 HC DEB, 27 March 1919, col. 573 (Carson, Law); 3 April 1919, col. 1482 (Carson).
47. PRO/T.1/12469/4046 no. 4046 (Headlam to Niemeyer, 7 July 1919).
48. BODLEIAN MSS, Ms. Eng. Hist. C. 1104, f. 127 (manifesto of Irish Centre Party, 1919): *Irish Times*, 3 February 1919, p. 4; 10 March 1919, p. 7; 17 March 1919, p. 5; 10 April 1919, p. 4; 28 August 1919, pp. 6–8: *Irish Builder*, 3 May 1919, pp. 215–16; 13 September 1919, p. 378.
49. 115 HC DEB, 13 May 1919, col. 1488 (Devlin).
50. F. S. L. Lyons, *Ireland since the Famine*, 1971, pp. 400–11: R. F. Foster, *Modern Ireland 1600–1972*, 1988, pp. 495–97.
51. Dáil Éireann, *Minutes of Proceedings*, pp. 21–23, quoted in F. S. L. Lyons, op. cit., p. 402.
52. E. Rumpf and A. C. Hepburn, *Nationalism and Socialism in Twentieth Century Ireland*, 1977, pp. 24–25: F. S. L. Lyons, op. cit., p. 403: A. Mitchell, *Labour in Irish Politics 1890–1930*, 1974, pp. 105–10: B. Chubb, *The Government and Politics of Ireland*, 1970/82, pp. 43–44: P. Lynch, 'The social revolution that never was', in T. D. Williams (ed.), *The Irish Struggle 1916–1926*, 1966, pp. 46–49.
53. *The Times*, 27 February 1919, p. 5, d.
54. SPO/DE/2/243 (Report of Activities of Local Government Committee, Dáil Éireann, unsigned and undated).
55. 115 HC DEB, 13 May 1919, cols 1473 (Macpherson), 1513 (Guinness): 118 HC DEB, 1 August 1919, cols 2479–91 (Henry, MacVeagh, Harbison, Dockrell): PRO/T.1/12286/8353 (note by Niemeyer, 7 March 1919; note by 'F. M. W.', 20 March 1919; Heath to Under Secretary, 25 March 1919): PP 1921 Cd.1432 xiv, '48th Annual Report of the ILGB for the year ending 31 March 1920', ff. 857–61: in Chapter 8 it will be seen that there was some housing built in Ulster under the Labourers Acts in the 1920s, but the measure lay unused in the Irish Free State until revived in 1936 by Fianna Fáil.
56. 115 HC DEB, 13 May 1919, col. 1473 (Macpherson): also 121 HC DEB, 21 November 1919, col. 1394 (Macpherson).
57. 114 HC DEB, 27 March 1919 col. 573 (Carson, Law); 3 April 1919 cols 1482 (Carson), 1538–39 (Macpherson): PP 1921 Cd.1432 xiv, 'Annual Report of the ILGB for year ended 31 March 1920', f. 837.
58. PRO/T.1/12469/4046 no. 4046 (Greer to Niemeyer, 14 July 1919; also Niemeyer to Bradbury, June 1919): *Irish Times*, 2 May 1919, p. 5; 14 May 1919, p. 4.
59. PRO/T.1/12469/4046 no. 4046 (Headlam to Niemeyer, 28 August 1919).
60. 115 HC DEB, 13 May 1919, cols 1500 (Dixon), 1508 (Redmond): also cols 1478–1518 (Carson, Devlin, et seq.).
61. PP 1919 Cd.181 xli. 685, 'Estimate of Probable Expenditure under the Housing of the Working Classes (Ireland) Bill'.
62. M. Swenarton, op. cit., p. 82.
63. 117 HC DEB, 26 June 1919, cols 500–01 (Banbury, Thompson, Craig).
64. PRO/T.1/12469/4046 no. 4046 (deputation to Macpherson, 2 July 1919): *Northern Whig*, 3 July 1919, p. 5.

65. PRO/T.1/12469/4046 no. 4046 (Greer to Niemeyer, 14 July 1919; Niemeyer to Bradbury, 14 July 1919).
66. PRO/T.1/12469/4046 no. 4046 (Niemeyer to Watt, 4 July 1919; also Watt to Niemeyer, 3 July 1919; note by Niemeyer, 3 July 1919; note by Bradbury, 3 July 1919; note by Chamberlain, 3 July 1919).
67. 117 HC DEB, 8 July 1919, cols 1771 (Williams), 1776 (Henry): 118 HC DEB, 18 July 1919, col. 847 (Henry).
68. 115 HC DEB, 13 May 1919, cols 1479–80 (Carson), 1485–86 (Devlin).
69. *Northern Whig*, 18 July 1919, p. 4; 22 August 1919, p. 4; 1 September 1919, p. 2; 12 September 1919, p. 4.
70. PRO/T.1/12469/4046 no. 4046 (Headlam to Niemeyer, 28 August 1919): *Irish Times*, 2 August 1919, p. 4; 28 August 1919, p. 6; 11 September 1919, p. 5.
71. PRO/T.1/12469/4046 no. 4046 (Niemeyer to Robinson, 8 September 1919): *Irish Times*, 2 August 1919, p. 6.
72. PRO/T.1/12469/4046 no. 4046 (Headlam to Niemeyer, 5 September 1919).
73. *Irish Times*, 8 August 1919, p. 6.
74. A. Mitchell, op. cit., p. 122.
75. SPO/DE/2/243 (Report of Activities of Local Government Committee, Dáil Éireann, unsigned and undated).
76. Ibid.
77. SPO/DE/2/243 (Scheme for Housing Conferences, unsigned and undated).
78. F. S. L. Lyons, op. cit., p. 423.
79. *Irish Times*, 30 August 1919, p. 6.
80. *Irish Times*, 2 September 1919, pp. 4–6; 3 September 1919, p. 4; 4 September 1919, p. 6; 5 September 1919, p. 6; 10 September 1919, p. 7; 12 September 1919, p. 5; 13 September 1919, p. 6; 7 October 1919, p. 3 : *Northern Whig*, 6 October 1919, p. 8: *Irish Builder*, 25 October 1919, pp. 473, 482.
81. PRO/T.1/12469/4046 no. 4046 (Headlam to Niemeyer, 28 August 1919).
82. PRO/T.1/12469/4046 no. 4046 (Niemeyer to Headlam, 2 September 1919).
83. *Irish Times*, 13 September 1919, p. 6; 7 July 1920, p. 5; 8 July 1920, p. 6; 18 November 1920, p. 5.
84. SPO/DE/2/243 (Report on Housing, unsigned but probably by Cosgrave, undated).
85. PP 1921 Cd.1432 xiv, 'Annual Report of the ILGB for year ended 31 March 1920', ff. 834–57.
86. SPO/CSO.RP (1921–22)/2503/8 (memo by ILGB Housing Committee, 16 July 1921).
87. M. Swenarton, op. cit., pp. 112–21.
88. PRO/T.1/12396/44750 no. 2407 (note by 'J. S.', 19 January 1920): PRO/T.1/12416/50108 no. 35694 (Devlin to Under Secretary, 9 August 1919; Taylor to Treasury, 14 August 1919): PRO/T.1/12434/52947 no. 50730 (interim report of the Treasury Committee on Housing Finance, 27 November 1919).
89. PRO/T.1/12396/44750 no. 2407 (note by 'A. P. J.', 19 January 1920).
90. This *ad hoc* measure aimed to help municipal housing by authorising the issue of 'Local Housing Bonds' to raise capital; allowing authorities to prohibit so-called 'luxury building' in their district; and allowing them to draw up 'agreed-price' contracts with local Builders' Federations in order to short-circuit the tendering

system: in addition, the subsidy to public utility societies was increased to 50 per cent of the loan charge for the first seven years: M. Swenarton, op. cit., pp. 123–24.
91. 121 HC DEB, 21 November 1919, cols 1390–93 (Moles).
92. 121 HC DEB, 21 November 1919, cols 1394–97 (Macpherson).
93. PRO/T.172/1044 (Macpherson to Chamberlain, 28 November 1919; also Robinson to Macpherson, 26 November 1919).
94. PRO/T.172/1044 (Niemeyer to Barstow, 1 December 1919; also Treasury to Watt, 3 December 1921): PRO/T.1172/1044 (Treasury note to Barstow, 2 December 1919).
95. PRO/T.1/12429/52124 no. 52124 (minutes of Cabinet Housing Committee meeting, 3 December 1919).
96. PRO/T.1/12429/52124 no. 52124 (draft clauses for Housing [Additional Powers] Act, section 2, subsection 1, undated).
97. SPO/CSO.RP (1921–22)/2503/2 (Robinson to Under Secretary, 23 January 1920; Barstow to Under Secretary, 1 March 1920).
98. SPO/CSO.RP (1921–22)/2503/2 (Codling to all Irish local authorities, 5 May 1920; also Robinson to Under Secretary, 5 July 1920).
99. M. Swenarton, op. cit., p. 136.
100. PRO/T.1/12286/8353 (O'Sullivan to Under Secretary, 18 February 1919).
101. PRO/T.1/12469/4046 no. 16386 (Headlam to Niemeyer, 4 March 1919; Niemeyer to Robinson, 8 March 1919).
102. PRO/T.1/12308/15462 (note by MacFadyean, 15 April 1919): 115 HC DEB, 13 May 1919, cols 1478–79 (Carson), 1484–86 (Devlin), 1513–14 (Guinness): *Irish Times*, 23 June 1919, p. 4.
103. M. Swenarton, op. cit., pp. 110, 136–41.
104. 116 HC DEB, 29 May 1919, col. 1391 (Barrie).
105. SPO/CSO.RP (1921–22)/3065/7 (Robinson to Anderson, 3 December 1920).
106. SPO/CSO.RP (1921–22)/3065/7 (agendas for Housing Committee meetings on 11 August/14 September/5 October/19 October/9 November 1920; Barlas to Under Secretary, 18 January 1921).
107. *Irish Builder*, 8 March 1919, p. 111: also 31 May 1919, p. 261; 5 May 1923, p. 317; 19 May 1923, pp. 373–74: C. O'Connor and J. O'Regan (Architectural Association of Ireland), *Public Works: The Architecture of the Office of Public Works 1831–1987*, 1987, pp. 31–32.
108. PP 1921 Cd.1432 xiv, 'Annual Report of the ILGB for the year ended 31 March 1920', f. 874.
109. M. Swenarton, op. cit., pp. 113–17.
110. PRO/T.1/12286/9306 no. 9306 (note by Vernon, March 1919): SPO/CPO. RP (1920)/19707 no. 4245 (Codling to Ministry of Munitions, 3 December 1919); no. 7705 (memo by Robinson, 23 March 1920); no. 10539 (Robinson to Under Secretary, 21 April 1920); no. 11238 (Treasury to Under Secretary, 27 April 1920); no. 13090 (note by Duggan to Under Secretary, 15 May 1920); no. 13863 (Macpherson to Inverforth, 13 May 1919; Inverforth to Macpherson, 15 May 1919.
111. M. Swenarton, op. cit., pp. 85–87.
112. *Irish Times*, 3 January 1919, p. 2.

113. *Irish Builder*, 11 January 1919, p. 15: also 25 January 1919, pp. 35–36; 10 April 1920, p. 218; 26 February 1921, p. 118.
114. *Irish Times*, 25 February 1919, p. 5.
115. 115 HC DEB, 13 May 1919, col. 1488 (Devlin).
116. 115 HC DEB, 13 May 1919, col. 1480 (Carson).
117. 115 HC DEB, 13 May 1919, cols 1492–93 (O'Neill).
118. 115 HC DEB, 13 May 1919, col. 1518 (Harbison): also cols 1487 (Devlin), 1492 (O'Neill).
119. 114 HC DEB, 3 April 1919, col. 1540 (Macpherson): also *Journal of the RIAI, 1920*, note on AGM, p. 15.
120. 115 HC DEB, 13 May 1919, col. 1514 (Guinness): also cols 1508–09 (Redmond, Dockrell).
121. Irish Local Government Board, *Housing of the Working Classes in Ireland*, 1919, p. 3.
122. *Journal of the RIAI, 1919*, 'Report of Council, 1918', p. 4: *Irish Builder*, 19 April 1919, p. 182; 11 October 1919, p. 450.
123. *Irish Builder*, 3 January 1920, p. 15: also 13 March 1920, p. 142: *Journal of the RIAI, 1921*, 'Report of Council, 1920', p. 2.
124. *Irish Builder*, 26 February 1921, p. 121.
125. *Journal of the RIAI, 1920*, 'Report of Council, 1919', p. 8.
126. *Journal of the RIAI, 1920*, note on Annual Dinner: *Irish Builder*, 28 February 1920, pp. 117–18.
127. For this tendency in Britain, see: M. Swenarton, op. cit., pp. 139–41.
128. PRO/T.1/12307/15191 no. 48348 (Barlas to Under Secretary, 10 December 1918): PRO/T.1/12469/4046 no. 16386 (note by Niemeyer, 24 March 1919; note by MacFadyean, 25 March 1919): *Journal of the RIAI, 1919*, note on Annual Dinner.
129. PRO/T.1/12307/15191 no. 48348 (Heath to Under Secretary, 9 January 1919): 114 HC DEB, 3 April 1919, col. 1540 (Macpherson).
130. PP 1920 Cd.578 xxi, 'Annual Report of the ILGB for year ended 31 March 1919', f. 55: see also: *Irish Times*, 28 February 1919, p. 5; 1 March 1919, p. 8: *Irish Builder*, 8 March 1919, p. 111.
131. *Journal of the RIAI, 1920*, 'Report of Council, 1919', p. 6.
132. PRO/T.1/12307/15191 no. 15191 (draft conditions for Irish Housing Competition, March 1919).
133. Ibid.
134. *Housing Journal*, November 1917, pp. 4–8; February/March 1918, pp. 1–8; May 1918, pp. 1–8.
135. *Journal of the RIAI, 1920*, 'Report of Council, 1919', p. 6.
136. Irish Local Government Board, op. cit., p. 10.
137. Ibid., plates xxxvii and xxxviii.
138. For the English LGB manual, see: M. Swenarton, op. cit., pp. 110–11, 141–47.
139. PRO/T.1/12469/4046 no. 4046 (ILGB Circular, 5 May 1919).
140. Ibid.
141. Irish Local Government Board, op. cit., plates xxxiii to xxxvi.
142. Ibid., p. 7.
143. Ibid., p. 4.
144. *Irish Builder*, 31 May 1919, p. 275.

145. *Irish Builder*, 14 February 1920, p. 95: see also 16 December 1922, p. 865.
146. RPDCD vol. 3, no. 210 (1919), p. 51: RPDCD vol. 2, no. 110 (1920), p. 396.
147. *Irish Builder*, 3 July 1920, p. 438.
148. *Northern Whig*, 31 October 1919, p. 8; 2 April 1920, p. 6; 13 May 1920, p, 6; 1 November 1920, p. 4; 2 November 1920, p. 3; 2 December 1920, p. 6; 12 March 1921, p. 6: H. A. Law, 'Irish housing in town and country', *Manchester Guardian Commercial*, 26 July 1923 ('Section 3: European Reconstruction Series: Ireland'), p. 39.
149. *Irish Times*, 11 September 1919, p. 5.
150. *Northern Whig*, 13 May 1920, p. 6: also 31 October 1919, pp. 4, 8; 4 November 1919, p. 6; 13 November 1919, pp. 4, 5; 26 November 1919, p. 4; 2 December 1919, p. 7; 16 December 1919, p. 5; 13 January 1920, p. 7; 2 March 1920, p. 6; 14 May 1920, p. 6; 15 May 1920, p. 6; 18 May 1920, pp. 5, 6; 12 March 1921, pp. 4, 6.
151. *Northern Whig*, 14 May 1920, p. 6; 15 May 1920, p. 6: see also: *Irish Times*, 23 October 1919, p. 6.
152. 121 HC DEB, 21 November 1919, col. 1391 (Moles).
153. In Britain the new type had L-shaped layouts and asymmetrical roofs: M. Swenarton, op. cit., pp. 157–60.
154. *Irish Times*, 25 January 1921, p. 4; 3 February 1921, p. 4; 12 March 1921, p. 8: *Irish Builder*, 6 September 1919, p. 354; 5 June 1920, p. 396; 19 June 1920, p. 418; 29 January 1921, p. 74; 26 March 1921, p. 198; 16 April 1921, p. 271.
155. *Irish Builder*, 18 December 1920, p. 774: also 6 December 1919, p. 546; 1 January 1921, p. 5; 12 February 1921, p. 105; 12 August 1922, pp. 349–350: 127 HC DEB, 31 March 1920, col. 1236 (Devlin, Macpherson).
156. RPDCD vol. 2, no. 110 (1920), p. 422: a further ILGB circular on 12 November 1919 set out the conditions and fees for employing an architect or other qualified person: Dublin Corporation Archives, UDC/2/C/39 (ILGB Circular, 12 November 1919).
157. *The Times*, 4 November 1919, p. 39, d.
158. 125 HC DEB, 19 February 1920, cols 1015–16 (Lynn, Macpherson): also 126 HC DEB, 11 March 1920, col. 1502 (Macpherson): for British progress, see: M. Swenarton, op. cit., p. 122.
159. PP 1921 Cd.1432 xiv, 'Annual Report of the ILGB for year ended 31 March 1920', f. 836: *Irish Builder*, 27 March 1920, p. 173.
160. F. S. L. Lyons, op. cit., p. 407: C. Townshend, op. cit., pp. 67–68.
161. *Irish Bulletin*, 31 March 1920, p. 2.
162. J. McColgan, *British Policy and the Irish Administration, 1920–22*, 1983. pp. 69–70.
163. PRO/T.1/12493/9332 no. 9332 (Robinson to Under Secretary, 13 February 1920).
164. PRO/T.1/12493/9332 no. 9332 (note by Gilbert, 16 April 1920).
165. PRO/T.1/12493/9332 no. 9332 (Gilbert to Strohmenger, 13 March 1920; Strohmenger to Gilbert, 29 March 1920).
166. F. S. L. Lyons, op. cit., pp. 413–14: J. McColgan, op. cit., pp. 3–4: E. O'Halpin, op. cit., pp. 193–94.
167. PRO/CAB.23/38 (Cabinet Meeting, 13 October 1920).
168. J. McColgan, op. cit., pp. 36–49.
169. PRO/CAB.23/18 (Cabinet Meeting, 3 December 1919, item 2).

374 *John Bull's Other Homes*

170. PRO/CAB.27/69 (C. I. 11, draft 'B' of Government of Ireland Bill, 16 October 1919; C. I. 14, draft 'C' of Government of Ireland Bill, 21 October 1921).
171. PRO/CAB.27/69 (C. I. 35, report of Sub-Committee on Irish Finance of Cabinet Committee on Ireland, 22 November 1919): for Chamberlain's altered views on the British campaign, see: M. Swenarton, op. cit., p. 130.
172. *Irish Times*, 29 May 1920, p. 8.
173. PRO/CAB.24/94 (C. P. 201, memo by Chamberlain to Cabinet, 26 November 1919): 127 HC DEB, 29 March 1920, col. 1037 (Worthington-Evans): *Irish Times*, 29 May 1920, p. 8.
174. PRO/CAB.27/69 (C. I. 19, note on drafts 'A' and 'B' of Government of Ireland Bill, 28 October 1919); (C. I. 37, note by Adams on Government of Ireland Bill, 26 November 1919): PRO/CAB.27/68 (C. P. 247, 4th report of Cabinet Committee on Ireland, 2 December 1919).
175. Quoted in J. McColgan, op. cit., p. 5: see also: C. Townshend, op. cit., pp. 73–83: E. O'Halpin, op. cit., pp. 201–03, 207–13.
176. J. McColgan, op. cit., p. 12.
177. Ibid., p. 31: R. F. Foster, op. cit., pp. 503–04.
178. *Irish Builder*, 22 May 1920, p. 361.
179. PRO/CAB.23/37 (Cabinet Meeting, 31 May 1920).
180. SPO/DE/2/243 (O'Higgins, Ministry of Local Government to Dáil Éireann, 19 June 1920): see also: D. Fitzpatrick, *Politics and Irish Life 1913–1921: Provincial Experience of War and Revolution*, 1977, pp. 187–88.
181. H. Robinson, *Memories: Wise and Otherwise*, 1923, pp. 307–08: D. Fitzpatrick, op. cit., pp. 187–88.
182. SPO/DE/2/243 (decree by Dáil Éireann, 12 August 1920).
183. BODLEIAN MSS, Ms. Eng. Hist. C. 1104, f. 196 (Kelly to Headlam, 13 October 1920).
184. SPO/DE/2/475 (Cosgrave to Lynn, 21 August 1921).
185. SPO/DE/2/45 (General Secretariat, Dáil Éireann to Acting Town Clerk, Nenagh UDC, 12 July 1920).
186. Quoted in *Irish Builder*, 31 July 1920, p. 500.
187. *Irish Builder*, 25 September 1920, p. 614: also *Irish Times*, 15 September 1920, p. 6; 16 September 1920, p. 6.
188. SPO/DE/2/516 (Cosgrave to Minister of Finance, Dáil Éireann, 17 August 1920; plus various other items).
189. *Irish Times*, 17 September 1920, pp. 5–6.
190. SPO/CSO.RP (1921–22)/2503 (Robinson to Greenwood, 16 July 1920; also memo by Housing Committee to Robinson, July 1920).
191. SPO/CSO.RP (1921–22)/2503 (Anderson to Duggan, 4 November 1920).
192. M. Swenarton, op. cit., pp. 129–35, 157–61.
193. 133 HC DEB, 28 October 1920, col. 1985 (Greenwood): SPO/CSO.RP (1921–22)/2503 (Duggan to Anderson, 3 November 1920).
194. SPO/CSO.RP (1921–22)/2503 (Duggan to Anderson, 3 November 1920; memo by Cowan to Robinson, 17 November 1920): PRO/T.161/94/S.7136 (Duggan to Assistant Secretary, Irish Treasury, 1 December 1920).
195. PRO/T.161/94/S.7136 (Anderson to Under Secretary, Chief Secretary's Office, 1 January 1921).

References (Chapter 6)   375

196. PRO/T.161/94/S.7136 (Waterfield to Under Secretary, Chief Secretary's Office, 27 January 1921).
197. PRO/T.161/94/S.7136 (memo by Cowan, 11 February 1921).
198. PRO/T.158/3 (Anderson to Robinson, 18 May 1921): PRO/T.161/94/S.7136 (Codling to Under Secretary, Chief Secretary's Office, 29 June 1921).
199. SPO/CSO.RP (1920)/19707 no. 19707 (Duggan to Assistant Secretary, Irish Treasury, 16 November 1920; Irish Treasury to Under Secretary, 1 December 1920; Barlas to Under Secretary, 17 December 1920; Duggan to Assistant Secretary, Irish Treasury, 23 December 1920; Irish Treasury to Under Secretary, 30 December 1920).
200. SPO/CSO.RP (1921–22)/2503/2 (Robinson to Under Secretary, 5 July 1920; Anderson to Under Secretary, 9 August 1920; Robinson to Under Secretary, 12 August 1920; memo by Cowan, 28 September 1920; Waterfield to Under Secretary, 19 January 1921: Robinson to Under Secretary, 19 May 1921): 130 HC DEB, 9 June 1920, col. 429 (McNeill, Henry); 21 June 1920, col. 1780 (McNeill, Henry).
201. 140 HC DEB, 4 April 1921, cols 16–17 (Henry).
202. 141 HC DEB, 28 April 1921, col. 445 (Greenwood).
203. SPO/CSO.RP (1921–22)/2503/8 (Robinson to Anderson, 16 July 1921): this was borne out by Dundalk UDC, which appears to have abandoned its housing plans because of Dáil Éireann's ruling on non-cooperation with the ILGB: *Irish Builder*, 9 October 1920, p. 645.
204. 140 HC DEB, 14 April 1921, col. 1274–75 (Henry): PRO/T.158/4 (Waterfield to Irish Board of Works, 21 July 1921): NLI MSS, Joseph Brennan Papers, Ms. 26312 (memo by Hurson for Committee of Inquiry into Banking, Currency and Credit, 25 February 1935): *Irish Builder*, 14 January 1922, p. 5; 18 November 1922, p. 777.
205. *Irish Times*, 16 September 1920, p. 4.
206. Examples of Ulster authorities which had loans approved were Amagh UDC, for £10 500; Portadown UDC for £70 000; and Tanderagee UDC, for £7700: PRO/T.158/3 (Waterfield to Irish Board of Works, 3 May 1921; Waterfield to Irish Board of Works, 3 May 1921): PRO/T.192/28 (Irish Board of Works to Irish Treasury, 19 October 1920; Waterfield to Irish Board of Works, 27 October 1920): PRO/T.192/48 (Irish Board of Works to Treasury, 15 April 1921; Waterfield to Irish Board of Works, 3 May 1921).
207. *Irish Builder*, 18 November 1922, p. 777.
208. *Northern Whig*, 12 March 1921, p. 6; 2 September 1921: *Irish Times*, 3 February 1921, p. 4; 12 March 1921, pp. 4, 8; 19 November 1921, p. 6: *Irish Builder*, 23 October 1920, pp. 665–67.
209. *Irish Times*, 19 November 1921, p. 6.
210. M. Swenarton, op. cit., pp. 122–29.
211. *Irish Times*, 8 July 1920, p. 8: *Irish Builder*, 17 July 1920, pp. 462–69; 21 May 1921, p. 354; 22 October 1921, p. 681: for contrary developments in Britain, see: M. Swenarton, op. cit., pp. 105–08.
212. *Irish Times*, 9 April 1920, p. 4; 15 January 1921, p. 5; 27 January 1921, p. 8; 30 June 1921, p. 2; 29 October 1921, pp. 6, 8; 1 December 1921, p. 6; 19 June 1924,

p. 4; 25 September 1924, p. 3; 30 September 1924, p. 6; 10 October 1924, p. 4; et seq.: *Irish Builder*, 17 April 1919, p. 273; 3 July 1920, p. 438; 2 July 1921, p. 449.

213. *Irish Times*, 3 April 1920, p. 4: *Northern Whig*, 2 April 1920, p. 6; 7 May 1920, p. 5; 13 May 1920, p. 6: H. Patterson, op. cit., p. 121: for the use of direct labour in Britain, see: M. Swenarton, op. cit., p. 127.

214. *Irish Times*, 2 August 1921, p. 3: see also 16 March 1920, p. 4; 17 March 1921, p. 3; 2 April 1924, p. 3; 23 April 1920, p. 4; 11 June 1920, p. 4; 5 August 1921, pp. 5–6; 22 September 1921, p. 2; 17 December 1921, p. 8: *Irish Builder*, 13 August 1921, p. 545; 19 November 1921, p. 749: C. Lincoln, 'Working class housing in Dublin, 1914–1939' (UCD MA Thesis 1979), pp. 38–42: there were also smaller guilds in Cork and Waterford: E. O'Connor, *Syndicalism in Ireland 1917–1923*, 1988, pp. 46–51: for guilds in Britain, see: M. Swenarton, *Artisans and Architects: The Ruskinian Tradition in Architectural Thought*, 1989, pp. 167–88.

215. F. S. L. Lyons, op. cit., pp. 423–38: R. F. Foster, op. cit., pp. 503–04.

216. M. Swenarton, op. cit. (1981), pp. 129–35, 160–61.

217. Ibid., pp. 130–32.

218. M. Daunton, *House and Home in the Victorian City*, 1983, pp. 297–98.

219. SPO/CSO.RP (1921–22)/2503/8 (memo by ILGB Housing Committee entitled 'The Government's housing policy in its relation to Ireland', 16 July 1921).

220. SPO/CSO.RP (1921–22)/2503/8 (ILGB Housing Committee to Robinson, 20 October 1921; also Robinson to Anderson, 16 July 1921; unsigned memo by Robinson to Greenwood, undated but probably October 1921).

221. SPO/CSO.RP (1921–22)/2503/8 (Anderson to Greenwood, 16 July 1921).

222. *Northern Whig*, 2 September 1921, pp. 4, 6.

223. SPO/CSO.RP (1921–22)/2503/8 (ILGB Housing Committee to Robinson, 6 September 1921; unsigned memo by Anderson, undated but probably 25 October 1921); 2503 (Codling to Under Secretary, 19 November 1921; Waterfield to Under Secretary, 9 January 1922): see also: *Irish Builder*, 18 November 1922, p. 777.

224. SPO/CSO.RP (1921–22)/2503/2 (ILGB circular to all Irish urban local authorities, 29 July 1921); 2503/8 (memo by ILGB Housing Committee, 16 July 1921; Robinson to Anderson, 16 July 1921; Anderson to Greenwood, 16 July 1921; ILGB Housing Committee to Robinson, 6 September 1921; Robinson to Greenwood, undated but probably October 1921; unsigned memo by Anderson, undated but probably 25 October 1921).

225. *Irish Times*, 20 October 1921, p. 3.

226. PRO/T.158/6 (Waterfield to Under Secretary, 22 December 1921; also Waterfield to Under Secretary, 30 November 1921; Waterfield to Robinson, 7 December 1921; Waterfield to Robinson, 16 December 1921; Waterfield to Robinson, 22 December 1921; Waterfield to Watt, NI Ministry of Home Affairs, 9 January 1922): PRO/T.158/5 (Waterfield to Johnson, 20 September 1921).

227. SPO/CSO.RP (1921–22)/3065/7 (Barlas to Under Secretary, 18 January 1922).

228. SPO/CSO.RP (1921–22)/2503/8 (unsigned memo by Anderson with note by Greenwood, 18 November 1921; Hemming to Duggan, 21 November 1921): *Northern Whig*, 2 November 1921, p. 6; 18 November 1921, p. 7; 9 December 1921, p. 6; 23 March 1922, pp. 5–6; 4 April 1922, p. 7; 2 May 1922, p. 9; 10 May 1922, p. 6.

7. POST-WAR HOUSING FOR IRISH EX-SERVICEMEN (240–271)

1. PRO/T.158/9 (Waterfield to Cuthbertson, 30 August 1922).
2. F. H. A. Aalen, 'Homes for Irish heroes: housing under the Irish Land (Provision for Soldiers and Sailors) Act 1919, and the Irish Sailors' and Soldiers' Land Trust', *Town Planning Review*, vol. 59, no. 3, 1988, pp. 305–23: for the campaign in Britain, see: P. B. Johnson, *Land Fit for Heroes: The Planning of British Reconstruction 1916–1919*, 1968, pp. 347–51: L. Leneman, *Fit for Heroes?: Land Settlement in Scotland after World War 1*, 1989.
3. E. O'Halpin, *The Decline of the Union: British Government in Ireland 1892–1920*, 1987, pp. 157–79: C. Townshend, *The British Campaign in Ireland 1919–1921: The Development of Political and Military Policies*, 1975: F. S. L. Lyons, *Ireland since the Famine*, 1971, pp. 395–96.
4. HLL Lloyd George Papers F/48/6/13 (French to Lloyd George, 30 May 1918): IWM, French Papers, 75/46/13 (French to Long, 28 May 1918; Long to French, 29 May 1918).
5. PRO/CAB.23/7 (Cabinet Meeting, 29 July 1918, item 6).
6. PRO/RECO.1/785 (internal Ministry of Reconstruction memos, 21 and 28 October 1918; Addison to Shortt, 6 December 1918): PRO/RECO.1/786 (Law to Addison, 6 December 1918; internal memo by Shortt, 3 January 1918; Plunkett, Irish Reconstruction Association to Hutchinson, Ministry of Reconstruction, 14 December 1918): WRO, Walter Long Papers, 947/231 (memo from Reconstruction Advisory Committee to French, 21 November 1918): IWM, French Papers, 75/46/12 (note on meeting of Reconstruction Advisory Committee on 28 November 1918): *The Times*, 30 November 1918, p. 30, c; 13 December 1918, p. 9, e; 14 December 1918, p. 9, e.
7. PRO/T.1/12427/51828 no. 5359 (Cabinet Paper G. T. 6527, 'Demobilization and resettlement in Ireland', 19 December 1919).
8. Figure calculated from data in F. H. A. Aalen, op. cit., p. 308.
9. PRO/T.172/1402 (internal Treasury memo, 7 March 1921): see also: E. O'Halpin, op. cit., p. 181.
10. IWM, French Papers, 75/46/13 (French to Long, 10 January 1919).
11. PRO/T.1/ 12427/51828 no. 5359 (Macpherson to Treasury, 3 February 1919).
12. BODLEIAN MSS, Ms. Eng. Hist. C. 490 (memorandum by Gwynn *et al.*, 14 January 1919): IWM, French Papers, 75/46/13 (Gwynn to Long, 6 January 1919).
13. PRO/CAB.24/72/1 GT. 6574 (Long to Cabinet, 31 December 1918).
14. WRO, Walter Long Papers, 947/231 (Long to Chamberlain, 12 January 1919; also Long to Chamberlain, 21 January 1919); 947/347 (Saunderson to Long, 12 June 1919; Long to Saunderson, 15 June 1919): IWM, French Papers, 75/46/13 (Long to French, 9 January 1919; Long to French, 21 January 1919): E. O'Halpin, op. cit., pp. 163–80: J. McColgan, op. cit., 1983, pp. 3–4: for Long's views on the political danger in Britain, see: C. Petrie, *Walter Long and his Times*, 1936, p. 219: M. Swenarton, *Homes Fit for Heroes: The Politics and Architecture of Early State Housing in Britain*, 1981, p. 77.
15. WRO, Walter Long Papers, 947/245 (Gwynn to Long, 19 February 1919; Long to Gwynn, 22 February 1919).
16. *Irish Times*, 11 January 1919, p. 4.

378   *John Bull's Other Homes*

17. PRO/T.1/12427/51828 no. 5359 (Headlam to Phillips, 5 February 1919).
18. P. B. Johnson, op. cit., pp. 347–51.
19. WRO, Walter Long Papers, 947/230 (French to Long, 28 May 1919): *Irish Times*, 14 June 1919, p. 7.
20. PRO/CAB.24/89 (G. T. 8227, memo by French and Macpherson entitled 'Ireland', 25 September 1919): see also: E. O'Halpin, op. cit., p. 181.
21. P. B. Johnson, op. cit., p. 351.
22. 121 HC DEB, 18 November 1919, col. 854 (Macpherson).
23. 121 HC DEB, 18 November 1919, cols 854–56 (Macpherson).
24. 121 HC DEB, 18 November 1919, cols 855–57 (Macpherson).
25. PRO/T.1/12497/10124 no. 48904 (note by Upcott, 17 October 1919).
26. 121 HC DEB, 18 November 1919, col. 858 (Macpherson).
27. 121 HC DEB, 18 November 1919, cols 859 (Carson), 863 (Williams): *Irish Times*, 19 November 1919, p. 4.
28. *Irish Bulletin*, 12 December 1919, p. 2.
29. PRO/T.1/12497/10124 no. 48904 (note by Chamberlain, 23 October 1919; also note by Barstow, 21 October 1919; Greer to Upcott, 6 November 1919).
30. PRO/T.1/12497/10124 no. 48904 (Healy to Treasury, 20 November 1919).
31. PRO/T.1/12497/10124 no. 48904 (Robinson to Greer, 28 October 1919).
32. 121 HC DEB, 25 November 1919, cols 1752–53 (Henry): 126 HC DEB, 18 March 1920, cols 2357–58 (Macpherson).
33. PP 1921 Cd.1432 xiv, 'Annual Report of the ILGB for year ended 31 March 1920', f. 861.
34. Ibid.
35. Cited in C. Townshend, op. cit., p. 22.
36. PRO/T.160/216/F.7958/1 (Stephenson to Barstow, 17 May 1920): PRO/T.160/216/F.7958/1 (note by 'J. M.', 28 May 1920; Robinson to Waterfield, 30 July 1920).
37. PRO/T.160/216/F.7958/1 (Robinson to Waterfield, 5 September 1920): also: PRO/T.1/158/1 (Waterfield to Robinson, 9 October 1920): SPO/CSO.RP (1921–22)/3434 (Robinson to Under Secretary, 11 July 1920; Duggan to Robinson, 19 August 1920).
38. SPO/CSO.RP (1921–22)/3434 (Robinson to Under Secretary, 5 July 1920): also: PRO/T.158/3 (Healy, Irish Board of Works to Irish Treasury, 3 May 1921).
39. PP 1921 Cd.1481 xvii, 'Annual Report of the Irish Commissioners of Works for year ended 31 March 1921', f. 47.
40. PRO/T.160/216/F.7958/1 (Waterfield to Anderson, 4 August 1920): PRO/T.160/216/F.7958/2 (note by 'N. W. S', 15 March 1921).
41. PRO/T.160/216/F.7958/1 (Waterfield to Anderson, 4 August 1920); also Waterfield to Stephenson, 4 November 1920; Robinson to Waterfield, 24 November 1920): PRO/T.158/1 (Waterfield to Irish Board of Works, 19 August 1920; Waterfield to O'Conor, ILGB, 25 August 1920).
42. PRO/T.160/216/F.7958/2 (Waterfield to Irish Board of Works, 11 December 1920).
43. *Irish Times*, 20 January 1921, p. 6; 25 January 1921, p. 2: HLL, Lloyd George Papers, F/37/4/29 (Duke to Lloyd George, 9 July 1917).
44. SPO/CSO.RP (1921–22)/3434 (Robinson to Under Secretary, 27 October 1920).

References (Chapter 7) 379

45. PRO/T.172/1402 (memo by Anderson to Fisher, 5 March 1921; also Anderson to Strohmenger, Ministry of Health, 21 January 1921; internal Treasury note, 7 March 1921; et seq.).
46. SPO/CSO.RP (1921–22)/3434 (Anderson to Duggan, 1 December 1920).
47. PRO/T.158/3 (Robinson to Anderson, 1 March 1921): also: PRO/T.158/2 (Anderson to Robinson, 25 February 1921).
48. PRO/T.158/1 (Waterfield to Robinson, 4 November 1920): ISSLT, *First Report: 1st January 1924 to 31st March 1926*, (HMSO) 1927, pp. 72–73 (Appendix viii): *Irish Builder*, 17 July 1920, pp. 462–69: N. O'Flanagan, 'Dublin City in an age of war and revolution, 1914–24' (UCD MA thesis 1985), p. 137.
49. PRO/T.160/216/F.7958/1 (Robinson to Waterfield, 5 September 1920; Robinson to Waterfield, 8 November 1920): *Irish Builder*, 25 September 1920, p. 614; 21 May 1921, p. 354.
50. PRO/T.158/1 (Ministry of Health to Waterfield, 31 August 1920; Waterfield to Stevenson, 15 October 1920): PRO/T.160/216/F.7958/1 (Waterfield to Robinson, 1 September 1920).
51. PP 1921 Cd.1481 xvii, 'Annual Report of the Irish Commissioners of Public Works for year ended 31 March 1921', f. 47: PRO/AP.3/28 (Report by IFS Board of Works to Treasury, 21 May 1925): see also: C. O'Connor and J. O'Regan (Architectural Association of Ireland), *Public Works: The Architecture of the Office of Public Works 1831–1987*, 1987, p. 30.
52. *Irish Times*, 20 January 1921, p. 6.
53. NLS MSS, Geddes Papers, Ms. 10573 (Mears to Geddes, 13 September 1920; Mears to Geddes, 27 October 1920; Mears to Geddes, 1 December 1920; Mears to Geddes, 15 December 1920; Mears to Geddes, 13 April 1921): SPO/CSO.RP (1921–22)/3434 (Duggan to Anderson, 4 November 1920): *Irish Times*, 27 January 1921, p. 8; 7 April 1921, p. 7; 28 July 1921, p. 8; 29 October 1921: *Builder*, 3 November 1922, p. 673: F. H. A. Aalen, op. cit., pp. 315–17.
54. NLS MSS, Geddes Papers, Ms. 10573 (Lady Aberdeen to Mears, 10 May 1922): PRO/T.158/9 (Waterfield to Cuthbertson, 2 October 1922).
55. ISSLT, op. cit., pp. 16–19, 72–73 (Appendix viii).
56. PRO/T.158/3 (Irish Treasury to Hanson, Irish Board of Works, 25 May 1921).
57. PRO/AP.3/36 (Browne, ISSLT to Ardee, 8 June 1929).
58. PRO/T.158/4 (Waterfield to Robinson, 5 August 1921): PRO/T.158/8 (Waterfield to Robinson, 16 March 1922; Waterfield to Anderson, 22 April 1922; Waterfield to Robinson, 4 April 1922; Waterfield to Robinson, 8 April 1922; Waterfield to Sturgis, 18 April 1922).
59. Account here based on: ISSLT, op. cit., 1927: many files, too numerous to list, in: PRO/AP.
60. *Irish Times*, 1 June 1922, p. 9.
61. *Irish Times*, 20 September 1923, p. 4.
62. E. O'Halpin, op. cit., pp. 181, 210.
63. 144 HC DEB, 7 July 1921, col. 604 (Brown).
64. SPO/CSO.RP (1921–22)/3504 (Barlas to Duggan, 20 August 1921): PP 1921 Cd.1481 xvii, 'Annual Report of the Irish Commissioners of Public Works for year ended 31 March 1921', f. 47.
65. 147 HC DEB, 27 October 1921, col. 1012 (Greenwood): PP 1921 Cd.1481 xvii,

'Annual Report of the Irish Commissioners of Public Works for year ended 31 March 1921', f. 47: SPO/CSO.RP (1921–22)/3504 (Barlas to Duggan, 20 August 1921).
66. P. B. Johnson, op. cit., pp. 442 et seq.
67. SPO/CSO.RP (1921–22)/3434 (Robinson to Greenwood, 5 March 1921; Waterfield to ILGB, 16 June 1921): PRO/T.158/4 (Sturgis, Irish Treasury to Under Secretary, 5 August 1921).
68. SPO/CSO.RP (1921–22)/3434 (Codling to Under Secretary, 6 July 1921).
69. *Irish Times*, 19 October 1921.
70. SPO/CSO.RP (1921–22)/2503/8 (Waterfield to Under Secretary, 30 November 1921): SPO/CSO.RP (1921–22)/3434 (MacMahon to Assistant Secretary, Irish Treasury, 15 August 1921).
71. SPO/CSO.RP (1921–22)/2503/8 (Robinson to Anderson, 16 July 1921; unsigned memo by Robinson to Greenwood, undated but probably October 1921).
72. SPO/CSO.RP (1921–22)/3434 (Waterfield to Under Secretary, 9 November 1921; also Corbitt to Under Secretary, 21 November 1921; Waterfield to Under Secretary, 5 December 1921; ILGB to Under Secretary, 10 December 1921): SPO/CSO.RP (1921–22)/2503/8 (unsigned memo by Anderson, undated but probably 25 October 1921): PRO/T.158/5 (Waterfield to Robinson, 16 November 1921).
73. PRO/CO.739/4 (paper by Finance Sub-Committee of Provisional Government of Ireland Committee to Cabinet, 6 March 1922).
74. PRO/T.158/8 (Waterfield to Whiskard, Irish Office, 4 April 1922).
75. PRO/T.158/8 (Waterfield to Sturgis, 18 April 1922; Waterfield to Niemeyer, 25 April 1922): PRO/T.158/9 (memo by Clark, NI Government, 13 July 1922; Waterfield to Cuthbertson, 30 August 1922; Waterfield to Niemeyer, 26 September 1922; Waterfield to Niemeyer, 4 October 1922): PRO/HO.45/11708 (internal Home Office memo, January 1923; draft memo by Technical Department Sub-Committee of Committee on Irish Affairs to Cabinet, 10 November 1922; Clark, NI Ministry of Finance to Sturgis, 5 September 1922).
76. SPO/DE/2/428 (Concubair to Minister of Defence, Dáil Éireann, 9 November 1921).
77. SPO/DE/2/428 (Concubair to Barton, Ministry of Defence, Dáil Éireann, 29 November 1921).
78. SPO/DE/2/243 (Robirg to Dáil Éireann Cabinet, 15 February 1922).
79. L. M. Cullen, *An Economic History of Ireland since 1660*, 1972, p. 172.
80. PRO/T.158/8 (Waterfield to Sturgis, 25 April 1922).
81. PRO/T.158/8 (Waterfield to Anderson, 7 April 1922; Waterfield to IFS Ministry of Finance, 15 April 1922; Waterfield to Sturgis, 18 April 1922; Waterfield to Sturgis, 25 April 1922).
82. PRO/T.158/8 (Waterfield to Niemeyer, 25 April 1922; Waterfield to Sturgis, 25 April 1922): PRO/T.158/9 (Waterfield to Niemeyer, 26 September 1922).
83. Section here based on: ISSLT, op. cit. (and subsequent, perfunctory annual reports): numerous files on ISSLT in PRO/AP: PRO/T.160/169/F.6511/014/1: PRO/T.160/169/F.6511/014/2: PRO/T.160/169/F.6511/028: PRO/T.160/377/F.6511/08: PRO/HO.45/14659: PRO/HO.45/14660: F. H. A. Aalen, op. cit., pp. 308–22.
84. H. A. Law, 'Irish housing in town and country' (special section on 'European

Reconstruction Series: Ireland'), *Manchester Guardian Commercial*, 26 July 1923, p. 39.
85. PRO/HO.45/14659 (internal Home Office note, 30 January 1925): also PRO/HO.45/14199 (Duckworth, RCHM to Sturgis, 8 November 1923): PRO/RECO.1/558 (letters and notes by Duckworth, Ministry of Munitions).
86. PRO/T.160/169/F.6511/028 (Duckworth to Lord Ardee, 31 August 1926; also Duckworth to Upcott, Treasury, 31 August 1926): PRO/HO.45/14660 (Duckworth to Markbreiter, 23 September 1927): PRO/AP.3/5 (Duckworth to Alexander, 25 May 1925): ISSLT, op. cit., p. 31: J. Leonard, 'Lest we forget', in D. Fitzpatrick (ed.), *Ireland and the First World War*, 1988, pp. 61–62.
87. PRO/HO.45/14659 (Guinness, Financial Secretary to Treasury, to Amery, Home Office, 16 March 1925): also PRO/AP.3/5 (Duckworth to Ross, 28 February 1925).
88. PRO/HO.45/14659 (internal Home Office memo on ISSLT conference held on 25 September 1925).
89. PRO/T.160/169/F.6511/014/1 (Waterfield to Tallents, 22 September 1924).
90. PRO/AP.3/5 (ISSLT Trustees to Duckworth, 8 June 1925).
91. PRO/T.172/1537 (Churchill to Devlin, 25 March 1926; also internal Treasury memo to Churchill, 24 March 1926): PRO/HO.45/14659 (minutes of interview between Guinness, Secretary to Treasury and ISSLT, February 1925).
92. PRO/AP.1/16 (Duckworth to Lefroy, 20 June 1924; also Duckworth to Lefroy, 15 July 1924; Duckworth to Southern Trustees, 21 August 1924).
93. ISSLT, op. cit., p. 19.
94. PRO/T.160/377/F.6511/08 (Waterfield to Ramsay, 21 May 1926).
95. *Irish Times*, 26 June 1926, pp. 6, 8; 13 July 1926, p. 5; 26 July 1926, p. 6.
96. PRO/AP.1/98 (Duckworth to Brise, British Legion, 10 December 1926; also note on ISSLT meeting on 30 March 1926): PRO/AP.3/32: PRO/HO.45/14199 (Cosgrave to Thomas, Colonial Office, 26 July 1924): PRO/HO.45/14659 (Healy to Secretary of State for Dominion Affairs, 26 August 1925; Amery to Healy, 30 December 1925).
97. PRO/T.160/169/F.6511/014/2 (internal Treasury memo, undated but probably 1928): PRO/T.160/416/F.6511/033 (Machtig, Dominions Office to Heath, British Legion, 17 March 1930).
98. PRO/AP.1/124 (Browne, ISSLT to Brunyate, 20 September 1928; also Mahon to Brunyate, 27 July 1928).
99. PRO/T.160/416/F.6511/033 (Machtig, Dominions Office to Heath, British Legion, 17 March 1930; Heath to Dominions Office, 18 June 1930; Alexander, ISSLT to Machtig, 8 August 1930; Machtig to Heath, 6 October 1930; Thomas, Dominions Office to Earl of Jellicoe, 17 February 1931).
100. See various correspondence in the following files: PRO/T.160/F.6511/017/1: PRO/T.160/F.6511/017/2: PRO/T.160/377/F.6511/08: PRO/T.160/1309/F.6511/034: PRO/HO.45/14660.
101. PRO/T.169/377/F.6511/08 (Strohmenger, Ministry of Health to Waley, 13 October 1931).

8. STATE HOUSING IN NORTHERN IRELAND AND THE IRISH FREE STATE (272–291)

1. B. Chubb, *The Government and Politics of Ireland*, 1970/82, p. 249: R. Foster, *Modern Ireland 1600–1972*, 1988, pp. 503–04: J. McColgan, *British Policy and the Irish Administration, 1920–22*, 1983, pp. 30–35, 56–86, 132–37.
2. PRO/T.161/94/S. 7136 (Waterfield to Under Secretary, 3 November 1921; Watt, NI Ministry of Home Affairs, to Waterfield, 11 November 1921; Watt to Waterfield, 17 November 1921; Anderson to Bates, NI Ministry of Home Affairs, 19 November 1921; internal Treasury note by 'D. W. S.', 29 November 1921): SPO/CSO.RP (1921–22)/2503 (Codling to Under Secretary, 22 December 1921; Waterfield to Under Secretary, 12 January 1922): *Northern Whig*, 23 March 1922, pp. 5–6; 4 April 1922, p. 7.
3. PRO/T.158/9 (Clark, NI Ministry of Finance, to Treasury, 13 July 1922): PRO/T.160/139/F.5074/01/1: CAB.27/154 (PG1. 48, proposals by Provisional Government of Ireland Committee of Cabinet, January 1922).
4. This account of Ulster socio-economic conditions from: P. J. Buckland, *The Factory of Grievances: Devolved Government in Northern Ireland 1921–39*, 1979: L. M. Cullen, *An Economic History of Ireland since 1660*, 1972, pp. 173–74, 180: R. Foster, op. cit., pp. 526–31, 555–59: R. J. Lawrence, *The Government of Northern Ireland: Public Finances and Public Services 1921–1964*, 1965: F. S. L. Lyons, *Ireland since the Famine*, 1971, pp. 695–727: D. S. Johnston, 'The Northern Ireland economy, 1914–39', in L. Kennedy and P. Ollerenshaw (eds), *An Economic History of Ulster, 1820–1940*, 1985a, pp. 184–223: D. S. Johnston, *The Interwar Economy in Ireland*, 1985b.
5. F. S. L. Lyons, op. cit., pp. 720–21: H. Patterson, *Class Conflict and Sectarianism: The Protestant Working Class and the Belfast Labour Movement 1868–1920*, 1980: G. Walker, 'Labour in Scotland and Northern Ireland: the inter-war experience', in R. Mitchison and P. Roebuck (eds), *Economy and Society in Scotland and Ireland 1500–1939*, 1988, pp. 267–75: E. Rumpf and A. C. Hepburn, *Nationalism and Socialism in Twentieth-Century Ireland*, 1977, pp. 174–218.
6. For the development of inter-war housing policy in Northern Ireland, see: W. D. Birrell, P. A. R. Hillyard, A. Murie and B. J. D. Roche, *Housing in Northern Ireland*, 1971, pp. 49–80: C. E. B. Brett, *Housing a Divided Community*, 1986, pp. 21–25: P. J. Buckland, op. cit., pp. 163–75: J. Hendry, 'The control of development and the origins of planning in Northern Ireland', in M. J. Bannon (ed.), *Planning: The Irish Experience 1922–1988*, 1989, pp. 109–11: R. J. Lawrence, op. cit., pp. 147–52: A. McCashin and M. Morrissey, 'Housing policy: North and South', *Administration*, vol. 33, no. 3, 1985, pp. 292–98.
7. The 1923 Chamberlain Housing Act in Britain gave a subsidy of £6 (later £4) per annum per dwelling for 20 years to private builders, although it was available to local authorities to use as a last resort; the 1924 Wheatley Housing Act was the response of the short-lived first Labour Government, and allowed a subsidy to both local authorities and private builders of £9 (later £7 10s) per annum per urban dwelling for 40 years (£13 10s per annum for rural dwellings), as well as permitting local authorities to provide a subsidy of another £4 10s per annum from their own revenues: M. Bowley, *Housing and the State 1919–1944*, 1945, pp. 36–47: J. Burnett, *A Social History of Housing 1815–1970*, 1978/85, pp. 227–29: the 1924 Wheatley Act,

with its intention to make housing a social service provided by local authorities, was never likely to be adopted in Northern Ireland.
8. The subsidy from the Northern Government varied from £60 in 1923; to £80 in 1925; £100 in 1927; £50 in 1931; £25 in 1932; and was withdrawn in 1937–local authority contributions were more stable: for discussions on variations in subsidy level, see for instance: *Irish Times*, 11 April 1924, p. 8: *Northern Whig*, 8 November 1923, pp. 7–8; 11 April 1924, pp. 6, 8; 24 October 1924, p. 10.
9. *Irish Builder*, 29 October 1927, p. 798: also 27 October 1928, pp. 912–13.
10. Ulster housing statistics here taken from: R. J. Lawrence, op. cit., pp. 147–52: M. Bowley, op. cit., pp. 263–67.
11. R. J. Lawrence, op. cit., pp. 152–54.
12. The account here based on: Belfast Corporation, *The Belfast Book (First Issue): Local Government in the City and Co. Borough of Belfast*, 1929, pp. 104–21: C. E. B. Brett, op. cit., pp. 21–22: P. Buckland, op. cit., 1979, pp. 163–75: I. Budge and C. O'Leary, *Belfast: Approach to Crisis. A Study of Belfast Politics 1613–1970*, 1973, pp. 145–49 : H. Patterson, op. cit., pp. 120–21: plus other individual references cited below.
13. D. S. Johnston, op. cit. (1985a), p. 215.
14. *Northern Whig*, 18 November 1921, p. 7; 2 October 1923, p. 9: also 26 March 1919, p. 6; 3 April 1919, p. 2; 21 June 1919, p. 6; 2 August 1919, p. 6; 31 October 1919, p. 8; 13 November 1919, p. 5; 2 March 1920, p. 6; 2 April 1920, p. 6; 12 March 1921, p. 6; 2 November 1923, p. 5; 2 February 1926, p. 6: *Irish Builder*, 7 April 1923, p. 252; 17 November 1923, p. 887.
15. Statistics here taken from: PRO/T.160/169/F.6511/014/1 (Tallents, NI Imperial Secretary's Office, to Waterfield, 3 October 1924, and appended tables): Belfast Corporation, op. cit., pp. 104–21: see also *Irish Times*, 19 November 1921, p. 6: *Northern Whig*, 11 October 1919, p. 5; 31 October 1919, pp. 4, 8; 18 November 1921, p. 7: *Irish Builder*, 27 August 1921, pp. 585–86.
16. *Irish Times*, 16 November 1922, p. 11: *Northern Whig*, 2 November 1922, p. 6; 2 December 1922, p. 6; 2 February 1923, p. 10; 30 March 1923, p. 7; 8 February 1924, p. 8; 11 July 1924, pp. 7–8: *Irish Builder*, 30 December 1922, p. 910; 10 February 1923, p. 90; 8 September 1923, p. 685.
17. PRO/T.160/169/F.6511/017/1 (Tallents, NI Imperial Secretary's Office, to Waterfield, 9 January 1925): *Irish Times*, 21 August 1923, p. 6: *Northern Whig*, 4 April 1923, p. 6; 3 July 1923, p. 9; 21 August 1923, p. 5; 2 October 1923, p. 9; 8 February 1924, p. 8: *Irish Builder*, 18 November 1922, p. 789; 5 May 1923, p. 326; 25 August 1923, p. 646.
18. *Northern Whig*, 2 May 1924, p. 9; 7 June 1924, p. 9; 17 March 1925, p. 10; 24 September 1925, p. 6; 2 March 1926, p. 9; 27 March 1926, p. 7; 2 April 1926, p. 5: *Irish Builder*, 14 June 1924, p. 516; 26 July 1924, p. 659; 20 February 1926, p. 129; 6 March 1926, p. 169.
19. *Irish Times*, 26 August 1925, p. 5; 16 September 1925, p. 8; 6 October 1925, p. 8; 3 November 1925, p. 5; 1 April 1926, pp. 6, 7–8; 9 April 1926, p. 7: *Northern Whig*, 6 October 1925, p. 9; et seq.: *Irish Builder*, 17 April 1926, pp. 304–05; 12 June 1926, pp. 466–67.
20. C. E. B. Brett, op. cit., p. 22.
21. PRO/CAB.23/26 (Cabinet Meeting, 26 July 1921; also Cabinet Meeting, 20 July 1921, appendix).

22. Quote by Kevin O'Higgins, given in: J. Lee, *Ireland 1912–85*, 1989, p. 105.
23. This account of Free State socio-economic conditions is based on: T. Brown, *Ireland: A Social and Cultural History 1922–79*, 1981, pp. 13–47: B. Chubb, op. cit.: L. M. Cullen, op. cit., pp. 171–80: R. Foster, op. cit., pp. 511–54: D. S. Johnston, op. cit. (1985b): J. Lee, op. cit.: F. S. L. Lyons, op. cit., pp. 471–558, 599–624, 635–82: O. MacDonagh, *Ireland: The Union and its Aftermath*, 1967/77, pp. 102–41: J. Meenan, *The Irish Economy since 1922*, 1970: E. Rumpf and A. C. Hepburn, op. cit., pp. 28–107, 219–21.
24. J. D. Clarkson, *Labour and Nationalism in Ireland*, 1925, pp. 435–78: F. S. L. Lyons, op. cit., pp. 673–78: A. Mitchell, *Labour in Irish Politics 1890–1930*, 1974, pp. 155, 180–99: C. Lincoln, 'Working class housing in Dublin, 1914–1939' (UCD MA Thesis 1979), pp. 54–57.
25. T. J. Barrington, 'Public administration 1927–36', in F. McManus (ed.), *The Years of the Great Test 1926–39*, 1967, pp. 80–91: B. Chubb, op. cit., pp. 9, 42, 240–41, 257: B. Chubb, 'Britain and Irish constitutional development', in P. J. Drudy (ed.), *Ireland and Britain since 1922 (Irish Studies 5)*, 1986, pp. 21–44: J. D. Clarkson, op. cit., p. 468: G. Cook, 'Britain's legacy to the Irish social security system', in P. J. Drudy, *Ireland and Britain since 1922 (Irish Studies 5)*, 1986, pp. 65–85: R. Fanning, *The Irish Department of Finance 1922–58*, 1978, pp. 34, 78, 120–75: R. Fanning, 'Britain's legacy: government and administration', in P. J. Drudy (ed.), *Ireland and Britain since 1922 (Irish Studies 5)*, 1986, pp. 45–64: B. Farrell, *The Founding of Dáil Éireann: Parliament and Nation Building*, 1971, pp. x–xv: A. McCashin and M. Morrissey, op. cit., p. 292: J. McColgan, op. cit., pp. 136–37: E. O'Halpin, *The Decline of the Union: British Government in Ireland 1892–1920*, 1987, pp. 212–13, 217.
26. O. MacDonagh, op. cit., pp. 126–27: see also: F. S. L. Lyons, op. cit., pp. 599–600: J. Meenan, op. cit., p. 76: D. McAleese, 'Anglo-Irish economic interdependence: from excessive intimacy to a wider embrace', in P. J. Drudy (ed.), *Ireland and Britain since 1922 (Irish Studies 5)*, 1986, p. 88.
27. A commonly-held view is that economic and cultural over-dependence on Britain did not really begin to change until the Republic of Ireland joined the EEC in 1972: M. A. G. O'Tuathaigh, 'Ireland and Britain under the Union, 1800–1921: an overview', in P. J. Drudy (ed.), *Ireland and Britain since 1922 (Irish Studies 5)*, 1986, pp. 15–20: B. Chubb, op. cit. (1970/82), pp. 5–8, 329: B. Chubb, op. cit. (1986), pp. 22, 41: D. McAleese, op. cit., pp. 93, 103–04.
28. The general account of Free State housing policy here based on: A. McCashin and M. Morrissey, op. cit., pp. 298–304: P. Meighen, *Housing in Ireland*, 1965: D. Roche (Institute of Public Administration), *Local Government in Ireland*, 1980, p. 222–26: C. Lincoln, op. cit.: plus other individual references cited below.
29. *Irish Times*, 3 February 1922, p. 4: also 20 January 1923, p. 6; 6 March 1923, p. 4; 6 April 1923, p. 4; 25 April 1923, p. 4.
30. *Irish Times*, 5 May 1923, p. 5: see also: J. Lee, op. cit., p. 124.
31. (IFS) Ministry of Local Government Housing Department, *Circulars to Urban Local Authorities*, 16 March 1922; 22 April 1922; 27 April 1922; 15 May 1922: D. Roche, op. cit., p. 222–23: *Irish Times*, 17 March 1922, p. 4; 4 January 1923, p. 10: *Irish Builder*, 18 November 1922, pp. 777–82.
32. *Irish Times*, 6 August 1923, p. 5; 20 August 1923, p. 7; 23 August 1923, p. 8.
33. *Irish Times*, 2 October 1925, p. 6: *Irish Builder*, 21 April 1923, p. 289–92.

34. SPO/S. 3366 (memo by Ministry of Local Government, 26 November 1923): C. O'Connor and J. O'Regan (Architectural Association of Ireland), *Public Works: The Architecture of the Office of Public Works 1831–1987*, 1987, pp. 31–32.
35. PRO/T.160/169/F.6511/014/1 (Waterfield to Hanson, IFS Board of Public Works, 8 September 1924; Le Fanu, IFS Board of Public Works, to Waterfield, 9 September 1924; Waterfield to McCarron, IFS Ministry of Local Government, 11 November 1924): PRO/T.160/169/F.6511/014/2 (McCarron, IFS Ministry of Local Government, to Waterfield, 17 November 1924; McCarron to Waterfield, 5 December 1924; Mosse, Ministry of Health, to Waterfield, 23 December 1924): R. Fanning, op. cit., pp. 120–75.
36. *Irish Times*, 15 December 1923, p. 8; 19 January 1924, pp. 6, 7; 26 January 1924, p. 8; 26 February 1924, pp. 4, 5–6; 19 March 1925, pp. 7–8; 2 April 1925, p. 8; 8 April 1925, pp. 5, 6; 17 June 1926, p. 7: *Irish Builder*, 12 January 1924, pp. 21–22; 26 January 1924, pp. 64–65; 19 February 1927, pp. 106–13: NLI MSS, Joseph Brennan Papers, Ms. 26312 (housing memo by Hudson for Committee of Inquiry into Banking, Currency and Credit, 25 February 1935): also D. Roche, op. cit., p. 223.
37. Developments in housing subsidy in the 1920s Free State were: the 1924 Housing (Building Facilities) Act provided an urban subsidy of £60 for a three-room house, £80 for a four-room house, and £100 for a five-room house; rural subsidy was £50 for a three-room house, £70 for a four-room house, and £90 for a five-room dwelling: the 1924 Housing (Amendment) Act extended these subsidy levels to local authorities: the 1925 Housing Act provided another £300 000, and kept the same subsidies for local authorities while reducing those for private builders to £45 for a three-room house, £60 for a four-room house, and £75 per five-room dwelling: this pattern was continued by subsequent legislation, although the 1929 Housing Act set a maximum subsidy of £60 to urban local authorities, £50 to rural authorities, and only £45 to private builders.
38. Department of Local Government 'White Paper', *Housing: Progress and Prospects*, 1964, Appendix 1: D. Roche, op. cit., p. 224.
39. SPO/S. 3366 (memo by IFS Ministry of Local Government and Public Health, 26 November 1923): D. Roche, op. cit., p. 222.
40. *Irish Builder*, 14 November 1925, p. 933.
41. *Irish Builder*, 29 September 1928, p. 824.
42. (IFS) Ministry of Local Government, *Housing of the Working Classes (Ireland) Acts: Memorandum for the Guidance of Local Authorities and Memorandum for the Guidance of Architects*, April 1922: (IFS) Ministry of Local Government, *The Housing (New Houses) Order*, 1924, and *The Housing (New Houses) Order*, 1925: (IFS) Ministry of Local Government, *House Designs: Book CL*, 1924: PRO/T.160/169/F.6511/014/2 (McCarron, IFS Ministry of Local Government, to Waterfield, 17 November 1924; McCarron to Waterfield, 5 December 1924; internal Treasury memo by Waterfield, December 1924): *Irish Builder*, 18 November 1922, pp. 778–82; 31 May 1924, pp. 473–74.
43. *Manchester Guardian Commercial*, 26 July 1923 (Section 3 'European Reconstruction Series: Ireland'), pp. 48–49: *Irish Times*, 7 June 1924, p. 7; 17 February 1926, pp. 7–8; 31 March 1926, p. 6: *Irish Builder*, 9 February 1924, pp. 101–02; 8 March 1924, p. 185; 10 January 1925, p. 18; 27 November 1926, p. 873; 11 December 1926,

pp. 905, 917: S. Rothery, *Ireland and the New Architecture 1900–1940*, 1991, pp. 140–41.
44. H. T. O'Rourke and the Dublin Civic Survey Committee, *The Dublin Civic Survey Report*, 1925, pp. 146–49: *Irish Times*, 16 September 1922, p. 7; 31 October 1922, pp. 3, 4; 12 December 1922, p. 7; 14 December 1922, pp. 3–4, 6, 9; 18 June 1924, pp. 4, 5; 25 September 1924, pp. 7–8; 20 November 1925, p. 7: *Builder*, 3 November 1922, p. 673: *Irish Builder*, 23 September 1922, pp. 642, 650; 7 October 1922, p. 674; 16 June 1923, pp. 461–63: M. J. Bannon, 'Irish planning from 1921 to 1945: an overview', in M. J. Bannon (ed.), *Planning: The Irish Experience 1920–1988*, 1989, pp. 14–21.
45. NLS MSS, Geddes Papers, Ms. 10573 (Mears to Geddes, 15 August 1922; Mears to Geddes, 5 June 1923; also Lady Aberdeen to Mears, 10 May 1922; Mears to Geddes, 19 July 1922; Mears to Geddes, 24 January 1923; Mears to Geddes, 12 April 1923); Ms.10502 (Geddes to Nora Geddes, 14 September 1922).
46. *Irish Times*, 4 May 1922, p. 6; 3 November 1922, p. 7; 4 November 1922, p. 8; 13 December 1922, p. 7; 16 December 1922, p. 8; 18 December 1922, p. 9; 21 December 1922, p. 8; 6 February 1923, pp. 3, 4; 10 February 1923, p. 5; 27 October 1923, p. 6; 6 November 1925, p. 6; 15 December 1926, pp. 6, 7: *Irish Builder*, 28 January 1922, p. 53; 10 March 1923, pp. 157–58; 3 November 1923, pp. 845, 849; 13 December 1924, p. 1024; 31 October 1925, p. 889; 26 December 1925, pp. 1046–49; 31 March 1928, pp. 262–66: BODLEIAN MSS, Nathan Papers, Ms.142 (Lady Aberdeen to Nathan, 27 November 1924; Lady Aberdeen to Nathan, 18 May 1926): Dublin Corporation Archives, Minute Book of meetings of Civics Institute, 1922–25: P. Abercombie/S. Kelly/A. Kelly, *Dublin of the Future: The New Town Plan*, 1923: H. T. O'Rourke, *Dublin Civic Survey: Why You Should Support a Work of National Importance*, 1925: H. T. O'Rourke and the Dublin Civic Survey Committee, op. cit.: M. J. Bannon, op. cit., pp. 21–29.
47. Cork Town Planning Association, *Cork: A Civic Survey*, 1926: M. Gough, 'Socio-economic conditions and the genesis of planning in Cork', in M. J. Bannon (ed.), *The Emergence of Irish Planning 1880–1920*, 1985, pp. 319–22.
48. Department of Local Government and Public Health, *Report of Inquiry into the Housing of the Working Classes of the City of Dublin 1939/43*, 1944, p. 25: D. Roche, op. cit., p. 224; C. Lincoln, op. cit., pp. 62–68: the 1930 Greenwood Housing Act in Britain offered £2 5s per annum over 40 years for every person rehoused in urban areas, and £2 10s per annum per person in rural areas; there was extra subsidy for expensive urban sites, and local authorities were allowed to offer another £3 15s per annum for every person rehoused: then the 1933 Housing Act in Britain pursued the policy of making local authorities take on a residual, sanitary policy of slum rehousing, leaving private enterprise to build new additional housing in the suburbs for the better-paid working class and the middle classes: M. Bowley, op. cit., pp. 135–68: J. Burnett, op. cit., pp. 234–42.
49. T. Brown, op. cit., pp. 141–70: R. Foster, op. cit., pp. 537–42: J. Lee, op. cit., pp. 170–87: N. Mansergh, *The Irish Free State: Its Government and Politics*, 1934, pp. 287–88: E. Rumpf and A. C. Hepburn, op. cit., pp. 82–128.
50. Department of Local Government and Public Health, op. cit. (1944): see also: Department of Local Government, *Housing: A Review of Past Operations and Immediate*

Requirements, 1948, pp. 8–9, 17, 21–22: D. Roche, op. cit., pp. 224–26: C. Lincoln, op. cit., pp. 62–68.
51. Department of Local Government 'White Paper', op. cit., Appendix 1: D. Roche, op. cit., p. 225.
52. For comparative Irish statistics, see above comparison between Ulster and Britain, plus: D. S. Johnston, op. cit. (1985b), pp. 40–41.
53. Department of Local Government, op. cit. (1948), pp. 9–10, 13–15, Appendix A: F. S. L. Lyons, op. cit., pp. 571–72.
54. This account based on: H. T. O'Rourke and the Dublin Civic Survey Committee, op. cit., pp. 57–80: Department of Local Government and Public Health, op. cit. (1944): C. Lincoln, op. cit.: N. O'Flanagan, 'Dublin City in an age of war and reconstruction, 1914–24' (UCD MA Thesis 1985), pp. 150–65: plus other individual references cited below.
55. RPDCD, vol. 2, no. 110 (1920), pp. 343–528.
56. RPDCD vol. 3, no. 221 (1918) pp. 403–14; vol. 3, no. 248 (1920), pp. 529–30; vol. 1, no. 22 (1921), pp. 83–86.
57. RPDCD, vol. 1, no. 24 (1921), pp. 115–17; vol. 2, no. 125 (1921), pp. 17–23; vol. 1, no. 68 (1922), pp. 411–16; vol. 2, no. 154 (1922), pp. 59–60; vol. 1, no. 48 (1923), pp. 209–12; vol. 2, no. 329 (1923), pp. 715–17: C. Lincoln, op. cit., pp. 38–42.
58. RPDCD, vol. 2, no. 177 (1924), pp. 15–20; no. 161 (1926), pp. 458–60: Department of Local Government and Public Health, op. cit. (1944), pp. 180–86, Appendix 1(A, C).
59. RPDCD vol. 3, no. 210 (1920), pp. 51–80; vol. 2, no. 162 (1922), pp. 95–97; vol. 1, no. 14 (1923), pp. 45–48; vol. 2, no. 105 (1925), pp. 51–54: *Irish Times*, 21 May 1925, pp. 4–5: *Irish Builder*, 21 February 1925, pp. 145–46; 11 July 1925, pp. 557–58: J. P. Moore, 'Marino housing estate' (UCD BA Thesis 1986).
60. J. Sheehy, *The Rediscovery of Ireland's Past: The Celtic Revival 1830–1930*, 1980, p. 134: S. Rothery, op. cit., p. 37.
61. *Irish Times*, 1 September 1925, p. 7: see also: *Irish Builder*, 5 September 1925, p. 715; 31 October 1925, p. 881: RPDCD, vol. 2, no. 196 (1925); no. 85 (1926), p. 254; Dublin Corporation Archives, C2/CAD/1925/1/E, F, K, U: J. Moore, op. cit.
62. B. Chubb, op. cit. (1970/82), p. 8: this counters the recent, erroneous portrayal of the Free State Government as a significant conduit for Continental modernism, as argued in: S. Rothery, op. cit., pp. 140–54.
63. *Irish Builder*, 16 June 1923, p. 457; 29 September 1928, pp. 825–26: RPDCD, vol. 2, no. 125 (1921), pp. 17–18; vol. 2, no. 184 (1925), p. 280.
64. An analysis of the Roehampton Estate is given in: M. Swenarton, *Homes Fit for Heroes: The Politics and Architecture of Early State Housing in Britain*, 1981, pp. 169–78.
65. *Irish Times*, 8 June 1925, p. 6.
66. Quoted in N. O'Flanagan, op. cit., p. 156.
67. Department of Local Government and Public Health, op. cit. (1944), pp. 117–33: D. Roche, op. cit., p. 225–26.
68. S. Rothery, op. cit., pp. 148–53: for the counter-view that stresses the British influence, see the review of Rothery's book by M. Fraser in: *AA Files*, no. 24, Autumn 1992, pp. 96–98.
69. Department of Local Government, op. cit. (1948), pp. 14–15, Appendix A.

70. Department of Local Government and Public Health, op. cit. (1944), pp. 15–23, 34–48.
71. M. Gough, op. cit., pp. 324–26.

CONCLUSION (292–302)

1. C. G. Pooley, 'Housing strategies in Europe 1880–1930: towards a comparative perspective', in C. G. Pooley (ed.), *Housing Strategies in Europe 1880–1930*, 1992, p. 346.
2. J. Lee, *Ireland 1912–85*, 1989, p. 628.
3. *Freemans Journal*, 29 April 1909, p. 8.
4. P. O'Farrell, *Ireland's English Question: Anglo-Irish Relations 1534–1970*, 1971, p. 124.
5. R. Wilson, 'Imperialism in crisis: the "Irish dimension" ', in M. Langan and B. Schwarz (eds), *Crises in the British State 1880–1930*, 1985, pp. 152, 153–55.
6. 97 HC DEB, 16 August 1917, col. 1575 (Duke).
7. R. Wilson, op. cit., pp. 152, 159–65.
8. O. MacDonagh, *States of Mind: A Study of Anglo-Irish Conflict 1780–1950*, 1983, p. 126.
9. J. Lee, op. cit., p. 627.
10. See, for instance: P. Greenhalgh, *Ephemeral Vistas: The Expositions Universelles, Great Exhibitions and World's Fairs 1851–1939*, 1989: C. McArthur, 'The dialectic of national identity: The Glasgow Empire Exhibition of 1938', in T. Bennett, C. Mercer and J. Woollacott (eds), *Popular Culture and Social Relations*, 1986, pp. 117–34: J. Sheehy, *The Rediscovery of Ireland's Past: The Celtic Revival 1830–1930*, 1980, pp. 131–34.
11. W. Baumgart, *Imperialism: The Idea and Reality of British and French Colonial Expansion, 1880–1914*, 1982, pp. 82–90, 165–77.
12. Quoted in: E. W. Said, *Culture and Imperialism*, 1993, pp. 123–25.
13. Quoted in: A. D. King, *Urbanism, Colonialism, and the World-Economy*, 1990, p. 44.
14. Ibid., pp. 9, 44–67.
15. A. Crawford, *C. R. Ashbee: Architect, Designer and Romantic Socialist*, 1985, p. 119.
16. T. Brown, *Ireland: A Social and Cultural History 1922–79*, 1981, p. 136.
17. Quoted in J. Morley, *The Life of William Ewart Gladstone: Vol. 1*, p. 383: see also: F. S. L. Lyons, *Ireland since the Famine*, 1971, p. 141.
18. PRO/CAB.23/9 (Item 2, Cabinet Meeting, 3 March 1919).
19. The main texts are: A. Offer, *Property and Politics 1870–1914: Landownership, Law, Ideology and Urban Development in England*, 1981: D. Englander, *Landlord and Tenant in Urban Britain 1838–1918*, 1983: M. Swenarton, *Homes Fit for Heroes: The Politics and Architecture of Early State Housing in Britain*, 1981.
20. RPDCD vol. 2, no. 120 (1914), p. 179.
21. See, for example: M. Daunton (ed.), *Councillors and Tenants: Local Authority Housing in English Cities, 1919–1939*, 1984, p. 10: M. Daunton, 'Housing', in F. M. L. Thompson (ed.), *The Cambridge Social History of Britain 1750–1950: Vol. 2 People and Their Environment*, 1990, p. 237.
22. See, for instance: W. Baumgart, op. cit.
23. For a wider view of this process, see: S. Hall and B. Schwarz (eds), 'State and society, 1880–1930', in M. Langan and B. Schwarz (eds), *Crises in the British State 1880–1930*, 1985, pp. 21–24.

24. O. MacDonagh, *Ireland: The Union and its Aftermath*, 1967/77, pp. 18, 43.
25. A. D. King, *The Bungalow: The Production of a Global Culture*, 1984: A. D. King, op. cit. (1990).
26. E. W. Said, op. cit.: for an earlier, detailed study of a specific aspect of the imperialist phenomenon, see: E. W. Said, *Orientalism*, 1978.
27. E. W. Said, op. cit. (1993), p. xxiv: also pp. 4, 43.
28. Ibid., p. xxix: also pp. 15, 130–31, 295, 384.

BIBLIOGRAPHY

1. OFFICIAL PAPERS

PUBLIC RECORDS OFFICE (KEW)/ AP.1
AP.2
AP.3
AP.4
AP.5
CAB.23
CAB.24
CAB.26
CAB.27
CAB.37
CAB.41
CAB.43
CO.739
CO.783
CO.784
CO.904
CO.906
HLG.29
HO.45
HO.246
RECO.1
T.1
T.14
T.103
T.143
T.158
T.160
T.161
T.172
T.192

STATE PAPER OFFICE (DUBLIN)/ CSO.RP
DE/2
S.1305
S.3366
S.3642
S.4102

| | S.4278 |
| | S.5738 |

DUBLIN CORPORATION ARCHIVES   B.12
Minute Book of Civics Institute of Ireland
C.2/CAD
UD/1/C
UDC/2
Dublin Corporation Minutes
Reports and Printed Documents of the Corporation of Dublin

2. PARLIAMENTARY PAPERS

PP 1880 xxx Cd.2605, 'Report of the Royal Commissioners appointed to inquire into the Sewerage and Drainage of the City of Dublin, and other matters connected therewith, together with Minutes of Evidence, Appendix, Index, etc.', ff. 1–325.

PP 1884 Cd.317 viii, 'Report from the Select Committee on Agricultural Labourers (Ireland): together with the Proceedings of the Committee, Minutes of Evidence, and Appendix', ff. 245–401.

PP 1884–85 Cd.32 vii, 'Report from the Select Committee on Agricultural Labourers (Ireland): together with the Proceedings of the Committee, and Minutes of Evidence', ff. 559–677

PP 1884–85 Cd.4547 xxxi, '3rd Report of Her Majesty's Commissioners for inquiring into the Housing of the Working Classes', ff. 185–202.

PP 1884–85 xxxi Cd.4547–1, 'Minutes of evidence, etc . . . of the 3rd Report of Her Majesty's Commissioners for inquiring into the Housing of the Working Classes (Ireland)', ff. 202–311.

PP 1900 Cd.243/244 xxxix, 'Report of Committee appointed by ILGB to inquire into the Public Health of the City of Dublin', ff. 681–1007.

PP 1902 Cd.1260 xxxvii, 'Supplement to 29th Annual Report of ILGB—Reports on the Sanitary Circumstances and Administration of Cities and Towns in Ireland', ff. 429–756.

PP 1906 Cd.337 xcvii, 'Housing of the Working Classes Acts: A Return showing Particulars as to the action of Local Authorities in Ireland under the Acts, compiled to the 31st day of March, 1906', ff. 843–73.

PP 1906 Cd.376 ix, 'Report and Special Report from the Select Committee on the Housing of the Working Classes Acts Amendment Act; with the Proceedings of the Committee, Minutes of Evidence, Appendix, and Index', ff. 1–658.

PP 1906 Cd.3202 li, 'Report of the Vice-Regal Commission on Poor Law Reform in Ireland: Volume 1', ff. 349–615.

PP 1908 Bills 6/268/389, 'Housing of the Working Classes (Ireland) Bill, 1908, and various amendments', ff. 825–50.

PP 1908 Cd.4128 xxxi, 'Report of Belfast Health Commission to ILGB', ff. 699–881.

PP 1912–13 Cd.6153 xxxiv, 'Report of the Committee on Irish Finance', ff. 5–40.

PP 1913 Cd.6955 lxvi, 'Report of an Enquiry by the Board of Trade into Working Class

Rents and Retail Prices together with the rates of Wages in Certain Occupations in Industrial Towns of the UK in 1912', ff. 395–755.

PP 1914 Cd.6708 xv, 'Report of the Departmental Committee appointed by the President of the Board of Agriculture and Fisheries to inquire and report as to Buildings for Small-Holdings in England and Wales', ff. 561–756.

PP 1914 Cd.7273 xix, 'Report of the Departmental Committee appointed by the ILGB to inquire into the Housing Conditions of the Working Classes in the City of Dublin', ff. 61–106.

PP 1914 Cd.7317 xix, 'Appendix to the Report of the Departmental Committee appointed by the ILGB to inquire into the Housing Conditions of the Working Classes in the City of Dublin: Minutes of Evidence, with appendices', ff. 107–505.

PP 1914 Cd.431 lxix, 'Loans for Housing Purposes, Ireland', ff. 521–29.

PP 1916 Cd.8279 xi, 'Report of Royal Commission on the Rebellion in Ireland', ff. 171–80.

PP 1917–18 Cd.8573 xxxviii, 'Letter from the Prime Minister [Lloyd George] regarding Ireland', ff. 247–50.

PP 1918 Cd.9019 x, 'Report of the Proceedings of Irish Convention', ff. 697–871.

PP 1919 Cd.129 i, '1919 Housing of the Working Classes (Ireland) Bill, as amended by Standing Committee "D" ', ff. 905–10.

PP 1919 Cd.181 xli, 'Estimate of Probable Expenditure under the Housing of the Working Classes (Ireland) Bill', ff. 685–90.

PP 1919 Cd.184 xli, 'Circular regarding financial assistance to local authorities', ff. 691–94.

PP 1919 Cd.225 xli, 'Draft Regulations for financial assistance to local authorities', ff. 695–702.

PP 1919 Cd.226 xli, 'Draft Regulations for financial assistance to Public Utility Societies', ff. 703–08.

Annual Reports of the ILGB, 1883–1921.
Annual Reports of the Irish Board of Works, 1883–1921.
Annual Reports of the Irish Land Commissioners, 1907–1920.

House of Commons Parliamentary Debates, 1875–1922.
House of Lords Parliamentary Debates, 1875–1883.

3. NEWSPAPERS AND PERIODICALS

Architect
Architects and Builders Journal
Architectural Record
Architectural Review
Builder
Building News
Cork Weekly Examiner
Daily Express
Dublin Evening Herald
Dundalk Democrat
Freemans Journal

Garden Cities and Town Planning
Glasgow Herald
Housing Journal
Irish Architect and Building Trades Journal (formerly *Irish Architect and Craftsman*)
Irish Builder and Engineer (formerly *Dublin Builder; Irish Builder and Engineering Record; Irish Builder; Irish Builder and Technical Builder*)
Irish Bulletin
Irish Times
Irish Weekly Independent
Irish Worker
Journal of the RIAI
Limerick Chronicle
Limerick Echo
Manchester Guardian
Municipal Journal
New York Times
Northern Whig and Belfast Post
Reports of RIAI Council and of Annual General Meeting
The Statist
The Times
Town Planning Review
Waterford News and General Advertiser
Worker

4. MANUSCRIPTS

BRITISH LIBRARY ADDITIONAL MSS
  Balfour Papers
  Burns Papers
  Campbell-Bannerman Mss
  Viscount Gladstone Papers
  Ripon Papers
  C. P. Scott Papers
  Long Papers

BODLEIAN MSS
  Asquith Mss
  Birrell Mss (Medley Deposit Dep.c.299–c.303)
  Duke Mss (Dep.c.714–c.717)
  Headlam Mss (Ms. Eng. Hist. c.1100–c.1105, c.1112–c.1113)
  Magill Mss (Ms. Eng. Lett. c.213)
  Nathan Mss
  Strathcarron Mss (Ms. Eng. Hist. c.490– c.491: Ms. Eng. Hist. d.309)

HOUSE OF LORDS LIBRARY
  Bonar Law Papers
  Lloyd George Papers (Series C, D, E, F)

Samuel Papers
Strachey Papers

IRISH ARCHITECTURAL ARCHIVE

IMPERIAL WAR MUSEUM
Sir John French Papers

NATIONAL LIBRARY OF IRELAND
Joseph Brennan Papers
Thomas Johnson Papers
Redmond Papers
Robertson Papers
Sheehy-Skeffington Papers

NATIONAL LIBRARY OF SCOTLAND
Geddes Papers

ROYAL SOCIETY OF ANTIQUARIES OF IRELAND
Darkest Dublin Collection

WILTSHIRE RECORDS OFFICE
Walter Long Papers (947)

5. CONTEMPORARY BOOKS AND ARTICLES

P. Abercrombie, 'Study before town planning', *Town Planning Review*, vol. 6, no. 3, January 1916, pp. 171–90.
P. Abercrombie, S. Kelly and A. Kelly, *Dublin of the Future: The New Town Plan* (Dublin, 1923).
Lord and Lady Aberdeen, *We Twa (2 Vols)* (London, 1925).
E. P. Alabaster, *New Dublin* (Dublin, 1905).
H. R. Aldridge, *The Case for Town Planning* (London, 1915).
J. G. Allen, *The Cheap Cottage and Small Home* (London, 1912/19).
AMAI, *Report of Conference held in City Hall Dublin on 11th and 12th December 1912* (Dublin, 1913).
C. R. Ashbee, *A Book of Cottages and Little Houses* (London, 1906).
C. R. Ashbee, *Where the Great City Stands: A Study in the New Civics* (London, 1917).
W. Barrett and H. J. McCann, *The Law of the Labourers and the Labourers Question* (Dublin, 1906).
Belfast Corporation, *The Belfast Book (First Issue): Local Government in the City and Co. Borough of Belfast* (Belfast, 1929).
F. J. Biggar, *Labourers' Cottages for Ireland* (Dublin, 1907).
Board of Public Works, Ireland, *Land Improvement: Instructions with the Rules and Conditions under which Loans are Made; and Addenda, containing Specimen Plans, Specifications, etc . . .* (Dublin, 1869).
A. D. Bolton, *The Labourers' (Ireland) Acts 1883–1906* (Dublin, 1908).
A. D. Bolton, *Housing of the Working Classes (Ireland) Acts 1890–1908* (Dublin, 1914).
C. Brady, *The Practicability of Improving the Dwellings of the Labouring Classes* (London, 1854).

J. V. Brady, *The Future of Dublin. Practical Slum Reform* (Dublin, 1917).
J. M. C. Briscoe, *Town Tenants' Case Stated* (Dublin, 1904).
R. Brown, 'The housing of the Irish artizan', in Irish International Exhibition, 1907, *Irish Rural Life and Industry, with Suggestions for the Future* (Dublin, 1907).
Sir C. Cameron, *Brief History of Municipal Health Administration in Dublin* (Dublin, 1914).
Sir C. Cameron, *Autobiography* (Dublin, 1921).
R. Caulfield Orpen, 'Architecture in Ireland', in *Manchester Guardian Commercial*, 26 July 1923, Section 3 'European Reconstruction Series: Ireland', p. 48.
D. A. Chart, *Unskilled Labour in Dublin: Its Housing and Living Conditions* (Dublin, 1914).
Citizens Housing League, *Dublin: Its Slums and Death Rate* (Dublin, 1914).
Civic Exhibition, Dublin, *Official Catalogue of the Civic Exhibition, Ireland, 1914* (Dublin, 1914).
Civic Exhibition, Dublin, *Summer School of Civics* (Dublin, 1914).
J. J. Clancy, *A Handbook of Local Government in Ireland* (Dublin, 1899).
J. J. Clancy, *The Housing Problem: How to Solve It* (Dublin, 1908).
Rev. P. Coffey, *The Social Question in Ireland: Some Principles and Problems of Reconstruction* (Dublin, 1930).
J. Collings, *The Colonisation of Rural Britain* (London, 1914).
Congested Districts Board of Ireland, *Plans for Houses* (Dublin, 1914).
J. Connolly, *Labour in Irish History* (Dublin, 1910).
Cork Town Planning Association, *Cork: A Civic Survey* (Liverpool/London, 1926).
J. Cornes, *Modern Housing in Town and Country* (London, 1905).
E. M. Cosgrave, *Dublin and County Dublin in the Twentieth Century* (Dublin, 1908).
P. C. Cowan, *Report on Dublin Housing* (Dublin, 1918).
M. Davitt, *The Fall of Feudalism in Ireland: or The Story of the Land League Revolution* (London/New York, 1904).
C. Dawson, *Improved Dwellings for the Working Classes* (Dublin, 1876).
C. Dawson, 'The housing of the people with special reference to Dublin', *JSSISI*, vol. 11, part 81, August 1901, pp. 45–56.
P. L. Dickinson, *The Dublin of Yesterday* (London, 1929).
D. S. Doyle, 'Housing', *JSSISI*, vol. 13, March 1915, pp. 255–68.
Dublin Sanitary Association, *Report of the Executive Committee of the Dublin Sanitary Association for the year ending 31st December 1885* (Dublin, 1886).
Dublin Tenants Association, *Stop: The Tragedy of Dublin* (Dublin, 1918).
C. J. Eason, 'The tenement houses of Dublin: their condition and regulation', *JSSISI*, vol. 10, part 79, August 1899, pp. 383–97.
M. G. Ellison, *Housing Legislation: Papers on the Law in Ireland Relating to the Housing of the Working Classes* (Dublin, 1913).
F. Engels, *The Condition of the Working Class in England* (Oxford, 1845/1958).
F. Engels, 'The housing question', in K. Marx and F. Engels, *Collected Works: Volume 23 (1871–74)* (London, 1988), pp. 317–91.
W. G. Fallon, 'The municipal problem of Dublin', *Studies*, vol. 4, 1915, pp. 601–21.
W. Field, *Housing Homily* (Dublin, 1916).
D. Figgis, *Planning for the Future* (Dublin, 1922).
P. Geddes, *Cities in Evolution* (London, 1915).
Sir I. G. Gibbon and R. W. Bell, *The History of the London County Council, 1889–1939* (London, 1939).

F. E. Green, 'The problem of providing cottages for rural labourers', in L. Weaver, *The 'Country Life' Book of Cottages, Costing from £150 to £600* (London, 1913), pp. 6–11.
F. E. Green, *The Tyranny of the Countryside* (London, 1913).
F. E. Green, *A History of the English Agricultural Labourer, 1870–1920* (London, 1920).
T. W. Grimshaw, *The House Accommodation of the Artisan and Labouring Classes in Ireland, with Special Reference to Dublin and Other Large Towns* (Dublin, 1885).
Dr W. N. Hancock, *Suggestions for Removing the Legal Impediments to the Erection of Dwelling-houses in Towns in Ireland* (Dublin, 1871).
S. C. Harrison, 'The housing of the poor', in Irish Inter-Collegiate Christian Union, *Ireland's Hope: A Call to Service* (London, 1913), pp. 80–85.
S. Harty, 'Some considerations on the working of the Artisans' Dwellings Acts, as illustrated in the case of the Coombe Area, Dublin', *JSSISI*, 37th session, part 62, July 1884, pp. 508–22.
O. Hill, *The Homes of the London Poor* (London, 1875).
J. J. Horgan, *The Cork City Management Act* (Cork, 1929).
HTPAI, *Housing and Town Improvement* (Dublin, 1912).
ILGB, *Labourers (Ireland) Acts, 1883 to 1906: Model Plans of Labourers' Cottages* (Dublin, 1907).
ILGB, *Labourers (Ireland) Acts, 1883 to 1906: General Form of Specification for the Erection of Labourers' Cottages* (Dublin, 1907).
ILGB, *Housing of the Working Classes in Ireland* (Dublin, 1919).
Irish International Exhibition, 1907, *Irish Rural Life and Industry: With Suggestions for the Future* (Dublin, 1907).
ISSLT, *First Report: 1st January 1924 to 31st March 1926* (London, 1927).
M. Kaufman, *The Housing of the Working Classes and of the Poor* (London, 1907).
D. B. King, *The Irish Question* (New York, 1882).
Land Enquiry Committee, *The Land: The Report of the Land Enquiry Committee—Vol. 1, Rural* (London, 1913).
Land Enquiry Committee, *The Land: The Report of the Land Enquiry Committee—Vol. 2, Urban* (London, 1914).
H. A. Law, 'Irish housing in town and country', Section 3, *Manchester Guardian Commercial*, 26 July 1923, pp. 39–40.
W. Lawson, 'Remedies for overcrowding in the City of Dublin', *JSSISI*, vol. 12, part 89, January 1909, pp. 230–48.
Local Government Board for England and Wales, *The Housing of the Working Classes Acts, 1890–1909: Memorandum with respect to the Provision and Arrangement of Houses for the Working Classes* (London, 1913).
Sir W. Long, *Memories* (London, 1923).
A. M. MacSweeney, 'A study of poverty in Cork City', *Studies*, vol. 4, 1915, pp. 93–104.
Dr A. G. Malcolm, *The Sanitary State of Belfast, with Suggestions for its Improvement* (Belfast, 1852).
Dr E. D. Mapother, 'The sanitary state of Dublin', *JSSISI*, 17th session, part 27, May 1864, pp. 62–76.
Dr E. D. Mapother, 'The unhealthiness of Irish towns, and the want of sanitary legislation', *JSSISI*, 19th session, part 31, January 1866, pp. 250–75.
Dr E. D. Mapother, *Lectures on Public Health* (Dublin, 1867).

R. E. Matheson, 'The housing of the people of Ireland during the period 1841–1901', *JSSISI*, vol. 11, no. 4, November 1903, pp. 196–212.
H. Mayhew, *London Labour and the London Poor* (London, 1849–52/1985).
J. S. Mill, *England and Ireland* (London, 1868).
S. Millin, ' "Slums": a sociological retrospect of the city of Dublin', *JSSISI*, vol. 13, part 93, January 1914, pp. 130–38.
(IFS) Ministry of Local Government, *Circulars to Urban Local Authorities* (Dublin, 1922).
(IFS) Ministry of Local Government, *Housing of the Working Classes (Ireland) Acts: Memorandum for the Guidance of Local Authorities* (Dublin, 1922).
(IFS) Ministry of Local Government, *Housing of the Working Classes (Ireland) Acts: Memorandum for the Guidance of Architects* (Dublin, 1922).
(IFS) Ministry of Local Government, *The Housing (New Houses) Order* (Dublin, 1924).
(IFS) Ministry of Local Government, *House Designs: Book CL* (Dublin, 1924).
(IFS) Ministry of Local Government, *The Housing (New Houses) Order* (Dublin, 1925).
J. Morley, *The Life of William Ewart Gladstone: Vol. 1* (London, 1903).
J. Muldoon and G. MacSweeny, *Guide to Irish Local Government* (Dublin, 1899).
National Unionist Association of Conservative and Liberal Unionist Associations, *The History of Housing Reform* (London, 1913).
National Unionist Association of Conservative and Liberal Unionist Associations, *The Campaign Guide: A Handbook for Unionist Speakers* (London, 1914).
J. S. Nettlefold, *Practical Housing* (Letchworth, 1908).
J. S. Nettlefold, *Practical Town Planning: A Land and Housing Policy* (London, 1914).
J. Nolen, 'Greater Dublin: competitive designs for the town plan of Dublin, Ireland', *Landscape Architecture*, vol. 7, October 1916–July 1917, pp. 73–77.
J. Nolen, *New Towns for Old* (Boston, 1927).
R. B. O'Brien, *Dublin Castle and the Irish People* (Dublin, 1909).
W. O'Brien, *An Olive Branch in Ireland and its History* (London, 1910).
J. R. O'Connell, 'The Catholic Church and the problem of the housing of the poor' (article from *Rosary*, October 1911), in *The Problem of the Dublin Slums* (Dublin, 1913).
H. T. O'Rourke, *Dublin Civic Survey: Why you should Support a Work of National Importance* (Dublin, 1925).
H. T. O'Rourke and The Dublin Civic Survey Committee, *The Dublin Civic Survey Report* (London, 1925).
M. O'Sullivan, *A Key to the Labourers (Ireland) Acts, 1883 to 1896* (Dublin, 1902).
Sir H. Plunkett, *The Irish Convention: Confidential Report to His Majesty the King*, 1918.
C. B. Purdom (ed.), *Town Theory and Practice* (London, 1921).
A. J. Rahilly, 'The social problem in Cork', *Studies*, vol. 6, 1917, pp. 177–88.
A. E. Richardson, *Monumental Classic Architecture in Great Britain and Ireland* (London, 1914).
Sir H. Robinson, *Memories: Wise and Otherwise* (London, 1923).
Sir H. Robinson, *Further Memories of Irish Life* (London, 1924).
N. Robinson, *The Conditions of the Dwellings of the Poor in Dublin, with a Glance at the Model Lodging Houses* (London, 1862).
N. Robinson, *Homes for the Working Poor* (Dublin, 1862).
A. Roche, 'The housing of the working classes', *Tracts on Social and Industrial Questions, 1896–1905*, no. 7 (Dublin, 1905).

Miss Rooney, 'Some remedies for overcrowded city districts', *JSSISI*, vol. 12, part 87, December 1906, pp. 52–61.
RIAI, *A Cautionary Guide to Dublin* (London, 1933).
Royal Institute of Public Health, *Programme and Guide to 1911 Congress* (Dublin, 1911).
W. G. Savage, *Rural Housing* (London, 1915).
D. D. Sheehan, *Ireland since Parnell* (London, 1921).
G. Slater, 'Rural housing—a lesson from Ireland', *Contemporary Review*, vol. 82, September 1902, pp. 401–10.
N. J. Synnott, *The Housing of the Rural Population in Ireland: A Review of the Labourers' Acts* (Dublin, 1904).
N. J. Synnott, *Proposals for a New Labourers' Bill* (Naas, 1906).
N. J. Synnott, *The Housing Question in Irish Towns* (Dublin, 1908).
W. Thompson, *The Housing Handbook* (London, 1903).
W. Thompson, *Housing Up-to-date (Companion Volume to the Housing Handbook)* (London, 1907).
W. Thompson, *The Housing Problem—Paper Presented to 1908 Pan-Anglican Congress* (London, 1908).
R. Unwin, *Town Planning in Practice* (London, 1909).
R. Unwin, *Nothing Gained by Overcrowding! How the Garden City Type of Development may Benefit both Owner and Occupier* (London, 1912).
R. D. Urlin, 'On the dwellings of working men in cities, and the efforts that have been made to improve them', *JSSISI*, 18th session, part 29, January 1865, pp. 158–64.
L. Weaver, *The 'Country Life' Book of Cottages, Costing from £150 to £600* (London, 1913).
L. Weaver, *The 'Country Life' Book of Cottages (2nd Edition)* (London, 1919).
S. Webb, 'Social movements', in A. W. Ward and G. W. Prothero and S. Leathes (eds), *The Cambridge Modern History: Vol. XII. The Latest Age* (Cambridge, 1910), pp. 730–65.
R. Williams and F. Knee, *The Labourer and his Cottage* (London, 1905).
C. Williams-Ellis, *Cottage Building in Cob, Pise, Chalk and Clay: A Renaissance* (London, 1919).
A. Wright, *Disturbed Dublin: The Story of the Great Strike of 1913–14* (London, 1914).
G. Wyndham, *The Development of the State* (London, 1904).

6. SECONDARY SOURCES ON IRISH AND GENERAL HISTORY

C. Antoni, *From History to Sociology: The Transition in German Historical Thinking* (London, 1940/59).
D. L. Armstrong, *An Economic History of Agriculture in Northern Ireland, 1850–1900* (Oxford, 1989).
T. J. Barrington, 'Public administration 1927–36', in F. McManus (ed.), *The Years of the Great Test 1926–39* (Cork, 1967), pp. 80–91.
W. Baumgart, *Imperialism: The Idea and Reality of British and French Colonial Expansion, 1880–1914* (Oxford, 1982).
J. C. Beckett, *The Making of Modern Ireland 1603–1923* (London, 1966).
C. Bellamy, *Administering Central–Local Relations, 1871–1919: The Local Government Board and its Fiscal and Cultural Context* (Manchester, 1988).
T. Bennett, 'Introduction', in T. Bennett, C. Mercer and J. Woollacott (eds), *Popular Culture and Social Relations* (Milton Keynes/Philadelphia, 1986), pp. xiv–xv.

G. F. A. Best, 'Another part of the island', in H. J. Dyos and M. Wolff (eds), *The Victorian City: Images and Realities, Vol. 2* (London, 1973), pp. 389–411.
P. Bew, *Land and the National Question in Ireland 1858–82* (Dublin, 1978).
P. Bew, *Conflict and Conciliation in Ireland 1890–1910: Parnellites and Radical Agrarians* (Oxford, 1987).
P. Bew, P. Gibbon and H. Patterson, *The State in Northern Ireland 1921–72: Political Forces and Social Classes* (Manchester, 1979).
D. G. Boyce, *Nationalism in Ireland* (London/Dublin, 1982).
D. G. Boyce and C. Hazlehurst, 'The unknown chief secretary; H. E. Duke and Ireland, 1916–18', *Irish Historical Studies*, no. 79, March 1977.
A. Boyd, *The Rise of the Irish Trade Unions* (Dublin, 1972/85).
J. W. Boyle, 'A marginal figure: the Irish rural labourer', in S. Clark and J. S. Donnelly (eds), *Irish Peasants: Violence and Political Unrest, 1780–1914* (Manchester, 1983), pp. 311–38.
J. W. Boyle (ed.), *Leaders and Workers* (Cork, 1966).
K. B. Brown, *John Burns* (London, 1977).
M. Brown, *The Politics of Irish Literature: From Thomas Davis to W. B. Yeats* (London, 1972).
T. Brown, *Ireland: A Social and Cultural History 1922–79* (London, 1981).
C. Buci-Glucksmann, *Gramsci and the State* (London, 1980).
P. J. Buckland, *The Factory of Grievances: Devolved Government in Northern Ireland 1921–39* (Dublin, 1979).
I. Budge and C. O'Leary, *Belfast: Approach to Crisis. A Study of Belfast Politics 1613–1970* (London, 1973).
W. L. Burn, 'Free trade in land: an aspect of the Irish question', *Transactions of the Royal Historical Society*, 4th Series, vol. 31, 1949.
D. Cairns and S. Richards, *Writing Ireland: Colonialism, Nationalism and Culture* (Manchester, 1988).
B. Chubb, *The Government and Politics of Ireland* (London, 1970/82).
B. Chubb, 'Britain and Irish constitutional development', in P. J. Drudy (ed.), *Ireland and Britain since 1922 (Irish Studies 5)* (Cambridge, 1986), pp. 21–44.
R. S. Churchill, *Winston Churchill 1874–1965 (Vol. 2 Companion Pt. 1, 1901–1907)* (London, 1969).
R. S. Churchill, *Winston Churchill 1874–1965 (Vol. 2 Companion Pt. 3, 1911–1914)* (London, 1969).
S. Clark, *The Social Origins of the Irish Land War* (Princeton, 1979).
J. D. Clarkson, *Labour and Nationalism in Ireland* (New York, 1925).
G. Cook, 'Britain's legacy to the Irish social security system', in P. J. Drudy, *Ireland and Britain since 1922 (Irish Studies 5)* (Cambridge, 1986), pp. 65–85.
L. M. Cullen, *An Economic History of Ireland since 1660* (London, 1972).
L. M. Cullen, *The Emergence of Modern Ireland 1600–1900* (London, 1981).
L. P. Curtis Jr, *Coercion and Conciliation in Ireland 1880–1892* (New Jersey/London, 1963).
M. Daly, *Social and Economic History of Ireland since 1800* (Dublin, 1981).
M. Daly, 'Late nineteenth- and early twentieth-century Dublin', in D. Harkness and M. O'Dowd (eds), *The Town in Ireland* (Belfast, 1981), pp. 221–52.
M. Daly, *Dublin, The Deposed Capital. A Social and Economic History, 1860–1914*, (Cork, 1984).
M. Daly, 'Industrial policy in Scotland and Ireland in the inter-war years', in R.

Mitchison and P. Roebuck (eds), *Economy and Society in Scotland and Ireland 1500–1939* (Edinburgh, 1988), pp. 288–96.
G. Dangerfield, *The Damnable Question* (Boston, 1976).
E. David (ed.), *Inside Asquith's Cabinet: From the Diaries of Charles Hobhouse* (London, 1977).
J. S. Donnelly Jr, *The Land and the People of Nineteenth-Century Cork* (London/Boston, 1975).
R. Douglas, 'God gave the land to the people', in A. J. A. Morris (ed.), *Edwardian Radicalism* (London, 1974), pp. 148–61.
J. P. Dunbabin, *Rural Discontent in Nineteenth-Century Britain* (London, 1974).
R. D. Edwards, *An Atlas of Irish History (2nd Edition)* (London/New York, 1981).
R. D. Edwards, *James Connolly* (Dublin, 1981).
R. Ellmann, *James Joyce* (Oxford, 1982/88).
R. Fanning, *The Irish Department of Finance 1922–58* (Dublin, 1978).
R. Fanning, 'Britain's legacy: government and administration', in P. J. Drudy (ed.), *Ireland and Britain since 1922 (Irish Studies 5)* (Cambridge, 1986), pp. 45–64.
R. Fanning, *Independent Ireland* (Dublin, 1986).
B. Farrell, *The Founding of Dáil Éireann: Parliament and Nation Building* (Dublin, 1971).
D. Fitzpatrick, *Politics and Irish Life 1913–1921: Provincial Experience of War and Revolution* (Dublin, 1977).
D. Fitzpatrick, 'The disappearance of the Irish agricultural labourer, 1841–1912', *Irish Economic and Social History*, vol. vii, 1980, pp. 66–92.
D. Fitzpatrick (ed.), *Ireland and the First World War* (Dublin, 1986).
R. F. Foster, *Charles Stewart Parnell: The Man and his Family* (Hassocks, 1976).
R. F. Foster, *Modern Ireland 1600–1972* (London, 1988).
A. L. H. Gailey, *Ireland and the Death of Kindness: The Experience of Constructive Unionism 1890–1905* (Cork, 1987).
L. M. Geary, *The Plan of Campaign 1886–1891* (Cork, 1986).
A. M. Gibbs, *Shaw* (Edinburgh, 1969).
J. M. Goldstrom and L. A. Clarkson (eds), *Irish Population, Economy and Society* (Oxford, 1981).
B. J. Graham and S. Hood, 'Town tenant protest in late-nineteenth and early-twentieth century Ireland', *Irish Economic and Social History*, vol. 21, 1994, pp. 39–57.
A. Gramsci, *Selections from the Prison Notebooks* (London, 1971).
A. Gramsci, *Selections from Political Writings (1910–1920)* (London, 1977).
A. Gramsci, *Selections from Political Writings (1921–1926)* (London, 1978).
A. Gramsci, *Selections from Cultural Writings* (London, 1985).
J. Gray, *City in Revolt: James Larkin and the Belfast Dock Strike of 1907* (Belfast, 1985).
C. D. Greaves, *The Life and Times of James Connolly* (Dublin, 1961).
S. Gribbon, 'An Irish city: Belfast 1911', in D. Harkness and M. O'Dowd (eds), *The Town in Ireland* (Belfast, 1981), pp. 203–20.
S. Gribbon, *Edwardian Belfast: A Social Profile* (Belfast, 1982).
A. R. G. Griffiths, *The Irish Board of Works, 1831–1878* (New York/London, 1987).
D. Grigg, *Lloyd George: From Peace to War 1912–1916* (London, 1985).
D. Gwynn, *The Life of John Redmond* (London, 1932).
S. Hall and B. Schwarz, 'State and society, 1880–1930', in M. Langan and B. Schwarz (eds), *Crises in the British State 1880–1930* (London, 1985), pp. 7–32.

D. Hardy, 'War, planning and social change', *Planning Perspectives*, vol. 4, 1989, pp. 191–94.
J. Harris, *Unemployment and Politics: A Study in English Social Policy 1886–1914* (Oxford, 1972).
M. Hechter, *Internal Colonialism: The Celtic Fringe in British National Development, 1536–1966* (London, 1975).
J. Hill, *The Building of Limerick* (Cork, 1991).
E. J. Hobsbawm, *Industry and Empire* (London, 1968).
K. T. Hoppen, *Elections, Politics, and Society in Ireland 1832–1885* (Oxford, 1984).
K. T. Hoppen, 'Landlords, society and electoral politics in mid-nineteenth century Ireland', in C. H. E. Philpin (ed.), *Nationalism and Popular Protest in Ireland* (Cambridge, 1987), pp. 284–319.
J. A. Jackson, *The Irish in Great Britain* (London, 1963).
P. Jalland, 'A Liberal Chief Secretary and the Irish question: Augustine Birrell, 1907–1914', *Historical Journal*, vol. 19, no. 2, 1976, pp. 421–51.
P. Jalland, *The Liberals and Ireland: The Ulster Question in British Politics to 1914* (Brighton, 1980).
P. B. Johnson, *Land Fit for Heroes: The Planning of British Reconstruction 1916–1919* (Chicago/London, 1968).
D. S. Johnston, 'The Northern Ireland economy, 1914–39', in L. Kennedy and P. Ollerenshaw (eds), *An Economic History of Ulster, 1820–1940* (Manchester, 1985), pp. 184–223.
D. S. Johnston, *The Interwar Economy in Ireland* (Dublin, 1985).
E. Jones, *A Social Geography of Belfast* (London, 1960).
E. Jones, 'Late Victorian Belfast: 1850–1900', in J. C. Beckett and R. E. Glasscock, *Belfast: The Origin and Growth of an Industrial City* (London, 1967), pp. 109–19.
P. R. Kaim-Caudle, *Social Policy in the Irish Republic* (Dublin, 1967).
L. Kennedy, 'The rural economy, 1820–1914', in L. Kennedy and P. Ollerenshaw, *An Economic History of Ulster, 1820–1940* (Manchester, 1985), pp. 1–61.
C. F. Kolbert and T. O'Brien, *Land Reform in Ireland* (Cambridge, Mass., 1975).
D. Krause (ed.), *The Letters of Sean O'Casey 1910–41: Volume 1* (New York, 1975).
E. Larkin, 'Socialism and Catholicism in Ireland', *Church History*, vol. 30, 1964, pp. 462–82.
E. Larkin, *James Larkin: Irish Labour Leader, 1876–1947* (London, 1965).
R. J. Lawrence, *The Government of Northern Ireland: Public Finances and Public Services 1921–1964* (Oxford, 1965).
J. Lee, *The Modernisation of Irish Society 1848–1918* (Dublin, 1973).
J. Lee, *Ireland 1912–85* (Cambridge, 1989).
L. Leneman, *Fit for Heroes?: Land Settlement in Scotland after World War 1* (Aberdeen, 1989).
J. Leonard, 'Lest we forget', in D. Fitzpatrick (ed.), *Ireland and the First World War* (Dublin, 1988), pp. 61–62.
I. Lustick, *State-Building Failure in British Ireland and French Algeria* (Berkeley, 1985).
P. Lynch, 'The social revolution that never was', in T. D. Williams (ed.), *The Irish Struggle 1916–1926* (London, 1966), pp. 41–54.
F. S. L. Lyons, *The Irish Parliamentary Party 1890–1910* (London, 1951).
F. S. L. Lyons, *The Fall of Parnell 1890–91* (London, 1960).

F. S. L. Lyons, *John Dillon* (London/Chicago, 1968).
F. S. L. Lyons, *Ireland since the Famine* (London, 1971).
F. S. L. Lyons, *Charles Stewart Parnell* (London, 1977).
F. S. L. Lyons, *Culture and Anarchy in Ireland 1890–1939* (Oxford, 1979).
F. S. L. Lyons and R. A. J. Hawkins (eds), *Ireland under the Union: Varieties of Tension* (Oxford, 1980).
D. McAleese, 'Anglo-Irish economic interdependence: from excessive intimacy to a wider embrace', in P. J. Drudy (ed.), *Ireland and Britain since 1922 (Irish Studies 5)* (Cambridge, 1986), pp. 87–106.
C. McArthur, 'The dialectic of national identity: The Glasgow Empire Exhibition of 1938', in T. Bennett, C. Mercer and J. Woollacott (eds), *Popular Culture and Social Relations* (Milton Keynes/Philadelphia, 1986), pp. 117–34.
J. McColgan, *British Policy and the Irish Administration, 1920–22* (London, 1983).
O. MacDonagh, *Ireland: The Union and its Aftermath* (London, 1967/77).
O. MacDonagh, *States of Mind: A Study of Anglo-Irish Conflict 1780–1950* (London, 1983).
R. B. McDowell, *The Irish Administration 1801–1914* (London/Toronto, 1964).
R. B. McDowell, *The Irish Convention 1917–18* (London/Toronto, 1970).
N. Mansergh, *The Irish Free State: Its Government and Politics* (London, 1934).
N. Mansergh, *The Government of Northern Ireland* (London, 1936).
N. Mansergh, *The Irish Question 1840–1921* (London, 1940/75).
J. Meenan, *The Irish Economy since 1922* (Liverpool, 1970).
W. L. Micks, *History of the Congested Districts Board* (Dublin, 1925).
D. W. Miller, *Queen's Rebels: Unionist Loyalism in Historical Perspective* (Dublin, 1978).
A. Mitchell, *Labour in Irish Politics 1890–1930* (Dublin, 1974).
R. Mitchison and P. Roebuck (eds), *Economy and Society in Scotland and Ireland 1500–1939* (Edinburgh, 1988).
W. J. Mommsen, *Theories of Imperialism* (London, 1980).
M. Murphy, 'The economic and social structure of nineteenth-century Cork', in D. Harkness and M. O'Dowd (eds), *The Town in Ireland* (Belfast, 1981), pp. 125–54.
C. C. O'Brien (ed.), *The Shaping of Modern Ireland* (London, 1960).
J. V. O'Brien, *William O'Brien and the Course of Irish Politics 1881–1918* (Berkeley, 1976).
J. V. O'Brien, *Dear Dirty Dublin: A City in Distress, 1899–1916* (London, 1982).
L. O'Broin, *The Chief Secretary: Augustine Birrell in Ireland* (London, 1969).
L. O'Broin, *Dublin Castle and the 1916 Rising* (New York, 1971).
S. O'Casey, *Autobiography Volume 4: Inishfallen, Fare Thee Well* (London, 1949/72).
S. O'Casey, *Three Plays* (London/New York, 1968).
E. O'Connor, *Syndicalism in Ireland 1917–1923* (Cork, 1988).
P. O'Farrell, *Ireland's English Question: Anglo-Irish Relations 1534–1970* (New York, 1971).
L. O'Flaherty, *Famine* (London, 1937).
E. O'Halpin, *The Decline of the Union: British Government in Ireland 1892–1920* (Dublin/Syracuse, 1987).
C. O'Leary, 'Belfast Urban Government in the age of reform', in D. Harkness and M. O'Dowd (eds), *The Town in Ireland* (Belfast, 1981), pp. 187–202.
D. J. O'Neill, 'Explaining Irish underdevelopment: Plunkett and Connolly prior to 1916', *Eire-Ireland*, vol. 22, no. 4, Winter 1987, pp. 47–71.
M. A. G. O'Tuathaigh, 'Ireland and Britain under the Union, 1800–1921: an overview',

in P. J. Drudy (ed.), *Ireland and Britain since 1922 (Irish Studies 5)* (Cambridge, 1986), pp. 1–20.
P. Ollerenshaw, 'Industry, 1820–1914', in L. Kennedy and P. Ollerenshaw (eds), *An Economic History of Ulster, 1820–1940* (Manchester, 1985), pp. 62–108.
H. Patterson, *Class Conflict and Sectarianism: The Protestant Working Class and the Belfast Labour Movement 1868–1920* (Belfast, 1980).
Sir C. Petrie, *Walter Long and his Times* (London, 1936).
F. Prill, *Ireland, Britain and Germany 1871–1914: Problems of Nationalism and Religion in Nineteenth Century Europe* (Dublin, 1975).
P. Rowland, *The Last Liberal Governments: The Promised Land, 1905–1910* (London/New York, 1969).
P. Rowland, *Lloyd George* (London, 1975).
E. Rumpf and D. Hepburn, *Nationalism and Socialism in Twentieth Century Ireland* (Liverpool, 1977).
D. Ryan, *The Workers' Republic: a Selection from the Writings of James Connolly* (Dublin, 1951).
E. W. Said, *Orientalism* (New York, 1978).
E. W. Said, *Culture and Imperialism* (London, 1993).
G. R. Searle, *The Quest for National Efficiency: A Study in British Politics and Political Thought, 1899–1914* (Oxford, 1971).
B. L. Solow, *The Land Question and the Irish Economy, 1870–1903* (Cambridge, Mass., 1971).
A. T. Q. Stewart, *The Ulster Crisis* (London, 1967).
R. Swift and S. Gilley (eds), *The Irish in the Victorian City* (London, 1985).
R. Swift and S. Gilley, *The Irish in Britain 1815–1939* (London, 1989).
C. Townshend, *The British Campaign in Ireland 1919–1921: the Development of Political and Military Policies* (Oxford, 1975).
C. Townshend, 'Modernisation and nationalism: perspectives in recent Irish history', *History*, vol. 66, 1981, pp. 233–43.
J. Turner, *Lloyd George's Secretariat* (Cambridge, 1980).
G. Walker, 'Labour in Scotland and Northern Ireland: the inter-war experience', in R. Mitchison and P. Roebuck (eds), *Economy and Society in Scotland and Ireland 1500–1939* (Edinburgh, 1988), pp. 267–75.
P. J. Waller, *Democracy and Sectarianism: A Political and Social History of Liverpool 1868–1939* (Liverpool, 1981).
R. Wilson, 'Imperialism in crisis: the "Irish dimension" ', in M. Langan and B. Schwarz (eds), *Crises in the British State 1880–1930* (London, 1985), pp. 151–78.
S. H. Zebel, *Balfour: A Political Biography* (Cambridge, 1977).

7. SECONDARY SOURCES ON HOUSING AND ARCHITECTURAL HISTORY

F. H. A. Aalen, 'Evolution of the traditional house in Western Ireland', *RSAI Journal*, 1966.
F. H. A. Aalen, *Man and the Landscape in Ireland* (London, 1978).
F. H. A. Aalen, 'Approaches to the working-class housing problem in late Victorian Dublin: the Dublin Artisans Dwellings Company and the Guinness (later Iveagh)

Trust', in R. J. Bender (ed.), *New Research on the Social Geography of Ireland*, 1984, pp. 161–90.

F. H. A. Aalen, 'The Working-Class Housing Movement in Dublin, 1850–1920', in M. J. Bannon (ed.), *The Emergence of Irish Planning 1880–1920* (Dublin, 1985), pp. 131–88.

F. H. A. Aalen, 'The rehousing of rural labourers in Ireland under the Labourers (Ireland) Acts, 1883–1919', *Journal of Historical Geography*, vol. 12, no. 3, 1986, pp. 287–306.

F. H. A. Aalen, 'Public housing in Ireland, 1880–1921', *Planning Perspectives*, vol. 2, 1987, pp. 175–93.

F. H. A. Aalen, 'Homes for Irish heroes: housing under the Irish Land (Provision for Soldiers and Sailors) Act 1919, and the Irish Sailors' and Soldiers' Land Trust', *Town Planning Review*, vol. 59, no. 3, 1988, pp. 305–23.

F. H. A. Aalen, 'Ebenezer Howard's Garden City: the rural context *c.* 1880–1920', paper to 1989 International Planning History Group Conference.

F. H. A. Aalen, 'Lord Meath, city improvement and social imperialism', *Planning Perspectives*, vol. 4, 1989, pp. 127–52.

F. H. A. Aalen, *The Iveagh Trust* (London/Dublin, 1990).

F. H. A. Aalen, 'Health and housing in Dublin *c.* 1850 to 1921', in F. H. A. Aalen and K. Whelan (eds), *Dublin City and County: From Prehistory to Present* (Dublin, 1990).

F. H. A. Aalen, 'Ireland', in C. G. Pooley (ed.), *Housing Strategies in Europe 1880–1930* (Leicester, 1992).

F. H. A. Aalen, 'Constructive Unionism and the shaping of rural Ireland, *c.* 1880–1921', *Rural History*, vol. 4, no. 2, 1993, pp. 137–64.

T. J. Baker and L. M. O'Brien, *The Irish Housing System: A Critical Overview* (Dublin, 1979).

M. J. Bannon (ed.), *The Emergence of Irish Planning 1880–1920* (Dublin, 1985).

M. J. Bannon (ed.), *Planning: The Irish Experience 1920–1988* (Dublin, 1989).

S. Beattie, *A Revolution in London Housing* (London, 1980).

W. D. Birrell, P. A. R. Hillyard, A. Murie and B. J. D. Roche, *Housing in Northern Ireland* (London, 1971).

J. M. Blackwell and E. Brangan, *Survey of the Housing Stock—1980: A Summary Report* (Dublin, 1984).

M. Bowley, *Housing and the State 1919–1944* (London, 1945).

M. C. Boyer, *Dreaming the Rational City: The Myth of American Town Planning* (Cambridge, Mass., 1983).

C. E. B. Brett, *Buildings of Belfast 1700–1914* (Belfast, 1967).

C. E. B. Brett, *Housing a Divided Community* (Dublin/Belfast, 1986).

J. Burnett, *A Social History of Housing 1815–1970* (Newton Abbot/London, 1978/85).

M. Castells, *The Urban Question: A Marxist Approach* (London, 1972/76).

M. Craig, *The Architecture of Ireland: From the Earliest Times to 1880* (London/Dublin, 1982).

A. Crawford, *Charles Robert Ashbee: Architect, Designer and Romantic Socialist* (New York/London, 1985).

W. L. Creese, *The Search for Environment: The Garden City. Before and After* (New Haven, 1966).

K. Danaher, *Ireland's Vernacular Architecture* (Cork, 1975/78).

G. Darley, *Octavia Hill* (London, 1990).

M. J. Daunton, *House and Home in the Victorian City* (London, 1983).

M. J. Daunton, *A Property Owning Democracy: Housing in Britain* (London, 1987).
M. J. Daunton, 'Housing', in F. M. L. Thompson (ed.), *The Cambridge Social History of Britain 1750–1950: Vol. 2. People and Their Environment* (Cambridge, 1990), pp. 195–250.
M. J. Daunton (ed.), *Councillors and Tenants: Local Authority Housing in English Cities, 1919–1939* (Leicester, 1984).
M. J. Daunton (ed.), *Housing the Workers, 1850–1914: A Comparative Perspective* (Leicester, 1990).
A. Defries, *The Interpreter Geddes: The Man and His Gospel* (London, 1927).
Department of Local Government and Public Health, *Report of Inquiry into the Housing of the Working Classes of the City of Dublin 1939/43* (Dublin, 1944).
Department of Local Government, *Housing: A Review of Past Operations and Immediate Requirements* (Dublin, 1948).
G. Dix, 'Patrick Abercrombie 1897–1957', in G. E. Cherry (ed.), *Pioneers in British Planning* (London, 1981), pp. 103–30.
H. Dixon, *Ulster Architecture 1800–1900* (Belfast, 1972).
H. Dixon, *An Introduction to Ulster Architecture* (Belfast, 1975).
J. Dyos, *Victorian Suburb: A Study of the Growth of Camberwell* (Leicester, 1961).
B. Edwards, 'The Glasgow Improvement Scheme as a model of urban renewal', *Planning History*, vol. 12, no. 3, 1990, pp. 7–14.
D. Englander, *Landlord and Tenant in Urban Britain 1838–1918* (Oxford, 1983).
B. Finnimore, *Houses from the Factory: System Building and the Welfare State* (London, 1989).
A. Forty, *Objects of Desire: Design and Society 1750–1980* (London, 1986).
D. Fraser, *The Evolution of the Welfare State* (London, 1973/84).
M. Fraser, 'Public building and colonial policy in Dublin, 1760–1800', *Architectural History*, vol. 28, 1985, pp. 102–22.
M. Fraser, review article on S. Rothery, *Ireland and the New Architecture 1900–1940, AA Files*, no. 24, Autumn 1992, pp. 96–98.
P. Froggatt, 'Industrialisation and health in Belfast', in D. Harkness and M. O'Dowd (eds), *The Town in Ireland* (Belfast, 1981), pp. 155–86.
A. Gailey, *Rural Houses of the North of Ireland* (Edinburgh, 1984).
A. Gailey, 'Traditional buildings in the landscape: conservation and preservation', in F. H. A. Aalen (ed.), *The Future of the Irish Rural Landscape* (Dublin, 1985), pp. 26–45.
A. Gailey, 'Changes in Irish rural housing, 1600–1900', in P. O'Flanagan, P. Ferguson and K. Whelan (eds), *Rural Ireland 1600–1900: Modernisation and Change* (Cork, 1987), pp. 86–103.
S. Martin Gaskell, *Model Housing: From the Great Exhibition to the Festival of Britain*, (London, 1987).
E. Gauldie, *Cruel Habitations: A History of Working Class Housing 1780–1918* (London, 1974).
M. Gough, 'Socio-economic conditions and the genesis of planning in Cork', in M. J. Bannon (ed.), *The Emergence of Irish Planning 1880–1920* (Dublin, 1985), pp. 307–32.
P. Greenhalgh, *Ephemeral Vistas: The Expositions Universelles, Great Exhibitions and World's Fairs 1851–1939* (Manchester, 1989).
E. Gribbin and P. Braniff, *Urban Housing Waterford: A Case Study of Two Areas* (Dublin, 1979).

P. Harbison, H. Potterton and J. Sheehy, *Irish Art and Architecture: From Prehistory to the Present* (London, 1978).
R. Hebblethwaite, 'The municipal housing programme in Sheffield before 1914', *Architectural History*, vol. 30, 1987, pp. 143–80
J. Hendry, 'The control of development and the origins of planning in Northern Ireland', in M. J. Bannon (ed.), *Planning: The Irish Experience 1922–1988* (Dublin, 1989), pp. 105–21.
Irish Government White Paper, *Housing—Progress and Prospects* (Dublin, 1964).
F. Jackson, *Sir Raymond Unwin: Architect, Planner and Visionary* (London, 1985).
A. D. King, *The Bungalow: The Production of a Global Culture* (London, 1984).
A. D. King, *Urbanism, Colonialism, and the World-Economy* (London/New York, 1990).
P. Kitchen, *A Most Unsettling Person: An Introduction to the Ideas and Life of Patrick Geddes* (London, 1975).
A. McCashin and M. Morrissey, 'Housing policy: North and South', *Administration*, vol. 33, no. 3, 1985, pp. 291–325.
N. McCullough and V. Mulvin, *A Lost Tradition: The Nature of Architecture in Ireland* (Dublin, 1988).
J. McGahey, 'Bolt-holes for weekenders: the press and the Cheap Cottages Exhibition, Letchworth Garden City 1905', *Planning History*, vol. 12, no. 2, 1990, pp. 17–18.
P. Mairet, *Pioneer of Sociology: Patrick Geddes* (London, 1952).
P. Meighen, *Housing in Ireland* (Dublin, 1965).
H. E. Meller, 'Cities and evolution: Patrick Geddes as an international prophet of town planning before 1914', in A. Sutcliffe (ed.), *The Rise of Modern Urban Planning, 1800–1914* (London, 1980), pp. 199–223.
H. E. Meller, 'Patrick Geddes 1854–1932', in G. E. Cherry (ed.), *Pioneers in British Planning* (London, 1981), pp. 46–71.
H. E. Meller, *Patrick Geddes: Social Evolutionist and City Planner* (London/New York, 1990).
S. Merrett, *State Housing in Britain* (London, 1979).
M. Miller, 'Raymond Unwin and the planning of Dublin', in M. J. Bannon (ed.), *The Emergence of Irish Planning 1880–1920* (Dublin, 1985), pp. 263–305.
M. Miller, *Raymond Unwin: Garden Cities and Town Planning* (Leicester, 1992).
C. O'Connor and J. O'Regan (Architectural Association of Ireland), *Public Works: The Architecture of the Office of Public Works 1831–1987* (Dublin, 1987).
D. O'Connor, *Housing in Dublin's Inner City* (Dublin, 1979).
A. Offer, *Property and Politics 1870–1914: Landownership, Law, Ideology, and Urban Development in England* (Cambridge, 1981).
S. Pepper and M. Swenarton, 'Neo-Georgian maison-type', *Architectural Review*, vol. 168, no. 1002, August 1980, pp. 87–92.
C. G. Pooley, 'Housing for the poorest poor: slum-clearance and rehousing in Liverpool, 1890–1918', *Journal of Historical Geography*, vol. 11, no. 1, 1985, pp. 70–88.
C. G. Pooley (ed.), *Housing Strategies in Europe 1880–1930* (Leicester, 1992).
D. Roche (Institute of Public Administration), *Local Government in Ireland* (Dublin, 1982).
S. Rothery, *Ireland and the New Architecture 1900–1940* (Dublin, 1991).
E. R. Scoffham, *The Shape of British Housing* (London/New York, 1984).
M. Scott, *American City Planning since 1890* (Berkeley, 1969).

P. Shaffrey, *The Irish Town: An Approach to Survival* (Dublin, 1975).
P. Shaffrey, 'Settlement patterns: rural housing, villages, small towns', in F. H. A. Aalen (ed.), *The Future of the Irish Rural Landscape* (Dublin, 1985), pp. 57–65.
P. and M. Shaffrey, *Irish Countryside Buildings* (Dublin, 1985).
J. Sheehy, *J. J. McCarthy and the Gothic Revival in Ireland* (Belfast, 1977).
J. Sheehy, *The Rediscovery of Ireland's Past: The Celtic Revival 1830–1930* (London, 1980).
P. J. Smith, 'Planning as environmental improvement: slum clearance in Victorian Edinburgh', in A. Sutcliffe (ed.), *The Rise of Modern Urban Planning, 1800–1914* (London, 1980), pp. 99–133.
G. Stedman Jones, *Outcast London: A Study in the Relationship between Classes in Victorian Society* (Oxford, 1971).
A. Sutcliffe, *Towards the Planned City: Germany, Britain, the United States, and France, 1780–1914* (Oxford, 1981).
A. Sutcliffe, 'Britain's first town planning act: A review of the 1909 achievement', *Town Planning Review*, vol. 59, no. 3, 1988, pp. 289–303.
A. Sutcliffe (ed.), *The Rise of Modern Urban Planning, 1800–1914* (London, 1980).
M. Swenarton, *Homes Fit for Heroes: The Politics and Architecture of Early State Housing in Britain* (London, 1981).
M. Swenarton, *Artisans and Architects: The Ruskinian Tradition in Architectural Thought* (London, 1989).
J. N. Tarn, *Working-Class Housing in Nineteenth-Century Britain* (London, 1971).
J. N. Tarn, *Five Per Cent Philanthropy: An Account of Housing in Urban Areas between 1840 and 1914* (Cambridge, 1973).
J. N. Tarn, 'Housing reform and the emergence of town planning in Britain before 1914', in A. Sutcliffe (ed.), *The Rise of Modern Urban Planning, 1800–1914* (London, 1980), pp. 71–97.
P. Wilding, 'Towards Exchequer subsidies for housing 1906–14', *Social and Economic Administration*, vol. 6, no. 1, January 1972, pp. 3–18.
A. S. Wohl, *The Eternal Slum: Housing and Social Policy in Victorian London* (London, 1977).
J. A. Yelling, *Slums and Slum Clearance in Victorian London* (London, 1986).

8. UNPUBLISHED THESES

T. C. Griffiths, 'Local Authority rural housing: a case study of the Tallaght Area' (TCD Dept of Geography BA Thesis, 1986).
C. Lincoln, 'Working class housing in Dublin, 1914–1939' (UCD MA Thesis, 1979).
B. McDonnell, 'The Dublin Labour Movement, 1894–1907' (UCD PhD Thesis, 1979).
J. P. Moore, 'Marino Housing Estate' (UCD BA Thesis, 1986).
S. C. Moore, 'The development of working-class housing in Ireland 1840–1912' (University of Ulster PhD Thesis, 1986).
N. O'Flanagan, 'Dublin City in an age of war and revolution, 1914–1924' (UCD MA Thesis, 1985).

INDEX

Aalen, Frederick 19, 241
Abercrombie, Patrick 132, 138–42, 147, 165, 252, 282, 296
Aberdeen, Lord and Lady 108–09, 111, 113–14, 133–34, 136–38, 145, 282
Adams, Professor W. S. G. 175–80, 183, 227
Addison, Christopher 108, 170, 174, 178, 183, 188, 206, 232, 237, 299
Anderson, Sir John 228–29, 232–33, 238, 248, 250, 259–60
Ashbee, Charles Robert 54, 138, 146, 296
Ashworth, Charles 72
Asquith, Herbert Henry 40–41, 86, 108, 123–24, 169
Association for Housing the Very Poor 73
Association of Municipal Authorities of Ireland (AMAI) 101–02, 134, 143, 171, 182, 190, 224, 229, 231
Aston, E. A. 106, 111, 128–29, 134, 136, 250–52, 282

Balfour, Arthur 30, 32–34, 35, 81–82, 187, 293–94, 298
Belfast, conditions in 62–63, 80–81, 182–83, 277–78
Belfast Corporation 94–95, 97, 99–100, 137, 182–83, 194–95, 200–01, 206, 224, 235, 239, 275–78
Birrell, Augustine 44, 46, 53, 86–89, 101, 108–09, 114, 124–26, 128, 149–50
Briscoe, Coughlan 83, 135, 205
Bryce, James 40–41, 45
Burns, John 86, 119–22, 297
Butler, R. M. 13–14, 54, 118, 212
Byrne, Thomas Joseph 54–58, 86, 118, 159–62, 210, 213, 223, 280

Cameron, Sir Charles 66, 69, 76, 110
Campbell-Bannerman, Henry 40–41, 87
Carson, Sir Edward 58, 182, 196, 211, 246

Chamberlain, Austen 119, 186, 189, 207, 227–28, 243
Citizens Housing League (CHL) 128–29, 142, 145, 162, 251
Clancy, J. J. 87, 89, 108, 110, 125, 129, 136, 149
Congested Districts Board (CDB) 30–33, 297
Connolly, James 87, 103–04, 154
Conservative Party, reactions to pre-war Irish housing policy 88, 119–21, 293–94, 297–98
Cosgrave, William 87, 129, 136, 203, 205, 226, 231, 236, 262, 270, 278–82, 284, 290
Cowan, Dr Peter 91, 94, 109, 134, 152, 164, 171–73, 178, 205, 209–10, 212, 214, 224, 233, 297
Craig, Sir James 236, 273–74, 277–78
Cross Housing Act, 1875 *see* Housing acts

Dáil Éireann 198, 203–04, 229–31, 234, 280
Daly, Mary 19, 105
Daunton, Martin 18, 299
Davitt, Michael 25, 36, 76, 81
Deane, Thomas Manly 9, 47, 49
De Valera, Eamonn 180, 198, 204, 236, 278, 282–83
Devlin, Joseph 94, 181, 211
Drew, Sir Thomas 9, 72
Dublin Artizans Dwellings Company (DADC) 71–72, 97
Dublin Civic Exhibition, 1914 136–38
Dublin, conditions in 63–67, 149–50, 154–59, 283–84, 290–91
Dublin Corporation 71, 76, 80, 84–85, 88, 93, 96–97, 110, 149–51, 153–54, 158–69, 194–95, 200, 205–06, 231, 283–91, 297
Dublin Housing Inquiry, 1913–14 103, 108–15, 124–25, 294, 298

Dublin Industrial Tenements Company 70
Dublin Town Plan Competition, 1914 138–42, 155
Duckworth, George 263–70
Duke, H. E. 155–59, 168–69, 171–75, 284, 294

Easter Rising, 1916, consequences of 154–59, 294, 299
Englander, David 17, 131, 298

Fairbrothers Fields Estate, Dublin 153, 164–69, 172, 236, 284–85, 297
Field, William 44, 82–83
Forty, Adrian 19
French Lord 180, 213, 228, 241–44, 249

Geddes, Patrick 111, 113, 129–30, 132–47, 282, 284–85, 295–96
Gladstone, William 6, 26, 29, 81, 297
Gramsci, Antonio 7, 293
Great Famine, 1845–49, consequences of 21–27
Greenwood, Sir Hamar 228–29, 234, 238, 248, 259
Griffith-Boscawen, Sir Arthur 119–20, 124, 127
Grimshaw, Dr Thomas 70, 75
Guinness, Sir Arthur Edward 69, 71
Guinness Trust 73

Headlam, Maurice 59, 114, 194–95, 197, 204, 244
Hicks, F. G. 285
Housing acts,
 Cross Housing Act, 1875 15, 70–71, 74
 Housing (Additional Powers) Act, 1919 206–08, 238
 Housing (Ireland) Act, 1919 199–205, 272–74, 276, 294
 Housing (No. 2) Act, 1914 147–50
 Housing of the Working Classes (Ireland) Act, 1908 ('Clancy Act') 88–95, 273, 293
 Housing, Town Planning, etc. (England and Wales) Act, 1909 ('Burns Act') 15, 116, 133, 146
Housing and Town Planning Association of Ireland (HTPAI) 108–09, 134, 143

Housing legislation for Irish towns, early measures 69–71, 77, 79–80

Irish Board of Works (IBoW) 23–25, 247–58, 265, 297
Irish Builders' Cooperative Society (IBCS) 129–31
Irish Convention, 1917–18 175–80, 183–85, 295, 297
Irish Free State, housing policy in after independence 261–62, 270, 278–83
Irish Labour Party 87, 181, 196, 203, 225, 279–80, 284
Irish Land (Provision for Sailors and Soldiers) Act, 1919 244–47
Irish Local Government Board (ILGB) 28, 37, 45–52, 91, 95–96, 151–54, 183, 208–10, 213–27, 230–39, 246–55, 297
Irish Parliamentry Party (IPP) 5, 25–27, 29, 34–36, 40–45, 58–60, 81–89, 100–02, 114, 116–17, 124–25, 128, 134–36, 158–59, 170–71, 175–76, 181–82, 197, 200–02, 246, 292–93, 298–300
Irish Soldiers' and Sailors' Land Trust (ISSLT) 262–71
Irish Trades Union Council (Irish TUC) 81, 91, 105, 170, 279
Irish Transport and General Workers Union (ITGWU) 87, 102–08, 111, 129–31

Kelly, Thomas 87, 129, 136, 162, 204–05, 226
Killester Estate, Dublin 235, 249–55, 259, 262, 265, 267, 270

Labour Party, reactions to pre-war Irish housing policy 88, 120–21, 297–98
Labourers (Ireland) Acts,
 Design 37–40, 45–58, 247, 297
 Policy 28–29, 31–37, 40–45, 58–60, 150, 199, 240, 245, 273, 293, 295
 Reactions to in Britain 117–24
Land Acts for Ireland 25–26, 31, 40
Land Improvement Acts for Ireland 22–25
Larkin, James 87, 102–08, 128–31, 137, 143
Law, Arthur Bonar 119–20, 158, 170
Liberal Party, reactions to pre-war Irish housing policy 88, 121–24, 293–94, 297–98

Index 411

Limerick Corporation 68, 94, 97–98
Liverpool Corporation 74, 85, 93, 95–96, 258, 277
Lloyd George, David 40, 58–59, 64, 89, 101, 121–23, 125–27, 137, 146, 148, 169, 175–80, 183–87, 226–27, 236, 241, 294, 298–99
Local Government (Ireland) Act, 1898 35, 82
London County Council (LCC) 54–56, 93, 289–91
Long, Sir Walter 36, 119–20, 179–80, 185–86, 227, 243–44, 297

MacCarthy, Charles 134, 159, 164
Macpherson, Ian 189–91, 193–95, 199–203, 206–07, 211–13, 224–25, 242–47
Marino Estate, Dublin 135, 142, 285–90
McCaffrey Estate, Dublin 159–62, 168, 172, 210, 231
McLaughlin, Sir Henry 249–51
Mears, Frank 134, 142, 147, 251–52, 282
Mill, John Stuart 4
Munitions housing in Ireland 150
Murphy, William Martin 102, 108

Nannetti, Joseph 82, 86
National Housing and Town Planning Council 117–18
Nettlefold, John 83, 118, 298
Nolen, John 137–38
Northern Ireland, housing policy in after partition 260, 264, 270, 272–75

O'Brien, William (Independent nationalist) 44–45, 54, 59
O'Brien, William (labour representative) 111, 128–31
O'Casey, Sean 113
O'Connor, George 100, 144, 250
Offer, Avner 16, 298
O'Rourke, Horace 164, 281, 285

Parnell, Charles Stuart 5, 26–27, 81–82
Pembroke Urban District Council (UDC) 79, 92–93, 100, 107, 135, 143–44, 157, 297
Plunkett, Sir Horace 133–34, 145, 176–78, 295

Redmond, John 30, 40–41, 44–45, 53, 83–84, 86–87, 90, 101, 126, 151–52, 158, 175, 227
Reilly, Professor Charles 12–14
Richardson, Professor Albert 13–14
Robinson, Sir Henry 114, 151, 153, 159, 193–94, 209, 226, 232–34, 243, 247–55, 259, 262
Royal Commission on Working Class Housing (Ireland), 1885 63–64, 75
Royal Institute of Architects of Ireland (RIAI) 39–40, 45–46, 182, 211–15

Said, Edward 301
Samuel, Herbert 120, 155–56
Scott, Anthony 54
Scott, William 10, 12, 14, 55, 58, 106, 223
Shankill Estate, County Dublin 56–57
Shaw, George Bernard 103, 113, 155
Sherlock, Lorcan 102, 129, 135
Shortt, Edward 180, 182–83, 188–89, 192, 241–42
Sinn Fein 6, 87, 96, 107–08, 112, 129, 136, 142, 154, 181–82, 191, 197–98, 203–05, 225–26, 229–32, 234, 236, 238, 240, 242–44, 246, 260–62, 284, 294
South Dublin Rural Distric Council (RDC) 54–58, 159, 210, 297
Stephenson, Sir George 114
Strachey, John St Loe 119, 123
Strachie, Lord 123–24, 297
Swenarton, Mark 17, 19, 127, 186–87, 205, 208, 210, 237, 299

Thompson, Robert 214–15, 218
Thompson, William 117–18, 298
Town Tenants League 83–84, 86, 114, 299
Treasury 88–90, 137, 149–54, 156–57, 168–70, 178–80, 191–95, 200–05, 208, 210, 226–28, 246–47, 262–71, 295
Tudor Walters Report 171–73, 210, 213, 217, 223, 276, 281, 285

Ulster Unionist Party 42, 88–89, 125, 182, 196–97, 200–02, 224, 228–29, 230, 234, 236, 246, 272–74, 294, 298
United Irish League 30, 90

Unwin, Raymond 54, 57–58, 123, 129, 132, 140, 142–43, 146, 155–56, 159–60, 164–65, 172, 213, 224, 235, 265, 284–85, 296–97
Urban housing in Ireland, pre-war design 95–100

Vernon, Roland 177–78

Waterford Corporation 74, 80, 94, 151–52, 158
Weaver, Laurence 117, 119
Webb, Sydney 16
Woodview Cottages, Rathfarnham 56–57
Wyndham, George 30, 35–36, 84, 293

Yeats, William Butler 9, 10, 12, 196, 281–82, 301